PLAYFAIR
CRIC▮▮▮▮▮AL

EDITED BY BILL FRINDALL

All statistics by the Editor unless otherwise credited

PLAYFAIR CRICKET COMPETITION 1994

TEST CRICKET QUIZ

£1500 TO BE WON

PLUS NATWEST FINAL TICKETS AND HOSPITALITY
PLUS 25 CONSOLATION PRIZES

First Prize   £500 + overnight accommodation (B and B) at the Regents Park Hilton Hotel (opposite Lord's) on 2 and 3 September + TWO tickets to the 1994 NatWest Trophy Final + NatWest hospitality

Second Prize   £400 + TWO tickets to the 1994 NatWest Trophy Final

Third Prize   £300 + TWO tickets to the 1994 NatWest Trophy Final

Fourth Prize   £200

Fifth Prize   £100

Consolation prizes

Senders of the next 25 correct entries will each receive a copy of THE INNINGS OF MY LIFE by Jack Bannister and published by Headline at £16.99.

Closing date for entries
is 12.00 noon on 26 July 1994

Winning entries will be drawn by the Man of the Match Adjudicator at one of the NatWest semi-finals on Tuesday 9 August.

PLAYFAIR CRICKET COMPETITION 1994

SOUTH AFRICAN TEST CRICKET QUIZ

ENTRY FORM

Please PRINT your answers in the spaces provided and answer every question.

1 Who was the first to score a hundred on Test debut for South Africa? ....

2 Which South African bowler is the only Test cricketer to climb Mount Kilimanjaro twice? ....

3 Who is the only cricketer to captain England in his only Test match? ....

4 Which South African Test cricketer was born at Zagazig in Egypt? ....

5 Which ground staged Johannesburg's first six post-war Tests? ....

6 Who overcame the discomfort of a fractured thumb to score 208 against England? ....

7 Who was the first wicket-keeper to make 25 dismissals in a Test series? ....

8 Who is the only bowler to take a hat-trick in a Test at Lord's? ....

9 What was the record number of runs scored by England on the second day at Lord's in 1930? ....

10 Who set a world Test record by bowling 137 consecutive balls without conceding a run? ....

Your name and address:

....

....

....

Your daytime telephone number: ....

Post to: PLAYFAIR CRICKET COMPETITION, Special Events, Corporate Affairs Department, National Westminster Bank PLC, 1st Floor, 2 Broadgate, London EC2M 2AD.

Entries must be received before noon on 26 July 1994. All-correct entries will go into the prize-winning draw on 9 August and an announcement detailing all prize-winners will appear in the October edition of *The Cricketer* magazine. A list of winners is available on request by writing to Mrs B.J.Quinn at the above address and enclosing a stamped addressed envelope.

Rules: All entries must be on this official form. Proof of posting is not proof of entry. The decision of the editor regarding the answers to this quiz shall be final and binding; no correspondence may be entered into.

1993 PLAYFAIR CRICKET COMPETITION

ASHES TEST CRICKET QUIZ ANSWERS

1 Who, at The Oval in 1948, bowled Don Bradman for nought in his final innings in Tests?	W.E.(Eric) HOLLIES
2 In which year did 27 wickets fall in a single day at an Ashes Test match?	1888
3 Who was the first England captain to regain and then successfully defend the Ashes?	Len HUTTON
4 Which Australian Test cricketer changed his surname from Durtanovich?	L.S.(Len) PASCOE
5 Who, at 50 years and 327 days, was the oldest Australian to appear in an Ashes Test?	H.(Bert) IRONMONGER
6 On which English ground was an Ashes Test completed in just six hours 34 minutes?	OLD TRAFFORD
7 Who, during an Ashes Test, became the first wicket-keeper to complete the Test 'double'?	W.A.S.(Bert) OLDFIELD
8 How many century opening partnerships did Hobbs and Sutcliffe share against Australia?	ELEVEN
9 Who, during an Ashes Test, became the first cricketer to appear in 100 Test matches?	M.C.(Colin) COWDREY
10 Which famous Australian fast bowler was known as 'Nugget'?	K.R.(Keith) MILLER

There were 603 sets of correct answers out of a total of 850 entries. The winners were drawn by Brian Luckhurst (Kent and England) at the 1993 NatWest Trophy semi-final between Sussex and Glamorgan at Hove.

First Prize:	£500 + two nights accommodation + two tickets to include hospitality at the 1993 NatWest Trophy Final	P.S.HARRIS (Hoddesdon)
Second Prize:	£400 + two tickets to the 1993 NatWest Trophy Final	R.T.HARPER (St Austell)
Third Prize:	£300 + two tickets to the 1993 NatWest Trophy Final	Ms V.RENSHAW (Shoreham-by-Sea)
Fourth Prize:	£200	M.PORTER (Swindon)
Fifth Prize:	£100	L.R.DELBRIDGE (Torquay)

25 Runners-up each received a copy of *Hitting Across The Line* by Viv Richards:

G.S.Astin (Lincoln)
P.Ashtonhurst (Manchester)
P.W.Burchett (South Ockendon)
R.Buxton (Sidcup)
D.Edney (Chelmsford)
E.F.Holstead (Pontefract)
S.Hudson (Leeds)
N.Hughes (Greasby)
A.R.Jonas (South India)
Mrs J.A.King (Wokingham)
R.Leech (Norwich)
G.Miller (Borehamwood)
M.Pope (Mexborough)

Mrs Y.Prigmore (Wellingborough)
D.E.Robinson (Rochdale)
N.Rogers (Coventry)
C.Schanschieff (Northampton)
P.J.Scott (Croxley Green)
C.A.Shearing (Bournemouth)
A.W.Smith (Hitchin)
Miss J.Standevan (Oldham)
G.Swarts (Dinas-Powis)
J.Walton (Epsom)
J.I.Weeks (Cirencester)
N.Wilkinson (Blackpool)

EDITORIAL PREFACE

Playfair makes its 47th appearance at the start of a season in which most interest will focus on the first visit by South Africa since 1965. Having witnessed the recent Adelaide Test, I can warmly recommend the early reservation of seats for the three Cornhill Tests and two Texaco Trophy internationals; just a glimpse of 'Jonty' Rhodes in the field will more than justify the outlay on tickets and travel. The batting skills of 'Hansie' Cronje, allied to the pace bowling of Allan Donald and Co, will provide a searching examination for Mike Atherton's young team.

The latter's selection for our cover profile needs no justification. Anyone witnessing his captaincy of the England Under-19 team in Sri Lanka in 1986-87 would have recognised a Test match leader in the making. Very much his own man, he is a resilient and highly intelligent competitor, equally adept at handling menacing barrages from fast bowlers and the media.

We also welcome New Zealand, who, after a difficult winter, will want their captain, Martin Crowe, and all their bowlers fully returned to fitness. Traditionally the most polite and agreeable of touring teams, they should never be underrated, even in their post-Hadlee rebuilding phase.

The 1993 season saw the retirement of far too many recent stalwarts of the international cricket scene: Ian Botham, Neil Foster, David Gower, Derek Pringle, Derek Randall and Chris Tavaré of England, together with Malcolm Marshall and Viv Richards of West Indies. My enjoyment of their long careers has been mainly from the 'Test Match Special' box in the company of Brian Johnston. His passing has been lamented universally and not merely within the world of cricket for, by transforming the commentary box into a cavalcade of comedy and cake, he made life fun for his colleagues and for millions of listeners. He was 81 years young, very special and Westminster Abbey will be a worthy setting for the celebration of his life on 16 May.

Only one statistic requires my comment and regrettably it involves the ICC's outrageous decision regarding the status of 'rebel' tours of South Africa. As predicted in the last edition, this so clearly flouts their own definition of a first-class match that the edict has been ignored by all statisticians and publications in Britain and South Africa. Hopefully, the ICC will soon amend its unfortunate and ill-judged ruling.

Once again the compilation of *Playfair* has been greatly assisted by the county secretaries and scorers, by Tony Brown, Tim Lamb and Kate Jenkins of the TCCB, by David Richards of the ICC, and by David Armstrong of the MCCA. Happily, *Playfair* continues to be indebted to NatWest for its sponsorship and to Barbara Quinn and her Special Events team for their continuing support, including the highly efficient administration of our competition. Thanks are also due to Philip Bailey for compiling the first-class career records, to Ian Marshall and colleagues at Headline for again seeing the manuscript safely through the hazardous process of production, and especially to Chris Leggett at our new typesetters, Letterpart, in my beloved Reigate.

BILL FRINDALL
Urchfont

NEW ZEALAND v AUSTRALIA (1st Test)

Played at Lancaster Park, Christchurch, on 25, 26, 27, 28 February 1993.
Toss: New Zealand.   Result: AUSTRALIA won by an innings and 60 runs.
Debuts: Nil.

AUSTRALIA

D.C.Boon c Parore b Owens	15
M.A.Taylor c Crowe b Morrison	82
J.L.Langer lbw b Morrison	63
M.E.Waugh c Parore b Patel	13
S.R.Waugh lbw b Owens	62
*A.R.Border c Parore b Morrison	88
†I.A.Healy c Morrison b Owens	54
M.G.Hughes c Cairns b Patel	45
P.R.Reiffel c Greatbatch b Su'a	18
S.K.Warne not out	22
C.J.McDermott c Jones b Cairns	4
Extras (B2, LB6, W5, NB6)	19
Total	**485**

NEW ZEALAND

M.J.Greatbatch c Healy b McDermott	4	c Reiffel b Hughes	0
J.G.Wright lbw b Warne	39	b McDermott	14
A.H.Jones lbw b McDermott	8	c Border b McDermott	10
*M.D.Crowe c Taylor b Hughes	15	lbw b Hughes	14
K.R.Rutherford b Warne	57	c Healy b Warne	102
C.L.Cairns c Boon b McDermott	0	c Taylor b Warne	21
†A.C.Parore c Boon b Reiffel	6	c Boon b Warne	5
D.N.Patel c McDermott b Hughes	35	b Warne	8
M.L.Su'a c Healy b Reiffel	0	b Hughes	44
D.K.Morrison not out	4	c Healy b Hughes	19
M.B.Owens lbw b Warne	0	not out	0
Extras (B2, LB4, W4, NB4)	14	(LB2, NB4)	6
Total	**182**		**243**

NEW ZEALAND	O	M	R	W	O	M	R	W	FALL OF WICKETS			
										A	NZ	NZ
Morrison	36	11	81	3					Wkt	1st	1st	2nd
Su'a	33	5	106	1					1st	33	4	0
Cairns	31.3	9	87	1					2nd	149	18	19
Owens	26	9	58	3					3rd	170	53	24
Patel	31	3	145	2					4th	217	124	51
									5th	264	128	92
AUSTRALIA									6th	363	138	110
McDermott	21	4	73	3	19	6	45	2	7th	435	150	144
Hughes	21	10	44	2	24.5	6	62	4	8th	441	152	190
Reiffel	18	8	27	2	18	3	59	0	9th	480	181	242
S.R.Waugh	4	2	9	0	2	2	0	0	10th	485	182	243
Warne	22	12	23	3	26	7	63	4				
M.E.Waugh					5	1	12	0				

Umpires: B.L.Aldridge (15) and C.E.King (1).   Test No. 1215/27

NEW ZEALAND v AUSTRALIA (2nd Test)

Played at Basin Reserve, Wellington, on 4, 5, 6, 7, 8 March 1993.
Toss: Australia.   Result: MATCH DRAWN.
Debuts: Nil.

NEW ZEALAND

M.J.Greatbatch c Taylor b Reiffel	61			b McDermott	0
J.G.Wright c Healy b Hughes	72	(6)		not out	46
A.H.Jones b Reiffel	4	(2)		lbw b Warne	42
*M.D.Crowe b McDermott	98	(3)		lbw b McDermott	3
K.R.Rutherford c Healy b Hughes	32	(4)		c Healy b Reiffel	11
†T.E.Blain b Hughes	13	(5)		c Healy b Warne	51
C.L.Cairns c Border b McDermott	13			lbw b McDermott	14
D.N.Patel not out	13			c Healy b M.E.Waugh	25
D.K.Morrison c Warne b McDermott	2			not out	0
W.Watson c Taylor b Warne	3				
M.B.Owens b Warne	0				
Extras (B7, LB11, W2, NB10)	30			(B8, LB8, W1, NB1)	18
Total	**329**			**(7 wickets)**	**210**

AUSTRALIA

M.A.Taylor run out	50
D.C.Boon c and b Morrison	37
J.L.Langer c Blain b Watson	24
M.E.Waugh c and b Owens	12
S.R.Waugh c Blain b Morrison	75
*A.R.Border lbw b Morrison	30
†I.A.Healy c Rutherford b Morrison	8
M.G.Hughes c Wright b Morrison	8
P.R.Reiffel lbw b Morrison	7
S.K.Warne c Greatbatch b Morrison	22
C.J.McDermott not out	7
Extras (LB14, NB4)	18
Total	**298**

AUSTRALIA	O	M	R	W	O	M	R	W
McDermott	31	8	66	3	23	9	54	3
Hughes	35	9	100	3	11	5	22	0
Reiffel	23	8	55	2	16	7	27	1
S.R.Waugh	15	7	28	0				
Warne	29	9	59	2	40	25	49	2
M.E.Waugh	2	1	3	0	8	3	12	1
Border					12	5	15	0
Taylor					4	2	15	0
Boon					1	1	0	0

NEW ZEALAND	O	M	R	W
Morrison	26.4	5	89	7
Cairns	24	3	77	0
Watson	29	12	60	1
Owens	21	3	54	1
Patel	1	0	4	0

FALL OF WICKETS

	NZ	A	NZ
Wkt	1st	1st	2nd
1st	111	92	4
2nd	120	105	9
3rd	191	128	30
4th	287	153	101
5th	289	229	131
6th	307	237	154
7th	308	251	202
8th	314	258	–
9th	329	271	–
10th	329	298	–

Umpires: B.L.Aldridge (16) and R.S.Dunne (10).   Test No. 1216/28

NEW ZEALAND v AUSTRALIA (3rd Test)

Played at Eden Park, Auckland, on 12, 13, 14, 15, 16 March 1993.
Toss: Australia.   Result: NEW ZEALAND won by 5 wickets.
Debuts: Nil.

AUSTRALIA

D.C.Boon lbw b Watson	20 (2)	lbw b Su'a	53
M.A.Taylor lbw b Morrison	13 (1)	st Blain b Patel	3
J.L.Langer c Blain b Morrison	0	lbw b Patel	0
D.R.Martyn c Blain b Watson	1	c Greatbatch b Patel	74
S.R.Waugh c Jones b Watson	41	lbw b Patel	0
*A.R.Border c Blain b Morrison	0	c Harris b Watson	71
†I.A.Healy c Jones b Morrison	0	c Blain b Patel	24
M.G.Hughes c Morrison b Patel	33	not out	31
P.R.Reiffel c Jones b Morrison	9	b Watson	1
S.K.Warne not out	3	c Jones b Morrison	2
C.J.McDermott b Morrison	6	c Wright b Watson	10
Extras (LB7, NB6)	13	(B1, LB7, NB8)	16
Total	**139**		**285**

NEW ZEALAND

J.G.Wright c Taylor b McDermott	33	run out	33
M.J.Greatbatch c Border b Hughes	32	b Hughes	29
A.H.Jones c Healy b Hughes	20	b Warne	26
*M.D.Crowe c Taylor b Waugh	31	c Langer b Warne	25
K.R.Rutherford st Healy b Warne	43	not out	53
C.Z.Harris c Taylor b Warne	13	lbw b Waugh	0
†T.E.Blain c Healy b McDermott	15	not out	24
D.N.Patel c Healy b Warne	2		
M.L.Su'a c Waugh b Warne	3		
D.K.Morrison not out	10		
W.Watson lbw b Hughes	0		
Extras (B7, LB10, NB5)	22	(LB10, NB1)	11
Total	**224**	**(5 wickets)**	**201**

NEW ZEALAND	O	M	R	W	O	M	R	W	FALL OF WICKETS				
										A	NZ	A	NZ
Morrison	18.4	5	37	6	33	8	81	1	Wkt	1st	1st	2nd	2nd
Su'a	14	3	27	0	18	4	56	1	1st	38	60	5	44
Watson	19	9	47	3	19	5	43	3	2nd	38	91	8	65
Patel	4	0	21	1	34	10	93	5	3rd	39	97	115	109
Harris					2	1	4	0	4th	39	144	119	129
									5th	43	178	160	134
AUSTRALIA									6th	48	200	225	–
McDermott	19	6	50	2	12	3	38	0	7th	101	205	261	–
Hughes	24.5	6	67	3	15.4	2	54	1	8th	121	206	271	–
Reiffel	22	6	63	0	6	1	19	0	9th	133	224	274	–
Warne	15	12	8	4	27	8	54	2	10th	139	224	285	–
Waugh	14	6	19	1	6	1	15	1					
Martyn	1	1	0	0									
Border					6	3	11	0					

Umpires: B.L.Aldridge (17) and C.E.King (2).   Test No. 1217/29

NEW ZEALAND v AUSTRALIA 1992-93

NEW ZEALAND – BATTING AND FIELDING

	M	I	NO	HS	Runs	Avge	100	50	Ct/St
K.R.Rutherford	3	6	1	102	298	59.60	1	2	1
J.G.Wright	3	6	1	72	237	47.40	–	1	2
M.D.Crowe	3	6	–	98	186	31.00	–	1	1
T.E.Blain	2	4	1	51	91	30.33	–	1	7/1
M.J.Greatbatch	3	6	–	61	126	21.00	–	1	3
D.N.Patel	3	5	1	35	83	20.75	–	–	–
A.H.Jones	3	6	–	42	110	18.33	–	–	4
D.K.Morrison	3	5	3	19	35	17.50	–	–	–
M.L.Su'a	2	3	–	44	47	15.66	–	–	–
C.L.Cairns	2	4	–	21	48	12.00	–	–	1
W.Watson	2	2	–	3	3	1.50	–	–	–
M.B.Owens	2	3	1	0*	0	0.00	–	–	1

Played in one Test: C.Z.Harris 13, 0 (1ct); A.C.Parore 6, 5 (3ct).

NEW ZEALAND – BOWLING

	O	M	R	W	Avge	Best	5wI	10wM
D.K.Morrison	114.2	29	288	17	16.94	7-89	2	–
W.Watson	67	26	150	7	21.42	3-43	–	–
M.B.Owens	47	12	112	4	28.00	3-58	–	–
D.N.Patel	70	13	263	8	32.87	5-93	1	–

Also bowled: C.L.Cairns 55.3-12-164-1; C.Z.Harris 2-1-4-0; M.L.Su'a 65-12-189-2.

AUSTRALIA – BATTING AND FIELDING

	M	I	NO	HS	Runs	Avge	100	50	Ct/St
A.R.Border	3	4	–	88	189	47.25	–	2	3
S.R.Waugh	3	4	–	75	178	44.50	–	2	1
M.G.Hughes	3	4	1	45	117	39.00	–	–	1
M.A.Taylor	3	4	–	82	148	37.00	–	2	7
D.C.Boon	3	4	–	53	125	31.25	–	1	3
S.K.Warne	3	4	2	22*	49	24.50	–	–	1
J.L.Langer	3	4	–	63	87	21.75	–	1	1
I.A.Healy	3	4	–	54	86	21.50	–	1	12/1
M.E.Waugh	2	2	–	13	25	12.50	–	–	1
C.J.McDermott	3	4	1	10	27	9.00	–	–	1
P.R.Reiffel	3	4	–	18	35	8.75	–	–	1

Played in one Test: D.R.Martyn 1, 74.

AUSTRALIA – BOWLING

	O	M	R	W	Avge	Best	5wI	10wM
S.K.Warne	159	73	256	17	15.05	4- 8	–	–
C.J.McDermott	125	36	326	13	25.07	3-54	–	–
M.G.Hughes	132.2	38	349	13	26.84	4-62	–	–
P.R.Reiffel	103	33	250	5	50.00	2-27	–	–

Also bowled: D.C.Boon 1-1-0-0; A.R.Border 18-8-26-0; D.R.Martyn 1-1-0-0; M.A.Taylor 4-2-15-0; M.E.Waugh 15-5-27-1; S.R.Waugh 41-18-71-2.

INDIA v ZIMBABWE (Only Test)

Played at Feroz Shah Kotla, Delhi, on 13, 14, 15, 16, 17 March 1993.
Toss: India.   Result: INDIA won by an innings and 13 runs.
Debuts: India – V.Yadav; Zimbabwe – G.A.Briant, U.Ranchod.

INDIA

M.Prabhakar c A.Flower b Brain	3
N.S.Sidhu lbw b Traicos	61
V.G.Kambli c and b Traicos	227
S.R.Tendulkar c Traicos b Ranchod	62
*M.Azharuddin run out	42
P.K.Amre not out	52
Kapil Dev st A.Flower b Traicos	16
†V.Yadav b Brain	30
A.Kumble not out	18
R.K.Chauhan ⎫ did not bat	
Maninder Singh ⎭	
Extras (B17, LB6, W2)	25
Total (7 wickets declared)	**536**

ZIMBABWE

K.J.Arnott lbw b Kapil Dev	0	b Maninder	21
G.W.Flower lbw b Maninder	96	lbw b Prabhakar	0
A.D.R.Campbell b Chauhan	32	c Amre b Kumble	61
*D.L.Houghton lbw b Kumble	18	c Amre b Kumble	1
†A.Flower st Yadav b Maninder	115	not out	62
G.A.Briant st Yadav b Kumble	1	c Kambli b Maninder	16
A.H.Shah run out	25	lbw b Kumble	6
E.A.Brandes c Sidhu b Kumble	8	c Chauhan b Maninder	1
D.H.Brain c Kambli b Maninder	0	lbw b Kumble	0
U.Ranchod b Chauhan	7	c Yadav b Maninder	1
A.J.Traicos not out	0	lbw b Kumble	1
Extras (B4, LB10, W1, NB5)	20	(B10, LB16, W2, NB3)	31
Total	**322**		**201**

ZIMBABWE	O	M	R	W	O	M	R	W	FALL OF WICKETS		
									I	*Z*	*Z*
Brandes	26	4	93	0					Wkt	1st	1st	2nd
Brain	34	1	146	2					1st	19	0	2
Shah	10	3	43	0					2nd	126	53	53
Traicos	50	4	186	3					3rd	263	83	62
Ranchod	12	0	45	1					4th	370	275	126
INDIA									5th	434	276	159
Kapil Dev	13	4	37	1	4	1	4	0	6th	464	276	167
Prabhakar	14	4	23	0	4	3	5	1	7th	507	286	176
Chauhan	28.1	4	68	2	14	5	30	0	8th	–	287	177
Kumble	43	12	90	3	38.5	16	70	5	9th	–	318	188
Maninder	32	4	79	3	35	8	66	4	10th	–	322	201
Tendulkar	5	1	11	0								

Umpires: S.K.Bansal (1) and S.Venkataraghavan (3).   Test No. 1218/2

SRI LANKA v ENGLAND (Only Test)

Played at Sinhalese Sports Club, Colombo, on 13, 14, 15, 17, 18 March 1993.
Toss: England.   Result: SRI LANKA won by 5 wickets.
Debuts: Sri Lanka – A.M.De Silva.

ENGLAND

R.A.Smith b Muralitharan	128	b Jayasuriya	35
M.A.Atherton lbw b Ramanayake	13	c Tillekeratne b Gurusinha	2
M.W.Gatting c Jayasuriya b Muralitharan	29	c Tillekeratne b Warnaweera	18
G.A.Hick c Tillekeratne b Muralitharan	68	c Ramanayake b Warnaweera	26
*†A.J.Stewart c Tillekeratne b Warnaweera	63	c Mahanama b Warnaweera	3
N.H.Fairbrother b Warnaweera	18	run out	3
C.C.Lewis run out	22	c Jayasuriya b Muralitharan	45
J.E.Emburey not out	1	b Gurusinha	59
P.W.Jarvis lbw b Warnaweera	0	st A.M.De Silva b Jayasuriya	3
P.C.R.Tufnell lbw b Muralitharan	1	c A.M.De Silva b Warnaweera	1
D.E.Malcolm c Gurusinha b Warnaweera	13	not out	8
Extras (B5, LB3, W1, NB15)	24	(B4, LB2, W1, NB18)	25
Total (130.1 overs; 560 minutes)	380	(66 overs; 293 minutes)	228

SRI LANKA

R.S.Mahanama c Smith b Emburey	64	c Stewart b Lewis	6
U.C.Hathurusinghe c Stewart b Lewis	59	c Stewart b Tufnell	14
A.P.Gurusinha st Stewart b Tufnell	43	b Emburey	29
P.A.De Silva c Stewart b Jarvis	80	c Jarvis b Emburey	7
*A.Ranatunga c Stewart b Lewis	64	c Gatting b Tufnell	35
H.P.Tillekeratne not out	93	not out	36
S.T.Jayasuriya c Atherton b Lewis	4	not out	6
†A.M.De Silva c Gatting b Emburey	9		
C.P.H.Ramanayake c Lewis b Jarvis	1		
M.Muralitharan b Lewis	19		
K.P.J.Warnaweera b Jarvis	1		
Extras (B2, LB13, W2, NB15)	32	(B1, LB2, NB6)	9
Total (156.5 overs; 684 minutes)	469	(42.4 overs; 204 minutes)	142-5

SRI LANKA	O	M	R	W	O	M	R	W
Ramanayake	17	2	66	1	3	0	16	0
Gurusinha	5	1	12	0	6	3	7	2
Warnaweera	40.1	11	90	4	25	4	98	4
Hathurusinghe	8	2	22	0				
Muralitharan	45	12	118	4	16	3	55	1
Jayasuriya	12	1	53	0	16	3	46	2
Ranatunga	3	0	11	0				

ENGLAND	O	M	R	W	O	M	R	W
Malcolm	25	7	60	0	3	1	11	0
Jarvis	25.5	1	76	3	8	2	14	0
Lewis	31	5	66	4	8	1	21	1
Tufnell	33	5	108	1	7.4	1	34	2
Emburey	34	6	117	2	14	2	48	2
Hick	8	0	27	0	2	0	11	0

FALL OF WICKETS

	E	SL	E	SL
Wkt	1st	1st	2nd	2nd
1st	40	99	16	8
2nd	82	153	38	48
3rd	194	203	83	61
4th	316	330	91	61
5th	323	339	96	136
6th	358	349	130	–
7th	366	371	153	–
8th	376	376	173	–
9th	367	459	188	–
10th	380	469	228	–

Umpires: K.T.Francis (8) and T.M.Samarasinghe (4).

Test No. 1219/5

WEST INDIES v PAKISTAN (1st Test)

Played at Queen's Park Oval, Port-of-Spain, Trinidad, on 16, 17, 18 April 1993.
Toss: West Indies.   Result: WEST INDIES won by 204 runs.
Debuts: Pakistan – Basit Ali.

WEST INDIES

Batsman	1st innings		2nd innings	
D.L.Haynes	c Moin b Rehman	31	not out	143
P.V.Simmons	c Moin b Rehman	27	c Asif b Aamir	22
*R.B.Richardson	b Mushtaq	7	c Wasim b Waqar	68
B.C.Lara	c Aamir b Waqar	6	b Asif	96
K.L.T.Arthurton	run out	3	(6) lbw b Wasim	1
C.L.Hooper	lbw b Waqar	9	(7) lbw b Waqar	0
†J.R.Murray	lbw b Waqar	0	lbw b Waqar	0
I.R.Bishop	c Inzamam b Rehman	4	(5) c Moin b Wasim	3
C.E.L.Ambrose	lbw b Wasim	4	lbw b Wasim	5
A.C.Cummins	not out	14	lbw b Wasim	0
C.A.Walsh	b Wasim	0	run out	6
Extras	(B6, LB3, W2, NB11)	22	(B1, LB18, W2, NB17)	38
Total		127		382

PAKISTAN

Batsman	1st innings		2nd innings	
Aamir Sohail	c Hooper b Bishop	55	lbw b Walsh	15
Ramiz Raja	lbw b Bishop	9	lbw b Ambrose	11
Inzamam-ul-Haq	lbw b Walsh	10	lbw b Walsh	6
Javed Miandad	lbw b Ambrose	20	c Murray b Bishop	4
Basit Ali	lbw b Bishop	0	c Richardson b Hooper	37
Asif Mujtaba	c Lara b Bishop	10	lbw b Hooper	20
*Wasim Akram	c Richardson b Ambrose	2	st Murray b Hooper	4
†Moin Khan	c Murray b Ambrose	0	c Bishop b Hooper	18
Waqar Younis	c Lara b Ambrose	16	lbw b Walsh	1
Mushtaq Ahmed	c Hooper b Bishop	3	not out	12
Ata-ur-Rehman	not out	3	c Ambrose b Hooper	19
Extras	(LB6, NB6)	12	(LB10, NB8)	18
Total		140		165

PAKISTAN	O	M	R	W	O	M	R	W
Wasim	10.2	2	32	2	27	6	75	4
Waqar	11	3	37	3	23	2	88	3
Mushtaq	8	1	21	1	13	1	45	0
Rehman	9	1	28	3	19	0	82	0
Aamir					5	1	30	1
Asif					10	1	43	1

FALL OF WICKETS

	WI	P	WI	P
Wkt	1st	1st	2nd	2nd
1st	63	17	57	17
2nd	76	52	160	34
3rd	85	100	329	41
4th	85	100	342	42
5th	95	102	356	109
6th	95	104	358	111
7th	102	108	358	114
8th	102	120	371	127
9th	127	136	371	134
10th	127	140	382	165

WEST INDIES	O	M	R	W	O	M	R	W
Ambrose	17	6	34	4	13	3	37	1
Bishop	15.5	6	43	5	11	2	28	1
Walsh	7	4	13	1	12	3	29	3
Cummins	5	0	19	0	5	1	16	0
Hooper	4	0	25	0	11.5	3	40	5
Simmons					1	0	5	0

Umpires: H.D.Bird (51) and S.U.Bucknor (8).   Test No. 1220/29

WEST INDIES v PAKISTAN (2nd Test)

Played at Kensington Oval, Bridgetown, Barbados, on 23, 24, 25, 27 April 1993.
Toss: Pakistan.   Result: WEST INDIES won by 10 wickets.
Debuts: Pakistan – Aamir Nazir.

WEST INDIES

D.L.Haynes b Aamir Nazir	125	not out	16
P.V.Simmons c Moin b Rehman	87	not out	8
*R.B.Richardson lbw b Waqar	31		
B.C.Lara c Moin b Rehman	51		
K.L.T.Arthurton b Wasim	56		
C.L.Hooper c Moin b Waqar	15		
†J.R.Murray st Moin b Aamir Sohail	35		
I.R.Bishop c Moin b Aamir Nazir	11		
C.E.L.Ambrose not out	12		
W.K.M.Benjamin b Waqar	0		
C.A.Walsh c and b Waqar	3		
Extras (B1, LB1, W2, NB25)	29	(W3, NB2)	5
Total	455	(0 wickets)	29

PAKISTAN

Aamir Sohail c Murray b Ambrose	10	c Benjamin b Ambrose	4
Ramiz Raja c Haynes b Ambrose	37	lbw b Walsh	25
Asif Mujtaba c Richardson b Walsh	13	lbw b Benjamin	41
Javed Miandad c Richardson b Benjamin	22	c Arthurton b Hooper	43
Inzamam-ul-Haq lbw b Bishop	7	(7) lbw b Benjamin	26
Basit Ali not out	92	lbw b Walsh	37
*Wasim Akram c Simmons b Hooper	29	(8) b Benjamin	0
†Moin Khan c Murray b Walsh	0	(5) c Murray b Hooper	17
Waqar Younis c Murray b Walsh	0	c Lara b Walsh	9
Ata-ur-Rehman c Benjamin b Walsh	0	c Simmons b Walsh	13
Aamir Nazir c Arthurton b Benjamin	1	not out	6
Extras (LB3, NB7)	10	(B12, LB5, NB4)	21
Total	221		262

PAKISTAN	O	M	R	W	O	M	R	W	FALL OF WICKETS			
										WI	P	P	WI
Wasim	32	2	95	1	2.3	0	18	0				
Waqar	25.5	3	132	4						Wkt	1st	1st	2nd	2nd
Aamir Nazir	20	1	79	2	2	0	11	0	1st	122	12	4	–
Rehman	21	1	103	2					2nd	200	31	47	–
Asif	3	0	30	0					3rd	303	62	113	–
Aamir Sohail	4	1	14	1					4th	337	79	133	–
									5th	363	109	141	–
WEST INDIES									6th	426	189	207	–
Ambrose	16	5	42	2	26	10	55	0	7th	440	190	207	–
Bishop	16	5	43	1	4	1	13	0	8th	440	190	215	–
Walsh	18	2	56	4	24	7	51	3	9th	445	200	238	–
Benjamin	19	5	55	2	17	7	30	3	10th	455	221	262	–
Hooper	7	0	22	1	32.3	6	96	3					

Umpires: L.H.Barker (18) and H.D.Bird (52).

Test No. 1221/30

WEST INDIES v PAKISTAN (3rd Test)

Played at Recreation Ground, St John's, Antigua, on 1, 2, 4, 5, 6‡ May 1993.
Toss: West Indies.   Result: MATCH DRAWN.
Debuts: Pakistan – Nadim Khan, Shakil Ahmed.   (‡ no play)

WEST INDIES

D.L.Haynes c Rashid b Nadim	23	not out	64
P.V.Simmons c Wasim b Rehman	28	b Waqar	17
*R.B.Richardson c Wasim b Waqar	52	lbw b Waqar	0
B.C.Lara st Rashid b Nadim	44	lbw b Waqar	19
K.L.T.Arthurton lbw b Waqar	30	lbw b Waqar	0
C.L.Hooper not out	178	not out	29
†J.R.Murray lbw b Waqar	4		
C.E.L.Ambrose lbw b Wasim	1		
A.C.Cummins lbw b Waqar	14		
W.K.M.Benjamin c Wasim b Waqar	12		
C.A.Walsh c Asif b Wasim	30		
Extras (LB6, NB16)	22	(B8, LB5, NB11)	24
Total	**438**	**(4 wickets)**	**153**

PAKISTAN

Shakil Ahmed lbw b Ambrose	0
Ramiz Raja c Murray b Walsh	0
Asif Mujtaba c Haynes b Hooper	59
Javed Miandad lbw b Benjamin	31
Basit Ali b Cummins	56
Inzamam-ul-Haq c Haynes b Cummins	123
†Rashid Latif lbw b Cummins	2
*Wasim Akram c Hooper b Benjamin	9
Waqar Younis c Hooper b Benjamin	4
Nadim Khan c Murray b Cummins	25
Ata-ur-Rehman not out	1
Extras (LB6, NB10)	16
Total	**326**

PAKISTAN	O	M	R	W	O	M	R	W	FALL OF WICKETS			
										WI	P	WI
Wasim	26.2	5	108	2	10	2	30	0	Wkt	1st	1st	2nd
Waqar	28	4	104	5	11	1	23	4	1st	35	0	36
Rehman	17	1	66	1	9	1	24	0	2nd	77	4	36
Nadim	38	5	147	2	14	0	48	0	3rd	153	85	68
Asif	1	0	7	0	4	1	9	0	4th	159	108	68
Basit					1	0	6	0	5th	218	196	–
									6th	241	206	–
WEST INDIES									7th	252	221	–
Ambrose	23	9	40	1					8th	312	227	–
Walsh	19	3	58	1					9th	332	323	–
Benjamin	20	4	53	3					10th	438	326	–
Cummins	20	4	54	4								
Hooper	28	2	98	1								
Simmons	5	0	17	0								

Umpires: H.D.Bird (53) and S.U.Bucknor (9).   Test No. 1222/31

WEST INDIES v PAKISTAN 1992-93

WEST INDIES – BATTING AND FIELDING

	M	I	NO	HS	Runs	Avge	100	50	Ct/St
D.L.Haynes	3	6	3	143*	402	134.00	2	1	3
C.L.Hooper	3	5	2	178*	231	77.00	1	–	4
B.C.Lara	3	5	–	96	216	43.20	–	2	3
P.V.Simmons	3	6	1	87	189	37.80	–	1	2
R.B.Richardson	3	5	–	68	158	31.60	–	2	4
K.L.T.Arthurton	3	5	–	56	90	18.00	–	1	2
A.C.Cummins	2	3	1	14*	28	14.00	–	–	–
C.A.Walsh	3	4	–	30	39	9.75	–	–	–
J.R.Murray	3	4	–	35	39	9.75	–	–	8/1
C.E.L.Ambrose	3	4	1	12*	22	7.33	–	–	1
W.K.M.Benjamin	2	2	–	12	12	6.00	–	–	2
I.R.Bishop	2	3	–	11	18	6.00	–	–	1

WEST INDIES – BOWLING

	O	M	R	W	Avge	Best	5wI	10wM
C.A.Walsh	80	19	207	12	17.25	4-56	–	–
W.K.M.Benjamin	56	16	138	8	17.25	3-30	–	–
I.R.Bishop	46.5	14	127	7	18.14	5-43	1	–
A.C.Cummins	30	5	89	4	22.25	4-54	–	–
C.E.L.Ambrose	95	33	208	9	23.11	4-34	–	–
C.L.Hooper	83.2	11	281	10	28.10	5-40	1	–

Also bowled: P.V.Simmons 6-0-22-0.

PAKISTAN – BATTING AND FIELDING

	M	I	NO	HS	Runs	Avge	100	50	Ct/St
Basit Ali	3	5	1	92*	222	55.50	–	2	–
Inzamam-ul-Haq	3	5	–	123	172	34.40	1	–	1
Asif Mujtaba	3	5	–	59	143	28.60	–	1	2
Javed Miandad	3	5	–	43	120	24.00	–	–	1
Aamir Sohail	2	4	–	55	84	21.00	–	1	1
Ramiz Raja	3	5	–	37	82	16.40	–	–	–
Ata-ur-Rehman	3	5	2	19	36	12.00	–	–	–
Waqar Younis	3	5	–	29	50	10.00	–	–	1
Wasim Akram	3	5	–	29	44	8.80	–	–	4
Moin Khan	3	5	–	18	35	8.75	–	–	7/1

Played in one Test: Aamir Nazir 1, 6*; Mushtaq Ahmed 3, 12*; Nadim Khan 25; Rashid Latif 2 (1ct, 1st); Shakil Ahmed 0.

PAKISTAN – BOWLING

	O	M	R	W	Avge	Best	5wI	10wM
Waqar Younis	98.5	13	384	19	20.21	5-105	1	–
Wasim Akram	108.1	17	358	9	39.77	4- 75	–	–
Ata-ur-Rehman	75	4	303	6	50.50	3- 28	–	–

Also bowled: Aamir Nazir 22-1-90-2; Aamir Sohail 9-2-44-2; Asif Mujtaba 18-2-89-1; Basit Ali 1-0-6-0; Mushtaq Ahmed 21-2-66-1; Nadim Khan 52-5-195-2.

ENGLAND v AUSTRALIA (1st Test)

Played at Old Trafford, Manchester, on 3, 4, 5, 6, 7 June 1993.
Toss: England.   Result: AUSTRALIA won by 179 runs.
Debuts: England – A.R.Caddick, P.M.Such; Australia – B.P.Julian, M.J.Slater.
‡(Lewis/Stewart)

AUSTRALIA

M.A.Taylor c and b Such	124	(2)	lbw b Such	9
M.J.Slater c Stewart b DeFreitas	58	(1)	c Caddick b Such	27
D.C.Boon c Lewis b Such	21		c Gatting b DeFreitas	93
M.E.Waugh c and b Tufnell	6		b Tufnell	64
*A.R.Border st Stewart b Such	17		c and b Caddick	31
S.R.Waugh b Such	3		not out	78
†I.A.Healy c Such b Tufnell	12		not out	102
B.P.Julian c Gatting b Such	0			
M.G.Hughes c DeFreitas b Such	2			
S.K.Warne not out	15			
C.J.McDermott run out ‡	8			
Extras (B8, LB8, NB7)	23		(B6, LB14, NB8)	28
Total (112.3 overs; 440 minutes)	**289**		(130 overs; 525 minutes)	**432-5d**

ENGLAND

*G.A.Gooch c Julian b Warne	65		Handled the ball	133
M.A.Atherton c Healy b Hughes	19		c Taylor b Warne	25
M.W.Gatting b Warne	4		b Hughes	23
R.A.Smith c Taylor b Warne	4		b Warne	18
G.A.Hick c Border b Hughes	34		c Healy b Hughes	22
†A.J.Stewart b Julian	27		c Healy b Warne	11
C.C.Lewis c Boon b Hughes	9		c Taylor b Warne	43
P.A.J.DeFreitas lbw b Julian	5		lbw b Julian	7
A.R.Caddick c Healy b Warne	7		c Warne b Hughes	25
P.M.Such not out	14		c Border b Hughes	9
P.C.R.Tufnell c Healy b Hughes	7		not out	0
Extras (B6, LB10, NB5)	21		(LB11, W1, NB4)	16
Total (74.5 overs; 305 minutes)	**210**		(120.2 overs; 474 minutes)	**332**

ENGLAND	O	M	R	W	O	M	R	W	FALL OF WICKETS				
										A	E	A	E
Caddick	15	4	38	0	20	3	79	1	Wkt	1st	1st	2nd	2nd
DeFreitas	23	8	46	1	24	1	80	1	1st	128	71	23	73
Lewis	13	2	44	0	9	0	43	0	2nd	183	80	46	133
Such	33.3	9	67	6	31	6	78	2	3rd	221	84	155	171
Tufnell	28	5	78	2	37	4	112	1	4th	225	123	234	223
Hick					9	1	20	0	5th	232	148	252	230
									6th	260	168	–	238
AUSTRALIA									7th	264	178	–	260
McDermott	18	2	50	0	30	9	76	0	8th	266	183	–	299
Hughes	20.5	5	59	4	27.2	4	92	4	9th	267	203	–	331
Julian	11	2	30	2	14	1	67	1	10th	289	210	–	332
Warne	24	10	51	4	49	26	86	4					
Border	1	0	4	0									

Umpires: H.D.Bird (54) and K.E.Palmer (21).   Test No. 1223/275

ENGLAND v AUSTRALIA (2nd Test)

Played at Lord's, London, on 17, 18, 19, 20, 21 June 1993.
Toss: Australia.   Result: AUSTRALIA won by an innings and 62 runs.
Debuts: Nil.

AUSTRALIA

M.A.Taylor st Stewart b Tufnell	111	
M.J.Slater c sub (B.F.Smith) b Lewis	152	
D.C.Boon not out	164	
M.E.Waugh b Tufnell	99	
*A.R.Border b Lewis	77	
S.R.Waugh not out	13	
†I.A.Healy		
M.G.Hughes		
S.K.Warne	} did not bat	
T.B.A.May		
C.J.McDermott		
Extras (LB1, W1, NB14)	16	
Total (196 overs; 766 minutes)	632-4 dec	

ENGLAND

*G.A.Gooch c May b Hughes	12	c Healy b Warne	29	
M.A.Atherton b Warne	80	run out (Hughes/Healy)	99	
M.W.Gatting b May	5	lbw b Warne	59	
R.A.Smith st Healy b May	22	c sub (M.L.Hayden) b May	5	
G.A.Hick c Healy b Hughes	20	c Taylor b May	64	
†A.J.Stewart lbw b Hughes	3	lbw b May	62	
C.C.Lewis lbw b Warne	0	st Healy b May	0	
N.A.Foster c Border b Warne	16	c M.E.Waugh b Border	20	
A.R.Caddick c Healy b Hughes	21	not out	0	
P.M.Such c Taylor b Warne	7	b Warne	4	
P.C.R.Tufnell not out	2	b Warne	0	
Extras (LB8, NB9)	17	(B10, LB13)	23	
Total (99 overs; 333 minutes)	205	(165.5 overs; 552 minutes)	365	

ENGLAND	O	M	R	W	O	M	R	W	FALL OF WICKETS			
										A	*E*	*E*
Caddick	38	5	120	0					Wkt	1st	1st	2nd
Foster	30	4	94	0					1st	260	33	71
Such	36	6	90	0					2nd	277	50	175
Tufnell	39	3	129	2					3rd	452	84	180
Lewis	36	5	151	2					4th	591	123	244
Gooch	9	1	26	0					5th	–	131	304
Hick	8	3	21	0					6th	–	132	312
									7th	–	167	361
AUSTRALIA									8th	–	174	361
Hughes	20	5	52	4	31	9	75	0	9th	–	189	365
M.E.Waugh	6	1	16	0	17	4	55	0	10th	–	205	365
S.R.Waugh	4	1	5	0	2	0	13	0				
May	31	12	64	2	51	23	81	4				
Warne	35	12	57	4	48.5	17	102	4				
Border	3	1	3	0	16	9	16	1				

Umpires: M.J.Kitchen (6) and D.R.Shepherd (18).   Test No. 1224/276

ENGLAND v AUSTRALIA (3rd Test)

Played at Trent Bridge, Nottingham, on 1, 2, 3, 5, 6 July 1993.
Toss: England.   Result: MATCH DRAWN.
Debuts: England – M.C.Ilott, M.N.Lathwell, M.J.McCague, G.P.Thorpe.

ENGLAND

Batsman	1st innings		2nd innings	
M.N.Lathwell	c Healy b Hughes	20	lbw b Warne	33
M.A.Atherton	c Boon b Warne	11	c Healy b Hughes	9
R.A.Smith	c and b Julian	86	c Healy b Warne	50
†A.J.Stewart	c M.E.Waugh b Warne	25	lbw b Hughes	6
*G.A.Gooch	c Border b Hughes	38	c Taylor b Warne	120
G.P.Thorpe	c S.R.Waugh b Hughes	6	(7) not out	114
N.Hussain	c Boon b Warne	71	(8) not out	47
A.R.Caddick	lbw b Hughes	15	(6) c Boon b Julian	12
M.J.McCague	c M.E.Waugh b Hughes	9		
M.C.Ilott	c Taylor b May	6		
P.M.Such	not out	0		
Extras	(B5, LB23, W4, NB2)	34	(B11, LB11, NB9)	31
Total	(118.4 overs; 452 minutes)	321	(155 overs; 563 minutes)	422-6d

AUSTRALIA

Batsman	1st innings		2nd innings	
M.J.Slater	lbw b Caddick	40	(2) b Such	26
M.A.Taylor	c Stewart b McCague	28	(1) c Atherton b Such	28
D.C.Boon	b McCague	101	c Stewart b Caddick	18
M.E.Waugh	c McCague b Such	70	b Caddick	1
S.R.Waugh	c Stewart b McCague	13	(6) not out	47
†I.A.Healy	c Thorpe b Ilott	9	(7) lbw b Ilott	5
B.P.Julian	c Stewart b Ilott	5	(8) not out	56
*A.R.Border	c Smith b Such	38	(5) c Thorpe b Caddick	2
M.G.Hughes	b Ilott	17		
S.K.Warne	not out	35		
T.B.A.May	lbw b McCague	1		
Extras	(B4, LB8, W4)	16	(B5, LB5, W4, NB5)	19
Total	(108.3 overs; 474 minutes)	373	(76 overs; 314 minutes)	202-6

AUSTRALIA	O	M	R	W	O	M	R	W
Hughes	31	7	92	5	22	8	41	2
Julian	24	3	84	1	33	10	110	1
Warne	40	17	74	3	50	21	108	2
May	14.4	7	31	1	38	6	112	0
S.R.Waugh	8	4	12	0	1	0	3	0
M.E.Waugh	1	1	0	0	6	3	15	0
Border					5	0	11	0
ENGLAND								
McCague	32.3	5	121	4	19	6	58	0
Ilott	34	8	108	3	18	5	44	1
Such	20	7	51	2	23	6	58	2
Caddick	22	5	81	1	16	6	32	3

FALL OF WICKETS

	E	A	E	A
Wkt	1st	1st	2nd	2nd
1st	28	55	11	46
2nd	63	74	100	74
3rd	153	197	109	75
4th	159	239	117	81
5th	174	250	159	93
6th	220	262	309	115
7th	290	284	–	–
8th	304	311	–	–
9th	321	356	–	–
10th	321	373	–	–

Umpires: B.J.Meyer (25) and R.Palmer (2).   Test No. 1225/277

ENGLAND v AUSTRALIA (4th Test)

Played at Headingley, Leeds, on 22, 23, 24, 25, 26 July 1993.
Toss: Australia.   Result: AUSTRALIA won by an innings and 148 runs.
Debuts: England – M.P.Bicknell.

AUSTRALIA

M.J.Slater b Ilott	67	
M.A.Taylor lbw b Bicknell	27	
D.C.Boon lbw b Ilott	107	
M.E.Waugh b Ilott	52	
*A.R.Border not out	200	
S.R.Waugh not out	157	
†I.A.Healy		
M.G.Hughes		
P.R.Reiffel } did not bat		
S.K.Warne		
T.B.A.May		
Extras (B8, LB22, W4, NB9)	43	

Total (193 overs; 822 minutes)   653-4 dec

ENGLAND

M.N.Lathwell c Healy b Hughes	0	b May	25
M.A.Atherton b Reiffel	55	st Healy b May	63
R.A.Smith c and b May	23	lbw b Reiffel	35
†A.J.Stewart c Slater b Reiffel	5	c M.E.Waugh b Reiffel	78
*G.A.Gooch lbw b Reiffel	59	st Healy b May	26
G.P.Thorpe c Healy b Reiffel	0	c Taylor b Reiffel	13
N.Hussain b Reiffel	15	not out	18
A.R.Caddick c M.E.Waugh b Hughes	9	lbw b Hughes	12
M.P.Bicknell c Border b Hughes	12	lbw b Hughes	0
M.J.McCague c Taylor b Warne	0	b Hughes	11
M.C.Ilott not out	0	c Border b May	4
Extras (B2, LB3, NB17)	22	(B5, LB3, W1, NB11)	20

Total (82.5 overs; 311 minutes)   200   (127 overs; 473 minutes)   305

ENGLAND	O	M	R	W	O	M	R	W	FALL OF WICKETS
McCague	28	2	115	0					
Ilott	51	11	161	3					
Caddick	42	5	138	0					
Bicknell	50	8	155	1					
Gooch	16	5	40	0					
Thorpe	6	1	14	0					
AUSTRALIA									
Hughes	15.5	3	47	3	30	10	79	3	
Reiffel	26	6	65	5	28	8	87	3	
May	15	3	33	1	27	6	65	4	
Warne	23	9	43	1	40	16	63	0	
M.E.Waugh	3	0	7	0	2	1	3	0	

	A	E	E
Wkt	1st	1st	2nd
1st	86	0	60
2nd	110	43	131
3rd	216	50	149
4th	321	158	202
5th	–	158	256
6th	–	169	263
7th	–	184	279
8th	–	195	279
9th	–	200	295
10th	–	200	305

Umpires: H.D.Bird (55) and N.T.Plews (6).   Test No. 1226/278

ALLAN BORDER'S 200 not out

KIRKSTALL LANE END

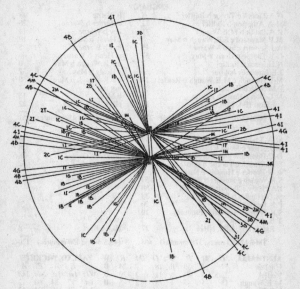

MAIN STAND END

BOWLER	SYMBOL	BALLS	1	2	3	4	TOTAL	PER 100 BALLS
BICKNELL	B	142	22	4	1	7	61	42.9
CADDICK	C	71	17	1	.	5	39	54.9
GOOCH	G	39	4	.	1	3	19	48.7
ILOTT	I	102	13	2	1	8	52	50.9
McCAGUE	M	30	4	2	1	3	23	76.6
THORPE	T	15	4	1	.	-	6	40.0
TOTALS		**399**	**64**	**10**	**4**	**26**	**200**	**50.1**

ENGLAND v AUSTRALIA
Fourth Test at Headingley on
22,23 and 24 JULY, 1993

in 569 minutes

BORDER'S 26th Test hundred
and highest score against England.

© BILL FRINDALL 1993

21

ENGLAND v AUSTRALIA (5th Test)

Played at Edgbaston, Birmingham, on 5, 6, 7, 8, 9 August 1993.
Toss: England.   Result: AUSTRALIA won by 8 wickets.
Debuts: Nil.   ‡(Maynard/Stewart)

ENGLAND

G.A.Gooch c Taylor b Reiffel	8	b Warne	48
*M.A.Atherton b Reiffel	72	c Border b Warne	28
R.A.Smith b M.E.Waugh	21	lbw b Warne	19
M.P.Maynard c S.R.Waugh b May	0	c Healy b Warne	10
†A.J.Stewart c and b Warne	45	lbw b Warne	5
G.P.Thorpe c Healy b May	37	st Healy b Warne	60
N.Hussain b Reiffel	3	c S.R.Waugh b May	0
J.E.Emburey not out	55	c Healy b May	37
M.P.Bicknell c M.E.Waugh b Reiffel	14	c S.R.Waugh b May	0
P.M.Such b Reiffel	1	not out	7
M.C.Ilott c Healy b Reiffel	3	b May	15
Extras (B4, LB6, NB7)	17	(B11, LB9, NB2)	22
Total (101.5 overs; 363 minutes)	276	(133.2 overs; 459 minutes)	251

AUSTRALIA

M.A.Taylor run out ‡	19	(2) c Thorpe b Such	4
M.J.Slater c Smith b Such	22	(1) c Thorpe b Emburey	8
D.C.Boon lbw b Emburey	0	not out	38
M.E.Waugh c Thorpe b Ilott	137	not out	62
*A.R.Border c Hussain b Such	3		
S.R.Waugh c Stewart b Bicknell	59		
†I.A.Healy c Stewart b Bicknell	80		
M.G.Hughes b Bicknell	38		
P.R.Reiffel b Such	20		
S.K.Warne c Stewart b Emburey	10		
T.B.A.May not out	3		
Extras (B7, LB8, NB2)	17	(B3, LB5)	8
Total (149.5 overs; 578 minutes)	408	(43.3 overs; 150 minutes)	120-2

AUSTRALIA	O	M	R	W	O	M	R	W
Hughes	19	4	53	0	18	7	24	0
Reiffel	22.5	3	71	6	11	2	30	0
M.E.Waugh	15	5	43	1	5	2	5	0
S.R.Waugh	5	2	4	0				
May	19	9	32	2	48.2	15	89	5
Warne	21	7	63	1	49	23	82	5
Border					2	1	1	0
ENGLAND								
Bicknell	34	9	99	3	3	0	9	0
Ilott	24	4	85	1	2	0	14	0
Such	52.5	18	90	3	20.3	4	58	1
Emburey	39	9	119	2	18	4	31	1

FALL OF WICKETS

	E	A	E	A
Wkt	1st	1st	2nd	2nd
1st	17	34	60	12
2nd	71	39	104	12
3rd	76	69	115	–
4th	156	80	115	–
5th	156	233	124	–
6th	160	263	125	–
7th	215	370	229	–
8th	262	379	229	–
9th	264	398	229	–
10th	276	408	251	–

Umpires: J.H.Hampshire (11) and D.R.Shepherd (19).   Test No. 1227/279

ENGLAND v AUSTRALIA (6th Test)

Played at Kennington Oval, London, on 19, 20, 21, 22, 23 August 1993.
Toss: England.   Result: ENGLAND won by 161 runs.
Debuts: Nil.

ENGLAND

G.A.Gooch	c Border b S.R.Waugh	56	c Healy b Warne	79
*M.A.Atherton	lbw b S.R.Waugh	50	c Warne b Reiffel	42
G.A.Hick	c Warne b May	80	c Boon b May	36
M.P.Maynard	b Warne	20	c Reiffel b Hughes	9
N.Hussain	c Taylor b Warne	30	c M.E.Waugh b Hughes	0
†A.J.Stewart	c Healy b Hughes	76	c M.E.Waugh b Reiffel	35
M.R.Ramprakash	c Healy b Hughes	6	c Slater b Hughes	64
A.R.C.Fraser	b Reiffel	28	c Healy b Reiffel	13
S.L.Watkin	c S.R.Waugh b Reiffel	13	lbw b Warne	4
P.M.Such	c M.E.Waugh b Hughes	4	lbw b Warne	10
D.E.Malcolm	not out	0	not out	0
Extras	(LB7, W1, NB9)	17	(B5, LB12, W1, NB3)	21
Total	**(101.5 overs; 423 minutes)**	**380**	**(119.2 overs; 472 minutes)**	**313**

AUSTRALIA

M.A.Taylor	c Hussain b Malcolm	70 (2)	b Watkin	8
M.J.Slater	c Gooch b Malcolm	4 (1)	c Stewart b Watkin	12
D.C.Boon	c Gooch b Malcolm	13	lbw b Watkin	0
M.E.Waugh	c Stewart b Fraser	10	c Ramprakash b Malcolm	49
*A.R.Border	c Stewart b Fraser	48	c Stewart b Malcolm	17
S.R.Waugh	b Fraser	20	lbw b Malcolm	26
†I.A.Healy	not out	83	c Maynard b Watkin	5
M.G.Hughes	c Ramprakash b Watkin	7	c Watkin b Fraser	12
P.R.Reiffel	c Maynard b Watkin	0	c and b Fraser	42
S.K.Warne	c Stewart b Fraser	16	lbw b Fraser	37
T.B.A.May	c Stewart b Fraser	15	not out	4
Extras	(B5, LB6, W2, NB4)	17	(B2, LB6, W2, NB7)	17
Total	**(94.4 overs; 409 minutes)**	**303**	**(81.1 overs; 336 minutes)**	**229**

AUSTRALIA	O	M	R	W	O	M	R	W
Hughes	30	7	121	3	31.2	9	110	3
Reiffel	28.5	4	88	2	24	8	55	3
S.R.Waugh	12	2	45	2				
Warne	20	5	70	2	40	15	78	3
M.E.Waugh	1	0	17	0				
May	10	3	32	1	24	6	53	1
ENGLAND								
Malcolm	26	5	86	3	20	3	84	3
Watkin	28	4	87	2	25	9	65	4
Fraser	26.4	4	87	5	19.1	5	44	3
Such	14	4	32	0	9	4	17	0
Hick					8	3	11	0

FALL OF WICKETS

	E	A	E	A
Wkt	1st	1st	2nd	2nd
1st	88	9	77	23
2nd	143	30	157	23
3rd	177	53	180	30
4th	231	132	180	92
5th	253	164	186	95
6th	272	181	254	106
7th	339	196	276	142
8th	363	196	283	143
9th	374	248	313	217
10th	380	303	313	229

Umpires: M.J.Kitchen (7) and B.J.Meyer (26).   Test No. 1228/280

ENGLAND v AUSTRALIA 1993

ENGLAND – BATTING AND FIELDING

	M	I	NO	HS	Runs	Avge	100	50	Ct/St
G.A.Gooch	6	12	–	133	673	56.08	2	4	2
M.A.Atherton	6	12	–	99	553	46.08	–	6	1
G.P.Thorpe	3	6	1	114*	230	46.00	1	1	5
G.A.Hick	3	6	–	80	256	42.66	–	2	–
A.J.Stewart	6	12	–	78	378	31.50	–	3	14/2
N.Hussain	4	8	2	71	184	30.66	–	1	2
R.A.Smith	5	10	–	86	283	28.30	–	2	2
M.W.Gatting	2	4	–	59	91	22.75	–	1	2
M.N.Lathwell	2	4	–	33	78	19.50	–	–	1
A.R.Caddick	4	8	1	25	101	14.42	–	–	2
C.C.Lewis	2	4	–	43	52	13.00	–	–	1
M.P.Maynard	2	4	–	20	39	9.75	–	–	2
P.M.Such	5	9	3	14*	56	9.33	–	–	2
M.C.Ilott	3	5	1	15	28	7.00	–	–	–
M.J.McCague	2	3	–	11	20	6.66	–	–	1
M.P.Bicknell	2	4	–	14	26	6.50	–	–	–
P.C.R.Tufnell	2	4	2	2*	3	1.50	–	–	1

Played in one Test: P.A.J.DeFreitas 5, 7 (1ct); J.E.Emburey 55*, 37; N.A.Foster 16, 20; A.R.C.Fraser 28, 13 (1ct); D.E.Malcolm 0*, 0*; M.R.Ramprakash 6, 64 (2ct); S.L.Watkin 13, 4 (1ct).

ENGLAND – BOWLING

	O	M	R	W	Avge	Best	5wI	10wM
A.R.C.Fraser	45.5	9	131	8	16.37	5- 87	1	–
S.L.Watkin	53	13	152	6	25.33	4- 65	–	–
D.E.Malcolm	46	8	170	6	28.33	3- 84	–	–
P.M.Such	239.5	64	541	16	33.81	6- 67	1	–
M.C.Ilott	129	28	412	8	51.50	3-108	–	–
P.C.R.Tufnell	104	12	319	5	63.80	2- 78	–	–
A.R.Caddick	153	28	488	5	97.60	3- 32	–	–

Also bowled: M.P.Bicknell 87-17-263-4; P.A.J.DeFreitas 47-9-126-2; J.E.Emburey 57-13-150-3; N.A.Foster 30-4-94-0; G.A.Hick 25-7-52-0; C.C.Lewis 58-7-238-2; M.J.McCague 79.3-13-294-4; G.P.Thorpe 6-1-14-0.

AUSTRALIA – BATTING AND FIELDING

	M	I	NO	HS	Runs	Avge	100	50	Ct/St
S.R.Waugh	6	9	4	157*	416	83.20	1	2	5
D.C.Boon	6	10	2	164*	555	69.37	3	1	5
M.E.Waugh	6	10	1	137	550	61.11	1	5	9
I.A.Healy	6	7	2	102*	296	59.20	1	2	21/5
A.R.Border	6	9	1	200*	433	54.12	1	1	8
M.A.Taylor	6	10	–	124	428	42.80	2	1	11
M.J.Slater	6	10	–	152	416	41.60	1	2	2
S.K.Warne	6	5	2	37	113	37.66	–	–	4
B.P.Julian	2	3	1	56*	61	30.50	–	1	2
P.R.Reiffel	3	3	–	42	62	20.66	–	–	1
M.G.Hughes	6	5	–	38	76	15.20	–	–	–
T.B.A.May	5	4	2	15	23	11.50	–	–	2
C.J.McDermott	2	2	–	8	8	8.00	–	–	–

AUSTRALIA – BOWLING

	O	M	R	W	Avge	Best	5wI	10wM
P.R.Reiffel	140.4	31	396	19	20.84	6-71	2	–
S.K.Warne	439.5	178	877	34	25.79	5-82	1	–
M.G.Hughes	296.2	78	845	31	27.25	5-92	1	–
T.B.A.May	278	90	592	21	28.19	5-89	1	–
B.P.Julian	82	16	291	5	58.20	2-30	–	–

Also bowled: A.R.Border 27-11-35-1; C.J.McDermott 48-11-126-0; M.E.Waugh 56-17-161-1; S.R.Waugh 32-9-82-2.

SRI LANKA v INDIA (1st Test)

Played at Asgiriya Stadium, Kandy, on 17‡, 18, 19‡, 21‡, 22‡ July 1993.
Toss: India.   Result: MATCH DRAWN.
Debuts: Nil.

(‡ no play)

SRI LANKA

R.S.Mahanama c More b Kapil Dev		0
U.C.Hathurusinghe c Kumble b Prabhakar		4
A.P.Gurusinha not out		10
P.A.De Silva c Kumble b Prabhakar		1
*A.Ranatunga not out		7
H.P.Tillekeratne		
†A.M.De Silva		
C.P.H.Ramanayake	did not bat	
D.K.Liyanage		
M.Muralitharan		
K.P.J.Warnaweera		
Extras (LB1, NB1)		2
Total (3 wickets)		24

INDIA

M.Prabhakar
N.S.Sidhu
V.G.Kambli
S.R.Tendulkar
*M.Azharuddin
P.K.Amre
Kapil Dev
†K.S.More
A.Kumble
R.K.Chauhan
J.Srinath

INDIA	O	M	R	W
Kapil Dev	5	1	10	1
Prabhakar	6	1	13	2
Srinath	1	1	0	0

FALL OF WICKETS

	SL
Wkt	1st
1st	0
2nd	6
3rd	8
4th	–
5th	–
6th	–
7th	–
8th	–
9th	–
10th	–

Umpires: K.T.Francis (9) and T.M.Samarasinghe (5).

Test No. 1229/9

SRI LANKA v INDIA (2nd Test)

Played at Sinhalese Sports Club, Colombo, on 27, 28, 29, 31 July, 1 August 1993.
Toss: India.   Result: INDIA won by 235 runs.
Debuts: Sri Lanka – R.S.Kalpage.   ‡(W.V.Raman)

INDIA

M.Prabhakar	lbw b Gurusinha	4	c Tillekeratne b Kalpage		95
N.S.Sidhu	c Tillekeratne b Warnaweera	82	c A.M.De Silva b Hathurusinghe		104
V.G.Kambli	c Mahanama b Hathurusinghe	125	c A.M.De Silva b Warnaweera		4
S.R.Tendulkar	c Tillekeratne b Kalpage	28	not out		104
*M.Azharuddin	lbw b Wickremasinghe	26	c Tillekeratne b Kalpage		21
P.K.Amre	c Kalpage b Warnaweera	21	not out		15
Kapil Dev	lbw b Gurusinha	35			
†K.S.More	c Mahanama b Warnaweera	4			
A.Kumble	lbw b Wickremasinghe	1			
R.K.Chauhan	c A.M.De Silva b Wickremasinghe	2			
J.Srinath	not out	0			
Extras	(B9, LB3, W10, NB16)	38	(B5, LB1, W2, NB8)		16
Total		**366**	(4 wickets declared)		**359**

SRI LANKA

R.S.Mahanama	c More b Prabhakar	22	lbw b Kapil Dev		9
U.C.Hathurusinghe	b Kumble	37	c Azharuddin b Prabhakar		43
A.P.Gurusinha	lbw b Prabhakar	4	c Chauhan b Kumble		39
P.A.De Silva	c Azharuddin b Kumble	22	c Azharuddin b Kumble		93
*A.Ranatunga	c Srinath b Kumble	88	c More b Prabhakar		14
H.P.Tillekeratne	c More b Srinath	28	c sub ‡ b Prabhakar		2
†A.M.De Silva	c Amre b Kumble	0	b Kapil Dev		1
R.S.Kalpage	c More b Srinath	1	c Amre b Srinath		5
D.K.Liyanage	b Kumble	2	c Azharuddin b Chauhan		8
G.P.Wickremasinghe	not out	11	lbw b Kumble		4
K.P.J.Warnaweera	b Prabhakar	20	not out		2
Extras	(B9, LB5, W4, NB1)	19	(B6, LB6, W3, NB1)		16
Total		**254**			**236**

SRI LANKA	O	M	R	W	O	M	R	W	FALL OF WICKETS				
Liyanage	19	3	64	0	10	2	31	0		I	SL	I	SL
Wickremasinghe	27	6	83	3	22	4	58	0	Wkt	1st	1st	2nd	2nd
Hathurusinghe	17	2	48	1	12	1	35	1	1st	25	48	171	44
Gurusinha	16	2	49	2	7	0	24	0	2nd	151	60	176	59
Warnaweera	20.1	1	76	3	20	1	86	1	3rd	219	85	263	127
Kalpage	8	1	34	1	38	3	97	2	4th	282	96	316	180
Ranatunga					2	1	5	0	5th	311	207	–	182
P.A.De Silva					7	0	17	0	6th	352	208	–	191
									7th	362	209	–	198
INDIA									8th	363	218	–	221
Kapil Dev	11	4	26	0	26	13	34	2	9th	366	218	–	229
Prabhakar	15.5	5	43	3	18	4	49	3	10th	366	254	–	236
Srinath	17	5	42	2	15	2	36	1					
Kumble	24	3	87	5	38.1	14	85	3					
Chauhan	10	1	42	0	24	18	20	1					

Umpires: S.Ponnadurai (3) and I Anandappa (3).   Test No. 1230/10

SRI LANKA v INDIA (3rd Test)

Played at P. Saravanamuttu Stadium, Colombo, on 4, 5, 7, 8, 9 August 1993.
Toss: Sri Lanka.   Result: MATCH DRAWN.
Debuts: Nil.

SRI LANKA

R.S.Mahanama lbw b Prabhakar	6	c Chauhan b Prabhakar	151
U.C.Hathurusinghe c Amre b Kapil Dev	6	c sub (W.V.Raman) b Raju	22
A.P.Gurusinha c Tendulkar b Kumble	56	c sub (W.V.Raman) b Kumble	35
P.A.De Silva c Raju b Kumble	148	c Kambli b Kumble	2
*A.Ranatunga c Kapil Dev b Raju	9	c Tendulkar b Prabhakar	13
H.P.Tillekeratne b Chauhan	51	c and b Kumble	86
S.T.Jayasuriya lbw b Chauhan	0	not out	31
†R.S.Kaluwitharana b Prabhakar	40		
G.P.Wickremasinghe c Tendulkar b Chauhan	0		
M.Muralitharan b Kapil Dev	7		
K.P.J.Warnaweera not out	1		
Extras (B3, LB20, W1, NB3)	27	(B6, LB4, W1, NB1)	12
Total	**351**	**(6 wickets)**	**352**

INDIA

M.Prabhakar c Jayasuriya b Wickremasinghe	55
N.S.Sidhu c Kaluwitharana b Wickremasinghe	39
V.G.Kambli lbw b Warnaweera	120
S.R.Tendulkar c Ranatunga b Hathurusinghe	71
*M.Azharuddin c Wickremasinghe b Muralitharan	50
P.K.Amre c Kaluwitharana b Wickremasinghe	21
A.Kumble b Muralitharan	9
Kapil Dev lbw b Warnaweera	27
†K.S.More c and b Muralitharan	4
R.K.Chauhan not out	15
S.L.V.Raju c Jayasuriya b Muralitharan	1
Extras (B5, LB12, W1, NB16)	34
Total	**446**

INDIA	O	M	R	W	O	M	R	W
Kapil Dev	27.1	10	56	2	24	11	33	0
Prabhakar	21	7	59	2	31	14	59	2
Raju	25	5	55	1	27	5	66	1
Tendulkar	3	0	4	0				
Kumble	40	12	95	2	38.2	7	108	3
Chauhan	26	7	59	3	33	5	76	0
SRI LANKA								
Wickremasinghe	38	8	95	3				
Gurusinha	11	1	27	0				
Warnaweera	23	2	86	2				
Hathurusinghe	20	6	53	1				
Ranatunga	4	2	2	0				
Muralitharan	47.1	12	136	4				
Jayasuriya	8	2	30	0				

FALL OF WICKETS

	SL	I	SL
Wkt	1st	1st	2nd
1st	13	86	75
2nd	29	109	142
3rd	165	271	144
4th	182	334	157
5th	281	384	289
6th	286	388	352
7th	309	397	–
8th	309	409	–
9th	347	437	–
10th	351	446	–

Umpires: B.C.Cooray (2) and P.Manuel (1).   Test No. 1231/11

SRI LANKA v INDIA 1993-94

SRI LANKA – BATTING

	M	I	NO	HS	Runs	Avge	100	50	Ct/St
P.A.De Silva	3	5	–	148	266	53.20	1	1	–
H.P.Tillekeratne	3	4	–	86	167	41.75	–	2	4
R.S.Mahanama	3	5	–	151	188	37.60	1	–	2
A.P.Gurusinha	3	5	1	56	144	36.00	–	1	–
A.Ranatunga	3	5	1	88	131	32.75	–	1	1
K.P.J.Warnaweera	3	3	2	20	23	23.00	–	–	–
U.C.Hathurusinghe	3	5	–	43	112	22.40	–	–	–
G.P.Wickremasinghe	2	3	1	11*	15	7.50	–	–	1
M.Muralitharan	2	1	–	7	7	7.00	–	–	1
D.K.Liyanage	2	2	–	8	10	5.00	–	–	–
A.M.De Silva	2	2	–	1	1	0.50	–	–	3

Played in one Test: S.T.Jayasuriya 0, 31* (2ct); R.S.Kalpage 1, 5 (1ct); R.S.Kaluwitharana 40 (2ct); C.P.H.Ramanayake did not bat.

SRI LANKA – BOWLING

	O	M	R	W	Avge	Best	5wI	10wM
M.Muralitharan	47.1	12	136	4	34.00	4-136	–	–
G.P.Wickremasinghe	87	18	236	6	39.33	3- 83	–	–
K.P.J.Warnaweera	63.1	4	248	6	41.33	3- 76	–	–
R.S.Kalpage	46	4	131	3	43.66	2- 97	–	–
U.C.Hathurusinghe	49	9	136	3	45.33	1- 35	–	–

Also bowled: P.A.De Silva 7-0-17-0; A.P.Gurusinha 34-3-100-2; S.T.Jayasuriya 8-2-30-0; D.K.Liyanage 29-5-95-0; A.Ranatunga 6-3-7-0.

INDIA – BATTING

	M	I	NO	HS	Runs	Avge	100	50	Ct/St
S.R.Tendulkar	3	3	1	104*	203	101.50	1	1	3
V.G.Kambli	3	3	–	125	249	83.00	2	–	1
N.S.Sidhu	3	3	–	104	225	75.00	1	1	–
M.Prabhakar	3	3	–	95	154	51.33	–	2	–
M.Azharuddin	3	3	–	50	97	32.33	–	1	4
Kapil Dev	3	2	–	35	62	31.00	–	–	3
P.K.Amre	3	3	1	21	57	28.50	–	–	3
R.K.Chauhan	3	2	1	15*	17	17.00	–	–	2
A.Kumble	3	2	–	9	10	5.00	–	–	5
K.S.More	3	2	–	4	8	4.00	–	–	3
J.Srinath	2	1	1	0*	0		–	–	1

Played in one Test: S.L.V.Raju 1 (1ct).

INDIA – BOWLING

	O	M	R	W	Avge	Best	5wI	10wM
M.Prabhakar	91.5	31	223	12	18.58	3-43	–	–
J.Srinath	33	8	78	3	26.00	2-42	–	–
A.Kumble	140.3	36	375	13	28.84	5-87	1	–
Kapil Dev	93.1	39	159	5	31.80	2-34	–	–
R.K.Chauhan	93	31	197	4	49.25	3-59	–	–

Also bowled: S.L.V.Raju 52-10-121-2; S.R.Tendulkar 3-0-4-0.

SRI LANKA v SOUTH AFRICA (1st Test)

Played at Tyronne Fernando Stadium, Moratuwa, on 25, 26, 28, 29, 30 August 1993.
Toss: Sri Lanka.   Result: MATCH DRAWN.
Debuts: Sri Lanka – P.B.Dassanayake, P.K.Wijetunge; South Africa – C.E.Eksteen,
P.L.Symcox.   ‡(S.T.Jayasuriya)

SRI LANKA

R.S.Mahanama b Schultz	53	lbw b Symcox		17
U.C.Hathurusinghe c Richardson b Donald	1	b Donald		9
A.P.Gurusinha c Richardson b Donald	26 (4)	b Schultz		27
P.A.De Silva c Wessels b Schultz	27 (5)	c Richardson b Symcox		68
*A.Ranatunga c Richardson b Donald	44 (6)	b Donald		131
H.P.Tillekeratne lbw b Schultz	92 (7)	not out		33
R.S.Kalpage c Richardson b Cronje	42 (8)	not out		0
†P.B.Dassanayake b Schultz	7			
P.K.Wijetunge b Donald	10 (3)	c Hudson b Symcox		0
G.P.Wickremasinghe c Rhodes b Donald	11			
M.Muralitharan not out	2			
Extras (LB11, W1, NB4)	16	(B3, LB6, NB6)		15
Total	331	(6 wickets declared)		300

SOUTH AFRICA

*K.C.Wessels c Tillekeratne b Muralitharan	47 (2)	c Wickremasinghe b Muralitharan		16
A.C.Hudson c Gurusinha b Wijetunge	90 (1)	c Dassanayake b Hathurusinghe		4
W.J.Cronje b Muralitharan	17	c sub ‡ b Wickremasinghe		1
D.J.Cullinan lbw b Hathurusinghe	33	lbw b Wickremasinghe		46
S.J.Cook b Wickremasinghe	7	c Tillekeratne b Wijetunge		24
J.N.Rhodes c Tillekeratne b Muralitharan	8	not out		101
†D.J.Richardson c and b Wickremasinghe	2	c Tillekeratne b De Silva		4
P.L.Symcox c Mahanama b Muralitharan	48	c Hathurusinghe b De Silva		21
C.E.Eksteen b Muralitharan	1	not out		4
A.A.Donald not out	0			
B.N.Schultz lbw b Kalpage	0			
Extras (LB4, W1, NB9)	14	(B10, LB4, W1, NB15)		30
Total	267	(7 wickets)		251

SOUTH AFRICA	O	M	R	W	O	M	R	W	FALL OF WICKETS				
										SL	SA	SL	SA
Donald	28	5	69	5	22	5	73	1	Wkt	1st	1st	2nd	2nd
Schultz	31.2	12	75	4	20	2	82	2	1st	5	104	26	13
Eksteen	14	4	44	0	9	2	34	0	2nd	77	152	26	15
Cronje	26	14	32	1	8	2	27	0	3rd	100	179	34	47
Symcock	28	3	100	0	21	2	75	3	4th	157	203	75	92
									5th	168	203	196	126
SRI LANKA									6th	258	206	299	138
Wickremasinghe	19	4	58	2	22	6	59	2	7th	273	240	–	199
Gurusinha	3	0	3	0					8th	285	262		
Kalpage	17.5	6	23	1	8	2	21	0	9th	313	267		
Wijetunge	29	2	58	1	23	3	60	1	10th	331	267		
Muralitharan	39	8	104	5	31	11	48	1					
De Silva	1	0	3	0	17	3	35	2					
Hathurusinghe	4	0	14	1	9	5	9	1					
Tillekeratne					2	0	5	0					

Umpires: B.L.Aldridge (18) and K.T.Francis (10).   Test No. 1232/1

SRI LANKA v SOUTH AFRICA (2nd Test)

Played at Sinhalese Sports Club Ground, Colombo, on 6, 7, 8, 10 September 1993.
Toss: Sri Lanka.   Result: SOUTH AFRICA won by an innings and 208 runs.
Debuts: Sri Lanka – H.D.P.K.Dharmasena.

SRI LANKA

R.S.Mahanama c Richardson b Schultz		7	b Schultz	0
U.C.Hathurusinghe c McMillan b Donald		34	c Cronje b Donald	0
H.P.Tillekeratne c Cronje b McMillan		9	c Richardson b Snell	9
P.A.De Silva c Richardson b Schultz		34	c and b Donald	24
*A.Ranatunga c Cullinan b Snell		11	(6) c Richardson b Schultz	14
S.T.Jayasuriya b Schultz		44	(7) b Schultz	16
†P.B.Dassanayake c Richardson b Donald		0	(8) c Richardson b Snell	10
H.D.P.K.Dharmasena c Richardson b Schultz		5	(9) c Richardson b Schultz	2
C.P.H.Ramanayake not out		1	(5) lbw b McMillan	0
G.P.Wickremasinghe b Schultz		17	c Donald b Snell	21
M.Muralitharan c Rhodes b Snell		0	not out	14
Extras (LB3, NB1)		4	(LB4, NB5)	9
Total		**168**		**119**

SOUTH AFRICA

*K.C.Wessels c Dassanayake b Muralitharan	92
A.C.Hudson lbw b Wickremasinghe	58
W.J.Cronje b De Silva	122
D.J.Cullinan c and b Muralitharan	52
J.N.Rhodes run out	10
B.M.McMillan b Muralitharan	0
†D.J.Richardson c Jayasuriya b Muralitharan	11
P.L.Symcox st Dassanayake b De Silva	50
R.P.Snell st Dassanayake b De Silva	48
A.A.Donald not out	4
B.N.Schultz st Dassanayake b Muralitharan	6
Extras (B5, LB20, W1, NB16)	42
Total	**495**

SOUTH AFRICA	O	M	R	W	O	M	R	W	FALL OF WICKETS			
										SL	SA	SL
Donald	12	4	22	2	10	7	6	2				
Schultz	20	8	48	5	16	4	58	4	Wkt	1st	1st	2nd
Snell	19	3	57	2	12	4	32	3	1st	7	137	1
McMillan	9	1	38	1	4	0	11	1	2nd	27	179	1
Symcox	2	2	0	0	1	0	8	0	3rd	72	284	30
									4th	85	306	31
SRI LANKA									5th	117	307	49
Ramanayake	20	5	63	0					6th	119	333	54
Wickremasinghe	31	6	111	1					7th	145	401	69
Hathurusinghe	7	4	12	0					8th	147	480	76
Dharmasena	45	12	91	0					9th	167	487	101
Muralitharan	54	17	101	5					10th	168	495	119
Jayasuriya	9	1	47	0								
De Silva	13	1	39	3								
Ranatunga	2	0	6	0								

Umpires: B.L.Aldridge (19) and T.M.Samarasinghe (6).   Test No. 1233/2

SRI LANKA v SOUTH AFRICA (3rd Test)

Played at P. Saravanamuttu Stadium, Colombo, on 14, 15, 16, 18, 19‡ September 1993.
Toss: South Africa.   Result: MATCH DRAWN.
Debuts: Nil.   # (D.P.Samaraweera) ‡(no play)

SOUTH AFRICA

A.C.Hudson c Tillekeratne b Dharmasena	22	(2) b Ramanayake	28
*K.C.Wessels b Liyanage	26	(1) c Mahanama b Hathurusinghe	7
W.J.Cronje b Ramanayake	24	not out	73
D.J.Cullinan c Ramanayake b Jayasuriya	102	c sub # b Dharmasena	4
J.N.Rhodes st Dassanayake b Muralitharan	7	b Muralitharan	19
B.M.McMillan c Jayasuriya b Muralitharan	2	not out	0
†D.J.Richardson c De Silva b Muralitharan	62		
P.L.Symcox c Tillekeratne b Ramanayake	30		
R.P.Snell not out	13		
A.A.Donald lbw b Ramanayake	1		
B.N.Schultz c De Silva b Muralitharan	0		
Extras (B6, LB10, NB11)	27	(B4, LB17, NB7)	28
Total	316	(4 wickets declared)	159

SRI LANKA

R.S.Mahanama c McMillan b Schultz	25
U.C.Hathurusinghe c Richardson b Donald	1
†P.B.Dassanayake run out	8
P.A.De Silva lbw b Symcox	82
*A.Ranatunga c Richardson b Schultz	50
H.P.Tillekeratne c Richardson b Schultz	37
S.T.Jayasuriya c Cronje b Schultz	65
H.D.P.K.Dharmasena c Richardson b Schultz	5
D.K.Liyanage b Donald	0
C.P.H.Ramanayake not out	0
M.Muralitharan did not bat	
Extras (B7, LB9, NB7)	23
Total (9 wickets declared)	296

SRI LANKA	O	M	R	W	O	M	R	W	FALL OF WICKETS			
Ramanayake	25	4	75	3	10	1	26	1		SA	SL	SA
Liyanage	21	4	58	1	4	1	17	0	Wkt	1st	1st	2nd
Hathurusinghe	6	4	6	0	8	4	7	1	1st	51	1	11
Dharmasena	28	5	79	1	18	8	29	1	2nd	53	27	58
Muralitharan	35.1	8	64	4	15	3	39	1	3rd	96	55	65
De Silva	1	0	9	0	3	1	3	0	4th	108	156	159
Jayasuriya	5	1	9	1	3	1	17	0	5th	128	202	–
									6th	250	263	–
SOUTH AFRICA									7th	281	273	–
Donald	30	12	62	2					8th	311	294	–
Schultz	36.5	9	63	5					9th	315	296	–
McMillan	30	8	64	0					10th	316	–	–
Snell	25	8	44	0								
Symcox	18	5	47	1								

Umpires: B.L.Aldridge (20) and B.C.Cooray (3).   Test No. 1234/3

SRI LANKA v SOUTH AFRICA 1993-94

SRI LANKA – BATTING

	M	I	NO	HS	Runs	Avge	100	50	Ct/St
A.Ranatunga	3	5	–	131	250	50.00	1	1	–
P.A.De Silva	3	5	–	82	235	47.00	–	2	2
H.P.Tillekeratne	3	5	1	92	180	45.00	–	1	6
S.T.Jayasuriya	2	3	–	65	125	41.66	–	1	2
R.S.Mahanama	3	5	–	53	102	20.40	–	1	2
G.P.Wickremasinghe	2	3	–	21	49	16.33	–	–	2
M.Muralitharan	3	3	2	14*	16	16.00	–	–	1
U.C.Hathurusinghe	3	5	–	34	45	9.00	–	–	1
P.B.Dassanayake	3	4	–	10	25	6.25	–	–	2/4
H.D.P.K.Dharmasena	2	3	–	12	12	4.00	–	–	–
C.P.H.Ramanayake	2	3	2	3*	3	3.00	–	–	1

Played in one Test: A.P.Gurusinha 26, 27 (1ct); R.S.Kalpage 42, 0*; D.K.Liyanage 0; P.K.Wijetunge 10, 0.

SRI LANKA – BOWLING

	O	M	R	W	Avge	Best	5wI	10wM
P.A.De Silva	35	5	89	5	17.80	3- 39	–	–
M.Muralitharan	174.1	47	356	16	22.25	5-101	2	–
C.P.H.Ramanayake	55	10	164	4	41.00	3- 75	–	–
G.P.Wickremasinghe	72	16	228	5	45.60	2- 58	–	–

Also bowled: H.D.P.K.Dharmasena 91-25-199-2; A.P.Gurusinha 3-0-3-0; U.C.Hathurusinghe 34-17-48-3; S.T.Jayasuriya 17-3-73-1; R.S.Kalpage 25.5-8-44-1; D.K.Liyanage 25-5-75-1; A.Ranatunga 2-0-6-0; H.P.Tillekeratne 2-0-5-0; P.K.Wijetunge 52-5-118-2.

SOUTH AFRICA – BATTING

	M	I	NO	HS	Runs	Avge	100	50	Ct/St
R.P.Snell	2	2	1	48	61	61.00	–	–	–
W.J.Cronje	3	5	1	122	237	59.25	1	1	3
D.J.Cullinan	3	5	–	102	237	47.40	1	1	1
A.C.Hudson	3	5	–	90	202	40.40	–	2	1
K.C.Wessels	3	5	–	92	188	37.60	–	1	1
P.L.Symcox	3	4	–	50	149	37.25	–	1	1
J.N.Rhodes	3	5	1	101*	145	36.25	1	–	2
D.J.Richardson	3	4	–	62	79	19.75	–	1	17
A.A.Donald	3	3	2	4*	5	5.00	–	–	2
B.N.Schultz	3	3	–	6	6	2.00	–	–	–
B.M.McMillan	2	3	1	2	2	1.00	–	–	–

Played in one Test: S.J.Cook 7, 24; C.E.Eksteen 1, 4*.

SOUTH AFRICA – BOWLING

	O	M	R	W	Avge	Best	5wI	10wM
B.N.Schultz	124.1	33	326	20	16.30	5-48	2	–
A.A.Donald	102	33	232	12	19.33	5-69	1	–
R.P.Snell	56	15	133	5	26.60	3-32	–	–
P.L.Symcox	70	12	230	4	57.50	3-75	–	–

Also bowled: W.J.Cronje 34-16-59-1; C.E.Eksteen 23-6-78-0; B.M.McMillan 43-9-113-2.

AUSTRALIA v NEW ZEALAND (1st Test)

Played at W.A.C.A. Ground, Perth, on 12, 13, 14, 15, 16 November 1993.
Toss: New Zealand.   Result: MATCH DRAWN.
Debuts: Australia – G.D.McGrath; New Zealand – B.A.Pocock.

AUSTRALIA

M.A.Taylor b Cairns		64	(2) not out	142
M.J.Slater c Patel b Cairns		10	(1) c Blain b Patel	99
D.C.Boon c Rutherford b Cairns		0	not out	67
M.E.Waugh lbw b Morrison		36		
*A.R.Border c Rutherford b Morrison		16		
S.R.Waugh c Blain b Patel		44		
†I.A.Healy not out		113		
P.R.Reiffel c Jones b Watson		51		
S.K.Warne c Patel b Cairns		11		
C.J.McDermott b Su'a		35		
G.D.McGrath lbw b Su'a		0		
Extras (B4, LB7, NB7)		18	(LB6, NB9)	15
Total		**398**	**(1 wicket declared)**	**323**

NEW ZEALAND

M.J.Greatbatch c Healy b McGrath		18	c Healy b McDermott	0
B.A.Pocock c Boon b McDermott		34	c Healy b McGrath	28
A.H.Jones c Healy b M.E.Waugh		143	lbw b M.E.Waugh	45
*M.D.Crowe c Taylor b Reiffel		42	not out	31
K.R.Rutherford c Healy b McDermott		17	lbw b S.R.Waugh	39
D.N.Patel c S.R.Waugh b Reiffel		20	not out	18
C.L.Cairns b Warne		78		
†T.E.Blain lbw b McDermott		36		
M.L.Su'a not out		14		
D.K.Morrison lbw McGrath		0		
W.Watson not out		0		
Extras (B1, LB6, NB10)		17	(LB1, NB4)	5
Total (9 wickets declared)		**419**	**(4 wickets)**	**166**

NEW ZEALAND	O	M	R	W	O	M	R	W	FALL OF WICKETS				
Morrison	35	4	113	2	25	5	80	0		A	NZ	A	NZ
Cairns	28	4	113	4	1	0	12	0	Wkt	1st	1st	2nd	2nd
Watson	24	11	52	1					1st	37	25	198	0
Su'a	19.5	2	72	2	20	0	71	0	2nd	37	100	–	66
Patel	8	0	37	1	39	4	144	1	3rd	100	199	–	85
Pocock					2	0	10	0	4th	129	239	–	145
									5th	164	275	–	–
AUSTRALIA									6th	198	292	–	–
McDermott	40	10	127	3	13	3	40	1	7th	291	394	–	–
McGrath	39	12	92	2	16	6	50	1	8th	329	413	–	–
Reiffel	24	2	75	2	7	2	25	0	9th	398	418	–	–
Warne	37.1	6	90	1	13	6	23	0	10th	398		–	–
M.E.Waugh	13	5	18	1	6	4	17	1					
S.R.Waugh	4	0	10	0	7	2	10	1					
Border	2	2	0	0									

Umpires: D.B.Hair (4) and A.J.McQuillan (1).   Test No. 1235/30

AUSTRALIA v NEW ZEALAND (2nd Test)

Played at Bellerive Oval, Hobart, on 26, 27, 28, 29 November 1993.
Toss: Australia.   Result: AUSTRALIA won by an innings and 222 runs.
Debuts: New Zealand – R.P.de Groen.

AUSTRALIA

M.A.Taylor c Jones b Su'a	27	
M.J.Slater c Morrison b Patel	168	
D.C.Boon c Jones b Doull	106	
M.E.Waugh c Doull b de Groen	111	
*A.R.Border c and b Morrison	60	
S.R.Waugh not out	25	
†I.A.Healy c Doull b de Groen	1	
P.R.Reiffel not out	23	
T.B.A.May		
S.K.Warne } did not bat		
C.J.McDermott		
Extras (B7, LB2, NB14)	23	
Total (6 wickets declared)	**544**	

NEW ZEALAND

M.J.Greatbatch c May b McDermott	12	c M.E.Waugh b McDermott	0
B.A.Pocock lbw b M.E.Waugh	9	st Healy b Warne	15
A.H.Jones c Healy b May	47	c Border b M.E.Waugh	18
*K.R.Rutherford c Taylor b May	17	b Warne	55
D.N.Patel c Taylor b Warne	18	lbw b May	16
C.Z.Harris c M.E.Waugh b May	0	b May	4
†T.E.Blain c Warne b May	40	c and b Warne	29
M.L.Su'a c Taylor b Warne	6	b Warne	5
D.K.Morrison c M.E.Waugh b May	0	b Warne	0
S.B.Doull lbw b Warne	0	c May b Warne	1
R.P.de Groen not out	0	not out	3
Extras (B2, LB1, NB9)	12	(B2, LB5, NB8)	15
Total	**161**		**161**

NEW ZEALAND	O	M	R	W	O	M	R	W	FALL OF WICKETS			
										A	NZ	NZ
Morrison	33	4	125	1					Wkt	1st	1st	2nd
Su'a	24	3	102	1					1st	65	15	1
Doull	21	0	99	1					2nd	300	47	29
de Groen	36	9	113	2					3rd	335	84	84
Patel	23	3	78	1					4th	485	105	103
Harris	2	0	18	0					5th	501	107	111
									6th	502	117	133
AUSTRALIA									7th	–	137	149
McDermott	15	3	29	1	17	8	42	1	8th	–	138	149
Reiffel	5	1	13	0	12	1	28	0	9th	–	139	158
S.R.Waugh	4	1	8	0					10th	–	161	161
M.E.Waugh	9	4	7	1	4	0	8	1				
May	31.3	10	65	5	25	13	45	2				
Warne	18	5	36	3	19.5	9	31	6				

Umpires: D.B.Hair (5) and W.P.Sheahan (1).   Test No. 1236/31

AUSTRALIA v NEW ZEALAND (3rd Test)

Played at Woolloongabba, Brisbane, on 3, 4, 5, 6, 7 December 1993.
Toss: New Zealand.   Result: AUSTRALIA won by an innings and 96 runs.
Debuts: New Zealand – B.A.Young.

NEW ZEALAND

B.A.Pocock	c Healy b McDermott	0	(2)	c Healy b McDermott	11
B.A.Young	c Healy b M.E.Waugh	38	(1)	b Warne	53
A.H.Jones	b Warne	56		c Border b Warne	15
*K.R.Rutherford	c Boon b McDermott	36		c Warne b McGrath	86
M.J.Greatbatch	c Healy b McDermott	35		lbw b McDermott	2
C.L.Cairns	c and b Warne	5		c Healy b McGrath	16
D.N.Patel	c Boon b May	1	(8)	b Warne	3
†T.E.Blain	not out	42	(7)	b McGrath	18
D.K.Morrison	c Healy b Warne	0		not out	20
S.B.Doull	c Healy b McDermott	10		c Taylor b Warne	24
R.P.de Groen	c Border b Warne	3		b May	6
Extras	(B2, LB3, NB2)	7		(B7, LB12, NB5)	24
Total		**233**			**278**

AUSTRALIA

M.J.Slater	c Blain b Patel	28
M.A.Taylor	c Pocock b Doull	53
D.C.Boon	c Blain b Doull	89
M.E.Waugh	c Greatbatch b Cairns	68
*A.R.Border	c Patel b de Groen	105
S.R.Waugh	not out	147
†I.A.Healy	run out	15
S.K.Warne	not out	74
C.J.McDermott		
T.B.A.May	} did not bat	
G.D.McGrath		
Extras	(B6, LB13, NB9)	28
Total (6 wickets declared)		**607**

AUSTRALIA	O	M	R	W	O	M	R	W
McDermott	23	11	39	4	25	4	63	2
McGrath	20	7	45	0	21	1	66	3
S.R.Waugh	3	0	13	0				
M.E.Waugh	10	4	14	1	6	1	30	0
May	21	7	51	0	16	3	41	1
Warne	28.3	12	66	4	35	11	59	4
NEW ZEALAND								
Morrison	33	3	104	0				
Cairns	36	7	128	1				
Doull	33	5	105	2				
de Groen	46	14	120	1				
Patel	33	4	125	1				
Jones	2	0	6	0				

FALL OF WICKETS

	NZ	A	NZ
Wkt	1st	1st	2nd
1st	2	80	34
2nd	96	102	80
3rd	98	227	81
4th	167	277	84
5th	170	436	138
6th	174	465	187
7th	174	–	218
8th	178	–	230
9th	193	–	265
10th	233	–	278

Umpires: P.D.Parker (1) and S.G.Randell (14).   Test No. 1237/32

AUSTRALIA v NEW ZEALAND 1993-94

AUSTRALIA – BATTING

	M	I	NO	HS	Runs	Avge	100	50	Ct/St
S.R.Waugh	3	3	2	147*	216	216.00	1	–	1
M.A.Taylor	3	4	1	142*	286	95.33	1	2	5
D.C.Boon	3	4	–	106	262	87.33	1	2	3
S.K.Warne	3	2	1	74*	85	85.00	–	1	4
M.J.Slater	3	4	–	168	305	76.25	1	1	–
P.R.Reiffel	2	2	1	51	74	74.00	–	1	1
M.E.Waugh	3	3	–	111	215	71.66	1	1	3
I.A.Healy	3	3	1	113*	129	64.50	1	–	13/1
A.R.Border	3	3	–	105	181	60.33	1	1	3
C.J.McDermott	3	1	–	35	35	35.00	–	–	–

Also played (2 Tests): G.D.McGrath O; T.B.A.May (2 ct) did not bat.

AUSTRALIA – BOWLING

	O	M	R	W	Avge	Best	5wI	10wM
S.K.Warne	151.3	49	305	18	16.94	6-31	1	–
M.E.Waugh	48	18	94	5	18.80	1- 7	–	–
T.B.A.May	93.3	33	202	9	22.44	5-65	1	–
C.J.McDermott	133	39	340	12	28.33	4-39	–	–
G.D.McGrath	96	26	253	6	42.16	3-66	–	–

Also bowled: A.R.Border 2-2-0-0; P.R.Reiffel 48-6-141-2; S.R.Waugh 18-3-41-1.

NEW ZEALAND – BATTING

	M	I	NO	HS	Runs	Avge	100	50	Ct/St
A.H.Jones	3	6	–	143	324	54.00	1	1	3
K.R.Rutherford	3	6	–	86	250	41.66	–	2	2
T.E.Blain	3	5	1	42*	165	41.25	–	–	4
C.L.Cairns	2	3	–	78	99	33.00	–	1	–
B.A.Pocock	3	6	–	34	97	16.16	–	–	1
D.N.Patel	3	6	1	20	76	15.20	–	–	3
M.L.Su'a	2	3	1	14*	25	12.50	–	–	–
M.J.Greatbatch	3	6	–	35	67	11.16	–	–	1
S.B.Doull	2	4	–	24	35	8.75	–	–	2
R.P.de Groen	2	4	2	6	12	6.00	–	–	–
D.K.Morrison	3	5	1	20*	20	5.00	–	–	2

Played in one Test: M.D.Crowe 42, 31*; C.Z.Harris 0, 4; W.Watson 0*; B.A.Young 38, 53.

NEW ZEALAND – BOWLING

	O	M	R	W	Avge	Best	5wI	10wM
C.L.Cairns	65	11	253	5	50.60	4-113	–	–
S.B.Doull	54	5	204	3	68.00	2-105	–	–
R.P.de Groen	82	23	233	3	77.66	2-113	–	–
M.L.Su'a	63.5	5	245	3	81.66	2- 72	–	–
D.N.Patel	103	11	384	4	96.00	1- 37	–	–
D.K.Morrison	126	16	422	3	140.66	2-113	–	–

Also bowled: C.Z.Harris 2-0-18-0; A.H.Jones 2-0-6-0; B.A.Pocock 2-0-10-0; W.Watson 24-11-52-1.

PAKISTAN v ZIMBABWE (1st Test)

Played at Defence Stadium, Karachi, on 1, 2, 3, 5, 6 December 1993.
Toss: Pakistan.   Result: PAKISTAN won by 131 runs.
Debuts: Zimbabwe – G.K.Bruk-Jackson, M.H.Dekker, S.G.Peall, J.A.Rennie,
  H.H.Streak, G.J.Whittal.

PAKISTAN

Aamir Sohail b Peall	63	run out	29
Shoaib Mohammad c A.Flower b Rennie	81		
Inzamam-ul-Haq c A.Flower b Brandes	21	(2) not out	57
Javed Miandad lbw b Brandes	70	run out	12
Basit Ali c A.Flower b Whittal	36	(3) c and b Brandes	12
Asif Mujtaba c Dekker b Brandes	4	(5) not out	10
†Rashid Latif not out	68		
*Waqar Younis c Peall b G.W.Flower	13		
Mushtaq Ahmed c A.Flower b Peall	18		
Tausif Ahmed not out	21		
Ata-ur-Rehman did not bat			
Extras (B15, LB12, NB1)	28	(B6, LB2, W1, NB1)	10
Total (8 wickets declared)	423	(3 wickets declared)	131

ZIMBABWE

G.W.Flower b Waqar	24	b Rehman	25
M.H.Dekker lbw b Waqar	5	lbw b Waqar	4
A.D.R.Campbell lbw b Mushtaq	53	c Inzamam b Mushtaq	8
D.L.Houghton lbw b Waqar	46	lbw b Waqar	18
*†A.Flower lbw b Rehman	63	c Inzamam b Mushtaq	21
G.J.Whittal run out	33	b Rehman	2
G.K.Bruk-Jackson b Waqar	31	lbw b Waqar	4
S.G.Peall c Aamir b Waqar	0	b Waqar	0
H.H.Streak b Waqar	0	not out	19
E.A.Brandes not out	0	b Waqar	17
J.A.Rennie lbw b Waqar	3	lbw b Waqar	0
Extras (B5, LB24, W1, NB1)	31	(B12, LB5, NB3)	20
Total	289		134

ZIMBABWE	O	M	R	W	O	M	R	W	FALL OF WICKETS			
										P	Z	P	Z
Brandes	35	4	106	3	13	0	59	1		*Wkt*	*1st*	*1st*	*2nd*	*2nd*
Streak	29	6	77	0	10	1	40	0	1st	95	16	47	1
Rennie	32	6	90	1	3	0	24	0	2nd	134	71	76	17
Whittal	12	4	26	1					3rd	217	132	108	61
Peall	41	10	89	2					4th	268	153	–	63
G.W.Flower	6	2	8	1					5th	280	230	–	65
									6th	305	280	–	78
PAKISTAN									7th	332	284	–	80
Waqar	34.1	8	91	7	21.5	7	44	6	8th	363	284	–	92
Rehman	15	5	28	1	16	6	20	2	9th	–	285	–	130
Mushtaq	39	11	89	1	17	7	24	2	10th	–	289	–	134
Tausif	23	7	49	0	6	2	13	0					
Shoaib	1	0	1	0									
Aamir	1	0	1	0	2	0	16	0					
Asif	3	2	1	0									

Umpires: Mahboob Shah (21) and Shakil Khan (4).   Test No. 1238/1

PAKISTAN v ZIMBABWE (2nd Test)

Played at Pindi Cricket Stadium, Rawalpindi, on 9, 10, 11, 13, 14 December 1993.
Toss: Zimbabwe.   Result: PAKISTAN won by 52 runs.
Debuts: Pakistan – Ashfaq Ahmed.

PAKISTAN

First innings		Second innings	
Aamir Sohail c Houghton b Streak	8	lbw b Streak	9
Shoaib Mohammad lbw b Brain	18	c A.Flower b Streak	13
Inzamam-ul-Haq b Brain	38	b Brandes	14
Javed Miandad b Streak	20	(5) b Streak	10
Basit Ali c Streak b Brandes	25	(6) lbw b Brandes	40
Asif Mujtaba not out	54	(7) c A.Flower b Brain	51
†Rashid Latif lbw b Brain	33	(8) c Houghton b Streak	61
*Wasim Akram c Campbell b Brandes	11	(9) lbw b Brandes	15
Waqar Younis lbw b Brandes	7	(10) c Campbell b Streak	17
Ata-ur-Rehman lbw b Brain	10	(4) lbw b Brain	0
Ashfaq Ahmed c A.Flower b Streak	0	not out	1
Extras (B4, LB12, W2, NB3)	21	(B1, LB11, W3, NB2)	17
Total	**245**		**248**

ZIMBABWE

First innings		Second innings	
G.W.Flower c Inzamam b Wasim	0	b Wasim	0
M.H.Dekker c Inzamam b Waqar	68	not out	68
A.D.R.Campbell lbw b Rehman	63	c Aamir b Rehman	75
D.L.Houghton c Asif b Ashfaq	5	lbw b Waqar	4
*†A.Flower c Wasim b Waqar	12	c Rashid b Waqar	0
G.J.Whittall c Inzamam b Ashfaq	29	lbw b Wasim	0
H.H.Streak c Inzamam b Waqar	2	(8) b Waqar	0
G.K.Bruk-Jackson c Aamir b Waqar	0	(7) c Rashid b Wasim	4
D.H.Brain c Rehman b Waqar	16	b Waqar	2
E.A.Brandes c Basit b Wasim	18	lbw b Wasim	1
S.G.Peall not out	11	c Inzamam b Wasim	10
Extras (B9, LB10, W1, NB10)	30	(B1, LB11, W1, NB10)	23
Total	**254**		**187**

ZIMBABWE	O	M	R	W	O	M	R	W
Brandes	32	5	82	3	31	9	71	3
Brain	32	9	41	4	34	6	73	2
Streak	23.2	5	58	3	20.3	3	56	5
Whittall	17	6	39	0	. 4	1	10	0
Peall	6	3	9	0	8	4	13	0
G.W.Flower					4	0	13	0
PAKISTAN								
Wasim	21	4	68	2	23.2	3	65	5
Waqar	19	3	88	5	21	4	50	4
Rehman	14	4	40	1	8	1	22	1
Ashfaq	17	8	31	2	6	1	22	0
Aamir	3	0	8	0				
Shoaib					4	1	16	0

FALL OF WICKETS

	P	Z	P	Z
Wkt	1st	1st	2nd	2nd
1st	29	0	25	0
2nd	33	102	38	135
3rd	99	110	39	140
4th	101	126	54	144
5th	131	131	58	147
6th	187	203	132	152
7th	209	203	209	153
8th	225	204	219	164
9th	241	225	240	168
10th	245	254	248	187

Umpires: Javed Akhtar (12) and Shakoor Rana (17).   Test No. 1239/2

PAKISTAN v ZIMBABWE (3rd Test)

Played at Gaddafi Stadium, Lahore, on 16, 17, 18, 20, 21 December 1993.
Toss: Zimbabwe.   Result: MATCH DRAWN.
Debuts: Zimbabwe – W.R.James.

PAKISTAN

Aamir Sohail	c Campbell b Brain	2	c James b Brain	32
Shoaib Mohammad	c Brandes b Rennie	14	not out	53
Inzamam-ul-Haq	b Brandes	33		
Javed Miandad	lbw b Brain	31		
Basit Ali	b Brain	29		
Asif Mujtaba	c James b Brain	0	(3) not out	65
†Rashid Latif	c Houghton b Brandes	7		
*Wasim Akram	not out	16		
Waqar Younis	b Brain	0		
Mushtaq Ahmed	b Brandes	1		
Ata-ur-Rehman	c James b Rennie	0		
Extras	(B4, LB6, NB4)	14	(B7, LB13, W1, NB3)	24
Total		**147**	**(1 wicket)**	**174**

ZIMBABWE

G.W.Flower	c Rashid b Rehman	30
M.H.Dekker	c Rashid b Wasim	2
A.D.R.Campbell	c Rashid b Waqar	6
D.L.Houghton	c Rashid b Waqar	50
*A.Flower	not out	62
G.J.Whittal	c Asif b Wasim	2
†W.R.James	c Shoaib b Waqar	8
H.H.Streak	b Waqar	0
D.H.Brain	c Aamir b Wasim	28
E.A.Brandes	lbw b Wasim	9
J.A.Rennie	c Rashid b Waqar	2
Extras	(B10, LB13, W1, NB7)	31
Total		**230**

ZIMBABWE	O	M	R	W	O	M	R	W	FALL OF WICKETS			
Brandes	14	3	45	3	16	5	31	0				
Brain	15	3	42	5	14	6	28	1	Wkt	1st	1st	2nd
Streak	12	3	28	0	16	4	25	0	1st	3	17	56
Rennie	10.4	3	22	2	14	6	35	0	2nd	50	35	–
G.W.Flower					10	2	15	0	3rd	54	88	–
Whittal					10.5	4	17	0	4th	107	121	–
Campbell					1	0	3	0	5th	111	126	–
A.Flower					0.1	0	0	0	6th	130	141	–
									7th	130	141	
PAKISTAN									8th	135	187	
Wasim	32	7	70	4					9th	140	215	
Waqar	34.4	9	100	5					10th	147	230	
Rehman	13	6	24	1								
Mushtaq	5	1	13	0								

Umpires: Athar Zaidi (4) and Khizer Hayat (28).   Test No. 1240/3

PAKISTAN v ZIMBABWE 1993-94

PAKISTAN – BATTING

	M	I	NO	HS	Runs	Avge	100	50	Ct/St
Asif Mujtaba	3	6	3	65*	184	61.33	–	3	2
Rashid Latif	3	4	1	68*	169	56.33	–	2	7
Shoaib Mohammad	3	5	1	81	179	44.75	–	2	1
Inzamam-ul-Haq	3	5	1	57*	163	40.75	–	1	7
Javed Miandad	3	5	–	70	143	28.60	–	1	–
Basit Ali	3	5	–	40	143	28.60	–	–	1
Aamir Sohail	3	6	–	63	143	23.83	–	1	4
Wasim Akram	2	3	1	16*	42	21.00	–	–	1
Mushtaq Ahmed	2	2	–	18	19	9.50	–	–	–
Waqar Younis	3	4	–	17	37	9.25	–	–	–
Ata-ur-Rehman	3	3	–	10	10	3.33	–	–	–

Played in one Test: Ashfaq Ahmed 0, 1*; Tausif Ahmed 21*.

PAKISTAN – BOWLING

	O	M	R	W	Avge	Best	5wI	10wM
Waqar Younis	130.4	31	373	27	13.81	7-91	4	1
Wasim Akram	76.2	14	203	11	18.45	5-65	1	–
Ata-ur-Rehman	66	22	134	6	22.33	2-20	–	–
Mushtaq Ahmed	61	19	126	3	42.00	2-24	–	–

Also bowled: Aamir Sohail 6-0-25-0; Ashfaq Ahmed 23-9-53-2; Asif Mujtaba 3-2-1-0; Shoaib Mohammad 5-1-17-0; Tausif Ahmed 29-9-62-0.

ZIMBABWE – BATTING

	M	I	NO	HS	Runs	Avge	100	50	Ct/St
A.D.R.Campbell	3	5	–	75	205	41.00	–	3	3
A.Flower	3	5	1	63	158	39.50	–	2	7
M.H.Dekker	3	5	1	68*	143	35.75	–	2	1
D.L.Houghton	3	5	–	50	123	24.60	–	1	3
G.W.Flower	3	5	–	30	79	15.80	–	–	–
D.H.Brain	2	3	–	28	46	15.33	–	–	–
G.J.Whittal	3	5	–	33	66	13.20	–	–	–
E.A.Brandes	3	5	1	18	45	11.25	–	–	2
G.K.Bruk-Jackson	2	4	–	31	39	9.75	–	–	–
S.G.Peall	2	4	1	11*	21	7.00	–	–	1
H.H.Streak	3	5	1	19*	21	5.25	–	–	1
J.A.Rennie	2	3	–	3	5	1.66	–	–	–

Played in one Test: W.R.James 8 (3 ct).

ZIMBABWE – BOWLING

	O	M	R	W	Avge	Best	5wI	10wM
D.H.Brain	95	24	184	12	15.33	5-42	1	–
E.A.Brandes	141	26	394	13	30.30	3-45	–	–
H.H.Streak	110.5	22	284	8	35.50	5-56	1	–
J.A.Rennie	59.4	15	171	3	57.00	2-22	–	–

Also bowled: A.D.R.Campbell 1-0-3-0; A.Flower 0.1-0-0-0; G.W.Flower 20-4-36-1; S.G.Peall 55-17-111-2; G.J.Whittal 43.5-15-92-1.

40

SRI LANKA v WEST INDIES (Only Test)

Played at Tyronne Fernando Stadium, Moratuwa, on 8‡, 9, 10, 11, 12‡, 13‡
December 1993.
Toss: Sri Lanka.   Result: MATCH DRAWN.
Debuts: Sri Lanka – D.P.Samaraweera.   (‡ no play)

SRI LANKA

R.S.Mahanama c Murray b Benjamin	11	c Simmons b Benjamin	11
D.P.Samaraweera c Harper b Hooper	16	run out	5
H.P.Tillekeratne c Lara b Harper	0	not out	9
P.A.De Silva b Benjamin	53	not out	15
*A.Ranatunga c Lara b Walsh	31		
S.T.Jayasuriya lbw b Benjamin	0		
R.S.Kalpage c Richardson b Ambrose	39		
†P.B.Dassanayake c Murray b Benjamin	18		
G.P.Wickremasinghe c Lara b Ambrose	0		
S.D.Anurasiri b Ambrose	1		
M.Muralitharan not out	1		
Extras (B1, LB9, NB10)	20	(LB2, NB1)	3
Total	190	(2 wickets)	43

WEST INDIES

D.L.Haynes lbw b Anurasiri	20
P.V.Simmons c Dassanayake b Kalpage	17
*R.B.Richardson c Dassanayake b Kalpage	51
B.C.Lara c Dassanayake b Muralitharan	18
K.L.T.Arthurton c Jayasuriya b Anurasiri	0
C.L.Hooper c Samaraweera b Muralitharan	62
R.A.Harper lbw b Jayasuriya	3
†J.R.Murray lbw b Anurasiri	7
W.K.M.Benjamin b Muralitharan	2
C.E.L.Ambrose not out	7
C.A.Walsh c Kalpage b Muralitharan	0
Extras (LB5, NB12)	17
Total	204

WEST INDIES	O	M	R	W	O	M	R	W	FALL OF WICKETS			
										SL	WI	SL
Ambrose	12.2	5	14	3	6	2	13	0	Wkt	1st	1st	2nd
Walsh	21	6	40	1	9.1	4	20	0	1st	18	42	17
Harper	24	12	36	1	1	0	3	0	2nd	20	42	18
Hooper	20	5	44	1					3rd	57	78	–
Benjamin	20	8	46	4	6	5	5	1	4th	106	84	–
Arthurton	1	1	0	0					5th	106	168	–
									6th	130	178	–
SRI LANKA									7th	181	191	–
Wickremasinghe	11	0	35	0					8th	182	191	–
Ranatunga	4	1	6	0					9th	188	204	–
Anurasiri	35	6	77	3					10th	190	204	–
Kalpage	10	2	27	2								
Muralitharan	15.5	4	47	4								
Jayasuriya	3	0	7	1								

Umpires: K.T.Francis (11) and T.M.Samarasinghe (7).   Test No. 1241/1

THE 1993 FIRST-CLASS SEASON
STATISTICAL HIGHLIGHTS

HIGHEST INNINGS TOTALS

653-4d	Australia v England (4th Test)	Leeds
632-4d	Australia v England (2nd Test)	Lord's
629	Nottinghamshire v Durham	Chester-le-St
591	Sussex v Essex	Hove
584	Middlesex v Glamorgan	Cardiff
568-7d	Worcestershire v Kent	Worcester
562-3d	Glamorgan v Middlesex	Cardiff
560	Worcestershire v Derbyshire	Kidderminster
560	Nottinghamshire v Lancashire	Manchester
559	Hampshire v Surrey	The Oval
558	Somerset v Sussex	Taunton
551-5d	Middlesex v Leicestershire	Lord's
524-6d	Kent v Glamorgan	Canterbury
521	Derbyshire v Gloucestershire	Cheltenham
520	Gloucestershire v Derbyshire	Cheltenham
515-9d	Durham v Lancashire	Manchester
501-7d	Gloucestershire v Hampshire	Bristol
500-6d	Somerset v Hampshire	Southampton
500-8d	Nottinghamshire v Derbyshire	Nottingham

HIGHEST FOURTH INNINGS TOTALS

412-3	Essex v Sussex (set 411)	Hove

LOWEST INNINGS TOTALS

68	Nottinghamshire v Surrey	The Oval
68	Middlesex v Worcestershire	Worcester
72	Lancashire v Somerset	Taunton
72	Leicestershire v Sussex	Horsham
83	Durham v Lancashire	Manchester
83	Zimbabweans v Kent	Canterbury
86	Oxford University v Durham	Oxford
88	Warwickshire v Surrey	Birmingham
88	Hampshire v Middlesex	Lord's
89	Derbyshire v Middlesex	Lord's
89	Durham v Northamptonshire	Northampton
90	Worcestershire v Australians	Worcester
95	Gloucestershire v Middlesex	Bristol
97	Leicestershire v Sussex	Horsham
97	Northamptonshire v Yorkshire	Harrogate
99	Oxford University v Glamorgan	Oxford

MATCH AGGREGATES OF 1400 RUNS

Runs-Wkts		
†1808-20	Sussex v Essex	Hove
1531-31	Kent v Essex	Maidstone
1497-38	Derbyshire v Lancashire	Derby
1457-35	Hampshire v Sussex	Portsmouth
1448-36	Somerset v Sussex	Taunton

†*Record first-class match aggregate in Britain*

VICTORY AFTER FOLLOWING-ON

Nottinghamshire (242 & 330-9d) beat Kent (394 & 104)	Nottingham

TIED MATCH

Worcestershire (203 & 325-8d) v Nottinghamshire (233 & 295)	Nottingham

FIRST TO INDIVIDUAL TARGETS

1000 RUNS	H.Morris	Glamorgan	July 1
2000 RUNS	G.A.Gooch	Essex and England	September 20
100 WICKETS	–. Highest aggregate: 92 by S.L.Watkin (Glamorgan and England)		

DOUBLE HUNDREDS (8)

R.J.Bailey	200	Northamptonshire v Sussex	Hove
A.R.Border	200*	Australia v England (4th Test)	Leeds
A.Dale	214*	Glamorgan v Middlesex	Cardiff
C.L.Hooper	236*	Kent v Glamorgan	Canterbury
C.C.Lewis	247	Nottinghamshire v Durham	Chester-le-St
J.E.Morris	229	Derbyshire v Gloucestershire	Cheltenham
P.J.Prichard	225*	Essex v Sussex	Hove
I.V.A.Richards	224*	Glamorgan v Middlesex	Cardiff

HUNDREDS IN THREE CONSECUTIVE INNINGS

D.C.Boon	112 v Durham, 107 v England (4th Test), 120 v Glamorgan	Durham/Leeds/ Neath

HUNDRED IN EACH INNINGS OF A MATCH (6)

D.C.Boon	108	106	Australians v Worcestershire	Worcester
N.A.Folland	101	108*	Somerset v Sussex	Taunton
G.A.Gooch	109	114	Essex v Hampshire	Chelmsford
H.Morris	102	133	Glamorgan v Nottinghamshire	Swansea
P.J.Prichard	104	106	Essex v Kent	Maidstone
R.T.Robinson	119	139*	Nottinghamshire v Glamorgan	Swansea

FASTEST AUTHENTIC HUNDREDS

P.Johnson	73 balls	Nottinghamshire v Glamorgan	Swansea
M.P.Maynard	73 balls	Glamorgan v Australians	Neath

In contrived circumstances, G.Chapple (Lancashire) scored 100 off 27 balls in 21 minutes against Glamorgan at Manchester.

HUNDRED ON FIRST-CLASS DEBUT

A.J.Hollioake	123	Surrey v Derbyshire	Ilkeston

HUNDRED BEFORE LUNCH (3)

		Day		
M.P.Maynard	132	2	Glamorgan v Australians	Neath
M.J.Slater	111*	1	Australians v Combined Us	Oxford
R.A.Smith	107*	2	Hampshire v Australians	Southampton

CARRYING BAT THROUGH COMPLETED INNINGS (3)

C.W.J.Athey	72*	Sussex (174) v Derbyshire	Derby
K.J.Barnett	108*	Derbyshire (214) v Glamorgan	Derby
K.J.Barnett	73*	Derbyshire (183) v Sussex	Derby

UNUSUAL DISMISSAL – HANDLED THE BALL

G.A.Gooch	England v Australia (1st Test)	Manchester

FIRST-WICKET PARTNERSHIP OF 100 IN EACH INNINGS (4)

127	179	G.D.Mendis/S.P.Titchard	Lancashire v Sussex	Manchester
135	143	N.J.Lenham/C.W.J.Athey	Sussex v Durham	Durham
291	150	P.R.Pollard/W.A.Dessaur	Nottinghamshire v Derbyshire	Nottingham
162	109	A.J.Moles/J.D.Ratcliffe	Warwickshire v Somerset	Birmingham

OTHER NOTABLE PARTNERSHIPS

First Wicket
291	P.R.Pollard/W.A.Dessaur	Nottinghamshire v Derbyshire	Nottingham
279	B.C.Broad/G.D.Hodgson	Gloucestershire v Hampshire	Bristol
260	M.A.Taylor/M.J.Slater	Australia v England (2nd Test)	Lord's

Second Wicket
313	J.W.Hall/C.M.Wells	Sussex v Cambridge University	Hove
299	D.J.Bicknell/G.P.Thorpe	Surrey v Worcestershire	Worcester
281	N.A.Felton/R.J.Bailey	Northamptonshire v Sussex	Hove
278	P.N.Hepworth/V.J.Wells	Leicestershire v Glamorgan	Leicester
275	P.D.Bowler/C.J.Adams	Derbyshire v Nottinghamshire	Nottingham
262	T.S.Curtis/G.R.Haynes	Worcestershire v Kent	Worcester

Third Wicket
321	M.W.Gatting/M.R.Ramprakash	Middlesex v Yorkshire	Scarborough
262	J.E.Emburey/M.W.Gatting	Middlesex v Glamorgan	Cardiff

Fourth Wicket
425*†	A.Dale/I.V.A.Richards	Glamorgan v Middlesex	Cardiff
290	Salim Malik/N.Hussain	Essex v Derbyshire	Chelmsford

Fifth Wicket
332*	A.R.Border/S.R.Waugh	Australia v England (4th Test)	Leeds
302*†	J.E.Morris/D.G.Cork	Derbyshire v Gloucestershire	Cheltenham

346 runs were added for this wicket in two separate partnerships.

Sixth Wicket
241	M.P.Speight/P.Moores	Sussex v Nottinghamshire	Eastbourne

Seventh Wicket
301†	C.C.Lewis/B.N.French	Nottinghamshire v Durham	Chester-le-St

†*County record.*

EIGHT OR MORE WICKETS IN AN INNINGS (6)
M.C.J.Ball	8-46	Gloucestershire v Somerset	Taunton
A.R.Caddick	9-32	Somerset v Lancashire	Taunton
J.E.Emburey	8-40	Middlesex v Hampshire	Lord's
M.A.Robinson	9-37	Yorkshire v Northamptonshire	Harrogate
P.C.R.Tufnell	8-29	Middlesex v Glamorgan	Cardiff
Wasim Akram	8-68	Lancashire v Yorkshire	Manchester

TEN OR MORE WICKETS IN A MATCH (28)
M.C.J.Ball		14-169	Gloucestershire v Somerset	Taunton
S.Bastien		12-105	Glamorgan v Essex	Cardiff
M.P.Bicknell	(2)	11-108	Surrey v Sussex	Hove
		11-192	Surrey v Worcestershire	Worcester
A.R.Caddick	(3)	10- 92	Somerset v Hampshire	Southampton
		12-120	Somerset v Lancashire	Taunton
		10-129	Somerset v Glamorgan	Taunton
M.Davies		10-141	Gloucestershire v Northamptonshire	Northampton
R.P.Davis		10-198	Kent v Nottinghamshire	Nottingham
P.A.J.DeFreitas		12-131	Lancashire v Somerset	Taunton
A.A.Donald		10-129	Warwickshire v Yorkshire	Birmingham
J.E.Emburey		12-115	Middlesex v Hampshire	Lord's
D.Gough		10- 96	Yorkshire v Somerset	Taunton

E.E.Hemmings		12- 58	Sussex v Leicestershire	Horsham
A.P.Igglesden		10-125	Kent v Durham	Darlington
A.D.Mullally		10-170	Leicestershire v Gloucestershire	Leicester
Mushtaq Ahmed (3)		10-145	Somerset v Worcestershire	Worcester
		12-175	Somerset v Sussex	Taunton
		10- 95	Somerset v Kent	Taunton
M.M.Patel		12-182	Kent v Lancashire	Lytham
M.A.Robinson		12-124	Yorkshire v Northamptonshire	Harrogate
P.M.Such	(3)	11-124	Essex v England A	Chelmsford
		10-146	Essex v Leicestershire	Southend
		10-160	Essex v Hampshire	Chelmsford
S.D.Udal	(2)	10-171	Hampshire v Nottinghamshire	Nottingham
		10-192	Hampshire v Warwickshire	Southampton
A.E.Warner		10-120	Derbyshire v Gloucestershire	Cheltenham
Wasim Akram		12-125	Lancashire v Yorkshire	Manchester

HAT-TRICK

| W.J.Holdsworth | | Australians v Derbyshire | Derby |

ELEVEN BOWLERS IN AN INNINGS

| Gloucestershire | Sussex (128-0) | Hove |

SIX OR MORE WICKET-KEEPING DISMISSALS IN AN INNINGS (3)

C.P.Metson	6ct	Glamorgan v Worcestershire	Worcester
A.J.Stewart	6ct	Surrey v Glamorgan	The Oval
T.J.Zoehrer	6ct, 2st	Australians v Surrey	The Oval

NINE OR MORE WICKET-KEEPING DISMISSALS IN A MATCH (4)

W.K.Hegg	8ct, 1st	Lancashire v Yorkshire	Manchester
C.P.Metson	9ct	Glamorgan v Worcestershire	Worcester
A.J.Stewart	9ct	Surrey v Glamorgan	The Oval
T.J.Zoehrer	7ct, 2st	Australians v Surrey	The Oval

NO BYES CONCEDED IN TOTAL OF 500 OR MORE

632-4d	A.J.Stewart	England v Australia (2nd Test)	Lord's
551-5d	P.A.Nixon	Leicestershire v Middlesex	Lord's
524-6d	C.P.Metson	Glamorgan v Kent	Canterbury
521	R.C.Russell	Gloucestershire v Derbyshire	Cheltenham
501-7d	A.N.Aymes	Hampshire v Gloucestershire	Bristol
500-8d	K.M.Krikken	Derbyshire v Nottinghamshire	Nottingham

FIFTY EXTRAS IN AN INNINGS

B	LB	W	NB†		
70	12	11	3	44	Nottinghamshire v Durham	Chester-le-St
59	13	14	–	32	Durham v Lancashire	Manchester
59	5	21	1	32	Surrey v Durham	The Oval
58	2	17	1	38	Sussex v Nottinghamshire	Eastbourne
56	2	18	–	36	Sussex v Somerset	Taunton
55	3	18	2	32	Durham v Warwickshire	Darlington
53	4	2	2	45	Hampshire v Australians	Southampton
53	9	7	1	36	Glamorgan v Warwickshire	Cardiff
53	6	20	4	23	Somerset v Derbyshire	Derby
53	5	14	–	34	Worcestershire (2nd inns) v Surrey	Worcester
50	–	18	–	32	Gloucestershire v Derbyshire	Cheltenham
50	9	12	1	28	Worcestershire (1st inns) v Surrey	Worcester

†*All instances under experimental no-ball law (penalty of 2 runs in addition to any scored or awarded).*

MIDDLESEX FIRST FOUR-DAY CHAMPIONS

Middlesex emerged worthy winners of the first 'pure' County Championship of this century; not since 1894, when there were only nine first-class counties, had the competition involved each team playing each of its opponents the same number of times.

Moreover, the four-day match programme produced a creditable increase in outright results with 104 wins and a tie from 153 matches (68.63%) compared with an identical number of wins from a hotchpotch of 197 three-and four-day games (52.79%) in 1992. Mercifully, there was only one outrageous instance of contrived trivia when Glamorgan's non-bowlers presented a Lancashire tail-ender with a 27-ball hundred.

Middlesex claimed the Britannic Assurance title and cricket's richest prize (£47,500) on 30 August, two days after trouncing holders Essex in just six sessions. It was the earliest the title had been resolved since 1979 (Essex – 21 August). Middlesex led the table from 7 June, at first jointly with Glamorgan who enjoyed their best season since 1970. Their encounter at Cardiff in early July provided the match of the season and a perfect exhibition of four-day cricket unencumbered by captains' manipulations. Hugh Morris terminated an unbroken record Glamorgan partnership (for any wicket) of 425 between Adrian Dale (214*) and Viv Richards (224*) by declaring at 562 for 3. Middlesex replied with 584, nightwatchman John Emburey (123) and Mike Gatting (173) adding 262 for the third wicket. Glamorgan (109) then collapsed against the spin of Phil Tufnell (8 for 29) and were defeated by ten wickets.

Gatting's third Championship title, which equalled the Middlesex record under Mike Brearley's captaincy, was gained without any batsman completing 1000 runs and owed much to the spin of Emburey and Tufnell who shared 127 wickets at 19.37 runs apiece. The highlight was the rehabilitation of Angus Fraser, whose 50 wickets were a tribute to the patience and perseverance of both the bowler and his mentor captain.

Worcestershire gained the runners-up prize of £23,750 by winning their last five matches, including a unique (two-day) defeat of the champions. Their rise of 15 places from the previous season is unmatched in the history of the Championship.

Essex secured most batting points but, deprived of the services of their guru, Keith Fletcher, their strike bowler, Neil Foster, and, for seven matches, their captain, Graham Gooch, they managed just four wins. Surrey mounted an early challenge but failed to win a match after July. Durham's mix of recruit and renegade proved unable to avoid another wooden spoon.

Bill Athey (1432 in his first summer with Sussex) scored most Championship runs and Mushtaq Ahmed (85 for Somerset) took most wickets. Nottinghamshire's erratic Chris Lewis recorded the season's highest innings (247), while 'Jack' Russell (60 dismissals for Gloucestershire) and John Carr, for the second successive year (39 catches for Middlesex), were the most successful wicket-keeper and fielder respectively.

BRITANNIC ASSURANCE
COUNTY CHAMPIONSHIP 1993
FINAL TABLE

		P	W	L	T	D	Bonus Bat	Points Bowl	Total Points
1	MIDDLESEX (11)	17	11	1	–	5	37	59	272
2	Worcestershire (17)	17	9	4	1	3	32	52	236
3	Glamorgan (14)	17	9	5	–	3	32	55	231
4	Northamptonshire (3)	17	8	4	–	5	35	59	222
5	Somerset (9)	17	8	7	–	2	26	59	213
6	Surrey (13)	17	6	6	–	5	40	60	196
7	Nottinghamshire (4)	17	6	3	1	7	34	56	194
8	Kent (2)	17	6	4	–	7	40	54	190
9	Leicestershire (8)	17	6	5	–	6	23	61	180
10	Sussex (7)	17	5	7	–	5	42	54	176
11	Essex (1)	17	4	6	–	7	44	55	163
12	Yorkshire (16)	17	5	4	–	8	21	56	157
13	Hampshire (15)	17	4	5	–	8	39	47	150
13	Lancashire (12)	17	4	8	–	5	38	48	150
15	Derbyshire (5)	17	4	7	–	6	33	50	147
16	Warwickshire (6)	17	4	8	–	5	24	49	137
17	Gloucestershire (10)	17	3	10	–	4	24	56	128
18	Durham (18)	17	2	10	–	5	29	52	113

1992 final positions are shown in brackets.

SCORING OF POINTS 1993

(a) For a win, 16 points, plus any points scored in the first innings.

(b) In a tie, each side to score eight points, plus any points scored in the first innings.

(c) If the scores are equal in a drawn match, the side batting in the fourth innings to score eight points, plus any points scored in the first innings.

(d) **First Innings Points** (awarded only for performances **in the first 120 overs** of each first innings and retained whatever the result of the match).

(i) A maximum of four batting points to be available as under—	(ii) A maximum of four bowling points to be available as under—
200 to 249 runs — 1 point	3 to 4 wickets taken — 1 point
250 to 299 runs — 2 points	5 to 6 wickets taken — 2 points
300 to 349 runs — 3 points	7 to 8 wickets taken — 3 points
350 runs or over — 4 points	9 to 10 wickets taken — 4 points

(e) If play starts when less than eight hours playing time remains and a one innings match is played, no first innings points shall be scored. The side winning on the one innings to score 12 points.

(f) A County which is adjudged to have prepared a pitch unsuitable for First-Class Cricket shall be liable to have 25 points deducted from its aggregate of points under the procedure agreed by the TCCB in December 1988.

(g) The side which has the highest aggregate of points gained at the end of the season shall be the Champion County. Should any sides in the Championship table be equal on points, the side with most wins will have priority.

COUNTY CHAMPIONS

The English County Championship was not officially constituted until December 1889. Prior to that date there was no generally accepted method of awarding the title; although the 'least matches lost' method existed, it was not consistently applied. Rules governing playing qualifications were not agreed until 1873, and the first unofficial points system was not introduced until 1888.

Research has produced a list of champions dating back to 1826, but at least seven different versions exist for the period from 1864 to 1889 (see *The Wisden Book of Cricket Records*). Only from 1890 can any authorised list of county champions commence.

That first official Championship was contested between eight counties: Gloucestershire, Kent, Lancashire, Middlesex, Nottinghamshire, Surrey, Sussex and Yorkshire. The remaining counties were admitted in the following seasons: 1891 – Somerset, 1895 – Derbyshire, Essex, Hampshire, Leicestershire and Warwickshire, 1899 – Worcestershire, 1905 – Northamptonshire, 1921 – Glamorgan, and 1992 – Durham.

The Championship pennant was introduced by the 1951 champions, Warwickshire, and the Lord's Taverners' Trophy was first presented in 1973. The first sponsors, Schweppes (1977 to 1983), were succeeded by BRITANNIC ASSURANCE in 1984.

Year	Champion	Year	Champion	Year	Champion
1890	Surrey	1927	Lancashire	1964	Worcestershire
1891	Surrey	1928	Lancashire	1965	Worcestershire
1892	Surrey	1929	Nottinghamshire	1966	Yorkshire
1893	Yorkshire	1930	Lancashire	1967	Yorkshire
1894	Surrey	1931	Yorkshire	1968	Yorkshire
1895	Surrey	1932	Yorkshire	1969	Glamorgan
1896	Yorkshire	1933	Yorkshire	1970	Kent
1897	Lancashire	1934	Lancashire	1971	Surrey
1898	Yorkshire	1935	Yorkshire	1972	Warwickshire
1899	Surrey	1936	Derbyshire	1973	Hampshire
1900	Yorkshire	1937	Yorkshire	1974	Worcestershire
1901	Yorkshire	1938	Yorkshire	1975	Leicestershire
1902	Yorkshire	1939	Yorkshire	1976	Middlesex
1903	Middlesex	1946	Yorkshire	1977	Kent / Middlesex
1904	Lancashire	1947	Middlesex		
1905	Yorkshire	1948	Glamorgan	1978	Kent
1906	Kent	1949	Middlesex / Yorkshire	1979	Essex
1907	Nottinghamshire			1980	Middlesex
1908	Yorkshire	1950	Lancashire / Surrey	1981	Nottinghamshire
1909	Kent			1982	Middlesex
1910	Kent	1951	Warwickshire	1983	Essex
1911	Warwickshire	1952	Surrey	1984	Essex
1912	Yorkshire	1953	Surrey	1985	Middlesex
1913	Kent	1954	Surrey	1986	Essex
1914	Surrey	1955	Surrey	1987	Nottinghamshire
1919	Yorkshire	1956	Surrey	1988	Worcestershire
1920	Middlesex	1957	Surrey	1989	Worcestershire
1921	Middlesex	1958	Surrey	1990	Middlesex
1922	Yorkshire	1959	Yorkshire	1991	Essex
1923	Yorkshire	1960	Yorkshire	1992	Essex
1924	Yorkshire	1961	Hampshire	1993	Middlesex
1925	Yorkshire	1962	Yorkshire		
1926	Lancashire	1963	Yorkshire		

WARWICKSHIRE WIN EPIC FINAL

Cricket's original cup final celebrated its thirtieth anniversary with a contest which may well come to be acclaimed as the greatest limited-overs match ever. Perhaps only Dermot Reeve, Warwickshire's unfazable captain, could have visualised a classic encounter after his bowlers had been ravaged for the highest total in any Lord's final. Certainly, most observers predicted a tedious second half and few challenged the bookmakers' odds of 7–1 on Sussex failing to defend their mammoth tally.

It was Martin Speight who inspired the day's batting feast. Called to arms when his side's most experienced batsman, Bill Athey, gloved a hook at the eighth ball of the innings, he evoked memories of Denis Compton as he danced down the pitch to drive and sweep two former Test bowlers as though they were slow trundlers. Speight's panache set the tempo for the match but, astonishingly, failed to earn him a winter tour. Spurred by his impetus, David Smith achieved the third highest score in a September show-piece and took the total beyond Yorkshire's record 317-4 in the 1965 final.

Warwickshire's gargantuan task of sustaining a run-rate of 5.36 for 60 overs appeared even more remote when both openers fell cheaply but Dominic Ostler and Paul Smith ignited a small spark of hope with a stand of 75 off 97 balls. Cue for Asif Din to play the innings of his life. His audacious wristy strokeplay blossomed in a run-a-ball partnership of 142 with his captain and was rewarded with a century, the match award, a new contract and a 1994 benefit. But it was Reeve, dropped by his opposite number when 2, who smote 4-2-2-4-1 off Franklyn Stephenson's final over in Stygian gloom.

Spare a thought for poor Sussex. The previous day they had been beaten in the highest-scoring first-class match ever staged in Britain.

GILLETTE CUP WINNERS

1963 Sussex	1969 Yorkshire	1975 Lancashire
1964 Sussex	1970 Lancashire	1976 Northamptonshire
1965 Yorkshire	1971 Lancashire	1977 Middlesex
1966 Warwickshire	1972 Lancashire	1978 Sussex
1967 Kent	1973 Gloucestershire	1979 Somerset
1968 Warwickshire	1974 Kent	1980 Middlesex

NATWEST TROPHY WINNERS

1981 Derbyshire	1986 Sussex	1991 Hampshire
1982 Surrey	1987 Nottinghamshire	1992 Northamptonshire
1983 Somerset	1988 Middlesex	1993 Warwickshire
1984 Middlesex	1989 Warwickshire	
1985 Essex	1990 Lancashire	

1993 NATWEST TROPHY FINAL

SUSSEX v WARWICKSHIRE

Played at Lord's, London, on 4 September.
Toss: Warwickshire.   Result: WARWICKSHIRE won by 5 wickets.
Match Award: Asif Din (Adjudicator: D.I.Gower).

SUSSEX	Runs	Min	Balls	6s	4s	Fall
D.M.Smith run out (Piper)	124	235	179	1	9	6-321
C.W.J.Athey c Piper b Munton	0	6	2	–	–	1-4
M.P.Speight c Piper b Reeve	50	73	51	1	8	2-107
*A.P.Wells b N.M.K.Smith	33	66	69	–	3	3-183
F.D.Stephenson c N.M.K.Smith b Twose	3	9	9	–	–	4-190
N.J.Lenham lbw b Reeve	58	65	51	–	6	5-309
K.Greenfield not out	8	7	7	–	1	–
†P.Moores						
I.D.K.Salisbury						
A.C.S.Pigott } did not bat						
E.S.H.Giddins						
Extras (LB11, W18, NB16)	45					
Total (60 overs; 235 minutes)	321-6 closed					

WARWICKSHIRE	Runs	Min	Balls	6s	4s	Fall
A.J.Moles c Moores b Pigott	2	18	7	–	–	2-18
J.D.Ratcliffe b Stephenson	13	14	17	–	2	1-18
D.P.Ostler c Smith b Salisbury	25	68	47	–	3	3-93
P.A.Smith c Moores b Stephenson	60	112	100	–	8	4-164
Asif Din c Speight b Giddins	104	145	106	–	6	5-306
*D.A.Reeve not out	81	108	85	–	6	–
R.G.Twose not out	2	8	1	–	–	–
N.M.K.Smith						
†K.J.Piper						
G.C.Small } did not bat						
T.A.Munton						
Extras (B3, LB13, W13, NB6)	35					
Total (60 overs; 241 minutes)	322-5					

WARWICKSHIRE	O	M	R	W	SUSSEX	O	M	R	W
Small	12	0	71	0	Giddins	12	0	57	1
Munton	9	0	67	1	Stephenson	12	2	51	2
P.A.Smith	7	0	45	0	Pigott	11	0	74	1
Reeve	12	1	60	2	Salisbury	11	0	59	1
N.M.K.Smith	12	1	37	1	Greenfield	7	0	31	0
Twose	8	1	30	1	Lenham	7	0	34	0

Umpires: H.D.Bird and M.J.Kitchen.

Congratulations
Warwickshire
on winning the 1993
NatWest Trophy.

THE NATWEST TROPHY 1993

FIRST ROUND 22 June	SECOND ROUND 7 July	QUARTER-FINALS 27, 28 July	SEMI-FINALS 10 August	FINAL 4 September
SUSSEX†	SUSSEX†			
Wales MC		SUSSEX		
HAMPSHIRE	Hampshire			
Staffordshire†			SUSSEX†	
NORTHAMPTONSHIRE†	NORTHAMPTONSHIRE			
Lancashire		Northamptonshire† (£3,750)		
ESSEX	Essex†			
Suffolk†				Sussex (£15,000)
GLAMORGAN†	GLAMORGAN†			
Oxfordshire		GLAMORGAN†		
DURHAM	Durham			
Wiltshire†			Glamorgan (£7,500)	
WORCESTERSHIRE	WORCESTERSHIRE†			
Scotland†		Worcestershire (£3,750)		
DERBYSHIRE	Derbyshire			
Devon†				
SURREY†	SURREY			
Dorset		Surrey (£3,750)		
LEICESTERSHIRE	Leicestershire†			
Buckinghamshire†			Somerset† (£7,500)	
SOMERSET	SOMERSET			
Shropshire†		SOMERSET†		
NOTTINGHAMSHIRE	Nottinghamshire†			
Cheshire†				WARWICKSHIRE (£30,000)
GLOUCESTERSHIRE†	Gloucestershire†			
Hertfordshire		Yorkshire† (£3,750)		
YORKSHIRE†	YORKSHIRE			
Ireland			WARWICKSHIRE	
KENT†	Kent			
Middlesex		WARWICKSHIRE		
WARWICKSHIRE	WARWICKSHIRE†			
Norfolk†				

† Home team. Winning teams are in capitals. Prize-money shown in brackets.

NATWEST TROPHY
PRINCIPAL RECORDS 1963-93
(Including The Gillette Cup)

Highest Total	413-4		Somerset v Devon	Torquay	1990
Highest Total in a Final	322-5		Warwicks v Sussex	Lord's	1993
Highest Total by a Minor County	305-9		Durham v Glam	Darlington	1991
Highest Total Batting Second	326-9		Hampshire v Leics	Leicester	1987
Highest Total to Win Batting 2nd	322-5		Warwicks v Sussex	Lord's	1993
Lowest Total	39		Ireland v Sussex	Lord's	1985
Lowest Total in a Final	118		Lancashire v Kent	Lord's	1974
Lowest Total to Win Batting First	98		Worcs v Durham	Chester-le-St	1968
Highest Score	206	A.I.Kallicharran	Warwicks v Oxon	Birmingham	1984
HS (Minor County)	132	G.Robinson	Lincs v Northumb	Jesmond	1971
Hundreds	232 have been scored in GC (93) and NWT (139) matches				
Fastest Hundred	36 balls – G.D.Rose		Somerset v Devon	Torquay	1990
Most Hundreds	7 C.L.Smith		Hampshire		1980-91

Highest Partnership for each Wicket

1st	248	D.M.Smith/C.W.J.Athey	Sussex v Hants	Hove	1993
2nd	286	I.S.Anderson/A.Hill	Derbys v Cornwall	Derby	1986
3rd	259*	H.Morris/M.P.Maynard	Glam v Durham	Darlington	1991
4th	234*	D.Lloyd/C.H.Lloyd	Lancashire v Glos	Manchester	1978
5th	166	M.A.Lynch/G.R.J.Roope	Surrey v Durham	The Oval	1982
6th	105	G.St A.Sobers/R.A.White	Notts v Worcs	Worcester	1974
	105	R.J.Blakey/C.White	Yorks v Warwicks	Leeds	1993
7th	160*	C.J.Richards/I.R.Payne	Surrey v Lincs	Sleaford	1983
8th	83	J.Hartley/D.A.Hale	Oxon v Glos	Oxford	1989
9th	87	M.A.Nash/A.E.Cordle	Glamorgan v Lincs	Swansea	1974
10th	81	S.Turner/R.E.East	Essex v Yorkshire	Leeds	1982
Most Runs	2287 (av 53.18)		G.A.Gooch	Essex	1973-93
Best Bowling	8-21	M.A.Holding	Derbys v Sussex	Hove	1988
	8-31	D.L.Underwood	Kent v Scotland	Edinburgh	1987
Hat-Tricks		J.D.F.Larter	Northants v Sussex	Northampton	1963
		D.A.D.Sydenham	Surrey v Cheshire	Hoylake	1964
		R.N.S.Hobbs	Essex v Middlesex	Lord's	1968
		N.M.McVicker	Warwicks v Lincs	Birmingham	1971
		G.S.Le Roux	Sussex v Ireland	Hove	1985
		M.Jean-Jacques	Derbyshire v Notts	Derby	1987
		J.F.M.O'Brien	Cheshire v Derbys	Chester	1988
Most Wickets	81 (av 14.85)		G.G.Arnold	Surrey	1963-80

Most Wicket-Keeping Dismissals in an Innings

6 (5ct, 1st)	R.W.Taylor	Derbyshire v Essex	Derby	1981
6 (4ct, 2st)	T.Davies	Glamorgan v Staffs	Stone	1986

Most Catches in an Innings

4 – A.S.Brown (Glos 1963), G.Cook (Northants 1972), C.G.Greenidge (Hants 1981), D.C.Jackson (Durham 1984), T.S.Smith (Herts 1984), H.Morris (Glam 1988), C.C.Lewis (Notts 1992).

Most Appearances	61		D.P.Hughes	Lancashire	1969-91
Most Match Awards	9		G.A.Gooch	Essex	1973-93
Most Match Wins	60 – Lancashire.		Most Cup/Trophy Wins	5 – Lancashire.

1993 BENSON AND HEDGES CUP FINAL

DERBYSHIRE v LANCASHIRE

Played at Lord's, London, on 10 July.
Toss: Lancashire.   Result: DERBYSHIRE won by 6 runs.
Match Award: D.G.Cork (Adjudicators: Cricket Writers' Club).

DERBYSHIRE	Runs	Min	Balls	6s	4s	Fall
*K.J.Barnett b Wasim Akram	19	43	41	–	3	2-32
P.D.Bowler lbw b DeFreitas	4	6	5	–	–	1-7
J.E.Morris c Hegg b Watkinson	22	56	37	–	4	3-61
C.J.Adams b Watkinson	11	23	12	–	1	4-66
T.J.G.O'Gorman c Hegg b DeFreitas	49	98	77	1‡	4	5-175
D.G.Cork not out	92	139	124	–	7	–
F.A.Griffith c Hegg b DeFreitas	0	11	1	–	–	6-175
†K.M.Krikken not out	37	41	35	–	3	–
A.E.Warner						
D.E.Malcolm } did not bat						
O.H.Mortensen						
Extras (B1, LB11, W1, NB5)	18		[‡ plus one 'five']			
Total (55 overs; 209 minutes)	252-6 closed					

LANCASHIRE	Runs	Min	Balls	6s	4s	Fall
M.A.Atherton c and b Griffith	54	144	111	–	4	3-150
S.P.Titchard c Adams b Warner	0	7	4	–	–	1-9
N.J.Speak b Mortensen	42	79	85	–	3	2-80
*N.H.Fairbrother not out	87	119	85	1	5	–
G.D.Lloyd lbw b Warner	5	9	12	–	–	4-159
Wasim Akram c and b Warner	12	15	13	–	1	5-184
M.Watkinson b Cork	10	18	12	–	1	6-218
P.A.J.DeFreitas c Krikken b Griffith	16	12	10	1	1	7-243
I.D.Austin not out	0	2	1	–	–	–
†W.K.Hegg } did not bat						
A.A.Barnett						
Extras (LB11, W3, NB6)	20					
Total (55 overs; 210 minutes)	246-7 closed					

LANCASHIRE	O	M	R	W	DERBYSHIRE	O	M	R	W
Austin	11	2	47	0	Malcolm	11	0	53	0
DeFreitas	11	2	39	3	Warner	11	1	31	3
Wasim Akram	11	0	65	1	Cork	11	1	50	2
Watkinson	11	2	44	2	Mortensen	11	0	41	1
Barnett	11	0	45	0	Griffith	11	0	60	2

Umpires: B.J.Meyer and D.R.Shepherd.

1993 BENSON AND HEDGES CUP

PRELIMINARY ROUND 27, 28 April	FIRST ROUND 11 May	QUARTER-FINALS 25, 26 May	SEMI-FINALS 8 June	FINAL 10 July
DERBYSHIRE	DERBYSHIRE†	DERBYSHIRE	DERBYSHIRE†	DERBYSHIRE (£30,000)
Gloucestershire†	Middlesex			
MIDDLESEX*				
SOMERSET*	SOMERSET	Somerset† (£3,750)		
NOTTINGHAMSHIRE*	Nottinghamshire†			
NORTHAMPTONSHIRE*	NORTHAMPTONSHIRE	NORTHAMPTONSHIRE	Northamptonshire (£7,500)	
YORKSHIRE*	Yorkshire†			
HAMPSHIRE†	HAMPSHIRE	Hampshire† (£3,750)	Leicestershire† (£7,500)	Lancashire (£15,000)
Combined Univs				
Minor Counties	Durham†			
DURHAM†				
WORCESTERSHIRE*	WORCESTERSHIRE†	Worcestershire (£3,750)		
ESSEX	Essex			
Scotland†				
LEICESTERSHIRE*	LEICESTERSHIRE†	LEICESTERSHIRE		
WARWICKSHIRE*	Warwickshire		LANCASHIRE	
GLAMORGAN	Glamorgan†	Sussex† (£3,750)		
Kent†	SUSSEX			
SUSSEX*				
SURREY*	Surrey†	LANCASHIRE		
LANCASHIRE*	LANCASHIRE			

† Home team. * Bye. Winning teams are in capitals. Prize-money shown in brackets.

BENSON AND HEDGES CUP
PRINCIPAL RECORDS 1972-93

Highest Total	388-7	Essex v Scotland	Chelmsford	1992
Highest Total Batting Second } Highest Losing Total	303-7	Derbys v Somerset	Taunton	1990
Lowest Total	50	Hampshire v Yorks	Leeds	1991
Highest Score	198* G.A.Gooch	Essex v Sussex	Hove	1982
Hundreds	228 have been scored in Benson and Hedges Cup matches			
Fastest Hundred	62 min – M.A.Nash	Glamorgan v Hants	Swansea	1976

Highest Partnership for each Wicket

1st	252	V.P.Terry/C.L.Smith	Hants v Comb Us	Southampton	1990
2nd	285*	C.G.Greenidge/D.R.Turner	Hants v Minor C (S)	Amersham	1973
3rd	269*	P.M.Roebuck/M.D.Crowe	Somerset v Hants	Southampton	1987
4th	184*	D.Lloyd/B.W.Reidy	Lancashire v Derbys	Chesterfield	1980
5th	160	A.J.Lamb/D.J.Capel	Northants v Leics	Northampton	1986
6th	121	P.A.Neale/S.J.Rhodes	Worcs v Yorkshire	Worcester	1988
7th	149*	J.D.Love/C.M.Old	Yorks v Scotland	Bradford	1981
8th	109	R.E.East/N.Smith	Essex v Northants	Chelmsford	1977
9th	83	P.G.Newman/M.A.Holding	Derbyshire v Notts	Nottingham	1985
10th	80*	D.L.Bairstow/M.Johnson	Yorkshire v Derbys	Derby	1981

Best Bowling	7-12	W.W.Daniel	Middx v Minor C (E)	Ipswich	1978
	7-22	J.R.Thomson	Middx v Hampshire	Lord's	1981
	7-32	R.G.D.Willis	Warwicks v Yorks	Birmingham	1981
Hat-Tricks		G.D.McKenzie	Leics v Worcs	Worcester	1972
		K.Higgs	Leics v Surrey	Lord's	1974
		A.A.Jones	Middlesex v Essex	Lord's	1977
		M.J.Procter	Glos v Hampshire	Southampton	1977
		W.Larkins	Northants v Comb Us	Northampton	1980
		E.A.Moseley	Glamorgan v Kent	Cardiff	1981
		G.C.Small	Warwickshire v Leics	Leicester	1984
		N.A.Mallender	Somerset v Comb Us	Taunton	1987
		W.K.M.Benjamin	Leics v Notts	Leicester	1987
		A.R.C.Fraser	Middlesex v Sussex	Lord's	1988

Most Wicket-Keeping Dismissals in an Innings

8 (8ct)	D.J.S.Taylor	Somerset v Comb Us	Taunton	1982

Most Catches in an Innings

5	V.J.Marks	Comb Us v Kent	Oxford	1976

Most Match Awards 20	G.A.Gooch	Essex	1973-93

BENSON AND HEDGES CUP WINNERS

1972	Leicestershire	1980	Northamptonshire	1988	Hampshire
1973	Kent	1981	Somerset	1989	Nottinghamshire
1974	Surrey	1982	Somerset	1990	Lancashire
1975	Leicestershire	1983	Middlesex	1991	Worcestershire
1976	Kent	1984	Lancashire	1992	Hampshire
1977	Gloucestershire	1985	Leicestershire	1993	Derbyshire
1978	Kent	1986	Middlesex		
1979	Essex	1987	Yorkshire		

SUNDAY LEAGUE
FINAL TABLE 1993

		P	W	L	T	NR	Pts
1	**GLAMORGAN** (16)	17	13	2	–	2	56
2	Kent (5)	17	12	3	–	2	52
3	Surrey (4)	17	11	4	–	2	48
4	Sussex (11)	17	10	5	1	1	44
5	Northamptonshire (13)	17	9	5	1	2	42
6	Lancashire (11)	17	8	5	1	3	40
7	Durham (8)	17	8	7	–	2	36
8	Middlesex (1)	17	7	6	2	2	36
9	Yorkshire (15)	17	8	8	–	1	34
10	Derbyshire (13)	17	7	8	–	2	32
11	Warwickshire (8)	17	7	8	–	2	32
12	Essex (2)	17	7	8	1	1	32
13	Gloucestershire (8)	17	5	9	1	2	26
14	Leicestershire (18)	17	5	10	–	2	24
15	Hampshire (3)	17	4	9	–	4	24
16	Worcestershire (7)	17	4	10	1	2	22
17	Nottinghamshire (17)	17	4	12	–	1	18
18	Somerset (5)	17	2	12	–	3	14

Win = 4 points. Tie/No Result = 2 points. When counties finish with an equal number of points, their places are decided by most wins or, if equal, by higher run-rate.

1992 final positions are shown in brackets.

The Sunday League's sponsors have been John Player & Sons (1969-1986), Refuge Assurance (1987-1991), TCCB (1992) and AXA Equity & Law Insurance (1993). The competition has been limited to 40 overs per innings, apart from 1993 when it was experimentally extended to 50.

WINNERS

1969 Lancashire	1978 Hampshire	1987 Worcestershire
1970 Lancashire	1979 Somerset	1988 Worcestershire
1971 Worcestershire	1980 Warwickshire	1989 Lancashire
1972 Kent	1981 Essex	1990 Derbyshire
1973 Kent	1982 Sussex	1991 Nottinghamshire
1974 Leicestershire	1983 Yorkshire	1992 Middlesex
1975 Hampshire	1984 Essex	1993 Glamorgan
1976 Kent	1985 Essex	
1977 Leicestershire	1986 Hampshire	

SUNDAY LEAGUE
PRINCIPAL RECORDS 1969-93

Highest Total		360-3	Somerset v Glam	Neath	1990
Highest Total Batting Second		317-6	Surrey v Notts	The Oval	1993
Lowest Total		23	Middlesex v Yorks	Leeds	1974
Highest Score		176	G.A.Gooch	Essex v Glamorgan	Southend	1983
Hundreds		457 have been scored in Sunday League matches			
Fastest Hundred		46 balls	G.D.Rose	Somerset v Glam	Neath	1990

Highest Partnership for each Wicket

1st	239	G.A.Gooch/B.R.Hardie	Essex v Notts	Nottingham	1985
2nd	273	G.A.Gooch/K.S.McEwan	Essex v Notts	Nottingham	1983
3rd	223	S.J.Cook/G.D.Rose	Somerset v Glam	Neath	1990
4th	219	C.G.Greenidge/C.L.Smith	Hampshire v Surrey	Southampton	1987
5th	190	R.J.Blakey/M.J.Foster	Yorkshire v Leics	Leicester	1993
6th	124*	J.J.Whitaker/P.A.Nixon	Leics v Surrey	The Oval	1992
7th	132	K.R.Brown/N.F.Williams	Middx v Somerset	Lord's	1988
8th	110*	C.L.Cairns/B.N.French	Notts v Surrey	The Oval	1993
9th	105	D.G.Moir/R.W.Taylor	Derbyshire v Kent	Derby	1984
10th	57	D.A.Graveney/J.B.Mortimore	Glos v Lancashire	Tewkesbury	1973

Best Bowling	8-26	K.D.Boyce	Essex v Lancashire	Manchester	1971
	7-15	R.A.Hutton	Yorkshire v Worcs	Leeds	1969
	7-39	A.Hodgson	Northants v Somerset	Northampton	1976
	7-41	A.N.Jones	Sussex v Notts	Nottingham	1986

Four Wkts in Four Balls A.Ward   Derbyshire v Sussex   Derby   1970

Hat-Tricks (22): Derbyshire – A.Ward (1970), C.J.Tunnicliffe (1979); Essex –
K.D.Boyce (1971); Glamorgan – M.A.Nash (1975), A.E.Cordle (1979), G.C.
Holmes (1987), A.Dale (1993); Gloucestershire – K.M.Curran (1989); Hampshire
– J.M.Rice (1975), M.D.Marshall (1981); Kent – R.M.Ellison (1983), M.J.
McCague (1992); Leicestershire – G.D.McKenzie (1972); Northamptonshire –
A.Hodgson (1976); Nottinghamshire – K.Saxelby (1987); Somerset – R.Palmer
(1970), I.V.A.Richards (1982); Surrey – M.P.Bicknell (1992); Sussex – A.Buss
(1974); Warwickshire – R.G.D.Willis (1973), W.Blenkiron (1974); Yorkshire –
P.W.Jarvis (1982).

Most Wicket-Keeping Dismissals in an Innings
7 (6ct, 1st) R.W.Taylor   Derbyshire v Lancs   Manchester   1975

Most Catches in an Innings
5   J.M.Rice   Hants v Warwicks   Southampton 1978

COUNTY CAPS AWARDED IN 1993

Derbyshire	D.G.Cork
Durham	D.M.Cox, A.C.Cummins, G.Fowler, J.P.Searle
Essex	M.C.Ilott
Glamorgan	R.P.Lefebvre
Gloucestershire	–
Hampshire	–
Kent	D.W.Headley, N.J.Llong
Lancashire	–
Leicestershire	A.D.Mullally
Middlesex	P.N.Weekes
Northamptonshire	–
Nottinghamshire	C.L.Cairns
Somerset	Mushtaq Ahmed
Surrey	J.E.Benjamin
Sussex	C.W.J.Athey, E.E.Hemmings
Warwickshire	N.M.K.Smith
Worcestershire	C.M.Tolley
Yorkshire	D.Gough, R.B.Richardson, C.White

MINOR COUNTIES CHAMPIONSHIP

FINAL TABLE 1993

		P	W	L	T	D	NR	Bonus Bat	Points Bowl	Total Points
EASTERN DIVISION										
Staffordshire	NW	9	5	1	0	3	0	22	18	120
Norfolk	NW	9	3	1	0	5	0	26	25	99
Cambridgeshire	NW	9	2	0	0	6	1	20	23	80
Northumberland	NW	9	2	3	0	4	0	17	20	69
Cumberland	NW	9	2	3	0	3	1	17	15	69
Lincolnshire	NW	9	2	3	0	4	0	18	17	67
Bedfordshire	NW	9	2	3	0	4	0	9	15	56
Hertfordshire		9	1	2	0	6	0	16	22	54
Buckinghamshire		9	1	2	0	6	0	20	16	52
Suffolk		9	1	3	0	4	0	10	17	43
WESTERN DIVISION										
Cheshire	NW	9	4	2	0	2	1	21	23	113
Oxfordshire	NW	9	4	0	0	4	1	19	22	110
Wales	NW	9	3	0	0	3	3	8	16	87
Berkshire	NW	9	2	3	0	4	0	17	24	73
Devon	NW	9	2	1	0	5	1	11	22	70
Wiltshire		9	1	0	0	6	2	20	19	*49
Shropshire		9	1	2	0	6	0	11	17	44
Herefordshire		9	0	3	0	5	1	17	21	43
Dorset		9	0	3	0	6	0	12	27	39
Cornwall		9	0	3	0	5	1	10	13	28

NW signifies qualification for 1994 NatWest Trophy.
*16 points deducted for breach of Regulations.

1993 CHAMPIONSHIP FINAL

CHESHIRE v STAFFORDSHIRE

Played at Worcester on 12, 13 September.
Toss: Cheshire.   Result: STAFFORDSHIRE won by 5 wickets.

CHESHIRE	Runs	Min	Balls	6s	4s	Fall
S.T.Crawley lbw b Newman	2	23	23	–	–	1-4
A.J.Hall c Humphries b Heap	9	44	35	–	1	2-15
T.J.Bostock b Myles	19	81	65	–	1	4-54
*I.Cockbain c Myles b Heap	8	21	23	–	1	3-29
J.D.Gray c Newman b Heap	54	125	100	–	6	5-167
R.G.Hignett b Newman	52	92	78	–	4	6-169
A.J.Murphy not out	6	6	6	–	–	–
J.F.M.O'Brien not out	1	3	1	–	–	–
G.Miller						
†T.P.A.Standing } did not bat						
N.D.Peel						
Extras (LB12, W9, NB2)	23					
Total (55 overs; 6 wickets)	174					

STAFFORDSHIRE	Runs	Min	Balls	6s	4s	Fall
S.J.Dean b Murphy	0	5	5	–	–	1-0
D.Cartledge c Crawley b Murphy	5	33	24	–	–	3-17
D.A.Banks b Miller	7	27	21	–	–	2-17
S.D.Myles not out	94	129	122	–	13	–
P.F.Shaw c Standing b Hignett	0	18	14	–	–	4-25
A.J.Dutton c Cockbain b Hignett	6	7	5	–	1	5-40
*P.G.Newman not out	33	118	88	–	1	–
†M.I.Humphries						
T.M.Heap						
R.A.Spiers } did not bat						
N.P.Hackett						
Extras (B2, LB12, W15, NB4)	33					
Total (46.1 overs; 5 wickets)	178					

STAFFORDSHIRE	O	M	R	W	CHESHIRE	O	M	R	W
Newman	11	4	34	2	Murphy	10	3	25	2
Hackett	11	2	20	0	Miller	9.1	2	23	1
Heap	11	3	37	3	Peel	7	1	24	0
Myles	11	0	38	1	Hignett	9	0	46	2
Dutton	11	2	33	0	O'Brien	9	1	36	0
					Crawley	2	0	10	0

Umpires: P.Adams and J.G.Wilson.

MINOR COUNTIES CHAMPIONS

Year	Champion	Year	Champion	Year	Champion
1895 {	Norfolk	1927	Staffordshire	1964	Lancashire II
	Durham	1928	Berkshire	1965	Somerset II
	Worcestershire	1929	Oxfordshire	1966	Lincolnshire
1896	Worcestershire	1930	Durham	1967	Cheshire
1897	Worcestershire	1931	Leicestershire II	1968	Yorkshire II
1898	Worcestershire	1932	Buckinghamshire	1969	Buckinghamshire
1899 {	Northamptonshire	1933	Undecided	1970	Bedfordshire
	Buckinghamshire	1934	Lancashire II	1971	Yorkshire II
	Glamorgan	1935	Middlesex II	1972	Bedfordshire
1900 {	Durham	1936	Hertfordshire	1973	Shropshire
	Northamptonshire	1937	Lancashire II	1974	Oxfordshire
1901	Durham	1938	Buckinghamshire	1975	Hertfordshire
1902	Wiltshire	1939	Surrey II	1976	Durham
1903	Northamptonshire	1946	Suffolk	1977	Suffolk
1904	Northamptonshire	1947	Yorkshire II	1978	Devon
1905	Norfolk	1948	Lancashire II	1979	Suffolk
1906	Staffordshire	1949	Lancashire II	1980	Durham
1907	Lancashire II	1950	Surrey II	1981	Durham
1908	Staffordshire	1951	Kent II	1982	Oxfordshire
1909	Wiltshire	1952	Buckinghamshire	1983	Hertfordshire
1910	Norfolk	1953	Berkshire	1984	Durham
1911	Staffordshire	1954	Surrey II	1985	Cheshire
1912	In abeyance	1955	Surrey II	1986	Cumberland
1913	Norfolk	1956	Kent II	1987	Buckinghamshire
1920	Staffordshire	1957	Yorkshire II	1988	Cheshire
1921	Staffordshire	1958	Yorkshire II	1989	Oxfordshire
1922	Buckinghamshire	1959	Warwickshire II	1990	Hertfordshire
1923	Buckinghamshire	1960	Lancashire II	1991	Staffordshire
1924	Berkshire	1961	Somerset II	1992	Staffordshire
1925	Buckinghamshire	1962	Warwickshire II	1993	Staffordshire
1926	Durham	1963	Cambridgeshire		

MINOR COUNTIES CHAMPIONSHIP RECORDS

Highest Total	621		Surrey II v Devon	The Oval 1928
Lowest Total	14		Cheshire v Staffs	Stoke 1909
Highest Score	282	E.Garnett	Berkshire v Wiltshire	Reading 1908
Most Runs – Season	1212	A.F.Brazier	Surrey II	1949

Record Partnership

2nd	388*	T.H.Clark and A.F.Brazier	Surrey II v Sussex II	The Oval	1949
Best Bowling – Innings	10- 11	S.Turner	Cambs v Cumberland	Penrith	1987
– Match	18-100	N.W.Harding	Kent II v Wiltshire	Swindon	1937
Most Wickets – Season	119	S.F.Barnes	Staffordshire		1906

1993 MINOR COUNTIES CHAMPIONSHIP

LEADING BATTING AVERAGES
(Qualification. 8 completed innings (or 500 runs), average 39.00)

		I	NO	HS	Runs	Avge
R.J.Evans	Lincs	13	4	153*	819	91.00
S.C.Goldsmith	Norfolk	17	4	200*	917	70.54
A.Needham	Herts	16	8	110	557	69.63
K.Sharp	Shropshire	15	5	136*	564	56.40
R.J.Bartlett	Cornwall	13	2	146*	598	54.36
C.K.Bullen	Beds	15	3	126*	613	51.08
S.N.Dutton	Cumberland	13	4	62	455	50.56
M.R.Gouldstone	Herts	17	5	116*	602	50.17
M.J.Roberts	Bucks	12	1	112*	547	49.73
S.N.V.Waterton	Oxon	16	2	100*	693	49.50
D.J.M.Mercer	Berkshire	14	3	118*	543	49.36
S.D.Myles	Staffs	14	4	91	494	49.40
B.Roberts	Cambs	12	3	87	444	49.33
R.J.Finney	Norfolk	15	4	107*	522	47.45
R.R.Savage	Wiltshire	15	4	114	519	47.18
D.J.Pearson	Cumberland	15	2	114*	590	45.38
S.J.Dean	Staffs	13	–	81	579	44.54
L.K.Smith	Wiltshire	16	–	119	702	43.88
T.J.A.Scriven	Bucks	17	2	94	656	43.73
J.J.E.Hardy	Dorset	18	5	75	557	42.85
S.G.Plumb	Norfolk	18	4	107*	586	41.86
A.W.Harris	Wales	11	1	88	405	40.50
G.W.Ecclestone	Cambs	16	4	104*	481	40.08
R.G.Hignett	Cheshire	14	5	71*	359	39.89
S.M.Willis	Devon	16	2	127*	551	39.36
J.D.Gray	Cheshire	13	3	72	390	39.00

LEADING BOWLING AVERAGES
(Qualification: 20 wickets, average 30.00)

		O	M	R	W	Avge
P.G.Newman	Staffs	308.2	88	672	50	13.44
D.R.Thomas	Norfolk	137.3	40	357	24	14.88
K.A.Arnold	Oxon	212.4	56	507	28	18.11
G.Miller	Cheshire	319.1	104	648	35	18.51
S.Turner	Cambs	245.1	76	523	28	18.68
I.J.Curtis	Oxon	209.2	49	630	33	19.09
P.J.Lewington	Berkshire	232.1	54	693	35	19.80
A.Smith	Wales	184.5	49	555	28	19.82
A.K.Golding	Suffolk	218.3	57	577	28	20.61
P.M.Roebuck	Devon	195.4	68	441	21	21.00
P.M.Blakeley	Shropshire	162.1	48	492	23	21.39
J.F.M.O'Brien	Cheshire	297.3	81	801	36	22.25
P.D.Thomas	Beds	119.1	18	501	22	22.77
A.Needham	Herts	245.2	62	734	32	22.94
R.A.Evans	Oxon	213.3	57	555	24	23.13
I.E.Conn	N'land	198.5	37	693	28	24.75
R.A.Bunting	Norfolk	254.4	45	895	36	24.86
S.R.Walbridge	Dorset	240	62	719	28	25.68
G.Angus	N'land	160.5	30	619	22	28.14
S.G.Plumb	Norfolk	196.3	52	602	21	28.67

SECOND XI CHAMPIONSHIP 1993
RAPID CRICKETLINE FINAL TABLE

	P	W	L	D	Bonus Points Bat	Bowl	Total Points
1 MIDDLESEX (6)	17	7	1	9	50	44	206
2 Lancashire (10)	17	6	2	9	42	47	185
3 Yorkshire (5)	17	6	1	10	45	45	182
4 Gloucestershire (3)	17	4	1	12	50	63	177
5 Nottinghamshire (14)	17	5	4	8	42	54	176
6 Surrey (1)	17	5	4	8	39	52	171
7 Essex (18)	17	5	7	5	34	54	168
8 Sussex (9)	17	4	7	6	42	45	151
9 Somerset (13)	17	4	4	9	44	42	150
10 Hampshire (4)	17	3	1	13	40	48	136
11 Kent (8)	17	3	4	10	40	37	125
12 Northamptonshire (2)	17	3	2	12	33	36	123
13 Leicestershire (15)	17	3	5	9	26	47	117
14 Durham (6)	17	2	6	9	38	46	116
15 Warwickshire (12)	17	2	4	11	38	43	113
16 Worcestershire (16)	17	3	3	11	28	34	110
17 Derbyshire (11)	17	1	2	14	35	39	86
18 Glamorgan (17)	17	1	9	7	28	39	83

Win = 16 points. One innings matches: Derbyshire, Leicestershire and Yorkshire totals include 12 points for winning; Northamptonshire's includes 6 points for drawing with the scores level. 1992 final positions are shown in brackets.

RAPID CRICKETLINE CHAMPIONSHIP PLAYER OF THE SEASON:
K.P.Dutch (Middlesex)

SECOND XI CHAMPIONS

1959 Gloucestershire	1971 Hampshire	1983 Leicestershire
1960 Northamptonshire	1972 Nottinghamshire	1984 Yorkshire
1961 Kent	1973 Essex	1985 Nottinghamshire
1962 Worcestershire	1974 Middlesex	1986 Lancashire
1963 Worcestershire	1975 Surrey	1987 Kent/Yorkshire
1964 Lancashire	1976 Kent	1988 Surrey
1965 Glamorgan	1977 Yorkshire	1989 Middlesex
1966 Surrey	1978 Sussex	1990 Sussex
1967 Hampshire	1979 Warwickshire	1991 Yorkshire
1968 Surrey	1980 Glamorgan	1992 Surrey
1969 Kent	1981 Hampshire	1993 Middlesex
1970 Kent	1982 Worcestershire	

BAIN CLARKSON TROPHY WINNERS

1986 Northamptonshire	1989 Middlesex	1992 Surrey
1987 Derbyshire	1990 Lancashire	1993 Leicestershire
1988 Yorkshire	1991 Nottinghamshire	

THE FIRST-CLASS COUNTIES HONOURS, REGISTER, RECORDS AND 1993 AVERAGES

To the end of the 1993 season
(Including Indian and South African tours of Sri Lanka, July-September 1993)

ABBREVIATIONS

General

*	not out/unbroken partnership	f-c	first-class
b	born	HS	Highest Score
BB	Best innings bowling analysis	LOI	Limited-Overs Internationals
Cap	Awarded 1st XI County Cap	Tests	Official Test Matches
Tours	Overseas tours involving first-class appearances		

Awards

BHC	Benson and Hedges Cup 'Gold' Award
NWT	NatWest Trophy/Gillette Cup 'Man of the Match' Award
Wisden 1993	One of Wisden Cricketers' Almanack's Five Cricketers of 1993
YC 1993	Cricket Writers' Club Young Cricketer of 1993

Competitions

BHC	Benson and Hedges Cup
GC	Gillette Cup
NWT	NatWest Trophy
SL	Sunday League

Playing Categories

LB	Bowls right-arm leg-breaks
LF	Bowls left-arm fast
LFM	Bowls left-arm fast-medium
LHB	Bats left-handed
LM	Bowls left-arm medium pace
LMF	Bowls left-arm medium-fast
OB	Bowls right-arm off-breaks
RF	Bowls right-arm fast
RFM	Bowls right-arm fast-medium
RHB	Bats right-handed
RM	Bowls right-arm medium pace
RMF	Bowls right-arm medium-fast
RSM	Bowls right-arm slow-medium
SLA	Bowls left-arm leg-breaks
WK	Wicket-keeper

Education

BHS	Boys' High School
BS	Boys' School
C	College
CE	College of Education
CFE	College of Further Education
CHE	College of Higher Education
CS	Comprehensive School
GS	Grammar School
HS	High School
IHE	Institute of Higher Education
LSE	London School of Economics
RGS	Royal Grammar School
S	School
SFC	Sixth Form College
SM	Secondary Modern School
SS	Secondary School
TC	Technical College
T(H)S	Technical (High) School
U	University

Teams (see also p 164)

Cav	Cavaliers	NSW	New South Wales
CD	Central Districts	NT	Northern Transvaal
DHR	D.H.Robins' XI	OFS	Orange Free State
DN	Duke of Norfolk's XI	PIA	Pakistan International Airlines
Eng Co	English Counties XI	RW	Rest of the World XI
EP	Eastern Province	SAB	South African Breweries XI
GW	Griqualand West	SAU	South African Universities
Int XI	International XI	WA	Western Australia
IW	International Wanderers	Zim	Zimbabwe (Rhodesia)
ND	Northern Districts		

DERBYSHIRE

Formation of Present Club: 4 November 1870
Colours: Chocolate, Amber and Pale Blue
Badge: Rose and Crown
Championships: (1) 1936
NatWest Trophy/Gillette Cup Winners: (1) 1981
Benson and Hedges Cup Winners: (1) 1993
Sunday League Champions: (1) 1990
Match Awards: NWT 31; BHC 57

Chief Executive: R.G.Taylor, County Cricket Ground, Nottingham Road, Derby DE2 6DA (☎ 0332-383211)
Captain: K.J.Barnett
Scorer: S.W.Tacey
1994 Beneficiary: O.H.Mortensen

ADAMS, Christopher John (Repton S), b Whitwell 6 May 1970. 6'0". RHB, OB. Debut 1988. Cap 1992. 1000 runs (1): 1109 (1992). HS 175 v Notts (Nottingham) 1993. BB 4-29 v Lancs (Derby) 1991. Award: BHC 1. **NWT:** HS 106* and BB 1-15 v Berks (Derby) 1992. **BHC:** HS 58 v Middx (Derby) 1993. **SL:** HS 141* v Kent (Chesterfield) 1992. BB 2-15 v Essex (Chelmsford) 1993.

BARNETT, Kim John (Leek HS), b Stoke-on-Trent, Staffs 17 Jul 1960. 6'1". RHB, LB. Debut 1979. Cap 1982. Captain 1983-. Boland 1982-83/1987-88. Staffordshire 1976. Wisden 1988. Benefit 1992. **Tests:** 4 (1988 to 1989); HS 80 v A (Leeds) 1989. LOI: 1 (HS 84). Tours: SA 1989-90 (Eng XI); NZ 1979-80 (DHR); SL 1985-86 (Eng B). 1000 runs (11); most – 1734 (1984). HS 239* v Leics (Leicester) 1988. BB 6-28 v Glam (Chesterfield) 1991. Awards: NWT 2; BHC 10. **NWT:** HS 88 v Middx (Derby) 1983. BB 6-24 v Cumberland (Kendal) 1984. **BHC:** HS 115 v Glos (Derby) 1987. BB 1-10. **SL:** HS 131* v Essex (Derby) 1984. BB 3-39 v Yorks (Chesterfield) 1979.

BASE, Simon John (Fish Hoek HS, Cape Town), b Maidstone, Kent 2 Jan 1960. 6'2". RHB, RMF. W Province 1981-82/1983-84. Glamorgan 1986-87. Boland 1987-88/1988-89. Border 1989-90 to date. Derbyshire debut 1988. Cap 1990. HS 58 v Yorks (Chesterfield) 1990. 50 wkts (1): 60 (1989). BB 7-60 v Yorks (Chesterfield) 1989. **NWT:** HS 4. BB 2-49 Gm v Sussex (Hove) 1986. **BHC:** HS 15* v Somerset (Taunton) 1990. BB 3-33 v Minor C (Wellington) 1990. **SL:** HS 31 v Kent (Canterbury) 1987. BB 4-14 v Northants (Derby) 1991 and v Glos (Cheltenham) 1993.

BISHOP, Ian Raphael (Belmont SS), b Port-of-Spain, Trinidad 24 Oct 1967. Nephew of R.J. (Trinidad 1986-87 to date). 6'5". RHB, RF. Trinidad 1986-87/1990-91. Derbyshire debut 1989. Cap 1990. **Tests** (WI): 18 (1988-89 to 1992-93); HS 30* v I (P-of-S) 1988-89; BB 6-40 v A (Perth) 1992-93. LOI (WI): 53 (HS 33*; BB 5-25). Tours (WI): E 1988; A 1988-89, 1992-93; P 1990-91. HS 103* v Yorks (Scarborough) 1990. 50 wkts (2); most – 64 (1992). BB 7-34 v Hants (Portsmouth) 1992. **NWT:** HS 6. BB-. **BHC:** HS 42 v Durham (Jesmond) 1992. BB 4-30 v Kent (Canterbury) 1992. **SL:** HS 36* v Notts (Derby) 1992. BB 3-18 v Glos (Derby) 1992.

BOWLER, Peter Duncan (Educated at Canberra, Australia), b Plymouth, Devon 30 Jul 1963. 6'1". RHB, OB, occ WK. Leicestershire 1986 – first to score hundred on f-c debut for Leics (100* and 62 v Hants). Tasmania 1986-87. Derbyshire debut 1988, scoring 155* v CU (Cambridge) – only instance of hundreds on debut for two counties. Cap 1989. 1000 runs (6) inc 2000 (1); most – 2044 (1992). HS 241* v Hants (Portsmouth) 1992. BB 3-41 v Leics (Leicester) 1991 and v Yorks (Chesterfield) 1991. Awards: BHC 3. **NWT:** HS 111 v Berks (Derby) 1992. **BHC:** HS 109 v Somerset (Taunton) 1990. BB 1-15. **SL:** HS 138* v Somerset (Derby) 1993. BB 3-31 v Glos (Cheltenham) 1991.

CORK, Dominic Gerald (St Joseph's C, Stoke-on-Trent), b Newcastle-under-Lyme, Staffs 7 Aug 1971. 6'2". RHB, RFM. Debut 1990. Cap 1993. Staffordshire 1989-90. LOI: 3 (HS 11; BB 1-37). Tours (Eng A): A 1992-93; WI 1991-92. HS 104 v Glos (Cheltenham) 1993. 50 wkts (1): 57 (1991). BB 8-53 (before lunch on his 20th birthday) v Essex (Derby) 1991. Awards: NWT 2; BHC 1. **NWT:** HS 23 v Worcs (Worcester) 1993. BB 5-18 v Berks (Derby) 1992. **BHC:** HS 92* v Lancs (Lord's) 1993. BB 4-26 v Durham (Jesmond) 1992. **SL:** HS 30 v Warwks (Birmingham) 1991. BB 3-26 v Glos (Derby) 1992.

GRIFFITH, Frank Alexander (Beaconsfield HS; Wm Morris HS; Haringey Cricket C), b Whipps Cross, Essex 15 Aug 1968. 6'0". RHB, RM. Debut 1988. HS 81 v Glam (Chesterfield) 1992. BB 4-33 v Leics (Ilkeston) 1992. **NWT:** HS 8. BB 1-13. **BHC:** HS 13* and BB 2-48 v Glos (Bristol) 1993. **SL:** HS 20 v Northants (Derby) 1991, v Kent (Canterbury) 1993 and v Worcs (Worcester) 1993. BB 4-48 v Glam (Derby) 1993.

HARRIS, Andrew James (Hadfield CS; Glossopdale Community C), b Ashton-under-Lyne, Lancs 26 Jun 1973. 6'1". RHB, RM. Derbyshire staff 1993 – awaiting f-c debut.

KRIKKEN, Karl Matthew (Rivington & Blackrod HS & SFC), b Bolton, Lancs 9 Apr 1969. Son of B.E. (Lancs and Worcs 1966-69). 5'9". RHB, WK. GW 1988-89. Derbyshire debut 1989. Cap 1992. HS 77* v Somerset (Taunton) 1990. **NWT:** HS 18 v Leics (Derby) 1992. **BHC:** HS 37* v Worcs (Worcester) 1992 and v Lancs (Lord's) 1993. **SL:** HS 44* v Essex (Chelmsford) 1991.

LOVELL, David John (Kelmscott HS, Perth, WA), b Adelaide, Australia 16 Feb 1969. 5'10". RHB, SLA. Derbyshire staff 1993 – awaiting f-c debut.

MAHER, Bernard Joseph Michael (Abbotsfield CS; Bishopshalt GS; Loughborough U), b Hillingdon, Middx 11 Feb 1958. 5'10". RHB, WK. Derbyshire debut 1981. Cap 1987. HS 126 v NZ (Derby) 1986. BAC HS 121* v Leics (Derby) 1988. BB 2-69 v Glam (Abergavenny) 1986. **NWT:** HS 44 v Hants (Derby) 1988. **BHC:** HS 50 v Northants (Derby) 1987. **SL:** HS 78 v Lancs (Manchester) 1987.

MALCOLM, Devon Eugene (Richmond C, Sheffield), b Kingston, Jamaica 22 Feb 1963. 6'2". RHB, RF. Debut 1984. Cap 1989. Tests: 25 (1989 to 1993). HS 15* v I (Oval) 1990; BB 6-77 v WI (P-of-S) 1989-90. LOI: 9 (HS 4; BB 3-40). Tours: A 1990-91; WI 1989-90, 1991-92 (Eng A); I 1992-93; SL 1992-93. HS 51 v Surrey (Derby) 1989. 50 wkts (2); most – 56 (1988). BB 7-74 v Australia XI (Hobart) 1990-91. De BB 6-57 v Sussex (Derby) 1993. Award: BHC 1. **NWT:** HS 10* v Leics (Derby) 1992. BB 3-29 v Devon (Exmouth) 1993. **BHC:** HS 15 v Comb Us (Oxford) 1991. BB 5-27 v Middx (Derby) 1988. **SL:** HS 18 v Essex (Chelmsford) 1991. BB 4-21 v Surrey (Derby) 1989 and v Leics (Knypersley) 1990.

MORTENSEN, Ole Henrek (Brondbyoster S; Abedore C, Copenhagen), b Vejle, Denmark 29 Jan 1958. 6'3". RHB, RFM. Debut 1983. Cap 1986. Benefit 1994. Denmark 1975-82. HS 74* v Yorks (Chesterfield) 1987. 50 wkts (2); most – 58 (1991). BB 6-27 v Yorks (Sheffield) 1983. Hat-trick 1987. Awards: NWT 2. **NWT:** HS 11 v Surrey (Derby) 1986. BB 6-14 v Ire (Derby) 1989. **BHC:** HS 5*. BB 3-17 v Leics (Chesterfield) 1986. **SL:** HS 11 v Worcs (Worcester) 1989. BB 4-10 v Leics (Chesterfield) 1985.

O'GORMAN, Timothy Joseph Gerard (St George's C, Weybridge; Durham U), b Woking, Surrey 15 May 1967. Grandson of J.G. (Surrey 1927). 6'2". RHB, OB. Debut 1987. Cap 1992. 1000 runs (2); most – 1116 (1991). HS 148 v Lancs (Manchester) 1991. BB 1-7. **NWT:** HS 68* v Devon (Exmouth) 1993. **BHC:** HS 49 v Northants (Derby) 1991 and v Lancs (Lord's) 1993. **SL:** HS 69 v Northants (Northampton) 1992.

RICHARDSON, Alastair William (Oundle S; Durham U), b Derby 23 Oct 1972. Son of G.W. (Derbys 1959-65); grandson of A.W. (Derbys 1928-36). 6'3". RHB, RFM. Debut 1992. HS 9. BB 2-38 v Glam (Cardiff) 1992.

ROLLINS, Adrian Stewart (Little Ilford CS), b Barking, Essex 8 Feb 1972. Brother of R.J. (see ESSEX). 6'5". RHB, WK, occ RM. Debut 1993. HS 85 v Somerset (Derby) 1993. **SL:** HS 57 v Notts (Nottingham) 1993.

SLADDIN, Richard William (Sowerby Bridge HS), b Halifax, Yorks 8 Jan 1969. 6'0". RHB, SLA. Debut 1991. HS 51* v Durham (Durham) 1993. BB 6-58 v CU (Cambridge) 1992. BAC BB 5-186 v Essex (Chelmsford) 1991. **SL:** HS 26 v Durham (Durham) 1993. BB 2-26 v Glos (Cheltenham) 1993.

STEER, Ian Gary Samuel (St Edmund Campion S), b Aston, Birmingham 17 Aug 1970. 5'7". RHB, RM. Warwickshire staff 1990-91. Debut 1993. HS 67 v Leics (Leicester) 1993. BB 3-23 v Surrey (Ilkeston) 1993. **SL:** HS 19 v Leics (Leicester) 1993. BB 1-33.

TWEATS, Timothy Andrew (Endon HS; Stoke-on-Trent SFC), b Stoke-on-Trent, Staffs 18 Apr 1974. 6'3". RHB, RM. Debut 1992. Staffordshire 1992. HS 24 v Glam (Cardiff) 1992.

VANDRAU, Matthew James (St Stithian's C, Johannesburg; St John's C, Jo'burg; Witwatersrand U), b Epsom, Surrey 22 Jul 1969. Son of B.M. (Transvaal B 1963). 6'3½". RHB, OB. Transvaal B (one match) 1990-91 (toured UK 1992 – not f-c). Derbyshire debut 1993. HS 58 v Northants (Derby) 1993. BB 2-8 v Middx (Lord's) 1993. **NWT:** HS 21 and BB 1-9 v Devon (Exmouth) 1993. **BHC:** HS-. BB 1-46. **SL:** HS 32* and BB 2-39 v Kent (Canterbury) 1993.

WARNER, Allan Esmond (Tabernacle S, St Kitts), b Birmingham 12 May 1957. 5'7". RHB, RFM. Worcestershire 1982-84. Derbyshire debut 1985. Cap 1987. Benefit 1995. HS 95* Kent (Canterbury) 1993. BB 5-27 Wo v Glam (Worcester) 1984 and 5-27 (10-120 match) v Glos (Cheltenham) 1993. Award: NWT 1. **NWT:** HS 32 v Kent (Canterbury) 1987. BB 4-39 v Salop (Chesterfield) 1990. **BHC:** HS 35* v Comb Us (Oxford) 1991. BB 4-36 v Notts (Nottingham) 1987. **SL:** HS 68 v Hants (Heanor) 1986. BB 5-39 v Worcs (Knypersley) 1985.

NEWCOMERS

DeFREITAS, Phillip Anthony Jason (Willesden HS, London), b Scotts Head, Dominica 18 Feb 1966. 6'0". RHB, RFM. UK resident since 1976. Leicestershire 1985-88 (cap 1986). Lancashire 1989-93 (cap 1989). Wisden 1991. MCC YC. **Tests:** 33 (1986-87 to 1993); HS 55* v WI (Nottingham) 1991; BB 7-70 v SL (Lord's) 1991. LOI: 85 (HS 49*; BB 4-35). Tours: a 1986-87, 1990-91; WI 1989-90; NZ 1987-88, 1991-92; P 1987-88; I 1992-93; Z 1988-89 (La). HS 113 Le v Notts (Worksop) 1988. 50 wkts (6); most – 94 (1986). BB 7-21 La v Middx (Lord's) 1989. Awards: NWT 3; BHC 4. **NWT:** HS 69 Le v Lancs (Leicester) 1986. BB 5-13 La v Cumberland (Kendal) 1989. **BHC:** HS 75* La v Hants (Manchester) 1990. BB 5-16 La v Essex (Chelmsford) 1992. **SL:** HS 49* La v Hants (Manchester) 1992. BB 5-26 La v Hants (Southampton) 1993.

RICHARDSON, Alan (Alleyne's HS; Stafford CFE), b Newcastle-under-Lyme, Staffs 6 May 1975. Not related to A.W. 6'2". RHB, RM.

TAYLOR, Matthew (Rivington & Blackrod HS; Bolton North SFC), b Bolton, Lancs 13 Nov 1973. 6'1". RHB, SLA.

WELLS, Colin Mark (Tideway CS, Newhaven), b Newhaven, Sussex 3 Mar 1960. Elder brother of A.P. (see SUSSEX). 5'11". RHB, RM. Sussex 1979-93 (cap 1982; benefit 1993). Border 1980-81. W Province 1984-85. LOI: 2 (HS 17). 1000 runs (6); most – 1456 (1987). HS 203 Sx v Hants (Hove) 1984. 50 wkts (2); most – 59 (1984). BB 7-42 Sx v Derbys (Derby) 1991. Awards: BHC 3. **NWT:** HS 76 Sx v Ire (Hove) 1985. BB 3-16 Sx v Scot (Edinburgh) 1991. **BHC:** HS 117 Sx v Glam (Swansea) 1989. BB 4-21 Sx v Middx (Lord's) 1980. **SL:** HS 104* Sx v Warwks (Hove) 1983. BB 4-15 Sx v Worcs (Worcester) 1983.

DEPARTURE

MORRIS, J.E. – see DURHAM.

DERBYSHIRE 1993

RESULTS SUMMARY

	Place	Won	Lost	Drew	Abandoned
Britannic Assurance Championship	15th	4	7	6	
All First-class Matches		4	7	8	
Sunday League	10th	7	8		2
NatWest Trophy	2nd Round				
Benson and Hedges Cup	Winners				

BRITANNIC ASSURANCE CHAMPIONSHIP AVERAGES

BATTING AND FIELDING

Cap		M	I	NO	HS	Runs	Avge	100	50	Ct/St
1982	K.J.Barnett	14	22	5	168	1067	62.76	4	5	6
1986	J.E.Morris	16	27	1	229	1323	50.88	4	6	8
–	A.S.Rollins	7	13	4	85	392	43.55	–	2	5/1
1989	P.D.Bowler	15	26	2	153*	1005	41.87	2	6	12
–	I.G.S.Steer	4	7	2	67	157	31.40	–	1	–
1992	C.J.Adams	16	27	–	175	818	30.29	1	7	16
1993	D.G.Cork	13	20	2	104	427	23.72	1	1	10
1992	T.J.G.O'Gorman	12	19	2	86	375	22.05	–	2	8
–	M.J.Vandrau	14	22	2	58	404	20.20	–	2	6
1987	A.E.Warner	11	14	1	95*	238	18.30	–	1	4
1992	K.M.Krikken	11	17	4	40	226	17.38	–	–	20/4
–	R.W.Sladdin	8	11	3	51*	131	16.37	–	1	2
–	F.A.Griffith	9	12	–	56	191	15.91	–	2	3
1989	D.E.Malcolm	9	11	4	19	69	9.85	–	–	4
1986	O.H.Mortensen	10	14	5	29	70	7.77	–	–	4
1990	S.J.Base	12	18	–	27	132	7.33	–	–	9
1987	B.J.M.Maher	5	5	1	17	22	5.50	–	–	9

Also played (1 match): A.W.Richardson 9, 0.

BOWLING

	O	M	R	W	Avge	Best	5wI	10wM
A.E.Warner	298.5	61	875	41	21.34	5-27	3	1
S.J.Base	286.1	64	972	34	28.58	5-59	3	–
D.E.Malcolm	278.5	48	1007	35	28.77	6-57	2	–
O.H.Mortensen	255	66	643	21	30.61	5-55	1	–
D.G.Cork	326.3	67	931	30	31.03	4-90	–	–
F.A.Griffith	147.1	22	546	12	45.50	3-32	–	–
R.W.Sladdin	272.5	70	941	18	52.27	3-30	–	–
M.J.Vandrau	281.4	61	910	16	56.87	2- 8	–	–

Also bowled: C.J.Adams 100.2-7-469-5; K.J.Barnett 33-9-78-2; P.D.Bowler 18-8-37-0; A.W.Richardson 22-5-74-0; I.G.S.Steer 9-2-34-3.

The First-Class Averages (pp 164-177) give the records of Derbyshire players in all first-class county matches (their other opponents being the Australians and Cambridge U), with the exception of:

D.G.Cork 15-22-2-104-539-26.95-1-3-11ct. 363.3-75-1024-34-30.11-4/90.

D.E.Malcolm 10-12-5-19-69-9.85-0-0-0ct. 290.5-48-1092-35-31.20-6/57-2-0.

DERBYSHIRE RECORDS

FIRST-CLASS CRICKET

Highest Total	For 645		v	Hampshire	Derby	1898
	V 662		by	Yorkshire	Chesterfield	1898
Lowest Total	For 16		v	Notts	Nottingham	1879
	V 23		by	Hampshire	Burton upon T	1958
Highest Innings	For 274	G.A.Davidson	v	Lancashire	Manchester	1896
	V 343*	P.A.Perrin	for	Essex	Chesterfield	1904

Highest Partnership for each Wicket

1st	322	H.Storer/J.Bowden	v	Essex	Derby	1929
2nd	349	C.S.Elliott/J.D.Eggar	v	Notts	Nottingham	1947
3rd	291	P.N.Kirsten/D.S.Steele	v	Somerset	Taunton	1981
4th	328	P.Vaulkhard/D.Smith	v	Notts	Nottingham	1946
5th	302*†	J.E.Morris/D.G.Cork	v	Glos	Cheltenham	1993
6th	212	G.M.Lee/T.S.Worthington	v	Essex	Chesterfield	1932
7th	241*	G.H.Pope/A.E.G.Rhodes	v	Hampshire	Portsmouth	1948
8th	182	A.H.M.Jackson/W.Carter	v	Leics	Leicester	1922
9th	283	A.Warren/J.Chapman	v	Warwicks	Blackwell	1910
10th	132	A.Hill/M.Jean-Jacques	v	Yorkshire	Sheffield	1986

† 346 runs were added for this wicket in two separate partnerships.

Best Bowling	For 10- 40	W.Bestwick	v	Glamorgan	Cardiff	1921
(Innings)	V 10- 47	T.F.Smailes	for	Yorkshire	Sheffield	1939
Best Bowling	For 17-103	W.Mycroft	v	Hampshire	Southampton	1876
(Match)	V 16-101	G.Giffen	for	Australians	Derby	1886

Most Runs – Season	2165	D.B.Carr	(av 48.11)		1959
Most Runs – Career	20516	D.Smith	(av 31.41)		1927-52
Most 100s – Season	8	P.N.Kirsten			1982
Most 100s – Career	43	K.J.Barnett			1979-93
Most Wkts – Season	168	T.B.Mitchell	(av 19.55)		1935
Most Wkts – Career	1670	H.L.Jackson	(av 17.11)		1947-63

LIMITED-OVERS CRICKET

Highest Total	NWT	365-3		v	Cornwall	Derby	1986
	BHC	366-4		v	Comb Us	Oxford	1991
	SL	292-9		v	Worcs	Knypersley	1985
Lowest Total	NWT	79		v	Surrey	The Oval	1967
	BHC	102		v	Yorkshire	Bradford	1975
	SL	61		v	Hampshire	Portsmouth	1990
Highest Innings	NWT	153	A.Hill	v	Cornwall	Derby	1986
	BHC	123	J.E.Morris	v	Somerset	Taunton	1990
	SL	141*	C.J.Adams	v	Kent	Chesterfield	1992
Best Bowling	NWT	8-21	M.A.Holding	v	Sussex	Hove	1988
	BHC	6-33	E.J.Barlow	v	Glos	Bristol	1978
	SL	6- 7	M.Hendrick	v	Notts	Nottingham	1972

DURHAM

Formation of Present Club: 10 May 1882
Colours: Navy blue, yellow and maroon
Badge: Coat of Arms of the County of Durham
Championships: (0) 18th 1992, 1993
NatWest Trophy/Gillette Cup Winners: (0) Quarter-Finalist 1992
Benson and Hedges Cup Winners: (0) Third in Group 1992
Sunday League Champions: (0) Seventh 1993
1994 Beneficiary: —
Match Awards: NWT 16; BHC 5.

Chief Executive: G.A.Wright, County Ground, Riverside, Chester-le-Street, Co Durham DH3 3QR. (☎ 091-387 1717)
Captain: P.Bainbridge
Scorer: B.Hunt

BAINBRIDGE, Philip (Hanley HS; Stoke-on-Trent SFC; Borough Road CE), b Sneyd Green, Stoke-on-Trent, Staffs 16 Apr 1958. 5'10". RHB, RM. Gloucestershire 1977-90 (cap 1981; benefit 1989). Durham debut/cap 1992. Captain 1994. Wisden 1985. Tours: SL 1986-87 (Gs); Z 1984-85 (EC). 1000 runs (9); most – 1644 (1985). HS 169 Gs v Yorks (Cheltenham) 1988. Du HS 150* v Essex (Chelmsford) 1993. BB 8-53 Gs v Somerset (Bristol) 1986. Du BB 5-53 v Yorks (Leeds) 1993. Awards: NWT 1; BHC 3. **NWT:** HS 89 Gs v Leics (Leicester) 1988. BB 3-49 Gs v Scot (Bristol) 1983. **BHC:** HS 96 Gs v Hants (Southampton) 1988. BB 4-38 v Worcs (Worcester) 1992. **SL:** HS 106* Gs v Somerset (Bristol) 1986. BB 5-22 Gs v Middx (Lord's) 1987.

BERRY, Philip John (Saltscar CS; Longlands CFE, Redcar), b Saltburn, Yorks 28 Dec 1966. 6'0". RHB, OB. Yorkshire 1986-90. Durham debut/cap 1992. HS 76 and BB 7-113 v Middx (Lord's) 1992. **NWT:** HS 9. BB 2-35 v Glam (Cardiff) 1993. **BHC:** HS-. **SL:** HS 6. BB 1-35.

BETTS, Melvyn Morris (Fyndoune CS, Sacriston), b Sacriston 26 Mar 1975. 5'10". RHB, RMF. Debut 1993 (summer contract – uncapped). HS 4. BB 1-19.

BLENKIRON, Darren Andrew (Bishop Barrington CS, Bishop Auckland), b Solihull, Warwks 4 Feb 1974. 5'10". Durham staff/cap 1992 – awaiting f-c debut. Son of W. (Warwks 1964-74, Durham 1975-76). LHB, RM. **NWT:** HS 56 v Glam (Darlington) 1991. **SL:** HS-.

BROWN, Simon John Emmerson (Boldon CS), b Cleadon 29 Jun 1969. 6'3". RHB, LFM. Northamptonshire 1987-90. Durham debut/cap 1992. HS 47* v Surrey (Durham) 1992. 50 wkts (1): 58 (1992). BB 7-70 v A (Durham) 1993. BAC BB 7-105 v Kent (Canterbury) 1992. **NWT:** HS 7*. BB 1-43. **BHC:** HS 4*. BB 2-32 v Minor C (Hartlepool) 1993. **SL:** HS 7. BB 3-26 Nh v Leics (Leicester) 1990.

COX, David Matthew (Greenford HS), b Southall, Middx 2 Mar 1972. 5'10". LHB, SLA. Hertfordshire 1992. MCC YC 1990-92. Durham staff/cap 1993 – awaiting f-c debut.

CUMMINS, Anderson Cleophas (Foundation S; Combermere S; Bridgetown U), b Packer's Valley, Barbados 7 May 1966. RHB, RFM. Barbados 1988-89/1991-92. Durham debut/cap 1993. **Tests** (WI): 3 (1992-93); HS 14* v P (P-o-S) 1992-93; BB 4-54 v P (St John's) 1992-93. LOI (WI): 29 (HS 24; BB 5-31). Tours (WI): A 1991-92, 1992-93. HS 70 v Worcs (Stockton) 1993. 50 wkts (1): 53 (1993). BB 6-115 v Sussex (Durham) 1993. **NWT:** HS 20* and BB 1-38 v Wilts (Trowbridge) 1993. **BHC:** HS 3* and BB 3-36 v Hants (Stockton) 1993. **SL:** HS 22 v Worcs (Stockton) 1993. BB 4-24 v Hants (Stockton) 1993.

DALEY, James Arthur (Hetton CS), b Sunderland 24 Sep 1973. 5'10". RHB, RM. Debut/cap 1992. MCC YC 1991. HS 88 v Somerset (Taunton) 1992 – on debut. **SL:** HS 10 v Leics (Leicester) 1993.

FOTHERGILL, Andrew Robert (Eastbourne CS, Darlington), b Newcastle upon Tyne, Northumberland 10 Feb 1962. 6'0". RHB, WK. Debut for Minor C v Indians (Trowbridge) 1990. Durham debut/cap 1992. HS 29 v Somerset (Hartlepool) 1993. Award: BHC 1. Soccer for Bishop Auckland 1986-91. **NWT:** HS 24 v Glam (Darlington) 1991. **BHC:** HS 45* Minor C v Somerset (Taunton) 1990. **SL:** HS 42* v Leics (Gateshead) 1992.

FOWLER, Graeme (Accrington GS; Durham U), b Accrington, Lancs 20 Apr 1957. 5'9½/2". LHB, RM. Lancashire 1979-92 (cap 1981; benefit 1991). Durham debut/cap 1993. **Tests:** 21 (1982 to 1984-85); HS 201 v I (Madras) 1984-85. LOI: 26 (HS 81*). Tours: A 1982-83; WI 1982-83 (Int); NZ 1983-84; I/SL 1984-85; P 1983-84; Z 1988-89 (La). 1000 runs (8); most – 1800 (1987). HS 226 La v Kent (Maidstone) 1984. Du HS 138 v Yorks (Leeds) 1993. BB 2-34 La v Warwks (Manchester) 1986. Awards: NWT 2; BHC 3. **NWT:** HS 122 La v Glos (Bristol) 1984. **BHC:** HS 136 La v Sussex (Manchester) 1991. **SL:** HS 124 v Derbys (Durham) 1993.

GRAVENEY, David Anthony (Millfield S), b Bristol 2 Jan 1953. Son of J.K. (Glos 1947-64); nephew of T.W. (Glos, Worcs, Queensland and England 1947/1971-72). 6'4". RHB, SLA. Gloucestershire 1972-90 (cap 1976; captain 1981-88; benefit 1986). Somerset 1991. Durham debut/cap 1992. Captain 1992-93. Tours: SA 1989-90 (Eng XI – manager); SL 1986-87 (Gs – capt). HS 119 Gs v OU (Oxford) 1980. BAC HS 105* Gs v Northants (Bristol) 1981. Du HS 36 v Surrey (Durham) 1992. 50 wkts (6); most – 73 (1976). BB 8-85 Gs v Notts (Cheltenham) 1974. Du BB 5-78 v Northants (Northampton) 1993. Hat-trick 1983. Awards: NWT 2. **NWT:** HS 44 Gs v Surrey (Bristol) 1973. BB 5-11 Gs v Ire (Dublin) 1981. **BHC:** HS 49* Gs v Somerset (Taunton) 1982. BB 3-13 Gs v Scot (Glasgow) 1983. **SL:** HS 56* Gs v Notts (Bristol) 1985. BB 4-22 Gs v Hants (Lydney) 1974.

HENDERSON, Paul William (Billingham Campus S; Bede SFC), b Stockton-on-Tees 22 Oct 1974. 6'0". RHB, RFM. Debut/cap 1992 – when aged 17. HS 46 v Glam (Cardiff) 1992 – on debut. BB 3-59 v Somerset (Darlington) 1992. **SL:** HS 10* and BB 3-47 v Notts (Nottingham) 1992.

HUTTON, Stewart (De Brus S, Skelton; Cleveland TC), b Stockton-on-Tees 30 Nov 1969. 6'0". LHB, RSM. Debut/cap 1992. HS 78 v Sussex (Horsham) 1992. Award: NWT 1. **NWT:** HS 95 v Wilts (Trowbridge) 1993. **SL:** HS 70 v Glam (Hartlepool) 1992.

LARKINS, Wayne (Bushmead SS, Eaton Socon), b Roxton, Beds 22 Nov 1953. 5'11". RHB, RM. Northamptonshire 1972-91 (cap 1976; benefit 1986). Durham debut/cap 1992. E Province 1982-83/1983-84. **Tests:** 13 (1979-80 to 1990-91); HS 64 v A (Melbourne) 1990-91. LOI: 25 (HS 124). Tours: A 1979-80, 1990-91; SA 1981-82 (SAB); WI 1989-90; I 1979-80, 1980-81 (Overseas XI). 1000 runs (13); most – 1863 (1982). HS 252 Nh v Glam (Cardiff) 1983. Du HS 151 v A (Durham) 1993. BB 5-59 Nh v Worcs (Worcester) 1984. Awards: NWT 2; BHC 7. **NWT:** HS 121* Nh v Essex (Chelmsford) 1987. BB 2-38 Nh v Glos (Bristol) 1985. **BHC:** HS 132 Nh v Warwks (Birmingham) 1982. BB 4-37 Nh v Comb Us (Northampton) 1980. **SL:** HS 172* Nh v Warwks (Luton) 1983. BB 5-32 Nh v Essex (Ilford) 1978.

LUGSDEN, Steven (St Edmund Campion S, Low Fell), b Gateshead 10 Jul 1976. 6'2". RHB, RFM. Debut 1993 aged 17yr 27d (youngest Durham player – summer contract – uncapped). HS 5* and BB 2-43 v Derbys (Durham) 1993.

SCOTT, Christopher Wilmot (Robert Pattinson CS, N Hykeham), b Thorpe-on-the-Hill, Lincs 23 Jan 1964. 5'8". RHB, WK. Nottinghamshire 1981-91 (cap 1988). Durham debut/cap 1992. HS 78 Nt v CU (Cambridge) 1983. BAC HS 69* Nt v Warwks (Nottingham) 1986. Du HS 64 v Glos (Bristol) 1993. Held 10 catches for Notts in match v Derbys (Derby) 1988. **NWT:** HS-. **BHC:** HS 18 Nt v Northants (Northampton) 1988. **SL:** HS 26 Nt v Yorks (Nottingham) 1988.

SEARLE, Jason Paul (John Bentley S, Calne; Swindon C), b Bath, Somerset 16 May 1976. 5'9". RHB, OB. Durham staff/cap 1993 – awaiting f-c debut.

SMITH, Ian (Ryton CS), b Shotley Bridge 11 Mar 1967. 6'2". RHB, RM. Glamorgan 1985-91. Durham debut/cap 1992. Tour: Z 1990-91 (Gm). HS 116 Gm v Kent (Canterbury) 1989. Du HS 110 v Somerset (Taunton) 1992. BB 3-48 Gm v Hants (Cardiff) 1989. Du BB 3-85 v Lancs (Gateshead) 1992. **NWT:** HS 33 Gm v Hants (Cardiff) 1989. BB 3-60 Gm v Durham (Darlington) 1991. **BHC:** HS 51 Gm v Hants (Southampton) 1991. BB 1-21. **SL:** HS 56* Gm v Warwks (Aberystwyth) 1989. BB 3-22 Gm v Hants (Cardiff) 1989.

WIGHAM, Gary (Bishop Barrington CS, Bishop Auckland), b Bishop Auckland 2 Mar 1973. 6'7½". RHB, RMF. MCC YC 1991. Durham staff/cap 1992 – awaiting f-c debut. **SL:** HS-. BB 1-43.

WOOD, John (Crofton HS; Wakefield District C; Leeds Poly), b Wakefield, Yorks 22 Jul 1970. 6'3". RHB, RFM. GW in Nissan Shield 1990-91. Debut/cap 1992. HS 63* v Notts (Chester-le-St) 1993. BB 5-68 v Hants (Southampton) 1992. **NWT:** HS 1. BB 2-22 v Ireland (Dublin) 1992. **BHC:** HS-. BB 1-19. **SL:** HS 11* v Worcs (Stockton) 1993. BB 2-39 v Glam (Colwyn Bay) 1993.

NEWCOMERS

BIRBECK, Shaun David (Hetton CS), b Sunderland 26 Jul 1972. Brother of A. (Durham 1983-90). 5'9". LHB, RM.

LONGLEY, Jonathan Ian (Tonbridge S; Durham U), b New Brunswick, New Jersey, USA 12 Apr 1969. 5'7". RHB. Kent 1989-93. Tour: Z 1992-93 (K). HS 110 K v CU (Cambridge) 1992. BAC HS 47 K v Northants (Canterbury) 1993. **BHC:** HS 57 K v Somerset (Canterbury) 1992. **SL:** HS 71 K v Northants (Northampton) 1992.

MORRIS, John Edward (Shavington CS; Dane Bank CFE), b Crewe, Cheshire 1 Apr 1964. 5'10". RHB, RM. Derbyshire 1982-93 (cap 1986). GW 1988-89. Tests: 3 (1990). HS 32 v I (Oval) 1990. LOI: 8 (HS 63*). Tour: A 1990-91. 1000 runs (8); most – 1739 (1986). HS 229 De v Glos (Cheltenham) 1993. BB 1-6. Awards: NWT 1; BHC 2. **NWT:** HS 94* De v Salop (Chesterfield) 1990. **BHC:** HS 123 De v Somerset (Taunton) 1990. **SL:** HS 134 De v Somerset (Taunton) 1990.

SAXELBY, Mark (Nottingham HS), b Worksop, Notts 4 Jan 1969. 6'3". LHB, RM. Younger brother of K. (Notts 1978-90). Nottinghamshire 1989-93. HS 77 Nt v Northants (Northampton) 1993. BB 3-41 Nt v Derbys (Derby) 1991. **NWT:** HS 41 Nt v Bucks (Marlow) 1990. BB 2-42 Nt v Lincs (Nottingham) 1991. **BHC:** HS 32 Nt v Hants (Southampton) 1991. BB 1-36. **SL:** HS 100* Nt v Durham (Chester-le-St) 1993. BB 4-29 Nt v Leics (Leicester) 1991.

WALKER, Alan (Shelley HS), b Emley, Yorks 7 Jul 1962. 5'11". LHB, RFM. Northamptonshire 1983-93 (cap 1987). Tour: SA 1991-92 (Nh). HS 41* Nh v Warwks (Birmingham) 1987. 50 wkts (1): 54 (1988). BB 6-50 Nh v Lancs (Northampton) 1986. Award: NWT 1. **NWT:** HS 11 Nh v Surrey (Oval) 1991. BB 4-7 Nh v Ire (Northampton) 1987. **BHC:** HS 15* Nh v Notts (Nottingham) 1987. BB 4-46 Nh v Glos (Northampton) 1985. **SL:** HS 30 Nh v Durham (Northampton) 1993. BB 4-21 Nh v Worcs (Worcester) 1985.

WILCOCK, Peter James (Balderstone CS; Hopwood Hall C), b Rochdale, Lancs 6 Aug 1974. 6'4". RHB, occ OB. Eng U-19 to India 1992-93.

DEPARTURES

BOTHAM, Ian Terence (Buckler's Mead SS, Yeovil), b Heswall, Cheshire 24 Nov 1955. 6'1". RHB, RMF. Somerset 1974-86 (cap 1976; captain 1984-85; benefit 1984). Worcestershire 1987-91 (cap 1987). Durham 1992-93 (cap 1992). Queensland 1987-88. Wisden 1977. YC 1977. MCC YC. OBE 1992. **Tests:** 102 (1977 to 1992, 12 as captain); HS 208 v I (Oval) 1982; BB 8-34 v P (Lord's) 1978. LOI: 116 (HS 79; BB 4-31). Tours: A 1978-79, 1979-80, 1982-83, 1986-87; WI 1980-81 (capt), 1985-86; NZ 1977-78, 1983-84, 1991-92; I 1979-80, 1981-82; P 1977-78, 1983-84; SL 1981-82; Z 1990-91 (Wo). 1000 runs (4); most – 1530 (1985). Hit 80 sixes 1985 (f-c record). HS 228 Sm v Glos (Taunton) 1980. Du HS 105 v Leics (Durham) 1992 (on Du debut). 50 wkts (8) inc 100 (1): 100 (1978). BB 8-34 (Tests). BAC BB 7-54 Warwks (Worcester) 1991. Du BB 4-11 v Glam (Colwyn Bay) 1993. Hat-trick 1978 (MCC). Awards: NWT 4; BHC 10. **NWT:** HS 101 Wo v Devon (Worcester) 1987. BB 5-51 Wo v Lancs (Worcester) 1989. **BHC:** HS 138* Wo v Glos (Bristol) 1990. BB 5-41 Wo v Yorks (Worcester) 1988. **SL:** HS 175* Sm v Northants (Wellingborough) 1986. BB 5-27 Wo v Glos (Gloucester) 1987.

BRIERS, Mark Paul (Hind Leys C, Shepshed; Loughborough TC), b Loughborough, Leics 21 Apr 1968. 6'0". RHB, LB. Worcestershire staff 1988. Bedfordshire 1990. Durham 1992-93 (cap 1992). HS 62* v Sussex (Horsham) 1992. BB 3-109 v Glos (Stockton) 1992. **NWT:** HS 54* v Ireland (Dublin) 1992. BB 1-0. **SL:** HS 69 v Surrey (Durham) 1992. BB 1-47.

GLENDENEN, John David (Ormesby SS), b Middlesbrough, Yorks 20 Jun 1965. 6'0". RHB, RM. Durham 1992-93 (cap 1992), scoring 117 v OU (Oxford) on debut. Scored 200* v Victoria (Durham) 1991 (not f-c). HS 117 (above). BAC HS 76 v Lancs (Gateshead) 1992. **NWT:** 109 v Glam (Darlington) 1991 – first 100 by Durham batsman in NWT/GC. **BHC:** HS 60 v Comb Us (Cambridge) 1992. **SL:** HS 78 v Warwks (Birmingham) 1992.

HUGHES, Simon Peter (Latymer Upper S, Hammersmith; Durham U), b Kingston upon Thames, Surrey 20 Dec 1959. 5'10". RHB, RFM. Middlesex 1980-91 (cap 1981; benefit 1991). Durham 1992-93 (cap 1992). N Transvaal 1982-83. Tours: I 1980-81 (Overseas XI); Z 1980-81 (M). HS 53 M v CU (Cambridge) 1988. BAC HS 47 M v Warwks (Uxbridge) 1986. Du HS 42 v Lancs (Gateshead) 1992. 50 wkts (2); most – 63 (1986). BB 7-35 M v Surrey (Oval) 1986. Du BB 5-25 v Yorks (Durham) 1992. Award: NWT 1. **NWT:** HS 11 and BB 4-20 M v Durham (Darlington) 1989. **BHC:** HS 22 M v Somerset (Taunton) 1990. BB 4-34 M v Somerset (Lord's) 1987. **SL:** HS 22* M v Surrey (Lord's) 1985. BB 5-23 M v Worcs (Worcester) 1989.

PARKER, Paul William Giles (Collyer's GS; St Catharine's C, Cambridge), b Bulawayo, Rhodesia 15 Jan 1956. 5'10". RHB, RM. Cambridge U 1976-78 (blue 1976-77-78). Sussex 1976-91 (cap 1979; captain 1988-91; benefit 1988). Durham 1992-93 (cap 1992). YC 1979. **Tests:** 1 (1981); HS 13 v A (Oval) 1981. 1000 runs (9); most – 1692 (1984). HS 215 CU v Essex (Cambridge) 1976. BAC/Du HS 159 v Warwicks (Darlington) 1993. BB 2-21 Sx v Surrey (Guildford) 1984. Awards: NWT 5; BHC 5. **NWT:** HS 109 Sx v Ire (Hove) 1985. BB 1-10. **BHC:** HS 87 Sx v Leics (Hove) 1991. BB 2-3 Sx v Minor C (Hove) 1987. **SL:** HS 121* Sx v Northants (Hastings) 1983. BB 1-2.

DURHAM 1993

RESULTS SUMMARY

	Place	Won	Lost	Drew	Abandoned
Britannic Assurance Championship	18th	2	10	5	
All First-class Matches		2	10	7	
Sunday League	7th	8	7		2
NatWest Trophy	2nd Round				
Benson and Hedges Cup	1st Round				

BRITANNIC ASSURANCE CHAMPIONSHIP AVERAGES

BATTING AND FIELDING

Cap		M	I	NO	HS	Runs	Avge	100	50	Ct/St
1992	P.Bainbridge	17	29	2	150*	1116	41.33	2	7	6
1992	W.Larkins	15	27	3	113*	837	34.87	2	5	21
1992	P.W.G.Parker	17	29	1	159	866	30.92	3	3	9
1992	S.Hutton	9	16	–	73	422	26.37	–	2	8
1992	J.A.Daley	12	20	–	79	521	26.05	–	3	7
1993	G.Fowler	12	21	–	138	540	25.71	1	–	7
1992	I.T.Botham	9	16	1	101	384	25.60	1	3	8
1992	D.A.Graveney	17	27	14	32	276	21.23	–	–	10
1993	A.C.Cummins	15	25	2	70	433	18.82	–	3	5
1992	J.Wood	8	15	2	63*	235	18.07	–	1	2
1992	C.W.Scott	12	21	3	64	320	17.77	–	2	24/2
1992	P.J.Berry	7	11	2	46	136	15.11	–	–	3
1992	I.Smith	5	10	–	39	143	14.30	–	–	1
1992	J.D.Glendenen	4	6	1	18	41	8.20	–	–	1
1992	S.J.E.Brown	14	23	4	31	150	7.89	–	–	4
1992	A.R.Fothergill	5	8	–	29	53	6.62	–	–	6/2
1992	S.P.Hughes	6	8	2	30	37	6.16	–	–	1

Also played (1 match each): M.M.Betts 0*, 4; M.P.Briers (cap 1992) 1, 1 (1 ct); S.Lugsden 5*.

BOWLING

	O	M	R	W	Avge	Best	5wI	10wM
P.Bainbridge	306.2	74	909	38	23.92	5- 53	2	–
A.C.Cummins	475.3	88	1527	51	29.94	6-115	3	–
I.T.Botham	168.5	42	450	13	34.61	4- 11	–	–
D.A.Graveney	531.1	163	1233	33	37.36	5- 78	1	–
P.J.Berry	154.1	28	474	11	43.09	3- 39	–	–
S.J.E.Brown	450.2	71	1687	37	45.59	5- 78	2	–
J.Wood	176	25	687	13	52.84	4-106	–	–

Also bowled: M.M.Betts 6-1-19-1; M.P.Briers 19-3-69-0; S.P.Hughes 211.3-61-552-8; S.Hutton 2-1-1-0; W.Larkins 4-0-18-0; S.Lugsden 26-2-85-2; P.W.G.Parker 16-3-38-0; I.Smith 24-6-74-1.

The First-Class Averages (pp 164-177) give the records of Durham players in all first-class county matches (their other opponents being the Australians and Oxford U).

DURHAM RECORDS

FIRST-CLASS CRICKET

Highest Total	For	521-9d		v	Glamorgan	Cardiff	1992
	V	629		by	Notts	Chester-le-St	1993
Lowest Total	For	83		v	Lancs	Manchester	1993
	V	86		by	Oxford U	Oxford	1993
Highest Innings	For	159	P.W.G.Parker	v	Warwicks	Darlington	1993
	V	247	C.C.Lewis	for	Notts	Chester-le-St	1993

Highest Partnership for each Wicket

1st	222	P.W.G.Parker/J.D.Glendenen	v	Oxford U	Oxford	1992
2nd	206	W.Larkins/D.M.Jones	v	Glamorgan	Cardiff	1992
3rd	205	G.Fowler/S.Hutton	v	Yorkshire	Leeds	1993
4th	201	W.Larkins/J.A.Daley	v	Somerset	Taunton	1992
5th	185	P.W.G.Parker/J.A.Daley	v	Warwicks	Darlington	1993
6th	152	I.T.Botham/A.C.Cummins	v	Worcs	Stockton	1993
7th	106	I.Smith/D.A.Graveney	v	Somerset	Taunton	1992
8th	91	C.W.Scott/S.P.Hughes	v	Surrey	The Oval	1993
9th	87	D.M.Jones/S.P.Hughes	v	Northants	Stockton	1992
10th	70	D.A.Graveney/S.J.E.Brown	v	Surrey	Durham	1992

Best Bowling	For	7- 70	S.J.E.Brown	v	Australians	Durham	1993
(Innings)	V	7- 37	A.A.Donald	for	Warwicks	Birmingham	1992
Best Bowling	For	10-191	P.J.Berry	v	Middlesex	Lord's	1992
(Match)	V	10- 87	D.J.Millns	for	Leics	Leicester	1992

Most Runs – Season	1536	W.Larkins	(av 37.46)		1992
Most Runs – Career	2581	W.Larkins	(av 37.95)		1992-93
Most 100s – Season	4	D.M.Jones			1992
	4	W.Larkins			1992
Most 100s – Career	7	W.Larkins			1992-93
Most Wkts – Season	58	S.J.E.Brown	(av 34.01)		1992
Most Wkts – Career	105	S.J.E.Brown	(av 36.51)		1992-93

LIMITED-OVERS CRICKET

Highest Total	NWT	320-5		v	Wiltshire	Trowbridge	1993
	BHC	271-6		v	Comb Us	Cambridge	1992
	SL	281-2		v	Derbyshire	Durham	1993
Lowest Total	NWT	82		v	Worcs	Chester-le-St	1968
	BHC	196-9	(55 overs)	v	Glamorgan	Durham	1992
		196-5	(55 overs)	v	Hampshire	Stockton	1993
	SL	105		v	Glamorgan	Colwyn Bay	1993
Highest Innings	NWT	113	W.Larkins	v	Ireland	Dublin	1992
	BHC	110*	W.Larkins	v	Hampshire	Stockton	1993
	SL	128	W.Larkins	v	Notts	Chester-le-St	1993
Best Bowling	NWT	7-32	S.P.Davis	v	Lancashire	Chester-le-St	1983
	BHC	4-38	P.Bainbridge	v	Worcs	Worcester	1992
	SL	4-24	A.C.Cummins	v	Hampshire	Stockton	1993

ESSEX

Formation of Present Club: 14 January 1876
Colours: Blue, Gold and Red
Badge: Three Seaxes above Scroll bearing 'Essex'
Championships: (6) 1979, 1983, 1984, 1986, 1991, 1992
NatWest Trophy/Gillette Cup Winners: (1) 1985
Benson and Hedges Cup Winners: (1) 1979
Sunday League Champions: (3) 1981, 1984, 1985
Match Awards: NWT 36; BHC 71

Secretary/General Manager: P.J.Edwards, County Ground, New Writtle Street, Chelmsford CM2 0PG (☎ 0245-252420)
Captain: G.A.Gooch
Scorer: C.F.Driver
1994 Beneficiary: J.H.Childs

ANDREW, Stephen Jon Walter (Milton Abbey S; Portchester SS), b London 27 Jan 1966. 6'3". RHB, RMF. Hampshire 1984-89. Essex debut 1990. HS 35 v Northants (Chelmsford) 1990. BB 7-47 v Lancs (Manchester) 1993. Awards: BHC 2. NWT: HS 1*. BB 2-34 v Scot (Chelmsford) 1990. BHC: HS 4*. BB 5-24 H v Essex (Chelmsford) 1987. SL: HS 14 v Kent (Maidstone) 1993. BB 4-50 H v Middx (Southampton) 1988.

BODEN, David Jonathan Peter (Alleynes HS, Stone; Stafford CFE), b Eccleshall, Staffs 26 Nov 1970. 6'3". RHB, RMF. Middlesex 1989. Essex debut 1992. HS 5, BB 4-11 M v OU (Oxford) 1989 – on debut. SL: HS 2. BB 2-48 v Durham (Chelmsford) 1993.

CHILDS, John Henry (Audley Park SM, Torquay), b Plymouth, Devon 15 Aug 1951. 6'0". LHB, SLA. Gloucestershire 1975-84 (cap 1977). Essex debut 1985. Cap 1986. Benefit 1994. Devon 1973-74. Wisden 1986. **Tests:** 2 (1988); HS 2*; BB 1-13. HS 43 v Hants (Chelmsford) 1992. 50 wkts (8); most – 89 (1986). BB 9-56 Gs v Somerset (Bristol) 1981. Ex BB 8-58 v Glos (Colchester) 1986. Awards: BHC 1. NWT: HS 14* Gs v Hants (Bristol) 1983. BB 2-15 Gs v Ire (Dublin) 1981. **BHC:** HS 10 Gs v Somerset (Bristol) 1979. BB 3-36 Gs v Glam (Bristol) 1982. SL: HS 16* Gs v Warwks (Bristol) 1981. BB 4-15 Gs v Northants (Northampton) 1976.

COUSINS, Darren Mark (Netherhall CS; Impington Village C), b Cambridge 24 Sep 1971. 6'2". RHB, RMF. Cambridgeshire 1990. Debut 1993. HS 0*. BB 1-51. SL: HS 1. BB 1-31.

DIWAN, Muneeb (Sir George Monoux S, Walthamstow), b St Stephens, Canada 20 Mar 1972. 5'9". RHB, RM. Essex staff 1993 – awaiting f-c debut.

GARNHAM, Michael Anthony (Camberwell GS, Melbourne; Scotch C, Perth; Barnstaple GS; N Devon SFC; East Anglia U), b Johannesburg, SA 20 Aug 1960. 5'10". RHB, WK. Gloucestershire 1979. Leicestershire 1980-85 and 1988. Essex debut 1989. Cap 1990. Cambridgeshire 1986-88. HS 123 v Leics (Leicester) 1991. Awards: NWT 2; BHC 1. NWT: HS 110 Cambs v Warwks (Birmingham) 1988. **BHC:** HS 55 Le v Derbys (Leicester) 1982. SL: HS 79* Le v Lancs (Leicester) 1982.

GOOCH, Graham Alan (Norlington Jr HS), b Leytonstone 23 Jul 1953. 6'0". RHB, RM. Debut 1973. Cap 1975. Captain 1986-87, 1989-. Benefit 1985. W Province 1982-83/1983-84. Wisden 1979. OBE 1991. **Tests:** 107 (1975 to 1993, 34 as captain); HS 333 and record match aggregate of 456 v I (Lord's) 1990; BB 3-39 v P (Manchester) 1992. LOI: 120 (HS 142; BB 3-19). Tours (C=captain): A 1978-79, 1979-80, 1990-91C; SA 1981-82 (SAB); WI 1980-81, 1985-86, 1989-90C; NZ 1991-92C; I 1979-80, 1981-82, 1992-93C; P 1987-88; SL 1981-82. 1000 runs (17+1) inc 2000 (5); most – 2746 (1990). HS 333 (Tests). Ex HS 275 v Kent (Chelmsford) 1988. BB 7-14 v Worcs (Ilford) 1982. Awards: NWT 9 (record); BHC 20 (record). **NWT:** HS 144 v Hants (Chelmsford) 1990. BB 3-31 v Warwks (Birmingham) 1986. **BHC:** HS 198* v Sussex (Hove) 1982. BB 3-24 v Sussex (Hove) 1982. **SL:** HS 176 v Glam (Southend) 1983. BB 4-33 v Worcs (Chelmsford) 1984.

HUSSAIN, Nasser (Forest S, Snaresbrook; Durham U), b Madras, India 28 Mar 1968. Brother of M. (Worcs 1985) 5'11". RHB, LB. Debut 1987. Cap 1989. YC 1989. **Tests:** 7 (1989-90 to 1993); HS 71 v A (Nottingham) 1993. LOI: 2 (HS 15*). Tours: WI 1989-90, 1991-92 (Eng A); P 1990-91 (Eng A); SL 1990-91 (Eng A). 1000 runs (2); most – 1604 (1993). HS 197 v Surrey (Oval) 1990. BB 1-38. Awards: NWT 1; BHC 1. **NWT:** HS 108 v Cumberland (Chelmsford) 1992. **BHC:** HS 118 Comb Us v Somerset (Taunton) 1989. **SL:** HS 66* v Yorks (Middlesbrough) 1990.

HYAM, Barry James (Havering SFC), b Romford 9 Sep 1975. RHB, WK. Debut 1993. HS 1. Not contracted.

ILOTT, Mark Christopher (Francis Combe S, Garston), b Watford, Herts 27 Aug 1970. 6'0½". LHB, LFM. Debut 1988. Cap 1993. Hertfordshire 1987-88. **Tests:** 3 (1993); HS 15 v A (Oval) 1993; BB 3-108 v A (Nottingham) 1993. Tours (Eng A): A 1992-93; SL 1990-91. HS 51 v Sussex (Hove) 1993. 50 wkts (2); most – 64 (1992). BB 7-85 v Surrey (Oval) 1993. Award: BHC 1. **NWT:** HS 10* v Leics (Leicester) 1992. BB 2-23 v Cumberland (Chelmsford) 1992. **BHC:** HS 14 v Worcs (Worcester) 1993. BB 5-21 v Scot (Forfar) 1993. **SL:** HS 17* v Glos (Bristol) 1993. BB 4-15 v Derbys (Derby) 1992.

KHAN, Gul Abbass (Valentine S, Ilford; Ipswich S; Swansea U), b Gujrat, Pakistan 31 Dec 1973. 5'8". RHB, LB. Essex staff 1993 – awaiting f-c debut.

KNIGHT, Nicholas Verity (Felsted S; Forest Court C, Loughborough U), b Watford, Herts 28 Nov 1969. 6'0". LHB. Debut 1991. HS 109 v Middx (Ilford) 1992. **NWT:** HS 81* v Cumberland (Chelmsford) 1992. **BHC:** HS 36 v Glos (Bristol) 1991. **SL:** HS 54 v Derbys (Chelmsford) 1993. BB 1-14.

LEWIS, Jonathan James Benjamin (King Edward VI S, Chelmsford; Roehampton IHE), b Isleworth, Middx 21 May 1970. 5'9". RHB, RSM. Debut 1990 v Surrey (Oval), scoring 116*. HS 136* v Notts (Nottingham) 1993. **NWT:** HS 21 v Leics (Leicester) 1992. **SL:** HS 19 v Lancs (Manchester) 1991.

PRICHARD, Paul John (Brentwood HS), b Billericay 7 Jan 1965. 5'10". RHB, RSM. Debut 1984. Cap 1986. Tour: A 1992-93 (Eng A). 1000 runs (6); most – 1485 (1992). HS 245 v Leics (Chelmsford) 1990. BB 1-28. Awards: BHC 2. **NWT:** HS 94 v Oxon (Chelmsford) 1985. **BHC:** HS 107 v Scot (Glasgow) 1990. **SL:** HS 107 v Notts (Nottingham) 1993.

ROBINSON, Darren David John (Tabor HS, Braintree; Chelmsford CFE), b Braintree 2 Mar 1973. 5'10½". RHB, RMF. Debut 1993. HS 67 v Glos (Bristol) 1993. **SL:** HS 2.

ROLLINS, Robert John (Little Ilford CS), b Plaistow 30 Jan 1974. 5'9". RHB, WK. Brother of A.S. (see DERBYSHIRE). Debut 1992. HS 13 v P (Chelmsford) 1992. **SL:** HS 0.

SHAHID, Nadeem (Ipswich S), b Karachi, Pakistan 23 Apr 1969. 6'0". RHB, LB. Debut 1989. Suffolk 1988. 1000 runs (1): 1003 (1990). HS 132 v Kent (Chelmsford) 1992. BB 3-91 v Surrey (Oval) 1990. **NWT:** HS 18 and BB 1-0 v Cumberland (Chelmsford) 1992. **BHC:** HS 42 v Hants (Chelmsford) 1991. **SL:** HS 64 v Sussex (Hove) 1993.

STEPHENSON, John Patrick (Felsted S; Durham U), b Stebbing 14 Mar 1965. 6'1". RHB, RM. Debut 1985. Cap 1989. Boland 1988-89. **Tests:** 1 (1989); HS 25 v A (Oval) 1989. Tours: WI 1991-92 (Eng A); Z 1989-90 (Eng A). 1000 runs (5); most – 1887 (1990). HS 202* v Somerset (Bath) 1990. BB 6-54 v Notts (Colchester) 1992. Awards: BHC 2. **NWT:** HS 90 v Northants (Chelmsford) 1993. BB 3-78 v Lancs (Chelmsford) 1992. **BHC:** HS 142 v Warwks (Birmingham) 1991. BB 3-22 v Northants (Northampton) 1990. **SL:** HS 109 v Lancs (Colchester) 1990. BB 5-58 v Glos (Chelmsford) 1992.

SUCH, Peter Mark (Harry Carlton CS, Ex Leake, Notts), b Helensburgh, Dunbartonshire 12 Jun 1964. 5'11". RHB, OB. Nottinghamshire 1982-86. Leicestershire 1987-89. Essex debut 1990. Cap 1991. **Tests:** 5 (1993); HS 14* and BB 6-67 v A (Manchester) 1993 – on debut. Tour: A 1992-93 (Eng A). HS 54 v Worcs (Chelmsford) 1993. 50 wkts (1): 76 (1993). BB 6-17 v Sussex (Southend) 1992. **NWT:** HS 0*. BB 2-29 v Devon (Exmouth) 1991. **BHC:** HS 4. BB 4-43 v Northants (Northampton) 1992. **SL:** HS 19 v Sussex (Hove) 1993. BB 5-32 v Yorks (Chelmsford) 1993.

TOPLEY, Thomas Donald (Royal Hospital S, Holbrook, Suffolk), b Canterbury, Kent 25 Feb 1964. Brother of P.A. (Kent 1972-75). 6'3". RHB, RMF. Surrey (v CU) and Essex debuts 1985. Cap 1988. GW 1987-88. Norfolk 1984-85. MCC YC. HS 66 v Yorks (Leeds) 1987. 50 wkts (1); most – 77 (1989). BB 7-75 v Derbys (Chesterfield) 1988. Awards: NWT 1; BHC 2. **NWT:** HS 19* v Leics (Leicester) 1992. BB 4-21 v Northumb (Jesmond) 1987. **BHC:** HS 10* v Notts (Chelmsford) 1990. BB 4-22 v Surrey (Chelmsford) 1988. **SL:** HS 38* v Lancs (Manchester) 1991. BB 6-33 v Notts (Colchester) 1988.

NEWCOMERS

AYRES, Duncan Wallace (Falmouth CS; Millfield S), b Basildon 8 Oct 1976. 5'11". RHB, RMF. Joined staff 1993.

COWAN, Ashley Preston (Framlingham C), b Hitchin, Herts 7 May 1975. 6'4". RHB, RM.

IRANI, Ronald Charles (Smithills CS, Bolton), b Leigh, Lancs 26 Oct 1971. 6'3". RHB, RM. Lancashire 1990-93. HS 44 La v Kent (Lytham) 1993. BB 2-21 La v Notts (Nottingham) 1992. **SL:** HS 34 La v Leics (Leicester) 1993. BB 1-7.

KASPROWICZ, Michael Scott (Brisbane State HS), b South Brisbane, Australia 10 Feb 1972. 6'4". RHB, RF. Queensland 1989-90 to date. Australian CA. Toured UK with Australia YC 1991. HS 49 Queensland v WA (Perth) 1989-90 – top-scored at No 11. 50 wkts (0+1): 51 (1992-93). BB 6-59 Queensland v Tasmania (Brisbane) 1992-93.

PEARSON, Richard Michael (Batley GS; St John's, Cambridge), b Batley, Yorks 27 Jan 1972. 6'3". RHB, OB. Cambridge U 1991-92 (blue 1991-92). Northamptonshire 1992. HS 33* CU v Surrey (Cambridge) 1992. BAC HS-. BB 5-108 CU v Warwks (Cambridge) 1992. BAC BB 2-90 Nh v Warwks (Northampton) 1992. **BHC:** HS 8. BB 2-31 Comb Us v Durham (Cambridge) 1992. **SL:** HS-. Joins on a three-month trial basis.

POWELL, Mark Geoffrey (Brentwood County HS; Southampton CHE), b Harold Wood, Romford 5 Aug 1972. 6'0". RHB, SLA. Joined staff 1993.

DEPARTURES – see p 156

78

ESSEX 1993

RESULTS SUMMARY

	Place	Won	Lost	Tied	Drew	Abandoned
Britannic Assurance Championship	11th	4	6		7	
All First-class Matches		5	6		9	
Sunday League	12th	7	8	1		1
NatWest Trophy	2nd Round					
Benson and Hedges Cup	1st Round					

BRITANNIC ASSURANCE CHAMPIONSHIP AVERAGES

BATTING AND FIELDING

Cap		M	I	NO	HS	Runs	Avge	100	50	Ct/St
1975	G.A.Gooch	10	18	2	159*	991	61.93	3	7	8
1989	N.Hussain	13	23	3	152	1102	55.10	5	5	12
1986	P.J.Prichard	17	32	3	225*	1237	42.65	4	6	15
–	J.J.B.Lewis	11	20	2	136*	706	39.22	1	5	11
1982	D.R.Pringle	12	14	4	76	575	38.33	–	6	10
1991	Salim Malik	14	25	2	132	861	37.43	2	3	11
1989	J.P.Stephenson	16	30	2	122	944	33.71	2	4	20
1990	M.A.Garnham	14	24	4	106	637	31.85	1	3	31/4
–	D.D.J.Robinson	2	4	–	67	112	28.00	–	1	2
–	N.Shahid	6	11	1	69*	258	25.80	–	2	8
1983	N.A.Foster	6	8	2	37	136	22.66	–	–	1
1993	M.C.Ilott	13	17	4	51	195	15.00	–	2	6
–	N.V.Knight	4	8	–	36	102	12.75	–	–	8
–	T.D.Topley	6	9	–	33	101	11.22	–	–	3
1986	J.H.Childs	14	15	8	23	76	10.85	–	–	3
1991	P.M.Such	12	14	1	54	131	10.07	–	1	5
–	S.J.W.Andrew	10	13	4	18	74	8.22	–	–	3
–	R.J.Rollins	3	4	1	7	14	4.66	–	–	3/3

Also played: D.J.P.Boden (2 matches) 0, 5; D.M.Cousins (1 match) 0*, 0; B.J.Hyam (1 match) 1, 0 (2 ct).

BOWLING

	O	M	R	W	Avge	Best	5wI	10wM
M.C.Ilott	452.4	95	1349	48	28.10	7-85	2	–
P.M.Such	478.1	110	1284	44	29.18	5-66	4	2
J.H.Childs	608.3	175	1466	49	29.91	6-37	3	–
J.P.Stephenson	257.5	51	866	28	30.92	5-31	2	–
Salim Malik	243.1	41	743	23	32.30	5-67	1	–
S.J.W.Andrew	255.4	46	886	25	35.44	7-47	2	–
D.R.Pringle	311.5	79	863	22	39.22	4-33	–	–
T.D.Topley	153.1	31	560	12	46.66	2-46	–	–
N.A.Foster	196.3	50	559	11	50.81	5-58	1	–

Also bowled: D.J.P.Boden 40-3-216-3; D.M.Cousins 27-4-109-1; G.A.Gooch 5-1-30-0; N.Hussain 10.3-0-108-1; P.J.Prichard 6-0-77-1; N.Shahid 7-1-22-0.

The First-Class Averages (pp 164-177) give the records of Essex players in all first-class county matches (their other opponents being England A, the Australians and Cambridge U), with the exception of:
N.A.Foster 7-10-3-37-199-28.42-0-0-1ct. 220.3-56-629-12-52.41-5/58-1-0.
G.A.Gooch 13-23-3-159*-1350-67.50-4-10-11ct. 1.1-3-44-0.
N.Hussain 16-27-3-152-1420-59.16-7-6-14ct. 10.3-0-108-1-108.00-0/1/75.
M.C.Ilott 15-20-4-51-252-15.75-0-2-7ct. 511.4-102-1550-51-30.39-7/85-2-0.
P.M.Such 15-18-2-54-172-10.75-0-1-6ct. 572.1-133-1607-60-26.78-6/98-6-3.

ESSEX RECORDS

FIRST-CLASS CRICKET

Highest Total	For 761-6d		v	Leics	Chelmsford 1990
	V 803-4d		by	Kent	Brentwood 1934
Lowest Total	For 30		v	Yorkshire	Leyton 1901
	V 14		by	Surrey	Chelmsford 1983
Highest Innings	For 343*	P.A.Perrin	v	Derbyshire	Chesterfield 1904
	332	W.H.Ashdown	for	Kent	Brentwood 1934

Highest Partnership for each Wicket

1st	270	A.V.Avery/T.C.Dodds	v	Surrey	The Oval 1946
2nd	403	G.A.Gooch/P.J.Prichard	v	Leics	Chelmsford 1990
3rd	347*	M.E.Waugh/N.Hussain	v	Lancashire	Ilford 1992
4th	314	Salim Malik/N.Hussain	v	Surrey	The Oval 1991
5th	316	N.Hussain/M.A.Garnham	v	Leics	Leicester 1991
6th	206	J.W.H.T.Douglas/J.O'Connor	v	Glos	Cheltenham 1923
	206	B.R.Knight/R.A.G.Luckin	v	Middlesex	Brentwood 1962
7th	261	J.W.H.T.Douglas/J.Freeman	v	Lancashire	Leyton 1914
8th	263	D.R.Wilcox/R.M.Taylor	v	Warwicks	Southend 1946
9th	251	J.W.H.T.Douglas/S.N.Hare	v	Derbyshire	Leyton 1921
10th	218	F.H.Vigar/T.P.B.Smith	v	Derbyshire	Chesterfield 1947

Best Bowling	For 10- 32	H.Pickett	v	Leics	Leyton 1895
(Innings)	V 10- 40	E.G.Dennett	for	Glos	Bristol 1906
Best Bowling	For 17-119	W.Mead	v	Hampshire	Southampton 1895
(Match)	V 17- 56	C.W.L.Parker	for	Glos	Gloucester 1925

Most Runs – Season	2559	G.A.Gooch	(av 67.34)	1984
Most Runs – Career	29434†	K.W.R.Fletcher	(av 36.88)	1962-88
Most 100s – Season	9	J.O'Connor		1934
	9	D.J.Insole		1955
Most 100s – Career	74	G.A.Gooch		1973-93
Most Wkts – Season	172	T.P.B.Smith	(av 27.13)	1947
Most Wkts – Career	1610	T.P.B.Smith	(av 26.68)	1929-51

† G.A.Gooch has scored 25334 runs.

LIMITED-OVERS CRICKET

Highest Total	NWT	386-5		v	Wiltshire	Chelmsford 1988
	BHC	388-7		v	Scotland	Chelmsford 1992
	SL	310-5		v	Glamorgan	Southend 1983
Lowest Total	NWT	100		v	Derbyshire	Brentwood 1965
	BHC	61		v	Lancashire	Chelmsford 1992
	SL	69		v	Derbyshire	Chesterfield 1974
Highest Innings	NWT	144	G.A.Gooch	v	Hampshire	Chelmsford 1990
	BHC	198*	G.A.Gooch	v	Sussex	Hove 1982
	SL	176	G.A.Gooch	v	Glamorgan	Southend 1983
Best Bowling	NWT	5- 8	J.K.Lever	v	Middlesex	Westcliff 1972
	BHC	5-13	J.K.Lever	v	Middlesex	Lord's 1985
	SL	8-26	K.D.Boyce	v	Lancashire	Manchester 1971

GLAMORGAN

Formation of Present Club: 6 July 1988
Colours: Blue and Gold
Badge: Gold Daffodil
Championships: (2) 1948, 1969
NatWest Trophy/Gillette Cup Winners: (0) Finalists 1977
Benson and Hedges Cup Winners: (0) Semi-Finalists 1988
Sunday League Champions: (1) 1993
Match Awards: NWT 31; BHC 42

Secretary: G.R.Stone. **Cricket Secretary:** M. Fatkin, Sophia Gardens, Cardiff, CF1 9XR (☎ 0222-343478)
Captain: H.Morris
Scorer: B.T.Denning
1994 Beneficiary: H.Morris

BARWICK, Stephen Royston (Cwrt Sart CS; Dwr-y-Felin CS), b Neath 6 Sep 1960. 6'2". RHB, RMF. Debut 1981. Cap 1987. HS 30 v Hants (Bournemouth) 1988. 50 wkts (2); most – 64 (1989). BB 8-42 v Worcs (Worcester) 1983. Award: BHC 1. **NWT:** HS 6. BB 5-26 v Surrey (Swansea) 1992. **BHC:** HS 18 v Kent (Canterbury) 1984. BB 4-11 v Minor C (Swansea) 1985. **SL:** HS 48* v Worcs (Worcester) 1989. BB 6-28 v Derbys (Derby) 1983.

BASTIEN, Steven (St Bonaventure S, Forest Gate; Haringey Cricket C), b Stepney, London 13 Mar 1963 (of Dominican parents). 6'1". RHB, RMF. Debut 1988. Tour: Z 1990-91 (Gm). HS 36* v Warwks (Birmingham) 1988 (his first innings). BB 6-52 (12-105 match) v Essex (Cardiff) 1993. **NWT:** HS 7*. BB 1-42. **BHC:** HS 7. BB 1-29. **SL:** HS 1. BB 2-42 v Kent (Maidstone) 1991.

BISHOP, Jamie (Pontardulais CS; Gorseinon Tertiary C; Cardiff IHE), b Swansea 14 Jan 1971. 5'11". LHB. Debut v OU (Oxford) 1992, scoring 51*. Wales (MC) 1991-92. HS 51* (above).

BUTCHER, Gary Paul (Trinity S; Riddlesdown S; Heath Clark C), b Clapham, London 11 Mar 1975. Son of A.R. (Surrey, Glam and England 1972-92); brother of M.A. (see SURREY). 5'9". RHB, RM. Glamorgan staff 1993 – awaiting f-c debut.

COTTEY, Phillip Anthony (Bishopston CS, Swansea), b Swansea 2 Jun 1966. 5'4". RHB, OB. Debut 1986. Cap 1992. E Transvaal 1991-92. Tour: Z 1990-91 (Gm). 1000 runs (3); most – 1076 (1992). HS 156 v OU (Oxford) 1990. BAC HS 141 v Kent (Canterbury) 1992. BB 2-42 E Transvaal v W Transvaal (Potchefstroom) 1991-92. **NWT:** HS 41 v Oxon (Swansea) 1993. **BHC:** HS 68 v Hants (Southampton) 1989. **SL:** 92* v Hants (Ebbw Vale) 1991. BB 2-30 v Sussex (Hove) 1992.

CROFT, Robert Damien Bale (St John Lloyd Catholic CS; W Glam IHE), b Morriston 25 May 1970. 5'10½". RHB, OB. Debut 1989. Cap 1992. Tours: WI 1991-92 (Eng A); Z 1990-91 (Gm). HS 107 v CU (Cambridge) 1993. BAC HS 91* v Worcs (Abergavenny) 1990. 50 wkts (2); most – 68 (1992). BB 8-66 (14-169 match) v Warwks (Swansea) 1992. **NWT:** HS 26 v Middx (Lord's) 1990. BB 2-28 v Worcs (Worcester) 1991. **BHC:** HS 30* v Durham (Durham) 1992. BB 3-28 v Comb Us (Cardiff) 1992. **SL:** HS 31* v Yorks (Ebbw Vale) 1992. BB 3-38 v Warwks (Neath) 1993.

DALE, Adrian (Chepstow CS; Swansea U), b Germiston, SA 24 Oct 1968 (to UK at 6 mths). 5'11½". RHB, RM. Debut 1989. Cap 1992. Tour: Z 1990-91 (Gm). 1000 runs (2); most – 1472 (1993). HS 214* v Middx (Cardiff) 1993. BB 6-18 v Warwicks (Cardiff) 1993. Award: NWT 1. **NWT:** HS 86 v Worcs (Worcester) 1991. BB 3-54 v Worcs (Swansea) 1993. **BHC:** HS 53 v Comb Us (Cardiff) 1992. BB 3-24 Comb Us v Surrey (Cambridge) 1989. **SL:** HS 67* v Derbys (Heanor) 1989. BB 6-22 v Durham (Colwyn Bay) 1993.

81

DALTON, Alistair John (Millfield S), b Bridgend 27 Apr 1973. 5'7". RHB, RM. Wales (MC) 1992. Glamorgan staff 1993 – awaiting f-c debut.

HEMP, David Lloyd (Olchfa CS; Millfield S; W Glamorgan C), b Bermuda 8 Nov 1970. UK resident since 1976. 6'0". LHB, RM. Debut 1991. Wales (MC) 1992. HS 90* v Essex (Cardiff) 1993. **SL:** HS 16 v Leics (Leicester) 1993.

JAMES, Stephen Peter (Monmouth S; Swansea U; Hughes Hall, Cambridge), b Lydney, Glos 7 Sep 1967. 6'0". RHB. Debut 1985. Cap 1992. Cambridge U 1989-90 (blue 1989-90). Tour: Z 1990-91 (Gm). 1000 runs (2); most – 1376 (1992). HS 152* v Lancs (Colwyn Bay) 1992. Award: BHC 1. **NWT:** HS 68 v Worcs (Swansea) 1993. **BHC:** HS 135 v Comb Us (Cardiff) 1992. **SL:** HS 107 v Sussex (Llanelli) 1993.

JONES, Andrew James (Monmouth S; Exeter U), b Swansea 5 Aug 1972. Son of A. (Glam, WA, NT and Natal 1957-83); nephew of E.W. (Glam 1961-83). 5'10". RHB. Wales (MC) 1992-93. Summer contract – awaiting f-c debut. **SL:** HS 3.

JONES, Robin Owen (Millfield S; Durham U), b Crewe, Cheshire 4 Oct 1973. Brother of G.W. (see CAMBRIDGE U). 5'10". RHB, OB. Glamorgan staff 1993 – awaiting f-c debut. **NWT:** HS 23 Wales (MC) v Sussex (Hove) 1993.

LEFEBVRE, Roland Philippe (Montessori Lyceum, Rotterdam; Hague Accademie of Physiotherapy), b Rotterdam, Holland 7 Feb 1963. 6'1". RHB, RMF. Somerset 1990-92 (cap 1991). Glamorgan debut/cap 1993. Holland 1983-90; ICC Trophy 1986 and 1989. Canterbury 1990-91. HS 100 Sm v Worcs (W-s-M) 1991. Gm HS 50 v Worcs (Worcester) 1993. BB 6-53 Canterbury v Auckland (Auckland) 1990-91. BAC BB 5-30 Sm v Glos (Taunton) 1990. Gm BB 4-70 v Surrey (Oval) 1993. **NWT:** HS 21* Sm v Warwks (Birmingham) 1991. BB 7-15 Sm v Devon (Torquay) 1990. **BHC:** HS 37 Sm v Middx (Lord's) 1990. BB 3-44 Sm v Surrey (Taunton) 1991. **SL:** HS 36* v Northants (Pentrych) 1993. BB 4-35 Sm v Northants (Taunton) 1990.

MAYNARD, Matthew Peter (David Hughes S, Anglesey), b Oldham, Lancs 21 Mar 1966. 5'10½". RHB, RM. Debut 1985 v Yorks (Swansea), scoring 102 out of 117 in 87 min, reaching 100 with 3 sixes off successive balls. Cap 1987. N Districts 1990-91/1991-92. YC 1988. **Tests:** 3 (1988 to 1993); HS 20 v A (Oval) 1993. Tour: SA 1989-90 (Eng XI). 1000 runs (8); most – 1803 (1991). HS 243 v Hants (Southampton) 1991. BB 3-21 v OU (Oxford) 1987. BAC BB 1-3. Awards: NWT 4; BHC 5. **NWT:** HS 151* v Durham (Darlington) 1991. **BHC:** HS 115 v Comb Us (Cardiff) 1988. **SL:** HS 122* v Leics (Swansea) 1992.

METSON, Colin Peter (Enfield GS; Stanborough S, Welwyn Garden City; Durham U), b Goffs Oak, Herts 2 Jul 1963. 5'5½". RHB, WK. Middlesex 1981-86. Glamorgan debut/cap 1987. HS 96 M v Glos (Uxbridge) 1984. Gm HS 84 v Kent (Maidstone) 1991. **NWT:** HS 21 v Notts (Nottingham) 1992. **BHC:** HS 23 v Kent (Swansea) 1990. **SL:** HS 30* v Hants (Bournemouth) 1990.

MORRIS, Hugh (Blundell's S), b Cardiff 5 Oct 1963. 5'8". LHB, RM. Debut 1981. Cap 1986. Captain 1986-89 and 1993-. Benefit 1994. **Tests:** 3 (1991); HS 44 v WI (Oval) 1991. Tours: WI 1991-92 (Eng A); SL 1990-91 (Eng A). 1000 runs (7) inc 2000 (1): 2276 – inc 10 hundreds – both Gm records (1990). HS 160* v Derbys (Cardiff) 1990. B 1-6. BAC BB 1-45. Awards: NWT 1; BHC 3. **NWT:** HS 154* v Staffs (Cardiff) 1989. **BHC:** HS 143* v Hants (Southampton) 1989. BB 1-14. **SL:** HS 104* v Derbys (Pontypridd) 1992.

PHELPS, Byron Stuart (Glanafan CS; Neath Tertiary C), b Neath 16 Dec 1975. 5'5". RHB, SLA. Debut 1993. Wales (MC) 1993. HS-. BB 1-105.

SHAW, Adrian David (Neath Tertiary C), b Neath 17 Feb 1972. 5'11". RHB, WK. Wales (MC) 1990-92. Glamorgan staff 1992 – awaiting f-c debut. **SL:** HS-.

THOMAS, Stuart Darren (Graig CS, Llanelli; Neath Tertiary C), b Morriston 25 Jan 1975. 6'0". LHB, RFM. Debut v Derbys (Chesterfield) 1992, taking 5-80 when aged 17yr 217d. HS 16* v Hants (Swansea) 1993. BB 5-76 v Worcs (Worcester) 1993. **SL:** HS-. BB 1-34.

WATKIN, Steven Llewellyn (Cymer Afan CS; S Glamorgan CHE), b Maesteg 15 Sep 1964. 6'3". RHB, RMF. Debut 1986. Cap 1989. Wisden 1993. **Tests:** 3 (1991 to 1993); HS 13 v A and BB 4-65 v A (Oval) 1993. Tours: WI 1991-92 (Eng A); P 1990-91 (Eng A); Z 1989-90 (Eng A), 1990-91 (Gm). HS 41 v Worcs (Worcester) 1992. 50 wkts (5); most – 94 (1989). BB 8-59 v Warwks (Birmingham) 1988. Award: NWT 1. **NWT:** HS 9. BB 3-18 v Sussex (Cardiff) 1990. **BHC:** HS 15 v Hants (Southampton) 1991. BB 3-28 v Minor C (Trowbridge) 1991. **SL:** 31* v Derbys (Checkley) 1991. BB 5-23 v Warwks (Birmingham) 1990.

WILLIAMS, James Robert Alexander (Clifton C), b Neath 20 Jul 1973. 5'11". RHB, OB. Debut 1993. HS 6.

NEWCOMERS

GIBSON, Ottis Delroy, b Barbados 16 Mar 1969. RHB, RF. Barbados 1990-91 to date. Border 1992-93. HS 83* Border v Transvaal (Johannesburg) 1992-93 – in 160 total. BB 7-78 Barbados v Trinidad (P-of-S) 1991-92.

PARKIN, Owen Thomas (Bournemouth GS), b Coventry, Warwks 24 Sep 1972. 6'2". RHB, RFM. Dorset 1992.

REES, Gareth Henry John (Clifton C), b Clifton, Bristol 24 Oct 1974. 6'1". RHB, RSM.

ROSEBERRY, Andrew (Durham S), b Sunderland, Co Durham 2 Apr 1971. 6'0". Younger brother of M.A. (see MIDDLESEX). RHB, RM. Leicestershire 1992. Northumberland 1993. HS 14 Le v P (Leicester) 1992. No BAC appearances.

DEPARTURES

FROST, Mark (Alexander HS, Tipton; St Peter's S, Wolverhampton; Durham U), b Barking, Essex 21 Oct 1962. 6'2". RHB, RMF. Surrey 1988-89. Glamorgan 1990-93 (cap 1991). Staffordshire 1987. Tour: Z 1990-91 (Gm). HS 12 v Warwks (Birmingham) 1990. 50 wkts (2); most – 65 (1991). BB 7-99 (11-143 match) v Glos (Cheltenham) 1991. Award: BHC 1. **NWT:** HS 3. BB 3-50 v Dorset (Swansea) 1990. **BHC:** HS 4. BB 4-25 v Worcs (Worcester) 1990. **SL:** HS 6*, BB 4-30 v Northants (Northampton) 1990.

RICHARDS, Isaac Vivian Alexander (Antigua GS), b St John's, Antigua 7 Mar 1952. 5'11". RHB, OB. Leeward Is 1971-72/1990-91 (captain 1981-82/1990-91). Somerset 1974-86 (cap 1974; benefit 1982). Queensland 1976-77. Glamorgan debut/cap 1990. Wisden 1976. **Tests:** (WI): 121 (1974-75 to 1991, 50 as captain); HS 291 v E (Oval) 1976; BB 2-17 v P (P-of-S) 1987-88. LOI (WI): 187 (HS 189*; BB 6-41). Tours (WI) (C=captain): E 1976, 1980, 1984, 1988C, 1991C; A 1975-76, 1979-80, 1981-82, 1984-85, 1986-87C, 1988-89C; NZ 1986-87C; I 1974-75, 1983-84, 1987-88C; P 1974-75, 1980-81, 1986-87C; SL 1974-75. 1000 runs (14+3) inc 2000 (1): 2161 (1977). Only West Indian to score 100 f-c hundreds (114). HS 322 (Sm record) v Warwks (Taunton) 1985. Gm HS 224* v Middx (Cardiff) 1993. BB 5-88 WI v Queensland (Brisbane) 1981-82. BAC BB 4-36 Sm v Derbys (Chesterfield) 1986. Gm BB 3-22 v Yorks (Middlesbrough) 1993. Awards: NWT 7; BHC 6. **NWT:** HS 162* v Oxon (Swansea) 1993. BB 3-15 Sm v Beds (Bedford) 1982. **BHC:** HS 132* Sm v Surrey (Lord's) 1981. BB 3-18 v Warwks (Birmingham) 1990. **SL:** HS 126* Sm v Glos (Bristol Imp) 1975. BB 6-24 Sm v Lancs (Manchester) 1983.

GLAMORGAN 1993

RESULTS SUMMARY

	Place	Won	Lost	Drew	Abandoned
Britannic Assurance Championship	3rd	9	5	3	
All First-class Matches		9	5	6	
Sunday League	1st	13	2		2
NatWest Trophy	Semi-Finalist				
Benson and Hedges Cup	1st Round				

BRITANNIC ASSURANCE CHAMPIONSHIP AVERAGES

BATTING AND FIELDING

Cap		M	I	NO	HS	Runs	Avge	100	50	Ct/St
1987	M.P.Maynard	14	24	–	145	1041	43.37	1	7	14
1990	I.V.A.Richards	16	31	5	224*	1126	43.30	1	7	16
1992	A.Dale	17	33	1	214*	1303	40.71	3	6	12
1986	H.Morris	16	31	1	134*	1146	38.20	4	5	14
1992	P.A.Cottey	16	29	4	105	855	34.20	2	6	13
–	D.L.Hemp	8	15	2	90*	400	30.76	–	5	4
1992	S.P.James	14	26	1	138*	726	29.04	1	4	16
1992	R.D.B.Croft	17	29	5	60	532	22.16	–	2	9
1991	M.Frost	2	4	3	7	19	19.00	–	–	–
1993	R.P.Lefebvre	17	25	2	50	426	18.52	–	1	9
–	S.D.Thomas	3	6	4	16*	37	18.50	–	–	–
1987	C.P.Metson	17	26	4	25*	269	12.22	–	–	47/4
1989	S.L.Watkin	16	20	6	31	161	11.50	–	–	6
1987	S.R.Barwick	10	11	3	23*	60	7.50	–	–	3
–	S.Bastien	4	5	3	14*	23				–

BOWLING

	O	M	R	W	Avge	Best	5wI	10wM
S.D.Thomas	103.3	17	368	16	23.00	5- 76	1	–
S.L.Watkin	669.4	144	1866	81	23.03	5- 71	2	–
S.Bastien	140.3	27	472	18	26.22	6- 52	2	1
R.P.Lefebvre	578.1	160	1304	41	31.80	4- 70	–	–
A.Dale	341.1	70	1071	31	34.54	6- 18	1	–
R.D.B.Croft	750.5	224	1947	54	36.05	5-112	2	–
S.R.Barwick	455	192	920	15	61.33	3- 28	–	–

Also bowled: P.A.Cottey 7-0-123-0; M.Frost 58.1-11-180-7; M.P.Maynard 6-0-110-1; I.V.A.Richards 84-18-235-4.

The First-Class Averages (pp 164-177) give the records of Glamorgan players in all first-class county matches (their other opponents being the Australians, Cambridge U and Oxford U), with the exception of:
  M.P.Maynard 17-28-1-145-1339-49.59-3-7-20ct. 6-0-110-1-110.00-1/110.
  S.L.Watkin 18-22-8-31-187-13.35-0-0-6ct. 713.4-160-1946-86-22.62-5/71-2-0.

GLAMORGAN RECORDS

FIRST-CLASS CRICKET

Highest Total	For	587-8d		v	Derbyshire	Cardiff	1951
	V	653-6d		by	Glos	Bristol	1928
Lowest Total	For	22		v	Lancashire	Liverpool	1924
	V	33		by	Leics	Ebbw Vale	1965
Highest Innings	For	287*	D.E.Davies	v	Glos	Newport	1939
	V	313*	S.J.Cook	for	Somerset	Cardiff	1990

Highest Partnership for each Wicket

1st	330	A.Jones/R.C.Fredericks	v	Northants	Swansea	1972
2nd	249	S.P.James/H.Morris	v	Oxford U	Oxford	1987
3rd	313	D.E.Davies/W.E.Jones	v	Essex	Brentwood	1948
4th	425*	A.Dale/I.V.A.Richards	v	Middlesex	Cardiff	1993
5th	264	M.Robinson/S.W.Montgomery	v	Hampshire	Bournemouth	1949
6th	230	W.E.Jones/B.L.Muncer	v	Worcs	Worcester	1953
7th	195*	W.Wooller/W.E.Jones	v	Lancashire	Liverpool	1947
8th	202	D.Davies/J.J.Hills	v	Sussex	Eastbourne	1928
9th	203*	J.J.Hills/J.C.Clay	v	Worcs	Swansea	1929
10th	143	T.Davies/S.A.B.Daniels	v	Glos	Swansea	1982

Best Bowling	For	10- 51	J.Mercer	v	Worcs	Worcester	1936
(Innings)	V	10- 18	G.Geary	for	Leics	Pontypridd	1929
Best Bowling	For	17-212	J.C.Clay	v	Worcs	Swansea	1937
(Match)	V	16- 96	G.Geary	for	Leics	Pontypridd	1929

Most Runs – Season	2276	H.Morris	(av 55.51)	1990
Most Runs – Career	34056	A.Jones	(av 33.03)	1957-83
Most 100s – Season	10	H.Morris		1990
Most 100s – Career	52	A.Jones		1957-83
Most Wkts – Season	176	J.C.Clay	(av 17.34)	1937
Most Wkts – Career	2174	D.J.Shepherd	(av 20.95)	1950-72

LIMITED-OVERS CRICKET

Highest Total	NWT	345-2		v	Durham	Darlington	1991
	BHC	302-6		v	Comb Us	Cardiff	1988
	SL	287-8		v	Middlesex	Cardiff	1993
Lowest Total	NWT	76		v	Northants	Northampton	1968
	BHC	68		v	Lancashire	Manchester	1973
	SL	42		v	Derbyshire	Swansea	1979
Highest Innings	NWT	162*	I.V.A.Richards	v	Oxfordshire	Swansea	1993
	BHC	143*	H.Morris	v	Hampshire	Southampton	1989
	SL	130*	J.A.Hopkins	v	Somerset	Bath	1983
Best Bowling	NWT	5-13	R.J.Shastri	v	Scotland	Edinburgh	1988
	BHC	5-17	A.H.Wilkins	v	Worcs	Worcester	1978
	SL	6-22	A.Dale	v	Durham	Colwyn Bay	1993

GLOUCESTERSHIRE

Formation of Present Club: 1871
Colours: Blue, Gold, Brown, Silver, Green and Red
Badge: Coat of Arms of the City and County of Bristol
Championships (since 1890): (0) Second 1930, 1931, 1947, 1959, 1969, 1986
NatWest Trophy/Gillette Cup Winners: (1) 1973
Benson and Hedges Cup Winners: (1) 1977
Sunday League Champions: (0) Second 1988
Match Awards: NWT 38; BHC 43

Secretary: P.G.M.August, Phoenix County Ground, Nevil Road, Bristol BS7 9EJ
(☎ 0272-245216)
Captain: C.A.Walsh
Scorer: B.H.Jenkins
1994 Beneficiary: R.C.Russell

ALLEYNE, Mark Wayne (Harrison C, Barbados; Cardinal Pole S, London E9; Haringey Cricket C), b Tottenham, London 23 May 1968. 5'10". RHB, RM. Debut 1986. Cap 1990. Tours (Gs): SL 1986-87, 1992-93. 1000 runs (2); most – 1121 (1991). HS 256 v Northants (Northampton) 1990. BB 4-48 v Glam (Bristol) 1988. Award: NWT 1. **NWT:** HS 73 v Herts (Bristol) 1993. BB 5-30 v Lincs (Gloucester) 1990. **BHC:** HS 36 v Derbys (Derby) 1987. BB 5-27 v Comb Us (Bristol) 1988. **SL:** HS 134* v Leics (Bristol) 1992. BB 4-35 v Lancs (Manchester) 1992.

BABINGTON, Andrew Mark (Reigate GS; Borough Road PE College), b Middlesex Hospital, London 22 Jul 1963. 6'2". LHB, RFM. Sussex 1986-90. Gloucestershire debut 1991. HS 58 v Sussex (Cheltenham) 1991. BB 8-107 v Kent (Bristol) 1992. Hat-trick 1986. **NWT:** HS 4* v Kent (Bristol) 1992. BHC: HS 27 v Leics (Cheltenham) 1992. BB 4-29 Sx v Surrey (Hove) 1988. **SL:** HS 11 v Essex (Cheltenham) 1991. BB 4-21 v Northants (Moreton) 1992.

BALL, Martyn Charles John (King Edmund SS; Bath CFE), b Bristol 26 Apr 1970. 5'8". RHB, OB. Debut 1988. Tour: SL 1992-93 (Gs). HS 72 v Notts (Bristol) 1993. BB 8-46 (14-169 match) v Somerset (Taunton) 1993. **NWT:** HS 16* v Essex (Cheltenham) 1992. BB 3-42 v Lancs (Gloucester) 1989. **BHC:** HS 13 v Middx (Lord's) 1992. BB 1-32. **SL:** HS 19 v Surrey (Bristol) 1992. BB 3-24 v Somerset (Taunton) 1993.

BROAD, Brian Christopher (Colston's S, Bristol; St Paul's C, Cheltenham), b Knowle, Bristol 29 Sep 1957. 6'4". LHB, RM. Gloucestershire 1979-83 and 1993- (cap 1981). Nottinghamshire 1984-92 (cap 1984). OFS 1985-86 (captain). **Tests:** 25 (1984 to 1989); HS 162 v A (Perth) 1986-87. LOI: 34 (HS 106). Tours: A 1986-87, 1987-88; SA 1989-90 (Eng XI); NZ 1987-88; P 1987-88; SL 1992-93 (Gs); Z 1984-85 (EC). 1000 runs (11) inc 2000 (1): 2226 (1990). HS 227* Nt v Kent (Tunbridge W) 1990. Gs HS 145 v Notts (Bristol) 1983. BB 2-14 v WI (Bristol) 1980. Awards: NWT 5; BHC 2. **NWT:** HS 115 Nt v Bucks (Marlow) 1990. **BHC:** HS 122 Nt v Derbys (Derby) 1984. BB 2-73 Nt v Lancs (Nottingham) 1984. **SL:** HS 108 Nt v Glam (Cardiff) 1991. BB 3-46 v Worcs (Bristol) 1982.

COOPER, Kevin Edwin (Hucknall National SS), b Hucknall, Notts 27 Dec 1957. 6'1". LHB, RFM. Nottinghamshire 1976-92 (cap 1980; benefit 1990). Gloucestershire debut v Board XI (Colombo) 1992-93. Tour: SL 1992-93 (Gs). HS 52 v Lancs (Cheltenham) 1993. 50 wkts (8) inc 100 (1): 101 (1988). BB 8-44 Nt v Middx (Lord's) 1984. Gs HS 5-83 v Yorks (Sheffield) 1993. Awards: NWT 1; BHC 2. **NWT:** HS 11 Nt v Glos (Nottingham) 1982. BB 4-49 Nt v Warwks (Nottingham) 1985. **BHC:** HS 25* Nt v Lancs (Manchester) 1983. BB 4-9 Nt v Yorks (Nottingham) 1989. **SL:** HS 31 Nt v Glos (Nottingham) 1984. BB 4-25 Nt v Hants (Nottingham) 1976.

CUNLIFFE, Robert John (Banbury S; Banbury TC), b Oxford 8 Nov 1973. 5'10". RHB, RM. Oxfordshire 1991-92. Gloucestershire staff 1993 – awaiting f-c debut. **SL:** HS 22 v Sussex (Hove) 1993.

DAVIES, Mark (Cwrt Sart CS; Neath Tertiary C), b Neath, Glam 18 Apr 1969. 5'6". RHB, SLA. Glamorgan 1990. Gloucestershire debut 1992. MCC YC. Tour: SL 1992-93 (Gs). HS 44* v Glam (Abergavenny) 1993. 50 wkts (1): 56 (1992). BB 5-57 (10-141 match) v Northants (Northampton) 1993. **SL:** HS 13* v Derbys (Cheltenham) 1993. BB 1-11.

DAWSON, Robert Ian (Millfield S; Newcastle Poly.), b Exmouth, Devon 29 Mar 1970. 5'11". RHB, RM. Debut 1992. Devon 1988-91. HS 58 v Notts (Bristol) 1993. **NWT:** HS 13 Devon v Essex (Exmouth) 1991. BB 1-37. **SL:** HS 35 v Sussex (Cheltenham) 1992.

HANCOCK, Timothy Harold Coulter (St Edward's S, Oxford; Henley C), b Reading, Berkshire 20 Apr 1972. 5'10". RHB, RM. Debut 1991. Oxfordshire 1990. Tour: SL 1992-93 (Gs). HS 102 v Somerset (Taunton) 1992. BB 3-10 v Glam (Abergavenny) 1993. **NWT:** HS 45 and BB 2-7 v Herts (Bristol) 1993. **BHC:** HS 23 v Derbys (Bristol) 1993. **SL:** HS 46 v Sussex (Hove) 1993.

HINKS, Simon Graham (St George's S, Gravesend), b Northfleet, Kent 12 Oct 1960. 6'2". LHB, RM. Kent 1982-91 (cap 1985). Gloucestershire debut 1992. Tour: SL 1992-93 (Gs). 1000 runs (3); most – 1588 (1990). HS 234 K v Middx (Canterbury) 1990. Gs HS 88* v Lancs (Manchester) 1992. BB 2-18 v Notts (Nottingham) 1989. Awards: NWT 1; BHC 1. **NWT:** HS 95 K v Surrey (Canterbury) 1985. **BHC:** HS 85 K v Sussex (Canterbury) 1987. BB 1-15. **SL:** HS 99 K v Glam (Maidstone) 1986. BB 1-3.

HODGSON, Geoffrey Dean (Nelson Thomlinson CS, Wigton; Loughborough U), b Carlisle, Cumberland 22 Oct 1966. 6'1". RHB. Debut 1989. Cap 1992. Cumberland 1984-88 (cap 1987 when aged 20 – county record). Warwickshire (SL only) 1987. 1000 runs (4); most – 1320 (1990). HS 166 v Hants (Bristol) 1993. Awards: BHC 2. **NWT:** HS 62 v Yorks (Bristol) 1993. **BHC:** HS 103* v Minor C (Cheltenham) 1992. **SL:** HS 104* v Durham (Bristol) 1993.

RUSSELL, Robert Charles (**Jack**) (Archway CS), b Stroud 15 Aug 1963. 5'8½". LHB, WK, occ OB. Debut 1981. Cap 1985. Benefit 1994. Wisden 1989. **Tests:** 31 (1988 to 1992); HS 128* v A (Manchester) 1989. LOI: 26 (HS 50). Tours: A 1990-91, 1992-93 (Eng A); WI 1989-90; NZ 1991-92; P 1987-88; SL 1986-87 (Gs). HS 128* (Tests). Gs HS 120 v Somerset (Bristol) 1990. BB 1-4. Award: BHC 1. **NWT:** HS 42* v Lancs (Gloucester) 1989. **BHC:** HS 51 v Worcs (Worcester) 1991. **SL:** HS 108 v Worcs (Hereford) 1986.

SMITH, Andrew Michael (Queen Elizabeth GS, Wakefield; Exeter U), b Dewsbury, Yorks 1 Oct 1967. 5'9". RHB, LM. Debut 1991. HS 51* v Warwks (Bristol) 1992. BB 4-41 v Leics (Hinckley) 1991. **NWT:** HS 8*. BB 3-45 v Somerset (Taunton) 1992. **BHC:** HS 15* Comb Us v Surrey (Oxford) 1990. BB 4-49 Comb Us v Somerset (Oxford) 1988. **SL:** HS 15* v Essex (Cheltenham) 1991. BB 4-38 v Leics (Bristol) 1992.

WALSH, Courtney Andrew (Excelsior HS), b Kingston, Jamaica 30 Oct 1962. 6'5½". RHB, RF. Jamaica 1981-82/1991-92 (captain 1990-91/1991-92). Gloucestershire debut 1984. Cap 1985. Captain 1993–. Benefit 1992. Wisden 1986. **Tests** (WI): 59 (1984-85 to 1992-93); HS 30* v A (Melbourne) 1988-89; BB 6-62 v I (Kingston) 1988-89. LOI (WI): 111 (HS 29*; BB 5-1). Tours (WI): E 1984, 1988, 1991; A 1984-85, 1986-87, 1988-89, 1992-93; NZ 1986-87; I 1987-88; P 1986-87, 1990-91; Z 1983-84 (Young WI). HS 63* v Yorks (Cheltenham) 1990. 50 wkts (7+1) inc 100 (1): 118 (1986). BB 9-72 v Somerset (Bristol) 1986. Hat-trick 1988-89 (WI). Awards: NWT 2. **NWT:** HS 37 v Herts (Bristol) 1993. BB 6-21 v Kent (Bristol) 1990 and v Cheshire (Bristol) 1992. **BHC:** HS 28 v Comb Us (Bristol) 1989. BB 2-19 v Scot 1985. **SL:** HS 35 v Glam (Cardiff) 1986. BB 4-19 v Kent (Cheltenham) 1987.

WIGHT, Robert Marcus (KCS, Wimbledon; Exeter U; Trinity Hall, Cambridge), b Kensington, London 12 Sep 1969. Distant cousin of P.B. (British Guiana, Somerset and Canterbury 1950/51-1965). 6'2". RHB, OB. Debut/blue Cambridge U 1992. Gloucestershire debut 1993. HS 62* CU v OU (Lord's) 1992. Gs HS 54 v Leics (Leicester) 1993. BB 3-65 CU v Kent (Cambridge) 1992. Gs BB 3-71 v Yorks (Sheffield) 1993. Hockey for Devon 1989-91; CU blue 1991-92 (captain 1992). **NWT:** HS 18 v Herts (Bristol) 1993. BB 1-24. **SL:** HS 11* v Middx (Moreton) 1993. BB 1-33.

WILLIAMS, Ricardo Cecil (Ellerslie SS, Barbados; Haringey Cricket C), b Camberwell, London 3 Feb 1968. 5'9". RHB, RM. Debut 1991. HS 44 v Notts (Worksop) 1992. BB 3-44 v P (Bristol) 1992. BAC BB 3-101 v Leics (Leicester) 1993. **SL:** HS 4. BB 3-46 v Durham (Bristol) 1993.

WILLIAMS, Richard Charles James (Millfield S). b Southmead, Bristol 8 Aug 1969. 5'8". LHB, WK. Debut 1990. Tour: SL 1992-93 (Gs). HS 55* v Derbys (Gloucester) 1991. **SL:** HS 17 v Warwks (Bristol) 1992.

WINDOWS, Matthew Guy Newman (Clifton C; Durham U), b Bristol 5 Apr 1973. Son of A.R. (Glos and CU 1960-68). 5'7". RHB, RSM. Debut 1992. HS 71 v Essex (Bristol) 1992 – on debut. **SL:** HS 24* v Notts (Bristol) 1993.

WRIGHT, Anthony John (Alleyn's GS) b Stevenage, Herts 27 Jun 1962. 6'0". RHB, RM. Gloucestershire debut 1982. Cap 1987. Captain 1990-93. Tours (Gs): SL 1986-87, 1992-93 (captain). 1000 runs (4); most – 1596 (1991). HS 161 v Glam (Bristol) 1987. BB 1-16. Awards: NWT 1; BHC 1. **NWT:** HS 107* v Cheshire (Bristol) 1992. **BHC:** HS 97 v Worcs (Bristol) 1990. **SL:** HS 93 v Durham (Stockton) 1992.

NEWCOMERS

CAWDRON, Michael John (Cheltenham C), b Luton, Beds 7 Oct 1974. 6'2". LHB, RM.

HEWSON, Dominic Robert (Cheltenham C), b Cheltenham 3 Oct 1974. 5'8". RHB, occ RM.

SHEERAZ, Kamran Pashah (Licensed Victuallers' S, Ascot; E Berkshire C, Langley), b Wellington, Shropshire 28 Dec 1973. 6'0". RHB, RMF. Bedfordshire 1992.

DEPARTURES

De la PENA, J.M. – see SURREY.

GERRARD, Martin James (Grittleton House S; St Brendan's SFC; Wales Poly) b Southmead, Bristol 19 May 1967. 6'3". RHB, LMF. Gloucestershire 1991-93. W Transvaal 1991-92. Tour: SL 1992-93 (Gs). HS 42 v Somerset (Bristol) 1991. BB 6-40 (10-60 match) v SL (Bristol) 1991. BAC BB 4-50 v Middx (Bristol) 1993. **NWT:** HS-. **BHC:** HS 1*. **SL:** HS 7. BB 2-35 v Surrey (Bristol) 1992.

SCOTT, Richard John (Queen Elizabeth S, Bournemouth), b Bournemouth, Hants 2 Nov 1963. 5'11". LHB, RM. Hampshire 1988-90. Gloucestershire 1991-93. Dorset 1981-85. Tour: SL 1992-93 (Gs). HS 127 v Worcs (Worcester) 1991 – on Gs debut. BB 3-43 v Sussex (Hove) 1991. **NWT:** HS 25 v Cheshire (Bristol) 1992. BB 4-22 v Norfolk (Bristol) 1991. **BHC:** HS 69 H v Sussex (Hove) 1989. BB 1-42. **SL:** HS 116* H v Yorks (Southampton) 1989. BB 3-23 v Northants (Moreton) 1992.

GLOUCESTERSHIRE 1993

RESULTS SUMMARY

	Place	Won	Lost	Tied	Drew	Abandoned
Britannic Assurance Championship	17th	3	10		4	
All First-class Matches		3	10		5	
Sunday League	13th	5	9	1		2
NatWest Trophy	2nd Round					
Benson and Hedges Cup	Preliminary Round					

BRITANNIC ASSURANCE CHAMPIONSHIP AVERAGES

BATTING AND FIELDING

Cap		M	I	NO	HS	Runs	Avge	100	50	Ct/St
1992	G.D.Hodgson	13	26	2	166	1063	44.29	2	7	7
1985	R.C.Russell	17	30	7	99*	826	35.91	–	5	53/7
1981	B.C.Broad	17	33	–	131	1081	32.75	2	6	6
1990	M.W.Alleyne	17	33	2	142*	992	32.00	3	2	10
–	R.C.Williams	3	6	3	38	90	30.00	–	–	–
–	T.H.C.Hancock	15	28	2	76	686	26.38	–	4	5
–	R.I.Dawson	8	16	1	58	349	23.26	–	1	12
–	S.G.Hinks	12	24	1	68	482	20.95	–	3	10
–	R.J.Scott	5	10	–	51	179	17.90	–	1	1
1987	A.J.Wright	10	20	2	75	299	16.61	–	1	8
–	R.M.Wight	7	11	1	54	152	15.20	–	1	1
1985	C.A.Walsh	13	20	2	57	262	14.55	–	1	4
–	M.C.J.Ball	4	8	–	71	113	14.12	–	1	13
–	M.Davies	14	23	5	44*	220	12.22	–	–	6
–	K.E.Cooper	14	25	6	52	218	11.47	–	1	5
–	A.M.Smith	6	10	1	33	84	9.33	–	–	1
–	M.J.Gerrard	3	5	2	9	20	6.66	–	–	1
–	A.M.Babington	7	9	3	23	40	6.66	–	–	1

Also played (1 match each): J.M.de la Pena 7*; M.G.N.Windows 21, 37.

BOWLING

	O	M	R	W	Avge	Best	5wI	10wM
C.A.Walsh	513.1	117	1466	62	23.64	5-59	3	–
M.C.J.Ball	157.3	35	439	18	24.38	8-46	2	1
K.E.Cooper	502.4	149	1233	47	26.23	5-83	1	–
M.W.Alleyne	238.1	50	652	24	27.16	3-25	–	–
M.Davies	515.1	141	1412	37	38.16	5-57	2	1
A.M.Babington	219.2	49	634	13	48.76	3-51	–	–
A.M.Smith	186.2	35	587	12	48.91	3-59	–	–

Also bowled: B.C.Broad 1-0-1-0; R.I.Dawson 1-0-2-0; J.M.de la Pena 14-1-79-0;
M.J.Gerrard 89.1-16-298-8; T.H.C.Hancock 42-11-128-6; S.G.Hinks 1-0-2-0;
R.C.Russell 1.5-0-15-0; R.J.Scott 60-14-157-2; R.M.Wight 181.2-47-478-9;
R.C.Williams 66-13-247-5; M.G.N.Windows 1-0-3-0.

The First-Class Averages (pp 164-177) give the records of Gloucestershire players
in all first-class county matches (their other opponents being the Australians), with
the exception of M.G.N.Windows, whose full county figures are as above, and:
  R.C.Russell 18-31-7-99*-852-35.50-0-5-54ct-7st. 1.5-0-15-0.

GLOUCESTERSHIRE RECORDS

FIRST-CLASS CRICKET

Highest Total	For	653-6d		v Glamorgan	Bristol	1928
	V	774-7d		by Australians	Bristol	1948
Lowest Total	For	17		v Australians	Cheltenham	1896
	V	12		by Northants	Gloucester	1907
Highest Innings	For	318*	W.G.Grace	v Yorkshire	Cheltenham	1876
	V	296	A.O.Jones	for Notts	Nottingham	1903

Highest Partnership for each Wicket

1st	395	D.M.Young/R.B.Nicholls	v Oxford U	Oxford	1962
2nd	256	C.T.M.Pugh/T.W.Graveney	v Derbyshire	Chesterfield	1960
3rd	336	W.R.Hammond/B.H.Lyon	v Leics	Leicester	1933
4th	321	W.R.Hammond/W.L.Neale	v Leics	Gloucester	1937
5th	261	W.G.Grace/W.O.Moberley	v Yorkshire	Cheltenham	1876
6th	320	G.L.Jessop/J.H.Board	v Sussex	Hove	1903
7th	248	W.G.Grace/E.L.Thomas	v Sussex	Hove	1896
8th	239	W.R.Hammond/A.E.Wilson	v Lancashire	Bristol	1938
9th	193	W.G.Grace/S.A.P.Kitcat	v Sussex	Bristol	1896
10th	131	W.R.Gouldsworthy/J.G.Bessant	v Somerset	Bristol	1923

Best Bowling	For	10-40	E.G.Dennett	v Essex	Bristol	1906
(Innings)	V	10-66	A.A.Mailey	for Australians	Cheltenham	1921
		10-66	K.Smales	for Notts	Stroud	1956
Best Bowling	For	17-56	C.W.L.Parker	v Essex	Gloucester	1925
(Match)	V	15-87	A.J.Conway	for Worcs	Moreton-in-M	1914

Most Runs – Season	2860	W.R.Hammond	(av 69.75)		1933
Most Runs – Career	33664	W.R.Hammond	(av 57.05)		1920-51
Most 100s – Season	13	W.R.Hammond			1938
Most 100s – Career	113	W.R.Hammond			1920-51
Most Wkts – Season	222	T.W.J.Goddard	(av 16.80)		1937
	222	T.W.J.Goddard	(av 16.37)		1947
Most Wkts – Career	3170	C.W.L.Parker	(av 19.43)		1903-35

LIMITED-OVERS CRICKET

Highest Total	NWT	327-7		v Berkshire	Reading	1966
	BHC	300-4		v Comb Us	Oxford	1982
	SL	281-2		v Hampshire	Swindon	1991
Lowest Total	NWT	82		v Notts	Bristol	1987
	BHC	62		v Hampshire	Bristol	1975
	SL	49		v Middlesex	Bristol	1978
Highest Innings	NWT	158	Zaheer Abbas	v Leics	Leicester	1983
	BHC	154*	M.J.Procter	v Somerset	Taunton	1972
	SL	134*	M.W.Alleyne	v Leics	Bristol	1992
Best Bowling	NWT	6-21	C.A.Walsh	v Kent	Bristol	1990
		6-21	C.A.Walsh	v Cheshire	Bristol	1992
	BHC	6-13	M.J.Procter	v Hampshire	Southampton	1977
	SL	6-52	J.N.Shepherd	v Kent	Bristol	1983

90

HAMPSHIRE

Formation of Present Club: 12 August 1863
Colours: Blue, Gold and White
Badge: Tudor Rose and Crown
Championships: (2) 1961, 1973
NatWest Trophy/Gillette Cup Winners: (1) 1991
Benson and Hedges Cup Winners: (2) 1988, 1992
Sunday League Champions: (3) 1975, 1978, 1986
Match Awards: NWT 49; BHC 55

Chief Executive: A.F.Baker, County Cricket Ground, Northlands Road, Southampton SO9 2TY (☎ 0703-333788/9)
Captain: M.C.J.Nicholas
Scorer: V.H Isaacs
1994 Beneficiary: V.P.Terry

AYMES, Adrian Nigel (Bellemoor SM, Southampton), b Southampton 4 Jun 1964. 6'0". RHB, WK. Debut 1987. Cap 1991. HS 107* v Sussex (Portsmouth) 1993. BB 1-75. **NWT:** HS 2. **BHC:** HS 23* v Durham (Stockton) 1993. **SL:** HS 44 v Essex (Chelmsford) 1993.

BOVILL, James Noel Bruce (Charterhouse; Durham U), b High Wycombe, Bucks 2 Jun 1971. Son of M.E. (Dorset 1957-60). 6'1". RHB, RFM. Debut 1993. Buckinghamshire 1990-92. HS 3* and BB 2-32 v Essex (Chelmsford) 1993. **BHC:** HS 14* and BB 1-39 Comb Us v Glam (Cardiff) 1992. **SL:** HS 7*. BB 3-40 v Surrey (Oval) 1993.

CONNOR, Cardigan Adolphus (The Valley SS, Anguilla; Langley C, Berkshire), b The Valley, Anguilla 24 Mar 1961. 5'9". RHB, RFM. Debut 1984. Cap 1988. Buckinghamshire 1979-83. HS 59 v Surrey (Oval) 1993. 50 wkts (3); most – 62 (1984). BB 7-31 v Glos (Portsmouth) 1989. **NWT:** HS 13 v Yorks (Southampton) 1990. BB 4-29 v Warwks (Birmingham) 1991. **BHC:** HS 5*. BB 4-19 v Sussex (Hove) 1989. **SL:** HS 25 v Middx (Lord's) 1993. BB 4-11 v Derbys (Portsmouth) 1990.

COX, Rupert Michael FIENNES- (Bradfield C), b Guildford, Surrey 20 Aug 1967. 5'9". LHB, OB. Debut 1990. HS 104* v Worcs (Worcester) 1990 – in second match. **SL:** 13 v Surrey (Oval) 1991.

FLINT, Darren Peter John (Queen Mary's SFC), b Basingstoke 14 Jun 1970. 6'0". RHB, SLA. Debut 1993. HS 14* v Worcs (Portsmouth) 1993. BB 5-32 v Glos (Bristol) 1993 – on debut.

GARAWAY, Mark (Sandown HS, IoW), b Swindon, Wilts 20 Jul 1973. 5'8". RHB, WK. MCC YC. Hampshire staff 1993 – awaiting f-c debut.

JAMES, Kevan David (Edmonton County HS), b Lambeth, London 18 Mar 1961. 6'0". RHB, LMF. Middlesex 1980-84. Wellington 1982-83. Hampshire debut 1985. Cap 1989. 1000 runs (2); most – 1274 (1991). HS 162 v Glam (Cardiff) 1989. BB 6-22 v **A** (Southampton) 1985. BAC BB 5-25 v Glos (Southampton) 1988. **NWT:** HS 42 v Glam (Cardiff) 1989. BB 3-22 v Dorset (Southampton) 1987. **BHC:** HS 45 v Essex (Chelmsford) 1989. BB 3-31 v Middx 1987 and v Glam (Southampton) 1989. **SL:** HS 66 v Glos (Trowbridge) 1989. BB 4-23 v Lancs (Southampton) 1986.

JEAN-JACQUES, Martin (Aylestone SS, London), b Soufriere, Dominica 2 Jul 1960. 6'0". RHB, RMF. Derbyshire 1986-92. Hampshire debut 1993. Buckinghamshire 1983-85. HS 73 De v Yorks (Sheffield) 1986 (on debut). H HS 21* v OU (Oxford) 1993. BB 8-77 De v Kent (Derby) 1986. H BB 2-117 v Derbys (Derby) 1993. **NWT:** HS 16 De v Surrey (Derby) 1986. BB 3-23 De v Cambs (Wisbech) 1987. **BHC:** HS 2*. BB 3-22 De v Notts (Nottingham) 1987. **SL:** HS 23 De v Lancs (Derby) 1991. BB 3-36 De v Worcs (Worcester) 1986.

91

LANEY, Jason Scott (Pewsey Vale SS; St John's SFC, Marlborough; Leeds U), b Winchester 27 Apr 1973. 5'10". RHB, OB. Hampshire staff 1993 – awaiting f-c debut. **SL:** HS 12 v Essex (Chelmsford) 1993.

MARU, Rajesh Jamandass (Rook's Heath HS, Harrow; Pinner SFC), b Nairobi, Kenya 28 Oct 1962. 5'6". RHB. SLA. Middlesex 1980-82. Hampshire debut 1984. Cap 1986. Tour: Z 1980-81 (Mx). HS 74 v Glos (Gloucester) 1988. 50 wkts (4); most – 73 (1985). BB 8-41 v Kent (Southampton) 1989. **NWT:** HS 22 v Yorks (Southampton) 1990. BB 3-46 v Leics (Leicester) 1990. **BHC:** HS 9. BB 3-46 v Comb Us (Southampton) 1990. **SL:** HS 33* v Glam (Ebbw Vale) 1991. BB 3-30 v Leics (Leicester) 1988.

MIDDLETON, Tony Charles (Montgomery of Alamein S, and Peter Symonds SFC, Winchester), b Winchester 1 Feb 1964. 5'10½". RHB, SLA. Debut 1984. Cap 1990. Tour: A 1992-93 (Eng A). 1000 runs (2); most – 1780 (1992). HS 221 v Surrey (Southampton) 1992. BB 2-41 v Kent (Canterbury) 1991. Award: BHC 1. **NWT:** HS 91* v Comb Us (Southampton) 1993. **BHC:** HS 65 v Middx (Southampton) 1992. **SL:** HS 98 v Northants (Bournemouth) 1992.

MORRIS, Robert Sean Millner (Stowe S; Durham U), b Great Horwood, Bucks 10 Sep 1968. RHB, OB. 6'0". Debut 1992. HS 92 v Glos (Bristol) 1993. **SL:** HS 4*.

NICHOLAS, Mark Charles Jefford (Bradfield C), b London 29 Sep 1957. Grandson of F.W.H. (Essex 1912-29). 5'11". RHB, RM. Debut 1978. Cap 1982. Captain 1985-. Benefit 1991. Tours (C=captain): SL 1985-86C (Eng B); Z 1984-85C (EC), 1989-90 (Eng A). 1000 runs (8); most – 1559 (1984). HS 206* v OU (Oxford) 1982. BAC HS 158 v Lancs (Portsmouth) 1984. BB 6-37 v Somerset (Southampton) 1989. Award: BHC 1. **NWT:** HS 71 v Surrey (Oval) 1989. BB 2-39 v Berks (Southampton) 1985. **BHC:** HS 74 v Glam (Southampton) 1985. BB 4-34 v Minor C (Reading) 1985. **SL:** HS 108 v Glos (Bristol) 1984. BB 4-30 v Glos (Trowbridge) 1989.

SMITH, Robin Arnold (Northlands HS), b Durban, SA 13 Sep 1963. Brother of C.L. (Natal, Glam, Hants and England 1977-78/1992) and grandson of Dr V.L.Shearer (Natal). 5'11". RHB, LB. Natal 1980-81/1984-85. Hampshire debut 1982. Cap 1985. Wisden 1989. **Tests:** 45 (1988 to 1993); HS 148* v WI (Lord's) 1991. LOI: 58 (HS 167* – Eng record). Tours: A 1990-91; WI 1989-90; NZ 1991-92; I/SL 1992-93. 1000 (7); most – 1577 (1989). HS 209* v Essex (Southend) 1987. BB 2-11 v Surrey (Southampton) 1985. Awards: NWT 6; BHC 3. **NWT:** HS 125* v Surrey (Oval) 1989. BB 2-13 v Berks (Southampton) 1985. **BHC:** HS 155* v Glam (Southampton) 1989. **SL:** HS 131 v Notts (Nottingham) 1989. BB 1-0.

TERRY, Vivian Paul (Millfield S), b Osnabruck, W Germany 14 Jan 1959. 6'0". RHB, RM. Debut 1978. Cap 1983. Benefit 1994. **Tests:** 2 (1984); HS 8. Tour: Z 1984-85 (EC). 1000 runs (9); most – 1469 (1993). HS 190 v SL (Southampton) 1988. BAC HS 180 v Derbys (Derby) 1990. Awards: NWT 4; BHC 4. **NWT:** HS 165* v Berks (Southampton) 1985. **BHC:** HS 134 v Comb Us (Southampton) 1990. **SL:** HS 142 v Leics (Southampton) 1986.

THURSFIELD, Martin John (Boldon CS), b South Shields, Co Durham 14 Dec 1971. 6'3". RHB, RM. Middlesex 1990. Hampshire debut 1992. MCC YC. HS 36* (his first f-c innings) and BB 4-78 v Middx (Lord's) 1993. **SL:** HS 9. BB 2-42 v Warwicks (Southampton) 1993.

UDAL, Shaun David (Cove CS), b Farnborough 18 Mar 1969. Grandson of G.F. (Middx 1932 and Leics 1946). 6'2". RHB, OB. Debut 1989. Cap 1992. HS 79* v Sussex (Portsmouth) 1993. 50 wkts (2); most – 74 (1993). BB 8-50 v Sussex (Southampton) 1992. Awards: NWT 1; BHC 1. **NWT:** HS 2. BB 3-39 v Kent (Southampton) 1992. **BHC:** HS 9*. BB 4-40 v Middx (Southampton) 1992. **SL:** HS 44 v Lancs (Southampton) 1993. BB 4-51 v Northants (Bournemouth) 1992.

BENJAMIN, Winston Keithroy Matthew (All Saints S, Antigua), b St John's, Antigua 31 Dec 1964. 6'3". RHB, RFM. Debut (Rest of World XI) 1985. Leicestershire 1986-90 (cap 1989) and 1992. Leeward Is 1985-86 to date. Cheshire 1985. **Tests** (WI): 10 (1987-88 to 1992-93); HS 40* v P (Bridgetown) 1987-88; BB 4-52 v Eng (Oval) 1988. LOI (WI): 60 (HS 31; BB 3-21). Tours: E 1988; A 1986-87, 1988-89; I 1987-88; P 1986-87. HS 101* Le v Derbys (Leicester) 1990. 50 wkts (1): 69 (1989). BB 7-54 (inc hat-trick) Le v A (Leicester) 1989. BAC BB 7-83 Le v Lancs (Leicester) 1993. Awards: BHC 2. **NWT:** HS 24* Le v Durham (Leicester) 1992. BB 5-32 Le v Derbys (Derby) 1992. **BHC:** HS 45 Le v Middx (Leicester) 1992. BB 5-17 Le v Minor C (Leicester) 1986. **SL:** HS 55 v Glos (Leicester) 1993. BB 4-19 Le v Lancs (Leicester) 1986.

BOTHAM, Liam James (Rossall S), b Doncaster, Yorks 26 Aug 1977. Son of I.T. (Somerset, Worcs, Durham, Queensland and England 1974-93). 6'0". RHB, RMF.

COWANS, Norman George (Park High SS, Stanmore), b Enfield St Mary, Jamaica 17 Apr 1961. 6'3". RHB, RFM. Middlesex 1980-93 (cap 1984; benefit 1993). YC 1982. MCC YC. **Tests:** 19 (1982-83 to 1985); HS 36 v A (Perth) 1982-83; BB 6-77 v A (Melbourne) 1982-83. LOI: 23 (HS 4*; BB 3-44). Tours: A 1982-83; NZ 1983-84; I 1984-85; P 1983-84; SL 1984-85, 1985-86 (Eng B); Z 1980-81 (Mx). HS 66 M v Surrey (Lord's) 1984. 50 wkts (6); most – 73 (1984, 1985). BB 6-31 M v Leics (Leicester) 1985. Awards: NWT 1; BHC 1. **NWT:** HS 12* M v Lancs (Lord's) 1984. BB 4-24 M v Yorks (Leeds) 1986. **BHC:** HS 12 M v Derbys (Derby) 1990. BB 4-33 M v Lancs (Lord's) 1983. **SL:** HS 27 M v Notts (Lord's) 1990. BB 6-9 M v Lancs (Lord's) 1991.

KEECH, Matthew (Northumberland Park S), b Hampstead 21 Oct 1970. 6'0". RHB, RM. Middlesex 1991-93. MCC YC. HS 58* M v Notts (Lord's) 1991. BB 2-28 M v Glos (Bristol) 1993. **NWT:** HS 3. **BHC:** HS 47 M v Warwks (Lord's) 1991. BB 1-37. **SL:** HS 49* M v Somerset (Taunton) 1991. BB 2-22 M v Northants (Lord's) 1993.

KENDALL, William Salwey (Bradfield C; Keble C, Oxford), b Wimbledon, Surrey 18 Dec 1973. 5'10". RHB, RM.

DEPARTURES

AYLING, Jonathan Richard (Portsmouth GS), b Portsmouth 13 Jun 1967. 6'4". RHB, RM. Hampshire 1988-93 (cap 1991). Took wicket of D.A.Polkinghorne (OU) with first ball in f-c cricket. HS 121 v OU (Oxford) 1992. BAC HS 90 v Durham (Darlington) 1992. BB 5-12 v Middx (Bournemouth) 1992. **NWT:** HS 29 v Leics (Leicester) 1990. BB 3-30 v Yorks (Southampton) 1990. **BHC:** HS 25 v Northants (Southampton) 1993. BB 2-22 v Lancs (Manchester) 1993. **SL:** HS 56 v Surrey (Oval) 1991. BB 4-37 v Notts (Southampton) 1990.

GOWER, David Ivon (King's S, Canterbury; London U), b Tunbridge Wells, Kent 1 Apr 1957. 6'0". LHB, OB. Leicestershire 1975-89 (cap 1977; captain 1984-86, 1988-89; benefit 1987). Hampshire 1990-93 (cap 1990). Wisden 1978. YC 1978. OBE 1992. **Tests:** 117 (1978 to 1992, 32 as captain); HS 215 v A (Birmingham) -1985; BB 1-1. LOI: 114 (HS 158). Tours (C=captain): A 1978-79, 1979-80, 1982-83, 1986-87, 1990-91; WI 1980-81, 1985-86C, 1989-90 (part); NZ 1983-84; I 1979-80, 1981-82, 1984-85C; P 1983-84; SL 1977-78 (DHR), 1981-82, 1984-85C. 1000 runs (13); most – 1530 (1982). HS 228 Le v Glam (Leicester) 1989. H HS 155 v Yorks (Basingstoke) 1992. BB 3-47 Le v Essex (Leicester) 1977. Awards: NWT 5; BHC 3. **NWT:** HS 156 Le v Derbys (Leicester) 1984. **BHC:** HS 118* v Northants (Southampton) 1992. **SL:** HS 135* Le v Warwks (Leicester) 1977.

continued on p 156

HAMPSHIRE 1993

RESULTS SUMMARY

	Place	Won	Lost	Drew	Abandoned
Britannic Assurance Championship	13th	4	5	8	
All First-class Matches		4	5	10	
Sunday League	15th	4	9		4
NatWest Trophy	2nd Round				
Benson and Hedges Cup	Quarter-Finalist				

BRITANNIC ASSURANCE CHAMPIONSHIP AVERAGES

BATTING AND FIELDING

Cap		M	I	NO	HS	Runs	Avge	100	50	Ct/St
1985	R.A.Smith	10	15	1	131	761	54.35	3	2	5
1983	V.P.Terry	17	29	2	174	1257	46.55	3	6	15
1990	D.I.Gower	15	26	–	153	1105	42.50	4	5	11
1991	A.N.Aymes	17	26	9	107*	682	40.11	1	5	29/4
1982	M.C.J.Nicholas	16	26	4	95	825	37.50	–	5	7
1989	K.D.James	15	26	3	71	630	27.39	–	4	4
–	R.S.M.Morris	8	14	–	92	372	26.57	–	2	14
–	R.M.F.Cox	6	10	1	63	204	22.66	–	1	4
1992	S.D.Udal	17	25	2	79*	503	21.86	–	2	8
1990	T.C.Middleton	10	18	–	90	377	20.94	–	2	11
1988	C.A.Connor	9	11	1	59	200	20.00	–	1	3
–	M.J.Thursfield	2	4	2	36*	36	18.00	–	–	–
1981	M.D.Marshall	13	16	2	75*	250	17.85	–	1	3
1991	J.R.Ayling	3	4	–	21	62	15.50	–	–	3
–	D.P.J.Flint	10	13	5	14*	47	5.87	–	–	7
–	K.J.Shine	11	13	5	12	47	5.87	–	–	4
–	I.J.Turner	3	4	1	8	12	4.00	–	–	2

Also played: J.N.B.Bovill (1 match) 3*, 0*; M.Jean-Jacques (3 matches) 11*, 10; J.R.Wood (1 match) 25.

BOWLING

	O	M	R	W	Avge	Best	5wI	10wM
K.D.James	276	73	806	31	26.00	4- 33	–	–
S.D.Udal	678.3	167	1889	65	29.06	6-141	5	2
M.D.Marshall	345.3	102	859	28	30.67	5- 62	1	–
D.P.J.Flint	388.2	95	1066	31	34.38	5- 32	1	–
K.J.Shine	256.3	49	1016	22	46.18	6- 62	2	–
C.A.Connor	226.4	62	671	12	55.91	3- 81	–	–

Also bowled: J.R.Ayling 33-6-138-3; J.N.B.Bovill 20-8-48-3; M.Jean-Jacques 25.3-5-120-2; T.C.Middleton 0.2-0-4-0; R.S.M.Morris 0.4-0-1-0; M.C.J.Nicholas 1-0-4-0; R.A.Smith 1-0-2-0; M.J.Thursfield 43-13-143-5; I.J.Turner 76.4-20-265-5.

The First-Class Averages (pp 164-177) give the records of Hampshire players in all first-class county matches (their other opponents being the Australians and Oxford U), with the exception of:
    R.A.Smith 12-19-2-191-970-57.05-4-2-6ct. 1-0-2-0.

HAMPSHIRE RECORDS

FIRST-CLASS CRICKET

Highest Total	For	672-7d		v	Somerset	Taunton	1899
	V	742		by	Surrey	The Oval	1909
Lowest Total	For	15		v	Warwicks	Birmingham	1922
	V	23		by	Yorkshire	Middlesbrough	1965
Highest Innings	For	316	R.H.Moore	v	Warwicks	Bournemouth	1937
	V	302*	P.Holmes	for	Yorkshire	Portsmouth	1920

Highest Partnership for each Wicket

1st	347	V.P.Terry/C.L.Smith	v	Warwicks	Birmingham	1987
2nd	321	G.Brown/E.I.M.Barrett	v	Glos	Southampton	1920
3rd	344	C.P.Mead/G.Brown	v	Yorks	Portsmouth	1927
4th	263	R.E.Marshall/D.A.Livingstone	v	Middlesex	Lord's	1970
5th	235	G.Hill/D.F.Walker	v	Sussex	Portsmouth	1937
6th	411	R.M.Poore/E.G.Wynyard	v	Somerset	Taunton	1899
7th	325	G.Brown/C.H.Abercrombie	v	Essex	Leyton	1913
8th	227	K.D.James/T.M.Tremlett	v	Somerset	Taunton	1985
9th	230	D.A.Livingstone/A.T.Castell	v	Surrey	Southampton	1962
10th	192	H.A.W.Bowell/W.H.Livsey	v	Worcs	Bournemouth	1921

Best Bowling	For	9- 25	R.M.H.Cottam	v	Lancashire	Manchester	1965
(Innings)	V	10- 46	W.Hickton	for	Lancashire	Manchester	1870
Best Bowling	For	16- 88	J.A.Newman	v	Somerset	Weston-s-Mare	1927
(Match)	V	17-119	W.Mead	for	Essex	Southampton	1895

Most Runs – Season	2854	C.P.Mead	(av 79.27)	1928
Most Runs – Career	48892	C.P.Mead	(av 48.84)	1905-36
Most 100s – Season	12	C.P.Mead		1928
Most 100s – Career	138	C.P.Mead		1905-36
Most Wkts – Season	190	A.S.Kennedy	(av 15.61)	1922
Most Wkts – Career	2669	D.Shackleton	(av 18.23)	1948-69

LIMITED-OVERS CRICKET

Highest Total	NWT	371-4		v	Glamorgan	Southampton	1975
	BHC	321-1		v	Minor C (S)	Amersham	1973
	SL	313-2		v	Sussex	Portsmouth	1993
Lowest Total	NWT	98		v	Lancashire	Manchester	1975
	BHC	50		v	Yorkshire	Leeds	1991
	SL	43		v	Essex	Basingstoke	1972
Highest Innings	NWT	177	C.G.Greenidge	v	Glamorgan	Southampton	1975
	BHC	173*	C.G.Greenidge	v	Minor C (S)	Amersham	1973
	SL	172	C.G.Greenidge	v	Surrey	Southampton	1987
Best Bowling	NWT	7-30	P.J.Sainsbury	v	Norfolk	Southampton	1965
	BHC	5-13	S.T.Jefferies	v	Derbyshire	Lord's	1988
	SL	6-20	T.E.Jesty	v	Glamorgan	Cardiff	1975

KENT

Formation of Present Club: 1 March 1859
Substantial Reorganisation: 6 December 1870
Colours: Maroon and White
Badge: White Horse on a Red Ground
Championships: (6) 1906, 1909, 1910, 1913, 1970, 1978
Joint Championship: (1) 1977
NatWest Trophy/Gillette Cup Winners: (2) 1967, 1974
Benson and Hedges Cup Winners: (3) 1973, 1976, 1978
Sunday League Champions: (3) 1972, 1973, 1976
Match Awards: NWT 44; BHC 70

Secretary: S.T.W.Anderson OBE, MC, St Lawrence Ground, Canterbury,
CT1 3NZ (☎ 0227-456886)
Captain: M.R.Benson
Scorer: J.C.Foley
1994 Beneficiary: –

BENSON, Mark Richard (Sutton Valence S), b Shoreham, Sussex 6 Jul 1958. 5'10".
LHB, OB. Debut 1980. Cap 1981. Captain 1991-. Benefit 1991. Tests: 1 (1986); HS
30 v I (Birmingham) 1986. LOI: 1 (HS 24). 1000 runs (11); most – 1725 (1987). HS
257 v Hants (Southampton) 1991. BB 2-55 v Surrey (Dartford) 1986. Awards:
NWT 2; BHC 4. **NWT:** HS 113* v Warwks (Birmingham) 1984. **BHC:** HS 118 v
Glam (Swansea) 1990. **SL:** HS 97 v Surrey (Oval) 1982.

COWDREY, Graham Robert (Tonbridge S; Durham U), b Farnborough 27 Jun
1964. Brother of C.S. (Kent, Glam and England 1977-92), son of M.C. (Kent and
England 1950-76), grandson of E.A. (Europeans). 5'11". RHB, RM. Debut 1984.
Cap 1988. 1000 runs (3); most – 1576 (1990). HS 147 v Glos (Bristol) 1992. BB 1-5.
Award: BHC 1. **NWT:** HS 37 v Glos (Bristol) 1990. BB 2-4 v Devon (Canterbury)
1992. **BHC:** HS 70* v Leics (Canterbury) 1991. BB 1-6. **SL:** HS 102* v Leics
(Folkestone) 1989. BB 4-15 v Essex (Ilford) 1987.

EALHAM, Mark Alan (Stour Valley SS, Chartham), b Willesborough, Ashford 27
Aug 1969. Son of A.G.E. (Kent 1966-82). 5'9". RHB, RMF. Debut 1989. Cap
1992. Tour: Z 1992-93 (K). HS 85 v Lancs (Lytham) 1993. Scored 7 fifties in his last
9 BAC innings in 1993. BB 5-14 v Z (Canterbury) 1993. BAC BB 5-39 v Sussex
(Hove) 1991. Award: NWT 1. **NWT:** HS 58* v Warwicks (Birmingham) 1993. **BB**
2-33 v Warwks (Birmingham) 1992. **BHC:** HS 26 v Yorks (Leeds) 1992. BB 4-29 v
Somerset (Canterbury) 1992. **SL:** HS 43* v Derbys (Chesterfield) 1992. BB 6-53 v
Hants (Basingstoke) 1993.

ELLISON, Richard Mark (Tonbridge S; Exeter U), b Willesborough, Ashford
21 Sep 1959. Brother of C.C. (Cambridge U 1982-83). 6'2". LHB, RMF. Debut
1981. Cap 1983. Benefit 1993. Tasmania 1986-87. Wisden 1985. Tests: 11 (1984
to 1986); HS 41 v SL (Lord's) 1984; BB 6-77 v A (Birmingham) 1985. LOI: 14
(HS 24; BB 3-42). Tours: SA 1989-90 (Eng XI); WI 1985-86; I/SL 1984-85. HS
108 v OU (Oxford) 1984. BAC HS 98 v Notts (Nottingham) 1985. 50 wkts (4);
most – 71 (1988). BB 7-33 v Warwks (Tunbridge W) 1991. Awards: NWT 1;
BHC 5. **NWT:** HS 49* v Warwks (Birmingham) 1984. BB 4-19 v Cheshire
(Canterbury) 1983. **BHC:** HS 72 v Middx (Lord's) 1984. BB 4-28 v Glam
(Canterbury) 1984. **SL:** HS 84 v Glos (Canterbury) 1984. BB 4-25 v Hants
(Canterbury) 1983.

FLEMING, Matthew Valentine (St Aubyns S, Rottingdean; Eton C), b Macclesfield, Cheshire 12 Dec 1964. 5'11½". RHB, RM. Debut 1989. Cap 1990. Tour: Z 1992-93 (K). HS 116 v WI (Canterbury) 1991. BAC HS 113 v Surrey (Canterbury) 1991. BB 4-31 v Glos (Tunbridge W) 1993. Awards: NWT 1; BHC 3. **NWT:** HS 53 v Devon (Canterbury) 1992. BB 3-34 v Hants (Southampton) 1992. **BHC:** HS 69 v Somerset (Canterbury) 1992. BB 3-52 v Glam (Canterbury) 1993. **SL:** HS 77 v Sussex (Hove) 1991. BB 4-45 v Somerset (Taunton) 1991.

FULTON, David Paul (The Judd S; Kent U), b Lewisham 15 Nov 1971. 6'2". RHB. Debut 1992. HS 75 v Northants (Canterbury) 1993. **SL:** HS 29 v Lancs (Manchester) 1993.

HEADLEY, Dean Warren (Worcester RGS), b Norton, Stourbridge, Worcs 27 Jan 1970. Son of R.G.A. (Worcs, Jamaica and WI 1958-74); grandson of G.A. (Jamaica and WI 1927-28/1953-54). 6'4". RHB, RFM. Middlesex 1991-92. Kent debut v Zimbabwe B (Harare) 1992-93. Cap 1993. Tour: Z 1992-93 (K). HS 91 M v Leics (Leicester) 1992. K HS 36 v Notts (Nottingham) 1993. BB 7-79 v Glos (Tunbridge W) 1993. Award: BHC 1. **NWT:** HS 11* M v Somerset (Taunton) 1991. BB 5-20 M v Salop (Telford) 1992. **BHC:** HS 26 M v Surrey (Lord's) 1991. BB 4-19 M v Sussex (Hove) 1992. **SL:** HS 10* v Glam (Canterbury) 1993. BB 4-23 M v Essex (Lord's) 1992.

HOOPER, Carl Llewellyn (Christchurch S, Georgetown), b Georgetown, Guyana 15 Dec 1966. 6'1". RHB, OB. Debut (Demerara) 1983-84. Guyana 1984-85/1991-92. Kent debut/cap 1992. **Tests** (WI): 39 (1987-88 to 1992-93); HS 178* v P (St John's) 1992-93; BB 5-40 v P (P-o-S) 1992-93. LOI (WI): 102 (HS 113* & BB 4-34). Tours (WI): E 1988, 1991; A 1988-89, 1991-92, 1992-93; NZ 1986-87; I 1987-88; P 1990-91; Z 1986-87 (WI B). 1000 runs (3); most – 1501 (1991). HS 236* v Glam (Canterbury) 1993. BB 5-33 WI v Queensland (Brisbane) 1988-89. K BB 4-35 v Northants (Canterbury) 1993. Award: BHC 1. **NWT:** HS 62 and BB 2-12 v Middx (Canterbury) 1993. **BHC:** HS 50 v Surrey (Canterbury) 1992. BB 3-28 v Yorks (Leeds) 1992. **SL:** HS 103 and BB 5-41 v Essex (Maidstone) 1993.

IGGLESDEN, Alan Paul (Churchill S, Westerham), b Farnborough 8 Oct 1964. 6'6". RHB, RFM. Debut 1986. Cap 1989. W Province 1987-88. Boland 1992-93. **Tests:** 1 (1989); HS 2* and BB 2-91 v A (Oval). Tours: Z 1989-90 (Eng A), 1992-93 (K). HS 41 v Surrey (Canterbury) 1988. 50 wkts (4); most – 56 (1989). BB 7-28 (12-66 match) Boland v GW (Kimberley) 1992-93. K BB 6-34 v Surrey (Canterbury) 1988. **NWT:** HS 12* v Oxon (Oxford) 1990. BB 4-29 v Cambs (Canterbury) 1991. **BHC:** HS 26* v Worcs (Worcester) 1991. BB 3-24 v Scot (Glasgow) 1991 and v Notts (Nottingham) 1992. **SL:** HS 13* (twice). BB 5-13 v Sussex (Hove) 1989.

LLONG, Nigel James (Ashford North S), b Ashford 11 Feb 1969. 6'0". LHB, OB. Debut 1990. Cap 1993. Tour: Z 1992-93 (K). HS 116* v CU (Cambridge) 1993. BAC HS 108 v Middx (Lord's) 1993. BB 3-29 v CU (Cambridge) 1993. BAC BB 3-70 v Worcs (Tunbridge W) 1992. **NWT:** HS 27* v Middx (Canterbury) 1993. BB 1-11. **BHC:** HS 5. **SL:** HS 64* v Northants (Canterbury) 1993. BB 4-24 v Sussex (Hove) 1993.

McCAGUE, Martin John (Hedland Sr HS; Carine Tafe C), b Larne, N Ireland 24 May 1969. 6'5". RHB, RF. W Australia 1990-91/1991-92. Kent debut 1991. Cap 1992. **Tests:** 2 (1993); HS 11 v A (Leeds) 1993; BB 4-121 v A (Nottingham) 1993. HS 34 WA v Victoria (Perth) 1991-92. K HS 29 v Leics (Leicester) 1991. 50 wkts (1): 53 (1992). BB 8-26 v Hants (Canterbury) 1992. Award: NWT 1. **NWT:** HS 14 v Warwks (Birmingham) 1992. BB 5-26 v Middx (Canterbury) 1993. **BHC:** HS 30 v Derbys (Canterbury) 1992. BB 5-43 v Somerset (Canterbury) 1993. **SL:** HS 22* v Glam (Swansea) 1992. BB 4-35 v Leics (Leicester) 1992.

MARSH, Steven Andrew (Walderslade SS; Mid-Kent CFE), b Westminster, London 27 Jan 1961. 5'10". RHB, WK. Debut 1982. Cap 1986. Benefit 1995. Tour: Z 1992-93 (K – captain). HS 125 v Yorks (Canterbury) 1992. BB 2-20 v Warwks (Birmingham) 1990. Set world f-c record by holding eight catches in an innings AND scoring a hundred (v Middx at Lord's) 1991. **NWT:** HS 24* v Middx (Lord's) 1988. **BHC:** HS 71 v Lancs (Manchester) 1991. **SL:** HS 59 v Leics (Canterbury) 1991.

PATEL, Minal Mahesh (Dartford GS; Erith TC), b Bombay, India 7 Jul 1970. 5'9". RHB, SLA. Debut 1989. HS 43 v Leics (Leicester) 1991. BB 7-75 (12-182 match) v Lancs (Lytham) 1993. NWT: HS-. BB 2-29 v Oxon (Oxford) 1990.

PENN, Christopher (Dover GS), b Dover 19 Jun 1963. 6'1". LHB, RFM. Debut 1982. Cap 1987. HS 115 v Lancs (Manchester) 1984. 50 wkts (2); most – 81 (1988). BB 7-70 v Middx (Lord's) 1988. NWT: HS 20* v Surrey (Oval) 1991. BB 3-30 v Warwks (Canterbury) 1988. BHC: HS 24* v Northants (Northampton) 1989. BB 4-34 v Surrey (Canterbury) 1982. SL: HS 40 v Sussex (Maidstone) 1982. BB 4-15 v Glos (Maidstone) 1989.

PRESTON, Nicholas William (Meopham SS; Gravesend GS; Exeter U), b Dartford 22 Jan 1972. 6'1". RHB, RFM. Kent staff 1991 – awaiting f-c debut.

SPENCER, Duncan John (Gosnells HS, W Australia), b Nelson, Lancs 5 Apr 1972. 5'8". RHB, RF. Debut 1993. HS 75 and BB 4-46 v Z (Canterbury) 1993. BAC HS 4. BAC BB 0-32. SL: HS 17* v Northants (Canterbury) 1993. BB 2-29 v Surrey (Canterbury) 1993.

TAYLOR, Neil Royston (Cray Valley THS), b Orpington 21 Jul 1959. 6'1". RHB, OB. Debut 1979 v SL (Canterbury), scoring 110 and 11. Cap 1982. Benefit 1992. 1000 runs (9); most – 1979 (1990). HS 204 v Surrey (Canterbury) 1990. BB 2-20 v Somerset (Canterbury) 1985. Awards: BHC 8. NWT: HS 85 v Derbys (Canterbury) 1987. BB 3-29 v Dorset (Canterbury) 1989. BHC: HS 137 v Surrey (Oval) 1988. SL: HS 95 v Hants (Canterbury) 1990.

WALKER, Matthew Jonathan (King's S, Rochester), b Gravesend 2 Jan 1974. Grandson of Jack (Kent 1949). 5'8". LHB, RM. England U-19 to Pakistan 1991-92, India 1992-93 (captain). Debut v Zimbabwe B (Harare) 1992-93. Awaiting f-c debut in UK. Tour: Z 1992-93 (K). HS 23* (on debut).

WARD, Trevor Robert (Hextable CS, nr Swanley), b Farningham 18 Jan 1968. 5'11". RHB, OB. Debut 1986. Cap 1989. Tour: Z 1992-93 (K). 1000 runs (3); most – 1648 (1992). HS 235* v Middx (Canterbury) 1991. BB 2-48 v Worcs (Canterbury) 1990. Awards: NWT 1; BHC 1. NWT: HS 92 v Hants (Southampton) 1992. BB 1-58. BHC: HS 94 v Worcs (Worcester) 1990. SL: HS 131 v Notts (Nottingham) 1993. BB 3-20 v Glam (Canterbury) 1989.

WILLIS, Simon Charles (Wilmington GS), b Greenwich, London 19 Mar 1974. 5'8". RHB, OB, WK. Debut 1993. HS 0*.

WREN, Timothy Neil (Harvey GS, Folkestone), b Folkestone 26 Mar 1970. 6'3". RHB, LM. Debut 1990. Tour: Z 1992-93 (K). HS 16 v Essex (Chelmsford) 1990. BB 3-14 v OU (Oxford) 1991. BAC BB 2-78 v Worcs (Canterbury) 1990. SL: HS 0*. BB 1-31.

NEWCOMER

THOMPSON, Dr Julian Barton deCourcy (The Judd S, Tonbridge; Guy's Hospital Med S, London U), b Cape Town, SA 28 Oct 1968. 6'4". RHB, RFM.

DEPARTURES

DAVIS, R.P. – see WARWICKSHIRE.

LONGLEY, J.I. – see DURHAM.

PARKS, Robert James (Eastbourne GS; Southampton Inst of Technology), b Cuckfield, Sussex 15 Jun 1959. Son of J.M. (Sussex, Somerset and England 1949-76) and grandson of J.H. (Sussex and England 1924-52). 5'8". RHB, WK. Hampshire 1980-92 (cap 1982; benefit 1992). Kent 1993. Tour: Z 1984-85 (EC). Held 10 catches in match H v Derbys (Portsmouth) 1981. Holds career record Hampshire aggregate of dismissals (700 – 630ct, 70st). HS 89 H v CU (Cambridge) 1984. BAC HS 80 H v Derbys (Portsmouth) 1986. K HS 13* v Essex (Maidstone) 1993. Award: BHC 1. NWT: HS 27* H v Yorks (Southampton) 1990. BHC: HS 23* H v Somerset (Taunton) 1988. SL: HS 38* H v Essex (Portsmouth) 1987.

KENT 1993

	Place	Won	Lost	Drew	Abandoned
Britannic Assurance Championship	8th	6	4	7	
All First-class Matches		8	5	7	
Sunday League	2nd	12	3		2
NatWest Trophy	2nd Round				
Benson and Hedges Cup	Preliminary Round				

BRITANNIC ASSURANCE CHAMPIONSHIP AVERAGES

BATTING AND FIELDING

Cap		M	I	NO	HS	Runs	Avge	100	50	Ct/St
1992	C.L.Hooper	16	24	2	236*	1304	59.27	3	6	22
1992	M.A.Ealham	10	14	3	85	604	54.90	–	8	3
1981	M.R.Benson	14	22	2	107	899	44.95	3	6	6
1993	N.J.Llong	15	23	4	108	810	42.63	1	6	12
1990	M.V.Fleming	16	26	4	100	805	36.59	1	6	6
1989	T.R.Ward	16	26	–	141	781	30.03	2	2	12
1982	N.R.Taylor	15	25	2	86	645	28.04	–	4	4
–	D.P.Fulton	5	9	–	75	221	24.55	–	2	10
1988	G.R.Cowdrey	9	17	–	139	379	22.29	1	–	6
1986	S.A.Marsh	16	23	1	63	469	21.31	–	3	52/3
1993	D.W.Headley	12	18	6	36	248	20.66	–	–	9
1987	C.Penn	3	4	–	23	63	15.75	–	–	1
1990	R.P.Davis	12	15	2	42	158	12.15	–	–	10
1992	M.J.McCague	7	8	3	22*	49	9.80	–	–	4
–	M.M.Patel	5	5	3	4	12	6.00	–	–	2
1989	A.P.Igglesden	11	12	6	10	32	5.33	–	–	1

Also played: R.M.Ellison (2 matches – cap 1983) 68, 2, 21* (1 ct); J.I.Longley (1 match) 47, 3 (2 ct); R.J.Parks (1 match) 13* (4 ct); D.J.Spencer (1 match) 4.

BOWLING

	O	M	R	W	Avge	Best	5wI	10wM
A.P.Igglesden	393	101	968	50	19.36	6- 58	3	1
M.J.McCague	218.4	54	594	27	22.00	5- 33	2	–
D.W.Headley	405.4	94	1125	41	27.43	7- 79	2	–
M.M.Patel	185.5	50	490	17	28.82	7- 75	2	1
R.P.Davis	404.4	114	946	30	31.53	7-127	1	1
M.A.Ealham	250.4	52	800	25	32.00	5- 66	1	–
M.V.Fleming	401	94	1043	32	32.59	4- 31	–	–
C.L.Hooper	545	126	1281	33	38.81	4- 35	–	–

Also bowled: R.M.Ellison 31-13-72-2; N.J.Llong 33.2-6-96-1; C.Penn 117-29-263-8; D.J.Spencer 24-3-94-0.

The First-Class Averages (pp 164-177) give the records of Kent players in all first-class county matches (their other opponents being the Australians, the Zimbabweans and Cambridge U) with the exception of M.J.McCague, whose full county figures are as above.

KENT RECORDS

FIRST-CLASS CRICKET

Highest Total	For 803-4d		v	Essex	Brentwood	1934
	V 676		by	Australians	Canterbury	1921
Lowest Total	For 18		v	Sussex	Gravesend	1867
	V 16		by	Warwicks	Tonbridge	1913
Highest Innings	For 332	W.H.Ashdown	v	Essex	Brentwood	1934
	V 344	W.G.Grace	for	MCC	Canterbury	1876

Highest Partnership for each Wicket

1st	300	N.R.Taylor/M.R.Benson	v	Derbyshire	Canterbury	1991
2nd	366	S.G.Hinks/N.R.Taylor	v	Middlesex	Canterbury	1990
3rd	321*	A.Hearne/J.R.Mason	v	Notts	Nottingham	1899
4th	297	H.T.W.Harding/A.P.F.Chapman	v	Hampshire	Southampton	1926
5th	277	F.E.Woolley/L.E.G.Ames	v	New Zealand	Canterbury	1931
6th	284	A.P.F.Chapman/G.B.Legge	v	Lancashire	Maidstone	1927
7th	248	A.P.Day/E.Humphreys	v	Somerset	Taunton	1908
8th	157	A.L.Hilder/A.C.Wright	v	Essex	Gravesend	1924
9th	161	B.R.Edrich/F.Ridgway	v	Sussex	Tunbridge W	1949
10th	235	F.E.Woolley/A.Fielder	v	Worcs	Stourbridge	1909

Best Bowling	For	10- 30	C.Blythe	v	Northants	Northampton	1907
(Innings)	V	10- 48	C.H.G.Bland	for	Sussex	Tonbridge	1899
Best Bowling	For	17- 48	C.Blythe	v	Northants	Northampton	1907
(Match)	V	17-106	T.W.J.Goddard	for	Glos	Bristol	1939

Most Runs – Season	2894	F.E.Woolley	(av 59.06)		1928
Most Runs – Career	47868	F.E.Woolley	(av 41.77)		1906-38
Most 100s – Season	10	F.E.Woolley			1928
	10	F.E.Woolley			1934
Most 100s – Career	122	F.E.Woolley			1906-38
Most Wkts – Season	262	A.P.Freeman	(av 14.74)		1933
Most Wkts – Career	3340	A.P.Freeman	(av 17.64)		1914-36

LIMITED-OVERS CRICKET

Highest Total	NWT	359-4		v	Dorset	Canterbury	1989
	BHC	319-8		v	Scotland	Glasgow	1991
	SL	327-6		v	Leics	Canterbury	1993
Lowest Total	NWT	60		v	Somerset	Taunton	1979
	BHC	73		v	Middlesex	Canterbury	1979
	SL	83		v	Middlesex	Lord's	1984
Highest Innings	NWT	129*	B.W.Luckhurst	v	Durham	Canterbury	1974
	BHC	143	C.J.Tavaré	v	Somerset	Taunton	1985
	SL	142	B.W.Luckhurst	v	Somerset	Weston-s-Mare	1970
Best Bowling	NWT	8-31	D.L.Underwood	v	Scotland	Edinburgh	1987
	BHC	5-21	B.D.Julien	v	Surrey	The Oval	1973
	SL	6- 9	R.A.Woolmer	v	Derbyshire	Chesterfield	1979

LANCASHIRE

Formation of Present Club: 12 January 1864
Colours: Red, Green and Blue
Badge: Red Rose
Championships (since 1890): (7) 1897, 1904, 1926, 1927, 1928, 1930, 1934
Joint Championship: (1) 1950
NatWest Trophy/Gillette Cup Winners: (5) 1970, 1971, 1972, 1975, 1990
Benson and Hedges Cup Winners: (2) 1984, 1990
Sunday League Champions: (3) 1969, 1970, 1989
Match Awards: NWT 55; BHC 58

Chief Executive: J.M.Bower. **Cricket Secretary:** Miss R.B.FitzGibbon, Old Trafford, Manchester M16 0PX (☎ 061-848 7021)
Captain: M.Watkinson
Scorer: W.Davies
1994 Beneficiary: –

ATHERTON, Michael Andrew (Manchester GS; Downing C, Cambridge), b Failsworth, Manchester 23 Mar 1968. 5'11". RHB, LB. Cambridge U 1987-89 (blue 1987-88-89; captain 1988-89). Lancashire debut 1987. Cap 1989. YC 1990. Wisden 1990. Tests: 29 (1989 to 1993, 2 as captain); HS 151 v NZ (Nottingham) 1990; BB 1-60. LOI: 10 (HS 74). Tours: A 1990-91; I/SL 1992-93; Z 1989-90 (Eng A). 1000 runs (5); most – 1924 (1990). Scored 1193 in season of f-c debut. HS 199 v Durham (Gateshead) 1992. BB 6-78 v Notts (Nottingham) 1990. Award: NWT 1. **NWT:** HS 109* v Oxon (Oxford) 1992. BB 2-15 v Glos (Manchester) 1990. **BHC:** HS 91 v Sussex (Manchester) 1991. BB 4-42 Comb Us v Somerset (Taunton) 1989. **SL:** HS 111 v Essex (Colchester) 1990. BB 3-33 v Notts (Nottingham) 1990.

AUSTIN, Ian David (Haslingden HS), b Haslingden 30 May 1966. 5'10". LHB, RM. Debut 1987. Cap 1990. Tour: Z 1988-89 (La). HS 115* v Derbys (Blackpool) 1992. BB 5-79 v Surrey (Oval) 1988. **NWT:** HS 38* v Northants (Northampton) 1993. BB 3-36 v Durham (Manchester) 1990. **BHC:** HS 80 v Worcs (Worcester) 1987. BB 4-25 v Surrey (Manchester) 1990. **SL:** HS 48 v Middx (Lord's) 1991. BB 5-56 v Derbys (Derby) 1991.

BARNETT, Alexander Anthony (William Ellis S), b Malaga, Spain, 11 Sep 1970. Great nephew of C.J. (Glos and England 1927-54). 5'11". RHB, SLA. Middlesex 1988-91. Lancashire debut 1992. HS 38 and BB 5-36 v Durham (Manchester) 1993. **NWT:** HS-. BB 2-29 v Northants (Northampton) 1993. **BHC:** HS-. BB 3-43 v Leics (Leicester) 1993. **SL:** HS 11* v Surrey (Oval) 1993. BB 3-15 v Derbys (Derby) 1993.

CHAPPLE, Glen (West Craven HS; Nelson & Colne C), b Skipton, Yorks 23 Jan 1974. 6'1". RHB, RMF. Debut 1992. HS 109* v Glam (Manchester) 1993 (100 off 27 balls in contrived circumstances). HS (authentic) 37* v Durham (Manchester) 1993. BB 3-40 v Warwks (Birmingham) 1992. **SL:** HS 9*. BB 1-4.

CRAWLEY, John Paul (Manchester GS; Trinity C, Cambridge), b Maldon, Essex 21 Sep 1971. Brother of M.A. (see NOTTS) and P.M. (CU 1992). 6'1". RHB, RM. Debut 1990. Cambridge U 1991-93 (blue 1991-92-93; captain 1992-93). 1000 runs (2); most – 1474 (1993). HS 187* CU v Sussex (Hove) 1993. La HS 172 v Surrey (Lytham) 1992. **BHC:** HS 42 Comb Us v Durham (Cambridge) 1992. **SL:** HS 44* v Notts (Manchester) 1993.

DERBYSHIRE, Nicholas Alexander (Ampleforth C; London U); b Ramsbottom 11 Sep 1970. 5'11½". RHB, RFM. Lancashire staff 1990 – awaiting f-c debut.

FAIRBROTHER, Neil Harvey (Lymm GS), b Warrington 9 Sep 1963. 5'8". LHB, LM. Debut 1982. Cap 1985. Captain 1992-93. Benefit 1995. **Tests:** 10 (1987 to 1992-93); HS 83 v I (Madras) 1992-93. LOI: 40 (Hs 113). Tours: NZ 1987-88, 1991-92; I/SL 1992-93; P 1987-88, 1990-91 (Eng A); SL 1990-91 (Eng A). 1000 runs (8); most – 1740 (1990). HS 366 v Surrey (Oval) 1990 (ground record), including 311 in a day and 100 or more in each session. BB 2-91 v Notts (Manchester) 1987. Awards: NWT 5; BHC 7. **NWT:** HS 93* v Leics (Leicester) 1986. **BHC:** HS 116* v Scot (Manchester) 1988. **SL:** HS 116* v Notts (Nottingham) 1988.

FIELDING, Jonathan Mark (Woodhey HS; Bury C), b Bury 13 Mar 1973. 6'1". RHB, SLA. Lancashire staff 1992 – awaiting f-c debut.

GALLIAN, Jason Edward Riche (Pittwater House S, Sydney; Keble C, Oxford), b Manly, Sydney, Australia 25 Jun 1971. 6'0". RHB, RM. Debut 1990, taking wicket of D.A.Hagan (OU) with his first ball. Eligible for England 1994. Oxford U 1992-93 (blue 1992-93; captain 1993). Captained Australia YC v England YC 1989-90, scoring 158* in 1st 'Test'. HS 141* OU v Notts (Oxford) 1993. La HS 42* v A (Manchester) 1993. BB 4-29 OU v Lancs (Oxford) 1992. La BB 1-50. **BHC:** HS 50 Comb Us v Derbys and v Durham 1992. BB 1-26.

HARVEY, Mark Edward (Habergham HS), b Burnley 26 Jun 1974. 5'9". RHB, RM/LB. Lancashire staff 1992 – awaiting f-c debut.

HEGG, Warren Kevin (Unsworth HS, Bury; Stand C, Whitefield), b Whitefield 23 Feb 1968. 5'8". RHB, WK. Debut 1986. Cap 1989. Tours: WI 1986-87 (La); SL 1990-91 (Eng A); Z 1988-89 (La). Held 130 v Northants (Northampton) 1987. Held 11 catches (equalling world f-c match record) v Derbys (Chesterfield) 1989. **NWT:** HS 29 v Glos (Gloucester) 1989. **BHC:** HS 31* v Worcs (Lord's) 1990. **SL:** HS 47* v Middx (Lord's) 1991.

HENDERSON, Jonathan Andrew Lloyd (Hulme GS, Oldham), b Cardiff, Glam 16 Jan 1975. Son of A.A. (Sussex 1972). 6'4". RHB, RFM. Lancashire staff 1993 – awaiting f-c debut.

LLOYD, Graham David (Hollins County HS), b Accrington 1 Jul 1969. Son of D. (Lancs and England 1965-83). 5'9". RHB, RM. Debut 1988. Cap 1992. Tour: A 1992-93 (Eng A). 1000 runs (2); most – 1389 (1992). HS 132 v Kent (Manchester) 1992. BB 1-57. **NWT:** HS 39 v Hants (Southampton) 1991. **BHC:** HS 34 v Leics (Leicester) 1993. **SL:** HS 100* v Kent (Maidstone) 1990.

MARTIN, Peter James (Danum S, Doncaster), b Accrington 15 Nov 1968. 6'4". RHB, RFM. Debut 1989. HS 133 v Durham (Gateshead) 1992. BB 5-35 v Yorks (Leeds) 1993 (not BAC). BAC BB 4-30 v Worcs (Blackpool) 1991. **NWT:** HS-. BB 2-19 v Dorset (Bournemouth) 1991. **BHC:** HS 10* v Surrey (Oval) 1993. BB 2-50 v Sussex (Hove) 1993. **SL:** HS 18* v Sussex (Hove) 1992. BB 3-52 v Essex (Manchester) 1993.

SPEAK, Nicholas Jason (Parrs Wood HS, Manchester), b Manchester 21 Nov 1966. 6'0". RHB, RM/OB. Debut v Jamaica (Kingston) 1986-87. Cap 1992. Tour: WI 1986-87 (La). 1000 runs (2); most – 1892 (1992). HS 232 v Leics (Leicester) 1992. BB 1-0. **NWT:** HS 60 v Essex (Chelmsford) 1992. **BHC:** HS 82 v Hants (Manchester) 1992. **SL:** HS 102* v Yorks (Leeds) 1992.

STANWORTH, John (Chadderton GS), b Oldham 30 Sep 1960. 5'10". RHB, WK. Debut 1983. Cap 1989. HS 50* v Glos (Bristol) 1985. **NWT:** HS 0. **BHC:** HS 8*. **SL:** HS 4*.

TITCHARD, Stephen Paul (Lymm County HS; Priestley C), b Warrington 17 Dec 1967. 6'3". RHB, RM. Debut 1990. HS 135 v Notts (Manchester) 1991. **NWT:** HS 20 v Oxon (Oxford) 1992. **BHC:** HS 82 v Surrey (Oval) 1992. **SL:** HS 84 v Leics (Leicester) 1993.

WASIM AKRAM (Islamia C), b Lahore, Pakistan 3 Jun 1966. 6'3". LHB, LF. PACO 1984-85/1985-86. Lahore 1985-86/1986-87. PIA 1987-88 to date. Lancashire debut 1988. Cap 1989. Wisden 1992. **Tests** (P): 48 (1984-85 to 1992-93); HS 123 v A (Adelaide) 1989-90; BB 6-62 v A (Melbourne) 1989-90. LOI (P): 153 (HS 86; BB 5-16). Tours (P): E 1987, 1992; A 1988-89, 1989-90, 1991-92, 1992-93; WI 1987-88, 1992-93 (captain); NZ 1984-85, 1992-93; I 1986-87; SL 1984-85 (P U-23), 1985-86. HS 123 (Tests). La HS 122 v Hants (Basingstoke) 1991. 50 wkts (4); most – 82 (1992). BB 8-68 (12-125 match) v Yorks (Manchester) 1993. Hat-trick 1988. Award: BHC 1. **NWT**: HS 29 v Hants (Southampton) 1991. BB 4-27 v Lincs (Manchester) 1988. **BHC**: HS 52 v Northants (Northampton) 1989. BB 5-10 v Leics (Leicester) 1993. **SL**: HS 51* v Yorks (Manchester) 1993. BB 4-19 v Yorks (Scarborough) 1990.

WATKINSON, Michael (Rivington and Blackrod HS, Horwich), b Westhoughton 1 Aug 1961. 6'1". RHB, RMF/OB. Debut 1982. Cap 1987. Captain 1994. Cheshire 1982. 1000 runs (1): 1016 (1993). HS 138 v Yorks (Manchester) 1990. 50 wkts (5); most – 66 (1992). BB 7-25 v Sussex (Lytham) 1987. Awards: NWT 2; BHC 2. Hat-trick 1992. **NWT**: HS 90 and BB 3-14 v Glos (Manchester) 1990. **BHC**: HS 76 v Northants (Northampton) 1992. BB 5-49 v Yorks (Manchester) 1991. **SL**: HS 83 v Sussex (Manchester) 1991. BB 5-46 v Warwks (Manchester) 1990.

WOOD, Nathan Theo (Wm Hulme's GS), b Thornhill Edge, Yorks 4 Oct 1974. Son of B. (Yorks, Lancs, Derbys and England 1964-83). 5'8". LHB, OB. Lancashire staff 1993 – awaiting f-c debut.

YATES, Gary (Manchester GS), b Ashton-under-Lyne 20 Sep 1967. 6'0". RHB, OB. Debut 1990. HS 134* v Northants (Manchester) 1993. BB 5-108 v Sussex (Manchester) 1993. **BHC**: HS-. BB 2-50 v Sussex (Manchester) 1991. **SL**: HS 8. BB 3-27 v Worcs (Worcester) 1993.

NEWCOMERS

BROWN, Christopher (Failsworth HS; Tameside TC), b Oldham 16 Aug 1974. 6'2". RHB, OB.

GREEN, Richard James (Bridgewater HS, Cheshire; Mid-Cheshire C), b Warrington 13 Mar 1976. 6'1". RHB, RM.

HARVEY, Nicholas Paul (Forest CS, Winnersh), b Ascot, Berks 21 Nov 1973. 5'7". RHB, WK. Berkshire 1993.

SEAL, Peter John (Haslingden HS; Rossendale & Accrington C), b Rawtenstall 16 Apr 1976. 6'0". RHB, RMF.

SHADFORD, Darren James (Breeze Hill HS; Oldham TC), b Oldham 4 Mar 1975. 6'3". RHB, RMF.

DEPARTURES

FLETCHER, Stuart David (Reins Wood SS), b Keighley, Yorks 8 Jun 1964. 5'10". RHB, RMF. Yorkshire 1983-91 (cap 1988). Lancashire 1992-93. HS 28* Y v Kent (Tunbridge Wells) 1984. 50 wkts (1): 59 (1988). BB 8-58 Y v Essex (Sheffield) 1988. La HS 23 and BB 2-53 v Notts (Nottingham) 1992. Award: NWT 1. **NWT**: HS 16* Y v Surrey (Oval) 1989. BB 3-20 Y v Berks (Finchampstead) 1988. **BHC**: HS 15* Y v Lancs (Leeds) 1990. BB 4-34 Y v Scot (Glasgow) 1987. **SL**: HS 11* Y v Essex (Chelmsford) 1991. BB 4-11 Y v Kent (Canterbury) 1988.

DeFREITAS, P.A.J. – see DERBYSHIRE.

IRANI, R.C. – see ESSEX.

MENDIS, Gehan Dixon (St Thomas C, Colombo; Brighton, Hove & Sussex GS; Durham U), b Colombo, Ceylon 24 Apr 1955. 5'9". RHB, RM. Sussex 1974-75 (cap 1980). Lancashire 1986-93 (cap 1986; benefit 1993). Tours: WI 1982-83 (Int), 1986-87 (La); P 1981-82 (Int); Z 1988-89 (La). 1000 runs (13); most – 1756 (1985). HS 209* Sx v Somerset (Hove) 1984. La HS 203* v Middx (Manchester) 1987. BB 1-65. Awards: NWT 4; BHC 5. **NWT**: HS 141* Sx v Warwks (Hove) 1980. **BHC**: HS 125* v Northants (Manchester) 1991. **SL**: HS 125* Sx v Glos (Hove) 1981.

LANCASHIRE 1993

RESULTS SUMMARY

	Place	Won	Lost	Tied	Drew	Abandoned
Britannic Assurance Championship	13th	4	8		5	
All First-class Matches		5	9		7	
Sunday League	6th	8	5	1		3
NatWest Trophy	1st Round					
Benson and Hedges Cup	Finalist					

BRITANNIC ASSURANCE CHAMPIONSHIP AVERAGES

BATTING AND FIELDING

Cap		M	I	NO	HS	Runs	Avge	100	50	Ct/St
–	G.Yates	7	10	6	134*	367	91.75	1	1	3
–	G.Chapple	6	11	6	109*	239	47.80	1	–	–
1987	M.Watkinson	15	24	2	107	936	42.54	2	4	6
1989	M.A.Atherton	10	16	–	137	557	34.81	2	3	9
1985	N.H.Fairbrother	16	28	3	110	855	34.20	1	4	11
–	J.P.Crawley	9	15	–	103	508	33.86	1	3	6
1992	N.J.Speak	17	29	1	122	931	33.25	1	7	10
1986	G.D.Mendis	14	27	–	94	875	32.40	–	7	3
–	S.P.Titchard	4	8	–	87	224	28.00	–	2	1
1992	G.D.Lloyd	13	22	1	80	574	27.33	–	3	10
–	P.J.Martin	12	18	6	43	310	25.83	–	–	2
1989	Wasim Akram	13	21	–	117	516	24.57	1	3	4
1989	W.K.Hegg	17	28	6	69*	488	22.18	–	1	45/7
1989	P.A.J.DeFreitas	16	25	3	51	426	19.36	–	1	13
–	R.C.Irani	2	4	–	44	44	11.00	–	–	1
–	A.A.Barnett	15	20	6	38	146	10.42	–	–	4

Also played (1 match): I.D.Austin (cap 1990) 1, 10.

BOWLING

	O	M	R	W	Avge	Best	5wI	10wM
Wasim Akram	409.2	93	1137	59	19.27	8- 68	5	1
P.A.J.DeFreitas	511.4	100	1578	49	32.20	7- 76	4	1
M.Watkinson	550.1	126	1621	44	36.84	5- 12	1	–
P.J.Martin	314.5	74	966	26	37.15	4- 63	–	–
G.Yates	233	46	692	16	43.25	5-108	1	–
G.Chapple	127	25	445	10	44.50	3- 50	–	–
A.A.Barnett	568.2	141	1618	35	46.22	5- 36	2	–

Also bowled: I.D.Austin 19.2-0-79-1; R.C.Irani 1-0-6-0.

The First-Class Averages (pp 164-177) give the records of Lancashire players in all first-class county matches (their other opponents being the Australians, Yorkshire in a non-Championship match, Cambridge U and Oxford U), with the exception of:

M.A.Atherton 13-20-1-137-811-42.68-3-3-13ct. 5-0-8-1-8.00-1/8.
J.P.Crawley 10-17-0-109-631-37.11-2-3-5ct. Did not bowl.
P.A.J.DeFreitas 20-29-3-51-453-17.42-0-1-14ct. 604.4-121-1844-58-31.79-7/76-4-1.
J.E.R.Gallian 1-2-1-42*-42-42.00-0-0-0ct. 9-0-22-0.
G.D.Lloyd 17-29-2-116-994-36.81-2-4-12ct. Did not bowl.

104

LANCASHIRE RECORDS

FIRST-CLASS CRICKET

Highest Total	For	863		v	Surrey	The Oval	1990
	V	707-9d		by	Surrey	The Oval	1990
Lowest Total	For	25		v	Derbyshire	Manchester	1871
	V	22		by	Glamorgan	Liverpool	1924
Highest Innings	For	424	A.C.MacLaren	v	Somerset	Taunton	1895
	V	315*	T.W.Hayward	for	Surrey	The Oval	1898

Highest Partnership for each Wicket

1st	368	A.C.MacLaren/R.H.Spooner	v	Glos	Liverpool	1903
2nd	371	F.B.Watson/G.E.Tyldesley	v	Surrey	Manchester	1928
3rd	364	M.A.Atherton/N.H.Fairbrother	v	Surrey	The Oval	1990
4th	324	A.C.MacLaren/J.T.Tyldesley	v	Notts	Nottingham	1904
5th	249	B.Wood/A.Kennedy	v	Warwicks	Birmingham	1975
6th	278	J.Iddon/H.R.W.Butterworth	v	Sussex	Manchester	1932
7th	245	A.H.Hornby/J.Sharp	v	Leics	Manchester	1912
8th	158	J.Lyon/R.M.Ratcliffe	v	Warwicks	Manchester	1979
9th	142	L.O.S.Poidevin/A.Kermode	v	Sussex	Eastbourne	1907
10th	173	J.Briggs/R.Pilling	v	Surrey	Liverpool	1885

Best Bowling	For	10-46	W.Hickton	v	Hampshire	Manchester	1870
(Innings)	V	10-40	G.O.B.Allen	for	Middlesex	Lord's	1929
Best Bowling	For	17-91	H.Dean	v	Yorkshire	Liverpool	1913
(Match)	V	16-65	G.Giffen	for	Australians	Manchester	1886

Most Runs – Season	2633	J.T.Tyldesley	(av 56.02)	1901
Most Runs – Career	34222	G.E.Tyldesley	(av 45.20)	1909-36
Most 100s – Season	11	C.Hallows		1928
Most 100s – Career	90	G.E.Tyldesley		1909-36
Most Wkts – Season	198	E.A.McDonald	(av 18.55)	1925
Most Wkts – Career	1816	J.B.Statham	(av 15.12)	1950-68

LIMITED-OVERS CRICKET

Highest Total	NWT	372-5		v	Glos	Manchester	1990
	BHC	330-4		v	Sussex	Manchester	1991
	SL	300-7		v	Leics	Leicester	1993
Lowest Total	NWT	59		v	Worcs	Worcester	1963
	BHC	82		v	Yorkshire	Bradford	1972
	SL	71		v	Essex	Chelmsford	1987
Highest Innings	NWT	131	A.Kennedy	v	Middlesex	Manchester	1978
	BHC	136	G.Fowler	v	Sussex	Manchester	1991
	SL	134*	C.H.Lloyd	v	Somerset	Manchester	1970
Best Bowling	NWT	5-13	P.A.J.DeFreitas	v	Cumberland	Kendal	1989
	BHC	6-10	C.E.H.Croft	v	Scotland	Manchester	1982
	SL	6-29	D.P.Hughes	v	Somerset	Manchester	1977

LEICESTERSHIRE

Formation of Present Club: 25 March 1879
Colours: Dark Green and Scarlet
Badge: Gold Running Fox on Green Ground
Championships: (1) 1975
NatWest Trophy/Gillette Cup Winners: (0) Finalist 1992
Benson and Hedges Cup Winners: (3) 1972, 1975, 1985
Sunday League Champions: (2) 1974, 1977
Match Awards: NWT 34; BHC 58

Chief Executive: A.O.Norman. **Administrative Secretary:** K.P.Hill, County Ground, Grace Road, Leicester LE2 8AD (☎ 0533-831880)
Captain: N.E.Briers
Scorer: G.R.Blackburn
1994 Beneficiaries: G.J.Parsons and L.Spence (Head Groundsman)

BOON, Timothy James (Edlington CS, Doncaster), b Doncaster, Yorks 1 Nov 1961. 6'0". RHB, RM. Debut 1980. Cap 1986. Tour: Z 1980-81 (Le). 1000 runs (7); most – 1539 (1990). HS 144 v Glos (Leicester) 1984. BB 3-40 v Yorks (Leicester) 1986. Awards: NWT 2; BHC 1. NWT: HS 117 v Bucks (Marlow) 1993. BHC: HS 103 v Scot (Leicester) 1991. SL: HS 135* v Kent (Canterbury) 1993. BB 1-23.

BRIERS, Nigel Edwin (Lutterworth GS; Borough Road CE), b Leicester 15 Jan 1955. 6'0". RHB, RM. Debut 1971 (aged 16yr 103d – youngest Leicestershire player). Cap 1981. Captain 1990-. Benefit 1990. Wisden 1992. Tour: Z 1980-81 (Le). 1000 runs (9); most – 1996 (1990). HS 201* v Warwks (Birmingham) 1983. BB 4-29 v Derbys (Leicester) 1985. Awards: NWT 1; BHC 5. NWT: HS 88 v Essex (Leicester) 1992. BHC: HS 102 v Minor C (Stone) 1992. BB 1-26. SL: HS 119* v Hants (Bournemouth) 1981. BB 3-29 v Middx (Leicester) 1984.

BRIMSON, Matthew Thomas (Chislehurst & Sidcup GS; Durham U), b Plumstead, London 1 Dec 1970. 6'0". RHB, SLA. Kent staff 1991. Debut 1993. HS 0. BB 2-66 v Glam (Leicester) 1993. SL: HS-. BB 1-28.

COBB, Russell Alan (Trent C), b Leicester 18 May 1961. 5'11". RHB, SLA. Leicestershire 1980-89 (cap 1986). Natal B 1988-89. Tours: NZ 1979-80 (DHR); Z 1980-81 (Le). 1000 runs (1): 1092 (1986). HS 91 v Northants (Leicester) 1986. Award: NWT 1. NWT: HS 66* v Oxon (Leicester) 1987. BHC: HS 22 v Warwks (Leicester) 1986. SL: HS 24 v Worcs (Leicester) 1981.

DAKIN, Jonathan Michael (King Edward VII S, Johannesburg) b Hitchin, Herts 28 Feb 1973. 6'4". LHB, RM. Debut 1993. HS 5 and BB 4-45 v CU (Cambridge) 1993 (on debut). Awaiting BAC debut. SL: HS 27 v Middx (Lord's) 1993. BB 3-45 v Glam (Leicester) 1993.

HEPWORTH, Peter Nash (Hemsworth HS), b Ackworth, Yorks 4 May 1967. 6'1". RHB, OB. Debut 1988. 1000 runs (1): 1119 (1991). HS 129 v Glam (Leicester) 1993. BB 3-51 v Kent (Canterbury) 1991. BHC: HS 33 v Sussex (Hove) 1991. BB 4-39 v Scot (Leicester) 1991. SL: HS 38 v Sussex (Leicester) 1988. BB 2-33 v Notts (Leicester) 1991.

MADDY, Darren Lee (Wreake Valley C), b Leicester 23 May 1974. 5'9". RHB, RM. Leicestershire staff 1993 – awaiting f-c debut. SL: HS 3.

MILLNS, David James (Garibaldi CS), b Clipstone, Notts 27 Feb 1965. 6'3". LHB, RF. Nottinghamshire 1988-89. Leicestershire debut 1990. Cap 1991. Tour: A 1992-93 (Eng A). HS 44 v Middx (Uxbridge) 1991. 50 wkts (2): most – 74 (1992). BB 9-37 (12-91 match) v Derbys (Derby) 1991. Award: NWT 1. **NWT:** HS 29* v Derbys (Derby) 1992. BB 3-22 v Norfolk (Leicester) 1992. **BHC:** HS 11* v Sussex (Hove) 1991. BB 4-51 v Minor C (Stone) 1992. **SL:** HS 20* v Notts (Leicester) 1991. BB 2-20 v Warwks (Leicester) 1991.

MULLALLY, Alan David (Cannington HS, Perth, Australia; Wembley TC), b Southend-on-Sea, Essex 12 Jul 1969. 6'5". RHB, LFM. W Australia 1987-88/1989-90. Victoria 1990-91. Hampshire (1 match) 1988. Leicestershire debut 1990. Cap 1993. HS 34 WA v Tasmania (Perth) 1989-90. Le HS 29 v Hants (Leicester) 1990. 50 wkts (1): 62 (1993). BB 7-72 (10-170 match) v Glos (Leicester) 1993. **NWT:** HS 19* v Bucks (Marlow) 1993. BB 2-22 v Derbys and Northants 1992. **BHC:** HS 11 v Surrey (Leicester) 1992. BB 1-8. **SL:** HS 10* (twice). BB 2-19 v Somerset (W-s-M) 1991.

NIXON, Paul Andrew (Ullswater HS, Penrith), b Carlisle, Cumberland 21 Oct 1970. 6'0". LHB, WK. Debut 1989. Cumberland 1987. MCC YC. HS 113* v Lancs (Leicester) 1993. **NWT:** HS 32 v Derbys (Derby) 1992. **BHC:** HS 27 v Worcs (Leicester) 1993. **SL:** HS 60 v Notts (Nottingham) 1992.

PARSONS, Gordon James (Woodside County SS, Slough), b Slough, Bucks 17 Oct 1959. Brother-in-law of W.J.Cronje (OFS and South Africa). 6'1". LHB, RMF. Leicestershire 1978-85 (cap 1984) and 1989-. Joint benefit 1994. Warwickshire 1986-88 (cap 1987). Boland 1983-84/1984-85. GW 1985-86/1986-87. OFS 1988-89/1990-91. Buckinghamshire 1977. Tours: NZ 1979-80 (DHR); Z 1980-81 (Le). HS 76 Boland v W Province B (Cape Town) 1984-85. Le HS 69 v Glos (Leicester) 1989. 50 wkts (2); most – 67 (1984). BB 9-72 Boland v Transvaal B (Johannesburg) 1984-85. Le BB 6-11 v OU (Oxford) 1985. BAC BB 6-70 v Surrey (Oval) 1992. Awards: BHC 2. **NWT:** HS 23 v Northants (Northampton) 1984. BB 2-11 v Wilts (Swindon) 1984. **BHC:** HS 63* and BB 4-12 v Scot (Leicester) 1989. **SL:** HS 38* v Lancs (Leicester) 1993. BB 4-19 v Essex (Harlow) 1982.

PIERSON, Adrian Roger Kirshaw (Kent C, Canterbury; Hatfield Poly), b Enfield, Middx 21 Jul 1963. 6'4". RHB, OB. Warwickshire 1985-91. Leicestershire debut 1993. Cambridgeshire 1992. MCC YC. HS 58 and Le BB 6-87 v Lancs (Leicester) 1993. BB 6-82 Wa v Derbys (Nuneaton) 1989. Award: BHC 1. **NWT:** HS 1*. BB 3-20 Wa v Wilts (Birmingham) 1989. **BHC:** HS 11 Wa v Minor C (Walsall) 1986. BB 3-34 Wa v Lancs (Birmingham) 1988. **SL:** HS 21* Wa v Hants (Birmingham) 1987. BB 3-21 Wa v Leics (Birmingham) 1988.

ROBINSON, Phillip Edward (Greenhead GS, Keighley), b Keighley, Yorks 3 Aug 1963. 5'9". RHB, LM. Yorkshire 1984-91 (cap 1988). Leicestershire debut 1992. Cumberland 1992. 1000 runs (3); most – 1402 (1990). HS 189 Y v Lancs (Scarborough) 1991. Le HS 71 v Essex (Southend) 1993. BB 1-10. Le BB 1-13. Awards: NWT 1; BHC 2. **NWT:** HS 73 v Norfolk (Leicester) 1992. **BHC:** HS 73* Y v Hants (Southampton) 1990. **SL:** HS 104 v Lancs (Manchester) 1992.

SHERIYAR, Alamgir (George Dixon SS; Joseph Chamberlain SFC), b Birmingham 15 Nov 1973. 6'1". RHB, LFM. Leicestershire staff 1993 – awaiting f-c debut. **SL:** HS-.

SMITH, Benjamin Francis (Kibworth HS), b Corby, Northants 3 Apr 1972. 5'9". RHB, RM. Debut 1990. HS 100* v Durham (Durham) 1992. BB 1-5. **NWT:** HS 49 v Norfolk (Leicester) 1992. **BHC:** HS 43 v Warwks (Leicester) 1993. **SL:** HS 97* v Derbys (Leicester) 1993.

WELLS, Vincent John (Sir William Nottidge S, Whitstable), b Dartford, Kent 6 Aug 1965. 6'0". RHB, RMF. Kent 1988-91. Leicestershire debut 1992. HS 167 v Glam (Leicester) 1993 BB 5-43 K v Leics (Leicester) 1990. Le BB 4-26 v Northants (Northampton) 1992. Awards: NWT 1; BHC 1. **NWT:** 100* K v Oxon (Oxford) 1990. BB 3-38 v Durham (Leicester) 1992. **BHC:** HS 25 K v Sussex (Canterbury) 1991. BB 4-37 v Worcs (Leicester) 1993. **SL:** HS 50 v Derbys (Leicester) 1993. BB 3-17 K v Somerset (Canterbury) 1988.

WHITAKER, John James (Uppingham S), b Skipton, Yorks 5 May 1962. 5'10". RHB, OB. Debut 1983. Cap 1986. Benefit 1993. Wisden 1986. YC 1986. **Tests:** 1 (1986-87); HS 11 v A (Adelaide) 1986-87. LOI: 2 (HS 44*). Tours: A 1986-87; Z 1989-90 (Eng A). 1000 runs (8); most – 1767 (1990). HS 200* v Notts (Leicester) 1986. BB 1-29. Awards: NWT 1; BHC 1. **NWT:** HS 155 v Wilts (Swindon) 1984. **BHC:** HS 100 v Kent (Canterbury) 1991. **SL:** HS 132 v Glam (Swansea) 1984.

WHITTICASE, Philip (Crestwood CS, Kingswinford), b Marston Green, Solihull 15 Mar 1965. 5'8". RHB, WK. Debut 1984. Cap 1987. HS 114* v Hants (Bournemouth) 1991. **NWT:** HS 32 v Lancs (Leicester) 1986. **BHC:** HS 45 v Notts (Nottingham) 1990. **SL:** HS 38 v Northants (Leicester) 1990.

NEWCOMERS

MASON, Timothy James (Denstone C), b Leicester 12 Apr 1975. 5'8". RHB, OB.

SIMMONS, Philip Verant (Holy Cross C, Arima), b Arima, Trinidad 18 Apr 1963. 6'3½". RHB, RM. Debut for N Trinidad 1982-83. Trinidad 1982-83/1991-92 (captain 1988-89). Durham 1989-90 (NWT only). **Tests** (WI): 16 (1987-88 to 1992-93); HS 110 and BB 2-34 v A (Melbourne) 1992-93. LOI (WI): 64 (HS 122; BB 4-3). Tours (WI): E 1988 (part), 1991, 1992 (RW), 1993 (RW) A 1992-93; I 1987-88; Z 1983-84 (Young WI), 1986-87 (Young WI). 1000 runs (1): 1031 (1991). HS 202 Trinidad v Guyana (Pointe-à-Pierre) 1991-92. BB 5-24 Trinidad v Windward Is (Pointe-à-Pierre) 1990-91. **NWT:** HS 33 and BB 1-43 Du v Middx (Darlington) 1989.

STANGER, Ian Michael (Hutcheson's GS, Glasgow; Duncan of Jordanstone Art C, Dundee), b Glasgow, Scotland 5 Oct 1971. 6'0". RHB, RFM.

SUTCLIFFE, Iain John (Leeds GS), b Leeds, Yorks 20 Dec 1974. LHB, OB.

DEPARTURES

BENJAMIN, W.K.M. – see HAMPSHIRE.

BENSON, Justin David Ramsay (The Leys S, Cambridge), b Dublin, Ireland 1 Mar 1967. 6'2". RHB, RM. Leicestershire 1988-93. Cambridgeshire 1984-87. HS 153 v Glos (Leicester) 1993. BB 2-24 v Yorks (Sheffield) 1992. Awards: NWT 2. **NWT:** HS 85 Cambs v Yorks (Leeds) 1986. BB 3-13 v Bucks (Marlow) 1993. **BHC:** HS 43 v Notts (Nottingham) 1990. BB 2-27 v Glos (Cheltenham) 1992. **SL:** HS 67 v Surrey (Oval) 1990. BB 4-27 v Glos (Leicester) 1993.

POTTER, Laurie (Kelmscott HS, Perth, Australia), b Bexleyheath, Kent 7 Nov 1962. 6'1". RHB, SLA. Kent 1981-85. Leicestershire 1986-93 (cap 1988). GW 1984-85/1985-86 (captain 1985-86). OFS 1987-88. 1000 runs (3); most – 1093 (1989). HS 165* GW v Border (East London) 1984-85. Le HS 121* v Notts (Leicester) 1989. BB 5-45 v Notts (Leicester) 1993. Award: BHC 1. **NWT:** HS 57 v Northants (Northampton) 1991. BB 2-40 v Surrey (Leicester) 1993. **BHC:** HS 112 v Minor C (Leicester) 1986. BB 2-37 v Warwks (Leicester) 1993. **SL:** HS 105 v Derbys (Leicester) 1986. BB 5-28 v Notts (Leicester) 1993.

LEICESTERSHIRE 1993

RESULTS SUMMARY

	Place	Won	Lost	Drew	Abandoned
Britannic Assurance Championship	9th	6	5	6	
All First-class Matches		6	6	7	
Sunday League	14th	5	10		2
NatWest Trophy	2nd Round				
Benson and Hedges Cup	Semi-Finalist				

BRITANNIC ASSURANCE CHAMPIONSHIP AVERAGES

BATTING AND FIELDING

Cap		M	I	NO	HS	Runs	Avge	100	50	Ct/St
–	J.D.R.Benson	5	6	–	153	232	38.66	1	–	9
1986	J.J.Whitaker	17	26	1	126	889	35.56	1	4	8
1986	T.J.Boon	17	27	1	110	878	33.76	2	5	8
–	V.J.Wells	13	20	2	167	575	31.94	1	2	10
1981	N.E.Briers	11	17	1	79	451	28.18	–	3	2
–	P.N.Hepworth	6	10	–	129	271	27.10	1	1	1
–	P.A.Nixon	17	25	6	113*	475	25.00	–	3	39/4
1984	G.J.Parsons	16	20	6	49*	338	24.14	–	–	9
1989	W.K.M.Benjamin	9	13	–	83	294	22.61	–	2	14
1988	L.Potter	11	16	1	62	301	20.06	–	1	11
–	P.E.Robinson	16	26	3	71	451	19.60	–	3	20
–	B.F.Smith	9	15	–	84	215	14.33	–	1	2
–	A.R.K.Pierson	16	21	5	58	223	13.93	–	1	3
1991	D.J.Millns	7	8	3	24	59	11.80	–	–	6
1993	A.D.Mullally	15	18	4	26	125	8.92	–	–	3

Also played (2 matches): M.T.Brimson 0.

BOWLING

	O	M	R	W	Avge	Best	5wI	10wM
W.K.M.Benjamin	281.3	81	702	32	21.93	7-83	3	–
A.D.Mullally	473.1	123	1371	59	23.23	7-72	2	1
D.J.Millns	184.3	51	584	25	23.36	5-21	2	–
G.J.Parsons	432.1	134	976	40	24.40	3-23	–	–
A.R.K.Pierson	466	125	1160	41	28.29	6-87	4	–
L.Potter	322.3	119	707	22	32.13	5-45	1	–
V.J.Wells	204.4	57	595	14	42.50	2- 5	–	–

Also bowled: T.J.Boon 8-1-38-0; M.T.Brimson 20-3-66-2; P.N.Hepworth 16-2-55-1; P.E.Robinson 13.3-1-78-1; B.F.Smith 6-2-8-0.

The First-Class Averages (pp 164-177) give the records of Leicestershire players in all first-class county matches (their other opponents being the Australians and Cambridge U).

LEICESTERSHIRE RECORDS

FIRST-CLASS CRICKET

Highest Total	For	701-4d	v Worcs	Worcester	1906
	V	761-6d	by Essex	Chelmsford	1990
Lowest Total	For	25	v Kent	Leicester	1912
	V	24	by Glamorgan	Leicester	1971
		24	by Oxford U	Oxford	1985
Highest Innings	For	252* S.Coe	v Northants	Leicester	1914
	V	341 G.H.Hirst	for Yorkshire	Leicester	1905

Highest Partnership for each Wicket

1st	390	B.Dudleston/J.F.Steele	v Derbyshire	Leicester	1979
2nd	289*	J.C.Balderstone/D.I.Gower	v Essex	Leicester	1981
3rd	316*	W.Watson/A.Wharton	v Somerset	Taunton	1961
4th	290*	P.Willey/T.J.Boon	v Warwicks	Leicester	1984
5th	233	N.E.Briers/R.W.Tolchard	v Somerset	Leicester	1979
6th	262	A.T.Sharpe/G.H.S.Fowke	v Derbyshire	Chesterfield	1911
7th	219*	J.D.R.Benson/P.Whitticase	v Hampshire	Bournemouth	1991
8th	164	M.R.Hallam/C.T.Spencer	v Essex	Leicester	1964
9th	160	W.W.Odell/R.T.Crawford	v Worcs	Leicester	1902
10th	228	R.Illingworth/K.Higgs	v Northants	Leicester	1977

Best Bowling	For	10- 18 G.Geary	v Glamorgan	Pontypridd	1929
(Innings)	V	10- 32 H.Pickett	for Essex	Leyton	1895
Best Bowling	For	16- 96 G.Geary	v Glamorgan	Pontypridd	1929
(Match)	V	16-102 C.Blythe	for Kent	Leicester	1909

Most Runs – Season	2446	L.G.Berry	(av 52.04)	1937
Most Runs – Career	30143	L.G.Berry	(av 30.32)	1924-51
Most 100s – Season	7	L.G.Berry		1937
	7	W.Watson		1959
	7	B.F.Davison		1982
Most 100s – Career	45	L.G.Berry		1924-51
Most Wkts – Season	170	J.E.Walsh	(av 18.96)	1948
Most Wkts – Career	2130	W.E.Astill	(av 23.19)	1906-39

LIMITED-OVERS CRICKET

Highest Total	NWT	354-7	v Wiltshire	Swindon	1984
	BHC	327-4	v Warwicks	Coventry	1972
	SL	291-5	v Glamorgan	Swansea	1984
Lowest Total	NWT	56	v Northants	Leicester	1964
	BHC	56	v Minor C	Wellington	1982
	SL	36	v Sussex	Leicester	1973
Highest Innings	NWT	156 D.I.Gower	v Derbyshire	Leicester	1984
	BHC	158* B.F.Davison	v Warwicks	Coventry	1972
	SL	152 B.Dudleston	v Lancashire	Manchester	1975
Best Bowling	NWT	6-20 K.Higgs	v Staffs	Longton	1975
	BHC	6-35 L.B.Taylor	v Worcs	Worcester	1982
	SL	6-17 K.Higgs	v Glamorgan	Leicester	1973

MIDDLESEX

Formation of Present Club: 2 February 1864
Colours: Blue
Badge: Three Seaxes
Championships (since 1890): (10) 1903, 1920, 1921, 1947,
1976, 1980, 1982, 1985, 1990, 1993
Joint Championships: (2) 1949, 1977
NatWest Trophy/Gillette Cup Winners: (4) 1977, 1980,
1984, 1988
Benson and Hedges Cup Winners: (2) 1983, 1986
Sunday League Champions: (1) 1992
Match Awards: NWT 47; BHC 52

Secretary: J.Hardstaff MBE, Lord's Cricket Ground, London NW8 8QN
(☎ 071-289 1300/071-286 1310)
Captain: M.W.Gatting
Scorer: M.J.Smith
1994 Beneficiary: N.F.Williams

BALLINGER, Richard John (Millfield S; Durham U), b Wimbledon, Surrey 18
Sep 1973. 6'2". RHB, RFM. Middlesex staff 1993 – awaiting f-c debut.

BROWN, Keith Robert (Chace S, Enfield), b Edmonton 18 Mar 1963. Brother of
G.K. (Middx 1986 and Durham 1992). 5'11". RHB, WK, RSM. Debut 1984. Cap
1990. MCC YC. 1000 runs (2); most – 1505 (1990). HS 200* v Notts (Lord's) 1990.
BB 2-7 v Glos (Bristol) 1987. Award: NWT 1. **NWT:** HS 103* v Surrey (Uxbridge)
1990. **BHC:** HS 56 v Minor C (Lord's) 1990. **SL:** HS 102 v Somerset (Lord's) 1988.

CARR, John Donald (Repton S; Worcester C, Oxford), b St John's Wood 15 Jun
1963. Son of D.B. (Derbys, OU and England 1945-63). 5'11". RHB, RM. Oxford
U 1983-85 (blue 1983-84-85). Middlesex 1983-89 (cap 1987) and 1992-. Hertford-
shire 1982-84 and 1991. 1000 runs (3); most – 1541 (1987). HS 192* v Warwks
(Birmingham) 1993. BB 6-61 v Glos (Lord's) 1985. **NWT:** HS 83 v Hants
(Southampton) 1989. BB 2-19 v Surrey (Oval) 1988. **BHC:** HS 70 v Leics
(Leicester) 1992. BB 3-22 Comb Us v Glos (Bristol) 1984. **SL:** HS 104* v Warwks
(Lord's) 1992. BB 4-21 v Surrey (Lord's) 1989.

DUTCH, Keith Philip (Nower Hill HS; Weald C), b Harrow 21 Mar 1973. 5'10".
RHB, OB. Debut 1993. MCC YC 1992. 2nd XI Championship Player of 1993. HS-.

EMBUREY, John Ernest (Peckham Manor SS), b Peckham, London 20 Aug 1952.
6'2". RHB, OB. Debut 1973. Cap 1977. Wisden 1983. W Province 1982-83/1983-84.
Benefit 1986. **Tests:** 63 (1978 to 1993, 2 as captain); HS 75 v NZ (Nottingham)
1986; BB 7-78 v A (Sydney) 1986-87. **LOI:** 61 (HS 34; BB 4-37). **Tours:** A 1978-79,
1979-80, 1986-87, 1987-88; SA 1981-82 (SAB), 1989-90 (Eng XI); WI 1980-81,
1985-86; NZ 1987-88; I 1979-80, 1981-82, 1992-93; P 1987-88; SL 1977-78 (DHR),
1981-82, 1991-92; Z 1980-81 (Mx). HS 133 v Essex (Chelmsford) 1983. 50 wkts (15)
inc 100 (1): 103 (1983). BB 8-40 (12-115 match) v Hants (Lord's) 1993. Awards:
NWT 1; BHC 6. **NWT:** HS 36* v Lancs (Manchester) 1978. BB 3-11 v Sussex
(Lord's) 1989. **BHC:** HS 50 v Kent (Lord's) 1984. BB 5-37 v Somerset (Taunton)
1991. **SL:** HS 50 v Lancs (Blackpool) 1988. BB 5-23 v Somerset (Taunton) 1991.

FARBRACE, Paul (Geoffrey Chaucer S, Canterbury), b Ash, Kent 7 Jul 1967.
5'10". RHB, WK. Kent 1987-89. Middlesex debut 1990. HS 79 v CU (Cambridge)
1990. BAC HS 75* K v Yorks (Canterbury) 1987. BB 1-64. **NWT:** HS 17 v Berks
(Lord's) 1990. **SL:** HS 26* v Lancs (Lord's) 1991.

FELTHAM, Mark Andrew (Tiffin S), b St John's Wood 26 June 1963. 6'2½".
RHB, RMF. Surrey 1983-92 (cap 1990). Middlesex debut 1994. MCC YC. HS 101
Sy v Middx (Oval) 1990. M HS 73 v Notts (Lord's) 1993. 50 wkts (1): 56 (1988). BB

111

FELTHAM – continued:
6-53 Sy v Leics (Oval) 1990. **M** BB 4-48 v Derbys (Lord's) 1993. Awards: BHC 2.
NWT: HS 19* Sy v Hants (Oval) 1989. BB 2-27 Sy v Cheshire (Birkenhead) 1986.
BHC: HS 35 Sy v Kent (Canterbury) 1992. BB 5-28 Sy v Comb Us (Cambridge)
1989. **SL:** HS 61 Sy v Warwks (Oval) 1990. BB 4-35 Sy v Sussex (Guildford) 1986.

FRASER, Angus Robert Charles (Gayton HS, Harrow), b Billinge, Lancs 8 Aug
1965. Brother of A.G.J. (Middlesex and Essex 1986-92). 6'5". RHB, RFM. Debut
1984. Cap 1988. **Tests:** 12 (1989 to 1993); HS 29 v A (Nottingham) 1989; BB 6-82 v
A (Melbourne) 1990-91. LOI: 24 (HS 38*; BB 3-22). Tours: A 1990-91; WI
1989-90. HS 92 v Surrey (Oval) 1990. 50 wkts (4); most – 92 (1989). BB 7-40 v Leics
(Lord's) 1993. **NWT:** HS 19 v Durham (Darlington) 1989. BB 4-34 v Yorks (Leeds)
1988. **BHC:** HS 13* v Essex (Lord's) 1988. 3-30 v Glos (Lord's) 1992. **SL:** HS
30* v Kent (Canterbury) 1988. BB 4-17 v Hants (Lord's) 1993.

GATTING, Michael William (John Kelly HS), b Kingsbury 6 Jun 1957. 5'10".
RHB, RM. Debut 1975. Cap 1977. Captain 1983-. Benefit 1988. YC 1981. Wisden
1983. OBE 1987. **Tests:** 74 (1977-78 to 1993, 23 as captain); HS 207 v I (Madras)
1984-85; BB 1-14. LOI: 92 (HS 115*; BB 3-32). Tours (C=captain): A 1986-87C,
1987-88C; SA 1989-90C (Eng XI); WI 1980-81, 1985-86; NZ 1977-78, 1983-84,
1987-88C; I/SL 1981-82, 1984-85, 1992-93; P 1977-78, 1983-84, 1987-88C; Z 1980-81
(Mx). 1000 runs (15+1) inc 2000 (3); most – 2257 (1984). HS 258 v Somerset (Bath)
1984. BB 5-34 v Glam (Swansea) 1982. Awards: NWT 6; BHC 11. **NWT:** HS 132* v
Sussex (Lord's) 1989. BB 2-14 (twice). **BHC:** HS 143* v Sussex (Hove) 1985. BB
4-49 v Sussex (Lord's) 1984. **SL:** HS 124* v Leics (Leicester) 1990. BB 4-30 v Glos
(Bristol) 1989.

HABIB, Aftab (Millfield S; Taunton S), b Reading, Berkshire 7 Feb 1972. 5'11".
Cousin of Zahid Sadiq (Surrey and Derbys 1988-90). RHB, RMF. Debut 1992. **SL:** HS
12 v Surrey (Oval) 1992. **SL:** HS 15 v Northants (Lord's) 1993.

HARRISON, Jason Christian (Great Marlow SM; Bucks CHE), b Amersham,
Bucks 15 Jan 1972. 6'3". RHB, OB. Middlesex staff 1992 – awaiting f-c debut.
Buckinghamshire 1991-92.

HAYNES, Desmond Leo (Barbados Academy; Federal HS), b Holder's Hill,
Barbados 15 Feb 1956. 5'11". RHB, RM/LB. Barbados 1976-77/1991-92 (captain
1990-91). Middlesex debut/cap 1989. Scotland (BHC) 1983. Wisden 1990. **Tests**
(WI): 111 (1977-78 to 1992-93, 4 as captain); HS 184 v E (Lord's) 1980; BB 1-2.
LOI (WI): 225 (HS 152*). Tours (WI): E 1980, 1984, 1988, 1991; A 1979-80,
1981-82, 1984-85, 1986-87, 1988-89, 1991-92, 1992-93; NZ 1979-80, 1986-87; I
1983-84, 1987-88; P 1980-81, 1986-87, 1990-91 (captain); Z 1981-82 (WI B). 1000
runs (3+4) inc 2000 (1): 2346 (1990). HS 255* v Sussex (Lord's) 1990. BB 1-2
(Tests). **M** BB 1-4. Awards: NWT 1; BHC 3. **NWT:** HS 149* v Lancs (Manchester)
1990. BB 1-41. **BHC:** HS 131 v Sussex (Hove) 1990. BB 1-9. **SL:** HS 142* v Warwks
(Birmingham) 1993. BB 1-17.

JOHNSON, Richard Leonard (Sunbury Manor S; S Pelthorne C), b Chertsey,
Surrey 29 Dec 1974. 6'2". RHB, RMF. Debut 1992. HS 4. BB 1-25. **NWT:** HS 5.
SL: HS 18 v Derbys (Lord's) 1993. BB 4-66 v Worcs (Worcester) 1993.

POOLEY, Jason Calvin (Acton HS), b Hammersmith 8 Aug 1969. 6'0". LHB.
Debut 1989. HS 88 v Derbys (Lord's) 1991. **BHC:** HS 8. **SL:** HS 109 v Derbys
(Lord's) 1991.

RADFORD, Toby Alexander (St Bartholomew's S, Newbury; Loughborough U), b
Caerphilly, Glam 3 Dec 1971. 5'10". RHB, OB. Middlesex staff 1990 – awaiting f-c
debut. **SL:** HS 38 v Worcs (Worcester) 1993.

RAMPRAKASH, Mark Ravin (Gayton HS; Harrow Weald SFC), b Bushey, Herts
5 Sep 1969. 5'9". RHB, RM. Debut 1987. Cap 1990. YC 1991. **Tests:** 10 (1991 to
1993); HS 64 v A (Oval) 1993. LOI: 2 (HS 6*). Tours: WI 1991-92 (Eng A); NZ
1991-92; P 1990-91 (Eng A); SL 1990-91 (Eng A). 1000 runs (4); most – 1541
(1990). HS 233 v Surrey (Lord's) 1992. BB 1-0. Awards: NWT 1; BHC 1. **NWT:** HS

RAMPRAKASH – continued:
104 v Surrey (Uxbridge) 1990. BB 2-15 v Ire (Dublin) 1991. **BHC:** HS 108* v Leics (Leicester) 1992. **SL:** HS 147* v Worcs (Lord's) 1990. BB 5-38 v Leics (Lord's) 1993.

ROSEBERRY, Michael Anthony (Durham S), b Houghton-le-Spring, Co Durham 28 Nov 1966. Elder brother of A. (see GLAMORGAN). 6'1". RHB, RM. Debut 1986. Cap 1990. Tour: A 1992-93 (Eng A). 1000 runs (3) inc 2000 (1): 2044 (1992). HS 185 v Leics (Lord's) 1993. BB 1-1. Award: BHC 1. **NWT:** HS 112 and BB 1-22 v Salop (Telford) 1992. **BHC:** HS 84 v Minor C (Lord's) 1992. **SL:** HS 106* v Yorks (Lord's) 1991.

SIMS, Robin Jason (Vyners SS), b Hillingdon 22 Nov 1970. 5'8". LHB, WK. Debut 1992. MCC YC (held long-leg catch as substitute to dismiss A.R.Border in Lord's Test 1989). HS 28 v OU (Oxford) 1993. BAC HS 0. **NWT:** HS 13* v Salop (Telford) 1992. **BHC:** HS-. **SL:** HS 27* v Derbys (Derby) 1992.

TAYLOR, Charles William (Spendlove S, Charlbury), b Banbury, Oxon 12 Aug 1966. 6'5½". LHB, LMF. Debut 1990. Oxfordshire 1986 and 1990. HS 28* v OU (Oxford) 1993. BAC HS 21 v Kent (Lord's) 1991. BB 5-33 v Yorks (Leeds) 1990. **NWT:** HS-. BB 1-54. **SL:** HS 3*. BB 2-33 v Northants (Lord's) 1993.

TUFNELL, Philip Clive Roderick (Highgate S), b Barnet, Herts 29 Apr 1966. 6'0". RHB, SLA. Debut 1986. Cap 1990. MCC YC. **Tests:** 15 (1990-91 to 1993); HS 22* v I (Madras) 1992-93; BB 7-47 (11-147 match) v NZ (Christchurch) 1991-92. LOI: 15 (HS 5*; BB 3-40). Tours: A 1990-91; NZ 1991-92; I/SL 1992-93. HS 37 v Leics (Leicester) and v Yorks (Leeds) 1990. 50 wkts (4); most – 88 (1991). BB 8-29 v Glam (Cardiff) 1993. Award: NWT 1. **NWT:** HS 8. BB 3-29 v Herts (Lord's) 1988. **BHC:** HS 18 v Warwks (Lord's) 1991. BB 3-50 v Surrey (Lord's) 1991. **SL:** HS 13* v Glam (Merthyr Tydfil) 1989. BB 5-28 v Leics (Lord's) 1993.

WEEKES, Paul Nicholas (Homerton House SS, Hackney), b Hackney, London 8 Jul 1969. 5'10". LHB, OB. Debut 1990. Cap 1993. MCC YC. HS 95 v OU (Oxford) 1992. BAC HS 89* v Surrey (Lord's) 1992. BB 3-57 v Worcs (Worcester) 1991. Award: BHC 1. **NWT:** HS 7. BB 2-36 v Kent (Canterbury) 1993. **BHC:** HS 44* v Glos (Lord's) 1992. BB 2-29 v Hants (Southampton) 1992. **SL:** HS 66* v Surrey (Lord's) 1993. BB 4-37 v Somerset (Lord's) 1992.

WILLIAMS, Neil FitzGerald (Acland Burghley CS), b Hope Well, St Vincent 2 Jul 1962. 5'11". RHB, RFM. Debut 1982. Cap 1984. Benefit 1994. Windward Is 1982-83 and 1989-90/1991-92. Tasmania 1983-84. MCC YC. **Tests:** 1 (1990); HS 38 and BB 2-148 v I (Oval) 1990. Tour: Z 1984-85 (EC). HS 77 v Warwks (Birmingham) 1991. 50 wkts (3); most – 63 (1983). BB 8-75 (12-139 match) v Glos (Lord's) 1992. Award: BHC 1. **NWT:** HS 10 v Northumb (Jesmond) 1984. BB 4-36 v Derbys (Derby) 1983. **BHC:** HS 29* v Surrey (Lord's) 1985. BB 3-16 v Comb Us (Cambridge) 1982. **SL:** HS 43 v Somerset (Lord's) 1988. BB 4-39 v Surrey (Oval) 1988.

NEWCOMERS

SHINE, Kevin James, (Maiden Erlegh CS), b Bracknell, Berks 22 Feb 1969. 6'2½". RHB, RFM. Hampshire 1989-93. Berkshire 1986. HS 26* H v Middx (Lord's) 1989. BB 8-47 (8 wkts in 38 balls inc hat-trick and 4 in 5; 13-105 match) H v Lancs (Manchester) 1992. **BHC:** HS 0. BB 4-68 H v Surrey (Oval) 1990. **SL:** HS 2*. BB 2-15 H v Northants (Northampton) 1993.

YEABSLEY, Richard Stuart (Haberdashers' Aske's S, Elstree; Keble C, Oxford), b St Albans, Herts 2 Nov 1973. Son of D.I. (Devon 1959-89; Minor Counties 1974-79). 6'4½". RHB, RMF. OU debut/blue 1993. Devon 1990. HS 36 OU v Worcs (Worcester) 1993. BB 3-30 OU v Lancs (Oxford) 1993.

DEPARTURES

COWANS, N.G. – see HAMPSHIRE.

KEECH, M. – see HAMPSHIRE.

MIDDLESEX 1993

RESULTS SUMMARY

	Place	Won	Lost	Tied	Drew	Abandoned
Britannic Assurance Championship	1st	11	1		5	
All First-class Matches		11	1		6	
Sunday League	8th	7	6	2		2
NatWest Trophy	1st Round					
Benson and Hedges Cup	1st Round					

BRITANNIC ASSURANCE CHAMPIONSHIP AVERAGES

BATTING AND FIELDING

Cap		M	I	NO	HS	Runs	Avge	100	50	Ct/St
1977	M.W.Gatting	13	19	4	182	981	65.40	3	4	11
1977	J.E.Emburey	16	19	6	123	638	49.07	2	4	18
1993	P.N.Weekes	3	4	1	47	144	48.00	–	–	2
1987	J.D.Carr	17	24	6	192*	848	47.11	2	3	39
1990	K.R.Brown	17	22	5	88*	714	42.00	–	5	37/6
1989	D.L.Haynes	15	24	4	115	793	39.65	2	4	8
1990	M.R.Ramprakash	16	22	1	140	813	38.71	2	4	15
1990	M.A.Roseberry	15	24	4	185	679	33.95	1	2	12
–	M.A.Feltham	16	19	4	73	288	19.20	–	1	4
–	M.Keech	4	8	–	35	137	17.12	–	–	4
1984	N.F.Williams	13	11	1	44	140	14.00	–	–	3
1990	P.C.R.Tufnell	15	13	4	30*	113	12.55	–	–	6
1988	A.R.C.Fraser	16	14	2	29	106	8.83	–	–	5
1984	N.G.Cowans	5	4	1	7	9	3.00	–	–	1

Also played: K.P.Dutch (1 match) did not bat (2 ct); R.L.Johnson (1 match) 4, 4;
J.C.Pooley (1 match) 33, 7; R.J.Sims (2 matches) 0 (2 ct); C.W.Taylor (1 match) 0, 0.

BOWLING

	O	M	R	W	Avge	Best	5wI	10wM
N.G.Cowans	69	15	202	15	13.46	4-43	–	–
J.E.Emburey	662.4	213	1251	68	18.39	8-40	2	1
P.C.R.Tufnell	583.5	176	1210	59	20.50	8-29	3	–
A.R.C.Fraser	472.5	121	1219	50	24.38	7-40	1	–
N.F.Williams	361	61	1097	39	28.12	6-61	1	–
M.A.Feltham	327.4	88	905	29	31.20	4-48	–	–

Also bowled: J.D.Carr 10.5-0-73-4; K.P.Dutch 5-1-18-0; M.W.Gatting 4-0-10-0;
D.L.Haynes 7-1-61-1; M.Keech 5-0-16-0; R.L.Johnson 16-5-58-1; M.R.
Ramprakash 8.4-1-39-1; C.W.Taylor 30-7-93-1; P.N.Weekes 34-6-95-1.

The First-Class Averages (pp 164-177) give the records of Middlesex players in all
first-class county matches (their other opponents being Oxford U), with the
exception of J.E.Emburey, M.R.Ramprakash and M.A.Roseberry, whose full
county figures are as above, and:
  A.R.C.Fraser 17-15-2-29-121-9.30-0-0-6ct. 486.5-122-1257-53-23.71-7/40-1-0.
  M.W.Gatting 14-20-4-182-1041-65.06-3-5-12ct. 4-0-10-0.
  P.C.R.Tufnell 16-14-4-30*-125-12.50-0-0-6ct. 584.5-177-1210-59-20.50-8/29-3-0.

MIDDLESEX RECORDS

FIRST-CLASS CRICKET

Highest Total	For	642-3d		v	Hampshire	Southampton 1923
	V	665		by	W Indians	Lord's 1939
Lowest Total	For	20		v	MCC	Lord's 1864
	V	31		by	Glos	Bristol 1924
Highest Innings	For	331*	J.D.B.Robertson	v	Worcs	Worcester 1949
	V	316*	J.B.Hobbs	for	Surrey	Lord's 1926

Highest Partnership for each Wicket

1st	367*	G.D.Barlow/W.N.Slack	v	Kent	Lord's	1981
2nd	380	F.A.Tarrant/J.W.Hearne	v	Lancashire	Lord's	1914
3rd	424*	W.J.Edrich/D.C.S.Compton	v	Hampshire	Lord's	1948
4th	325	J.W.Hearne/E.H.Hendren	v	Hampshire	Lord's	1919
5th	338	R.S.Lucas/T.C.O'Brien	v	Sussex	Hove	1895
6th	227	C.T.Radley/F.J.Titmus	v	S Africans	Lord's	1965
7th	271*	E.H.Hendren/F.T.Mann	v	Notts	Nottingham	1925
8th	182*	M.H.C.Doll/H.R.Murrell	v	Notts	Lord's	1913
9th	160*	E.H.Hendren/T.J.Durston	v	Essex	Leyton	1927
10th	230	R.W.Nicholls/W.Roche	v	Kent	Lord's	1899

Best Bowling	For	10- 40	G.O.B.Allen	v	Lancashire	Lord's 1929
(Innings)	V	9- 38	R.C.Glasgow†	for	Somerset	Lord's 1924
Best Bowling	For	16-114	G.Burton	v	Yorkshire	Sheffield 1888
(Match)		16-114	J.T.Hearne	v	Lancashire	Manchester 1898
	V	16-109	C.W.L.Parker	for	Glos	Cheltenham 1930

Most Runs – Season	2669	E.H.Hendren	(av 83.41)	1923
Most Runs – Career	40302	E.H.Hendren	(av 48.81)	1907-37
Most 100s – Season	13	D.C.S.Compton		1947
Most 100s – Career	119	E.H.Hendren		1907-37
Most Wkts – Season	158	F.J.Titmus	(av 14.63)	1955
Most Wkts – Career	2361	F.J.Titmus	(av 21.27)	1949-82

LIMITED-OVERS CRICKET

Highest Total	NWT	296-4		v	Lancashire	Manchester 1990
	BHC	325-5		v	Leics	Leicester 1992
	SL	290-6		v	Worcs	Lord's 1990
Lowest Total	NWT	41		v	Essex	Westcliff 1972
	BHC	73		v	Essex	Lord's 1985
	SL	23		v	Yorkshire	Leeds 1974
Highest Innings	NWT	158	G.D.Barlow	v	Lancashire	Lord's 1984
	BHC	143*	M.W.Gatting	v	Sussex	Hove 1985
	SL	147*	M.R.Ramprakash	v	Worcs	Lord's 1990
Best Bowling	NWT	6-15	W.W.Daniel	v	Sussex	Hove 1980
	BHC	7-12	W.W.Daniel	v	Minor C	Ipswich 1978
	SL	6- 6	R.W.Hooker	v	Surrey	Lord's 1969

† R.C.Robertson-Glasgow

NORTHAMPTONSHIRE

Formation of Present Club: 31 July 1878
Colours: Maroon
Badge: Tudor Rose
Championships: (0) Second 1912, 1957, 1965, 1976
NatWest Trophy/Gillette Cup Winners: (2) 1976, 1992
Benson and Hedges Cup Winners: (1) 1980
Sunday League Champions: (0) Third 1991
Match Awards: NWT 44; BHC 43

Chief Executive: S.P.Coverdale, County Ground, Wantage Road, Northampton, NN1 4TJ (☎ 0604-32917)
Captain: A.J.Lamb
Scorer: A.C.Kingston
1994 Beneficiary: D.J.Capel

AMBROSE, Curtly Elconn Lynwall (All Saints Village SS), b Swetes Village, Antigua 21 Sep 1963. Cousin of R.M.Otto (Leeward Is 1979-80/1990-91). 6'7". LHB, RF. Leeward Is 1985-86/1991-92. Northamptonshire debut 1989. Cap 1990. Wisden 1991. **Tests** (WI): 42 (1987-88 to 1992-93); HS 53 v A (P-of-S) 1990-91; BB 8-45 v E (Bridgetown) 1989-90. **LOI** (WI): 91 (HS 26*; BB 5-17). **Tours** (WI): E 1988, 1991; A 1988-89, 1992-93; P 1990-91. HS 59 WI v Sussex (Hove) 1988. Nh HS 55* v Leics (Leicester) 1990. 50 wkts (4+1); most – 61 (1990). BB 8-45 (Tests). Nh BB 7-89 v Leics (Leicester) 1990. **Award:** NWT 1. **NWT:** HS 48 v Lancs (Lord's) 1990. BB 4-7 v Yorks (Northampton) 1992. **BHC:** HS 17* v Kent (Northampton) 1989. BB 4-31 v Essex (Northampton) 1992. **SL:** HS 26 v Durham (Northampton) 1993. BB 3-15 v Notts (Finedon) 1989.

BAILEY, Robert John (Biddulph HS), b Biddulph, Staffs 28 Oct 1963. 6'3". RHB, OB. Debut 1982. Cap 1985. Benefit 1993. Staffordshire 1980. YC 1984. **Tests:** 4 (1988 to 1989-90); HS 43 v WI (Oval) 1988. **LOI:** 4 (HS 43*). **Tours:** SA 1991-92 (Nh); WI 1989-90. 1000 runs (10); most – 1987 (1990). HS 224* v Glam (Swansea) 1986. BB 5-54 v Notts (Northampton) 1993. **Awards:** NWT 4; BHC 5. **NWT:** HS 145 v Staffs (Stone) 1991. BB 3-47 v Notts (Northampton) 1990. **BHC:** HS 134 v Glos (Northampton) 1987. BB 1-22. **SL:** HS 125* v Derbys (Derby) 1987. BB 3-23 v Leics (Leicester) 1987.

BOWEN, Mark Nicholas (Sacred Heart, Redcar; St Mary's C; Teesside Poly), b Redcar, Yorks 6 Dec 1967. 6'2". RHB, RM. Debut v Natal (Durban) 1991-92. **Tour:** SA 1991-92 (Nh). HS 23* v Durham (Northampton) 1993. BB 4-124 v Kent (Canterbury) 1993. **SL:** HS 20 v Kent (Canterbury) 1993. BB 3-35 v Derbys (Derby) 1993.

CAPEL, David John (Roade CS), b Northampton 6 Feb 1963. 5'11". RHB, RMF. Debut 1981. Cap 1986. Benefit 1994. E Province 1985-86/1986-87. **Tests:** 15 (1987 to 1989-90); HS 98 v P (Karachi) 1987-88; BB 3-88 v WI (Bridgetown) 1989-90. **LOI:** 23 (HS 50*; BB 3-38). **Tours:** A 1987-88, 1992-93 (Eng A); WI 1989-90; NZ 1987-88; P 1987-88. 1000 runs (3); most – 1311 (1989). HS 134 EP v W Province (Port Elizabeth) 1986-87. Nh HS 126 v Sussex (Hove) 1987. 50 wkts (3); most – 63 (1986). BB 7-46 v Yorks (Northampton) 1987. **Awards:** NWT 3. **NWT:** HS 101 v Notts (Northampton) 1990. BB 3-21 v Glam (Swansea) 1992. **BHC:** HS 97 v Yorks (Lord's) 1987. BB 4-29 v Warwks (Birmingham) 1986. **SL:** HS 121 v Glam (Northampton) 1990. BB 4-30 v Yorks (Middlesbrough) 1982.

116

COOK, Nicholas Grant Billson (Lutterworth GS), b Leicester 17 Jun 1956. 6'0". RHB, SLA. Leicestershire 1978-85 (cap 1982). Northamptonshire debut 1986. Cap 1987. **Tests:** 15 (1983 to 1989); HS 31 v A (Oval) 1989; BB 6-65 (11-83 match) v P (Karachi) 1983-84. LOI: 3 (HS-; BB 2-18). Tours: NZ 1979-80 (DHR), 1983-84; P 1983-84, 1987-88; SL 1985-86 (Eng B); Z 1980-81 (Le), 1984-85 (EC). HS 75 Le v Somerset (Taunton) 1980. Nh HS 64 v Lancs (Manchester) 1987. 50 wkts (8); most – 90 (1982). BB 7-34 (10-97 match) v Essex (Chelmsford) 1992. **NWT:** HS 13 v Middx (Northampton) 1986. BB 4-24 v Ire (Northampton) 1987. **BHC:** HS 23 Le v Warwks (Leicester) 1984. BB 3-35 v Kent (Northampton) 1989. **SL:** HS 20 v Yorks (Leeds) 1993. BB 4-22 v Glam (Pentrych) 1993.

CURRAN, Kevin Malcolm (Marandellas HS), b Rusape, S Rhodesia 7 Sep 1959. Son of K.P. (Rhodesia 1947-48/1953-54). 6'1". RHB, RMF. Zimbabwe 1980-81/1987-88. Natal 1988-89. Gloucestershire 1985-90 (cap 1985). Northamptonshire debut 1991. Cap 1992. Eligible for England 1994. LOI (Z): 11 (HS 73; BB 3-65). Tours (Z): E 1982; SL 1983-84. 1000 runs (5); most – 1353 (1986). HS 144* Gs v Sussex (Bristol) 1990. Nh HS 91 v Somerset (Luton) 1993. 50 wkts (5); most – 67 (1993). BB 7-47 Natal v Transvaal (Johannesburg) 1988-89 and v Yorks (Harrogate) 1993. Nh BB 6-45 v Hants (Bournemouth) 1992. Awards: NWT 2; BHC 2. **NWT:** HS 78* v Cambs (Northampton) 1992. BB 4-34 Gs v Northants (Bristol) 1985. **BHC:** HS 57 Gs v Derbys (Derby) 1987. BB 4-41 Gs v Notts (Bristol) 1989. **SL:** HS 92 Gs v Northants (Northampton) 1990. BB 5-15 Gs v Leics (Gloucester) 1988.

FELTON, Nigel Alfred (Millfield S; Loughborough U), b Guildford, Surrey 24 Oct 1960. 5'8". LHB, OB. Somerset 1982-88 (cap 1986). Northamptonshire debut 1989. Cap 1990. Tour: SA 1991-92 (Nh). 1000 runs (5); most – 1538 (1990). HS 173* Sm v Kent (Taunton) 1983. Nh HS 122 v Glam (Northampton) 1990. BB 1-48. Awards: NWT 2; BHC 2. **NWT:** HS 87 Sm v Kent (Taunton) 1984. **BHC:** HS 82 v Lancs (Northampton) 1992. **SL:** HS 96 Sm v Essex (Chelmsford) 1986.

FORDHAM, Alan (Bedford Modern S; Durham U), b Bedford 9 Nov 1964. 6'1". RHB, RM. Debut 1986. Cap 1990. Bedfordshire 1982-85. Tour: SA 1991-92 (Nh). 1000 runs (4); most – 1840 (1991). HS 206* v Yorks (Leeds) 1990. BB 1-25. Nh 2nd XI record score: 236 (158 balls) v Worcs (Kidderminster) 1989. Awards: NWT 4; BHC 3. **NWT:** HS 132* v Leics (Northampton) 1991. BB 1-3. **BHC:** HS 103 v Scot (Forfar) 1992. **SL:** HS 89 v Notts (Nottingham) 1992.

HUGHES, John Gareth (Sir Christopher Hatton SS, Wellingborough; Sheffield City Poly), b Wellingborough 3 May 1971. 6'1". RHB, RM. Debut 1990. Tour: SA 1991-92 (Nh). HS 6 and BB 3-56 v Natal (Durban) 1991-92. BAC HS 2. BAC BB 2-57 v Derbys (Chesterfield) 1990. **SL:** 21 v Kent (Canterbury) 1993.

INNES, Kevin John (Weston Favell Upper S), b Wellingborough 24 Sep 1975. 5'10". RHB, RM. 2nd XI debut 1990 (aged 14yr 8mth – Northamptonshire record). Northamptonshire staff 1992 – awaiting f-c debut.

LAMB, Allan Joseph (Wynberg HS; Abbotts C) b Langebaanweg, Cape Province, SA 20 Jun 1954. 5'8". RHB, RM. W Province 1972-73/1981-82 and 1992-93. OFS 1987-88. Northamptonshire debut/cap 1978. Benefit 1988. Captain 1989-. Wisden 1980. **Tests:** 79 (1982 to 1992, 3 as captain); HS 142 v NZ (Wellington) 1991-92; BB 1-6. LOI: 122 (HS 118). Tours: A 1982-83, 1986-87, 1990-91; WI 1985-86, 1989-90; NZ 1983-84, 1991-92; I/SL 1984-85; P 1983-84, 1987-88. 1000 runs (12) inc 2000 (1): 2049 (1981). HS 294 OFS v E Province (Bloemfontein) 1987-88 – sharing record SA 5th wkt stand of 355 with J.J.Strydom. Nh HS 235 v Yorks (Leeds) 1990. BB 2-29 v Lancs (Lytham) 1991. Awards: NWT 3; BHC 9. **NWT:** HS 124* v Essex (Chelmsford) 1993. BB 1-4. **BHC:** HS 126* v Kent (Canterbury) 1987. BB 1-11. **SL:** HS 132* v Surrey (Guildford) 1985.

LOYE, Malachy Bernhard (Moulton S), b Northampton 27 Sep 1972. 6'2". RHB, OB. Debut 1991. HS 153* v Kent (Canterbury) 1993. **NWT:** HS 65 v Essex (Chelmsford) 1993. **BHC:** HS 31* v Hants (Southampton) 1993. **SL:** HS 122 v Somerset (Luton) 1993.

MONTGOMERIE, Richard Robert (Rugby S; Worcester C, Oxford), b Rugby, Warwks 3 Jul 1971. 5'10½". RHB, OB. Oxford U 1991-93 (blue 1991-92-93; captain 1994). Northamptonshire debut 1991. Half blues for rackets and real tennis. HS 109 OU v Worcs (Worcester) 1993. Nh HS 35 v Durham (Northampton) 1993. **BHC:** HS 75 Comb Us v Worcs (Oxford) 1992. **SL:** HS 0.

PENBERTHY, Anthony Leonard (Camborne CS), b Troon, Cornwall 1 Sep 1969. 6'1". LHB, RM. Debut 1989. Cornwall 1987-89. Tour: SA 1991-92 (Nh). HS 101* v CU (Cambridge) 1990. BAC HS 83 v Essex (Chelmsford) 1990. BB 5-37 v Glam (Swansea) 1993. Dismissed M.A.Taylor with his first ball in f-c cricket. **NWT:** HS 41* v Essex (Chelmsford) 1993. BB 2-29 v Glam (Swansea) 1992. **BHC:** HS 10 v Notts (Nottingham) 1990. BB 2-22 v Comb Us (Northampton) 1991. **SL:** HS 43 v Warwks (Northampton) 1992. BB 5-36 v Glos (Northampton) 1993.

RIKA, Craig Justin (Woodhouse Grove S, Bradford), b Staincliffe, Yorks 18 Jan 1974. 6'2½". RHB, RM. Northamptonshire staff 1993 – awaiting f-c debut.

RIPLEY, David (Royds SS, Leeds), b Leeds, Yorks 13 Sep 1966. 5'9". RHB, WK. Debut 1984. Cap 1987. Tour: SA 1991-92 (Nh). HS 134* v Yorks (Scarborough) 1986. BB 2-89 v Essex (Ilford) 1987. Award: BHC 1. **NWT:** HS 27* v Durham (Darlington) 1984. **BHC:** HS 36* v Glos (Bristol) 1991. **SL:** HS 52* v Surrey (Northampton) 1993.

ROBERTS, Andrew Richard (Bishop Stopford CS, Kettering), b Kettering 16 Apr 1971. 5'6". RHB, LB. Debut 1989. Tour: SA 1991-92 (Nh). HS 62 v Notts (Nottingham) 1992. BB 6-72 v Lancs (Lytham) 1991. **NWT:** HS-. BB 1-23. **SL:** HS 14 v Worcs (Northampton) 1991. BB 3-26 v Hants (Northampton) 1991.

SNAPE, Jeremy Nicholas (Denstone C; Durham U), b Stoke-on-Trent, Staffs 27 Apr 1973. 5'8½". RHB, OB. Debut 1992. HS 18 and BB 2-49 Comb Us v A (Oxford) 1993. Nh HS-. Nh BB 1-20. Award: BHC 1. **NWT:** HS 5*. **BHC:** HS 52 Comb Us v Hants (Southampton) 1993. BB 3-35 Comb Us v Worcs (Oxford) 1992. **SL:** HS 6. BB 3-25 v Essex (Northampton) 1993.

TAYLOR, Jonathan Paul (Pingle S, Swadlincote), b Ashby-de-la-Zouch 8 Aug 1964. 6'2". LHB, LFM. Derbyshire 1984-86. Northamptonshire debut 1991. Cap 1992. Staffordshire 1989-90 (cap 1989). **Tests:** 1 (1992-93); HS 17* and BB 1-65 v I (Calcutta) 1992-93. LOI: 1 (HS 1). Tour: I 1992-93. HS 74* v Notts (Northampton) 1992, 50 wkts (2); most – 69 (1993). BB 7-23 v Hants (Bournemouth) 1992. **NWT:** HS 9. BB 3-41 v Glam (Swansea) 1992. **BHC:** HS 6*. BB 3-38 v Lancs (Northampton) 1992. **SL:** HS 24 v Worcs (Northampton) 1993. BB 3-14 De v Glos (Gloucester) 1986.

WALTON, Timothy Charles (Leeds GS), b Low Head, Yorks 8 Nov 1972. 6'0½". RHB, RM. Northamptonshire staff 1991 – awaiting f-c debut. **SL:** HS-. BB 2-27 v Leics (Leicester) 1993.

WARREN, Russell John (Kingsthorpe Upper S), b Northampton 10 Sep 1971. 6'1". RHB, OB. Debut 1992. HS 37* v Derbys (Derby) 1993. **SL:** HS 71* v Leics (Northampton) 1993.

NEWCOMERS/DEPARTURES – see p 157

118

NORTHAMPTONSHIRE 1993

RESULTS SUMMARY

	Place	Won	Lost	Tied	Drew	Abandoned
Britannic Assurance Championship	4th	8	4		5	
All First-class Matches		8	4		6	
Sunday League	5th	9	5	1		2
NatWest Trophy	Quarter-Finalist					
Benson and Hedges Cup	Semi-Finalist					

BRITANNIC ASSURANCE CHAMPIONSHIP AVERAGES

BATTING AND FIELDING

Cap		M	I	NO	HS	Runs	Avge	100	50	Ct/St
1985	R.J.Bailey	17	29	5	200	1191	49.62	2	8	15
1978	A.J.Lamb	17	27	1	172	1046	40.23	2	6	12
1990	A.Fordham	16	28	1	193	1024	37.92	3	5	12
1990	N.A.Felton	17	29	2	109	1010	37.40	2	7	16
–	M.B.Loye	17	26	1	153*	879	35.16	–	3	18
1992	K.M.Curran	16	23	4	91	612	32.21	–	5	6
–	M.N.Bowen	5	6	2	23*	72	18.00	–	–	1
1986	D.J.Capel	5	8	2	54	102	17.00	–	1	1
–	A.L.Penberthy	8	12	2	54*	161	16.10	–	1	5
1987	D.Ripley	17	22	4	54	286	15.88	–	1	50/3
1990	C.E.L.Ambrose	13	15	2	38	197	15.15	–	–	3
–	R.J.Warren	5	6	1	37*	56	11.20	–	–	3
–	A.R.Roberts	9	15	1	19*	116	8.28	–	–	3
1992	J.P.Taylor	17	20	10	14*	79	7.90	–	–	5
1987	N.G.B.Cook	7	8	1	18	48	6.85	–	–	2

Also played (1 match): R.R.Montgomerie 35.

BOWLING

	O	M	R	W	Avge	Best	5wI	10wM
K.M.Curran	458	123	1293	67	19.29	7- 47	3	–
C.E.L.Ambrose	543.4	150	1207	59	20.45	6- 49	2	–
D.J.Capel	117.4	37	252	12	21.00	3- 15	–	–
M.N.Bowen	147.5	30	554	22	25.18	4-124	–	–
J.P.Taylor	573.5	169	1590	61	26.06	6- 82	2	–
A.L.Penberthy	151	38	462	16	28.87	5- 37	1	–
R.J.Bailey	238.3	68	590	18	32.77	5- 54	1	–
A.R.Roberts	258.4	64	705	16	44.06	3- 51	–	–

Also bowled: N.G.B.Cook 175.5-60-371-5; M.B.Loye 0.1-0-1-0.

The First-Class Averages (pp 164-177) give the records of Northamptonshire players in all first-class county matches (their other opponents being Oxford U) with the exception of R.R.Montgomerie, whose full county figures are as above, and:

J.P.Taylor 18-20-10-14*-79-7.90-0-0-5ct. 603.5-181-1649-65-25.36-6/82-2-0.

NORTHAMPTONSHIRE RECORDS

FIRST-CLASS CRICKET

Highest Total	For 636-6d		v	Essex	Chelmsford 1990
	V 670-9d		by	Sussex	Hove 1921
Lowest Total	For 12		v	Glos	Gloucester 1907
	V 33		by	Lancashire	Northampton 1977
Highest Innings	For 300	R.Subba Row	v	Surrey	The Oval 1958
	V 333	K.S.Duleepsinhji	for	Sussex	Hove 1930

Highest Partnership for each Wicket

1st	361	N.Oldfield/V.Broderick	v	Scotland	Peterborough 1953
2nd	344	G.Cook/R.J.Boyd-Moss	v	Lancashire	Northampton 1986
3rd	393	A.Fordham/A.J.Lamb	v	Yorkshire	Leeds 1990
4th	370	R.T.Virgin/P.Willey	v	Somerset	Northampton 1976
5th	347	D.Brookes/D.W.Barrick	v	Essex	Northampton 1952
6th	376	R.Subba Row/A.Lightfoot	v	Surrey	The Oval 1958
7th	229	W.W.Timms/F.A.Walden	v	Warwicks	Northampton 1926
8th	164	D.Ripley/N.G.B.Cook	v	Lancashire	Manchester 1987
9th	156	R.Subba Row/S.Starkie	v	Lancashire	Northampton 1955
10th	148	B.W.Bellamy/J.V.Murdin	v	Glamorgan	Northampton 1925

Best Bowling	For 10-127	V.W.C.Jupp	v	Kent	Tunbridge W 1932
(Innings)	V 10- 30	C.Blythe	for	Kent	Northampton 1907
Best Bowling	For 15- 31	G.E.Tribe	v	Yorkshire	Northampton 1958
(Match)	V 17- 48	C.Blythe	for	Kent	Northampton 1907

Most Runs – Season	2198	D.Brookes	(av 51.11)	1952
Most Runs – Career	28980	D.Brookes	(av 36.13)	1934-59
Most 100s – Season	8	R.A.Haywood		1921
Most 100s – Career	67	D.Brookes		1934-59
Most Wkts – Season	175	G.E.Tribe	(av 18.70)	1955
Most Wkts – Career	1097	E.W.Clark	(av 21.31)	1922-47

LIMITED-OVERS CRICKET

Highest Total	NWT	360-2	v	Staffs	Northampton 1990
	BHC	300-9	v	Derbyshire	Derby 1987
	SL	306-2	v	Surrey	Guildford 1985
Lowest Total	NWT	62	v	Leics	Leicester 1974
	BHC	85	v	Sussex	Northampton 1978
	SL	41	v	Middlesex	Northampton 1972
Highest Innings	NWT	145	R.J.Bailey	v Staffs	Stone 1991
	BHC	134	R.J.Bailey	v Glos	Northampton 1987
	SL	172*	W.Larkins	v Warwicks	Luton 1983
Best Bowling	NWT	7-37	N.A.Mallender	v Worcs	Northampton 1984
	BHC	5-21	Sarfraz Nawaz	v Middlesex	Lord's 1980
	SL	7-39	A.Hodgson	v Somerset	Northampton 1976

NOTTINGHAMSHIRE

Formation of Present Club: March/April 1841
Substantial Reorganisation: 11 December 1866
Colours: Green and Gold
Badge: County Badge of Nottinghamshire
Championships (since 1890): (4) 1907, 1929, 1981, 1987
NatWest Trophy/Gillette Cup Winners: (1) 1987
Benson and Hedges Cup Winners: (1) 1989
Sunday League Champions: (1) 1991
Match Awards: NWT 35; BHC 57

Secretary/General Manager: B.Robson, Trent Bridge, Nottingham NG2 6AG
(☎ 0602-821525)
Captain: R.T.Robinson
Scorer: G.Stringfellow
1994 Beneficiary: Nottinghamshire C.C.C.

AFFORD, John Andrew (Spalding GS; Stamford CFE), b Crowland, Lincs 12 May 1964. 6'1½". RHB, SLA. Debut 1984. Cap 1990. Tour: Z 1989-90 (Eng A). HS 22* v Leics (Nottingham) 1989. 50 wkts (4); most – 57 (1991, 1993). BB 6-68 (10-185 match) v Sussex (Nottingham) 1992. Award: BHC 1. **NWT:** HS 2*. BB 3-32 v Herts (Hitchin) 1989. **BHC:** HS 1*. BB 4-38 v Kent (Nottingham) 1989. **SL:** HS 1. BB 3-33 v Northants (Northampton) 1991.

ARCHER, Graeme Francis (Heron Brook Middle S; King Edward VI HS, Stafford), b Carlisle, Cumberland 26 Sep 1970. 6'1". RHB, OB. Debut 1992. Staffordshire 1990. HS 117 v Derbys (Nottingham) 1992. **NWT:** HS 39 v Cheshire (Warrington) 1993. **SL:** HS 18 v Essex (Nottingham) 1993.

BATES, Richard Terry (Bourne GS; Stamford CFE), b Stamford, Lincs 17 Jun 1972. 6'1". RHB, OB. Lincolnshire 1990-91. Debut 1993. HS 33* v OU (Oxford) 1993. BAC HS 18* v Glos (Bristol) 1993. BB 2-43 v Sussex (Eastbourne) 1993. **SL:** HS 1. BB 3-43 v Derbys (Nottingham) 1993.

CHAPMAN, Robert James (Farnborough CS; S Notts CFE), b Nottingham 28 Jul 1972. Son of footballer R.O. ('Sammy') Chapman (Nottingham Forest, Notts County and Shrewsbury Town). 6'1". RHB, RFM. Debut 1992. HS-. BB 1-38.

CRAWLEY, Mark Andrew (Manchester GS; Oriel C, Oxford), b Newton-le-Willows, Lancs 16 Dec 1967. Brother of J.P. (see LANCASHIRE and CU) and P.M. (CU 1992). 6'3". RHB, RM. Oxford U 1987-90 (blue 1987-88-89-90; captain 1989). Lancashire 1990. Nottinghamshire debut 1991. 1000 runs (1): 1297 (1992). HS 160* v Derbys (Derby) 1992. BB 6-92 OU v Glam (Oxford) 1990. Nt BB 3-18 v OU (Oxford) 1992. BAC BB 3-21 v Derbys (Derby) 1991. Awards: NWT 1; BHC 1. **NWT:** HS 74* and 4-26 v Lincs (Nottingham) 1991 (on debut). **BHC:** HS 58 v Glam (Cardiff) 1991. BB 2-72 Comb Us v Worcs (Worcester) 1989. **SL:** HS 94* and BB 3-41 v Leics (Nottingham) 1992.

DESSAUR, Wayne Anthony (Loughborough GS), b Nottingham 4 Feb 1971. 6'0". RHB, RM. Debut 1992. HS 148 v CU (Nottingham) 1992. BAC HS 104 v Derbys (Nottingham) 1993. **SL:** HS 13* v Somerset (Bath) 1992.

DOWMAN, Mathew Peter (St Hugh's CS; Grantham CFE), b Grantham, Lincs 10 May 1974. 5'10". LHB, RMF. Awaiting f-c debut. Scored 267 for England YC v WI YC (Hove) 1993 – record score in youth 'Tests'. **SL:** HS 31 and BB 1-33 v Durham (Chester-le-St) 1993.

121

EVANS, Kevin Paul (Colonel Frank Seely S) b Calverton 10 Sep 1963. Elder brother of R.J. (Notts 1987-90). 6'2". RHB, RMF. Debut 1984. Cap 1990. HS 104 v Surrey (Nottingham) 1992. BB 6-67 v Yorks (Nottingham) 1993. **NWT:** HS 20 v Hants (Southampton) 1991. BB 4-30 v Kent (Nottingham) 1986. **BHC:** HS 31* v Northants (Northampton) 1988. BB 4-43 v Glam (Cardiff) 1991. **SL:** HS 30 v Kent 1990 and v Hants 1992. BB 4-28 v Derbys (Nottingham) 1989.

FIELD-BUSS, Michael Gwyn (Wanstead HS), b Mtarfa, Malta 23 Sep 1964. 5'10". RHB, OB. Essex 1987. Nottinghamshire debut 1989. HS 34* Ex v Middx (Lord's) 1987. Nt HS 25 v Middx (Lord's) 1991. BB 6-42 v Kent (Nottingham) 1993. **NWT:** HS 5*. BB 4-62 v Worcs (Nottingham) 1992. **SL:** HS 10* v Hants (Southampton) 1992. BB 3-25 v Worcs (Nottingham) 1993.

FRENCH, Bruce Nicholas (The Meden CS), b Warsop 13 Aug 1959. 5'6". RHB, WK. Debut 1976 (aged 16yr 287d). Cap 1980. Benefit 1991. **Tests:** 16 (1986 to 1987-88); HS 59 v P (Manchester) 1987. **LOI:** 13 (HS 9*). **Tours:** A 1986-87, 1987-88; SA 1989-90 (Eng XI); WI 1985-86; NZ 1987-88; I/SL 1984-85; P 1987-88. HS 123 v Durham (Chester-le-St) 1993. BB 1-37. Award: BHC 1. **NWT:** HS 49 v Staffs (Nottingham) 1985. **BHC:** HS 48* v Worcs (Nottingham) 1984. **SL:** HS 37 v Glos (Bristol) 1985.

HINDSON, James Edward (Toot Hill CS, Bingham), b Huddersfield, Yorks 13 Sep 1973. 6'1". RHB, SLA. Debut 1992. HS 1. BB 5-42 v CU (Nottingham) 1992. BAC BB 1-24.

JOHNSON, Paul (Grove CS, Balderton), b Newark 24 Apr 1965. 5'7". RHB, RM. Debut 1982. Cap 1986. **Tour:** WI 1991-92 (Eng A). 1000 runs (7); most – 1518 (1990). HS 187 v Lancs (Manchester) 1993. BB 1-9. BAC BB 1-14. Awards: NWT 1; BHC 3. **NWT:** HS 101* v Staffs (Nottingham) 1985. **BHC:** HS 104* v Essex (Chelmsford) 1990. **SL:** HS 167* v Kent (Nottingham) 1993.

LEWIS, Clairmonte Christopher (Willesden HS, London), b Georgetown, Guyana 14 Feb 1968. 6'2½". RHB, RFM. Leicestershire 1987-91 (cap 1990). Nottinghamshire debut 1992. **Tests:** 20 (1990 to 1993); HS 117 v I (Madras) 1992-93; BB 6-111 v WI (Birmingham) 1991. **LOI:** 40 (HS 33; BB 4-30). **Tours:** A 1990-91 (part); WI 1989-90 (part); NZ 1991-92; I/SL 1992-93. HS 247 v Durham (Chester-le-St) 1993. 50 wkts (2); most – 56 (1990). BB 6-22 Le v OU (Oxford) 1988. BAC BB 6-55 Le v Glam (Cardiff) 1990. Nt BB 6-90 v Surrey (Nottingham) 1992. Award: NWT 1. **NWT:** HS 53 Le v Glos (Leicester) 1988. BB 3-24 v Somerset (Nottingham) 1993. **BHC:** HS 28 Le v Essex (Chelmsford) 1990. BB 5-46 v Kent (Nottingham) 1992. **SL:** HS 93* Le v Essex (Leicester) 1990. BB 4-13 Le v Essex (Leicester) 1988.

MIKE, Gregory Wentworth (Claremont CS; Basford Hall C) b Nottingham 14 Jul 1966. 6'0". RHB, RMF. Debut 1989. HS 61* v Warwks (Birmingham) 1992. BB 5-65 v Worcs (Nottingham) 1993. **BHC:** HS 29 v Kent (Nottingham) 1989. BB 4-44 v Somerset (Nottingham) 1993. **SL:** HS 51* v Middx (Lord's) 1993. BB 3-30 v Glos (Nottingham) 1990.

NEWELL, Michael (West Bridgford CS), b Blackburn, Lancs 25 Feb 1965. 5'8". RHB, LB. Debut 1984. Cap 1987. 1000 runs (1): 1054 (1987). HS 203* v Derbys (Derby) 1987. BB 2-38 v SL (Nottingham) 1988. BAC BB 1-0. **NWT:** HS 60 v Derbys (Derby) 1987. **BHC:** HS 39 v Somerset (Taunton) 1989. **SL:** HS 109* v Essex (Southend) 1990.

PENNETT, David Barrington (Benton Park GS, Rawdon), b Leeds, Yorks 26 Oct 1969. 6'0". RHB, RMF. Debut 1992. Yorks Cricket Academy. HS 29 v Derbys (Nottingham) 1992. BB 5-36 v Durham (Chester-le-St) 1993. **SL:** HS 12* v Durham (Nottingham) 1992. BB 3-32 v Warwks (Nottingham) 1993.

PICK, Robert Andrew (Alderman Derbyshire CS; High Pavement SFC), b Nottingham 19 Nov 1963. 5'10". LHB, RFM. Debut 1983. Cap 1987. Wellington 1989-90. Tours: WI 1991-92 (Eng A); SL 1990-91 (Eng A). HS 63 v Warwks (Nuneaton) 1985. 50 wkts (3); most – 67 (1991). BB 7-128 v Leics (Leicester) 1990. Awards: NWT 1; BHC 1. **NWT:** HS 34* v Sussex (Hove) 1983. BB 5-22 v Glos (Bristol) 1987. **BHC:** HS 25* v Hants (Southampton) 1991. BB 4-42 v Northants (Nottingham) 1987. **SL:** HS 24 v Yorks (Sheffield) 1986 and v Hants 1992. BB 4-32 v Glos (Moreton) 1987.

POLLARD, Paul Raymond (Gedling CS), b Carlton, Nottingham 24 Sep 1968. 5'11". LHB, RM. Debut 1987. Cap 1992. 1000 runs (3); most – 1463 (1993). HS 180 v Derbys (Nottingham) 1993. BB 2-79 v Glos (Bristol) 1993. **NWT:** HS 28 v Worcs (Nottingham) 1992. **BHC:** HS 80 v Somerset (Nottingham) 1993. **SL:** HS 123* v Surrey (Oval) 1989.

ROBINSON, Robert Timothy (Dunstable GS; High Pavement SFC; Sheffield U), b Sutton in Ashfield 21 Nov 1958. 6'0". RHB, RM. Debut 1978. Cap 1983. Captain 1988-. Benefit 1992. Wisden 1985. Tests: 29 (1984-85 to 1989); HS 175 v A (Leeds) 1985. LOI: 26 (HS 83). Tours: A 1987-88; SA 1989-90 (Eng XI); NZ 1987-88; WI 1985-86; I/SL 1984-85; P 1987-88. 1000 runs (11) inc 2000 (1): 2032 (1984). HS 220* v Yorks (Nottingham) 1990. BB 1-22. Awards: NWT 4; BHC 6. **NWT:** HS 139 v Worcs (Worcester) 1985. **BHC:** HS 120 v Scot (Glasgow) 1985. **SL:** HS 116 v Derbys (Derby) 1990.

SYLVESTER, Steven Antony (Wellesbourne, SM; Buckinghamshire C; Goldsmiths' C, London U), b Chalfont St Giles, Bucks 26 Sep 1968. 5'11". RHB, LFM. Middlesex 1991-92. Buckinghamshire 1991-92. HS 0*. BB 2-34 M v CU (Cambridge) 1992. BAC BB 2-35 M v Lancs (Lord's) 1992. No f-c appearances for Nottinghamshire. **BHC:** HS 0. BB 1-31. **SL:** HS 1*.

NEWCOMERS

ADAMS, James Clive (Jamaica C, Kingston), b Port Maria, Jamaica 9 Jan 1968. 5'11". LHB, SLA, WK. Jamaica 1984-85 to date. Tests (WI): 4 (1991-92 to 1992-93); HS 79* and BB 4-43 v SA (Bridgetown) 1991-92 – on debut. LOI (WI): 110 (HS 27; BB 1-2). Tours (WI): E 1993 (RW); A 1992-93; Z 1986-87 (Young WI), 1989-90 (Young WI). HS 128* Jamaica v Windward Is (Kingston) 1991-92. BB 4-43 (Tests).

NOON, Wayne Michael (Caistor S), b Grimsby, Lincs 5 Feb 1971. 5'9". RHB, WK. Northamptonshire 1989-93. Worcs 2nd XI debut when aged 15yr 199d. Tour: SA 1991-92 (Nh). HS 37 Nh v A (Northampton) 1989. BAC HS 36 Nh v Glos (Bristol) 1991. **BHC:** HS-. **SL:** HS 21 Nh v Surrey (Oval) 1990.

DEPARTURES

BRAMHALL, Stephen (Stockton Heath CHS; Newcastle U), b Warrington, Lancs 26 Nov 1967. 6'1". RHB, WK. Lancashire 1990. Nottinghamshire 1992-93. Cheshire 1988-91. HS 37* v Surrey (Nottingham) 1992. **SL:** HS 1.

CAIRNS, Christopher Lance (Christchurch BHS), b Picton, NZ 13 Jun 1970. Son of B.L. (CD, Otago, ND and NZ 1971-86). 6'2". RHB, RFM. Nottinghamshire 1988-89 and 1992-93 (cap 1993). N Districts 1988-89. Canterbury 1990-91 to date. Tests (NZ): 7 (1989-90 to 1992-93); HS 61 v E (Christchurch) 1991-92; BB 6-52 v E (Auckland) 1991-92. LOI (NZ): 10 (HS 42; BB 4-55). Tour (NZ): A 1989-90. HS 110 ND v Auckland (Hamilton) 1988-89. Nt HS 107* v Glos (Worksop) 1992. 50 wkts (2); most – 56 (1992). BB 7-34 (11-100 match) Canterbury v CD (New Plymouth) 1991-92. Nt BB 6-70 v Lancs (Nottingham) 1992 and v Lancs (Manchester) 1993. Awards: NWT 2. **NWT:** HS 77 v Glam (Nottingham) 1992. BB 4-18 v Cheshire (Warrington) 1993. **BHC:** HS 16 v Kent (Nottingham) 1992. BB 2-63 v Somerset (Nottingham) 1993. **SL:** HS 126* v Surrey (Oval) 1993. BB 6-52 v Kent (Nottingham) 1993. Not available 1994.

continued on p 157

123

NOTTINGHAMSHIRE 1993

RESULTS SUMMARY

	Place	Won	Lost	Tied	Drew	Abandoned
Britannic Assurance Championship	7th	6	3	1	7	
All First-class Matches		6	4	1	8	
Sunday League	17th	4	12			1
NatWest Trophy	2nd Round					
Benson and Hedges Cup	1st Round					

BRITANNIC ASSURANCE CHAMPIONSHIP AVERAGES

BATTING AND FIELDING

Cap		M	I	NO	HS	Runs	Avge	100	50	Ct/St
1992	P.R.Pollard	17	29	1	180	1273	45.46	2	8	25
1986	P.Johnson	15	25	1	187	1089	45.37	5	3	7
1993	C.L.Cairns	15	23	1	93	962	43.72	–	9	8
1983	R.T.Robinson	17	29	4	139*	1092	43.68	3	6	12
–	W.A.Dessaur	6	9	–	104	325	36.11	1	2	2
–	C.C.Lewis	12	18	2	247	577	36.06	1	1	7
–	G.F.Archer	4	6	1	59*	163	32.60	–	1	4
–	M.Saxelby	10	15	–	77	464	30.93	–	4	5
1973	D.W.Randall	5	10	–	98	280	28.00	–	2	6
1990	K.P.Evans	8	12	3	56	206	22.88	–	1	8
–	M.A.Crawley	9	16	2	81	306	21.85	–	1	8
–	G.W.Mike	7	12	1	50	237	21.54	–	1	3
1980	B.N.French	17	24	3	123	420	20.00	1	1	40/5
–	R.T.Bates	4	4	2	18*	37	18.50	–	–	2
1987	R.A.Pick	11	12	4	22	109	13.62	–	–	4
–	M.G.Field-Buss	9	13	5	16	79	9.87	–	–	4
1990	J.A.Afford	13	17	8	11	50	5.55	–	–	6
–	D.B.Pennett	6	4	2	10*	11	5.50	–	–	4

Also played (2 matches): J.E.Hindson 1.

BOWLING

	O	M	R	W	Avge	Best	5wI	10wM
C.L.Cairns	411.5	74	1242	53	23.43	6-70	3	
M.G.Field-Buss	305.3	111	747	28	26.67	6-42	1	
J.A.Afford	718.5	223	1659	57	29.10	5-64	3	
K.P.Evans	238.3	57	623	21	29.66	6-67	1	
D.B.Pennett	166	33	506	16	31.62	5-36	1	
C.C.Lewis	467.2	110	1280	36	35.55	4-34	–	
R.A.Pick	312	73	956	25	38.24	5-53	1	
G.W.Mike	200	40	698	17	41.05	5-65	1	

Also bowled: G.F.Archer 6.3-0-72-0; R.T.Bates 83-27-215-5; M.A.Crawley 27-6-72-1; W.A.Dessaur 17-2-94-0; J.E.Hindson 39.5-10-114-1; P.R.Pollard 14-0-135-2.

The First-Class Averages (pp 164-177) give the records of Nottinghamshire players in all first-class county matches (their other opponents being Cambridge U and Oxford U), with the exception of:
C.C.Lewis 13-20-2-247-653-36.27-1-2-9ct. 503.1-115-1381-40-34.52-4/34.

NOTTINGHAMSHIRE RECORDS

FIRST-CLASS CRICKET

Highest Total	For	739-7d		v	Leics	Nottingham	1903
	V	706-4d		by	Surrey	Nottingham	1947
Lowest Total	For	13		v	Yorkshire	Nottingham	1901
	V	16		by	Derbyshire	Nottingham	1879
		16		by	Surrey	The Oval	1880
Highest Innings	For	312*	W.W.Keeton	v	Middlesex	The Oval	1939
	V	345	C.G.Macartney	for	Australians	Nottingham	1921

Highest Partnership for each Wicket

1st	391	A.O.Jones/A.Shrewsbury	v	Glos	Bristol	1899
2nd	398	A.Shrewsbury/W.Gunn	v	Sussex	Nottingham	1890
3rd	369	W.Gunn/J.R.Gunn	v	Leics	Nottingham	1903
4th	361	A.O.Jones/J.R.Gunn	v	Essex	Leyton	1905
5th	266	A.Shrewsbury/W.Gunn	v	Sussex	Hove	1884
6th	303*	F.H.Winrow/P.F.Harvey	v	Derbyshire	Nottingham	1947
7th	301	C.C.Lewis/B.N.French	v	Durham	Chester-le-St	1993
8th	220	G.F.H.Heane/R.Winrow	v	Somerset	Nottingham	1935
9th	165	W.McIntyre/G.Wootton	v	Kent	Nottingham	1869
10th	152	E.B.Alletson/W.Riley	v	Sussex	Hove	1911

Best Bowling	For	10-66	K.Smales	v	Glos	Stroud	1956
(Innings)	V	10-10	H.Verity	for	Yorkshire	Leeds	1932
Best Bowling	For	17-89	F.C.Matthews	v	Northants	Nottingham	1923
(Match)	V	17-89	W.G.Grace	for	Glos	Cheltenham	1877

Most Runs – Season	2620	W.W.Whysall	(av 53.46)	1929
Most Runs – Career	31592	G.Gunn	(av 35.69)	1902-32
Most 100s – Season	9	W.W.Whysall		1928
	9	M.J.Harris		1971
	9	B.C.Broad		1990
Most 100s – Career	65	J.Hardstaff, jr		1930-55
Most Wkts – Season	181	B.Dooland	(av 14.96)	1954
Most Wkts – Career	1653	T.G.Wass	(av 20.34)	1896-1920

LIMITED-OVERS CRICKET

Highest Total	NWT	312-9		v	Bucks	Marlow	1990
	BHC	296-6		v	Kent	Nottingham	1989
	SL	329-6		v	Derbyshire	Nottingham	1993
Lowest Total	NWT	123		v	Yorkshire	Scarborough	1969
	BHC	74		v	Leics	Leicester	1987
	SL	66		v	Yorkshire	Bradford	1969
Highest Innings	NWT	149*	D.W.Randall	v	Devon	Torquay	1988
	BHC	130*	C.E.B.Rice	v	Scotland	Glasgow	1982
	SL	167*	P.Johnson	v	Kent	Nottingham	1993
Best Bowling	NWT	6-18	C.E.B.Rice	v	Sussex	Hove	1982
	BHC	6-22	M.K.Bore	v	Leics	Leicester	1980
		6-22	C.E.B.Rice	v	Northants	Northampton	1981
	SL	6-12	R.J.Hadlee	v	Lancashire	Nottingham	1980

SOMERSET

Formation of Present Club: 18 August 1875
Colours: Black, White and Maroon
Badge: Somerset Dragon
Championships: (0) Third 1892, 1958, 1963, 1966, 1981
NatWest Trophy/Gillette Cup Winners: (2) 1979, 1983
Benson and Hedges Cup Winners: (2) 1981, 1982
Sunday League Champions: (1) 1979
Match Awards: NWT 44; BHC 55

Chief Executive: P.W.Anderson, The County Ground, Taunton TA1 1JT
(☎ 0823-272946)
Captain: A.N.Hayhurst
Scorer: D.A.Oldam
1994 Beneficiary: N.A.Mallender

BURNS, Neil David (Moulsham HS, Chelmsford), b Chelmsford, Essex 19 Sep 1965. 5'10". LHB, WK, occ SLA. W Province B 1985-86. Essex 1986. Somerset debut/cap 1987. HS 166 v Glos (Taunton) 1990. **NWT:** HS 31 v Warwks (Taunton) 1993. **BHC:** HS 51 v Middx (Lord's) 1987. **SL:** HS 58 v Sussex (Hove) 1990.

CADDICK, Andrew Richard (Papanui HS), b Christchurch, NZ 21 Nov 1968. Son of English emigrants – qualified for England 1992. 6'5". RHB, RFM. Debut 1991. Cap 1992. Represented NZ in 1987-88 Youth World Cup. **Tests:** 4 (1993); HS 25 v A (Manchester) 1993; BB 3-32 v A (Nottingham) 1993. **LOI:** 3 (HS 2*; BB 3-39). Tour: A 1992-93 (Eng A). HS 54* v Worcs (W-s-M) 1992. 50 wkts (2); most – 71 (1992). BB 9-32 (12-120 match) v Lancs (Taunton) 1993. Award: NWT 1. **NWT:** HS 8. BB 6-30 v Glos (Taunton) 1992. **BHC:** HS 6*. BB 2-20 v Yorks (Taunton) 1992. **SL:** HS 36* v Durham (Hartlepool) 1993. BB 4-18 v Lancs (Manchester) 1992.

CLIFFORD, Paul Robert (Sheldon CS, Chippenham), b Swindon, Wilts 19 Sep 1976. 6'4". RHB, RFM. Somerset staff 1993 – awaiting f-c debut.

FLETCHER, Ian (Millfield S; Loughborough U), b Sawbridgeworth, Herts 31 Aug 1971. 5'11". RHB, RM. Debut 1991. Hertfordshire 1990. HS 65* v Middx (Bath) 1993. **NWT:** (Herts) HS 1. **BHC:** HS 9. **SL:** HS 26 v Derbys (Derby) 1993.

FOLLAND, Nicholas Arthur (Exmouth S; Loughborough U), b Bristol 17 Sep 1963. 6'0½". LHB, RM. Debut for Minor Counties v Indians (Trowbridge) 1990 scoring 26 and 82. Somerset debut 1992. Devon 1981-92. England Amateurs 1992. Master at Blundell's S. HS 108* v Sussex (Taunton) 1993. Awards: NWT 1; BHC 1. **NWT:** HS 63 v Notts (Nottingham) 1993. **BHC:** HS 100* Minor C v Notts (Nottingham) 1991. **SL:** HS 107* v Leics (W-s-M) 1993.

HALLETT, Jeremy Charles (Millfield S; Durham U), b Yeovil 18 Oct 1970. 6'2". RHB, RMF. Debut 1990. HS 15 v Glos (Bristol) 1991. BB 3-85 Comb Us v A (Oxford) 1993. Sm BB 3-154 v Worcs (Worcester) 1991. **BHC:** HS 5*. BB 3-36 Comb Us v Worcs (Cambridge) 1991. **SL:** HS 26 v Sussex (Taunton) 1993. BB 3-41 v Glam (Neath) 1990.

HARDEN, Richard John (King's C, Taunton), b Bridgwater 16 Aug 1965. 5'11". RHB, SLA. Debut 1985. Cap 1989. C Districts 1987-88. 1000 runs (5); most – 1460 (1990). HS 187 v Notts (Taunton) 1992. BB 2-7 CD v Canterbury (Blenheim) 1987-88. Sm BB 2-24 v Hants (Taunton) 1986. Award: NWT 1. **NWT:** HS 108* v Scot (Taunton) 1992. **BHC:** HS 76 v Kent (Canterbury) 1992. **SL:** HS 90* v Surrey (Bath) 1992.

HAYHURST, Andrew Neil (Worsley Wardley HS; Eccles SFC; Leeds Poly), b Davyhulme, Manchester 23 Nov 1962. 5'11". RHB, RM. Lancashire 1985-89. Somerset debut/cap 1990. Captain 1994. Tours: WI 1986-87 (La); Z 1988-89 (La). 1000 runs (2); most – 1559 (1990). YC 1993. MCC YC. **Tests:** 2 (1993); HS 172* v Glos (Bath) 1991. BB 4-27 La v Middx (Manchester) 1987. Sm BB 3-27 v Yorks (Middlesbrough) 1992. Awards: NWT 1; BHC 2. **NWT:** HS 91* and BB 5-60 v Warwks (Birmingham) 1991. **BHC:** HS 95 v Notts (Nottingham) 1992. BB 4-50 La v Worcs (Worcester) 1987. **SL:** HS 84 La v Leics (Manchester) 1988. BB 4-37 La v Glam (Pontypridd) 1988 and Sm v Sussex (Hove) 1990.

KERR, Jason Ian Douglas (Withins HS; Bolton C), b Bolton, Lancs 7 Apr 1974. 6'2". RHB, RMF. Debut 1993. HS 19* and BB 3-47 v Essex (Chelmsford) 1993. **SL:** HS 17 v Northants (Luton) 1993. BB 3-34 v Essex (Chelmsford) 1993.

LATHWELL, Mark Nicholas (Braunton S, Devon), b Bletchley, Bucks 26 Dec 1971. 5'8". RHB, RM. Debut 1991. Cap 1992. YC 1993. MCC YC. **Tests:** 2 (1993); HS 33 v A (Nottingham) 1993. Tour: A 1992-93 (Eng A). 1000 runs (2); most – 1176 (1992). HS 175 Eng A v Tasmania (Launceston) 1992-93. Sm HS 132 v Essex (Chelmsford) 1993. BB 1-9. Awards: NWT 1; BHC 1. **NWT:** HS 103 and BB 1-23 v Salop (Telford) 1993. **BHC:** HS 93 v Worcs (Worcester) 1992. **SL:** HS 96 v Leics (Leicester) 1992.

MALLENDER, Neil Alan (Beverley GS), b Kirk Sandall, Yorks 13 Aug 1961. 6'0". RHB, RFM. Northamptonshire 1980-86 (cap 1984). Somerset debut/cap 1987. Benefit 1994. Otago 1983-84/1992-93 (captain 1990-91/1992-93). **Tests:** 2 (1992); HS 4; BB 5-50 v P (Leeds) 1992 – on debut. HS 100* Otago v CD (Palmerston N) 1991-92. Sm HS 87* v Sussex (Hove) 1990. 50 wkts (6); most – 56 (1983). BB 7-27 Otago v Auckland (Auckland) 1984-85. BAC BB 7-41 Nh v Derbys (Northampton) 1982. Sm BB 7-61 v Derbys (Taunton) 1987. Award: NWT 1. **NWT:** HS 11* (twice). BB 7-37 Nh v Worcs (Northampton) 1984. **BHC:** HS 16* v Hants (Taunton) 1988. BB 5-53 Nh v Leics (Northampton) 1986. **SL:** HS 31* v Durham (Hartlepool) 1993. BB 5-34 Nh v Middx (Tring) 1981.

MUSHTAQ AHMED, b Sahiwal, Pakistan 28 Jun 1970. 5'5". RHB, LB. Multan 1986-87/1990-91. United Bank 1986-87 to date. Somerset debut/cap 1993. **Tests** (P): 10 (1989-90 to 1992-93); HS 12* v WI (P-o-S) 1992-93; BB 3-32 v E (Lord's) 1992. LOI (P): 70 (HS 17*; BB 3-14). Tours (P): E 1992; A 1989-90, 1991-92, 1992-93; WI 1992-93; NZ 1992-93. HS 90 and Sm BB 7-91 (12-175 match) v Sussex (Taunton) 1993. 50 wkts (2+1); most – 85 (1993). BB 9-93 Multan v Peshawar (Sahiwal) 1990-91. Award. NWT 1. **NWT:** HS 35 v Surrey (Taunton) 1993. BB 2-16 v Salop (Telford) 1993. **BHC:** HS 7. **SL:** HS 32 v Middx (Bath) 1993. BB 3-17 v Glos (Taunton) 1993.

PARSONS, Keith Alan (The Castle S, Taunton; Richard Huish SFC), b Taunton 2 May 1973. Identical twin brother of Kevin (Somerset staff). 6'1". RHB, RM. Debut 1992. HS 63 v Sussex (Taunton) 1993. **NWT:** HS 33 v Notts (Nottingham) 1993. BB 2-47 v Salop (Telford) 1993. **SL:** HS 34 v Sussex (Taunton) 1993. BB 1-19.

PARSONS, Kevin John (The Castle S, Taunton; Richard Huish SFC), b Taunton 2 May 1973. Identical twin brother of Keith. 6'1". RHB, OB. Somerset staff 1992 – awaiting f-c debut. **SL:** HS-.

PAYNE, Andrew (Accrington & Rossendale C), b Rawtenstall, Lancs 20 Oct 1973. 5'10". RHB, RMF. Debut 1992. HS 51* v Glos (Taunton) 1992. BB 2-15 v Worcs (Worcester) 1993. **SL:** HS 55* v Kent (Taunton) 1993. BB 2-43 v Lancs (Taunton) 1993.

ROSE, Graham David (Northumberland Park S, Tottenham), b Tottenham, London 12 Apr 1964. 6'4". RHB, RM. Middlesex 1985-86. Somerset debut 1987. Cap 1988. 1000 runs (1): 1000 (1990). HS 138 v Sussex (Taunton) 1993. 50 wkts (2); most – 57 (1988). BB 6-41 M v Worcs (Worcester) 1985 – on debut. Sm BB 6-47 v Warwks (Bath) 1988. Awards: BHC 2. NWT: HS 110 v Devon (Torquay) 1990. BB 3-11 v Salop (Telford) 1993. BHC: HS 65 v Hants (Southampton) 1992. BB 4-37 v Sussex (Hove) 1990. SL: HS 148 v Glam (Neath) 1990. BB 4-26 v Kent (Taunton) 1993.

TRESCOTHICK, Marcus Edward (Sir Bernard Lovell S), b Keynsham 25 Dec 1975. 6'2". LHB, RM. Debut 1993. HS 6. SL: HS 28 v Sussex (Taunton) 1993.

TRUMP, Harvey Russell John (Millfield S), b Taunton 11 Oct 1968. 6'0". RHB, OB. Debut 1988. HS 48 v Notts (Taunton) 1988 – on debut. 50 wkts (1): 51 (1991). BB 7-52 (inc hat-trick; 14-104 match) v Glos (Gloucester) 1992. NWT: HS 1*. BB 2-44 v Essex (Taunton) 1989. BHC: HS 1. BB 2-23 v Yorks (Taunton) 1992. SL: HS 19 v Kent (Taunton) 1991. BB 2-8 v Lancs (Manchester) 1992.

TURNER, Robert Julian (Millfield S; Magdalene C, Cambridge), b Malvern, Worcs 25 Nov 1967. 6'1½". RHB, WK. Brother of S.J. (Somerset 1984-85). Cambridge U 1988-91 (blue 1988-89-90-91; captain 1991). Somerset debut 1991. HS 101* v Notts (Taunton) 1992. BHC: HS 25* Comb Us v Surrey (Oxford) 1990. SL: HS 33 v Derbys (Derby) 1993.

Van TROOST, Adrianus Pelrus (Spieringshoek C, Schiedam), b Schiedam, Holland 2 Oct 1972. 6'7". RHB, RF. Debut 1991. Eligible for England 1998. Holland 1990 (opened bowling in ICC Trophy final v Zimbabwe). HS 35 v Lancs (Taunton) 1993. BB 6-48 v Essex (Taunton) 1992. NWT: HS 17* v Surrey (Taunton) 1993. BB 3-57 v Warwks (Taunton) 1993. BHC: HS 9* and BB 2-38 v Notts (Nottingham) 1993. SL: HS 8. BB 3-17 v Leics (W-s-M) 1993.

WHITE, Giles William (Millfield S), b Barnstaple, Devon 23 Mar 1972. 6'0". RHB, LB. Debut 1991. Devon 1988-93. HS 42 and BB 1-30 v SL (Taunton) 1991 – on debut. Awaiting BAC debut. NWT: HS 11 and BB 1-45 Devon v Kent (Canterbury) 1992. SL: HS 40 v Durham (Hartlepool) 1993.

NEWCOMERS

BIRD, Paul, b Bristol 7 May 1971. RHB, RFM.

BOND, Ian, b Barnstaple, Devon 7 Nov 1973. RHB, RFM.

CLARKE, Vincent, b Liverpool, Lancs 11 Nov 1971. RHB, LB.

DIMOND, Matthew, b Taunton 24 Sep 1975. RHB, RFM.

HOLLOWAY, Piran Christopher Laity (Millfield S; Taunton S; Loughborough U), b Helston, Cornwall 1 Oct 1970. 5'8". LHB, WK. Warwickshire 1988-93. HS 102* Wa v Worcs (Birmingham) 1992. NWT: HS 16 Wa v Norfolk (Lakenham) 1993. BHC: HS 27 Comb Us v Derbys (Oxford) 1991. SL: HS 51 Wa v Northants (Northampton) 1992.

DEPARTURES

COTTAM, A.C. – see NORTHAMPTONSHIRE.

TAVARÉ, Christopher James (Sevenoaks S; St John's, Oxford), b Orpington, Kent 27 Oct 1954. 6'1½". RHB, RM. Kent 1974-88 (cap 1978; captain 1983-84; benefit 1988). Oxford U 1975-77 (blue 1975-76-77). Somerset 1989-93 (cap 1989; captain 1990-93). **Tests**: 31 (1980 to 1989); HS 149 v I (Delhi) 1981-82. LOI: 29 (HS 83*). Tours: A 1982-83; NZ 1983-84; I/SL 1981-82; P 1983-84. 1000 runs (16); most – 1770 (1981). HS 219 v Sussex (Hove) 1990. BB 1-3. Awards: NWT 4; BHC 9. NWT: HS 162* v Devon (Torquay) 1990. BHC: HS 143 K v Somerset (Taunton) 1985. SL: HS 136* K v Glos (Canterbury) 1978.

SOMERSET 1993

RESULTS SUMMARY

	Place	Won	Lost	Drew	Abandoned
Britannic Assurance Championship	5th	8	7	2	
All First-class Matches		8	8	2	
Sunday League	18th	2	12		3
NatWest Trophy	Semi-Finalist				
Benson and Hedges Cup	Quarter-Finalist				

BRITANNIC ASSURANCE CHAMPIONSHIP AVERAGES

BATTING AND FIELDING

Cap		M	I	NO	HS	Runs	Avge	100	50	Ct/St
1989	R.J.Harden	17	30	3	132	1092	40.44	3	4	32
1992	M.N.Lathwell	13	23	1	132	802	36.45	2	3	16
–	N.A.Folland	16	28	3	108*	839	33.56	2	4	12
1988	G.D.Rose	17	29	2	138	865	32.03	2	2	10
–	H.R.J.Trump	7	10	7	22*	79	26.33	–	–	5
1990	A.N.Hayhurst	13	21	–	169	531	25.28	2	–	7
1987	N.A.Mallender	13	16	6	46	250	25.00	–	–	1
–	I.Fletcher	7	10	1	65*	223	24.77	–	2	1
1989	C.J.Tavaré	12	23	1	141*	535	24.31	1	1	22
1987	N.D.Burns	12	21	1	102*	466	23.30	1	1	35/3
–	R.J.Turner	6	10	1	70	195	21.66	–	1	15/3
1993	Mushtaq Ahmed	16	25	–	90	498	19.92	–	3	14
–	K.A.Parsons	4	8	1	63	133	19.00	–	1	2
1992	A.R.Caddick	10	15	3	35*	201	16.75	–	–	2
–	A.P.van Troost	13	16	6	35	100	10.00	–	–	2
–	J.I.D.Kerr	6	10	3	19*	55	7.85	–	–	3
–	M.E.Trescothick	3	6	–	6	14	2.33	–	–	4

Also played (2 matches): A Payne 17, 22* (2 ct).

BOWLING

	O	M	R	W	Avge	Best	5wI	10wM
A.R.Caddick	319	79	968	56	17.28	9-32	5	3
Mushtaq Ahmed	694.3	212	1773	85	20.85	7-91	8	3
N.A.Mallender	329.5	102	772	32	24.12	5-49	–	–
G.D.Rose	324.3	62	1090	43	25.34	6-83	3	–
J.I.D.Kerr	96	12	320	12	26.66	3-47	–	–
A.P.van Troost	259	46	931	27	34.48	5-47	1	–
H.R.J.Trump	215.4	76	488	13	37.53	4-74	–	–

Also bowled: R.J Harden 0 3-0-0-0; A N Hayhurst 44-15-118-3; M.N Lathwell
23-8-61-1; K.A Parsons 1-0-14-0; A Payne 18.2-4-62-4; C.J.Tavaré 1-0-2-0.

The First-Class Averages (pp 164-177) give the records of Somerset players in all
first-class county matches (their other opponents being the Australians), with the
exception of:
    A.R.Caddick 11-16-3-35*-214-16.46-0-0-2ct. 347-81-1072-57-18.80-9/32-5-3
    M.N.Lathwell 14-25-1-132-817-34.04-2-3-19ct 25-8-73-1-73.00-1/40.

SOMERSET RECORDS

FIRST-CLASS CRICKET

Highest Total	For	675-9d		v Hampshire	Bath	1924
	V	811		by Surrey	The Oval	1899
Lowest Total	For	25		v Glos	Bristol	1947
	V	22		by Glos	Bristol	1920
Highest Innings	For	322	I.V.A.Richards	v Warwicks	Taunton	1985
	V	424	A.C.MacLaren	for Lancashire	Taunton	1895

Highest Partnership for each Wicket

1st	346	H.T.Hewett/L.C.H.Palairet	v Yorkshire	Taunton	1892
2nd	290	J.C.W.MacBryan/M.D.Lyon	v Derbyshire	Buxton	1924
3rd	319	P.M.Roebuck/M.D.Crowe	v Leics	Taunton	1984
4th	310	P.W.Denning/I.T.Botham	v Glos	Taunton	1980
5th	235	J.C.White/C.C.C.Case	v Glos	Taunton	1927
6th	265	W.E.Alley/K.E.Palmer	v Northants	Northampton	1961
7th	240	S.M.J.Woods/V.T.Hill	v Kent	Taunton	1898
8th	172	I.V.A.Richards/I.T.Botham	v Leics	Leicester	1983
9th	183	C.H.M.Greetham/H.W.Stephenson	v Leics	Weston-s-Mare	1963
	183	J.J.Tavaré/N.A.Mallender	v Sussex	Hove	1990
10th	143	J.J.Bridges/A.H.D.Gibbs	v Essex	Weston-s-Mare	1919

Best Bowling	For	10- 49	E.J.Tyler	v Surrey	Taunton	1895
(Innings)	V	10- 35	A.Drake	for Yorkshire	Weston-s-Mare	1914
Best Bowling	For	16- 83	J.C.White	v Worcs	Bath	1919
(Match)	V	17-137	W.Brearley	for Lancashire	Manchester	1905

Most Runs – Season	2761	W.E.Alley	(av 58.74)	1961
Most Runs – Career	21142	H.Gimblett	(av 36.96)	1935-54
Most 100s – Season	11	S.J.Cook		1991
Most 100s – Career	49	H.Gimblett		1935-54
Most Wkts – Season	169	A.W.Wellard	(av 19.24)	1938
Most Wkts – Career	2166	J.C.White	(av 18.02)	1909-37

LIMITED-OVERS CRICKET

Highest Total	NWT	413-4		v Devon	Torquay	1990
	BHC	321-5		v Sussex	Hove	1990
	SL	360-3		v Glamorgan	Neath	1990
Lowest Total	NWT	59		v Middlesex	Lord's	1977
	BHC	98		v Middlesex	Lord's	1982
	SL	58		v Essex	Chelmsford	1977
Highest Innings	NWT	162*	C.J.Tavaré	v Devon	Torquay	1990
	BHC	177	S.J.Cook	v Sussex	Hove	1990
	SL	175*	I.T.Botham	v Northants	Wellingborough	1986
Best Bowling	NWT	7-15	R.P.Lefebvre	v Devon	Torquay	1990
	BHC	5-14	J.Garner	v Surrey	Lord's	1981
	SL	6-24	I.V.A.Richards	v Lancashire	Manchester	1983

SURREY

Formation of Present Club: 22 August 1845
Colours: Chocolate
Badge: Prince of Wales' Feathers
Championships (since 1890): (15) 1890, 1891, 1892, 1894, 1895, 1899, 1914, 1952, 1953, 1954, 1955, 1956, 1957, 1958, 1971. **Joint:** (1) 1950
NatWest Trophy/Gillette Cup Winners: (1) 1982
Benson and Hedges Cup Winners: (1) 1974
Sunday League Champions: (0) Third 1993
Match Awards: NWT 37; BHC 51

Chief Executive: G.A.Woodman, Kennington Oval, London, SE11 5SS
(☎ 071-582 6660)
Captain: A.J.Stewart
Scorer: M.R.L.W.Ayers
1994 Beneficiary: A.J.Stewart

BAINBRIDGE, Mark Robert (Teddington S; Richmond upon Thames C), b Isleworth, Middx 11 May 1973 5'9½". RHB, SLA. Surrey staff 1992 – awaiting f-c debut.

BENJAMIN, Joseph Emmanuel (Cayon HS, St Kitts; Mount Pleasant S, Highgate, Birmingham), b Christ Church, St Kitts 2 Feb 1961. 6'2". RHB, RMF. Warwickshire 1988-91. Surrey debut 1992. Cap 1993. Staffordshire 1986-88. HS 42 v Kent (Guildford) 1992. 50 wkts (1): 64 (1993). BB 6-19 v Notts (Oval) 1993. **NWT:** HS 19 and BB 2-37 Staffs v Glam (Stone) 1986. **BHC:** HS 20 Wa v Worcs (Birmingham) 1990. BB 2-32 Wa v Glos (Bristol) 1990. **SL:** HS 24 Wa v Lancs (Manchester) 1990. BB 4-44 v Middx (Oval) 1992.

BICKNELL, Darren John (Robert Haining SS; Guildford TC), b Guildford 24 Jun 1967. Elder brother of M.P. 6'4". LHB, LM. Debut 1987. Cap 1990. Tours (Eng A): WI 1991-92; P 1990-91; SL 1990-91; Z 1989-90. 1000 runs (5); most – 1888 (1991). HS 190 v Sussex (Hove) 1993. BB 2-62 v Northants (Northampton) 1991. Awards: NWT 1; BHC 2. **NWT:** HS 135* v Yorks (Oval) 1989. **BHC:** HS 119 v Hants (Oval) 1990. **SL:** HS 125 v Durham (Durham) 1992.

BICKNELL, Martin Paul (Robert Haining SS), b Guildford 14 Jan 1969. Younger brother of D.J. 6'3". RHB, RFM. Debut 1986. Cap 1989. **Tests:** 2 (1993); HS 14 and BB 3-99 v A (Birmingham) 1993. LOI: 7 (HS 31*; BB 3-55). Tours: A 1990-91; Z 1989-90 (Eng A). HS 88 v Hants (Southampton) 1992. 50 wkts (5); most – 71 (1992). BB 9-45 v CU (Oval) 1988. BAC BB 7-52 v Sussex (Oval) 1991. Award: BHC 1. **NWT:** HS 66* v Northants (Oval) 1991. BB 4-35 v Somerset (Taunton) 1993. **BHC:** HS 27* v Lancs (Manchester) 1990. BB 3-27 v Lancs (Oval) 1993. **SL:** HS 20* v Northants (Tring) 1991. BB 4-14 v Middx (Oval) 1990.

BOILING, James (Rutlish S, Merton; Durham U), b New Delhi, India 8 Apr 1968. 6'4". RHB, OB. Debut 1988. Tour: A 1992-93 (Eng A). HS 29 v Glam (Neath) 1992. BB 6-84 (10-203 match) v Glos (Bristol) 1991. Award: BHC 1. **NWT:** HS 22 and BB 2-22 v Northants (Oval) 1991. **BHC:** HS 9*. BB 3-9 Comb Us v Surrey (Cambridge) 1989. **SL:** HS 23* v Worcs (Worcester) 1993. BB 5-24 v Hants (Basingstoke) 1992.

BROWN, Alistair Duncan (Caterham S), b Beckenham, Kent 11 Feb 1970. 5'10". RHB, occ LB. Debut 1992. 1000 runs (1): 1382 (1993). HS 175 v Durham (Durham) 1992. **NWT:** HS 26 v Somerset (Taunton) 1993. **BHC:** HS 41 v Lancs (Oval) 1992. **SL:** HS 113 v Glam (Llanelli) 1992.

BUTCHER, Mark Alan (Trinity S; Archbishop Tenison's S, Croydon), b Croydon 23 Aug 1972. Son of A.R. (Surrey, Glamorgan and England 1972-92); brother of G.P. (see GLAMORGAN). 5'11". LHB, RM. Debut 1992. HS 66* v Yorks (Oval) 1993. BB 4-51 v Z (Oval) 1993. BAC BB 3-51 v Northants (Northampton) 1993. **NWT:** HS 15 and BB 2-57 v Somerset (Taunton) 1993. **BHC:** HS 1 and BB 2-41 v Lancs (Oval) 1993. **SL:** HS 48* v Glam (Oval) 1991 (on 1st XI debut and against team captained by his father). BB 3-23 v Sussex (Oval) 1992.

HOLLIOAKE, Adam John (St George's S, Weybridge), b Melbourne, Australia 5 Sep 1971. 5'11". RHB, RMF. Debut 1993, scoring 13 and 123 v Derbys (Ilkeston). Qualified for England 1992. HS 123 and BB 2-75 v Derbys (Ilkeston) 1993 (on debut). **SL:** HS 58 v Kent (Canterbury) 1993. BB 4-33 v Lancs (Oval) 1993.

KENDRICK, Neil Michael (Wilson's GS), b Bromley, Kent 11 Nov 1967. 5'11". RHB, SLA. Debut 1988. HS 55 v Middx (Lord's) 1992. 50 wkts (1): 51 (1992). BB 7-115 v Notts (Oval) 1992. **NWT:** HS-. BB 1-51. **BHC:** HS 24 and BB 2-47 v Kent (Canterbury) 1992. **SL:** HS 2*. BB 1-45.

KERSEY, Graham James (Bexley & Erith Technical HS), b Plumstead, London 19 May 1971. 5'7". RHB, WK. Kent 1991-92. Surrey debut 1993. HS 38* v Leics (Leicester) 1993 – on Sy debut. **SL:** HS 50 v Durham (Oval) 1993.

LYNCH, Monte Alan (Ryden's S, Walton-on-Thames), b Georgetown, British Guiana 21 May 1958. 5'8". RHB, OB. Debut 1977. Cap 1982. Benefit 1991. Guyana 1982-83. LOI: 3 (HS 6). Tours: SA 1983-84 (WI XI); P 1981-82 (Int). 1000 (8); most – 1714 (1985). HS 172* v Kent (Oval) 1989. BB 3-6 v Glam (Swansea) 1981. Awards: NWT 1; BHC 4. **NWT:** HS 129 v Durham (Oval) 1982. BB 2-28 v Glam (Swansea) 1992. **BHC:** HS 112* v Kent (Oval) 1987. **SL:** HS 136 v Yorks (Bradford) 1985. BB 2-2 v Northants 1987 and v Sussex 1990.

MURPHY, Anthony John (Xaverian C; Swansea U), b Manchester 6 Aug 1962. 6'0". RHB, RMF. Lancashire 1985-88. Surrey debut 1989. Cheshire 1984-85. Tour: WI 1986-87 (La). HS 38 v Glos (Oval) 1989. 50 wkts (1): 65 (1989). BB 6-97 v Derbys (Derby) 1989. **NWT:** HS 1*. BB 2-27 v Dorset (Oval) 1993. **BHC:** HS 5*. BB 2-23 v Middx (Lord's) 1991. **SL:** HS 9*. BB 4-22 Glos (Oval) 1989.

SARGEANT, Neil Frederick (Whitmore HS), b Hammersmith 8 Nov 1965. 5'8". RHB, WK. Debut 1989. HS 49 v Lancs (Manchester) 1991. BB 1-88. **SL:** HS 22 v Glos (Cheltenham) 1990.

SMITH, Andrew William (Sutton Manor HS), b Sutton 30 May 1969. Son of W.A. (Surrey 1961-70). 5'8". RHB, OB. Debut 1993. HS 68 v Derbys (Ilkeston) 1993. BB 2-7 v Northants (Northampton) 1993. Award: NWT 1. **NWT:** HS-. BB 3-25 v Leics (Leicester) 1993. **SL:** HS 58 v Derbys (Ilkeston) 1993.

STEWART, Alec James (Tiffin S), b Merton 8 Apr 1963. Son of M.J. (Surrey and England 1954-72). 5'11". RHB, WK. Debut 1981. Cap 1985. Captain 1992-. Benefit 1994. Wisden 1992. **Tests:** 32 (1989-90 to 1993, 2 as captain); HS 190 v P (Birmingham) 1992. LOI: 51 (HS 103). Tours: A 1990-91; WI 1989-90; NZ 1991-92; Z 1992-93; SL 1992-93 (captain). 1000 runs (8); most – 1665 (1986). HS 206* v Essex (Oval) 1989. BB 1-7. Held 11 catches (equalling all-time f-c match record) v Leics (Leicester) 1989. Awards: NWT 2; BHC 3. **NWT:** HS 107* v Middx (Oval) 1988. **BHC:** HS 110* v Somerset (Taunton) 1991. **SL:** HS 125 v Lancs (Oval) 1990.

THORPE, Graham Paul (Weydon CS; Farnham C), b Farnham 1 Aug 1969. 5'11". LHB, RM. Debut 1988. Cap 1991. **Tests:** 3 (1993); HS 114* v A (Nottingham) 1993 – on debut. LOI: 3 (HS 36). Tours (Eng A): A 1992-93; WI 1991-92; P 1990-91; SL 1990-91; Z 1989-90. 1000 runs (4); most – 1895 (1992). HS 216 v Somerset (Oval) 1992. BB 4-40 v A (Oval) 1993. BAC BB 2-31 v Essex (Oval) 1989. **NWT:** HS 93 v Hants (Lord's) 1991. **BHC:** HS 103 v Lancs (Oval) 1993. BB 3-35 v Middx (Lord's) 1989. **SL:** HS 115* v Lancs (Manchester) 1991. BB 3-21 v Somerset (Oval) 1991.

WAQAR YOUNIS (Government C, Vehari), b Vehari, Pakistan 16 Nov 1971. 6'0". RHB, RF. Multan 1987-88/1990-91. United Bank 1988-89 to date. Surrey debut/ cap 1990. Wisden 1991. **Tests** (P): 23 (1989-90 to 1992-93); HS 29 v WI (Bridgetown) 1992-93; BB 7-76 v NZ (Faisalabad) 1990-91. LOI (P): 74 (HS 37; BB 6-26). Tours (P): E 1992; A 1989-90; WI 1992-93; NZ 1992-93. HS 51 United Bank v PIA (Lahore) Qaid-e-Azam Final. Sy HS 31 v Yorks (Guildford) 1991. 50 wkts (3+2) inc 100 (1): 113 (1991). BB 7-64 United Bank v ADBP (Lahore) 1990-91. Sy BB 7-73 v Warwks (Oval) 1990. Awards: NWT 2. **NWT:** HS 26 v Essex (Oval) 1991. BB 5-40 v Northants (Oval) 1991. **BHC:** HS 5*. BB 3-29 v Somerset (Taunton) 1991. **SL:** HS 39 v Hants (Oval) 1993. BB 5-26 v Kent (Oval) 1990.

WARD, David Mark (Haling Manor HS), b Croydon 10 Feb 1961. 6'1". RHB, OB, occ WK. Debut 1985. Cap 1990. 1000 runs (2) inc 2000 (1): 2072 (1990). HS 263 v Kent (Canterbury) 1990. BB 2-66 v Glos (Guildford) 1991. Award: NWT 1. **NWT:** HS 101* v Glam (Swansea) 1992. **BHC:** HS 46* v Yorks (Oval) 1990. **SL:** HS 102* v Hants (Southampton) 1990.

NEWCOMERS

De la PENA, Jason Michael (Stowe S; Bournside S), b London 16 Sep 1972. 6'4". RHB, RFM. Gloucestershire 1991-93. HS 7*. BB 4-77 Gs v A (Bristol) 1993.

KENNIS, Gregor John (Tiffin S), b Yokohama, Japan 9 Mar 1974. 6'1". RHB, OB.

PIGOTT, Anthony Charles Shackleton (Harrow S), b Fulham, London 4 Jun 1958. 6'1". RHB, RFM. Sussex 1978-92 (cap 1982; benefit 1991). Wellington 1982-83/ 1983-84. **Tests:** 1 (1983-84); HS 8* and BB 2-75 v NZ (Christchurch) 1983-84. Tours: NZ 1979-80 (DHR), 1983-84 (part). HS 104* Sx v Warwks (Birmingham) 1986. 50 wkts (5); most – 74 (1988). BB 7-74 Sx v Northants (Eastbourne) 1982. Hat-trick 1978 (Sx – his first f-c wkts). **NWT:** HS 53 Sx v Derbys (Hove) 1988. BB 3-4 Sx v Ire (Hove) 1985. **BHC:** HS 49* Sx v Essex (Hove) 1989. BB 3-29 Sx v Leics (Hove) 1991. **SL:** HS 51* Sx v Northants (Hove) 1989. BB 5-24 Sx v Lancs (Manchester) 1986.

THOMPSON, David James, b London 11 Mar 1976. RHB, RMF.

DEPARTURES

ALIKHAN, Rehan Iqbal ('Ray') (KCS, Wimbledon), b Westminster Hospital, London 28 Dec 1962. 6'1½". RHB, OB. Sussex 1986-88. PIA 1986-87. Surrey 1989-93. 1000 runs (1): 1055 (1991). HS 138 v Essex (Oval) 1990. BB 2-19 Sx v WI (Hove) 1988. Sy BB 2-43 v Northants (Northampton) 1991. **NWT:** HS 41 Sx v Worcs (Worcester) 1986. **BHC:** HS 71 Sx v Glam (Swansea) 1987. **SL:** HS 23 Sx v Essex (Chelmsford) 1987.

ATKINS, Paul David (Aylesbury GS), b Aylesbury, Bucks 11 Jun 1966. 6'1". RHB, OB. Surrey 1988-93. Buckinghamshire 1985-90 (cap 1986). HS 114* v CU (Oval) 1988 – on debut. BAC HS 99 v Lancs (Southport) 1988 and v Notts (Oval) 1992. Award: NWT 1. **NWT:** HS 82 v Glam (Oval) 1988. **BHC:** HS 9. **SL:** HS 55 v Somerset (Oval) 1993.

BILL FRINDALL'S SCORING SHEETS AND BINDERS

For illustrated instructions and price list send a S.A.E. to

THE BEECHES, URCHFONT, DEVIZES, WILTSHIRE SN10 4RD

SURREY 1993

RESULTS SUMMARY

	Place	Won	Lost	Drew	Abandoned
Britannic Assurance Championship	6th	6	6	5	
All First-class Matches		6	7	6	
Sunday League	3rd	11	4		2
NatWest Trophy	Quarter-Finalist				
Benson and Hedges Cup	1st Round				

BRITANNIC ASSURANCE CHAMPIONSHIP AVERAGES

BATTING AND FIELDING

Cap		M	I	NO	HS	Runs	Avge	100	50	Ct/St
1985	A.J.Stewart	10	16	1	127	716	47.73	2	5	20
1990	D.J.Bicknell	17	31	2	190	1383	47.68	4	8	8
–	A.D.Brown	17	30	3	150*	1188	44.00	2	4	15
–	A.J.Hollioake	4	7	–	123	304	43.42	1	2	3
1991	G.P.Thorpe	11	19	1	171	721	40.05	2	4	10
–	M.A.Butcher	4	7	2	66*	181	36.20	–	1	3
1990	D.M.Ward	11	18	1	151*	530	31.17	1	3	6
1989	M.P.Bicknell	10	15	2	57	372	28.61	–	2	9
–	A.W.Smith	13	21	2	68	491	25.84	–	2	7
1982	M.A.Lynch	14	26	1	90	596	23.84	–	3	24
–	P.D.Atkins	7	12	–	62	228	19.00	–	1	4
–	R.I.Alikhan	3	6	–	41	101	16.83	–	–	1
–	G.J.Kersey	10	16	1	38*	221	14.73	–	–	30/3
–	N.M.Kendrick	11	18	5	39*	191	14.69	–	–	5
–	A.J.Murphy	9	11	8	17*	43	14.33	–	–	5
1990	Waqar Younis	13	18	1	28	214	12.58	–		3
–	J.Boiling	7	10	3	28	69	9.85	–	–	3
1993	J.E.Benjamin	16	24	9	22	122	7.17	–	–	3

BOWLING

	O	M	R	W	Avge	Best	5wI	10wM
M.P.Bicknell	415.2	120	1078	63	17.11	6- 43	6	2
Waqar Younis	449.4	89	1407	62	22.69	6- 42	4	–
J.E.Benjamin	616.2	150	1764	62	28.45	6- 19	2	–
N.M.Kendrick	324	103	810	26	31.15	7-115	1	–
A.J.Murphy	259	69	802	22	36.45	3- 38	–	–
J.Boiling	180.1	55	467	11	42.45	5-100	1	–

Also bowled: D.J.Bicknell 1-0-21-0; A.D.Brown 1-0-6-0; M.A.Butcher 93-19-288-9; A.J.Hollioake 89.3-17-263-4; M.A.Lynch 1-1-0-0; A.W.Smith 80-10-346-5; G.P.Thorpe 48-9-165-3.

The First-Class Averages (pp 164-177) give the records of Surrey players in all first-class county matches (their other opponents being the Australians and the Zimbabweans), with the exception of M.P.Bicknell and A.J.Stewart, whose full county figures are as above, and:

G.P.Thorpe 13-23-1-171-787-35.77-2-4-12ct. 69.3-14-246-7-35.14-4/40.

SURREY RECORDS

FIRST-CLASS CRICKET

Highest Total	For	811	v	Somerset	The Oval	1899
	V	863	by	Lancashire	The Oval	1990
Lowest Total	For	14	v	Essex	Chelmsford	1983
	V	16	by	MCC	Lord's	1872
Highest Innings	For	357* R.Abel	v	Somerset	The Oval	1899
	V	366 N.H.Fairbrother	for	Lancashire	The Oval	1990

Highest Partnership for each Wicket

1st	428	J.B.Hobbs/A.Sandham	v	Oxford U	The Oval	1926
2nd	371	J.B.Hobbs/E.G.Hayes	v	Hampshire	The Oval	1909
3rd	413	D.J.Bicknell/D.M.Ward	v	Kent	Canterbury	1990
4th	448	R.Abel/T.W.Hayward	v	Yorkshire	The Oval	1899
5th	308	J.N.Crawford/F.C.Holland	v	Somerset	The Oval	1908
6th	298	A.Sandham/H.S.Harrison	v	Sussex	The Oval	1913
7th	262	C.J.Richards/K.T.Medlycott	v	Kent	The Oval	1987
8th	205	I.A.Greig/M.P.Bicknell	v	Lancashire	The Oval	1990
9th	168	E.R.T.Holmes/E.W.J.Brooks	v	Hampshire	The Oval	1936
10th	173	A.Ducat/A.Sandham	v	Essex	Leyton	1921

Best Bowling	For	10-43	T.Rushby	v	Somerset	Taunton	1921
(Innings)	V	10-28	W.P.Howell	for	Australians	The Oval	1899
Best Bowling	For	16-83	G.A.R.Lock	v	Kent	Blackheath	1956
(Match)	V	15-57	W.P.Howell	for	Australians	The Oval	1899

Most Runs – Season	3246	T.W.Hayward	(av 72.13)	1906
Most Runs – Career	43554	J.B.Hobbs	(av 49.72)	1905-34
Most 100s – Season	13	T.W.Hayward		1906
	13	J.B.Hobbs		1925
Most 100s – Career	144	J.B.Hobbs		1905-34
Most Wkts – Season	252	T.Richardson	(av 13.94)	1895
Most Wkts – Career	1755	T.Richardson	(av 17.87)	1892-1904

LIMITED-OVERS CRICKET

Highest Total	NWT	313-5		v	Northumb	Jesmond	1989
	BHC	331-5		v	Hampshire	The Oval	1990
	SL	330-6		v	Durham	Durham	1992
Lowest Total	NWT	74		v	Kent	The Oval	1967
	BHC	89		v	Notts	Nottingham	1984
	SL	64		v	Worcs	Worcester	1978
Highest Innings	NWT	146	G.S.Clinton	v	Kent	Canterbury	1985
	BHC	121*	G.S.Clinton	v	Kent	The Oval	1988
	SL	136	M.A.Lynch	v	Yorkshire	Bradford	1985
Best Bowling	NWT	7-33	R.D.Jackman	v	Yorkshire	Harrogate	1970
	BHC	5-21	P.H.L.Wilson	v	Comb Us	The Oval	1979
	SL	6-25	Intikhab Alam	v	Derbyshire	The Oval	1974

SUSSEX

Formation of Present Club: 1 March 1839
Substantial Reorganisation: August 1857
Colours: Dark Blue, Light Blue and Gold
Badge: County Arms of Six Martlets
Championships: (0) Second 1902, 1903, 1932, 1933, 1934, 1953, 1981
NatWest Trophy/Gillette Cup Winners: (4) 1963, 1964, 1978, 1986
Benson and Hedges Cup Winners: (0) Semi-Finalists 1982
Sunday League Champions: (1) 1982
Match Awards: NWT 49; BHC 48

Secretary: N.Bett, County Ground, Eaton Road, Hove BN3 3AN
(☎ 0273-732161)
Captain: A.P.Wells
Scorer: L.V.Chandler
1994 Beneficiary: D.M.Smith (testimonial)

ATHEY, Charles William Jeffrey (Stainsby SS; Acklam Hall HS), b Middlesbrough, Yorks 27 Sep 1957. 5'9½". RHB, RM. Yorkshire 1976-83 (cap 1980). Gloucestershire 1984-92 (cap 1985; captain 1989; benefit 1990). Sussex debut/cap 1993. Tests: 23 (1980 to 1988); HS 123 v P (Lord's) 1987. LOI: 31 (HS 142*). Tours: A 1986-87, 1987-88; SA 1989-90 (Eng A); WI 1980-81; NZ 1979-80 (DHR), 1987-88; P 1987-88; SL 1985-86 (Eng B). 1000 runs (11); most – 1812 (1984). HS 184 Eng B v Sri Lanka (Galle) 1985-86. BAC HS 181 Gs v Sussex (Cheltenham) 1992. Sx HS 137 v Somerset (Taunton) 1993. BB 3-3 Gs v Hants (Bristol) 1985. Sx BB 2-40 v Notts (Eastbourne) 1993. Awards: NWT 4; BHC 5. **NWT:** HS 115 Y v Kent (Leeds) 1980. BB 1-18. **BHC:** HS 95 Gs v Northants (Northampton) 1987. BB 4-48 Gs v Comb Us (Bristol) 1984. **SL:** HS 121* Gs v Worcs (Moreton) 1985. BB 5-35 Y v Derbys (Chesterfield) 1981.

DEAN, Jacob Winston (Chailey S; Haywards Heath SFC), b Cuckfield 23 Aug 1970. 5'10½". RHB, SLA. Sussex staff 1991 – awaiting f-c debut.

GIDDINS, Edward Simon Hunter (Eastbourne C), b Eastbourne 20 Jul 1971. 6'4½". RHB, RMF. Debut 1991. MCC YC. HS 14* v Middx (Lord's) 1991. BB 5-32 v Derbys (Eastbourne) 1992. **NWT:** HS 0* and BB 2-21 v Northants (Northampton) 1993. **BHC:** HS 0. BB 2-42 v Glam (Cardiff) 1993. **SL:** HS 9*. BB 4-36 v Glos (Hove) 1993.

GREENFIELD, Keith (Falmer HS), b Brighton 6 Dec 1968. 6'0". RHB, RM. Debut 1987. HS 127* v CU (Hove) 1991. BB 2-40 and BAC HS 107 v Essex (Hove) 1993. Award: NWT 1. **NWT:** HS 96* v Wales (Hove) 1993. BB 2-35 v Glam (Hove) 1993. **BHC:** HS 62 v Leics (Leicester) 1992. BB 1-35. **SL:** HS 79 v Glam (Hove) 1992. BB 3-44 v Worcs (Hove) 1993.

HALL, James William (Chichester HS), b Chichester 30 Mar 1968. 6'3". RHB, OB. Debut 1987. Cap 1990. 1000 runs (2); most – 1140 (1990 – debut season). HS 140* v Lancs (Hove) 1992. Award: BHC 1. **NWT:** HS 47 v Bucks (Beaconsfield) 1992. **BHC:** HS 81 v Surrey (Hove) 1992. **SL:** HS 77 v Notts (Nottingham) 1992.

HEMMINGS, Edward Ernest (Campion S), b Leamington Spa, Warwks 20 Feb 1949. 5'10". RHB, OB. Warwickshire 1966-78 (cap 1974). Nottinghamshire 1979-92 (cap 1980; benefit 1987). Sussex debut/cap 1993. Tests: 16 (1982 to 1990-91); HS 95 v A (Sydney) 1982-83; BB 6-58 v NZ (Birmingham) 1990. LOI: 33 (HS 8*; BB 4-52). Tours: A 1982-83, 1987-88, 1990-91; SA 1974-75 (DHR); WI 1982-83 (Int), 1989-90; NZ 1987-88; P 1981-82 (Int), 1987-88. HS 127* Nt v Yorks (Worksop)

1982. Sx HS 17* v Middx (Lord's) 1993. 50 wkts (15); most – 94 (1984). BB 10-175 Int XI v WI XI (Kingston) 1982-83. BAC BB 7-23 Nt v Lancs (Nottingham) 1983. Sx BB 7-31 (12-58 match) v Leics (Horsham) 1993. 2 hat-tricks: 1977 (Wa), 1984 (Nt). Awards: NWT 1; BHC 1. **NWT:** HS 31* Nt v Staffs (Nottingham) 1985. BB 3-27 Nt v Warwks (Nottingham) 1985. **BHC:** HS 61* Wa v Leics (Birmingham) 1974. BB 4-47 Nt v Glos (Bristol) 1989. **SL:** HS 44* Wa v Kent (Birmingham) 1971. BB 5-22 Wa v Notts (Birmingham) 1974.

HUMPHRIES, Shaun (The Weald, Billingshurst; Kingston C, London), b Horsham 11 Jan 1973. 5'9". RHB, WK. Debut 1993. HS- Awaiting BAC debut.

LAW, Danny Richard (Steyning GS), b Lambeth, London 15 Jul 1975. 6'5". RHB, RFM. Debut 1993. HS 11 v Glos (Hove) 1993. BB 2-38 v Worcs (Hove) 1993.

LENHAM, Neil John (Brighton C), b Worthing 17 Dec 1965. Son of L.J. (Sussex 1956-70). 5'11". RHB, RM. Debut 1984. Cap 1990. 1000 runs (3); most – 1663 (1990). HS 222* v Kent (Hove) 1992. BB 4-13 v Durham (Durham) 1993. Awards: NWT 1; BHC 1. **NWT:** HS 66 v Scot (Edinburgh) 1991. BB 2-12 v Ire (Downpatrick) 1990. **BHC:** HS 82 v Somerset (Hove) 1986. BB 1-3. **SL:** HS 86 v Kent (Hove) 1991. BB 5-28 v Durham (Durham) 1993.

MOORES, Peter (King Edward VI S, Macclesfield), b Macclesfield, Cheshire 18 Dec 1962. 6'0". RHB, WK. Worcestershire 1983-84. Sussex debut 1985. Cap 1989. OFS 1988-89. HS 116 v Somerset (Hove) 1989. **NWT:** HS 26 v Scot (Edinburgh) 1991. **BHC:** HS 76 v Middx (Hove) 1990. **SL:** HS 57 v Hants (Hove) 1992.

NEWELL, Keith (Ifield Community C), b Crawley 25 Mar 1972. 6'0". RHB, RM. Sussex staff 1993 – awaiting f-c debut. **SL:** HS-.

NORTH, John Andrew (Chichester HS), b Slindon 19 Nov 1970. 5'9". RHB, RM. Debut 1990. HS 114 v Essex (Hove) 1993. BB 4-47 v SL (Hove) 1991. BAC BB 3-32 v Worcs (Hove) 1993. **NWT:** HS 20 v Wales (Hove) 1993. **BHC:** HS 22 v Scot (Hove) 1991. BB 3-24 v Leics (Leicester) 1992. **SL:** 56 v Durham (Horsham) 1992. BB 3-29 v Kent (Hove) 1991.

PEIRCE, Michael Toby Edward (Ardingly C; Durham U), b Maidenhead, Berks 14 Jun 1973. 5'10". LHB, SLA. Sussex staff 1993 – awaiting f-c debut.

PHILLIPS, Nicholas Charles (Wm Parker S, Hastings), b Pembury, Kent 10 May 1974. 5'10 1/2". RHB, OB. Debut 1993. HS-. BB 3-39 v CU (Hove) 1993. Awaiting BAC debut.

REMY, Carlos Charles (St Aloyous C; Haringey Cricket C), b Castries, St Lucia 24 Jul 1968. 5'9". RHB, RM. Debut 1989. HS 47 v Derbys (Eastbourne) 1992. BB 4-63 v CU (Hove) 1990. BAC BB 3-27 v Lancs (Hove) 1992. **NWT:** HS 1. **SL:** HS 19 v Essex (Hove) 1993. BB 4-31 v Lancs (Hove) 1992.

SALISBURY, Ian David Kenneth (Moulton CS), b Northampton 21 Jan 1970. 5'11". RHB, LB. Debut 1989. Cap 1991. MCC YC. YC 1992. Wisden 1992. **Tests:** 4 (1992 to 1992-93); HS 50 v P (Manchester) 1992; BB 3-49 v P (Lord's) 1992. LOI: 2 (HS 2*; BB 2-36). Tours: WI 1991-92 (Eng A); I 1992-93; P 1990-91 (Eng A); SL 1990-91 (Eng A). HS 68 v Derbys (Hove) 1990. 50 wkts (2); most – 87 (1992). BB 7-54 (12-138 match) v Yorks (Hove) 1992. Award: BHC 1. **NWT:** HS 14* v Essex (Hove) 1991. BB 3-28 v Bucks (Beaconsfield) 1992. **BHC:** HS 17* and BB 3-40 v Kent (Canterbury) 1991. **SL:** HS 27* v Glos (Cheltenham) 1992. BB 5-30 v Leics (Leicester) 1992.

SMITH, David Mark (Battersea GS), b Balham, London 9 Jan 1956. 6'4". LHB, RM. Surrey 1973-83 and 1987-88 (cap 1980). Worcestershire 1984-86 (cap 1984). Sussex debut/cap 1989. Testimonial 1994. **Tests:** 2 (1985-86); HS 47 v WI (P-of-S) 1985-86. LOI: 2 (HS 10*). Tour: WI 1985-86. 1000 runs (7); most – 1305 (1989). HS 213 v Essex (Southend) 1992. BB 3-40 Sy v Sussex (Oval) 1976. Sx BB-. Awards: NWT 4; BHC 4. **NWT:** HS 124 v Warwks (Lord's) 1993. BB 3-39 Sy v Derbys (Ilkeston) 1976. **BHC:** HS 126 Wo v Warwks (Worcester) 1985. BB 4-29 Sy v Kent (Oval) 1980. **SL:** HS 87* Sy v Hants (Oval) 1980. BB 2-21 Sy v Worcs (Byfleet) 1973.

SPEIGHT, Martin Peter (Hurstpierpoint C; Durham U), b Walsall, Staffs 24 Oct 1967. 5'9". RHB, WK. Debut 1986. Cap 1991. Wellington 1989-90 to date. 1000 runs (3); most – 1375 (1990). HS 184 v Notts (Eastbourne) 1993. BB 1-2. Award: BHC 1. **NWT:** HS 50 v Warwks (Lord's) 1989. **BHC:** HS 83 Comb Us v Glos (Bristol) 1988. **SL:** HS 126 v Somerset (Taunton) 1993.

STEPHENSON, Franklyn Dacosta (Samuel Jackson Prescod Poly), b St James, Barbados 8 Apr 1959. 6'3 1/2". RHB, RFM. Barbados 1981-82 and 1989-90. Tasmania 1981-82. Gloucestershire 1982-83. Nottinghamshire 1988-91 (cap 1988). OFS 1991-92 to date. Sussex debut/cap 1992. Staffordshire 1980. Wisden 1988. Tours (WI XI): SA 1982-83, 1983-84. 1000 runs (1): 1018 (1988). HS 165 Barbados v Leeward Is (Basseterre) 1981-82. Sx HS 133 v Somerset (Hove) 1992. 50 wkts (4) inc 100 (1): 125 (1988). BB 8-47 (15-106 match) Nt v Essex (Nottingham) 1989. Sx BB 7-29 (11-107 match) v Worcs (Worcester) 1992. Scored 111 and 117 and took 11-222 Nt v Yorks (Nottingham) 1988. Double 1988. Awards: NWT 1; BHC 3. **NWT:** HS 40 v Warwks (Birmingham) 1992. BB 3-8 v Bucks (Beaconsfield) 1992. **BHC:** HS 98* Nt v Worcs (Nottingham) 1990. BB 5-30 Nt v Yorks (Nottingham) 1991. **SL:** HS 103 v Surrey (Hove) 1993. BB 5-23 v Essex (Hove) 1993.

WELLS, Alan Peter (Tideway CS, Newhaven), b Newhaven 2 Oct 1961. Younger brother of C.M. (see DERBYSHIRE). 6'0". RHB, RM. Debut 1981. Cap 1986. Captain 1992-. Border 1981-82. Tour: SA 1989-90 (Eng XI). 1000 runs (8); most – 1784 (1991). HS 253* v Yorks (Middlesbrough) 1991. BB 3-67 v Worcs (Worcester) 1987. Awards: NWT 2. **NWT:** HS 119 v Bucks (Beaconsfield) 1992. **BHC:** HS 74 v Middx (Hove) 1990. BB 1-17. **SL:** HS 127 v Hants (Portsmouth) 1993. BB 1-0.

NEWCOMERS

JARVIS, Paul William (Bydales CS, Marske), b Redcar, Yorks 29 Jun 1965. 5'10". RHB, RFM. Yorkshire 1981-93 (cap 1986; youngest Yorkshire debutant at 16yr 75d). **Tests:** 9 (1987-88 to 1992-93); HS 29* and BB 4-107 v WI (Lord's) 1988. LOI: 16 (HS 16*; BB 5-35). Tours: SA 1989-90 (Eng XI); WI 1986-87 (Y); NZ 1987-88; I/SL 1992-93; P 1987-88. HS 80 Y v Northants (Scarborough) 1992. 50 wkts (3); most – 81 (1987). BB 7-55 Y v Surrey (Leeds) 1986. Hat-trick 1985 (Y). **NWT:** HS 16 Y v Somerset (Leeds) 1985. BB 4-41 Y v Leics (Leeds) 1987. **BHC:** HS 42 Y v Lancs (Leeds) 1990. BB 4-34 Y v Warwks (Birmingham) 1992. **SL:** HS 38* Y v Glam (Middlesbrough) 1993. BB 6-27 Y v Somerset (Taunton) 1989.

LEWRY, Jason David (Durrington HS, Worthing), b Worthing 2 Apr 1971. LHB, LFM.

DEPARTURES

DONELAN, Bradleigh Thomas Peter (Finchley Catholic HS), b Park Royal Hospital, Middx 3 Jan 1968. 6'1". RHB, OB. Sussex 1989-93. MCC YC. HS 68* v Hants (Southampton) 1992. BB 6-62 (10-136 match) v Glos (Hove) 1991. **BHC:** HS 9*. BB 1-41. **SL:** HS 19 v Glos (Hove) 1991 and v Lancs (Manchester) 1993. BB 2-39 v Surrey (Oval) 1992.

JONES, Adrian Nicholas (Seaford C), b Woking, Surrey 22 Jul 1961. 6'2". LHB, RFM. Sussex 1981-86 (cap 1986) and 1991-93. Somerset 1987-90 (cap 1987). Border 1981-82. HS 43* Sm v Leics (Taunton) 1989. Sx HS 35 v Middx (Hove) 1984. 50 wkts (5); most – 71 (1989). BB 7-30 Sm v Hants (Southampton) 1988. Sx BB 5-29 v Glos (Hove) 1984. Awards: BHC 3. **NWT:** HS 7. BB 4-26 v Yorks (Leeds) 1986. **BHC:** HS 25 Sm v Essex (Taunton) 1989. BB 5-53 Sm v Notts (Taunton) 1989. **SL:** HS 37 Sm v Surrey (Oval) 1989. BB 7-41 v Notts (Nottingham) 1986.

PIGOTT, A.C.S. – see SURREY.

WELLS, C.M. – see DERBYSHIRE.

SUSSEX 1993

RESULTS SUMMARY

	Place	Won	Lost	Tied	Drew	Abandoned
Britannic Assurance Championship	10th	5	7		5	
All First-class Matches		5	7		7	
Sunday League	4th	10	5	1		1
NatWest Trophy	Finalist					
Benson and Hedges Cup	Quarter-Finalist					

BRITANNIC ASSURANCE CHAMPIONSHIP AVERAGES

BATTING AND FIELDING

Cap		M	I	NO	HS	Runs	Avge	100	50	Ct/St
1993	C.W.J.Athey	15	26	5	137	1432	68.19	4	9	16
1986	A.P.Wells	17	26	2	144	1339	55.79	6	4	20
1991	M.P.Speight	12	20	1	184	1009	53.10	3	5	11
–	K.Greenfield	7	10	3	107	295	42.14	1	2	5
1990	N.J.Lenham	11	20	1	149	769	40.47	2	5	3
1989	D.M.Smith	15	23	1	150	802	36.45	1	4	15
1992	F.D.Stephenson	14	21	2	90	538	28.31	–	3	5
1989	P.Moores	17	23	2	85*	523	24.90	–	2	38/3
1991	I.D.K.Salisbury	13	19	4	63*	303	20.20	–	1	10
–	J.A.North	6	10	2	114	158	19.75	1	–	2
1992	J.W.Hall	8	14	–	53	275	19.64	–	1	5
1982	A.C.S.Pigott	10	12	2	52	148	14.80	–	1	3
1993	E.E.Hemmings	15	20	4	17*	78	4.87	–	–	10
1986	A.N.Jones	4	5	1	10*	19	4.75	–	–	–
–	E.S.H.Giddins	14	18	7	4	12	1.09	–	–	2

Also played: B.T.P.Donelan (3 matches) 41, 2, 36* (1 ct); D.R.Law (2 matches) 0, 11; C.C.Remy (3 matches) 39, 17, 0 (1 ct); C.M.Wells (1 match – cap 1982) 3, 0 (1 ct).

BOWLING

	O	M	R	W	Avge	Best	5wI	10wM
E.E.Hemmings	683.2	208	1541	63	24.46	7- 31	2	1
F.D.Stephenson	397	77	1155	41	28.17	5- 55	1	–
I.D.K.Salisbury	519.5	113	1736	49	35.42	5- 81	2	–
A.C.S.Pigott	229.3	32	844	20	42.20	4- 51	–	–
E.S.H.Giddins	358	52	1395	28	49.82	5-120	1	–

Also bowled: C.W.J.Athey 39.7-1-154-2; B.T.P.Donelan 94.3-8-450-9; K.Greenfield 39-7-136-5; A.N.Jones 66-7-283-2; D.R.Law 43.4-7-155-4; N.J.Lenham 93-23-255-9; J.A.North 88-11-357-7; C.C.Remy 11-2-66-0; C.M.Wells 15-4-36-2.

The First-Class Averages (pp 164-177) give the records of Sussex players in all first-class county matches (their other opponents being the Australians and Cambridge U), with the exception of:
I.D.K.Salisbury 15-21-4-63*-372-21.88-0-2-11ct. 580.5-122-1910-52-36.73-5/81-2-0.

SUSSEX RECORDS

FIRST-CLASS CRICKET

Highest Total	For	705-8d	v Surrey	Hastings	1902
	V	726	by Notts	Nottingham	1895
Lowest Total	For	19	v Surrey	Godalming	1830
		19	v Notts	Hove	1873
	V	18	by Kent	Gravesend	1867
Highest Innings	For	333	K.S.Duleepsinhji	v Northants	Hove	1930
	V	322	E.Paynter	for Lancashire	Hove	1937

Highest Partnership for each Wicket

1st	490	E.H.Bowley/J.G.Langridge	v Middlesex	Hove	1933
2nd	385	E.H.Bowley/M.W.Tate	v Northants	Hove	1921
3rd	298	K.S.Ranjitsinhji/E.H.Killick	v Lancashire	Hove	1901
4th	326*	J.Langridge/G.Cox	v Yorkshire	Leeds	1949
5th	297	J.H.Parks/H.W.Parks	v Hampshire	Portsmouth	1937
6th	255	K.S.Duleepsinhji/M.W.Tate	v Northants	Hove	1930
7th	344	K.S.Ranjitsinhji/W.Newham	v Essex	Leyton	1902
8th	229*	C.L.A.Smith/G.Brann	v Kent	Hove	1902
9th	178	H.W.Parks/A.F.Wensley	v Derbyshire	Horsham	1930
10th	156	G.R.Cox/H.R.Butt	v Cambridge U	Cambridge	1908

Best Bowling	For	10- 48	C.H.G.Bland	v Kent	Tonbridge	1899
(Innings)	V	9- 11	A.P.Freeman	for Kent	Hove	1922
Best Bowling	For	17-106	G.R.Cox	v. Warwicks	Horsham	1926
(Match)	V	17- 67	A.P.Freeman	for Kent	Hove	1922

Most Runs – Season	2850	J.G.Langridge	(av 64.77)	1949
Most Runs – Career	34152	J.G.Langridge	(av 37.69)	1928-55
Most 100s – Season	12	J.G.Langridge		1949
Most 100s – Career	76	J.G.Langridge		1928-55
Most Wkts – Season	198	M.W.Tate	(av 13.47)	1925
Most Wkts – Career	2211	M.W.Tate	(av 17.41)	1912-37

LIMITED-OVERS CRICKET

Highest Total	NWT	327-6		v Bucks	Beaconsfield	1992
	BHC	305-6		v Kent	Hove	1982
	SL	312-8		v Hampshire	Portsmouth	1993
Lowest Total	NWT	49		v Derbyshire	Chesterfield	1969
	BHC	61		v Middlesex	Hove	1978
	SL	61		v Derbyshire	Derby	1978
Highest Innings	NWT	141*	G.D.Mendis	v Warwicks	Hove	1980
	BHC	117	R.D.V.Knight	v Surrey	The Oval	1977
		117	C.M.Wells	v Glamorgan	Swansea	1989
	SL	129	A.W.Greig	v Yorkshire	Scarborough	1976
Best Bowling	NWT	6- 9	A.I.C.Dodemaide	v Ireland	Downpatrick	1990
	BHC	5- 8	Imran Khan	v Northants	Northampton	1978
	SL	7-41	A.N.Jones	v Notts	Nottingham	1986

WARWICKSHIRE

Formation of Present Club: 8 April 1882
Substantial Reorganisation: 19 January 1884
Colours: Dark Blue, Gold and Silver
Badge: Bear and Ragged Staff
Championships: (3) 1911, 1951, 1972
NatWest Trophy/Gillette Cup Winners: (4) 1966, 1968, 1989, 1993
Benson and Hedges Cup Winners: (0) Finalists 1984
Sunday League Champions: (1) 1980
Match Awards: NWT 49; BHC 44

General Secretary: D.L.Amiss, County Ground, Edgbaston, Birmingham, B5 7QU (☎ 021-446 4422)
Captain: D.A.Reeve
Scorer: A.E.Davis
1994 Beneficiary: Asif Din

ASIF DIN, Mohamed (Ladywood CS, Birmingham), b Kampala, Uganda 21 Sep 1960. 5'9½". RHB, LB. Debut 1981. Cap 1987. Benefit 1994. MCC YC. Tours (Wa): SA 1991-92, 1992-93. 1000 runs (2); most – 1425 (1988). HS 158* v CU (Cambridge) 1988. BAC HS 140 v Leics (Leicester) 1991. BB 5-61 v Boland (Brackenfell) 1992-93. BAC BB 5-100 v Glam (Birmingham) 1982. Awards: NWT 3; BHC 1. **NWT:** HS 104 v Sussex (Lord's) 1993. BB 5-40 v Herts (St Albans) 1990. **BHC:** HS 137 v Somerset (Birmingham) 1991. BB 1-26. **SL:** HS 132* v Hants (Southampton) 1993. BB 1-11.

BELL, Michael Anthony Vincent (Bishop Milner CS; Dudley TC), b Birmingham 19 Dec 1966. 6'2". RHB, LMF. Debut 1992. MCC YC. HS 22* and BB 7-48 v Glos (Birmingham) 1993. **SL:** HS 6*. BB 5-21 v Notts (Nottingham) 1993.

BROWN, Douglas Robert (Alloa Academy; W London IHE), b Stirling, Scotland 29 Oct 1969. 6'2". RHB, RFM. Debut for Scotland 1989. Warwickshire debut v Boland (Brackenfell) 1991-92. Tour: SA 1991-92 (Wa). HS 44* Scot v Ire (Dublin) 1989. Wa HS 5*. BB 3-27 v CU (Cambridge) 1992. Awaiting BAC debut. **BHC:** HS 24 Scot v Notts (Glasgow) 1990. BB 3-50 Scot v Northants (Northampton) 1990. **SL:** HS 14 v Middx (Lord's) 1990. BB 3-21 v Hants (Birmingham) 1992.

BURNS, Michael (Walney CS), b Barrow-in-Furness, Lancs 6 Jun 1969. 6'0". RHB, WK, occ RM. Cumberland 1988-90. Debut 1992. HS 78 v CU (Cambridge) 1992. BAC HS 22 v Sussex (Birmingham) 1993. **BHC:** HS 22 v Leics (Leicester) 1993. **SL:** HS 26 v Notts (Nottingham) 1993.

GILES, Ashley Fraser (George Abbot S, Guildford), b Chertsey, Surrey 19 Mar 1973. 6'3". RHB, SLA. Debut 1993. HS 23 v Kent (Canterbury) 1993. BB 1-27.

KHAN, Wasim Gulzar (Small Heath CS; Josiah Mason SFC, Erdington), b Birmingham 26 Feb 1971. 6'1". LHB, LB. Warwickshire staff 1991 – awaiting f-c debut. **SL:** HS 7.

MOLES, Andrew James (Finham Park CS; Butts CHE), b Solihull 12 Feb 1961. 5'10". RHB, RM. Debut 1986. Cap 1987. GW 1986-87/1988-89. Tours (Wa): SA 1991-92, 1992-93. 1000 runs (6); most – 1854 (1990). HS 230* GW v N Transvaal B (Verwoerdburg) 1988-89. Wa HS 224* v Glam (Swansea) 1990. BB 3-21 v OU (Oxford) 1987. BAC BB 3-50 v Essex (Chelmsford) 1987. Awards: NWT 1; BHC 1. **NWT:** HS 127 v Bucks (Birmingham) 1987. **BHC:** HS 72 v Scot (Perth) 1987. BB 1-11. **SL:** HS 96* v Glam (Birmingham) 1992. BB 2-24 v Worcs (Worcester) 1987.

MULRAINE, Charles Edward (Warwick S), b Leamington Spa 24 Dec 1973. 5'7". LHB, SLA. Warwickshire staff 1993 – awaiting f-c debut.

141

MUNTON, Timothy Alan (Sarson HS; King Edward VII Upper S), b Melton Mowbray, Leics 30 Jul 1965. 6'5". RHB, RMF. Debut 1985. Cap 1989. **Tests:** 2 (1992); HS 25* v P (Manchester) 1992; BB 2-22 v P (Leeds) 1992. Tours: SA 1992-93 (Wa); WI 1991-92 (Eng A); P 1990-91 (Eng A); SL 1990-91 (Eng A). HS 47 v Kent (Birmingham) 1992. 50 wkts (4); most – 78 (1990). BB 8-89 (11-128 match) v Middx (Birmingham) 1991. **NWT:** HS 5. BB 3-36 v Kent (Canterbury) 1989. **BHC:** HS 13 v Leics (Leicester) 1989. BB 4-35 v Surrey (Oval) 1991. **SL:** HS 13 v Kent (Canterbury) 1993. BB 5-23 v Glos (Moreton) 1990.

OSTLER, Dominic Piers (Princethorpe C; Solihull TC), b Solihull 15 Jul 1970. 6'3". RHB, RM. Debut 1990. Cap 1991. Tour: SA 1992-93 (Wa). 1000 runs (3); most – 1284 (1991). HS 192 v Surrey (Guildford) 1992. Awards: NWT 2. **NWT:** HS 104 and BB 1-4 v Norfolk (Lakenham) 1993. **BHC:** HS 65* v Somerset (Taunton) 1992. **SL:** HS 83 v Middx (Birmingham) 1993.

PENNEY, Trevor Lionel (Prince Edward S, Salisbury), b Salisbury, Rhodesia 12 Jun 1968. 6'0". RHB, RM. Qualified for England 1992. Debut for Boland 1991-92. Warwickshire debut v Boland (Brackenfell) 1991-92. UK debut v Cambridge U (Cambridge) scoring 102*. Tours (Wa): SA 1991-92, 1992-93. HS 151 v Middx (Lord's) 1992. **NWT:** HS 14 v Norfolk (Lakenham) 1993. **BHC:** HS 22 v Leics (Leicester) 1993. **SL:** HS 83* v Kent (Canterbury) 1993.

PIPER, Keith John (Haringey Cricket C), b Leicester 18 Dec 1969. 5'6". RHB, WK. Debut 1989. Cap 1992. Tours (Wa): SA 1991-92, 1992-93. HS 111 v Somerset (Birmingham) 1990. BB 1-57. **NWT:** HS 12 v Northants (Birmingham) 1992. **BHC:** HS 11* v Surrey (Oval) 1991. **SL:** HS 30 v Lancs (Manchester) 1990.

RATCLIFFE, Jason David (Sharman's Cross SS; Solihull SFC), b Solihull 19 Jun 1969. Son of D.P. (Warwks 1957-68). 6'4". RHB, RM. Debut 1988. Tours (Wa): SA 1991-92, 1992-93. HS 127* v CU (Cambridge) 1989. BAC HS 101 v Sussex (Birmingham) 1993. BB 1-6. Awards: NWT 2. **NWT:** HS 105 v Yorks (Leeds) 1993. **BHC:** HS 29 v Surrey (Oval) 1991. **SL:** HS 37 v Somerset (Birmingham) 1989. BB 2-11 v Glam (Neath) 1993.

REEVE, Dermot Alexander (King George V S, Kowloon), b Kowloon, Hong Kong 2 Apr 1963. 6'0". RHB, RMF. Sussex 1983-87 (cap 1986). Warwickshire debut 1988. Cap 1989. Captain 1993- . Hong Kong 1982 (ICC Trophy). MCC YC. **Tests:** 3 (1991-92); HS 59 v NZ (Christchurch) 1991-92 (on debut); BB 1-4. LOI: 24 (HS 33*; BB 3-20). Tours: SA 1992-93 (Wa – captain); NZ 1991-92; I 1992-93. 1000 runs (2); most – 1412 (1990). HS 202* v Northants (Northampton) 1990. 50 wkts (2); most – 55 (1984). BB 7-37 Sx v Lancs (Lytham) 1987. Wa BB 6-73 v Kent (Tunbridge W) 1991. Awards: NWT 4; BHC 1. **NWT:** HS 81* v Sussex (Lord's) 1991. BB 4-20 Sx v Lancs (Lord's) 1986. **BHC:** HS 80 v Essex (Birmingham) 1991. BB 4-42 Sx v Kent (Canterbury) 1987. **SL:** HS 100 v Lancs (Birmingham) 1991. BB 5-23 v Essex (Birmingham) 1988.

SMALL, Gladstone Cleophas (Moseley S; Hall Green TC), b St George, Barbados 18 Oct 1961. 5'11". RHB, RFM. Debut 1979-80 (DHR XI in NZ). Warwickshire debut 1980. Cap 1982. Benefit 1992. S Australia 1985-86. **Tests:** 17 (1986 to 1990); HS 59 v A (Oval) 1989; BB 5-48 v A (Melbourne) 1986-87. LOI: 53 (HS 18*; BB 4-31). Tours: A 1986-87, 1990-91; SA 1992-93 (Wa); WI 1990-91; NZ 1979-80 (DHR); P 1981-82 (Int). HS 70 v Lancs (Manchester) 1988. 50 wkts (6); most – 80 (1988). BB 7-15 v Notts (Birmingham) 1988. Award: NWT 1. **NWT:** HS 33 v Surrey (Lord's) 1982. BB 3-22 v Glam (Cardiff) 1982. **BHC:** HS 22 v Kent (Canterbury) 1990. BB 4-22 v Glam (Birmingham) 1990. **SL:** HS 40* v Essex (Ilford) 1984. BB 5-29 v Surrey (Birmingham) 1980.

SMITH, Neil Michael Knight (Warwick S), b Birmingham 27 Jul 1967. Son of M.J.K. (Leics, Warwks and England 1951-75). 6'0". RHB, OB. Debut 1987. Cap 1993. MCC YC. Tour: SA 1991-92 (Wa). HS 161 v Yorks (Leeds) 1989. BB 6-122 v Kent (Canterbury) 1993. Award: BHC 1. **NWT:** HS 52 v Yorks (Leeds) 1990. BB 5-17 v Norfolk (Lakenham) 1993. **BHC:** HS 32 and BB 3-45 v Somerset (Taunton) 1992. **SL:** HS 54 v Glos (Birmingham) 1993. BB 5-26 v Lancs (Manchester) 1993.

SMITH, Paul Andrew (Heaton GS), b Jesmond, Northumb 15 Apr 1964. Son of K.D. sr (Leics 1950-51) and brother of K.D. jr (Warwks 1973-85). 6'2". RHB, RFM. Debut 1982. Cap 1986. Benefit 1995. MCC YC. Tour: SA 1991-92 (Wa). 1000 runs (2); most – 1508 (1986). HS 140 v Worcs (Worcester) 1989. BB 6-91 v Derbys (Birmingham) 1992. 2 hat-tricks: 1989, 1990. Awards: BHC 2. **NWT:** HS 79 v Durham (Birmingham) 1986. BB 4-37 v Yorks (Leeds) 1993. **BHC:** HS 74 v Northants (Birmingham) 1989. BB 3-28 v Middx (Lord's) 1991. **SL:** HS 93* v Middx (Birmingham) 1989. BB 5-36 v Worcs (Birmingham) 1993.

TWOSE, Roger Graham (King's C, Taunton), b Torquay, Devon 17 Apr 1968. Nephew of R.W.Tolchard (Leics and England 1965-83). 6'0". LHB, RM. Debut 1989. Cap 1992. N Districts 1989-90. C Districts 1991-92 to date. Devon 1988-89. MCC YC. Tours (Wa): SA 1991-92, 1992-93. 1000 runs (1): 1412 (1992). HS 233 v Leics (Birmingham) 1992. BB 6-63 v Middx (Coventry) 1992. Award: NWT 1. **NWT:** HS 107* v Staffs (Birmingham) 1992. BB 3-39 v Sussex (Birmingham) 1992. **BHC:** HS 62 v Yorks (Birmingham) 1992. **SL:** HS 100 v Leics (Birmingham) 1992. BB 3-31 v Durham (Darlington) 1993.

WELCH, Graeme (Hetton CS), b Durham 21 Mar 1972. 5'11½". RHB, RM. Warwickshire staff 1990 – awaiting f-c debut. **SL:** HS 3 v Durham (Birmingham) 1992. BB 1-24.

NEWCOMERS

ALTREE, Darren Anthony, b Rugby 30 Sep 1974. RHB, LFM.

DAVIS, Richard Peter (King Ethelbert's S, Birchington; Thanet TC), b Westbrook, Margate, Kent 18 Mar 1966. 6'3". RHB, SLA. Kent 1986-93 (cap 1990). Tour: Z 1992-93 (K). HS 67 K v Hants (Southampton) 1989. 50 wkts (2); most – 74 (1992). BB 7-64 K v Durham (Gateshead) 1992. Award: BHC 1. **NWT:** HS 22 K v Warwks (Birmingham) 1992. BB 3-19 K v Bucks (Canterbury) 1988. **BHC:** HS 18* K v Glam (Canterbury) 1993. BB 2-33 K v Sussex (Hove) 1988. **SL:** HS 40* K v Northants (Canterbury) 1991. BB 5-52 K v Somerset (Bath) 1989.

FROST, Tony, b Stoke-on-Trent, Staffs 17 Nov 1975. RHB, WK.

POWELL, Michael James (Lawrence Sheriff S, Rugby), b Bolton, Lancs 5 Apr 1975. 5'11". RHB, RM.

PRABHAKAR, Manoj (Delhi U), b Ghaziabad, India 15 Apr 1963. 5'8". RHB, RM. Delhi 1982-83 to date. **Tests** (I): 30 (1984-85 to 1993-94); HS 95 v NZ (Napier) 1989-90; BB 6-132 v P (Faisalabad) 1989-90. LOI (I): 94 (HS 106; BB 4-19). Tours (I): E 1986, 1990; A 1991-92; SA 1992-93; NZ 1989-90; P 1989-90; SL 1993-94; Z 1992-93. HS 229* and BB 6-36 Delhi v Himachal Pradesh (Delhi) 1988-89.

DEPARTURES

BOOTH, Paul Antony (Honley HS), b Huddersfield, Yorks 5 Sep 1965. 5'10". LHB, SLA. Yorkshire 1982-89. Warwickshire 1990-93. Tours (Wa): SA 1991-92, 1992-93. HS 62 v Somerset (Taunton) 1991. BB 5-98 Y v Lancs (Manchester) 1988. Wa BB 4-29 v Somerset (Taunton) 1992. **NWT:** HS 6*. **BHC:** HS 13* v Glam (Birmingham) 1990. BB 2-28 Y v Worcs (Bradford) 1985. **SL:** HS 5*. BB 1-33.

DEAN, Steven John (Cheadle HS), b Cosford, Staffs 16 Nov 1960. RHB. Staffordshire 1982-93 (cap 1986). No f-c appearances. **NWT:** HS 72 Staffs v Warwks (Burton) 1987. **BHC:** HS 46 Minor C v Leics (Stone) 1992. **SL:** HS 17 v Notts (Nottingham) 1993.

DONALD, Allan Anthony (Grey College HS), b Bloemfontein, SA 20 Oct 1966. 6'2". RHB, RF. OFS 1985-86 to date. Warwickshire debut 1987. Cap 1989. Wisden 1991. **Tests** (SA): 8 (1991-92 to 1993-94); HS 14* v I (Jo'burg) 1992-93; BB 7-84 (12-139 match) v I (Pt Eliz) 1992-93. LOI (SA): 30 (HS 5*; BB 5-29). Tours (SA): WI 1991-92; SL 1993-94. HS 46* OFS v W Province (Cape Town) 1990-91. Wa HS 41 v Notts (Birmingham) 1992. 50 wkts (3); most – 86 (1989). BB 8-37 OFS v Transvaal (Johannesburg) 1986-87. Wa BB 7-37 v Durham (Birmingham) 1992. Awards: NWT 3. **NWT:** HS 14* v Northants (Birmingham) 1992. BB 5-12 v Wilts (Birmingham) 1989. **BHC:** HS 23* v Leics (Leicester) 1989. BB 4-28 v Scot (Perth) 1987. **SL:** HS 18* v Middx (Lord's) 1988. BB 4-23 v Surrey (Oval) 1992. Not available 1994.

HOLLOWAY, P.C. – see SOMERSET.

WARWICKSHIRE 1993

RESULTS SUMMARY

	Place	Won	Lost	Drew	Abandoned
Britannic Assurance Championship	16th	4	8	5	
All First-class Matches		4	8	7	
Sunday League	11th	7	8		2
NatWest Trophy	Winners				
Benson and Hedges Cup	1st Round				

BRITANNIC ASSURANCE CHAMPIONSHIP AVERAGES

BATTING AND FIELDING

Cap		M	I	NO	HS	Runs	Avge	100	50	Ct/St
1987	A.J.Moles	17	32	3	117	1100	37.93	2	7	2
1989	D.A.Reeve	16	27	7	87*	742	37.10	–	5	22
–	T.L.Penney	15	27	5	135*	761	34.59	1	4	10
1991	D.P.Ostler	17	32	2	174	1024	34.13	1	6	17
1987	Asif Din	6	9	–	66	291	32.33	–	3	4
–	J.D.Ratcliffe	17	32	–	101	960	30.00	1	6	12
–	P.C.L.Holloway	2	4	1	44	68	22.66	–	–	6
1993	N.M.K.Smith	16	25	2	51*	420	18.26	–	1	2
–	P.A.Booth	6	11	3	49*	144	18.00	–	–	4
–	A.F.Giles	2	4	1	23	53	17.66	–	–	–
1986	P.A.Smith	9	15	–	55	253	16.86	–	1	2
1992	K.J.Piper	10	14	1	52	183	14.07	–	1	14
1992	R.G.Twose	9	16	–	37	184	11.50	–	–	1
–	M.Burns	5	9	–	22	89	9.88	–	–	9/1
1982	G.C.Small	12	18	3	39	140	9.33	–	–	5
–	M.A.V.Bell	8	12	5	22*	60	8.57	–	–	2
1989	A.A.Donald	9	11	3	19	63	7.87	–	–	7
1989	T.A.Munton	11	13	5	18	51	6.37	–	–	4

BOWLING

	O	M	R	W	Avge	Best	5wI	10wM
D.A.Reeve	261.1	103	473	20	23.65	3- 38	–	–
A.A.Donald	258.1	59	744	30	24.80	7- 98	2	1
M.A.V.Bell	207.1	52	627	25	25.08	7- 48	3	–
T.A.Munton	309.3	105	677	25	27.08	7- 41	1	–
G.C.Small	238.4	68	589	20	29.45	4- 39	–	–
P.A.Booth	163.5	44	380	11	34.54	2- 16	–	–
P.A.Smith	124.5	18	484	14	34.57	4- 35	–	–
N.M.K.Smith	562.2	143	1522	44	34.59	6-122	3	–

Also bowled: Asif Din 4-1-12-0; M.Burns 7-4-8-0; A.F.Giles 41.3-6-128-3; A.J.Moles 14-2-97-4; D.P Ostler 6-1-16-0; T.L Penney 2.1-0-13-0; J.D.Ratcliffe 18.3-3-106-2; R.G.Twose 88.2-13-241-8.

The First-Class Averages (pp 164-177) give the records of Warwickshire players in all first-class county matches (their other opponents being the Australians and Oxford U).

WARWICKSHIRE RECORDS

FIRST-CLASS CRICKET

Highest Total	For 657-6d		v Hampshire	Birmingham	1899
	V 887		by Yorkshire	Birmingham	1896
Lowest Total	For 16		v Kent	Tonbridge	1913
	V 15		by Hampshire	Birmingham	1922
Highest Innings	For 305*	F.R.Foster	v Worcs	Dudley	1914
	V 322	I.V.A.Richards	for Somerset	Taunton	1985

Highest Partnership for each Wicket

1st	377*	N.F.Horner/K.Ibadulla	v Surrey	The Oval	1960
2nd	465*	J.A.Jameson/R.B.Kanhai	v Glos	Birmingham	1974
3rd	327	S.P.Kinneir/W.G.Quaife	v Lancashire	Birmingham	1901
4th	470	A.I.Kallicharran/G.W.Humpage	v Lancashire	Southport	1982
5th	268	W.Quaife/W.G.Quaife	v Essex	Leyton	1900
6th	220	H.E.Dollery/J.Buckingham	v Derbyshire	Derby	1938
7th	250	H.E.Dollery/J.S.Ord	v Kent	Maidstone	1953
8th	228	A.J.W.Croom/R.E.S.Wyatt	v Worcs	Dudley	1925
9th	154	G.W.Stephens/A.J.W.Croom	v Derbyshire	Birmingham	1925
10th	128	F.R.Santall/W.Sanders	v Yorkshire	Birmingham	1930

Best Bowling	For 10-41	J.D.Bannister	v Comb Servs	Birmingham	1959
(Innings)	V 10-36	H.Verity	for Yorkshire	Leeds	1931
Best Bowling	For 15-76	S.Hargreave	v Surrey	The Oval	1903
(Match)	V 17-92	A.P.Freeman	for Kent	Folkestone	1932

Most Runs – Season	2417 M.J.K.Smith	(av 60.42)	1959
Most Runs – Career	35146 D.L.Amiss	(av 41.64)	1960-87
Most 100s – Season	9 A.I.Kallicharran		1984
Most 100s – Career	78 D.L.Amiss		1960-87
Most Wkts – Season	180 W.E.Hollies	(av 15.13)	1946
Most Wkts – Career	2201 W.E.Hollies	(av 20.45)	1932-57

LIMITED-OVERS CRICKET

Highest Total	NWT	392-5		v Oxfordshire	Birmingham	1984
	BHC	308-4		v Scotland	Birmingham	1988
	SL	301-6		v Essex	Colchester	1982
Lowest Total	NWT	109		v Kent	Canterbury	1971
	BHC	96		v Leics	Leicester	1972
	SL	65		v Kent	Maidstone	1979
Highest Innings	NWT	206	A.I.Kallicharran	v Oxfordshire	Birmingham	1984
	BHC	137*	T.A.Lloyd	v Lancashire	Birmingham	1985
	SL	132*	Asif Din	v Hampshire	Southampton	1993
Best Bowling	NWT	6-32	K.Ibadulla	v Hampshire	Birmingham	1965
		6-32	A.I.Kallicharran	v Oxfordshire	Birmingham	1984
	BHC	7-32	R.G.D.Willis	v Yorkshire	Birmingham	1981
	SL	6-20	N.Gifford	v Northants	Birmingham	1985

145

WORCESTERSHIRE

Formation of Present Club: 11 March 1865
Colours: Dark Green and Black
Badge: Shield Argent a Fess between three Pears Sable
Championships: (5) 1964, 1965, 1974, 1988, 1989
NatWest Trophy/Gillette Cup Winners: (0) Finalists 1963, 1966, 1988
Benson and Hedges Cup Winners: (1) 1991
Sunday League Champions: (3) 1971, 1987, 1988
Match Awards: NWT 37; BHC 55

Secretary: Revd M.D.Vockins, County Ground, New Road, Worcester, WR2 4QQ (☎ 0905-422694)
Captain: T.S.Curtis
Scorer: J.W.Sewter
1994 Beneficiary: T.S.Curtis

BRINKLEY, James Edward (Marist C, Canberra; Trinity C, Perth), b Helensburgh, Scotland 13 Mar 1974. 6'3". RHB, RFM. Worcestershire staff 1993 – awaiting f-c debut.

CURTIS, Timothy Stephen (Worcester RGS; Durham U; Magdalene C, Cambridge), b Chislehurst, Kent 15 Jan 1960. 5'11". RHB, LB. Debut 1979. Cap 1984. Captain 1992-. Benefit 1994. Cambridge U 1983 (blue). **Tests:** 5 (1988 to 1989), HS 41 v A (Birmingham) 1989. Tour: Z 1990-91 (Wo). 1000 runs (10); most – 1829 (1992). HS 248 v Somerset (Worcester) 1991. BB 2-17 v OU (Oxford) 1991. BAC BB 2-72 v Warwks 1987 and v Derbys 1992. Awards: NWT 6; BHC 2. **NWT:** HS 120 v Notts (Nottingham) 1988. BB 1-6. **BHC:** HS 97 v Warwks (Birmingham) 1990. **SL:** HS 124 v Somerset (Taunton) 1990.

D'OLIVEIRA, Damian Basil (Blessed Edward Oldcorne SS), b Cape Town, SA 19 Oct 1960. Son of B.L. (Worcs and England 1964-80) 5'9". RHB, OB. Debut 1982. Cap 1985. Joint benefit 1993. MCC YC. Tours: Z 1984-85 (EC), 1990-91 (Wo). 1000 runs (4); most – 1263 (1990). HS 237 v OU (Oxford) 1991. BAC HS 155 v Lancs (Manchester) 1990. BB 3-36 v Essex (Chelmsford) 1993. Awards: NWT 2; BHC 2. **NWT:** HS 99 v Oxon (Worcester) 1986. BB 2-17 v Suffolk (Bury St E) 1990. **BHC:** HS 66 v Yorks (Leeds) 1986. BB 3-12 v Scot (Glasgow) 1986. **SL:** HS 103 v Surrey (Worcester) 1985. BB 3-23 v Derbys (Derby) 1983.

EDWARDS, Timothy (Mounts Bay S), b Penzance, Cornwall 24 Jun 1974. 5'3". RHB, WK. Somerset staff 1991-92 (YTS trainee). Debut 1993. HS-.

EYERS, Christopher John (Worcester RGS, Staffordshire U), b Aylesbury, Bucks 28 Mar 1972. 6'1". RHB, RM. Worcestershire staff 1993 – awaiting f-c debut.

HAYNES, Gavin Richard (High Park S; King Edward VI S, Stourbridge), b Stourbridge 29 Sep 1969. 5'10". RHB, RM. Debut 1991. HS 158 and BB 2-29 v Kent (Worcester) 1993. **NWT:** HS 5. **BHC:** HS 19* v Somerset (Worcester) 1992. BB 2-22 v Glam (Cardiff) 1992. **SL:** HS 48 v Middx (Worcester) 1993. BB 2-21 v Warwks (Birmingham) 1993.

HICK, Graeme Ashley (Prince Edward HS, Salisbury), b Salisbury, Rhodesia 23 May 1966. 6'3". RHB, OB. Zimbabwe 1983-84/1985-86. Worcestershire debut 1984. Cap 1986. N Districts 1987-88/1988-89. Queensland 1990-91. Wisden 1986. **Tests:** 18 (1991 to 1993); HS 178 v I (Bombay) 1992-93; BB 4-126 v NZ (Wellington) 1991-92. LOI: 32 (HS 105*; BB 2-7). Tours: E 1985 (Z); NZ 1991-92; I 1992-93; SL 1983-84 (Z), 1992-93; Z 1990-91 (Wo). 1000 runs (9+1) inc 2000 (3); most – 2713 (1988); youngest to score 2000 (1986). 1019 runs before June 1988. HS 405* (Worcs record and second highest in UK f-c matches) v Somerset (Taunton) 1988. BB 5-37 v Glos (Worcester) 1990. Awards: NWT 3; BHC 8. **NWT:** HS 172* v Devon (Worcester) 1987. BB 4-54 v Hants (Worcester) 1988. **BHC:** HS 109 v Comb Us (Worcester) 1989. BB 3-36 v Warwks (Birmingham) 1990. **SL:** HS 120* v Essex (Chelmsford) 1993. BB 4-42 v Sussex (Worcester) 1988.

ILLINGWORTH, Richard Keith (Salts GS), b Bradford, Yorks 23 Aug 1963. 5'11". RHB, SLA. Debut 1982. Cap 1986. Natal 1988-89. **Tests:** 2 (1991); HS 13 (twice) and BB 3-110 (including wicket of P.V.Simmons with first ball) v WI (Nottingham) 1991 – on debut. LOI: 18 (HS 14; BB 3-33). Tours: NZ 1991-92; P 1990-91 (Eng A); SL 1990-91 (Eng A); Z 1989-90 (Eng A), 1990-91 (Wo). HS 120* v Warwks (Worcester) 1987. 50 wkts (4); most – 75 (1990). BB 7-50 v OU (Oxford) 1985. BAC BB 6-28 v Glos (Gloucester) 1993. **NWT:** HS 22 v Northants (Northampton) 1984. BB 4-20 v Devon (Worcester) 1987. **BHC:** HS 36* v Kent (Worcester) 1990. BB 4-36 v Yorks (Bradford) 1985. **SL:** HS 30 v Leics (Worcester) 1993. BB 5-24 v Somerset (Worcester) 1983.

LAMPITT, Stuart Richard (Kingswinford S; Dudley TC), b Wolverhampton, Staffs 29 Jul 1966. 5'11". RHB, RMF. Debut 1985. Cap 1989. Tour: Z 1990-91 (Wo). HS 93 v Derbys (Kidderminster) 1991. 50 wkts (2); most – 58 (1990). BB 5-32 v Kent (Worcester) 1989. Awards: NWT 1; BHC 2. **NWT:** HS 17 v Glam (Swansea) 1993. BB 5-22 v Suffolk (Bury St E) 1990. **BHC:** HS 41 v Glam (Worcester) 1990. BB 4-46 v Glos (Worcester) 1991. **SL:** HS 41* v Leics (Worcester) 1993. BB 5-67 v Middx (Lord's) 1990.

LEATHERDALE, David Anthony (Pudsey Grangefield S), b Bradford, Yorks 26 Nov 1967. 5'10½". RHB, RM. Debut 1988. HS 157 v Somerset (Worcester) 1991. BB 1-12. **NWT:** HS 43 v Hants (Worcester) 1988. **BHC:** HS 14 (thrice in 1992). **SL:** HS 62* v Kent (Folkestone) 1988.

MOODY, Thomas Masson (Guildford GS, WA), b Adelaide, Australia 2 Oct 1965. 6'6½". RHB, RM. W Australia 1985-86 to date. Warwickshire 1990 (cap 1990). Worcestershire 1992 (cap 1991). **Tests:** 8 (1989-90 to 1992-93); HS 106 v SL (Brisbane) 1989-90; BB 1-17. LOI (A): 34 (HS 89; B-56). Tours (A): E 1989; I 1989-90 (WA); SL 1992-93. 1000 runs (2+1); most – 1887 (1991). HS 210 v Warwks (Worcester) 1991. BB 7-43 (10-109 match) WA v Victoria (Perth) 1990-91. BAC BB 4-50 v Warwks (Birmingham) 1992. Awards: BHC 5. **NWT:** HS 58 Wa v Herts (St Albans) 1990. BB 1-7. **BHC:** HS 110* v Derbys (Worcester) 1991. BB 4-59 v Somerset (Worcester) 1992. **SL:** HS 160 v Kent (Worcester) 1991 (on Wo 1st XI debut). BB 2-33 v Yorks (Worcester) 1992.

NEWPORT, Philip John (High Wycombe RGS; Portsmouth Poly), b High Wycombe, Bucks 11 Oct 1962. 6'3". RHB, RFM. Debut 1982. Cap 1986. Boland 1987-88. N Transvaal 1992-93. Buckinghamshire 1981-82. **Tests:** 3 (1988 to 1990-91); HS 40* v A (Perth) 1990-91. LOI (A): 4-87 v SL (Lord's) 1988 (on debut). Tours: A 1990-91 (part); P 1990-91 (Eng A); SL 1990-91 (Eng A). HS 98 v NZ (Worcester) 1990. BAC HS 96 v Essex (Worcester) 1990. 50 wkts (6); most – 93 (1988). BB 8-52 v Middx (Lord's) 1988. **NWT:** HS 25 v Northants (Northampton) 1984. BB 4-46 v Northants (Northampton) 1990. **BHC:** HS 28 v Kent (Worcester) 1990. BB 5-22 v Warwks (Birmingham) 1987. **SL:** HS 26* v Leics (Leicester) 1987 and v Surrey (Worcester) 1993. BB 4-18 v Glam (Worcester) 1989.

147

RADFORD, Neal Victor (Athlone BHS, Johannesburg), b Luanshya, N Rhodesia 7 Jun 1957. Brother of W.R. (OFS). 5'11". RHB, RFM. Transvaal 1978-79/1988-89. Lancashire 1980-84 Worcestershire debut/cap 1985. Wisden 1985. **Tests:** 3 (1986 to 1987-88); HS 12* v NZ (Lord's) 1986; BB 2-131 v I (Birmingham) 1986. LOI: 6 (HS 0*; BB 1-32). Tours: NZ 1987-88; Z 1990-91 (Wo). HS 76* La v Derbys (Blackpool) 1981. Wo HS 73* v Notts (Nottingham) 1992. 50 wkts (6) inc 100 (2); most – 109 (1987). BB 9-70 v Somerset (Worcester) 1986. Award: NWT 1. **NWT:** HS 37 v Essex (Chelmsford) 1987. BB 7-19 v Beds (Bedford) 1991. **BHC:** HS 40 v Glam (Worcester) 1990. BB 4-25 v Northants (Northampton) 1988. **SL:** HS 70 v Durham (Stockton) 1993. BB 5-32 v Warwks (Worcester) 1987.

RHODES, Steven John (Lapage Middle S; Carlton-Bolling S, Bradford), b Bradford, Yorks 17 Jun 1964. Son of W.E. (Notts 1961-64). 5'7". RHB, WK. Yorkshire 1981-84. Worcestershire debut 1985. Cap 1986. LOI: 3 (HS 8). Tours: WI 1991-92 (Eng A); SL 1985-86 (Eng B), 1990-91 (Eng A); Z 1989-90 (Eng A), 1990-91 (Wo). HS 116* v Warwks (Worcester) 1992. Award: BHC 1. **NWT:** HS 61 v Derbys (Worcester) 1989. **BHC:** HS 51* v Warwks (Birmingham) 1987. **SL:** HS 48* v Kent (Worcester) 1989.

SEYMOUR, Adam Charles Hylton (Millfield S), b Royston, Cambs 7 Dec 1967. 6'2". LHB, RM. Essex 1988-91. Worcestershire debut 1992. HS 157 Ex v Glam (Cardiff) 1991. Wo HS 113 v OU (Oxford) 1992 – on Wo debut. **NWT:** HS 0. **BHC:** HS 23 v Comb Us (Oxford) 1992. **SL:** HS 25 Ex v Lancs (Manchester) 1991.

SOLANKI, Vikram Singh (Regis S, Wolverhampton), b Udaipur, India 1 Apr 1976. 6'0". RHB, OB. Worcestershire staff 1993 – awaiting f-c debut. **SL:** HS 22 v Middx (Worcester) 1993.

SPIRING, Karl Ruben (Monmouth S), b Southport, Lancs 13 Nov 1974. 5'11". RHB, OB. Worcestershire staff 1993 – awaiting f-c debut. **SL:** HS 7.

TOLLEY, Christopher Mark (King Edward VI C, Stourbridge; Loughborough U), b Kidderminster 30 Dec 1967. 5'9". RHB, LMF. Debut 1989. Cap 1993. Tour: Z 1990-91 (Wo). HS 78 v Surrey (Worcester) 1993. BB 5-55 v Kent (Worcester) 1993. Award: BHC 1. **NWT:** HS 12* v Glam (Swansea) 1993. BB 3-25 v Derbys (Worcester) 1993. **BHC:** HS 77 Comb Us v Lancs (Cambridge) 1990. BB 1-12. **SL:** HS 5*. BB 4-50 v Hants (Portsmouth) 1993.

WESTON, William Philip Christopher (Durham S), b Durham 16 Jun 1973. Son of M.P. (Durham; England RFU). 6'3". LHB, LM. Debut 1991. HS 113 v OU (Worcester) 1993. BAC HS 109 v Derbys (Kidderminster) 1993. BB 2-39 v P (Worcester) 1992. BAC BB-. **NWT:** HS 31 v Scot (Edinburgh) 1993. **BHC:** HS 32* v Essex (Worcester) 1993. **SL:** HS 26 v Lancs (Worcester) 1993.

WYLIE, Alex (Bromsgrove S; Warwick C of Ag), b Tamworth, Staffs 20 Feb 1973. 6'2½". LHB, RF. Boland 1992-93. Worcestershire debut 1993. HS 0. BB 1-50.

NEWCOMERS

BROOKE, Matthew Peter (Bruntcliffe HS, Morley), b Morley, Yorks 14 Apr 1972. 6'2". RHB, RMF.

MIRZA, Parvaz (Small Heath S), b Birmingham 17 Dec 1970. 5'11". RHB, RM. Herefordshire 1992.

DEPARTURES – see p 157

WORCESTERSHIRE 1993

RESULTS SUMMARY

	Place	Won	Lost	Tied	Drew	Abandoned
Britannic Assurance Championship	2nd	9	4	1	3	
All First-class Matches		9	5	1	4	
Sunday League	16th	4	10	1		2
NatWest Trophy	Quarter-Finalist					
Benson and Hedges Cup	Quarter-Finalist					

BRITANNIC ASSURANCE CHAMPIONSHIP AVERAGES

BATTING AND FIELDING

Cap		M	I	NO	HS	Runs	Avge	100	50	Ct/St
1986	G.A.Hick	14	22	2	182	1074	53.70	3	5	22
1984	T.S.Curtis	17	28	2	127	1354	52.07	4	7	12
1986	S.J.Rhodes	17	26	3	101	848	36.86	2	2	39/6
1986	P.J.Newport	16	25	6	79*	623	32.78	–	6	7
–	G.R.Haynes	8	12	–	158	334	27.83	1	2	2
1986	R.K.Illingworth	16	22	8	109	376	26.85	1	1	7
–	W.P.C.Weston	11	17	1	109	383	23.93	1	–	3
1986	M.J.Weston	7	13	1	59	277	23.08	–	2	3
1993	C.M.Tolley	16	22	5	78	381	22.41	–	2	7
1985	D.B.D'Oliveira	13	21	–	94	464	22.09	–	3	10
–	D.A.Leatherdale	10	15	1	119*	303	21.64	1	1	17
–	A.C.H.Seymour	5	8	–	49	157	19.62	–	–	–
1989	S.R.Lampitt	14	22	1	58	344	16.38	–	1	18
1985	N.V.Radford	11	13	5	29	102	12.75	–	–	3
–	K.C.G.Benjamin	11	11	3	26	85	10.62	–	–	1

Also played (1 match): A.Wylie 0.

BOWLING

	O	M	R	W	Avge	Best	5wI	10wM
P.J.Newport	509	128	1337	56	23.87	6-63	1	–
K.C.G.Benjamin	283.5	42	911	37	24.62	6-70	2	–
R.K.Illingworth	574.1	200	1192	48	24.83	6-28	1	–
N.V.Radford	222.5	36	797	29	27.48	6-49	1	–
C.M.Tolley	395.5	102	1060	38	27.89	5-55	1	–
S.R.Lampitt	282	52	910	26	35.00	3- 9	–	–
G.A.Hick	172.4	52	518	10	51.80	2-15	–	–

Also bowled: T.S.Curtis 1-0-7-0; D.B.D'Oliveira 38-8-107-5; G.R.Haynes
76-17-200-5; M.J.Weston 29-9-96-2; W.P.C.Weston 2-0-2-0; A.Wylie 22-3-73-1.

The First-Class Averages (pp 164-177) give the records of Worcestershire players in
all first-class county matches (their other opponents being the Australians and
Oxford U), with the exception of:
G.A.Hick 15-24-2-187-1266-57.54-4-5-24ct. 178.4-52-551-10-55.10-2/15.

WORCESTERSHIRE RECORDS

FIRST-CLASS CRICKET

Highest Total	For	633		v Warwicks	Worcester	1906
	V	701-4d		by Leics	Worcester	1906
Lowest Total	For	24		v Yorkshire	Huddersfield	1903
	V	30		by Hampshire	Worcester	1903
Highest Innings	For	405*	G.A.Hick	v Somerset	Taunton	1988
	V	331*	J.D.B.Robertson	for Middlesex	Worcester	1949

Highest Partnership for each Wicket

1st	309	F.L.Bowley/H.K.Foster	v	Derbyshire	Derby	1901
2nd	287*	T.S.Curtis/G.A.Hick	v	Glamorgan	Neath	1986
3rd	314	M.J.Horton/T.W.Graveney	v	Somerset	Worcester	1962
4th	281	J.A.Ormrod/Younis Ahmed	v	Notts	Nottingham	1979
5th	393	E.G.Arnold/W.B.Burns	v	Warwicks	Birmingham	1909
6th	265	G.A.Hick/S.J.Rhodes	v	Somerset	Taunton	1988
7th	205	G.A.Hick/P.J.Newport	v	Yorkshire	Worcester	1988
8th	184	S.J.Rhodes/S.R.Lampitt	v	Derbyshire	Kidderminster	1991
9th	181	J.A.Cuffe/R.D.Burrows	v	Glos	Worcester	1907
10th	119	W.B.Burns/G.A.Wilson	v	Somerset	Worcester	1906

Best Bowling	For	9- 23	C.F.Root	v Lancashire	Worcester	1931
(Innings)	V	10- 51	J.Mercer	for Glamorgan	Worcester	1936
Best Bowling	For	15- 87	A.J.Conway	v Glos	Moreton-in-M	1914
(Match)	V	17-212	J.C.Clay	for Glamorgan	Swansea	1937

Most Runs – Season	2654	H.H.I.Gibbons	(av 52.03)		1934
Most Runs – Career	33490	D.Kenyon	(av 33.19)		1946-67
Most 100s – Season	10	G.M.Turner			1970
	10	G.A.Hick			1988
Most 100s – Career	72	G.M.Turner			1967-82
Most Wkts – Season	207	C.F.Root	(av 17.52)		1925
Most Wkts – Career	2143	R.T.D.Perks	(av 23.73)		1930-55

LIMITED-OVERS CRICKET

Highest Total	NWT	404-3		v Devon	Worcester	1987
	BHC	314-5		v Lancashire	Manchester	1980
	SL	307-4		v Derbyshire	Worcester	1975
Lowest Total	NWT	98		v Durham	Chester-le-St	1968
	BHC	81		v Leics	Worcester	1983
	SL	86		v Yorkshire	Leeds	1969
Highest Innings	NWT	172*	G.A.Hick	v Devon	Worcester	1987
	BHC	143*	G.M.Turner	v Warwicks	Birmingham	1976
	SL	160	T.M.Moody	v Kent	Worcester	1991
Best Bowling	NWT	7-19	N.V.Radford	v Beds	Bedford	1991
	BHC	6- 8	N.Gifford	v Minor C (S)	High Wycombe	1979
	SL	6-26	A.P.Pridgeon	v Surrey	Worcester	1978

YORKSHIRE

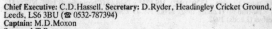

Formation of Present Club: 8 January 1863
Substantial Reorganisation: 10 December 1891
Colours: Dark Blue, Light Blue and Gold
Badge: White Rose
Championships (since 1890): (29) 1893, 1896, 1898, 1900, 1901, 1902, 1905, 1908, 1912, 1919, 1922, 1923, 1924, 1925, 1931, 1932, 1933, 1935, 1937, 1938, 1939, 1946, 1959, 1960, 1962, 1963, 1966, 1967, 1968. **Joint:** (1) 1949
NatWest Trophy/Gillette Cup Winners: (2) 1965, 1969
Benson and Hedges Cup Winners: (1) 1987
Sunday League Champions: (1) 1983
Match Awards: NWT 26; BHC 55

Chief Executive: C.D.Hassell. **Secretary:** D.Ryder, Headingley Cricket Ground, Leeds, LS6 3BU (☎ 0532-787394)
Captain: M.D.Moxon
Scorer: J.T.Potter
1994 Beneficiary: P.Carrick (testimonial)

BATTY, Jeremy David (Bingley GS; Horsforth C), b Bradford 15 May 1971. 6'1". RHB, OB. Debut 1989. Tours (Y): SA 1991-92, 1992-93. HS 51 v SL (Leeds) 1991. BAC HS 50 v Notts (Nottingham) 1993. BB 6-48 v Notts (Worksop) 1991. **NWT:** HS 4. BB 1-17. **BHC:** HS 2*. BB 1-34. **SL:** HS 13* and BB 4-33 v Kent (Scarborough) 1991.

BLAKEY, Richard John (Rastrick GS), b Huddersfield 15 Jan 1967. 5'9". RHB, WK. Debut 1985. Cap 1987. YC 1987. Tests: 2 (1992-93); HS 6. LOI: 3 (HS 25). Tours: SA 1991-92 (Y); WI 1986-87 (Y); I 1992-93; P 1990-91 (Eng A); SL 1990-91 (Eng A); Z 1989-90 (Eng A). 1000 runs (4); most – 1361 (1987). HS 221 Eng A v Z (Bulawayo) 1989-90. Y HS 204* v Glos (Leeds) 1987. BB 1-68. Awards: BHC 2. **NWT:** HS 75 v Warwks (Leeds) 1993. **BHC:** HS 79 v Surrey (Oval) 1990. **SL:** HS 130* v Kent (Scarborough) 1991.

BROADHURST, Mark (Kingstone S, Barnsley), b Worsborough Common, Barnsley 20 Jun 1974. 6'0". RHB, RFM. Debut 1991. Tour: SA 1992-93 (Y). Awaiting BAC debut. HS 1. BB 3-61 v OU (Oxford) 1991. **SL:** HS-.

BYAS, David (Scarborough C), b Kilham 26 Aug 1963. 6'4". LHB, RM. Debut 1986. Cap 1991. Tours (Y): SA 1991-92, 1992-93. 1000 runs (2); most – 1557 (1991). HS 156 v Essex (Chelmsford) 1993. BB 3-55 v Derbys (Chesterfield) 1990. **NWT:** HS 54 v Scot (Leeds) 1993. BB 1-23. **BHC:** HS 92 v Hants (Leeds) 1991. BB 2-38 v Somerset (Leeds) 1989. **SL:** HS 106* v Derbys (Chesterfield) 1993. BB 3-19 v Notts (Leeds) 1989.

CHAPMAN, Colin Anthony (Beckfoot GS, Bingley; Bradford & Ilkley Art C), b Bradford 8 Jun 1971. 5'8½". RHB, WK. Debut 1990. Tour: SA 1992-93 (Y). HS 20 v Middx (Uxbridge) 1990. **SL:** HS 36* v Middx (Scarborough) 1990.

FOSTER, Michael James (New C, Pontefract), b Leeds 17 Sep 1972. 6'1". RHB, RFM. Debut 1993. HS 6 and BB 3-39 v Hants (Southampton) 1993 (on debut). **SL:** HS 118 v Leics (Leicester) 1993. BB 1-20.

GOUGH, Darren (Priory CS, Lundwood), b Barnsley 18 Sep 1970. 5'11". RHB, RFM. Debut 1989. Cap 1993. Tours (Y): SA 1991-92, 1992-93. HS 72 v Northants (Northampton) 1991. 50 wkts (1): 57 (1993). BB 7-42 (10-96 match) v Somerset (Taunton) 1993. **NWT:** HS 16 and BB 3-31 v Warwks (Leeds) 1993. **BHC:** HS 7*. BB 2-29 v Somerset and v Kent 1992. **SL:** HS 72* v Leics (Leicester) 1991. BB 4-25 v Hants (Southampton) 1993.

GRAYSON, Adrian Paul (Bedale CS), b Ripon 31 Mar 1971. 6'1". RHB, SLA. Debut 1990. Tour: SA 1991-92 (Y). HS 64 v Lancs (Manchester) 1993. BB 1-3. **NWT:** HS 12 v Glos (Bristol) 1993. **BHC:** HS 22 v Warwks (Birmingham) 1992. **SL:** HS 36 v Surrey (Oval) 1993. BB 2-18 v Durham (Leeds) 1993.

HARTLEY, Peter John (Greenhead GS; Bradford C), b Keighley 18 Apr 1960. 6'0". RHB, RMF. Warwickshire 1982. Yorkshire debut 1985. Cap 1987. Tours (Y): SA 1991-92; WI 1986-87. HS 127* v Lancs (Manchester) 1988. 50 wkts (3); most – 56 (1992). BB 8-111 v Sussex (Hove) 1992. Awards: NWT 1; BHC 1. **NWT:** HS 52 and BB 5-46 v Hants (Southampton) 1990. **BHC:** HS 29* v Notts (Nottingham) 1986. BB 5-43 v Scot (Leeds) 1986. **SL:** HS 51 v Northants (Tring) 1990. BB 5-36 v Sussex (Scarborough) 1993.

KELLETT, Simon Andrew (Whitcliffe Mount S), b Mirfield 16 Oct 1967. 6'2". RHB. Debut 1989. Cap 1992. Wellington 1991-92. Tours (Y): SA 1991-92, 1992-93. 1000 runs (2); most – 1326 (1992). HS 125* v Derbys (Chesterfield) 1991. **NWT:** HS 38 v Northumb (Leeds) 1992. **BHC:** HS 45 v Surrey (Oval) 1990. **SL:** HS 118* v Derbys (Leeds) 1992.

KETTLEBOROUGH, Richard Allan (Worksop C), b Sheffield 15 Mar 1973. 6'0". LHB, RM. Yorkshire staff 1993 – awaiting f-c debut.

METCALFE, Ashley Anthony (Bradford GS; University C, London), b Horsforth 25 Dec 1963. 5'8". RHB, OB. Debut 1983 v Notts (Bradford), scoring 122. Cap 1986. YC 1986. OFS 1988-89. Tours (Y): SA 1991-92, 1992-93; WI 1986-87. 1000 runs (6) inc 2000 (1): 2047 (1990). HS 216* v Middx (Leeds) 1988. BB 2-18 v Warwks (Scarborough) 1987. Awards: NWT 2; BHC 5. **NWT:** HS 127* v Warwks (Leeds) 1990. BB 2-44 v Wilts (Trowbridge) 1987. **BHC:** HS 114 v Lancs (Manchester) 1991. **SL:** HS 116 v Middx (Lord's) 1991.

MILBURN, Stuart Mark (Upper Nidderdale HS), b Harrogate 29 Sep 1972. 6'1". RHB, RMF. Debut 1992. HS 5. BB 1-54.

MOXON, Martyn Douglas (Holgate GS, Barnsley), b Barnsley 4 May 1960. 6'0". RHB, RM. Debut 1981 v Essex (Leeds), scoring 5 and 116. Cap 1984. Captain 1990-. Benefit 1993. GW 1982-83/1983-84. Wisden 1992. Tests: 10 (1986 to 1989); HS 99 v NZ (Auckland) 1987-88. LOI: 8 (HS 70). Tours (C=captain): A 1987-88, 1992-93C (Eng A); SA 1992-93C (Y); WI 1986-87 (Y); NZ 1987-88; I 1984-85; SL 1984-85, 1985-86 (Eng B). 1000 runs (9); most – 1669 (1991). HS 218* v Sussex (Eastbourne) 1990. BB 3-24 v Hants (Southampton) 1989. Awards: NWT 4; BHC 7. **NWT:** HS 107* v Warwks (Leeds) 1990. BB 2-19 v Norfolk (Leeds) 1990. **BHC:** HS 141* v Glam (Cardiff) 1991. BB 5-31 v Warwks (Leeds) 1991. **SL:** HS 129* v Surrey (Oval) 1991. BB 3-29 v Sussex (Hove) 1990.

PARKER, Bradley (Bingley GS), b Mirfield 23 Jun 1970. 5'11". RHB, RM. Debut 1992. HS 30 v Kent (Canterbury) 1992. **SL:** HS 5.

RICHARDSON, Richard Benjamin ('Richie'), b Five Islands, Antigua 12 Jan 1962. RHB, RM. Leeward Is 1981-82/1991-92. Yorkshire debut/cap 1993. Tests (WI): 71 (1983-84 to 1992-93, 9 as captain); HS 194 v I (Georgetown) 1988-89. LOI (WI): 185 (HS 122; BB 1-4). Tours (WI): E 1984, 1988, 1990 (RW), 1991; A 1984-85, 1986-87, 1988-89, 1992-93 (captain); NZ 1986-87; I 1983-84, 1987-88; P 1986-87, 1990-91. 1000 runs (1+2); most – 1403 (1991). HS 194 (Tests). WI HS 112 v Warwicks (Birmingham) 1993. BB 5-40 Leeward Is v E (St John's) 1985-86 (his first f-c wkts). Y BB 1-5. **NWT:** HS 90 v Glos (Bristol) 1993. **BHC:** HS 52 v Northants (Leeds) 1993. **SL:** HS 103 v Notts (Nottingham) 1993.

ROBINSON, Mark Andrew (Hull GS), b Hull 23 Nov 1966. 6'3". RHB, RFM. Northamptonshire 1987-90 (cap 1990). Canterbury 1988-89. Yorkshire debut 1991. Cap 1992. Tours (Y): SA 1991-92, 1992-93. Failed to score in 12 successive f-c innings 1990 – world record. HS 19* Nh v Essex (Chelmsford) 1988. Y HS 16* v Essex (Chelmsford) 1993. 50 wkts (1): 50 (1992). BB 9-37 (12-124 match) v Northants (Harrogate) 1993. Award: BHC 1. **NWT:** HS 3*. BB 4-32 Nh v Somerset (Taunton) 1989. **BHC:** HS 3*. BB 3-20 Nh v Scot (Glasgow) 1989. **SL:** HS 6*. BB 4-23 v Northants (Leeds) 1993.

SILVERWOOD, Christopher Eric Wilfred (Garforth CS), b Pontefract 5 Mar 1975. 6'1". RHB, RFM. Debut 1993. HS 0. BB 1-19. **BHC:** HS 2. BB 1-19. **SL:** HS 0. BB 1-40.

STEMP, Richard David (Brittania HS, Rowley Regis), b Erdington, Birmingham 11 Dec 1967. 6'0". RHB, SLA. Worcestershire 1990-92. Yorkshire debut 1993. Tour: SA 1992-93 (Y). HS 37 v Essex (Chelmsford) 1993. BB 6-67 (11-146 match) Wo v Glos (Gloucester) 1992. Y BB 6-92 v Lancs (Leeds) 1993 (not BAC). **NWT:** HS 1*. **BHC:** HS-. **SL:** HS 23* v Warwks (Birmingham) 1993. BB 3-18 Wo v Derbys (Worcester) 1991.

VAUGHAN, Michael Paul (Silverdale CS, Sheffield), b Manchester, Lancs 29 Oct 1974. 6'2". RHB, OB. Debut 1993. HS 64 v Lancs (Manchester) 1993 (on debut). BB 1-23. **SL:** HS 11 v Leics (Leicester) 1993.

WHITE, Craig (Flora Hill HS, Bendigo, Australia; Bendigo HS), b Morley Hall 16 Dec 1969. 6'0". RHB, OB. Debut 1990. Cap 1993. Victoria 1990-91. Tours (Y): SA 1991-92, 1992-93. HS 146 v Durham (Leeds) 1993. BB 5-74 v Surrey (Harrogate) 1990. **NWT:** HS 46 and BB 2-41 v Warwks (Leeds) 1993. **BHC:** HS 26 v Notts (Leeds) 1992. BB 2-30 v Northants (Leeds) 1993. **SL:** HS 63 v Surrey (Scarborough) 1992. BB 3-52 v Leics (Leicester) 1993.

NEWCOMERS

KEEDY, Gary (Garforth CS), b Wakefield 27 Nov 1974. 6'0". LHB, SLA.

McGRATH, Anthony (Yorkshire Martyrs Collegiate S), b Bradford 6 Oct 1975. 6'2". RHB, OB.

DEPARTURES

CARRICK, Phillip (Bramley SS; Intake SS; Park Lane CPE), b Armley 16 Jul 1952. 5'11½". RHB, SLA. Yorkshire 1970-93 (cap 1976; captain 1987-89; benefit 1985; testimonial 1994). E Province 1976-77. N Transvaal 1982-83. Tours: SA 1975-76 (DHR), 1991-92 (Y); WI 1986-87 (Y – captain); SL 1977-78 (DHR). HS 131* v Northants (Northampton) 1980. 50 wkts (11): most – 79 (1975). BB 8-33 v CU (Cambridge) 1973. BAC BB 8-72 v Derbys (Scarborough) 1975. Awards: NWT 1; BHC 1. **NWT:** HS 54 v Sussex (Leeds) 1986. BB 3-8 v Norfolk (Leeds) 1990. **BHC:** HS 53 v Warwks (Leeds) 1985. BB 3-22 v Warwks (Leeds) 1991. **SL:** HS 48* v Worcs (Scarborough) 1989. BB 5-22 v Glam (Leeds) 1991.

JARVIS, P.W. – see SUSSEX.

YORKSHIRE 1993

RESULTS SUMMARY

	Place	Won	Lost	Drew	Abandoned
Britannic Assurance Championship	12th	5	4	8	
All First-class Matches		6	4	9	
Sunday League	9th	8	8		1
NatWest Trophy	Quarter-Finalist				
Benson and Hedges Cup	1st Round				

BRITANNIC ASSURANCE CHAMPIONSHIP AVERAGES

BATTING AND FIELDING

Cap		M	I	NO	HS	Runs	Avge	100	50	Ct/St
1984	M.D.Moxon	16	27	2	171*	1081	43.24	1	8	8
1993	C.White	17	28	6	146	816	37.09	1	4	12
1993	R.B.Richardson	14	23	1	112	759	34.50	1	6	9
1991	D.Byas	17	30	3	156	891	33.00	1	8	15
–	M.P.Vaughan	2	4	–	64	118	29.50	–	1	–
1992	S.A.Kellett	3	6	–	85	167	27.83	–	2	3
1987	P.J.Hartley	13	21	6	102	400	26.66	1	1	3
1987	R.J.Blakey	17	28	–	74	712	25.42	–	4	38/3
1986	A.A.Metcalfe	8	13	–	76	320	24.61	–	3	2
–	A.P.Grayson	10	17	–	64	386	22.70	–	2	6
1986	P.W.Jarvis	8	12	1	76	189	17.18	–	1	1
–	R.D.Stemp	15	21	6	37	254	16.93	–	–	11
–	J.D.Batty	13	17	2	50	208	13.86	–	1	6
1993	D.Gough	14	21	3	39	227	12.61	–	–	2
1992	M.A.Robinson	16	20	8	16*	43	3.58	–	–	–

Also played: P.Carrick (2 matches – cap 1976) 15, 0, 14*; M.J.Foster (1 match) 6 (1 ct); C.E.W.Silverwood (1 match) 0 (1 ct).

BOWLING

	O	M	R	W	Avge	Best	5wI	10wM
C.White	120	35	292	12	24.33	3- 9	–	–
D.Gough	458.5	96	1416	55	25.74	7-42	3	1
M.A.Robinson	500	127	1324	48	27.58	9-37	3	1
P.J.Hartley	351.4	91	1027	37	27.75	5-51	1	–
P.W.Jarvis	238.1	56	644	23	28.00	4-51	–	–
R.D.Stemp	472.3	165	1060	31	34.19	5-89	1	–
J.D.Batty	302.2	78	861	20	43.05	4-27	–	–

Also bowled: P.Carrick 60-24-108-2; M.J.Foster 17-3-50-3; A.P.Grayson 5-3-7-0; R.B.Richardson 7-0-23-1; C.E.W.Silverwood 20-3-75-1; M.P.Vaughan 13-4-42-1.

The First-Class Averages (pp 164-177) give the records of Yorkshire players in all first-class county matches (their other opponents being Lancashire in a non-Championship match and Cambridge U), with the exception of:
M.D.Moxon 18-31-2-171*-1251-43.13-1-9-9ct. 4-2-7-0.

YORKSHIRE RECORDS

FIRST-CLASS CRICKET

Highest Total	For 887		v Warwicks	Birmingham	1896
	V 630		by Somerset	Leeds	1901
Lowest Total	For 23		v Hampshire	Middlesbrough	1965
	V 13		by Notts	Nottingham	1901
Highest Innings	For 341	G.H.Hirst	v Leics	Leicester	1905
	V 318*	W.G.Grace	for Glos	Cheltenham	1876

Highest Partnerships for each Wicket

1st	555	P.Holmes/H.Sutcliffe	v Essex	Leyton	1932
2nd	346	W.Barber/M.Leyland	v Middlesex	Sheffield	1932
3rd	323*	H.Sutcliffe/M.Leyland	v Glamorgan	Huddersfield	1928
4th	312	D.Denton/G.H.Hirst	v Hampshire	Southampton	1914
5th	340	E.Wainwright/G.H.Hirst	v Surrey	The Oval	1899
6th	276	M.Leyland/E.Robinson	v Glamorgan	Swansea	1926
7th	254	W.Rhodes/D.C.F.Burton	v Hampshire	Dewsbury	1919
8th	292	R.Peel/Lord Hawke	v Warwicks	Birmingham	1896
9th	192	G.H.Hirst/S.Haigh	v Surrey	Bradford	1898
10th	149	G.Boycott/G.B.Stevenson	v Warwicks	Birmingham	1982

Best Bowling (Innings)	For 10-10	H.Verity	v Notts	Leeds	1932
	V 10-37	C.V.Grimmett	for Australians	Sheffield	1930
Best Bowling (Match)	For 17-91	H.Verity	v Essex	Leyton	1933
	V 17-91	H.Dean	for Lancashire	Liverpool	1913

Most Runs – Season	2883	H.Sutcliffe	(av 80.08)	1932
Most Runs – Career	38561	H.Sutcliffe	(av 50.20)	1919-45
Most 100s – Season	12	H.Sutcliffe		1932
Most 100s – Career	112	H.Sutcliffe		1919-45
Most Wkts – Season	240	W.Rhodes	(av 12.72)	1900
Most Wkts – Career	3608	W.Rhodes	(av 16.00)	1898-1930

LIMITED-OVERS CRICKET

Highest Total	NWT	317-4		v Surrey	Lord's	1965
	BHC	317-5		v Scotland	Leeds	1986
	SL	318-7		v Leics	Leicester	1993
Lowest Total	NWT	76		v Surrey	Harrogate	1970
	BHC	111		v Notts	Nottingham	1989
	SL	74		v Warwicks	Birmingham	1972
Highest Innings	NWT	146	G.Boycott	v Surrey	Lord's	1965
	BHC	142	G.Boycott	v Worcs	Worcester	1980
	SL	130*	R.J.Blakey	v Kent	Scarborough	1991
Best Bowling	NWT	6-15	F.S.Trueman	v Somerset	Taunton	1965
	BHC	6-27	A.G.Nicholson	v Minor C (N)	Middlesbrough	1972
	SL	7-15	R.A.Hutton	v Worcs	Leeds	1969

FOSTER, Neil Alan (Philip Morant CS), b Colchester 6 May 1962. 6'3". RHB, RFM. Essex 1980-93 (cap 1983; benefit 1993). YC 1983. Wisden 1987. Transvaal 1991-92. **Tests:** 29 (1983 to 1993); HS 39 v P (Lahore) 1987-88 and v A (Manchester) 1989; BB 8-107 v P (Leeds) 1987. LOI: 48 (HS 24; BB 3-20). Tours: A 1986-87, 1987-88; SA 1989-90 (Eng XI); WI 1985-86; NZ 1983-84, 1987-88; I/SL 1984-85; P 1983-84, 1987-88. HS 107* v Sussex (Horsham) 1991. 50 wkts (9) inc 100 (2); most – 105 (1986). BB 8-99 v Lancs (Manchester) 1991. Awards: NWT 1; BHC 3. **NWT:** HS 26 v Worcs (Chelmsford) 1987. BB 4-9 v Northumb (Jesmond) 1987. **BHC:** HS 62 v Scot (Chelmsford) 1992. BB 5-32 v Surrey (Oval) 1985. **SL:** HS 57 v Northants (Northampton) 1991. BB 5-17 v Derbys (Derby) 1986.

PRINGLE, Derek Raymond (Felsted S; Fitzwilliam C, Cambridge), b Nairobi, Kenya 18 Sep 1958. Son of D.J. (East Africa). 6'4½". RHB, RMF. Essex 1978-93 (cap 1982; benefit 1992). Cambridge U 1979-82 (blue 1979-80-81; capt 1982). **Tests:** 30 (1982 to 1992); HS 63 v I (Lord's) 1986; BB 5-95 v WI (Leeds) 1988. LOI: 44 (HS 49*; BB 4-42). Tours: A 1982-83; NZ 1991-92; SL 1985-86 (Eng B); Z 1989-90 (Eng A). HS 128 v Kent (Chelmsford) 1988. 50 wkts (6); most – 94 (1989). BB 7-18 v Glam (Swansea) 1989. Awards: NWT 2; BHC 4. **NWT:** HS 80* v Wilts (Chelmsford) 1988. BB 5-12 v Oxon (Chelmsford) 1985. **BHC:** HS 77* v Scot (Glasgow) 1990. BB 5-35 v Lancs (Chelmsford) 1984. **SL:** HS 81* v Warwks (Birmingham) 1985. BB 5-41 v Glos (Southend) 1985.

SALIM MALIK (Government C, Lahore), b Lahore, Pakistan 16 Apr 1963. 5'9". RHB, RSM. Lahore 1978-79/1985-86. Habib Bank 1982-83 to date. Essex 1991-93 (cap 1991). **Tests** (P): 72 (1981-82 to 1992-93); HS 165 v E (Birmingham) 1992; BB 1-3. LOI (P): 170 (HS 102; BB 5-35). Tours (P): E 1982, 1987, 1992; A 1981-82, 1983-84, 1989-90, 1991-92; WI 1987-88; NZ 1984-85, 1988-89, 1992-93; I 1983-84, 1986-87; SL 1984-85 (P U-23), 1985-86. 1000 runs (2+1); most – 1972 (1991). HS 215 v Leics (Ilford) 1991. BB 5-19 Habib Bank v Karachi (Karachi) 1985-86. Ex BB 5-67 v Warwicks (Ilford) 1993. Awards: NWT 1; BHC 1. **NWT:** HS 74 and BB 4-25 v Suffolk (Bury St Edmunds) 1993. **BHC:** HS 90* v Surrey (Oval) 1991. BB 1-7. **SL:** HS 89 v Worcs (Ilford) 1991. BB 3-36 v Middx (Colchester) 1993.

MARSHALL, Malcolm Denzil (Parkinson CS, Barbados), b St Michael, Barbados 18 Apr 1958. 5'11". RHB, RF. Barbados 1977-78/1990-91 (capt 1987-88). Hampshire 1979-93 (cap 1981; benefit 1987). Natal 1992-93. Wisden 1982. **Tests** (WI): 81 (1978-79 to 1991); HS 92 v I (Kanpur) 1983-84; BB 7-22 v E (Manchester) 1988. LOI (WI): 136 (HS 66; BB 4-18). Tours (WI): E 1980, 1984, 1988, 1991; A 1979-80, 1981-82, 1984-85, 1988-89; NZ 1979-80, 1986-87; I 1978-79, 1983-84; P 1980-81, 1986-87, 1990-91; SL 1978-79; Z 1981-82 (Young WI). HS 117 v Yorks (Leeds) 1990. 50 wkts (8+5) inc 100 (2); most – 134 (1982). 2 hat-tricks: 1978-79 (Barbados), 1983 (4 wkts in 5 balls). BB 8-71 v Worcs (Southampton) 1982. Awards: NWT 1; BHC 1. **NWT:** HS 77 v Northants (Southampton) 1990. BB 4-15 v Kent (Canterbury) 1983. **BHC:** HS 34 v Essex (Chelmsford) 1987. BB 4-20 v Essex (Southampton) 1992. **SL:** HS 59 v Yorks (Southampton) 1993. BB 5-13 v Glam (Portsmouth) 1979.

SHINE, K.J. – see MIDDLESEX.

TURNER, Ian John (Cowplain SS; Southdown C), b Denmead 18 Jul 1968. 6'1". RHB, SLA. Hampshire 1989-93. HS 39* v Glam (Swansea) 1991. BB 5-81 v Essex (Chelmsford) 1992. **NWT:** HS-. BB 1-41. **SL:** HS 2. BB 3-58 v Somerset (Southampton) 1993.

WOOD, Julian Ross (Leighton Park S, Reading), b Winchester 21 Nov 1968. 5'8". LHB, RM. Hampshire 1989-93. MCC YC. HS 96 v Northants (Northampton) 1989. BB 1-5. Award: BHC 1. **NWT:** HS 3*. **BHC:** HS 70* v Minor C (Trowbridge) 1991. **SL:** HS 92* v Northants (Northampton) 1993.

COTTAM, Andrew Colin (Axminster SS), b Northampton 14 Jul 1973. Son of R.M.H. (Hants, Northants and England 1963-76). 6'1". RHB, SLA. Somerset 1992-93. Devon 1993. HS 31 Sm v Glos (Gloucester) 1992. BB 1-1. **NWT:** HS 2. BB 1-45. **BHC:** HS-. **SL:** HS-.

DAWOOD, Ismail (Batley GS), b Dewsbury, Yorks 23 Jul 1976. 5'8". RHB, WK.

HARRISON, Tom William (Oundle S; Manchester U), b Peterborough, Cambs 11 Dec 1972. 6'2". LHB, LFM.

LEWIS, Jonathan (Churchfields S, Swindon; Swindon C), b Aylesbury, Bucks 26 Aug 1975. 6'2". RHB, RFM. Wiltshire 1993.

ROBERTS, David James (Mullion CS), b Truro, Cornwall 29 Dec 1976. Cousin of C.K.Bullen (Surrey 1982-91). 5'11". RHB, RSM.

DEPARTURES

NOON, W.M. – see NOTTINGHAMSHIRE.

PEARSON, R.M. – no 1st XI appearances 1993 – see ESSEX.

STANLEY, Neil Alan (Bedford Modern S), b Bedford 16 May 1968. 6'2". RHB, RM. Northamptonshire 1988-93. Bedfordshire 1987. Tour: SA 1991-92 (Nh). HS 132 v Lancs (Lytham) 1991. **BHC:** HS 8. BB 1-3. **SL:** HS 18 v Warwks (Birmingham) 1988.

WALKER, A. – see DURHAM.

RANDALL, Derek William (Sir Frederick Milner SS), b Retford 24 Feb 1951. 5'9". RHB, RM. Nottinghamshire 1972-93 (cap 1973; benefit 1983; testimonial 1993). Wisden 1979. **Tests:** 47 (1976-77 to 1984); HS 174 v A (Melbourne) 1976-77. LOI: 49 (HS 88; BB 1-2). Tours: A 1976-77, 1978-79, 1979-80, 1982-83; SA 1975-76 (DHR); NZ 1977-78, 1983-84; I/SL 1976-77; P 1977-78, 1983-84; Z 1985-86 (Eng B). 1000 runs (13) inc 2000 (1): 2151 (1985). HS 237 v Derbys (Nottingham) 1988. BB 3-15 v MCC (Lord's) 1982. BAC BB 3-43 v Sussex (Hove) 1984. Awards: NWT 3; BHC 6. **NWT:** HS 149* v Devon (Torquay) 1988. **BHC:** HS 103* v Minor C(N) (Nottingham) 1979. **SL:** HS 123 v Yorks (Nottingham) 1987.

SAXELBY, M. – see DURHAM.

BENJAMIN, Kenneth Charlie Griffith (All Saints Secondary S), b St John's, Antigua 8 Apr 1967. RHB, RFM. Leeward Is 1988-89/1991-92. Worcestershire 1993. **Tests** (WI): 2 (1991-92 to 1992-93); HS 15 v A (Adelaide) 1992-93; BB 2-87 v SA (Bridgetown) 1991-92. LOI (WI): 6 (HS 17; BB 2-16). Tours (WI): A 1992-93; E 1992 (RW). HS 52* Leeward Is v Trinidad (Basseterre) 1991-92. Wo HS 26 v Northants (Northampton) 1993. BB 7-51 Leeward Is v Jamaica (Basseterre) 1990-91. Wo BB 6-70 v Somerset (Worcester) 1993. **NWT:** HS-. BB 2-38 v Derbys (Worcester) 1993. **BHC:** HS 2. BB 2-28 v Essex (Worcester) 1993. **SL:** HS 20 v Glos (Gloucester) 1993. BB 3-25 v Notts (Nottingham) 1993.

WESTON, Martin John (Samuel Southall SS), b Worcester 8 Apr 1959. 6'1". RHB, RM. Worcestershire 1979-93 (cap 1986; joint benefit 1993). 1000 runs (1): 1061 (1984). HS 145* v Northants (Worcester) 1984. BB 4-24 v Warwks (Birmingham) 1988. Awards: NWT 1; BHC 1. **NWT:** HS 98 v Somerset (Taunton) 1990. BB 4-30 v Suffolk (Worcester) 1985. **BHC:** HS 99* v Notts (Nottingham) 1990. BB 2-27 v Yorks (Bradford) 1985. **SL:** HS 109 v Somerset (Taunton) 1982. BB 4-11 v Hants (Worcester) 1984.

UNIVERSITY MATCH RESULTS

Played: 148. Wins: Cambridge 55; Oxford 47. Drawn: 46. Abandoned: 1.
This, the oldest surviving first-class fixture, dates from 1827 and, wartime interruptions apart, has been played annually since 1838. With the exception of five matches played in the area of Oxford (1829, 1843, 1846, 1848 and 1850), all the fixtures have been played at Lord's.

1827	Drawn	1885	Cambridge	1939	Oxford
1829	Oxford	1886	Oxford	1946	Oxford
1836	Oxford	1887	Oxford	1947	Drawn
1838	Oxford	1888	Drawn	1948	Oxford
1839	Cambridge	1889	Cambridge	1949	Cambridge
1840	Cambridge	1890	Cambridge	1950	Drawn
1841	Cambridge	1891	Cambridge	1951	Oxford
1842	Cambridge	1892	Oxford	1952	Drawn
1843	Cambridge	1893	Cambridge	1953	Cambridge
1844	Drawn	1894	Oxford	1954	Drawn
1845	Cambridge	1895	Cambridge	1955	Drawn
1846	Oxford	1896	Oxford	1956	Drawn
1847	Cambridge	1897	Cambridge	1957	Cambridge
1848	Oxford	1898	Oxford	1958	Cambridge
1849	Cambridge	1899	Drawn	1959	Oxford
1850	Oxford	1900	Drawn	1960	Drawn
1851	Cambridge	1901	Drawn	1961	Drawn
1852	Oxford	1902	Cambridge	1962	Drawn
1853	Oxford	1903	Oxford	1963	Drawn
1854	Oxford	1904	Drawn	1964	Drawn
1855	Oxford	1905	Cambridge	1965	Drawn
1856	Cambridge	1906	Cambridge	1966	Oxford
1857	Oxford	1907	Cambridge	1967	Drawn
1858	Oxford	1908	Oxford	1968	Drawn
1859	Cambridge	1909	Drawn	1969	Drawn
1860	Cambridge	1910	Oxford	1970	Drawn
1861	Cambridge	1911	Oxford	1971	Drawn
1862	Cambridge	1912	Cambridge	1972	Cambridge
1863	Oxford	1913	Cambridge	1973	Drawn
1864	Oxford	1914	Oxford	1974	Drawn
1865	Oxford	1919	Oxford	1975	Drawn
1866	Oxford	1920	Drawn	1976	Oxford
1867	Cambridge	1921	Cambridge	1977	Drawn
1868	Cambridge	1922	Cambridge	1978	Drawn
1869	Cambridge	1923	Oxford	1979	Cambridge
1870	Cambridge	1924	Cambridge	1980	Drawn
1871	Oxford	1925	Drawn	1981	Drawn
1872	Cambridge	1926	Cambridge	1982	Cambridge
1873	Oxford	1927	Cambridge	1983	Drawn
1874	Oxford	1928	Drawn	1984	Oxford
1875	Oxford	1929	Drawn	1985	Drawn
1876	Cambridge	1930	Cambridge	1986	Cambridge
1877	Oxford	1931	Oxford	1987	Drawn
1878	Cambridge	1932	Drawn	1988	Abandoned
1879	Cambridge	1933	Drawn	1989	Drawn
1880	Cambridge	1934	Drawn	1990	Drawn
1881	Oxford	1935	Cambridge	1991	Drawn
1882	Cambridge	1936	Cambridge	1992	Cambridge
1883	Cambridge	1937	Oxford	1993	Oxford
1884	Oxford	1938	Drawn		

CAMBRIDGE v OXFORD
(148th UNIVERSITY MATCH)

Played at Lord's, London, on 30 June, 1, 2, July.
Toss: Cambridge.   Result: OXFORD won by 9 wickets.

OXFORD UNIVERSITY

R.R.Montgomerie	run out	1	c Cake b Pearson	23
*J.E.R.Gallian	c Cake b Whittall	115	not out	53
G.I.Macmillan	c Cake b Whittall	63	not out	15
G.B.T.Lovell	c Haste b Pitcher	114		
C.L.Keey	b Pearson	33		
C.M.Gupte	not out	43		
†C.W.J.Lyons	run out	2		
R.S.Yeabsley	not out	20		
M.P.W.Jeh				
R.H.Macdonald	} did not bat			
P.W.Trimby				
Extras	(B2, LB5, NB2)	9	(B4, LB1, W4)	9
Total	(6 wickets declared)	**400**	(1 wicket)	**100**

CAMBRIDGE UNIVERSITY

*J.P.Crawley	lbw b Jeh	63	lbw b Gallian	49
G.W.Jones	c Trimby b Macmillan	39	lbw b Gallian	2
M.E.D.Jarrett	b Trimby	22	c Lyons b Trimby	25
R.Q.Cake	c Macmillan b Trimby	0	c Lyons b Gallian	0
G.M.Charlesworth	lbw b Jeh	49	b Macdonald	17
J.P.Carroll	c Lovell b Macmillan	0	c Gallian b Jeh	21
†J.P.Arscott	c Keey b Macmillan	0	c Gupte b Trimby	14
N.J.Haste	b Jeh	36	c Gallian b Trimby	0
R.M.Pearson	c Yeabsley b Jeh	1	c Lovell b Jeh	31
C.M.Pitcher	lbw b Trimby	0	not out	27
A.R.Whittall	not out	0	c Macmillan b Yeabsley	40
Extras	(B4, LB8, W1, NB18)	31	(LB8, W5, NB16)	29
Total		**241**		**255**

CAMBRIDGE	O	M	R	W	O	M	R	W
Pitcher	27	3	90	1	1	0	13	0
Charlesworth	25.5	4	104	0				
Pearson	30	10	77	1	9	1	51	1
Haste	13	1	61	0				
Whittall	20	0	61	2	8.2	2	31	0
OXFORD								
Jeh	14	2	61	4	18	2	90	2
Gallian	5	0	14	0	16	2	52	3
Yeabsley	5	0	40	0	1.4	1	0	1
Trimby	24.2	8	79	3	15	1	72	3
Macdonald	10	2	22	0	8	3	23	1
Macmillan	9	5	13	3	2	1	10	0

FALL OF WICKETS				
	OU	CU	OU	CU
Wkt	1st	1st	2nd	2nd
1st	3	95	59	44
2nd	170	136	–	67
3rd	186	144	–	67
4th	276	160	–	103
5th	356	168	–	138
6th	371	168	–	138
7th	–	229	–	138
8th	–	238	–	181
9th	–	241	–	185
10th	–	241	–	255

Umpires: G.I.Burgess and G.Sharp.

CAMBRIDGE UNIVERSITY

ARSCOTT, Jonathan Paul (Tonbridge S; Magdalene C), b Tooting, London 4 Jul 1970. 5'10". RHB, RM, WK. Debut 1990; blue 1991-92-93. HS 79 v Surrey (Cambridge) 1992. BB 1-17.

CAKE, Russell Quentin (KCS, Wimbledon; St John's C), b Chertsey, Surrey 16 May 1973. 5'7". RHB. Debut/blue 1993. HS 108 Comb Us v A (Oxford) 1993. CU HS 83 v Leics (Cambridge) 1993. Hockey blue 1993.

CARROLL, John Paul (Rendcomb C, Cirencester; Homerton C), b Bebington, Cheshire 14 Jul 1972. 6'2". RHB, RM. Debut 1992; blue 1992-93. HS 92 v Kent (Cambridge) 1992.

CHARLESWORTH, Graham Michael (Bablake S, Coventry; Durham U; Hughes Hall), b Ashow, Warwicks 15 Feb 1965. 6'4". LHB, RM. Griqualand West 1989-90/1990-91 (captain 1990-91). CU debut/blue 1993. HS 83 GW v Boland (Stellenbosch) 1990-91. CU HS 49 v Leics (Cambridge) 1993 and v OU (Lord's) 1993. BB 3-33 v Leics (Cambridge) 1993.

CRAWLEY, John Paul (Manchester GS; Trinity C), b Maldon, Essex 21 Sep 1971. Brother of M.A. (see NOTTS) and P.M. (CU 1992). 6'1". RHB, RM. Lancashire 1990-. CU debut 1991; blue 1991-92-93; captain 1992-93. 1000 runs (2); most – 1474 (1993). HS 187* v Sussex (Hove) 1993. BB 1-90.

HASTE, Nicholas John (Wellingborough S; Pembroke C), b Northampton 13 Nov 1972. 6'0". RHB, RM. Debut/blue 1993. HS 36 v OU (Lord's) 1993. BB 2-44 v Leics (Cambridge) 1993.

JARRETT, Michael Eugene Dominic (Harrow S; Girton C), b St Thomas' Hospital, London 18 Sep 1972. 5'9". RHB, RM. Debut 1992; blue 1992-93. HS 51 v Leics (Cambridge) 1993.

JENKINS, Rory Harry John (Oundle S; Downing C), b Leicester 29 Jun 1970. 6'2". RHB, RM. Debut 1990; blue 1990-91. HS 20 v Northants (Cambridge) 1991. BB 5-100 v Middx (Cambridge) 1990. Athletics and Rugby blue.

JONES, Garri Wyn (King's S, Chester; Gonville & Caius C), b Birmingham 1 May 1970. Brother of R.O. (see GLAMORGAN). 5'7". LHB, OB. Debut 1991; blue 1992-93. HS 45* v Sussex (Hove) 1993.

LEPPARD, Joshua (Wm Ellis S, Highgate; W London IHE; Hughes Hall), b South Benfleet, Essex 24 Nov 1962. 5'6". RHB, OB. Debut 1993. HS 20 v Leics (Cambridge) 1993.

MILLAR, Piers Malcolm Charles (Eton C; Downing C), b Westminster, London 30 Dec 1971. 6'0". RHB, RFM. Debut 1993. HS 2.

PEARSON, Richard Michael (Batley GS; St John's C), b Batley, Yorks 27 Jan 1972. 6'3". RHB, OB. Debut 1991; blue 1991-92-93. Northamptonshire 1992. HS 33* v Surrey (Cambridge) 1992. BB 5-108 v Warwks (Cambridge) 1992.

PITCHER, Christopher Michael (St Edward's S, Oxford; Selwyn C), b Croydon, Surrey 26 Aug 1973. 6'2". RHB, RM. Debut 1992; blue 1992-93. HS 32* v Leics (Cambridge) 1992 – on debut. BB 3-50 v Glam (Cambridge) 1993.

WHITTALL, Andrew Richard (Falcon C, Zimbabwe; Trinity C), b Mutare, Zimbabwe 28 Mar 1973. 6'3". RHB, OB. Debut/blue 1993; captain 1994. HS 40 v OU (Lord's) 1993. BB 3-79 v Sussex (Hove) 1993.

OXFORD UNIVERSITY

ELLISON, Bruce Charles Aurelius (Rugby S; Durham U; Keble C), b King's Lynn, Norfolk 10 Dec 1969. 6'0". RHB, RMF. Debut 1993. Norfolk 1991-92. Hockey blue 1993. HS-. BB 2-40 v Warwicks (Oxford) 1993.

FOWLER, Edward Richard (Uppingham S; St Peter's C), b Northampton 28 Oct 1971. 6'0". RHB, RM. Debut 1993. HS 9.

GALLIAN, Jason Edward Riche (Pittwater House S, Sydney; Keble C), b Manly, Sydney, Australia 25 Jun 1971. 6'0". RHB, RM. Lancashire 1990-, taking wicket of D.A.Hagan (OU) with his first ball. Eligible for England 1994. Captained Australia YC v England YC 1989-90 scoring 158* in 1st 'Test'. OU debut 1992; blue 1992-93; captain 1993. HS 141* v Notts (Oxford) 1993. BB 4-29 v Lancs (Oxford) 1992.

GUPTE, Chinmay Madhukar (John Lyon S, Harrow; Pembroke C), b Poona, India 5 Jul 1972. Son of M.S. (Maharashtra). 5'7". RHB, SLA. Debut 1991; blue 1991-93. HS 61 v Middx (Oxford) 1993. BB 2-41 v Notts (Oxford) 1991.

JEH, Michael Pradeep Williams (Brisbane State HS; Griffith U, Brisbane; Keble C), b Colombo, Ceylon 21 Apr 1968. 6'1". RHB, RFM. Debut 1992; blue 1992-93. HS 23 Comb Us v P (Cambridge) 1992. OU HS 16 v Hants (Oxford) 1992. BB 5-63 v Hants (Oxford) 1993.

KEEY, Christopher Leyton (Harrow S; Durham U; Keble C), b Johannesburg, SA 27 Dec 1969. 5'10". RHB, OB. Debut 1992; blue 1992-93. HS 111 v Northants (Oxford) 1993.

LOVELL, Geoffrey Bruce Tasman (Sydney C of E GS; Sydney U; Exeter C), b Sydney, Australia 11 Jul 1966. 5'10½". RHB, RM. Debut 1991; blue 1991-92-93; captain 1992. Inaugural Bradman Scholarship. HS 114 v CU (Lord's) 1993. BB 1-13.

LYONS, Craig Warwick John (King Edward VIII S, Johannesburg; Witwatersrand U, Keble C), b Johannesburg, SA 18 Jun 1970. Brother of R.J. (Cambridge U 1991). 5'9". RHB, WK. Debut/blue 1993. HS 28 v Lancs (Oxford) 1993 – on debut.

MACDONALD, Robert Hepburn (Rondebosch BHS; Cape Town U; Durham U; Keble C), b Cape Town, SA 18 Jul 1965. 6'2". RHB, RMF. Debut 1991; blue 1991-92-93. HS 20 v Hants (Oxford) 1991. BB 5-20 v Middx (Oxford) 1993. Squash blue 1990.

MACLAY, Alasdair Worsfold (Horris Hill S; Winchester C; St Edmund Hall), b Salisbury, Wiltshire 15 Oct 1973. 6'3". RHB, RMF. Debut 1993. HS 0*. BB 1-11.

MACMILLAN, Gregor Innes (Guildford County S; Charterhouse; Southampton U; Keble C), b Guildford, Surrey 7 Aug 1969. 6'5". RHB, OB. Debut/blue 1993. HS 63 and BB 3-13 v CU (Lord's) 1993.

MALIK, Hasnain Siddiq (KCS, Wimbledon; Keble C), b Sargodha, Pakistan 21 Apr 1973. 5'11". LHB, OB. Debut 1992. HS 64* v Hants (Oxford) 1993. BB 2-18 v Durham (Oxford) 1993.

MONTGOMERIE, Richard Robert (Rugby S; Worcester C), b Rugby, Warwicks 3 Jul 1971. 5'10½". RHB, OB. Debut 1991; blue 1991-92-93; captain 1994. Northamptonshire 1991-. HS 109 v Worcs (Worcester) 1993. Half blues for rackets and real tennis.

OLIPHANT-CALLUM, Ralph David (Brighton C; Brasenose C), b Twickenham, Middx 26 Sep 1971. 5'8". RHB, WK. Debut 1992. HS 19 v Worcs (Oxford) 1992.

TOWNSEND, Christopher James (Dean Close S; Brasenose C), b Wokingham, Berks 1 Dec 1972. 6'0". RHB, WK. Grandson of W.D.Wickson (Surrey President 1992). Debut 1992; blue 1992. HS 8.

TRIMBY, Patrick William (Shrewbury S; Worcester C), b Shrewsbury, Shropshire 31 Jan 1972. 6'1½". LHB, LB. Debut/blue 1993. HS 2*. BB 3-72 v CU (Lord's) 1993.

YEABSLEY, Richard Stuart (Haberdashers' Aske's S, Elstree; Keble C), b St Albans, Herts 2 Nov 1973. Son of D.I. (Devon 1959-89; Minor Counties 1974-79). 6'4½". RHB, RMF. Debut/blue 1993. Devon 1990. HS 36 v Worcs (Worcester) 1993. BB 3-30 v Lancs (Oxford) 1993.

CAMBRIDGE UNIVERSITY 1993

RESULTS SUMMARY

	Played	Won	Lost	Drew
All first-class matches	10	0	2	8

FIRST-CLASS AVERAGES

BATTING AND FIELDING

	M	I	NO	HS	Runs	Avge	100	50	Ct/St
J.P.Crawley	9	15	3	187*	828	69.00	1	5	6
R.Q.Cake	10	17	6	83	348	31.63	–	3	5
M.E.D.Jarrett	8	13	1	51	277	23.08	–	1	3
G.M.Charlesworth	10	15	3	49	250	20.83	–	–	3
G.W.Jones	10	16	1	45*	241	16.06	–	–	1
J.P.Arscott	10	12	3	22*	105	11.66	–	–	12/1
R.M.Pearson	9	9	1	31	93	11.62	–	–	3
A.R.Whittall	10	9	2	40	80	11.42	–	–	2
C.M.Pitcher	9	8	2	27*	61	10.16	–	–	5
N.J.Haste	10	9	1	36	76	9.50	–	–	5
J.Leppard	5	6	–	20	55	9.16	–	–	–
J.P.Carroll	8	12	1	21	69	6.27	–	–	1

Also played (1 match each): R.H.J.Jenkins did not bat; P.M.C.Millar 2.

BOWLING

	O	M	R	W	Avge	Best	5wI	10wM
R.M.Pearson	310.3	67	876	20	43.80	3-61	–	–
C.M.Pitcher	203.1	35	698	14	49.85	3-50	–	–
A.R.Whittall	309.3	63	969	19	51.00	3-79	–	–
G.M.Charlesworth	229.5	52	645	12	53.75	3-33	–	–
N.J.Haste	225	43	715	10	71.50	2-44	–	–

Also bowled: R.H.J.Jenkins 16-1-77-0; J.Leppard 11-0-40-0; P.M.C.Millar 20-4-61-0.

The following appeared in other first-class matches in 1993: R.Q.Cake and R.M.Pearson for Combined Universities v Australians; J.P.Crawley also appeared for England A v Essex and in ten matches for Lancashire. Their records in all first-class matches appear on pp 164-177.

OXFORD UNIVERSITY 1993

RESULTS SUMMARY

	Played	Won	Lost	Drew
All first-class matches	10	2	0	8

FIRST-CLASS AVERAGES

BATTING AND FIELDING

	M	I	NO	HS	Runs	Avge	100	50	Ct/St
J.E.R.Gallian	9	15	2	141*	643	49.46	2	3	4
R.R.Montgomerie	9	11	1	109	371	37.10	1	2	2
G.B.T.Lovell	7	11	1	114	365	36.50	1	1	8
C.M.Gupte	9	16	3	61	397	30.53	–	1	3
G.I.Macmillan	9	14	1	63	336	25.84	–	3	5
H.S.Malik	9	13	3	64*	234	23.40	–	1	6
C.L.Keey	10	16	1	111	341	22.73	1	1	4

	M	I	NO	HS	Runs	Avge	100	50	Ct/St
R.S.Yeabsley	10	13	4	36	138	15.33	–	–	5
C.W.J.Lyons	9	12	4	28	108	13.50	–	–	22/2
R.D.Oliphant-Callum	2	3	–	13	20	6.66	–	–	–
E.R.Fowler	2	3	–	9	19	6.33	–	–	–
M.P.W.Jeh	10	10	4		26	4.33	–	–	2
R.H.Macdonald	9	7	2	11	18	3.60	–	–	–
P.W.Trimby	6	2	2	2*	3	–	–	–	2

Also played (1 match each): B.C.A.Ellison did not bat; A.W.MacLay 0*; C.J.Townsend 0* (2 ct).

BOWLING

	O	M	R	W	Avge	Best	5wI	10wM
R.H.Macdonald	216	64	562	16	35.12	5-20	1	–
R.S.Yeabsley	237.1	53	762	20	38.10	3-30	–	–
P.W.Trimby	143.2	31	469	12	39.08	3-72	–	–
J.E.R.Gallian	166	43	464	10	46.40	3-52	–	–
M.P.W.Jeh	297	48	1140	24	47.50	5-63	1	–

Also bowled: B.C.A.Ellison 11-1-40-2; C.M.Gupte 1-0-7-0; A.W.MacLay 12-0-51-1; G.I.Macmillan 67.2-14-211-7; H.S.Malik 117.5-28-414-7; R.R. Montgomerie 2-0-6-0.

The following appeared in other first-class matches in 1993: J.E.R.Gallian, G.B.T.Lovell, R.H.Macdonald and R.R.Montgomerie for Combined Universities v Australians; J.E.R.Gallian also appeared in one match for Lancashire and R.R.Montgomerie in one match for Northamptonshire. Their records in all first-class matches appear on pp 164-177.

YOUNG CRICKETER OF THE YEAR

This annual award, made by The Cricket Writers' Club (founded in 1946), is currently restricted to players qualified for England and under the age of 23 on 1 April. In 1986 their ballot resulted in a dead heat. Only six of their selections (marked†) have failed to win an England cap.

1950	R.Tattersall	1973	M.Hendrick
1951	P.B.H.May	1974	P.H.Edmonds
1952	F.S.Trueman	1975	A.Kennedy†
1953	M.C.Cowdrey	1976	G.Miller
1954	P.J.Loader	1977	I.T.Botham
1955	K.F.Barrington	1978	D.I.Gower
1956	B.Taylor†	1979	P.W.G.Parker
1957	M.J.Stewart	1980	G.R.Dilley
1958	A.C.D.Ingleby-Mackenzie†	1981	M.W.Gatting
1959	G.Pullar	1982	N.G.Cowans
1960	D.A.Allen	1983	N.A.Foster
1961	P.H.Parfitt	1984	R.J.Bailey
1962	P.J.Sharpe	1985	D.V.Lawrence
1963	G.Boycott	1986 {	A.A.Metcalfe†
1964	J.M.Brearley		J.J.Whitaker
1965	A.P.E.Knott	1987	R.J.Blakey
1966	D.L.Underwood	1988	M.P.Maynard
1967	A.W.Greig	1989	N.Hussain
1968	R.M.H.Cottam	1990	M.A.Atherton
1969	A.Ward	1991	M.R.Ramprakash
1970	C.M.Old	1992	I.D.K.Salisbury
1971	J.Whitehouse†	1993	M.N.Lathwell
1972	D.R.Owen-Thomas†		

These averages involve the 437 cricketers who played in the 199 first-class matches staged in the British Isles during the 1993 season.

'Cap' denotes the season in which the player was awarded a 1st XI cap by the county he represented in 1993. Durham do not award caps on merit; each player receives his cap on joining the staff.

Team abbreviations: A – Australia(ns); CU – Cambridge University; De – Derbyshire; Du – Durham; E – England; EA – England A; Ex – Essex; Gm – Glamorgan; Gs – Gloucestershire; H – Hampshire; Ire – Ireland; K – Kent; La – Lancashire; Le – Leicestershire; M – Middlesex; Nh – Northamptonshire; Nt – Nottinghamshire; OU – Oxford University; Sc – Scotland; Sm – Somerset; Sy – Surrey; Sx – Sussex; Us – Combined Universities; W – President's (World) XI; Wa – Warwickshire; Wo – Worcestershire; Y – Yorkshire; Z – Zimbabweans.

† Left handed batsman.

BATTING AND FIELDING

	Cap	M	I	NO	HS	Runs	Avge	100	50	Ct/St
Adams, C.J.(De)	1992	18	30	–	175	843	28.10	1	7	16
†Adams, J.C.(W)	–	1	1	–	15	15	15.00	–	–	1
Afford, J.A.(Nt)	1990	14	17	8	11	50	5.55	–	–	6
Alikhan, R.I.(Sy)	–	4	8	–	41	149	18.62	–	–	1
Alleyne, M.W.(Gs)	1990	18	34	2	142*	994	31.06	3	2	10
†Ambrose, C.E.L.(Nh)	1990	13	15	2	38	197	15.15	–	–	3
Andrew, S.J.W.(Ex)	–	11	14	4	18	75	7.50	–	–	3
Archer, G.F.(Nt)	–	6	9	2	59*	208	29.71	–	1	5
Arnott, K.J.(Z)	–	1	2	1	111*	129	129.00	1	–	–
Arscott, J.P.(CU)	–	10	12	3	22*	105	11.66	–	–	12/1
†Arthurton, K.L.T.(W)	–	1	1	–	103	103	103.00	1	–	–
Asif Din (Wa)	1987	6	9	–	66	291	32.33	–	3	4
Atherton, M.A.(La/E)	1989	19	32	1	137	1364	44.00	3	9	14
Athey, C.W.J.(Sx)	1993	17	30	5	137	1600	64.00	5	9	16
Atkins, P.D.(Sy)	–	7	12	–	62	228	19.00	–	1	4
†Austin, I.D.(La)	1990	2	3	–	20	31	10.33	–	–	–
Ayling, J.R.(H)	1991	4	6	1	27*	89	17.80	–	–	3
Aymes, A.N.(H)	1991	19	29	11	107*	709	39.38	1	5	34/5
†Babington, A.M.(Gs)	–	7	9	3	23	40	6.66	–	–	1
Bailey, R.J.(Nh)	1985	18	30	5	200	1282	51.28	2	9	15
Bainbridge, P.(Du)	1992	19	32	2	150*	1150	38.33	2	7	7
Ball, M.C.J.(Gs)	–	4	8	–	71	113	14.12	–	1	13
Barnett, A.A.(La)	–	19	23	7	38	157	9.81	–	–	4
Barnett, K.J.(De)	1982	16	24	5	168	1223	64.36	5	5	6
Barwick, S.R.(Gm)	1987	12	11	3	23*	60	7.50	–	–	3
Base, S.J.(De)	1990	14	19	–	27	139	7.31	–	–	9
Bastien, S.(Gm)	–	5	5	5	14*	23	–	–	–	–
Bates, R.T.(Nt)	–	5	5	3	33*	70	35.00	–	–	2
Batty, J.D.(Y)	–	15	19	2	50	221	13.00	–	1	7
Bee, A.(Sc)	–	1	1	1	12*	12	–	–	–	1
Bell, M.A.V.(Wa)	–	9	12	5	22*	60	8.57	–	–	2
Benjamin, J.E.(Sy)	1993	17	26	7	23	128	6.73	–	–	3
Benjamin, K.C.G.(Wo)	–	11	11	3	26	85	10.62	–	–	1
Benjamin, W.K.M.(Le)	1989	9	13	–	83	294	22.61	–	2	14
Benson, J.D.R.(Le)	–	6	7	–	153	243	34.71	1	–	13
†Benson, M.R.(K)	1981	15	23	2	107	913	43.47	3	6	6
Berry, D.S.(W)	–	1	1	–	4	4	4.00	–	–	1

	Cap	M	I	NO	HS	Runs	Avge	100	50	Ct/St
Berry, P.J.(Du)	1992	9	14	4	46	232	23.20	–	–	3
Betts, M.M.(Du)	—	1	2	1	4	4	4.00	–	–	–
†Beven, I.R.(Sc)	—	1	1	–	16	16	16.00	–	–	–
†Bicknell, D.J.(Sy)	1990	19	35	2	190	1418	42.96	4	8	11
Bicknell, M.P.(Sy/E)	1989	12	19	2	57	398	23.41	–	2	9
Blakey, R.J.(Y)	1987	19	32	2	95	859	28.63	–	5	41/5
Boden, D.J.P.(Ex)	—	2	2	–	5	5	2.50	–	–	–
Boiling, J.(Sy)	—	9	13	5	28	100	12.50	–	–	3
Boon, D.C.(A)	—	14	23	4	164*	1437	75.63	9	2	10
Boon, T.J.(Le)	1986	18	29	1	110	921	32.89	2	5	8
†Booth, P.A.(Wa)	—	7	11	3	49*	144	18.00	–	–	4
Border, A.R.(A)	—	16	21	3	200*	823	45.72	1	4	15
Botham, I.T.(Du)	1992	10	17	1	101	416	26.00	1	3	8
Bovill, J.N.B.(H)	—	1	2	2	3*	3	–	–	–	–
Bowen, M.N.(Nh)	—	5	6	2	23*	72	18.00	–	–	1
Bowler, P.D.(De)	1989	17	29	3	153*	1123	43.19	2	7	13
Brain, D.H.(Z)	—	3	3	1	31	65	32.50	–	–	1
Bramhall, S.(Nt)	—	2	–	–	–	–	–	–	–	1
Brandes, E.A.(Z)	—	3	3	–	9	9	3.00	–	–	2
Briant, G.A.(Z)	—	2	3	–	54	94	31.33	–	1	3
Briers, M.P.(Du)	1992	1	2	–	1	2	1.00	–	–	1
Briers, N.E.(Le)	1981	12	19	1	79	487	27.05	–	3	2
Brimson, M.T.(Le)	—	2	1	–	0	0	0.00	–	–	–
Broad, B.C.(Gs)	1981	18	34	–	131	1161	34.14	2	7	6
Broadhurst, M.(Y)	—	1	–	–	–	–	–	–	–	–
Brown, A.D.(Sy)	—	19	34	3	150*	1382	44.58	3	4	18
Brown, K.R.(M)	1990	18	24	6	88*	725	40.27	–	5	38/6
Brown, S.J.E.(Du)	1992	16	24	5	31	152	8.00	–	–	5
Burns, M.(Wa)	—	6	10	–	22	96	9.60	–	–	9/1
†Burns, N.D.(Sm)	1987	13	23	2	102*	479	22.80	1	2	37/4
†Butcher, M.A.(Sy)	—	6	11	3	66*	218	27.25	–	1	4
†Byas, D.(Y)	1991	19	33	3	156	1073	35.76	1	9	21
Caddick, A.R.(Sm/E/EA)	1992	16	26	4	35*	318	14.45	–	–	6
Cairns, C.L.(Nt)	1993	15	23	1	93	962	43.72	–	9	8
Cake, R.Q.(CU/Us)	—	11	19	6	108	472	36.30	1	3	5
†Campbell, A.D.R.(Z)	—	3	5	1	31	69	17.25	–	–	–
Capel, D.J.(Nh)	1986	5	8	2	54	102	17.00	–	1	1
Carr, J.D.(M)	1987	17	24	6	192*	848	47.11	2	3	39
Carrick, P.(Y)	1976	3	4	2	16*	45	22.50	–	–	1
Carroll, J.P.(CU)	—	8	12	1	21	69	6.27	–	–	1
Chapple, G.(La)	—	8	13	7	109*	256	42.66	1	–	–
*Charlesworth, G.M.(CU)	—	10	15	3	49	250	20.83	–	–	3
†Childs, J.H.(Ex)	1986	19	19	11	23	89	11.12	–	–	5
Cohen, M.F.(Ire)	—	1	2	1	37	38	38.00	–	–	–
Connor, C.A.(H)	1988	10	11	1	59	200	20.00	–	1	3
Cook, N.G.B.(Nh)	1987	8	9	1	18	50	6.25	–	–	3
†Cooper, K.E.(Gs)	—	14	25	6	52	218	11.47	–	1	5
Cork, D.G.(De/EA)	1993	16	24	2	104	606	27.54	1	4	11
Cottey, P.A.(Gm)	1992	19	34	5	105	1039	35.82	2	8	15
Cousins, D.M.(Ex)	—	1	2	1	0*	0	0.00	–	–	–
Cowans, N.G.(M)	1984	6	5	1	14	23	5.75	–	–	1
Cowdrey, G.R.(K)	1988	12	21	–	139	478	22.76	1	1	7
†Cox, R.M.F.(H)	—	6	10	1	63	204	22.66	–	1	4
Crawley, J.P.(CU/La/EA)	—	20	34	3	187*	1474	47.54	3	8	12
Crawley, M.A.(Nt)	—	10	18	2	81	306	19.12	–	1	8
Croft, R.D.B.(Gm)	1992	20	34	7	107	718	26.59	1	2	12

	Cap	M	I	NO	HS	Runs	Avge	100	50	Ct/St
Cummins, A.C.(Du)	1993	16	26	2	70	502	20.91	–	4	5
Curran, K.M.(Nh)	1992	16	23	4	91	612	32.21	–	5	6
†Curry, D.J.(Ire)	–	1	2	–	41	45	22.50	–	–	–
Curtis, T.S.(Wo)	1984	19	32	3	127	1553	53.55	5	8	14
†Dakin, J.M.(Le)	–	1	1	–	5	5	5.00	–	–	–
Dale, A.(Gm)	1992	20	38	1	214*	1472	39.78	3	7	12
Daley, J.A.(Du)	1992	13	22	–	79	563	25.59	–	3	7
Davies, M.(Gs)	–	14	23	5	44*	220	12.22	–	–	6
Davis, R.P.(K)	1990	14	16	2	42	164	11.71	–	–	14
Dawson, R.I.(Gs)	–	9	17	1	58	350	21.87	–	1	12
DeFreitas, P.A.J.(La/E)	1989	21	31	3	51	465	16.60	–	1	15
De la Pena, J.M.(Gs)	–	2	2	1	7*	7	7.00	–	–	–
Dessaur, W.A.(Nt)	–	7	10	–	104	325	32.50	1	2	2
Doak, N.G.(Ire)	–	1	2	–	25	27	13.50	–	–	2
D'Oliveira, D.B.(Wo)	1985	15	24	–	94	513	21.37	–	3	12
Donald, A.A.(Wa)	1989	10	12	4	19	68	8.50	–	–	8
Donelan, B.T.P.(Sx)	–	3	3	1	41	79	39.50	–	–	1
Dutch, K.P.(M)	–	1	–	–	–	–	–	–	–	2
Ealham, M.A.(K)	1992	12	16	3	85	666	51.23	–	8	3
Edwards, T.(Wo)	–	1	–	–	–	–	–	–	–	1
Ellison, B.C.A.(OU)	–	1	–	–	–	–	–	–	–	–
†Ellison, R.M.(K)	1983	3	4	1	68	92	30.66	–	1	1
Emburey, J.E.(M/E)	1977	17	21	7	123	730	52.14	2	5	18
Evans, K.P.(Nt)	1990	10	14	4	56	231	23.10	–	1	9
†Fairbrother, N.H.(La)	1985	18	31	4	110	901	33.37	1	4	11
Feltham, M.A.(M)	–	16	19	4	73	288	19.20	–	1	4
Felton, N.A.(Nh)	1990	18	30	2	109	1026	36.64	2	7	16
Field-Buss, M.G.(Nt)	–	10	14	6	20*	99	12.37	–	–	4
Fleming, M.V.(K)	1990	18	28	4	100	826	34.41	1	6	7
Fletcher, I.(Sm)	–	7	10	1	65*	223	24.77	–	2	1
Fletcher, S.D.(La)	–	1	–	–	–	–	–	–	–	–
Flint, D.P.J.(H)	–	10	13	5	14*	47	5.87	–	–	7
†Flower, A.(Z)	–	2	3	–	82	94	31.33	–	1	6/2
Flower, G.W.(Z)	–	3	6	1	130	224	44.80	1	1	1
†Folland, N.A.(Sm)	–	17	30	3	108*	872	32.29	2	4	13
Fordham, A.(Nh)	1990	17	29	1	193	1052	37.57	3	5	12
Foster, M.J.(Y)	–	1	1	–	6	6	6.00	–	–	1
Foster, N.A.(Ex/E)	1983	8	12	3	37	235	26.11	–	–	1
Fothergill, A.R.(Du)	1992	5	8	–	29	53	6.62	–	–	6/2
Fowler, E.R.(OU)	–	2	3	–	9	19	6.33	–	–	–
†Fowler, G.(Du)	1993	14	24	–	138	663	26.37	1	3	7
Fraser, A.R.C.(M/E)	1988	18	17	2	29	162	10.80	–	–	7
French, B.N.(Nt)	1980	17	24	3	123	420	20.00	1	1	40/5
Frost, M.(Gm)	1991	2	4	3	7	19	19.00	–	–	–
Fulton, D.P.(K)	–	7	13	1	75	307	25.58	–	2	11
Gallian, J.E.R.(OU/Us/La)	–	11	19	3	141*	702	43.87	3	3	5
Garnham, M.A.(Ex)	1990	17	29	4	106	694	27.76	1	3	34/5
Gatting, M.W.(M/E)	1977	16	24	4	182	1132	56.60	3	6	14
Gerrard, M.J.(Gs)	–	3	5	2	9	20	6.66	–	–	1
Giddins, E.S.H.(Sx)	–	15	19	8	4	12	1.09	–	–	4
Giles, A.F.(Wa)	–	2	4	1	23	53	17.66	–	–	1
Glendenen, J.D.(Du)	1992	4	6	1	18	41	8.20	–	–	1
Gooch, G.A.(Ex/E)	1975	19	35	3	159*	2023	63.21	6	14	13
Gough, D.(Y)	1993	16	24	3	39	248	11.80	–	–	3
Govan, J.W.(Sc)	–	1	1	–	50	50	50.00	–	1	–
†Gower, D.I.(H)	1990	16	28	1	153	1136	42.07	4	5	11

	Cap	M	I	NO	HS	Runs	Avge	100	50	Ct/St
Graveney, D.A.(Du)	1992	19	28	14	32	289	20.64	–	–	12
Grayson, A.P.(Y)	–	10	17	–	64	386	22.70	–	2	6
Greenfield, K.(Sx)	–	8	12	3	107	353	39.22	1	3	5
Griffith, F.A.(De)	–	11	14	–	56	257	18.35	–	2	4
Gupte, C.M.(OU)	–	9	16	3	61	397	30.53	–	1	3
Hall, J.W.(Sx)	1992	9	16	1	114	390	26.00	1	1	6
Hallett, J.C.(Us)	–	1	1	1	6*	6	–	–	–	1
Hamilton, G.M.(Sc)	–	1	1	–	0	0	0.00	–	–	–
Hancock, T.H.C.(Gs)	–	16	29	2	76	723	26.77	–	4	5
Harden, R.J.(Sm)	1989	18	32	3	132	1133	39.06	3	4	33
Harper, R.A.(W)	–	1	1	1	76*	76	–	–	1	1
Harrison, G.D.(Ire)	–	1	1	–	32	32	32.00	–	–	–
Hartley, P.J.(Y)	1987	13	21	6	102	400	26.66	1	1	3
Haste, N.J.(CU)	–	10	9	1	36	76	9.50	–	–	5
†Hayden, M.L.(A)	–	13	21	1	151*	1150	57.50	3	7	9
Hayhurst, A.N.(Sm)	1990	14	23	1	169	669	30.40	2	1	7
Haynes, D.L.(M)	1989	15	24	4	115	793	39.65	2	4	8
Haynes, G.R.(Wo)	–	9	13	–	158	383	29.46	1	2	3
Headley, D.W.(K)	1993	14	20	7	36	281	21.61	–	–	9
Healy, I.A.(A)	–	16	20	7	102*	499	38.38	1	3	42/11
Hegg, W.K.(La)	1989	21	34	9	69*	566	22.64	–	2	49/9
Hemmings, E.E.(Sx)	1993	15	20	4	17*	78	4.87	–	–	10
†Hemp, D.L.(Gm)	–	10	19	2	90*	508	29.88	–	5	4
Hepworth, P.N.(Le)	–	8	13	1	129	328	27.33	1	1	2
Hick, G.A.(Wo/E)	1986	18	30	2	187	1522	54.35	4	7	24
Hindson, J.E.(Nt)	–	2	1	1	1	1	1.00	–	–	–
†Hinks, S.G.(Gs)	–	12	24	1	68	482	20.95	–	3	10
Hodgson, G.D.(Gs)	1992	14	27	2	166	1079	43.16	2	7	9
Hoey, C.J.(Ire)	–	1	1	–	5	5	5.00	–	–	1
Holdsworth, W.J.(A)	–	9	3	–	12	17	5.66	–	–	2
Hollioake, A.J.(Sy)	–	5	9	–	123	352	39.11	1	2	4
†Holloway, P.C.L.(Wa)	–	3	4	1	44	68	22.66	–	–	6
Hooper, C.L.(K)	1992	16	24	2	236*	1304	59.27	3	6	22
Houghton, D.L.(Z)	–	2	3	–	36	82	27.33	–	–	1
Hughes, M.G.(A)	–	14	12	3	71	299	33.22	–	2	3
Hughes, S.P.(Du)	1992	6	8	2	30	37	6.16	–	–	1
Humphries, S.(Sx)	–	1	–	–	–	–	–	–	–	2
Hussain, N.(Ex/E)	1989	20	35	5	152	1604	53.46	7	7	16
†Hutton, S.(Du)	1992	10	17	–	73	469	27.58	–	2	8
Hyam, B.J.(Ex)	–	1	2	–	1	1	0.50	–	–	2
Igglesden, A.P.(K)	1989	13	13	7	10	32	5.33	–	–	2
Illingworth, R.K.(Wo)	1986	18	24	8	58	401	25.06	–	1	7
†Ilott, M.C.(Ex/E)	1993	18	25	5	51	280	14.00	–	2	7
Irani, R.C.(La)	–	2	4	–	44	44	11.00	–	–	1
Jackson, P.B.(Ire)	–	1	1	–	0	0	0.00	–	–	3
†James, K.D.(H)	1989	17	29	4	71	694	27.76	–	4	5
James, S.P.(Gm)	1992	16	30	1	138*	819	28.24	1	4	17
Jarrett, M.E.D.(CU)	–	8	13	1	51	277	23.08	–	1	3
Jarvis, P.W.(Y)	1986	9	14	1	76	207	15.92	–	1	1
Jean-Jacques, M.(H)	–	4	3	2	21*	42	42.00	–	–	1
Jeh, M.P.W.(OU)	–	10	10	4	9	26	4.33	–	–	2
Jenkins, R.H.J.(CU)	–	1	–	–	–	–	–	–	–	–
Johnson, P.(Nt/EA)	1986	16	27	1	187	1099	42.26	5	3	7
Johnson, R.L.(M)	–	1	2	–	4	8	4.00	–	–	–
†Jones, A.N.(Sx)	1986	5	6	1	20	39	7.80	–	–	–
Jones, D.M.(W)	–	1	1	–	32	32	32.00	–	–	–

167

	Cap	M	I	NO	HS	Runs	Avge	100	50	Ct/St
†Jones, G.W.(CU)	—	10	16	1	45*	241	16.06	–	–	1
Julian, B.P.(A)	—	13	17	6	66	284	25.81	–	2	7
Keech, M.(M)	—	5	10	1	35	164	18.22	–	–	5
Keey, C.L.(OU)	—	10	16	1	111	341	22.73	1	1	4
Kellett, S.A.(Y)	1992	5	9	–	85	301	33.44	–	4	4
Kendrick, N.M.(Sy)	—	12	20	5	41	237	15.80	–	–	6
Kerr, J.I.D.(Sm)	—	7	11	3	19*	67	8.37	–	–	3
Kersey, G.J.(Sy)	—	12	20	2	38*	272	15.11	–	–	34/3
†Knight, N.V.(Ex)	—	7	13	–	94	295	22.69	–	2	15
Krikken, K.M.(De)	1992	13	18	4	40	227	16.21	–	–	22/5
Lamb, A.J.(Nh)	1978	18	28	1	172	1092	40.44	2	6	13
†Lambert, C.B.(W)	—	1	1	–	9	9	9.00	–	–	–
Lampitt, S.R.(Wo)	1989	16	25	2	68*	438	19.04	–	2	21
Larkins, W.(Du)	1992	17	30	3	151	1045	38.70	3	5	24
Lathwell, M.N.(Sm/E/EA)	1992	17	31	1	132	1009	33.63	2	4	19
Law, D.R.(Sx)	—	3	2	–	11	11	5.50	–	–	–
Leatherdale, D.A.(Wo)	—	11	16	2	119*	354	25.28	1	2	18
Lefebvre, R.P.(Gm)	1993	19	28	3	50	484	19.36	–	1	11
Lenham, N.J.(Sx)	1990	12	22	1	149	799	38.04	2	5	3
Leppard, J.(CU)	—	5	6	–	20	55	9.16	–	–	–
Lewis, C.C.(Nt/E)	—	15	24	2	247	705	32.04	1	2	10
Lewis, D.A.(Ire)	—	1	2	1	73	129	129.00	–	2	1
Lewis, J.J.B.(Ex)	—	13	24	4	136*	736	36.80	1	5	15
†Llong, N.J.(K)	1993	18	27	5	116*	943	42.86	2	6	13
Lloyd, G.D.(La/EA)	1992	18	31	2	116	1095	37.75	2	5	12
Longley, J.I.(K)	—	2	3	–	47	52	17.33	–	–	4
Love, J.D.(Sc)	—	1	2	1	14*	28	28.00	–	–	–
Lovell, G.B.T.(OU/Us)	—	8	13	2	114	389	35.36	1	1	8
Loye, M.B.(Nh)	—	18	28	3	153*	956	38.24	2	4	19
Lugsden, S.(Du)	—	1	1	1	5*	5	–	–	–	–
Lynch, M.A.(Sy)	1982	15	28	1	90	666	24.66	–	3	28
Lyons, C.W.J.(OU)	—	9	12	4	28	108	13.50	–	–	22/2
McCague, M.J.(K/E)	1992	9	11	3	22*	69	8.62	–	–	5
McCrum, P.(Ire)	—	1	1	–	5	5	5.00	–	–	–
McDermott, C.J.(A)	—	6	3	–	23	42	14.00	–	–	3
Macdonald, R.H.(OU/Us)	—	10	8	2	11	22	3.66	–	–	–
MacLay, A.W.(OU)	—	1	1	–	0*	0	–	–	–	–
Macmillan, G.I.(OU)	—	9	14	1	63	336	25.84	–	3	5
Maher, B.J.M.(De)	1987	5	5	1	17	22	5.50	–	–	9
Malcolm, D.E.(De/E)	1989	11	14	7	19	69	9.85	–	–	–
†Malik, H.S.(OU)	—	9	13	3	64*	234	23.40	–	1	6
Mallender, N.A.(Sm)	1987	13	16	6	46	250	25.00	–	–	1
Marsh, S.A.(K)	1986	19	27	2	111	667	26.68	1	4	57/4
Marshall, M.D.(H)	1981	13	16	2	75*	250	17.85	–	1	3
Martin, P.J.(La)	—	16	21	7	43	399	28.50	–	–	9
Martyn, D.R.(A)		12	15	3	138*	838	69.83	4	3	9/1
Maru, R.J.(H)	1986	1	–	–	–	–	–	–	–	2
May, T.B.A.(A)	—	17	9	5	15	31	7.75	–	–	5
Maynard, M.P.(Gm/E)	1987	19	32	1	145	1378	44.45	3	7	22
Mendis, G.D.(La)	1986	18	34	1	106	1099	32.32	1	7	5
Metcalfe, A.A.(Y)	1986	10	16	1	133*	467	31.13	1	3	2
Metson, C.P.(Gm)	1987	20	31	8	25*	338	14.69	–	–	50/4
Middleton, T.C.(H)	1990	12	22	–	90	571	25.95	–	5	13
Mike, G.W.(Nt)	—	8	13	1	50	240	20.00	–	1	3
Milburn, S.M.(Y)	—	1	–	–	–	–	–	–	–	–
Millar, P.M.C.(CU)	—	1	1	–	2	2	2.00	–	–	–

	Cap	M	I	NO	HS	Runs	Avge	100	50	Ct/St
†Millns, D.J.(Le)	1991	7	8	3	24	59	11.80	–	–	6
Moles, A.J.(Wa)	1987	19	34	3	117	1228	39.61	2	8	2
Montgomerie, R.R.(OU/Us/Nh)	—	8	14	1	109	462	35.53	1	3	5
Moore, E.R.(Ire)	—	1	–	–	–	–	–	–	–	–
Moores, P.(Sx)	1989	19	27	4	85*	583	25.34	–	2	39/5
†Morris, H.(Gm)	1986	19	35	2	134*	1326	40.18	5	6	16
Morris, J.E.(De)	1986	18	29	1	229	1461	52.17	5	6	8
Morris, R.S.M.(H)	—	8	14	–	92	372	26.57	–	2	14
Morrison, D.K.(W)	—	1	–	–	–	–	–	–	–	–
Mortensen, O.H.(De)	1986	10	14	5	29	70	7.77	–	–	4
Moxon, M.D.(Y/EA)	1984	19	33	2	171*	1317	42.48	1	9	9
Mudassar Nazar (W)	—	1	1	1	2*	2	–	–	–	1
Mullally, A.D.(Le)	1993	17	20	4	26	132	8.25	–	–	4
Munton, T.A.(Wa)	1989	13	13	5	18	51	6.37	–	–	4
Murphy, A.J.(Sy)	—	11	14	10	24*	88	22.00	–	–	5
Mushtaq Ahmed (Sm)	1993	16	25	–	90	498	19.92	–	3	14
Newport, P.J.(Wo)	1986	17	26	6	79*	630	31.50	–	6	8
Nicholas, M.C.J.(H)	1982	18	29	4	95	918	36.72	–	6	8
†Nixon, P.A.(Le)	—	19	28	6	113*	501	22.77	1	3	42/6
North, J.A.(Sx)	—	7	11	3	114	228	28.50	1	1	2
O'Gorman, T.J.G.(De)	1992	14	21	3	130*	511	28.38	1	2	9
Oliphant-Callum, R.D.(OU)	—	2	3	–	13	20	6.66	–	–	–
Orr, D.A.(Sc)	—	1	1	–	14	14	14.00	–	–	1/2
Ostler, D.P.(Wa)	1991	19	34	1	174	1052	33.93	1	6	20
Parker, P.W.G.(Du)	1992	19	32	1	159	924	29.80	3	3	13
Parks, R.J.(K)	—	1	1	1	13*	13	–	–	–	4
†Parsons, G.J.(Le)	1984	18	23	7	59	405	25.31	–	1	11
Parsons, K.A.(Sm)	—	5	9	1	63	134	16.75	–	1	3
Patel, M.M.(K)	—	7	7	3	4	14	3.50	–	–	3
Patterson, B.M.W.(Sc)	—	1	2	–	43	43	21.50	–	–	–
Payne, A.(Sm)	—	2	2	1	22*	39	39.00	–	–	2
†Peall, S.G.(Z)	—	3	5	1	33	64	16.00	–	–	1
Pearson, R.M.(CU/Us)	—	10	10	1	31	94	10.44	–	–	3
†Penberthy, A.L.(Nh)	—	9	14	2	54*	164	13.66	–	1	5
†Penn, C.(K)	1987	4	4	–	23	63	15.75	–	–	2
Pennett, D.B.(Nt)	—	7	4	2	10*	11	5.50	–	–	–
Penney, T.L.(Wa)	—	17	29	6	135*	788	34.26	1	4	10
Phelps, B.S.(Gm)	—	1	–	–	–	–	–	–	–	–
Philip, I.L.(Sc)	—	1	2	–	16	30	15.00	–	–	–
Phillips, N.C.(Sx)	—	1	–	–	–	–	–	–	–	–
†Pick, R.A.(Nt)	1987	13	12	4	22	109	13.62	–	–	4
Pierson, A.R.K.(Le)	—	18	23	6	58	238	14.00	–	1	3
Pigott, A.C.S.(Sx)	1982	12	13	2	52	153	13.90	–	1	4
Piper, K.J.(Wa)	1992	10	14	1	52	183	14.07	–	1	14
Pitcher, C.M.(CU)	—	9	8	2	27*	61	10.16	–	–	5
†Pollard, P.R.(Nt)	1992	19	32	3	180	1463	50.44	3	9	26
†Pooley, J.C.(M)	—	2	3	–	49	89	29.66	–	–	1
Potter, L.(Le)	1988	12	17	2	103*	404	26.93	1	1	12
Prichard, P.J.(Ex)	1986	19	36	3	225*	1319	39.96	4	7	15
Pringle, D.R.(Ex)	1982	14	22	4	76	610	33.88	–	6	11
Radford, N.V.(Wo)	1985	13	14	5	29	106	11.77	–	–	3
Ramprakash, M.R.(M/E)	1990	17	24	1	140	883	38.39	2	5	17
Ranchod, U.(Z)	—	2	2	1	12*	14	14.00	–	–	1
Randall, D.W.(Nt)	1973	5	10	–	98	280	28.00	–	2	6
Ratcliffe, J.D.(Wa)	—	19	34	–	101	999	29.38	1	6	12
Rea, M.P.(Ire)	—	1	2	–	115	117	58.50	1	–	1

	Cap	M	I	NO	HS	Runs	Avge	100	50	Ct/St
Reeve, D.A.(Wa)	1989	17	28	7	87*	765	36.42	–	5	22
Reiffel, P.R.(A)	–	13	9	1	52	181	22.62	–	1	3
Remy, C.C.(Sx)	–	4	5	1	39	85	21.25	–	–	2
Rennie, J.A.(Z)	–	1	1	–	0	0	0.00	–	–	–
Rhodes, S.J.(Wo)	1986	18	27	3	101	848	35.33	2	2	40/7
Richards, I.V.A.(Gm)	1990	17	32	6	224*	1235	47.50	2	7	17
Richardson, A.W.(De)	–	1	2	–	9	9	4.50	–	–	–
Richardson, R.B.(Y)	1993	14	23	1	112	759	34.50	1	6	9
Ripley, D.(Nh)	1987	18	24	6	62*	398	22.11	–	3	52/4
Roberts, A.R.(Nh)	–	10	16	1	19*	119	7.93	–	–	3
Robinson, D.D.J.(Ex)	–	2	4	–	67	112	28.00	–	1	2
Robinson, M.A.(Y)	1992	17	22	10	16*	53	4.41	–	–	–
Robinson, P.E.(Le)	–	18	29	3	71	526	20.23	–	3	21
Robinson, R.T.(Nt)	1983	18	30	4	139*	1152	44.30	3	7	13
Rollins, A.S.(De)	–	7	13	4	85	392	43.55	–	2	5/1
Rollins, R.J.(Ex)	–	3	4	1	7	14	4.66	–	–	3/3
Rose, G.D.(Sm)	1988	17	29	2	138	865	32.03	2	2	10
Roseberry, M.A.(M/EA)	1990	16	26	4	185	685	31.13	1	2	12
Rowett, D.J.(Z)	–	2	2	–	8*	8	–	–	–	3
Russell, A.B.(Sc)	–	1	1	–	9	9	9.00	–	–	–
†Russell, R.C.(Gs/EA)	1985	19	33	7	99*	863	33.19	–	5	56/7
Salim Malik (Ex)	1991	15	27	2	132	917	36.68	2	3	12
Salisbury, I.D.K.(Sx/EA)	1991	16	23	5	63*	390	21.66	–	2	11
†Salmon, G.(Sc)	–	1	2	–	39	45	22.50	–	–	–
†Saxelby, M.(Nt)	–	12	18	–	77	558	31.00	–	5	5
Scott, C.W.(Du)	1992	14	24	3	64	343	16.33	–	2	27/4
†Scott, R.J.(Gs)	–	5	10	–	51	179	17.90	–	1	1
†Seymour, A.C.H.(Wo)	–	7	11	1	54*	237	23.70	–	1	2
Shahid, N.(Ex)	–	7	13	1	69*	270	22.50	–	2	9
Shephard, S.F.(Us)	–	1	2	–	5	5	2.50	–	–	1
Shine, K.J.(H)	–	13	14	5	12	54	6.00	–	–	4
Silverwood, C.E.W.(Y)	–	1	1	–	0	0	0.00	–	–	2
Simmons, P.V.(W)	–	1	1	–	46	46	46.00	–	–	2
†Sims, R.J.(M)	–	3	2	–	28	28	14.00	–	–	1
Sladdin, R.W.(De)	–	9	11	3	51*	131	16.37	–	1	2
Slater, M.J.(A)	–	17	28	4	152	1275	53.12	4	8	6
Sleep, P.R.(W)	–	1	1	–	151	151	151.00	1	–	1
Small, G.C.(Wa)	1982	13	19	4	39	147	9.80	–	–	5
Smith, A.M.(Gs)	–	7	11	1	33	87	8.70	–	–	1
Smith, A.W.(Sy)	–	14	23	2	68	560	26.66	–	3	7
Smith, B.F.(Le)	–	11	18	–	84	263	14.61	–	1	2
†Smith, D.M.(Sx)	1989	15	23	1	150	802	36.45	1	4	15
Smith, I.(Du)	1992	6	12	–	39	192	16.00	–	–	6
Smith, N.M.K.(Wa)	1993	18	26	2	51*	420	17.50	–	1	2
Smith, P.A.(Wa)	1986	10	15	–	55	253	16.86	–	1	3
Smith, R.A.(H/E)	1985	17	29	2	191	1253	46.40	4	4	8
Snape, J.N.(Us)	–	1	2	–	18	18	9.00	–	–	–
Speak, N.J.(La)	1992	21	35	2	122	1185	35.90	1	8	10
Speight, M.P.(Sx)	1991	13	22	1	184	1009	48.04	3	5	11
Spencer, D.J.(K)	–	2	2	–	75	79	39.50	–	1	1
Steer, I.G.S.(De)	–	4	7	2	67	157	31.40	–	1	–
Stemp, R.D.(Y)	–	16	23	6	37	265	15.58	–	–	11
Stephenson, F.D.(Sx)	1992	14	21	2	90	538	28.31	–	3	5
Stephenson, J.P.(Ex)	1989	17	32	2	122	1011	33.70	2	4	20
Stewart, A.J.(Sy/E)	1985	16	28	1	127	1094	40.51	2	8	34/2
Storie, A.C.(Sc)	–	1	2	1	40*	59	59.00	–	–	2

	Cap	M	I	NO	HS	Runs	Avge	100	50	Ct/St
Streak, H.H.(Z)	—	3	5	2	12	29	9.66	—	—	—
Such, P.M.(Ex/E)	1991	20	27	5	54	228	10.36	—	1	8
Tavaré, C.J.(Sm)	1989	13	25	1	141*	628	26.16	1	2	22
†Taylor, C.W.(M)	—	2	3	1	28*	28	14.00	—	—	—
†Taylor, J.P.(Nh/EA)	1992	19	22	11	21	100	9.09	—	—	5
†Taylor, M.A.(A)	—	15	25	2	124	972	42.26	3	4	25
Taylor, N.R.(K)	1982	16	26	2	86	679	28.29	—	4	4
Terry, V.P.(H)	1983	19	33	2	174	1469	47.38	4	7	15
†Thomas, S.D.(Gm)	—	4	7	4	16*	46	15.33	—	—	2
†Thorpe, G.P.(Sy/E/EA)	1991	17	31	2	171	1043	35.96	3	5	17
Thursfield, M.J.(H)	—	2	4	2	36*	36	18.00	—	—	1
Titchard, S.P.(La)	—	5	10	—	87	237	23.70	—	2	1
Tolley, C.M.(Wo)	1993	18	24	7	78	381	22.41	—	2	8
Topley, T.D.(Ex)	1988	8	12	1	33	155	14.09	—	—	3
Townsend, C.J.(OU)	—	1	1	1	0*	0	—	—	—	2
†Trescothick, M.E.(Sm)	—	3	6	—	6	14	2.33	—	—	4
†Trimby, P.W.(OU)	—	6	2	2	2*	3	—	—	—	2
Trump, H.R.J.(Sm)	—	8	11	8	22*	79	26.33	—	—	5
Tufnell, P.C.R.(M/E)	1990	18	18	6	30*	128	10.66	—	—	7
Turner, I.J.(H)	—	4	5	1	8	17	4.25	—	—	3
Turner, R.J.(Sm)	—	6	10	1	70	195	21.66	—	1	15/3
†Twose, R.G.(Wa)	1992	11	18	—	37	224	12.44	—	—	4
Udal, S.D.(H)	1992	19	27	2	79*	509	20.36	—	2	8
Vandrau, M.J.(De)	—	15	23	2	58	404	19.23	—	2	7
Van Troost, A.P.(Sm)	—	14	17	6	35	108	9.81	—	—	4
Vaughan, M.P.(Y)	—	2	4	—	64	118	29.50	—	1	—
†Walker, A.(Nh)	1987	1	—	—	—	—	—	—	—	1
Walsh, C.A.(Gs)	1985	14	21	3	57	266	14.77	—	1	4
Waqar Younis (Sy)	1990	13	18	1	28	214	12.58	—	—	3
Ward, D.M.(Sy)	1990	13	22	1	151*	580	27.61	1	3	6
Ward, T.R.(K)	1989	19	30	1	141	903	31.13	2	3	13
Warke, S.J.S.(Ire)	—	1	2	—	47	61	30.50	—	—	1
Warne, S.K.(A)	—	16	15	4	47	246	22.36	—	—	8
Warner, A.E.(De)	1987	12	14	1	95*	238	18.30	—	1	4
Warren, R.J.(Nh)	—	5	6	1	37*	56	11.20	—	—	3
†Wasim Akram (La)	1989	13	21	—	117	516	24.57	1	1	3
Watkin, S.L.(Gm/E)	1989	19	24	8	31	204	12.75	—	—	7
Watkinson, M.(La)	1987	19	30	4	107	1016	39.07	2	4	9
Waugh, M.E.(A)	—	16	25	4	178	1361	71.63	4	9	18
Waugh, S.R.(A)	—	16	21	8	157*	875	67.30	3	2	7
Weekes, P.N.(M)	1993	4	5	1	47	148	37.00	—	—	2
Wells, A.P.(Sx)	1986	18	27	2	144	1432	57.28	6	5	20
Wells, C.M.(Sx)	1982	3	5	1	185	198	49.50	1	—	1
Wells, V.J.(Le)	—	15	23	2	167	602	28.66	1	2	11
Weston, M.J.(Wo)	1986	7	13	1	59	277	23.08	—	2	3
†Weston, W.P.C.(Wo)	—	13	21	2	113	610	32.10	2	1	6
Whitaker, J.J.(Le)	1986	18	28	1	126	925	34.25	1	4	8
White, C.(Y)	1993	19	32	6	146	896	34.46	1	4	14
Whittal, G.J.(Z)	—	3	5	—	20	48	9.60	—	—	—
Whittall, A.R.(CU)	—	10	9	2	40	80	11.42	—	—	2
Wight, R.M.(Gs)	—	7	11	1	54	152	15.20	—	1	8
Wileman, J.R.(Us)	—	1	2	1	48	58	58.00	—	—	1
Williams, J.R.A.(Gm)	—	1	2	—	6	6	3.00	—	—	—
Williams, N.F.(M)	1984	14	12	1	44	146	13.27	—	—	3
Williams, R.C.(Gs)	—	4	7	3	38	92	23.00	—	—	1
Willis, S.C.(K)	—	1	1	1	0*	0	—	—	—	2

	Cap	M	I	NO	HS	Runs	Avge	100	50	Ct/St
Windows, M.G.N.(Us/Gs)	—	2	4	—	44	138	34.50	–	–	1
Wood, J.(Du)	1992	9	17	3	63*	250	17.85	–	1	2
†Wood, J.R.(H)	—	1	1	—	25	25	25.00	–	–	–
Wright, A.J.(Gs)	1987	11	21	2	75	322	16.94	–	1	9
†Wylie, A.(Wo)	—	1	1	—	0	0	0.00	–	–	–
Yates, G.(La)	—	7	10	6	134*	367	91.75	1	1	3
Yeabsley, R.S.(OU)	—	10	13	4	36	138	15.33	–	5	–
Zoehrer, T.J.(A/W)	—	9	9	1	38	115	14.37	–	–	17/4

BOWLING

See BATTING and FIELDING section for details of caps and teams.

	Cat	O	M	R	W	Avge	Best	5wI	10wM
Adams, C.J.	OB	111.2	9	492	5	98.40	2- 88	–	–
Adams, J.C	SLA	26	10	66	2	33.00	2- 66	–	–
Afford, J.A.	SLA	720.5	225	1659	57	29.10	5- 64	3	–
Alikhan, R.I.	OB	3	0	15	1	15.00	1- 15	–	–
Alleyne, M.W.	RM	246.3	50	707	26	27.19	3- 25	–	–
Ambrose, C.E.L.	RF	543.4	150	1207	59	20.45	6- 49	2	–
Andrew, S.J.W.	RMF	281.4	55	934	28	33.35	7- 47	2	–
Archer, G.F.	OB	6.3	0	72	0	–	–	–	–
Arthurton, K.L.T.	SLA	6	5	5	0	–	–	–	–
Asif Din	LB	4	1	12	0	–	–	–	–
Atherton, M.A.	LB	5	0	8	1	8.00	1- 8	–	–
Athey, C.W.J.	RM	50	7	200	2	100.00	2- 40	–	–
Austin, I.D.	RM	31.2	2	133	1	133.00	1- 66	–	–
Ayling, J.R.	RM	48	13	151	3	50.33	3- 68	–	–
Babington, A.M.	RFM	219.2	49	634	13	48.76	3- 51	–	–
Bailey, R.J.	OB	244.3	69	612	18	34.00	5- 54	1	–
Bainbridge, P.	RM	333.1	76	1021	40	25.52	5- 53	2	–
Ball, M.C.J.	OB	157.3	35	439	18	24.38	8- 46	2	1
Barnett, A.A.	SLA	713.2	177	2005	47	42.65	5- 36	3	–
Barnett, K.J.	LB	33	9	78	2	39.00	2- 40	–	–
Barwick, S.R.	RMF	506.4	208	1016	21	48.38	3- 26	–	–
Base, S.J.	RMF	310.1	69	1080	36	30.00	5- 59	3	–
Bastien, S.	RMF	167.3	27	573	19	30.15	6- 52	2	1
Bates, R.T.	OB	113	40	278	6	46.33	2- 43	–	–
Batty, J.D.	OB	383.2	97	1065	31	34.35	5- 36	1	–
Bee, A.	RMF	38	4	141	1	141.00	1- 86	–	–
Bell, M.A.V.	LMF	212.1	52	649	25	25.96	7- 48	3	–
Benjamin, J.E.	RMF	625.2	154	1783	64	27.85	6- 19	2	–
Benjamin, K.C.G.	RFM	283.5	42	911	37	24.62	6- 70	2	–
Benjamin, W.K.M.	RFM	281.3	81	702	32	21.93	7- 83	3	–
Berry, P.J.	OB	200.1	33	648	15	43.20	3- 39	–	–
Betts, M.M.	RMF	6	1	19	1	19.00	1- 19	–	–
Beven, I.R.	OB	45	14	107	2	53.50	2- 93	–	–
Bicknell, D.J.	LM	1	0	21	0	–	–	–	–
Bicknell, M.P.	RFM	502.2	137	1341	67	20.01	6- 43	6	2
Boden, D.J.P.	RMF	40	3	216	3	72.00	2-118	–	–
Boiling, J.	OB	221.1	61	669	11	60.81	5-100	1	–
Boon, T.J.	RM	8	1	38	0	–	–	–	–
Booth, P.A.	SLA	174.5	49	396	12	33.00	2- 36	–	–
Border, A.R.	SLA	65	17	177	3	59.00	1- 12	–	–
Botham, I.T.	RMF	185.5	46	516	13	39.69	4- 11	–	–
Bovill, J.N.B.	RFM	20	8	48	3	16.00	2- 32	–	–
Bowen, M.N.	RM	147.5	30	554	22	25.18	4-124	–	–

	Cat	O	M	R	W	Avge	Best	5wI	10wM
Bowler, P.D.	OB	20	8	45	0	–	–	–	–
Brain, D.H.	LFM	53.4	12	169	8	21.12	6- 48	1	–
Brandes, E.A.	RFM	73	7	312	5	62.40	2- 60	–	–
Briers, M.P.	LB	19	3	69	0	–	–	–	–
Brimson, M.T.	SLA	20	3	66	2	33.00	2- 66	–	–
Broad, B.C.	RM	1	0	1	0	–	–	–	–
Broadhurst, M.	RFM	1.1	0	7	0	–	–	–	–
Brown, A.D.	LB	1	0	6	0	–	–	–	–
Brown, S.J.E.	LFM	509	78	1861	47	39.59	7- 70	3	–
Burns, M.	RM	7	4	8	0	–	–	–	–
Butcher, M.A.	RM	134	24	436	15	29.06	4- 51	–	–
Byas, D.	RM	2	0	18	0	–	–	–	–
Caddick, A.R.	RFM	541	115	1678	63	26.63	9- 32	5	3
Cairns, C.L.	RFM	411.5	74	1242	53	23.43	6- 70	3	–
Capel, D.J.	RMF	117.4	37	252	12	21.00	3- 15	–	–
Carr, J.D.	RM	10.5	0	73	4	18.25	4- 73	–	–
Carrick, P.	SLA	77	35	122	3	40.66	1- 14	–	–
Chapple, G.	RMF	155	34	507	11	46.09	3- 50	–	–
Charlesworth, G.M.	RM	229.5	52	645	12	53.75	3- 33	–	–
Childs, J.H.	SLA	709	207	1729	62	27.88	6- 37	3	–
Cohen, M.F.	RSM	1	1	0	0	–	–	–	–
Connor, C.A.	RFM	261.4	65	803	16	50.18	4- 77	–	–
Cook, N.G.B.	SLA	199.5	68	412	8	51.50	3- 34	–	–
Cooper, K.E.	RFM	502.4	149	1233	47	26.23	5- 83	1	–
Cork, D.G.	RFM	396.5	85	1102	37	29.78	4- 90	–	–
Cottey, P.A.	OB	7	0	123	0	–	–	–	–
Cousins, D.M.	RMF	27	4	109	1	109.00	1- 51	–	–
Cowans, N.G.	RFM	81	16	234	16	14.62	4- 43	–	–
Crawley, M.A.	RM	61.3	14	171	6	28.50	3- 86	–	–
Croft, R.D.B.	OB	850.5	265	2158	61	35.37	5-112	2	–
Cummins, A.C.	RFM	504.3	95	1614	53	30.45	6-115	3	–
Curran, K.M.	RMF	458	123	1293	67	19.29	7- 47	3	–
Curry, D.J.	OB	10	7	16	1	16.00	1- 12	–	–
Curtis, T.S.	LB	7	2	22	0	–	–	–	–
Dakin, J.M.	RM	34	10	84	4	21.00	4- 45	–	–
Dale, A.	RM	393.1	81	1238	37	33.45	6- 18	1	–
Davies, M.	SLA	515.1	141	1412	37	38.16	5- 57	2	1
Davis, R.P.	SLA	479.4	141	1118	36	31.05	7-127	2	1
Dawson, R.I.	RM	1	0	2	0	–	–	–	–
DeFreitas, P.A.J.	RFM	651.4	130	1970	60	32.83	7- 76	4	1
De la Pena, J.M.	RFM	34	3	156	4	39.00	4- 77	–	–
Dessaur, W.A.	RM	17	2	94	0	–	–	–	–
Doak, N.G.	OB	1	1	0	0	–	–	–	–
D'Oliveira, D.B.	OB	55	13	155	5	31.00	3- 36	–	–
Donald, A.A.	RF	268.1	59	811	30	27.03	7- 98	2	1
Donelan, B.T.P.	OB	94.3	8	450	9	50.00	5-112	1	–
Dutch, K.P.	OB	5	1	18	0	–	–	–	–
Ealham, M.A.	RMF	281.2	56	917	31	29.58	5- 14	1	–
Ellison, B.C.A.	RMF	11	1	40	2	20.00	2- 40	–	–
Ellison, R.M.	RMF	61	19	169	4	42.25	2- 30	–	–
Emburey, J.E.	OB	719.4	226	1401	71	19.73	8- 40	2	1
Evans, K.P.	RMF	265.3	69	660	25	26.40	6- 67	1	–
Feltham, M.A.	RMF	327.4	88	905	29	31.20	4- 48	–	–
Field-Buss, M.G.	OB	307.3	112	748	28	26.71	6- 42	1	–
Fleming, M.V.	RM	422	103	1086	34	31.94	4- 31	–	–
Flint, D.P.J.	SLA	388.2	95	1066	31	34.38	5- 32	1	–

173

	Cat	O	M	R	W	Avge	Best	5wI	10wM
Flower, G.W.	SLA	26	5	99	1	99.00	1- 35	–	–
Foster, M.J.	RFM	17	3	50	3	16.66	3- 39	–	–
Foster, N.A.	RFM	250.3	60	723	12	60.25	5- 58	1	–
Fraser, A.R.C.	RFM	532.4	131	1388	61	22.75	7- 40	2	–
Frost, M.	RMF	58.1	11	180	7	25.71	3- 25	–	–
Gallian, J.E.R.	RM	195	43	585	11	53.18	3- 52	–	–
Gatting, M.W.	RM	4	0	10	0	–	–	–	–
Gerrard, M.J.	LMF	89.1	16	298	8	37.25	4- 50	–	–
Giddins, E.S.H.	RMF	379	55	1490	29	51.37	5-120	1	–
Giles, A.F.	SLA	41.3	6	128	3	42.66	1- 27	–	–
Gooch, G.A.	RM	36	9	110	0	–	–	–	–
Gough, D.	RFM	507.3	115	1517	57	26.61	7- 42	3	1
Govan, J.W.	OB	34.5	7	96	5	19.20	4- 34	–	–
Graveney, D.A.	SLA	579.1	187	1306	38	34.36	5- 78	1	–
Grayson, A.P.	SLA	5	3	7	0	–	–	–	–
Greenfield, K.	RM	39	7	136	5	27.20	2- 40	–	–
Griffith, F.A.	RM	170.5	29	593	14	42.35	3- 32	–	–
Gupte, C.M.	SLA	1	0	7	0	–	–	–	–
Hallett, J.C.	RMF	26	2	111	3	37.00	3- 85	–	–
Hamilton, G.M.	RMF	35.3	9	100	5	20.00	5- 65	1	–
Hancock, T.H.C.	RM	44	12	136	6	22.66	3- 10	–	–
Harden, R.J.	SLA	0.3	0	0	0	–	–	–	–
Harper, R.A.	OB	47	14	98	6	16.33	6- 71	1	–
Harrison, G.D.	OB	29	9	51	4	12.75	2- 20	–	–
Hartley, P.J.	RMF	351.4	91	1027	37	27.75	5- 51	1	–
Haste, N.J.	RM	225	43	715	10	71.50	2- 44	–	–
Hayden, M.L.	RM	8.4	1	31	1	31.00	1- 24	–	–
Hayhurst, A.N.	RM	58	19	168	3	56.00	1- 13	–	–
Haynes, D.L.	RM/LB	7	1	61	1	61.00	1- 61	–	–
Haynes, G.R.	RM	87	18	250	5	50.00	2- 29	–	–
Headley, D.W.	RFM	439.4	106	1191	42	28.35	7- 79	2	–
Hemmings, E.E.	OB	683.2	208	1541	63	24.46	7- 31	2	1
Hepworth, P.N.	OB	30	3	114	2	57.00	1- 17	–	–
Hick, G.A.	OB	203.4	59	603	10	60.30	2- 15	–	–
Hindson, J.E.	SLA	39.5	10	114	1	114.00	1- 24	–	–
Hinks, S.G.	RM	1	0	2	0	–	–	–	–
Hoey, C.J.	LB	46.1	12	111	4	27.75	3- 68	–	–
Holdsworth, W.J.	RF	204.5	32	833	23	36.21	5-117	1	–
Hollioake, A.J.	RMF	102.3	17	305	5	61.00	2- 75	–	–
Hooper, C.L.	OB	545	126	1281	33	38.81	4- 35	–	–
Hughes, M.G	RF	470.2	113	1420	48	29.58	5- 92	1	–
Hughes, S.P.	RFM	211.3	61	552	8	69.00	3- 48	–	–
Hussain, N.	LB	10.3	0	108	1	108.00	1- 75	–	–
Hutton, S.	RSM	2	1	1	0	–	–	–	–
Igglesden, A.P.	RFM	438.5	111	1068	54	19.77	6- 58	3	1
Illingworth, R.K.	SLA	645	219	1404	55	25.52	6- 28	1	–
Ilott, M.C.	LFM	640.4	130	1962	59	33.25	7- 85	2	–
Irani, R.C.	RM	1	0	6	0	–	–	–	–
James, K.D.	LMF	323.2	83	942	36	26.16	4- 33	–	–
Jarvis, P.W.	RFM	267.4	62	705	26	27.11	4- 51	–	–
Jean-Jacques, M.	RMF	52.3	11	181	4	45.25	2-117	–	–
Jeh, M.P.W.	RFM	297	48	1140	24	47.50	5- 63	1	–
Jenkins, R.H.J.	RM	16	1	77	0	–	–	–	–
Johnson, R.L.	RMF	16	5	58	1	58.00	1- 58	–	–
Jones, A.N.	RFM	84	8	373	2	186.50	2-108	–	–
Julian, B.P.	LFM	318.5	58	1158	29	39.93	5- 63	1	–

	Cat	O	M	R	W	Avge	Best	5wI	10wM
Keech, M.	RM	52	17	113	5	22.60	2- 28	–	–
Kendrick, N.M.	SLA	368	113	960	29	33.10	7-115	1	–
Kerr, J.I.D.	RMF	109.1	15	405	15	27.00	3- 47	–	–
Lambert, C.B.	OB	3	0	11	0	–	–	–	–
Lampitt, S.R.	RMF	333	62	1062	34	31.23	3- 9	–	–
Larkins, W.	RM	4	0	18	0	–	–	–	–
Lathwell, M.N.	RM	25	8	73	1	73.00	1- 40	–	–
Law, D.R.	RFM	63.4	12	216	5	43.20	2- 38	–	–
Leatherdale, D A.	RM	1	1	0	0	–	–	–	–
Lefebvre, R.P.	RMF	619.1	177	1379	44	31.34	4- 70	–	–
Lenham, N.J.	RM	93	23	255	9	28.33	4- 13	–	–
Leppard, J.	OB	11	0	40	0	–	–	–	–
Lewis, C.C.	RFM	561.1	122	1619	42	38.54	4- 34	–	–
Lewis, D.A.	RM	2	0	17	0	–	–	–	–
Llong, N.J.	OB	62.2	17	152	4	38.00	3- 29	–	–
Loye, M.B.	OB	0.1	0	1	0	–	–	–	–
Lugsden, S.	RFM	26	2	85	2	42.50	2- 43	–	–
Lynch, M.A.	OB	1	1	0	0	–	–	–	–
McCague, M.J.	RF	298.1	67	888	31	28.64	5- 33	2	–
McCrum, P.	RFM	27	7	82	3	27.33	3- 56	–	–
McDermott, C.J.	RF	143	26	449	6	74.83	2- 36	–	–
Macdonald, R.H.	RMF	250	66	710	20	35.50	5- 20	1	–
MacLay, A.W.	RMF	12	0	51	1	51.00	1- 11	–	–
Macmillan, G.I.	OB	67.2	14	211	7	30.14	3- 13	–	–
Malcolm, D.E.	RF	336.5	56	1262	41	30.78	6- 57	2	–
Malik, H.S.	OB	117.5	28	414	7	59.14	2- 18	–	–
Mallender, N.A.	RFM	329.5	102	772	32	24.12	5- 49	1	–
Marshall, M.D.	RF	345.3	102	859	28	30.67	5- 62	1	–
Martin, P.J.	RFM	406.5	105	1188	38	31.26	5- 35	1	–
Martyn, D.R.	RM/OB	8	2	21	0	–	–	–	–
Maru, R.J.	SLA	30	4	119	1	119.00	1- 62	–	–
May, T.B.A.	OB	562.5	156	1429	53	26.96	5- 89	1	–
Maynard, M.P.	RM	6	0	110	1	110.00	1-110	–	–
Middleton, T.C.	SLA	0.2	0	4	0	–	–	–	–
Mike, G.W.	RMF	205	42	708	17	41.64	5- 65	1	–
Milburn, S.M.	RMF	17.5	8	35	0	–	–	–	–
Millar, P.M.C.	RFM	20	4	61	0	–	–	–	–
Millns, D.J.	RF	184.3	51	584	25	23.36	5- 21	2	–
Moles, A.J.	RM	14	2	97	4	24.25	3- 87	–	–
Montgomerie, R.R.	OB	2	0	6	0	–	–	–	–
Moore, E.R.	LFM	29	15	53	1	53.00	1- 34	–	–
Moores, P.	(WK)	1	1	0	0	–	–	–	–
Morris, J.E.	RM	6	1	6	1	6.00	1- 6	–	–
Morris, R.S.M.	OB	0.4	0	1	0	–	–	–	–
Morrison, D.K.	RFM	33	10	91	1	91.00	1- 36	–	–
Mortensen, O.H.	RFM	255	66	643	21	30.61	5- 55	1	–
Moxon, M.D.	RM	4	2	7	0	–	–	–	–
Mudassar Nazar	RM	13	6	30	1	30.00	1- 9	–	–
Mullally, A.D.	LFM	528.1	141	1506	62	24.29	7- 72	2	1
Munton, T.A.	RMF	334.3	112	740	27	27.40	7- 41	1	–
Murphy, A.J.	RMF	333.4	79	1043	32	32.59	5- 58	1	–
Mushtaq Ahmed	LB	694.3	212	1773	85	20.85	7- 91	8	3
Newport, P.J.	RFM	546.5	135	1454	60	24.23	6- 63	1	–
Nicholas, M.C.J.	RM	1	0	4	0	–	–	–	–
North, J.A.	RM	104	14	413	7	59.00	3- 32	–	–
Ostler, D.P.	RM	6	1	16	0	–	–	–	–

	Cat	O	M	R	W	Avge	Best	5wI	10wM
Parker, P.W.G.	RM	21	3	70	0	–	–	–	–
Parsons, G.J.	RMF	490.1	151	1111	45	24.68	3- 23	–	–
Parsons, K.A.	RM	1	0	14	0	–	–	–	–
Patel, M.M.	SLA	199.5	52	533	17	31.35	7- 75	2	1
Payne, A.	RMF	18.2	4	62	4	15.50	2- 15	–	–
Peall, S.G.	OB	75	13	271	9	30.11	3- 46	–	–
Pearson, R.M.	OB	335.3	68	1020	21	48.57	3- 61	–	–
Penberthy, A.L.	RM	171	43	522	18	29.00	5- 37	1	–
Penn, C.	RFM	142	39	296	12	24.66	4- 12	–	–
Pennett, D.B.	RMF	172	34	520	17	30.58	5- 36	1	–
Penney, T.L.	RM	2.1	0	13	0	–	–	–	–
Phelps, B.S.	SLA	26	3	122	1	122.00	1-105	–	–
Phillips, N.C.	OB	43	13	103	3	34.33	3- 39	–	–
Pick, R.A.	RFM	346	78	1070	25	42.80	5- 53	1	–
Pierson, A.R.K.	OB	528.5	141	1371	44	31.15	6- 87	4	–
Pigott, A.C.S.	RFM	282.3	43	1001	21	47.66	4- 51	–	–
Pitcher, C.M.	RM	203.1	35	698	14	49.85	3- 50	–	–
Pollard, P.R.	RM	14	0	135	2	67.50	2- 79	–	–
Potter, L.	SLA	352.1	123	758	24	31.58	5- 45	1	–
Prichard, P.J.	RSM	6	0	77	1	77.00	1- 77	–	–
Pringle, D.R.	RMF	378.5	98	1041	29	35.89	4- 33	–	–
Radford, N.V.	RFM	269.5	46	1012	33	30.66	6- 49	1	–
Ramprakash, M.R.	RM	8.4	1	39	1	39.00	1- 22	–	–
Ranchod, U.	OB	17	3	66	2	33.00	2- 18	–	–
Ratcliffe, J.D.	RM	18.3	3	106	2	53.00	1- 6	–	–
Reeve, D.A.	RMF	284.1	108	528	22	24.00	3- 38	–	–
Reiffel, P.R.	RFM	375.4	85	1113	37	30.08	6- 71	2	–
Remy, C.C.	RM	24	7	103	2	51.50	2- 37	–	–
Rennie, J.A.	RM	15	4	60	1	60.00	1- 40	–	–
Richards, I.V.A.	OB	84	18	235	4	58.75	3- 22	–	–
Richardson, A.W.	RFM	22	5	74	0	–	–	–	–
Richardson, R.B.	RM	7	0	23	1	23.00	1- 5	–	–
Roberts, A.R.	LB	289.5	75	760	19	40.00	3- 51	–	–
Robinson, M.A.	RFM	514	131	1346	49	27.46	9- 37	3	1
Robinson, P.E.	LM	14.3	1	91	2	45.50	1- 13	–	–
Rose, G.D.	RM	324.3	62	1090	43	25.34	6- 83	3	–
Rowett, D.J.	RM	17	6	67	1	67.00	1- 28	–	–
Russell, A.B.	RM	6	0	22	0	–	–	–	–
Russell, R.C.	(WK)	1.5	0	15	0	–	–	–	–
Salim Malik	RSM	255.1	41	792	24	33.00	5- 67	1	–
Salisbury, I.D.K.	LB	616.3	132	2007	54	37.16	5- 81	2	–
Scott, R.J.	RM	60	14	157	2	78.50	2- 48	–	–
Shahid, N.	LB	13	5	28	0	–	–	–	–
Shine, K.J.	RFM	296.1	57	1172	24	48.83	6- 62	2	–
Silverwood, C.E.W.	RFM	20	3	75	1	75.00	1- 19	–	–
Simmons, P.V.	RM	18	11	20	0	–	–	–	–
Sladdin, R.W.	SLA	326.5	96	1017	23	44.21	3- 30	–	–
Sleep, P.R.	LB	5	1	17	0	–	–	–	–
Small, G.C.	RFM	251.4	71	629	21	29.95	4- 39	–	–
Smith, A.M.	LM	205.2	36	672	12	56.00	3- 59	–	–
Smith, A.W.	OB	93	15	387	5	77.40	2- 7	–	–
Smith, B.F.	RM	13	4	30	0	–	–	–	–
Smith, I.	RM	35	7	109	2	54.50	1- 10	–	–
Smith, N.M.K.	OB	588.1	151	1593	48	33.18	6-122	3	–
Smith, P.A.	RFM	130.5	18	505	14	36.07	4- 35	–	–
Smith, R.A.	LB	1	0	2	0	–	–	–	–

	Cat	O	M	R	W	Avge	Best	5wI	10wM
Snape, J.N.	OB	19.5	2	113	2	56.50	2- 49	–	–
Spencer, D.J.	RF	42	8	160	4	40.00	4- 46	–	–
Steer, I.G.S.	RM	9	2	34	3	11.33	3- 23	–	–
Stemp, R.D.	SLA	540	188	1207	40	30.17	6- 92	2	–
Stephenson, F.D.	RFM	397	77	1155	41	28.17	5- 55	1	–
Stephenson, J.P.	RM	265.5	52	908	30	30.26	5- 31	2	–
Streak, H.H.	RM	53	11	187	4	46.75	3- 87	–	–
Such, P.M.	OB	812	197	2148	76	28.26	6- 67	7	3
Tavaré, C.J.	RM	1	0	2	0	–	–	–	–
Taylor, C.W.	LMF	48	12	134	2	67.00	1- 25	–	–
Taylor, J.P.	LFM	646.5	191	1789	69	25.92	6- 82	2	–
Taylor, M.A.	RM	9	0	31	1	31.00	1- 4	–	–
Thomas, S.D.	RFM	141.3	21	556	20	27.80	5- 76	1	–
Thorpe, G.P.	RM	77.3	15	270	7	38.57	4- 40	–	–
Thursfield, M.J.	RM	43	13	143	5	28.60	4- 78	–	–
Tolley, C.M.	LMF	442.5	115	1194	42	28.42	5- 55	1	–
Topley, T.D.	RMF	181.5	41	627	15	41.80	3- 15	–	–
Trimby, P.W.	LB	143.2	31	469	12	39.08	3- 72	–	–
Trump, H.R.J.	OB	237.4	79	589	15	39.26	4- 74	–	–
Tufnell, P.C.R.	SLA	688.5	189	1529	64	23.89	8- 29	3	–
Turner, I.J.	SLA	111.4	34	337	8	42.12	3- 51	–	–
Twose, R.G.	RM	102.2	16	302	11	27.45	4- 85	–	–
Udal, S.D.	OB	763.2	183	2232	74	30.16	6-141	5	2
Vandrau, M.J.	OB	288.4	62	937	16	58.56	2- 8	–	–
Van Troost, A.P.	RF	282	49	1036	31	33.41	5- 47	1	–
Vaughan, M.P.	OB	13	4	42	1	42.00	1- 23	–	–
Walker, A.	RFM	24.5	6	78	3	26.00	3- 62	–	–
Walsh, C.A.	RF	528.1	119	1516	64	23.68	5- 59	3	–
Waqar Younis	RF	449.4	89	1407	62	22.69	6- 42	4	–
Warne, S.K.	LB	765.5	281	1698	75	22.64	5- 61	2	–
Warner, A.E.	RFM	322.5	76	900	41	21.95	5- 27	3	1
Wasim Akram	LF	409.2	93	1137	59	19.27	8- 68	5	1
Watkin, S.L.	RMF	766.4	173	2098	92	22.80	5- 71	2	–
Watkinson, M.	RMF	662.5	146	1950	51	38.23	5- 12	1	–
Waugh, M.E.	RM	121.1	28	403	6	67.16	3- 26	–	–
Waugh, S.R.	RM	73.1	19	229	7	32.71	2- 9	–	–
Weekes, P.N.	OB	55	7	151	3	50.33	2- 55	–	–
Wells, C.M.	RM	33	4	103	4	25.75	2- 36	–	–
Wells, V.J.	RMF	241.4	66	705	18	39.16	2- 5	–	–
Weston, M.J.	RM	29	9	96	2	48.00	1- 15	–	–
Weston, W.P.C.	LM	7	0	25	1	25.00	1- 13	–	–
White, C.	OB	130	36	310	15	20.66	3- 9	–	–
Whittall, A.R.	OB	309.3	63	969	19	51.00	3- 79	–	–
Wight, R.M.	OB	181.2	47	478	9	53.11	3- 71	–	–
Williams, N.F.	RFM	372	65	1131	39	29.00	6- 61	1	–
Williams, R.C.	RM	90	15	362	6	60.33	3-101	–	–
Windows, M.G.N.	RSM	1	0	3	0	–	–	–	–
Wood, J.	RFM	192	26	735	16	45.93	4-106	–	–
Wylie, A.	RF	22	3	73	1	73.00	1- 50	–	–
Yates, G.	OB	233	46	692	16	43.25	5-108	1	–
Yeabsley, R.S.	RMF	237.1	53	762	20	38.10	3- 30	–	–
Zoehrer, T.J.	LB	126.1	33	335	14	23.92	3- 16	–	–

FIRST-CLASS CAREER RECORDS

Compiled by Philip Bailey

The following career records are for all players who appeared in first-class cricket during the 1993 season, and are complete to the end of that season. Some players who did not appear in 1993 but may do so in 1994, are also included. The tours of Sri Lanka by India and South Africa in August and September 1993 are included.

BATTING AND FIELDING

'1000' denotes instances of scoring 1000 runs in a season. Where these have been achieved outside the UK, they are shown after a plus sign.

	M	I	NO	HS	Runs	Avge	100	1000	Ct/St
Adams, C.J.	87	133	13	175	3857	32.14	9	1	87
Adams, J.C.	53	87	15	128*	2697	37.45	4	–	48
Afford, J.A.	129	116	49	22*	448	3.85	–	–	42
Alikhan, R.I.	105	181	14	138	4696	28.11	2	1	57
Alleyne, M.W.	143	230	27	256	6102	30.05	8	2	114/2
Ambrose, C.E.L.	133	170	42	59	1873	14.63	–	–	31
Andrew, S.J.W.	111	83	35	35	367	7.64	–	–	24
Archer, G.F.	13	22	5	117	683	40.17	1	–	11
Arnott, K.J.	27	50	7	121	1404	32.65	3	–	17
Arscott, J.P.	31	42	8	79	678	19.94	–	–	30/9
Arthurton, K.L.T.	65	107	15	157*	4100	44.56	12	–	37
Asif Din	206	336	44	158*	8734	29.91	8	2	112
Atherton, M.A.	147	253	28	199	10041	44.62	29	5	127
Athey, C.W.J.	404	669	67	184	21729	36.09	47	11	385/2
Atkins, P.D.	24	44	3	114*	1081	26.36	1	–	9
Austin, I.D.	53	69	17	115*	1280	24.61	2	–	7
Ayling, J.R.	60	90	12	121	2082	26.69	1	–	17
Aymes, A.N.	69	92	28	107*	2111	32.98	1	–	155/14
Babington, A.M.	94	101	40	58	515	8.44	–	–	32
Bailey, R.J.	251	420	85	224*	15007	42.27	31	10	181
Bainbridge, P.	293	486	71	169	14426	34.76	24	9	125
Ball, M.C.J.	37	54	9	71	523	11.62	–	–	36
Barnett, A.A.	44	43	19	38	249	10.37	–	–	11
Barnett, K.J.	349	557	52	239*	19718	39.04	43	11	222
Barwick, S.R.	185	173	65	30	784	7.25	–	–	40
Base, S.J.	117	149	33	58	1274	10.98	–	–	54
Bastien, S.	49	38	18	36*	175	8.75	–	–	5
Bates, R.T.	5	5	3	33*	70	35.00	–	–	2
Batty, J.D.	61	61	15	51	625	13.58	–	–	22
Bee, A.	4	4	4	29*	53	–	–	–	2
Bell, M.A.V.	12	17	7	22*	70	7.00	–	–	2
Benjamin, J.E.	60	66	23	42	469	10.90	–	–	15
Benjamin, K.C.G.	40	48	15	52*	438	13.27	–	–	5
Benjamin, W.K.M.	140	172	35	101*	3128	22.83	1	–	79
Benson, J.D.R.	56	83	8	153	2097	27.96	4	–	65
Benson, M.R.	263	442	33	257	16948	41.43	45	11	126
Berry, D.S.	47	62	9	98	857	16.16	–	–	156/14
Berry, P.J.	25	36	13	76	513	22.30	–	–	9
Betts, M.M.	1	2	1	4	4	4.00	–	–	–
Beven, I.R.	19	35	1	57	605	17.79	–	–	13
Bicknell, D.J.	141	248	24	190	8782	39.20	21	5	56

178

	M	I	NO	HS	Runs	Avge	100	1000	Ct/St
Bicknell, M.P.	131	152	42	88	1961	17.82	–	–	47
Bishop, I.R.	96	127	33	103*	1452	15.44	1	–	21
Blakey, R.J.	179	291	38	221	8171	32.29	9	4	296/30
Boden, D.J.P.	4	3	–	5	10	3.33	–	–	2
Boiling, J.	39	50	21	29	360	12.41	–	–	31
Boon, D.C.	220	372	36	227	15940	47.44	51	2+5	186
Boon, T.J.	226	379	40	144	11038	32.56	14	7	114
Booth, P.A.	60	80	18	62	830	13.38	–	–	19
Border, A.R.	350	570	89	205	24770	51.49	66	3+8	335
Botham, I.T.	402	617	46	228	19399	33.97	38	4	354
Bovill, J.N.B.	1	2	2	3*	3	–	–	–	–
Bowen, M.N.	8	9	4	23*	98	19.60	–	–	1
Bowler, P.D.	145	252	25	241*	9379	41.31	20	6	95/1
Brain, D.H.	9	14	2	58	213	17.75	–	–	3
Bramhall, S.	12	13	5	37*	115	14.37	–	–	19/6
Brandes, E.A.	36	51	6	94	495	11.00	–	–	19
Briant, G.A.	7	11	–	69	262	23.81	–	–	7
Briers, M.P.	17	30	4	62*	462	17.76	–	–	8
Briers, N.E.	347	566	56	201*	16464	32.28	26	9	146
Brimson, M.T.	2	1	–	0	0	0.00	–	–	–
Broad, B.C.	330	593	38	227*	21396	38.55	49	11	180
Broadhurst, M.	4	2	–	1	1	0.50	–	–	–
Brown, A.D.	30	50	4	175	2122	46.13	6	1	24
Brown, D.R.	3	3	2	44*	54	54.00	–	–	2
Brown, K.R.	154	236	42	200*	6784	34.96	10	2	218/17
Brown, S.J.E.	51	62	24	47*	419	11.02	–	–	14
Burns, M.	8	13	–	78	181	13.92	–	–	16/2
Burns, N.D.	156	234	52	166	5349	29.39	5	–	316/32
Butcher, A.R.	8	13	4	66*	270	30.00	–	–	4
Byas, D.	119	196	21	156	5589	31.93	9	2	123
Caddick, A.R.	40	49	10	54*	595	15.25	–	–	13
Cairns, C.L.	82	114	16	110	3163	32.27	3	–	36
Cake, R.Q.	11	19	6	108	472	36.30	1	–	5
Campbell, A.D.R.	15	28	5	100*	730	31.73	1	–	8
Capel, D.J.	270	408	61	134	10279	29.62	12	3	128
Carr, J.D.	155	247	34	192*	7471	35.07	14	3	162
Carrick, P.	444	572	104	131*	10300	22.00	3	–	197
Carroll, J.P.	13	21	1	92	244	12.20	–	–	2
Chapman, C.A.	4	7	1	20	72	12.00	–	–	5/2
Chapman, R.J.	1	–	–	–	–	–	–	–	–
Chapple, G.	10	15	8	109*	275	39.28	1	–	4
Charlesworth, G.M.	18	30	3	83	803	29.74	–	–	11
Childs, J.H.	343	309	147	43	1480	9.13	–	–	108
Cohen, M.F.	10	18	1	60	320	18.82	–	–	4
Connor, C.A.	170	140	39	59	1089	10.78	–	–	50
Cook, N.G.B.	345	353	95	75	3039	11.77	–	–	194
Cooper, K.E.	288	308	73	52	2359	10.03	–	–	90
Cork, D.G.	61	84	14	104	1656	23.65	1	–	34
Cottam, A.C.	6	8	1	31	43	6.14	–	–	1
Cottey, P.A.	107	170	27	156	4621	32.31	7	3	60
Cousins, D.M.	1	2	1	0*	0	0.00	–	–	–
Cowans, N.G.	227	233	62	66	1554	9.08	–	–	60
Cowdrey, G.R.	136	214	27	147	6487	34.68	12	3	73
Cox, R.M.F.	15	22	3	104*	491	25.84	1	–	9
Crawley, J.P.	52	86	9	187*	3601	46.76	6	2	37
Crawley, M.A.	72	112	21	160*	3206	35.23	8	1	60

179

	M	I	NO	HS	Runs	Avge	100	1000	Ct/St
Croft, R.D.B.	93	134	34	107	2620	26.20	1	–	40
Cummins, A.C.	33	48	7	70	759	18.51	–	–	9
Curran, K.M.	226	343	57	144*	10053	35.15	18	5	124
Curry, D.J.	1	2	–	41	45	22.50	–	–	–
Curtis, T.S.	268	455	57	248	16864	42.37	32	10	153
Dakin, J.M.	1	1	–	5	5	5.00	–	–	–
Dale, A.	73	121	13	214*	3981	36.86	7	2	35
Daley, J.A.	15	26	1	88	753	30.12	–	–	9
Davies, M.	35	49	16	44*	382	11.57	–	–	18
Davis, R.P.	125	153	39	67	1795	15.74	–	–	108
Dawson, R.I.	15	25	1	58	438	18.25	–	–	14
DeFreitas, P.A.J.	191	259	27	113	4830	20.81	4	–	60
De la Pena, J.M.	4	4	2	7*	8	4.00	–	–	–
Dessaur, W.A.	9	13	–	148	489	37.61	2	–	3
Doak, N.G.	1	2	–	25	27	13.50	–	–	2
D'Oliveira, D.B.	227	355	22	237	9180	27.56	10	4	199
Donald, A.A.	173	202	80	46*	1391	11.40	–	–	67
Donelan, B.T.P.	52	65	21	68*	1105	25.11	–	–	14
Dutch, K.P.	1	–	–	–	–	–	–	–	2
Ealham, M.A.	38	57	11	85	1350	29.34	–	–	10
Edwards, T.	1	–	–	–	–	–	–	–	1
Ellison, B.C.A.	1	–	–	–	–	–	–	–	–
Ellison, R.M.	207	284	72	108	5046	23.80	1	–	86
Emburey, J.E.	467	589	120	133	11192	23.86	7	–	423
Evans, K.P.	99	137	34	104	2605	25.29	2	–	78
Fairbrother, N.H.	245	386	60	366	13315	40.84	27	8	153
Farbrace, P.	38	48	11	79	694	18.75	–	–	86/12
Feltham, M.A.	130	161	42	101	2814	23.64	1	–	52
Felton, N.A.	201	342	20	173*	9797	30.42	15	5	117
Field-Buss, M.G.	28	32	10	34*	235	10.68	–	–	11
Fleming, M.V.	87	138	19	116	3787	31.82	5	–	41
Fletcher, I.	8	12	2	65*	281	28.10	–	–	1
Fletcher, S.D.	114	96	32	28*	476	7.43	–	–	27
Flint, D.P.J.	10	13	5	14*	47	5.87	–	–	7
Flower, A.	22	38	5	121*	1164	35.27	2	–	33/5
Flower, G.W.	17	32	2	130	915	30.50	1	–	12
Folland, N.A.	19	34	4	108*	1084	36.13	2	–	14
Fordham, A.	120	211	17	206*	7811	40.26	17	4	77
Foster, M.J.	1	1	–	6	6	6.00	–	–	1
Foster, N.A.	230	269	59	107*	4343	20.68	2	–	116
Fothergill, A.R.	12	17	1	29	127	7.93	–	–	16/3
Fowler, E.R.	2	3	–	9	19	6.33	–	–	–
Fowler, G.	288	488	27	226	16436	35.65	36	8	150/5
Fraser, A.R.C.	137	151	36	92	1402	12.19	–	–	26
French, B.N.	357	468	91	123	7141	18.94	2	–	812/100
Frost, M.	64	52	19	12	106	3.21	–	–	7
Fulton, D.P.	8	15	1	75	365	26.07	–	–	13
Gallian, J.E.R.	21	35	4	141*	1187	38.29	3	–	11
Garnham, M.A.	188	250	50	123	5650	28.25	5	–	395/36
Gatting, M.W.	455	713	113	258	30114	50.19	76	15+1	395
Gerrard, M.J.	20	26	10	42	107	6.68	–	–	7
Gibson, O.D.	18	27	5	83*	445	20.22	–	–	6
Giddins, E.S.H.	28	28	15	14*	41	3.15	–	–	7
Giles, A.F.	2	4	1	23	53	17.66	–	–	–
Glendenen, J.D.	21	34	2	117	648	20.25	1	–	6
Gooch, G.A.	508	859	70	333	38427	48.70	106	17+1	495

180

	M	I	NO	HS	Runs	Avge	100	1000	Ct/St
Gough, D.	58	73	18	72	798	14.50	–	–	10
Govan, J.W.	11	14	1	50	137	10.53	–	–	6
Gower, D.I.	448	727	70	228	26339	40.08	53	13	280/1
Graveney, D.A.	444	558	172	119	6790	17.14	2	–	236
Grayson, A.P.	24	35	5	64	677	22.56	–	–	13
Greenfield, K.	33	54	8	127*	1348	29.30	4	–	32
Griffith, F.A.	31	45	4	81	724	17.65	–	–	16
Gupte, C.M.	22	31	5	61	633	24.34	–	–	6
Habib, A.	1	2	1	12	19	19.00	–	–	–
Hall, J.W.	64	113	10	140*	3341	32.43	5	2	27
Hallett, J.C.	12	7	2	15	41	8.20	–	–	5
Hamilton, G.M.	1	1	–	0	0	0.00	–	–	–
Hancock, T.H.C.	32	57	5	102	1257	24.17	1	–	21
Harden, R.J.	173	277	44	187	9035	38.77	18	5	132
Harper, R.A.	180	234	41	234	6446	33.39	8	–	229
Harrison, G.D.	10	16	1	86	445	29.66	–	–	2
Hartley, P.J.	138	161	42	127*	2679	22.51	2	–	46
Haste, N.J.	10	9	1	36	76	9.50	–	–	5
Hayden, M.L.	38	68	5	161*	3427	54.39	8	1+2	35
Hayhurst, A.N.	120	191	22	172*	5520	32.66	11	2	38
Haynes, D.L.	323	552	65	255*	22727	46.66	54	3+4	177/1
Haynes, G.R.	22	30	3	158	722	26.74	1	–	8
Headley, D.W.	44	49	11	91	753	19.81	–	–	19
Healy, I.A.	114	164	33	102*	3987	30.43	1	–	343/30
Hegg, W.K.	148	213	43	130	4264	25.08	2	–	333/44
Hemmings, E.E.	497	647	150	127*	9375	18.85	1	–	206
Hemp, D.L.	23	38	5	90*	846	25.63	–	–	12
Henderson, P.W.	5	7	–	46	119	17.00	–	–	1
Hepworth, P.N.	54	88	8	129	2000	25.00	3	1	30
Hick, G.A.	251	407	44	405*	21106	58.14	72	9+1	304
Hindson, J.E.	3	1	–	1	1	1.00	–	–	–
Hinks, S.G.	177	309	19	234	8473	29.21	11	3	110
Hodgson, G.D.	85	146	9	166	4784	34.91	7	4	39
Hoey, C.J.	3	4	1	8	21	7.00	–	–	1
Holdsworth, W.J.	55	50	14	33*	269	7.47	–	–	25
Hollioake, A.J.	5	9	–	123	352	39.11	1	–	4
Holloway, P.C.L.	14	21	7	102*	504	36.00	1	–	31/1
Hooper, C.L.	144	220	27	236*	8523	44.16	20	3	153
Houghton, D.L.	86	152	10	202	4867	34.27	9	–	142/16
Hughes, J.G.	6	9	–	6	11	1.22	–	–	1
Hughes, M.G.	153	181	41	72*	2488	17.77	–	–	52
Hughes, S.P.	205	226	70	53	1775	11.37	–	–	50
Humphries, S.	1	–	–	–	–	–	–	–	2
Hussain, N.	119	177	27	197	6767	45.11	17	2	137
Hutton, S.	18	32	–	78	875	27.34	–	–	11
Hyam, B.J.	1	2	–	1	1	0.50	–	–	2
Igglesden, A.P.	123	126	44	41	731	8.91	–	–	34
Illingworth, R.K.	261	288	78	120*	4495	21.40	3	–	112
Ilott, M.C.	62	67	18	51	649	13.24	–	–	18
Irani, R.C.	9	11	1	44	143	14.30	–	–	5
Jackson, P.B.	11	15	3	59	244	20.33	–	–	19/5
James, K.D.	157	226	40	162	6073	32.65	8	2	52
James, S.P.	93	161	12	152*	4886	32.79	11	2	70
Jarrett, M.E.D.	17	26	3	51	383	16.65	–	–	5
Jarvis, P.W.	156	183	52	80	2127	16.23	–	–	39
Jean-Jacques, M.	57	69	16	73	629	11.86	–	–	14

181

	M	I	NO	HS	Runs	Avge	100	1000	Ct/St
Jeh, M.P.W.	19	21	6	23	107	7.13	–	–	5
Jenkins, R.H.J.	18	21	6	20	123	8.20	–	–	4
Johnson, P.	231	380	38	187	12566	36.74	27	7	151/1
Johnson, R.L.	2	3	–	4	9	3.00	–	–	1
Jones, A.N.	175	153	62	43*	1037	11.39	–	–	42
Jones, D.M.	170	278	30	248	12500	50.40	35	2+3	128
Jones, G.W.	19	33	2	45*	509	16.41	–	–	2
Julian, B.P.	37	54	13	87	875	21.34	–	–	14
Kasprowicz, M.S.	22	32	4	49	373	13.32	–	–	8
Keech, M.	20	34	4	58*	584	19.46	–	–	9
Keey, C.L.	18	29	2	111	649	24.03	1	–	5
Kellett, S.A.	72	122	9	125*	3740	33.09	2	2	61
Kendrick, N.M.	48	61	17	55	750	17.04	–	–	41
Kerr, J.I.D.	7	11	3	19*	67	8.37	–	–	3
Kersey, G.J.	16	23	4	38*	341	17.94	–	–	48/4
Knight, N.V.	34	53	7	109	1510	32.82	3	–	37
Krikken, K.M.	87	122	20	77*	1903	18.65	–	–	197/17
Lamb, A.J.	435	722	103	294	30223	48.82	84	12	336
Lambert, C.B.	69	117	11	263*	4910	46.32	12	–	101
Lampitt, S.R.	105	124	24	93	2103	21.03	–	–	56
Larkins, W.	453	792	51	252	25429	34.31	56	13	284
Lathwell, M.N.	42	74	2	175	2580	35.83	5	2	34
Law, D.R.	3	2	–	11	11	5.50	–	–	–
Leatherdale, D.A.	60	91	8	157	2218	26.72	3	–	56
Lefebvre, R.P.	62	72	13	100	1199	20.32	1	–	31
Lenham, N.J.	140	240	22	222*	7266	33.33	15	3	56
Leppard, J.	5	6	–	20	55	9.16	–	–	–
Lewis, C.C.	113	167	20	247	4286	29.15	5	–	81
Lewis, D.A.	6	11	2	122*	389	43.22	1	–	2
Lewis, J.J.B.	29	47	9	136*	1671	43.97	3	–	20
Llong, N.J.	28	41	8	116*	1226	37.15	2	–	22
Lloyd, G.D.	83	136	16	132	4713	39.27	9	2	56
Longley, J.I.	10	17	–	110	361	21.23	1	–	8
Love, J.D.	250	393	60	170*	10355	31.09	13	2	125
Lovell, G.B.T.	26	39	6	114	1061	32.15	2	–	21
Loye, M.B.	29	43	5	153*	1154	30.36	2	–	27
Lugsden, S.	1	1	1	5*	5	–	–	–	–
Lynch, M.A.	315	511	59	172*	16043	35.49	34	8	317
Lyons, C.W.J.	9	12	4	28	108	13.50	–	–	22/2
McCague, M.J.	44	52	13	34	455	11.66	–	–	25
McCrum, P.	3	4	1	5	5	1.66	–	–	–
McDermott, C.J.	141	175	29	74	2392	16.38	–	–	40
Macdonald, R.H.	20	17	6	20	76	6.90	–	–	–
MacLay, A.W.	1	1	1	0*	0	–	–	–	–
Macmillan, G.I.	9	14	1	63	336	25.84	–	–	5
Maher, B.J.M.	133	205	36	126	3689	21.82	4	–	289/14
Malcolm, D.E.	147	164	49	51	922	8.01	–	–	26
Malik, H.S.	10	14	3	64*	238	21.63	–	–	6
Mallender, N.A.	326	370	116	100*	4287	16.87	1	–	106
Marsh, S.A.	192	269	47	125	6202	27.93	7	–	428/35
Marshall, M.D.	384	488	64	117	10200	24.05	6	–	138
Martin, P.J.	66	67	24	133	1040	24.18	1	–	17
Martyn, D.R.	43	70	12	139	3092	53.31	10	0+1	27/2
Maru, R.J.	201	190	46	74	2353	16.34	–	–	212
May, T.B.A.	106	127	37	128	1489	16.54	1	–	32
Maynard, M.P.	207	338	37	243	12740	42.32	28	8	183/2

	M	I	NO	HS	Runs	Avge	100	1000	Ct/St
Mendis, G.D.	366	643	61	209*	21436	36.83	41	13	145/1
Metcalfe, A.A.	188	325	19	216*	10677	34.89	24	6	68
Metson, C.P.	186	243	54	96	3339	17.66	–	–	437/34
Middleton, T.C.	94	160	13	221	5181	35.24	12	2	70
Mike, G.W.	18	26	5	61*	486	23.14	–	–	9
Milburn, S.M.	2	2	1	5	7	7.00	–	–	–
Millar, P.M.C.	1	1	–	2	2	2.00	–	–	–
Millns, D.J.	73	81	32	44	658	13.42	–	–	36
Moles, A.J.	184	331	34	230*	12101	40.74	24	6	119
Montgomerie, R.R.	26	42	6	109	1248	34.66	2	–	17
Moody, T.M.	146	243	19	210	10227	45.65	32	2+1	121
Moore, E.R.	1	–	–	–	–	–	–	–	–
Moores, P.	155	215	29	116	4516	24.27	4	–	309/39
Morris, H.	235	402	40	160*	13905	38.41	36	7	142
Morris, J.E.	236	388	27	229	14267	39.52	34	8	100
Morris, R.S.M.	13	23	1	92	581	26.40	–	–	21
Morrison, D.K.	102	102	33	36	575	8.33	–	–	37
Mortensen, O.H.	155	173	94	74*	709	8.97	–	–	47
Moxon, M.D.	259	442	32	218*	16843	41.08	34	9	195
Mudassar Nazar	220	355	34	241	14080	43.86	42	0+4	142
Mullally, A.D.	74	75	21	34	446	8.25	–	–	17
Munton, T.A.	161	163	63	47	943	9.43	–	–	58
Murphy, A.J.	83	85	38	38	313	6.65	–	–	17
Mushtaq Ahmed	77	92	11	90	1116	13.77	–	–	47
Newell, M.	102	178	26	203*	4636	30.50	6	1	93/1
Newport, P.J.	214	244	72	98	4403	25.59	–	–	64
Nicholas, M.C.J.	339	555	80	206*	15870	33.41	29	8	203
Nixon, P.A.	64	87	25	113*	1582	25.51	2	–	151/15
Noon, W.M.	12	16	2	37	150	10.71	–	–	23/3
North, J.A.	23	31	6	114	513	20.52	1	–	4
O'Gorman, T.J.G.	85	141	19	148	3739	30.64	6	2	54
Oliphant-Callum, R.D.	5	5	–	19	48	9.60	–	–	1
Orr, D.A.	2	2	1	23*	37	37.00	–	–	2/3
Ostler, D.P.	75	131	12	192	4127	34.68	5	3	71
Parker, B.	1	2	–	30	37	18.50	–	–	1
Parker, P.W.G.	371	633	79	215	19419	35.05	47	9	257
Parks, R.J.	256	285	83	89	3957	19.58	–	–	642/72
Parsons, G.J.	278	364	84	76	5334	19.05	–	–	89
Parsons, K.A.	6	11	1	63	135	13.50	–	–	3
Patel, M.M.	22	27	10	43	197	11.58	–	–	8
Patterson, B.M.W.	6	10	–	108	505	50.50	2	–	8
Payne, A.	3	3	2	51*	90	90.00	–	–	1
Peall, S.G.	10	17	5	41*	246	20.50	–	–	4
Pearson, R.M.	31	35	7	33*	260	9.29	–	–	9
Penberthy, A.L.	48	70	9	101*	1069	17.52	1	–	30
Penn, C.	127	145	36	115	2048	18.78	1	–	56
Pennett, D.B.	19	15	3	29	80	6.66	–	–	3
Penney, T.L.	40	63	17	151	2051	44.58	5	–	17
Phelps, B.S.	1	–	–	–	–	–	–	–	–
Philip, I.R.	8	13	1	145	604	50.33	3	–	7
Phillips, N.C.	1	–	–	–	–	–	–	–	–
Pick, R.A.	151	147	43	63	1539	14.79	–	–	36
Pierson, A.R.K.	75	87	35	58	656	12.78	–	–	20
Pigott, A.C.S.	246	295	65	104*	4605	20.02	1	–	119
Piper, K.J.	75	100	16	111	1586	18.88	1	–	174/9
Pitcher, C.M.	15	16	5	32*	123	11.18	–	–	5

	M	I	NO	HS	Runs	Avge	100	1000	Ct/St
Pollard, P.R.	100	175	10	180	5519	33.44	9	3	101
Pooley, J.C.	19	33	2	88	717	23.12	–	–	10
Potter, L.	223	354	42	165*	9027	28.93	8	3	190
Prabhakar, M.	108	146	27	229*	5077	42.66	12	–	40
Prichard, P.J.	215	346	41	245	10977	35.99	20	6	140
Pringle, D.R.	295	405	78	128	9243	28.26	10	–	153
Radford, N.V.	270	267	67	76*	3246	16.23	–	–	124
Ramprakash, M.R.	134	217	33	233	7210	39.18	14	4	65
Ranchod, U.	3	4	1	12*	22	7.33	–	–	1
Randall, D.W.	488	827	81	237	28456	38.14	52	13	361
Ratcliffe, J.D.	74	137	8	127*	3754	29.10	3	–	46
Rea, M.P.	7	14	1	115	424	32.62	1	–	2
Reeve, D.A.	209	280	71	202*	7313	34.99	5	2	153
Reiffel, P.R.	61	67	20	86	1029	21.89	–	–	26
Remy, C.C.	14	16	2	47	281	20.07	–	–	4
Rennie, J.A.	3	4	1	27*	33	11.00	–	–	1
Rhodes, S.J.	231	304	90	116*	6787	31.71	5	–	544/69
Richards, I.V.A.	507	796	62	322	36212	49.33	114	14+3	464/1
Richardson, A.W.	2	3	–	9	14	4.66	–	–	1
Richardson, R.B.	175	290	23	194	11330	42.43	31	1+2	162
Ripley, D.	196	253	63	134*	4666	24.55	6	–	424/59
Roberts, A.R.	43	58	14	62	696	15.81	–	–	18
Robinson, D.D.J.	2	4	–	67	112	28.00	–	–	2
Robinson, M.A.	118	118	52	19*	179	2.71	–	–	22
Robinson, P.E.	151	248	34	189	7213	33.70	7	3	117
Robinson, R.T.	330	574	75	220*	21361	42.80	49	11	212
Rollins, A.S.	7	13	4	85	392	43.55	–	–	5/1
Rollins, R.J.	4	6	1	13	33	6.60	–	–	5/3
Rose, G.D.	139	188	38	138	4591	30.60	5	1	67
Roseberry, M.A.	139	233	30	185	7596	37.41	16	3	97
Rowett, D.J.	2	2	2	8*	8	–	–	–	3
Russell, A.B.	7	9	1	51	209	26.12	–	–	10
Russell, R.C.	274	390	88	128*	8300	27.48	4	–	626/92
Salim Malik	206	318	48	215	12806	47.42	33	2+1	136
Salisbury, I.D.K.	100	115	35	68	1404	17.55	–	–	66
Salmond, G.	3	5	–	118	324	64.80	1	–	2
Sargeant, N.F.	41	52	9	49	612	14.23	–	–	91/16
Saxelby, M.	36	58	7	77	1540	30.19	–	–	9
Scott, C.W.	95	120	26	78	2039	21.69	–	–	189/15
Scott, R.J.	72	123	9	127	2719	23.85	3	–	34
Seymour, A.C.H.	32	56	5	157	1490	29.21	2	–	17
Shahid, N.	56	81	12	132	2236	32.40	2	1	51
Shepard, S.F.	1	2	–	5	5	2.50	–	–	1
Shine, K.J.	54	47	21	26*	258	9.92	–	–	7
Silverwood, C.E.W.	1	1	1	0	0	0.00	–	–	1
Simmons, P.V.	97	172	9	202	5748	34.83	12	1	98
Sims, R.J.	4	3	–	28	31	10.33	–	–	2
Sladdin, R.W.	30	36	9	51*	330	12.22	–	–	14
Slater, M.J.	29	50	6	152	2392	54.36	7	1+1	17
Sleep, P.R.	174	284	49	182	8122	34.56	15	–	104/1
Small, G.C.	286	370	86	70	4180	14.71	–	–	90
Smith, A.M.	33	38	8	51*	316	10.53	–	–	4
Smith, A.W.	14	23	2	68	560	26.66	–	–	7
Smith, B.F.	43	63	9	100*	1397	25.87	1	–	15
Smith, D.M.	312	499	88	213	14939	36.34	28	7	198
Smith, I.	81	111	14	116	2350	24.22	4	–	35

	M	I	NO	HS	Runs	Avge	100	1000	Ct/St
Smith, N.M.K.	58	87	12	161	1819	24.25	1	–	16
Smith, P.A.	203	326	38	140	7630	26.49	4	2	56
Smith, R.A.	254	431	72	209*	16059	44.73	39	7	164
Snape, J.N.	2	2	–	18	18	9.00	–	–	1
Speak, N.J.	74	127	9	232	4565	38.68	7	2	45
Speight, M.P.	95	156	13	184	5309	37.12	11	3	71
Spencer, D.J.	2	2	–	75	79	39.50	–	–	1
Stanley, N.A.	21	35	4	132	1019	32.87	1	–	9
Stanworth, J.	44	40	11	50*	266	9.17	–	–	63/10
Steer, I.G.S.	4	7	2	67	157	31.40	–	–	–
Stemp, R.D.	39	40	18	37	389	17.68	–	–	16
Stephenson, F.D.	162	246	30	165	6023	27.88	8	1	67
Stephenson, J.P.	172	297	31	202*	9695	36.44	17	5	104
Stewart, A.J.	246	409	47	206*	13998	38.66	25	8	317/12
Storie, A.C.	54	88	14	106	1554	21.00	1	–	36
Streak, H.H.	4	6	2	12	29	7.25	–	–	–
Such, P.M.	155	137	47	54	561	6.23	–	–	59
Sylvester, S.A.	5	2	1	0*	0	0.00	–	–	2
Tavaré, C.J.	431	717	75	219	24906	38.79	48	16	418
Taylor, C.W.	29	24	9	28*	175	11.66	–	–	5
Taylor, J.P.	65	62	27	74*	375	10.71	–	–	21
Taylor, M.A.	146	252	11	219	10739	44.56	28	1+4	203
Taylor, N.R.	280	476	63	204	16301	39.46	38	9	147
Terry, V.P.	246	412	40	190	13750	36.96	31	9	265
Thomas, S.D.	10	14	6	16*	71	8.87	–	–	3
Thorpe, G.P.	116	193	29	216	6908	42.12	13	4	79
Thursfield, M.J.	5	4	2	36*	36	18.00	–	–	–
Titchard, S.P.	30	54	4	135	1580	31.60	1	–	17
Tolley, C.M.	51	56	18	78	813	21.39	–	–	22
Topley, T.D.	119	137	29	66	1691	15.65	–	–	70
Townsend, C.J.	6	5	2	8	8	2.66	–	–	10
Trescothick, M.E.	3	6	–	6	14	2.33	–	–	4
Trimby, P.W.	6	2	2	2*	3	–	–	–	2
Trump, H.R.J.	74	77	26	48	508	9.96	–	–	47
Tufnell, P.C.R.	139	139	56	37	888	10.69	–	–	57
Turner, I.J.	24	27	8	39*	159	8.36	–	–	12
Turner, R.J.	47	74	15	101*	1440	24.40	1	–	57/15
Tweats, T.A.	1	1	–	24	24	24.00	–	–	1
Twose, R.G.	76	130	12	233	3620	30.67	4	1	44
Udal, S.D.	51	63	14	79*	988	20.16	–	–	14
Vandrau, M.J.	16	23	2	58	404	19.23	–	–	8
Van Troost, A.P.	29	27	12	35	150	10.00	–	–	6
Vaughan, M.P.	2	4	–	64	118	29.50	–	–	–
Walker, A.	97	91	45	41*	664	14.43	–	–	38
Walker, M.J.	1	2	1	23*	39	39.00	–	–	1
Walsh, C.A.	275	341	78	63*	3316	12.60	–	–	73
Waqar Younis	101	108	33	51	988	13.17	–	–	24
Ward, D.M.	134	214	32	263	7010	38.51	15	2	106/3
Ward, T.R.	113	192	14	235*	6671	37.47	15	3	86
Warke, S.J.S.	12	22	2	144*	893	44.65	2	–	8
Warne, S.K.	44	52	13	69	729	18.69	–	–	18
Warner, A.E.	175	235	41	95*	3402	17.53	–	–	43
Warren, R.J.	7	9	2	37*	83	11.85	–	–	3
Wasim Akram	143	191	24	123	3624	21.70	4	–	49
Watkin, S.L.	136	146	41	41	942	8.97	–	–	31
Watkinson, M.	219	322	40	138	7208	25.56	5	1	108

	M	I	NO	HS	Runs	Avge	100	1000	Ct/St
Waugh, M.E.	172	270	41	229*	13008	56.80	43	4+2	208
Waugh, S.R.	168	253	42	216*	9626	45.62	27	2	143
Weekes, P.N.	30	40	9	95	1011	32.61	–	–	25
Wells, A.P.	252	413	66	253*	13913	40.09	32	8	151
Wells, C.M.	279	441	70	203	12401	33.42	21	6	87
Wells, V.J.	46	71	9	167	1610	25.96	1	–	24
Weston, M.J.	161	258	24	145*	5597	23.91	3	1	76
Weston, W.P.C.	29	47	7	113	1313	32.82	2	–	8
Whitaker, J.J.	243	385	44	200*	12928	37.91	25	8	150
White, C.	52	75	16	146	1954	33.11	1	–	34
White, G.W.	1	1	–	42	42	42.00	–	–	–
Whittal, G.J.	6	10	1	42	155	17.22	–	–	1
Whittall, A.R.	10	9	2	40	80	11.42	–	–	2
Whitticase, P.	129	169	39	114*	2963	22.79	1	–	302/13
Wight, R.M.	17	28	4	62*	540	22.50	–	–	11
Wileman, J.R.	2	3	1	109	167	83.50	1	–	3
Williams, J.R.A.	1	2	–	6	6	3.00	–	–	–
Williams, N.F.	212	244	47	77	3775	19.16	–	–	57
Williams, R.C.	12	20	4	44	222	13.87	–	–	1
Williams, R.C.J.	24	27	8	55*	284	14.94	–	–	54/12
Willis, S.C.	1	1	1	0*	0	–	–	–	2
Windows, M.G.N.	3	5	–	71	209	41.80	–	–	2
Wood, J.	17	23	4	63*	330	17.36	–	–	3
Wood, J.R.	27	36	3	96	960	29.09	–	–	13
Wren, T.N.	8	6	2	16	24	6.00	–	–	5
Wright, A.J.	217	375	28	161	9661	27.84	12	4	151
Wylie, A.	1	1	–	0	0	0.00	–	–	–
Yates, G.	32	40	21	134*	847	44.57	3	–	13
Yeabsley, R.S.	10	13	4	36	138	15.33	–	–	5
Zoehrer, T.J.	136	190	22	168	4926	29.32	7	–	386/37

BOWLING

'50wS' denotes instances of taking 50 or more wickets in a season. Where these have been achieved outside the UK, they are shown after a plus sign.

	Runs	Wkts	Avge	Best	5wI	10wM	50wS
Adams, C.J.	867	15	57.80	4- 29	–	–	–
Adams, J.C.	727	17	42.76	4- 43	–	–	–
Afford, J.A.	11559	353	32.74	6- 68	12	2	4
Alikhan, R.I.	289	8	36.12	2- 19	–	–	–
Alleyne, M.W.	3212	88	36.50	4- 48	–	–	–
Ambrose, C.E.L.	11397	526	21.66	8- 45	24	4	4+1
Andrew, S.J.W.	9283	288	32.23	7- 47	7	–	–
Archer, G.F.	72	0	–	–	–	–	–
Arscott, J.P.	252	7	36.00	1- 17	–	–	–
Arthurton, K.L.T.	407	13	31.30	3- 14	–	–	–
Asif Din	4366	79	55.26	5- 61	2	–	–
Atherton, M.A.	4674	107	43.68	6- 78	3	–	–
Athey, C.W.J.	2539	47	54.02	3- 3	–	–	–
Austin, I.D.	3052	79	38.63	5- 79	1	–	–
Ayling, J.R.	3405	134	25.41	5- 12	1	–	–
Aymes, A.N.	75	1	75.00	1- 75	–	–	–
Babington, A.M.	7545	207	36.44	8-107	3	–	–
Bailey, R.J.	2973	73	40.72	5- 54	1	–	–
Bainbridge, P.	11575	327	35.39	8- 53	10	–	–

	Runs	Wkts	Avge	Best	5wI	10wM	50wS
Ball, M.C.J.	2991	90	33.23	8- 46	4	1	–
Barnett, A.A.	4564	103	44.31	5- 36	5	–	–
Barnett, K.J.	5402	139	38.86	6- 28	2	–	–
Barwick, S.R.	13947	399	34.95	8- 42	9	1	2
Base, S.J.	9995	359	27.84	7- 60	15	1	1
Bastien, S.	4288	115	37.28	6- 52	7	1	–
Bates, R.T.	278	6	46.33	2- 43	–	–	–
Batty, J.D.	5027	134	37.51	6- 48	3	–	–
Bee, A.	360	4	90.00	2- 20	–	–	–
Bell, M.A.V.	896	33	27.15	7- 48	3	–	–
Benjamin, J.E.	5583	173	32.27	6- 19	8	–	1
Benjamin, K.C.G.	3128	127	24.62	7- 51	4	–	–
Benjamin, W.K.M.	10142	403	25.16	7- 54	21	2	1
Benson, J.D.R.	488	8	61.00	2- 24	–	–	–
Benson, M.R.	493	5	98.60	2- 55	–	–	–
Berry, P.J.	1698	39	43.53	7-113	1	1	–
Betts, M.M.	19	1	19.00	1- 19	–	–	–
Beven, I.R.	816	12	68.00	2- 31	–	–	–
Bicknell, D.J.	286	3	95.33	2- 62	–	–	–
Bicknell, M.P.	11639	450	25.86	9- 45	19	2	5
Bishop, I.R.	7404	358	20.68	7- 34	20	1	2
Blakey, R.J.	68	1	68.00	1- 68	–	–	–
Boden, D.J.P.	284	7	40.57	4- 11	–	–	–
Boiling, J.	3187	77	41.38	6- 84	2	1	–
Boon, D.C.	363	6	60.50	1- 12	–	–	–
Boon, T.J.	563	11	51.18	3- 40	–	–	–
Booth, P.A.	4301	107	40.19	5- 98	1	–	–
Border, A.R.	3836	99	38.74	7- 46	3	1	–
Botham, I.T.	31902	1172	27.22	8- 34	59	8	8
Bovill, J.N.B.	48	3	16.00	2- 32	–	–	–
Bowen, M.N.	801	24	33.37	4-124	–	–	–
Bowler, P.D.	1494	20	74.70	3- 41	–	–	–
Brain, D.H.	682	22	31.00	6- 48	1	–	–
Brandes, E.A.	3168	91	34.81	6- 59	5	–	–
Briers, M.P.	690	12	57.50	3-109	–	–	–
Briers, N.E.	988	32	30.87	4- 29	–	–	–
Brimson, M.T.	66	2	33.00	2- 66	–	–	–
Broad, B.C.	1037	16	64.81	2- 14	–	–	–
Broadhurst, M.	179	6	29.83	3- 61	–	–	–
Brown, A.D.	84	0	–	–	–	–	–
Brown, D.R.	204	8	25.50	3- 27	–	–	–
Brown, K.R.	162	5	32.40	2- 7	–	–	–
Brown, S.J.E.	4648	130	35.75	7- 70	6	–	1
Burns, M.	8	0	–	–	–	–	–
Burns, N.D.	8	0	–	–	–	–	–
Butcher, M.A.	551	16	34.43	4- 51	–	–	–
Byas, D.	630	10	63.00	3- 55	–	–	–
Caddick, A.R.	3990	144	27.70	9- 32	8	4	2
Cairns, C.L.	7401	260	28.46	7- 34	9	2	2
Campbell, A.D.R.	38	1	38.00	1- 38	–	–	–
Capel, D.J.	18451	457	32.49	7- 46	12	–	3
Carr, J.D.	2939	68	43.22	6- 61	3	–	–
Carrick, P.	32237	1081	29.82	8- 33	47	5	11
Chapman, R.J.	77	2	38.50	1- 38	–	–	–
Chapple, G.	635	16	39.68	3- 40	–	–	–
Charlesworth, G.M.	990	18	55.00	3- 33	–	–	–

	Runs	Wkts	Avge	Best	5wI	10wM	50wS
Childs, J.H.	26824	902	29.73	9- 56	48	8	8
Cohen, M.F.	0	0	–	–	–	–	–
Connor, C.A.	14129	421	33.56	7- 31	10	1	3
Cook, N.G.B.	24792	862	28.76	7- 34	31	4	8
Cooper, K.E.	20605	761	27.07	8- 44	26	1	8
Cork, D.G.	4401	155	28.39	8- 53	3	1	1
Cottam, A.C.	280	6	46.66	1- 1	–	–	–
Cottey, P.A.	426	6	71.00	2- 42	–	–	–
Cousins, D.M.	109	1	109.00	1- 51	–	–	–
Cowans, N.G.	15475	636	24.33	6- 31	23	1	6
Cowdrey, G.R.	749	11	68.09	1- 5	–	–	–
Cox, R.M.F.	1	0	–	–	–	–	–
Crawley, J.P.	104	1	104.00	1- 90	–	–	–
Crawley, M.A.	2853	63	45.28	6- 92	1	–	–
Croft, R.D.B.	8234	204	40.36	8- 66	8	1	2
Cummins, A.C.	3043	102	29.83	6-115	3	–	1
Curran, K.M.	11882	476	24.96	7- 47	15	4	5
Curry, D.J.	16	1	16.00	1- 12	–	–	–
Curtis, T.S.	679	11	61.72	2- 17	–	–	–
Dakin, J.M.	84	4	21.00	4- 45	–	–	–
Dale, A.	2785	75	37.13	6- 18	1	–	–
Davies, M.	3220	98	32.85	5- 57	3	1	1
Davis, R.P.	11208	320	35.02	7- 64	13	2	2
Dawson, R.I.	2	0	–	–	–	–	–
DeFreitas, P.A.J.	17011	602	28.25	7- 21	31	3	6
De la Pena, J.M.	294	7	42.00	4- 77	–	–	–
Dessaur, W.A.	94	0	–	–	–	–	–
Doak, N.G.	0	0	–	–	–	–	–
D'Oliveira, D.B.	1867	42	44.45	3- 36	–	–	–
Donald, A.A.	14403	615	23.41	8- 37	35	5	3
Donelan, B.T.P.	4568	105	43.50	6- 62	4	1	–
Dutch, K.P.	18	0	–	–	–	–	–
Ealham, M.A.	2788	90	30.97	5- 14	4	–	–
Ellison, B.C.A.	40	2	20.00	2- 40	–	–	–
Ellison, R.M.	13773	475	28.99	7- 33	18	2	4
Emburey, J.E.	37442	1444	25.92	8- 40	65	10	15
Evans, K.P.	7065	207	34.13	6- 67	4	–	–
Fairbrother, N.H.	423	5	84.60	2- 91	–	–	–
Farbrace, P.	64	1	64.00	1- 64	–	–	–
Feltham, M.A.	10171	321	31.68	6- 53	6	–	1
Felton, N.A.	345	2	172.50	1- 48	–	–	–
Field-Buss, M.G.	1752	50	35.04	6- 42	1	–	–
Fleming, M.V.	3915	103	38.00	4- 31	–	–	–
Fletcher, S.D.	8375	240	34.89	8- 58	5	–	1
Flint, D.P.J.	1066	31	34.38	5- 32	1	–	–
Flower, G.W.	598	12	49.83	2- 6	–	–	–
Fordham, A.	238	3	79.33	1- 25	–	–	–
Foster, M.J.	50	3	16.66	3- 39	–	–	–
Foster, N.A.	22196	908	24.44	8- 99	50	8	9
Fowler, G.	366	10	36.60	2- 34	–	–	–
Fraser, A.R.C.	10764	416	25.87	7- 40	18	2	4
French, B.N.	70	1	70.00	1- 37	–	–	–
Frost, M.	6005	169	35.53	7- 99	4	2	2
Gallian, J.E.R.	1278	30	42.60	4- 29	–	–	–
Garnham, M.A.	39	0	–	–	–	–	–
Gatting, M.W.	4495	154	29.18	5- 34	2	–	–

	Runs	Wkts	Avge	Best	5wI	10wM	50wS
Gerrard, M.J.	1381	36	38.36	6- 40	1	1	–
Gibson, O.D.	1883	73	25.79	7- 78	3	1	–
Giddins, E.S.H.	2533	62	40.85	5- 32	3	–	–
Giles, A.F.	128	3	42.66	1- 27	–	–	–
Gooch, G.A.	8146	233	34.96	7- 14	3	–	–
Gough, D.	4688	138	33.97	7- 42	4	1	1
Govan, J.W.	942	40	23.55	6- 70	2	–	–
Gower, D.I.	227	4	56.75	3- 47	–	–	–
Graveney, D.A.	28620	950	30.12	8- 85	39	7	6
Grayson, A.P.	530	3	176.66	1- 3	–	–	–
Greenfield, K.	269	5	53.80	2- 40	–	–	–
Griffith, F.A.	1610	47	34.25	4- 33	–	–	–
Gupte, C.M.	260	4	65.00	2- 41	–	–	–
Hall, J.W.	14	0	–	–	–	–	–
Hallett, J.C.	986	21	46.95	3- 85	–	–	–
Hamilton, G.M.	100	5	20.00	5- 65	1	–	–
Hancock, T.H.C.	272	10	27.20	3- 10	–	–	–
Harden, R.J.	952	19	50.10	2- 7	–	–	–
Harper, R.A.	13426	499	26.90	6- 24	22	2	2
Harrison, G.D.	525	23	22.82	9-113	2	–	–
Hartley, P.J.	11890	355	33.49	8-111	13	–	3
Haste, N.J.	715	10	71.50	2- 44	–	–	–
Hayden, M.L.	67	1	67.00	1- 24	–	–	–
Hayhurst, A.N.	4086	89	45.91	4- 27	–	–	–
Haynes, D.L.	262	8	32.75	1- 2	–	–	–
Haynes, G.R.	460	5	92.00	2- 29	–	–	–
Headley, D.W.	3734	102	36.60	7- 79	4	–	–
Healy, I.A.	1	0	–	–	–	–	–
Hegg, W.K.	7	0	–	–	–	–	–
Hemmings, E.E.	43002	1467	29.31	10-175	68	15	15
Henderson, P.W.	405	10	40.50	3- 59	–	–	–
Hepworth, P.N.	1016	21	48.38	3- 51	–	–	–
Hick, G.A.	6493	161	40.32	5- 37	4	1	–
Hindson, J.E.	188	9	20.88	5- 42	1	–	–
Hinks, S.G.	383	8	47.87	2- 18	–	–	–
Hodgson, G.D.	65	0	–	–	–	–	–
Hoey, C.J.	255	9	28.33	3- 38	–	–	–
Holdsworth, W.J.	5589	180	31.05	7- 41	10	1	0+1
Hollioake, A.J.	305	5	61.00	2- 75	–	–	–
Hooper, C.L.	8404	246	34.16	5- 33	7	–	–
Houghton, D.L.	31	0	–	–	–	–	–
Hughes, J.G.	450	7	64.28	3- 56	–	–	–
Hughes, M.G.	15894	556	28.58	8- 87	20	3	0+3
Hughes, S.P.	15139	466	32.48	7- 35	10	–	2
Hussain, N.	306	2	153.00	1- 38	–	–	–
Hutton, S.	5	0	–	–	–	–	–
Igglesden, A.P.	10853	430	25.23	7- 28	21	4	4
Illingworth, R.K.	18153	580	31.29	7- 50	20	4	4
Ilott, M.C.	6129	178	34.43	7- 85	7	–	2
Irani, R.C.	298	5	59.60	2- 21	–	–	–
James, K.D.	8170	255	32.03	6- 22	7	–	–
Jarvis, P.W.	13611	495	27.49	7- 55	18	3	3
Jean-Jacques, M.	4272	119	35.89	8- 77	2	1	–
Jeh, M.P.W.	1986	41	48.43	5- 63	1	–	–
Jenkins, R.H.J.	1687	24	70.29	5-100	1	–	–
Johnson, P.	510	5	102.00	1- 9	–	–	–

	Runs	Wkts	Avge	Best	5wI	10wM	50wS
Johnson, R.L.	129	2	64.50	1- 25	–	–	–
Jones, A.N.	13516	410	32.96	7- 30	12	1	5
Jones, D.M.	1011	16	63.18	1- 0	–	–	–
Julian, B.P.	3359	99	33.92	5- 26	5	–	–
Kasprowicz, M.S.	1961	61	32.14	6- 59	3	–	0+1
Keech, M.	149	5	29.80	2- 28	–	–	–
Kellett, S.A.	19	0	–	–	–	–	–
Kendrick, N.M.	4219	124	34.02	7-115	6	1	1
Kerr, J.I.D.	405	15	27.00	3- 47	–	–	–
Knight, N.V.	32	0	–	–	–	–	–
Krikken, K.M.	40	0	–	–	–	–	–
Lamb, A.J.	199	8	24.87	2- 29	–	–	–
Lambert, C.B.	115	4	28.75	2- 33	–	–	–
Lampitt, S.R.	6735	220	30.61	5- 32	8	–	2
Larkins, W.	1876	42	44.66	5- 59	1	–	–
Lathwell, M.N.	396	6	66.00	1- 9	–	–	–
Law, D.R.	216	5	43.20	2- 38	–	–	–
Leatherdale, D.A.	59	1	59.00	1- 12	–	–	–
Lefebvre, R.P.	4324	118	36.64	6- 53	2	–	–
Lenham, N.J.	1650	38	43.42	4- 13	–	–	–
Leppard, J.	40	0	–	–	–	–	–
Lewis, C.C.	9854	327	30.13	6- 22	13	3	2
Lewis, D.A.	249	4	62.25	2- 39	–	–	–
Llong, N.J.	424	11	38.54	3- 29	–	–	–
Lloyd, G.D.	186	1	186.00	1- 57	–	–	–
Love, J.D.	835	12	69.58	2- 0	–	–	–
Lovell, G.B.T.	141	1	141.00	1- 13	–	–	–
Loye, M.B.	1	0	–	–	–	–	–
Lugsden, S.	85	2	42.50	2- 43	–	–	–
Lynch, M.A.	1360	26	52.30	3- 6	–	–	–
McCague, M.J.	3885	132	29.43	8- 26	9	1	1
McCrum, P.	255	4	63.75	3- 56	–	–	–
McDermott, C.J.	15152	548	27.64	8- 44	30	4	1+4
Macdonald, R.H.	1355	35	38.71	5- 20	1	–	–
MacLay, A.W.	51	1	51.00	1- 11	–	–	–
Macmillan, G.I.	211	7	30.14	3- 13	–	–	–
Maher, B.J.M.	234	4	58.50	2- 69	–	–	–
Malcolm, D.E.	14154	445	31.80	7- 74	12	1	2
Malik, H.S.	502	7	71.71	2- 18	–	–	–
Mallender, N.A.	23420	900	26.02	7- 27	36	5	6
Marsh, S.A.	227	2	113.50	2- 20	–	–	–
Marshall, M.D.	29821	1580	18.87	8- 71	85	13	8+5
Martin, P.J.	5002	134	37.32	5- 35	1	–	–
Martyn, D.R.	285	3	95.00	1- 10	–	–	–
Maru, R.J.	15657	480	32.61	8- 41	15	1	4
May, T.B.A.	11548	331	34.88	7- 93	12	–	1+1
Maynard, M.P.	676	6	112.66	3- 21	–	–	–
Mendis, G.D.	158	1	158.00	1- 65	–	–	–
Metcalfe, A.A.	316	4	79.00	2- 18	–	–	–
Metson, C.P.	0	0	–	–	–	–	–
Middleton, T.C.	241	5	48.20	2- 41	–	–	–
Mike, G.W.	1392	31	44.90	5- 65	1	–	–
Milburn, S.M.	150	1	150.00	1- 54	–	–	–
Millar, P.M.C.	61	0	–	–	–	–	–
Millns, D.J.	6076	221	27.49	9- 37	13	2	2
Moles, A.J.	1860	40	46.50	3- 21	–	–	–

	Runs	Wkts	Avge	Best	5wI	10wM	50wS
Montgomerie, R.R.	37	0	–	–	–	–	–
Moody, T.M.	2716	82	33.12	7- 43	1	1	–
Moore, E.R.	53	1	53.00	1- 34	–	–	–
Moores, P.	16	0	–	–	–	–	–
Morris, H.	380	2	190.00	1- 6	–	–	–
Morris, J.E.	759	6	126.50	1- 6	–	–	–
Morris, R.S.M.	1	0	–	–	–	–	–
Morrison, D.K.	9484	305	31.09	7- 82	13	–	–
Mortensen, O.H.	10316	432	23.87	6- 27	16	1	2
Moxon, M.D.	1481	28	52.89	3- 24	–	–	–
Mudassar Nazar	5251	153	34.32	6- 32	2	–	–
Mullally, A.D.	6207	181	34.29	7- 72	3	1	1
Munton, T.A.	11617	421	27.59	8- 89	16	3	4
Murphy, A.J.	7884	206	38.27	6- 97	6	–	1
Mushtaq Ahmed	7697	321	23.97	9- 93	21	5	2+1
Newell, M.	282	7	40.28	2- 38	–	–	–
Newport, P.J.	17576	639	27.50	8- 52	29	3	6
Nicholas, M.C.J.	3212	72	44.61	6- 37	2	–	–
North, J.A.	1577	44	35.84	4- 47	–	–	–
O'Gorman, T.J.G.	207	3	69.00	1- 7	–	–	–
Ostler, D.P.	109	0	–	–	–	–	–
Parker, P.W.G.	769	11	69.90	2- 21	–	–	–
Parks, R.J.	166	0	–	–	–	–	–
Parsons, G.J.	19547	651	30.02	9- 72	18	1	2
Parsons, K.A.	14	0	–	–	–	–	–
Patel, M.M.	1861	51	36.49	7- 75	4	2	–
Payne, A.	133	5	26.60	2- 15	–	–	–
Peall, S.G.	1018	17	59.88	3- 46	–	–	–
Pearson, R.M.	3389	56	60.52	5-108	1	–	–
Penberthy, A.L.	2431	68	35.75	5- 37	1	–	–
Penn, C.	9789	295	33.18	7- 70	12	–	2
Pennett, D.B.	1501	43	34.90	5- 36	1	–	–
Penney, T.L.	52	0	–	–	–	–	–
Phelps, B.S.	122	1	122.00	1-105	–	–	–
Phillips, N.C.	103	3	34.33	3- 39	–	–	–
Pick, R.A.	12591	377	33.39	7-128	12	3	3
Pierson, A.R.K.	5124	129	39.72	6- 82	7	–	–
Pigott, A.C.S.	19427	621	31.28	7- 74	23	1	5
Piper, K.J.	57	1	57.00	1- 57	–	–	–
Pitcher, C.M.	1151	17	67.71	3- 50	–	–	–
Pollard, P.R.	248	3	82.66	2- 79	–	–	–
Pooley, J.C.	11	0	–	–	–	–	–
Potter, L.	6879	177	38.86	5- 45	1	–	–
Prabhakar, M.	8184	281	29.12	6- 36	9	1	–
Prichard, P.J.	486	2	243.00	1- 28	–	–	–
Pringle, D.R.	20230	761	26.58	7- 18	25	3	6
Radford, N.V.	24481	933	26.23	9- 70	46	7	6
Ramprakash, M.R.	622	7	88.85	1- 0	–	–	–
Ranchod, U.	111	3	37.00	2- 18	–	–	–
Randall, D.W.	413	13	31.76	3- 15	–	–	–
Katcliffe, J.D.	231	3	77.00	1- 6	–	–	–
Reeve, D.A.	11019	397	27.75	7- 37	6	–	2
Reiffel, P.R.	6074	202	30.06	6- 57	7	2	–
Remy, C.C.	696	14	49.71	4- 63	–	–	–
Rennie, J.A.	218	6	36.33	2- 33	–	–	–
Rhodes, S.J.	30	0	–	–	–	–	–

	Runs	Wkts	Avge	Best	5wI	10wM	50wS
Richards, I.V.A.	10070	223	45.15	5- 88	1	–	–
Richardson, A.W.	112	2	56.00	2- 38	–	–	–
Richardson, R.B.	235	6	39.16	5- 40	1	–	–
Ripley, D.	103	2	51.50	2- 89	–	–	–
Roberts, A.R.	3331	80	41.63	6- 72	1	–	–
Robinson, M.A.	9026	278	32.46	9- 37	6	2	1
Robinson, P.E.	329	3	109.66	1- 10	–	–	–
Robinson, R.T.	254	3	84.66	1- 22	–	–	–
Rose, G.D.	9430	307	30.71	6- 41	7	–	2
Roseberry, M.A.	382	4	95.50	1- 1	–	–	–
Rowett, D.J.	67	1	67.00	1- 28	–	–	–
Russell, A.B.	120	3	40.00	2- 27	–	–	–
Russell, R.C.	53	1	53.00	1- 4	–	–	–
Salim Malik	2506	81	30.93	5- 19	3	–	–
Salisbury, I.D.K.	10537	273	38.59	7- 54	11	2	2
Sargeant, N.F.	88	1	88.00	1- 88	–	–	–
Saxelby, M.	765	9	85.00	3- 41	–	–	–
Scott, C.W.	10	0	–	–	–	–	–
Scott, R.J.	2031	43	47.23	3- 43	–	–	–
Seymour, A.C.H.	27	0	–	–	–	–	–
Shahid, N.	975	24	40.62	3- 91	–	–	–
Shine, K.J.	4556	119	38.28	8- 47	7	1	–
Silverwood, C.E.W.	75	1	75.00	1- 19	–	–	–
Simmons, P.V.	1762	40	44.05	5- 24	1	–	–
Sladdin, R.W.	3378	89	37.95	6- 58	2	–	–
Sleep, P.R.	14290	363	39.36	8-133	9	–	–
Small, G.C.	22178	772	28.72	7- 15	27	2	6
Smith, A.M.	2490	65	38.30	4- 41	–	–	–
Smith, A.W.	387	5	77.40	2- 7	–	–	–
Smith, B.F.	121	1	121.00	1- 5	–	–	–
Smith, D.M.	1574	30	52.46	3- 40	–	–	–
Smith, I.	2801	62	45.17	3- 48	–	–	–
Smith, N.M.K.	4356	105	41.48	6-122	4	–	–
Smith, P.A.	9273	257	36.08	6- 91	7	–	–
Smith, R.A.	693	12	57.75	2- 11	–	–	–
Snape, J.N.	175	3	58.33	2- 49	–	–	–
Speak, N.J.	92	2	46.00	1- 0	–	–	–
Speight, M.P.	32	2	16.00	1- 2	–	–	–
Spencer, D.J.	160	4	40.00	4- 46	–	–	–
Stanley, N.A.	19	0	–	–	–	–	–
Steer, I.G.S.	34	3	11.33	3- 23	–	–	–
Stemp, R.D.	2915	89	32.75	6- 67	5	1	–
Stephenson, F.D.	14613	594	24.60	8- 47	33	8	4
Stephenson, J.P.	3811	119	32.02	6- 54	4	–	–
Stewart, A.J.	352	3	117.33	1- 7	–	–	–
Storie, A.C.	199	2	99.50	1- 17	–	–	–
Streak, H.H.	263	6	43.83	3- 87	–	–	–
Such, P.M.	11453	383	29.90	6- 17	16	3	1
Sylvester, S.A.	320	4	80.00	2- 34	–	–	–
Tavaré, C.J.	722	5	144.40	1- 3	–	–	–
Taylor, C.W.	2178	61	35.70	5- 33	1	–	–
Taylor, J.P.	5485	181	30.30	7- 23	7	1	2
Taylor, M.A.	57	1	57.00	1- 4	–	–	–
Taylor, N.R.	891	16	55.68	2- 20	–	–	–
Terry, V.P.	58	0	–	–	–	–	–
Thomas, S.D.	960	38	25.26	5- 76	3	–	–

	Runs	Wkts	Avge	Best	5wI	10wM	50wS
Thorpe, G.P.	1014	20	50.07	4- 40	–	–	–
Thursfield, M.J.	308	9	34.22	4- 78	–	–	–
Tolley, C.M.	2835	84	33.75	5- 55	1	–	–
Topley, T.D.	10100	366	27.59	7- 75	15	2	3
Trimby, P.W.	469	12	39.08	3- 72	–	–	–
Trump, H.R.J.	6627	173	38.30	7- 52	6	1	1
Tufnell, P.C.R.	14250	455	31.31	8- 29	22	2	4
Turner, I.J.	1965	54	36.38	5- 81	1	–	–
Turner, R.J.	26	0	–	–	–	–	–
Twose, R.G.	2405	82	29.32	6- 63	1	–	–
Udal, S.D.	5282	156	33.85	8- 50	7	2	2
Vandrau, M.J.	960	16	60.00	2- 8	–	–	–
Van Troost, A.P.	2069	58	35.67	6- 48	3	–	–
Vaughan, M.P.	42	1	42.00	1- 23	–	–	–
Walker, A.	6949	224	31.02	6- 50	2	–	1
Walsh, C.A.	24509	1078	22.73	9- 72	58	11	7+1
Waqar Younis	9501	470	20.21	7- 64	41	9	3+2
Ward, D.M.	113	2	56.50	2- 66	–	–	–
Ward, T.R.	537	6	89.50	2- 48	–	–	–
Warne, S.K.	4338	156	27.80	7- 49	5	–	1
Warner, A.E.	11491	367	31.31	5- 27	5	1	–
Wasim Akram	12137	549	22.10	8- 68	43	9	4
Watkin, S.L.	13630	466	29.24	8- 59	18	3	5
Watkinson, M.	17436	511	34.12	7- 25	22	1	5
Waugh, M.E.	4590	118	38.89	5- 37	1	–	–
Waugh, S.R.	6336	192	33.00	6- 51	4	–	–
Weekes, P.N.	1198	26	46.07	3- 57	–	–	–
Wells, A.P.	690	9	76.66	3- 67	–	–	–
Wells, C.M.	13513	396	34.12	7- 42	7	–	2
Wells, V.J.	1870	69	27.10	5- 43	1	–	–
Weston, M.J.	3204	82	39.07	4- 24	–	–	–
Weston, W.P.C.	262	3	87.33	2- 39	–	–	–
Whitaker, J.J.	268	2	134.00	1- 29	–	–	–
White, C.	1010	30	33.66	5- 74	1	–	–
White, G.W.	30	1	30.00	1- 30	–	–	–
Whittall, A.R.	969	19	51.00	3- 79	–	–	–
Whitticase, P.	7	0	–	–	–	–	–
Wight, R.M.	1226	28	43.78	3- 65	–	–	–
Williams, N.F.	16272	554	29.37	8- 75	17	2	3
Williams, R.C.	743	12	61.91	3- 44	–	–	–
Windows, M.G.N.	3	0	–	–	–	–	–
Wood, J.	1269	33	38.45	5- 68	1	–	–
Wood, J.R.	38	1	38.00	1- 5	–	–	–
Wren, T.N.	667	15	44.46	3- 14	–	–	–
Wright, A.J.	68	1	68.00	1- 16	–	–	–
Wylie, A.	73	1	73.00	1- 50	–	–	–
Yates, G.	3026	55	55.01	5-108	1	–	–
Yeabsley, R.S.	762	20	38.10	3- 30	–	–	–
Zoehrer, T.J.	1578	37	42.44	5- 58	1	–	–

LEADING CURRENT PLAYERS

The leading career records of players currently registered for first-class county cricket. All figures are to the end of the 1993 English season.

BATTING
(Qualification: 100 innings)

	Runs	Avge
G.A.Hick	21106	58.14
M.W.Gatting	30114	50.19
A.J.Lamb	30223	48.82
G.A.Gooch	38427	48.70
D.L.Haynes	22727	46.66
T.M.Moody	10227	45.65
N.Hussain	6767	45.11
R.A.Smith	16059	44.73
M.A.Atherton	10041	44.62
C.L.Hooper	8523	44.16
R.T.Robinson	21361	42.80
M.Prabhakar	5077	42.66
R.B.Richardson	11330	42.43
T.S.Curtis	16864	42.37
M.P.Maynard	12740	42.32
R.J.Bailey	15007	42.27
G.P.Thorpe	6908	42.12
M.R.Benson	16948	41.43
P.D.Bowler	9379	41.31
M.D.Moxon	16843	41.08
N.H.Fairbrother	13315	40.84
A.J.Moles	12101	40.74
A.Fordham	7811	40.26
A.P.Wells	13913	40.09
J.E.Morris	14267	39.52
N.R.Taylor	16301	39.46
G.D.Lloyd	4713	39.27
D.J.Bicknell	8782	39.20
M.R.Ramprakash	7210	39.18
K.J.Barnett	19718	39.04
R.J.Harden	9035	38.77
N.J.Speak	4565	38.68
A.J.Stewart	13998	38.66
B.C.Broad	21396	38.55
D.M.Ward	7010	38.51
H.Morris	13905	38.41

BOWLING
(Qualification: 100 wickets)

	Wkts	Avge
Waqar Younis	470	20.21
I.R.Bishop	358	20.68
C.E.L.Ambrose	526	21.66
Wasim Akram	549	22.10
C.A.Walsh	1078	22.73
O.H.Mortensen	432	23.87
Mushtaq Ahmed	321	23.97
N.G.Cowans	636	24.33
F.D.Stephenson	594	24.60
K.M.Curran	476	24.96
W.K.M.Benjamin	403	25.16
A.P.Igglesden	430	25.23
M.P.Bicknell	450	25.86
A.R.C.Fraser	416	25.87
J.E.Emburey	1444	25.92
N.A.Mallender	900	26.02
N.V.Radford	933	26.23
K.E.Cooper	761	27.07
D.J.Millns	221	27.493
P.W.Jarvis	495	27.496
P.J.Newport	639	27.50
T.A.Munton	421	27.593
T.D.Topley	366	27.595
A.R.Caddick	144	27.70
D.A.Reeve	397	27.75
P.A.J.DeFreitas	602	28.25
D.G.Cork	155	28.39
G.C.Small	772	28.72
N.G.B.Cook	862	28.76
R.M.Ellison	475	28.99
M.Prabhakar	281	29.12
M.W.Gatting	154	29.18
S.L.Watkin	466	29.24
E.E.Hemmings	1467	29.31
N.F.Williams	554	29.37
M.J.McCague	132	29.43

WICKET-KEEPING

	Total	Ct	St
B.N.French	912	812	100
R.C.Russell	718	626	92
S.J.Rhodes	613	544	69
D.Ripley	483	424	59
C.P.Metson	471	437	34
S.A.Marsh	463	428	35
M.A.Garnham	431	395	36

FIELDING

	Ct
G.A.Gooch	495
J.E.Emburey	423
M.W.Gatting	395
C.W.J.Athey	385
A.J.Lamb	336
M.A.Lynch	317
G.A.Hick	304

TEST CAREER RECORDS

These records are complete to the end of the 1993 English season and also include the two three-match series hosted by Sri Lanka against India and South Africa between 17 July and 19 September 1993. Except for the England figures, which include everyone who appeared in first-class cricket in 1993, these records are restricted to those who have played Test cricket since 17 August 1992. Career records for all Tests prior to that date are published in *The Wisden Book of Cricket Records (Third Edition)*.

ENGLAND

BATTING AND FIELDING

	M	I	NO	HS	Runs	Avge	100	50	Ct/St
M.A.Atherton	29	55	1	151	1927	35.68	3	15	24
C.W.J.Athey	23	41	1	123	919	22.97	1	4	13
R.J.Bailey	4	8	–	43	119	14.87	–	–	–
K.J.Barnett	4	7	–	80	207	29.57	–	2	1
M.R.Benson	1	2	–	30	51	25.50	–	–	–
M.P.Bicknell	2	4	–	14	26	6.50	–	–	–
R.J.Blakey	2	4	–	6	7	1.75	–	–	2
I.T.Botham	102	161	6	208	5200	33.54	14	22	120
B.C.Broad	25	44	2	162	1661	39.54	6	6	10
A.R.Caddick	4	8	1	25	101	14.42	–	–	2
D.J.Capel	15	25	1	98	374	15.58	–	2	6
J.H.Childs	2	4	4	2*	2	–	–	–	1
N.G.B.Cook	15	25	4	31	179	8.52	–	–	5
N.G.Cowans	19	29	7	36	175	7.95	–	–	9
T.S.Curtis	5	9	–	41	140	15.55	–	–	3
P.A.J.DeFreitas	33	50	4	55*	562	12.21	–	1	9
R.M.Ellison	11	16	1	41	202	13.46	–	–	2
J.E.Emburey	63	95	20	75	1705	22.73	–	10	33
N.H.Fairbrother	10	15	1	83	219	15.64	–	1	4
N.A.Foster	29	45	7	39	446	11.73	–	–	7
G.Fowler	21	37	–	201	1307	35.32	3	8	10
A.R.C.Fraser	12	16	1	29	129	8.60	–	–	2
B.N.French	16	21	4	59	308	18.11	–	1	38/1
M.W.Gatting	74	129	14	207	4227	36.75	9	21	56
G.A.Gooch	107	195	6	333	8293	43.87	19	45	99
D.I.Gower	117	204	18	215	8231	44.25	18	39	74
E.E.Hemmings	16	21	4	95	383	22.52	–	2	5
G.A.Hick	18	31	–	178	972	31.35	1	5	27
N.Hussain	7	13	2	71	284	25.81	–	1	3
A.P.Igglesden	1	1	–	2*	2	–	–	–	1
R.K.Illingworth	2	4	2	13	31	15.50	–	–	1
M.C.Ilott	3	5	1	15	28	7.00	–	–	–
P.W.Jarvis	9	15	2	29*	132	10.15	–	–	2
A.J.Lamb	79	139	10	142	4656	36.09	14	18	75
W.Larkins	13	25	1	64	493	20.54	–	3	8
M.N.Lathwell	2	4	–	33	78	19.50	–	–	–
C.C.Lewis	20	31	1	117	771	25.70	1	3	18
M.J.McCague	2	3	–	11	20	6.66	–	–	1
D.E.Malcolm	25	37	13	15*	130	5.41	–	–	3
N.A.Mallender	2	3	–	4	8	2.66	–	–	–
M.P.Maynard	3	6	–	20	52	8.66	–	–	2

ENGLAND

BATTING AND FIELDING (continued)

	M	I	NO	HS	Runs	Avge	100	50	Ct/St
H.Morris	3	6	–	44	115	19.16	–	–	3
J.E.Morris	3	5	2	32	71	23.66	–	–	3
M.D.Moxon	10	17	1	99	455	28.43	–	3	10
T.A.Munton	2	2	1	25*	25	25.00	–	–	–
P.J.Newport	3	5	1	40*	110	27.50	–	–	1
P.W.G.Parker	1	2	–	13	13	6.50	–	–	–
A.C.S.Pigott	1	2	1	8*	12	12.00	–	–	–
D.R.Pringle	30	50	4	63	695	15.10	–	1	10
N.V.Radford	3	4	1	12*	21	7.00	–	–	–
M.R.Ramprakash	10	17	1	64	311	19.43	–	1	7
D.W.Randall	47	79	5	174	2470	33.37	7	12	31
D.A.Reeve	3	5	–	59	124	24.80	–	1	1
R.T.Robinson	29	49	5	175	1601	36.38	4	6	8
R.C.Russell	31	49	10	128*	1060	27.17	1	3	80/8
I.D.K.Salisbury	4	7	–	50	136	19.42	–	1	2
G.C.Small	17	24	7	59	263	15.47	–	1	9
D.M.Smith	2	4	–	47	80	20.00	–	–	–
R.A.Smith	45	84	14	148*	3237	46.24	8	22	31
J.P.Stephenson	1	2	–	25	36	18.00	–	–	–
A.J.Stewart	32	60	4	190	2083	37.19	4	11	46/4
P.M.Such	5	9	3	14*	56	9.33	–	–	2
C.J.Tavaré	31	56	2	149	1755	32.50	2	12	20
J.P.Taylor	1	2	1	17*	34	34.00	–	–	–
V.P.Terry	2	3	–	8	16	5.33	–	–	2
G.P.Thorpe	3	6	1	114*	230	46.00	1	1	5
P.C.R.Tufnell	15	23	13	22*	56	5.60	–	–	5
S.L.Watkin	3	5	–	13	25	5.00	–	–	1
J.J.Whitaker	1	1	–	11	11	11.00	–	–	1
N.F.Williams	1	1	–	38	38	38.00	–	–	–

BOWLING

	O	R	W	Avge	Best	5wI	10wM
M.A.Atherton	61	282	1	282.00	1- 60	–	–
K.J.Barnett	6	32	0	–	–	–	–
M.P.Bicknell	87	263	4	65.75	3- 99	–	–
I.T.Botham	3635.5	10878	383	28.40	8- 34	27	4
B.C.Broad	1	4	0	–	–	–	–
A.R.Caddick	153	488	5	97.60	3- 32	–	–
D.J.Capel	333.2	1064	21	50.66	3- 88	–	–
J.H.Childs	86	183	3	61.00	1- 13	–	–
N.G.B.Cook	695.4	1689	52	32.48	6- 65	4	1
N.G.Cowans	575.2	2003	51	39.27	6- 77	2	–
T.S.Curtis	3	7	0	–	–	–	–
P.A.J.DeFreitas	1171.4	3218	95	33.87	7- 70	3	1
R.M.Ellison	377.2	1048	35	29.94	6- 77	3	1
J.E.Emburey	2535.1	5564	147	37.85	7- 78	6	–
N.H.Fairbrother	2	9	0	–	–	–	–
N.A.Foster	1043.3	2891	88	32.85	8-107	5	1
G.Fowler	3	11	0	–	–	–	–
A.R.C.Fraser	563.3	1386	55	25.20	6- 82	5	–
M.W.Gatting	125.2	317	4	79.25	1- 14	–	–

ENGLAND

BOWLING (continued)

	O	R	W	Avge	Best	5wI	10wM
G.A.Gooch	407.3	960	22	43.63	3- 39	–	–
D.I.Gower	6	20	1	20.00	1- 1	–	–
E.E.Hemmings	739.3	1825	43	42.44	6- 58	1	–
G.A.Hick	240.5	598	14	42.71	4-126	–	–
A.P.Igglesden	37	146	3	48.66	2- 91	–	–
R.K.Illingworth	56.4	213	4	53.25	3-110	–	–
M.C.Ilott	129	412	8	51.50	3-108	–	–
P.W.Jarvis	318.4	965	21	45.95	4-107	–	–
A.J.Lamb	5	23	1	23.00	1- 6	–	–
C.C.Lewis	692	2068	52	39.76	6-111	2	–
M.J.McCague	79.3	294	4	73.50	4-121	–	–
D.E.Malcolm	934.3	3084	83	37.15	6- 77	4	1
N.A.Mallender	74.5	215	10	21.50	5- 50	1	–
M.D.Moxon	8	30	0	–	–	–	–
T.A.Munton	67.3	200	4	50.00	2- 22	–	–
P.J.Newport	111.3	417	10	41.70	4- 87	–	–
A.C.S.Pigott	17	75	2	37.50	2- 75	–	–
D.R.Pringle	881.1	2518	70	35.97	5- 95	3	–
N.V.Radford	113	351	4	87.75	2-131	–	–
M.R.Ramprakash	1.1	8	0	–	–	–	–
D.W.Randall	2.4	3	0	–	–	–	–
D.A.Reeve	24.5	60	2	30.00	1- 4	–	–
R.T.Robinson	1	0	0	–	–	–	–
I.D.K.Salisbury	122.1	536	8	67.00	3- 49	–	–
G.C.Small	654.3	1871	55	34.01	5- 48	2	–
R.A.Smith	4	6	0	–	–	–	–
P.M.Such	239.5	541	16	33.81	6- 67	1	–
C.J.Tavaré	5	11	0	–	–	–	–
J.P.Taylor	22	74	1	74.00	1- 65	–	–
G.P.Thorpe	6	14	0	–	–	–	–
P.C.R.Tufnell	687.2	1826	50	36.52	7- 47	4	1
S.L.Watkin	89	305	11	27.72	4- 65	–	–
N.F.Williams	41	148	2	74.00	2-148	–	–

AUSTRALIA

BATTING AND FIELDING

	M	I	NO	HS	Runs	Avge	100	50	Ct/St
J.Angel	1	2	1	4*	4	4.00	–	–	–
D.C.Boon	80	145	16	200	5869	45.49	17	25	78
A.R.Border	147	252	43	205	10695	51.17	26	61	148
A.I.C.Dodemaide	10	15	6	50	202	22.44	–	1	6
I.A.Healy	53	78	7	102*	1730	24.36	1	9	167/12
M.G.Hughes	51	67	7	72*	999	16.65	–	2	22
D.M.Jones	52	89	11	216	3631	46.55	11	14	34
B.P.Julian	2	3	1	56*	61	30.50	–	1	2
J.L.Langer	5	8	–	63	172	21.50	–	2	2
C.J.McDermott	49	67	8	42*	699	11.84	–	–	11
D.R.Martyn	5	9	1	74	244	30.50	–	2	1
G.R.J.Matthews	33	53	8	130	1849	41.08	4	12	17
T.B.A.May	13	16	7	42*	161	17.88	–	–	3

197

AUSTRALIA

BATTING AND FIELDING (continued)

	M	I	NO	HS	Runs	Avge	100	50	Ct/St
T.M.Moody	8	14	–	106	456	32.57	2	3	9
B.A.Reid	27	34	14	13	93	4.65	–	–	5
P.R.Reiffel	7	8	–	42	106	13.25	–	–	3
M.J.Slater	6	10	–	152	416	41.60	1	2	2
M.A.Taylor	46	84	5	219	3588	45.41	10	20	62
S.K.Warne	17	23	5	37	298	16.55	–	–	10
M.E.Waugh	27	44	3	139*	1613	39.34	4	10	39
S.R.Waugh	58	89	15	177*	2919	39.44	5	17	43
M.R.Whitney	12	19	8	13	68	6.18	–	–	2

BOWLING

	O	R	W	Avge	Best	5wI	10wM
J.Angel	19	72	1	72.00	1- 72	–	–
D.C.Boon	3	5	0	–	–	–	–
A.R.Border	650.1	1499	39	38.43	7- 46	2	1
A.I.C.Dodemaide	364	953	34	28.02	6- 58	1	–
M.G.Hughes	1977.3	5780	208	27.78	8- 87	7	1
D.M.Jones	33	64	1	64.00	1- 5	–	–
B.P.Julian	82	291	5	58.20	2- 30	–	–
C.J.McDermott	1856.5	5738	198	28.97	8- 97	9	2
D.R.Martyn	1	0	0	–	–	–	–
G.R.J.Matthews	1045.1	2942	61	48.22	5-103	2	1
T.B.A.May	631.4	1537	53	29.00	5- 9	2	–
T.M.Moody	72	147	2	73.50	1- 17	–	–
B.A.Reid	1040.4	2784	113	24.63	7- 51	5	2
P.R.Reiffel	271.4	726	26	27.92	6- 71	2	–
M.A.Taylor	4	15	0	–	–	–	–
S.K.Warne	813.2	1832	65	28.18	7- 52	2	–
M.E.Waugh	224	664	17	39.05	4- 80	–	–
S.R.Waugh	810.2	2295	51	45.00	5- 69	2	–
M.R.Whitney	445.2	1325	39	33.97	7- 27	2	1

SOUTH AFRICA

BATTING AND FIELDING

	M	I	NO	HS	Runs	Avge	100	50	Ct/St
S.J.Cook	3	6	–	43	107	17.83	–	–	–
W.J.Cronje	7	13	2	135	451	41.00	2	1	3
D.J.Cullinan	4	7	–	102	311	44.42	1	1	2
A.A.Donald	8	10	5	14*	34	6.80	–	–	2
C.E.Eksteen	1	2	1	4*	5	5.00	–	–	–
O.Henry	3	3	–	34	53	17.66	–	–	2
A.C.Hudson	8	15	–	163	610	40.66	1	5	7
P.N.Kirsten	5	9	1	52	139	17.37	–	1	4
B.M.McMillan	6	9	2	98	196	28.00	–	2	10
C.R.Matthews	3	4	1	31	94	31.33	–	–	–
M.W.Pringle	3	4	1	33	55	18.33	–	–	–
J.N.Rhodes	7	12	2	101*	420	42.00	1	3	3

SOUTH AFRICA

BATTING AND FIELDING (continued)

	M	I	NO	HS	Runs	Avge	100	50	Ct/St
D.J.Richardson	8	12	1	62	195	17.72	–	2	39
B.N.Schultz	5	5	2	6	6	2.00	–	–	–
R.P.Snell	3	4	1	48	67	22.33	–	–	–
P.L.Symcox	3	4	–	50	149	37.25	–	1	–
K.C.Wessels	8	15	1	118	616	44.00	1	4	7
K.C.Wessels (A/SA)	32	57	2	179	2377	43.21	5	13	25

BOWLING

	O	R	W	Avge	Best	5wI	10wM
W.J.Cronje	90.4	130	4	32.50	2-17	–	–
A.A.Donald	322	770	38	20.26	7-84	3	1
C.E.Eksteen	23	78	0	–	–	–	–
O.Henry	71.1	189	3	63.00	2-56	–	–
P.N.Kirsten	5	13	0	–	–	–	–
B.M.McMillan	198	420	15	28.00	4-74	–	–
C.R.Matthews	109	190	9	21.11	3-32	–	–
M.W.Pringle	68.4	171	3	57.00	2-61	–	–
J.N.Rhodes	1	5	0	–	–	–	–
B.N.Schultz	175.5	427	24	17.79	5-48	2	–
R.P.Snell	90	291	13	22.38	4-74	–	–
P.L.Symcox	70	230	4	57.50	3-75	–	–
K.C.Wessels (A/SA)	15	42	0	–	–	–	–

WEST INDIES

BATTING AND FIELDING

	M	I	NO	HS	Runs	Avge	100	50	Ct/St
J.C.Adams	4	6	2	79*	238	59.50	–	2	4
C.E.L.Ambrose	42	63	12	53	582	11.41	–	1	9
K.L.T.Arthurton	14	23	3	157*	641	32.05	1	4	10
K.C.G.Benjamin	2	4	–	15	23	5.75	–	–	–
W.K.M.Benjamin	10	12	1	40*	136	12.36	–	–	5
I.R.Bishop	18	28	8	30*	231	11.55	–	–	3
A.C.Cummins	3	4	1	14*	31	10.33	–	–	–
R.A.Harper	24	31	3	74	532	19.00	–	3	35
D.L.Haynes	111	194	24	184	7250	42.64	18	38	65
C.L.Hooper	39	66	6	178*	1770	29.50	4	7	40
B.C.Lara	10	17	–	277	812	47.76	1	6	15
J.R.Murray	6	8	1	49*	136	19.42	–	–	27/1
B.P.Patterson	28	38	16	21*	145	6.59	–	–	5
R.B.Richardson	71	122	10	194	5231	46.70	15	23	77
P.V.Simmons	16	30	1	110	740	25.51	1	2	14
C.A.Walsh	59	81	25	30*	518	9.25	–	–	8
D.Williams	3	6	–	15	21	3.50	–	–	15/1

WEST INDIES

BOWLING

	O	R	W	Avge	Best	5wI	10wM
J.C.Adams	53.4	162	5	32.40	4-43	–	–
C.E.L.Ambrose	1725.3	4070	190	21.42	8-45	9	2
K.L.T.Arthurton	26	68	0	–	–	–	–
K.C.G.Benjamin	52	162	4	40.50	2-87	–	–
W.K.M.Benjamin	264	702	34	20.64	4-52	–	–
I.R.Bishop	653	1698	83	20.45	6-40	5	–
A.C.Cummins	45	144	5	28.80	4-54	–	–
R.A.Harper	577.3	1252	45	27.82	6-57	1	–
D.L.Haynes	3	8	1	8.00	1- 2	–	–
C.L.Hooper	739.5	1966	35	56.17	5-40	1	–
B.C.Lara	2	4	0	–	–	–	–
B.P.Patterson	804.5	2875	93	30.91	5-24	5	–
R.B.Richardson	11	18	0	–	–	–	–
P.V.Simmons	63	154	2	77.00	2-34	–	–
C.A.Walsh	1942	5118	202	25.33	6-62	5	1

NEW ZEALAND

BATTING AND FIELDING

	M	I	NO	HS	Runs	Avge	100	50	Ct/St
T.E.Blain	5	9	1	51	164	20.50	–	1	8/1
G.E.Bradburn	5	9	2	30*	105	15.00	–	–	4
C.L.Cairns	7	12	–	61	213	17.75	–	1	5
M.D.Crowe	66	112	10	299	4777	46.83	15	16	60
S.B.Doull	1	1	–	2	2	2.00	–	–	–
M.J.Greatbatch	26	45	5	146*	1626	40.65	3	9	21
C.Z.Harris	4	8	1	56	112	16.00	–	1	2
B.R.Hartland	6	12	–	52	237	19.75	–	1	2
M.J.Haslam	2	1	–	3	3	3.00	–	–	3
A.H.Jones	31	58	7	186	2276	44.62	6	7	21
R.T.Latham	4	7	–	119	219	31.28	1	–	6
D.K.Morrison	29	42	14	27*	184	6.57	–	–	11
D.J.Nash	2	2	1	11*	15	15.00	–	–	2
M.B.Owens	5	8	4	8*	8	2.00	–	–	3
A.C.Parore	8	13	1	60	169	14.08	–	1	25/2
D.N.Patel	22	41	5	99	772	21.44	–	3	5
C.Pringle	7	12	2	24*	103	10.30	–	–	4
K.R.Rutherford	38	65	7	107*	1529	26.36	3	10	26
M.L.Su'a	9	12	3	44	106	11.77	–	–	6
J.T.C.Vaughan	1	2	1	17	17	17.00	–	–	1
W.Watson	14	17	5	11	60	5.00	–	–	4
J.G.Wright	82	148	7	185	5334	37.82	12	23	38

NEW ZEALAND

BOWLING

	O	R	W	Avge	Best	5wI	10wM
G.E.Bradburn	102.4	336	5	67.20	3-134	–	–
C.L.Cairns	243.3	864	21	41.14	6- 52	2	–
M.D.Crowe	229.3	676	14	48.28	2- 25	–	–
S.B.Doull	19	37	1	37.00	1- 29	–	–
M.J.Greatbatch	1	0	0	–	–	–	–
C.Z.Harris	20	85	0	–	–	–	–
M.J.Haslam	50	153	1	153.00	1- 33	–	–
A.H.Jones	39.4	138	1	138.00	1- 40	–	–
R.T.Latham	3	6	0	–	–	–	–
D.K.Morrison	1014.5	3382	103	32.83	7- 89	8	–
D.J.Nash	54	140	3	46.66	1- 19	–	–
M.B.Owens	119	379	12	31.58	4-101	–	–
D.N.Patel	572	1646	41	40.14	6- 50	3	–
C.Pringle	255	785	19	41.31	7- 52	1	1
K.R.Rutherford	42.4	161	1	161.00	1- 38	–	–
M.L.Su'a	319.1	813	29	28.03	5- 73	2	–
J.T.C.Vaughan	14	56	0	–	–	–	–
W.Watson	557	1335	39	34.23	6- 78	1	–
J.G.Wright	5	5	0	–	–	–	–

INDIA

BATTING AND FIELDING

	M	I	NO	HS	Runs	Avge	100	50	Ct/St
P.K.Amre	11	13	3	103	425	42.50	1	3	9
M.Azharuddin	58	84	3	199	3650	45.06	12	12	50
R.K.Chauhan	7	4	1	15*	34	11.33	–	–	3
A.D.Jadeja	3	5	1	43	99	24.75	–	–	–
V.G.Kambli	7	8	1	227	793	113.28	4	1	3
Kapil Dev	127	180	14	163	5131	30.90	8	26	63
A.Kumble	13	12	2	21*	106	10.60	–	–	5
Maninder Singh	36	39	12	104	203	7.51	1	–	9
S.V.Manjrekar	26	42	4	218	1523	40.07	4	5	15
K.S.More	49	64	14	73	1285	25.70	–	7	110/20
M.Prabhakar	30	45	7	95	1289	33.92	–	9	13
S.L.V.Raju	14	19	6	31	180	13.84	–	–	4
W.V.Raman	8	13	1	96	367	30.58	–	3	5
R.J.Shastri	80	121	14	206	3830	35.79	11	12	36
N.S.Sidhu	27	41	2	116	1415	36.28	4	7	4
J.Srinath	11	14	8	21	90	15.00	–	–	5
S.R.Tendulkar	28	40	4	165	1725	47.91	6	9	21
V.Yadav	1	1	–	30	30	30.00	–	–	1/2

INDIA

BOWLING

	O	R	W	Avge	Best	5wI	10wM
M.Azharuddin	1.1	12	0	–	–	–	–
R.K.Chauhan	304.5	618	15	41.20	3- 30	–	–
Kapil Dev	4541.4	12619	425	29.69	9- 83	23	2
A.Kumble	762.1	1684	66	25.51	6- 53	4	–
Maninder Singh	1369.4	3288	88	37.36	7- 27	3	2
S.V.Manjrekar	2.5	15	0	–	–	–	–
K.S.More	2	12	0	–	–	–	–
M.Prabhakar	1123.1	3186	84	37.92	6-132	3	–
S.L.V.Raju	710.3	1513	42	36.02	6- 12	1	–
W.V.Raman	43	66	2	33.00	1- 7	–	–
R.J.Shastri	2625.1	6185	151	40.96	5- 75	2	–
N.S.Sidhu	1	9	0	–	–	–	–
J.Srinath	417	1048	28	37.42	4- 33	–	–
S.R.Tendulkar	64	165	4	41.25	2- 10	–	–

PAKISTAN

BATTING AND FIELDING

	M	I	NO	HS	Runs	Avge	100	50	Ct/St
Aamir Nazir	1	2	1	6*	7	7.00	–	–	–
Aamir Sohail	8	15	1	205	497	35.50	1	2	6
Aqib Javed	14	12	3	10	29	3.22	–	–	1
Asif Mujtaba	12	20	–	59	446	22.30	–	4	10
Ata-ur-Rehman	4	5	2	19	36	12.00	–	–	–
Basit Ali	3	5	1	92*	222	55.50	–	2	–
Inzamam-ul-Haq	8	13	1	123	336	28.00	1	1	5
Javed Miandad	121	184	21	280*	8689	53.30	23	42	93/1
Moin Khan	11	15	2	32	169	13.00	–	–	24/2
Mushtaq Ahmed	10	15	3	12*	76	6.33	–	–	1
Nadim Khan	1	1	–	25	25	25.00	–	–	–
Ramiz Raja	48	78	5	122	2243	30.72	2	16	27
Rashid Latif	3	4	1	50	117	39.00	–	1	6/3
Salim Malik	72	103	18	165	3757	44.20	10	21	48
Shakil Ahmed	1	1	–	0	0	0.00	–	–	–
Shoaib Mohammad	39	58	6	203*	2443	46.98	7	10	20
Tausif Ahmed	33	37	19	33*	297	16.50	–	–	9
Waqar Younis	23	28	6	29	194	8.81	–	–	2
Wasim Akram	48	63	9	123	1057	19.57	1	4	16

BOWLING

	O	R	W	Avge	Best	5wI	10wM
Aamir Nazir	22	90	2	45.00	2- 79	–	–
Aamir Sohail	19	70	2	35.00	1- 14	–	–
Aqib Javed	349	1051	25	42.04	4-100	–	–
Asif Mujtaba	34	121	2	60.50	1- 0	–	–
Ata-ur-Rehman	93	372	9	41.33	3- 28	–	–
Basit Ali	1	6	0	–	–	–	–
Javed Miandad	245	682	17	40.11	3- 74	–	–
Mushtaq Ahmed	323.4	869	23	37.78	3- 32	–	–
Nadim Khan	52	195	2	97.50	2-147	–	–
Salim Malik	45.2	118	5	23.60	1- 3	–	–

PAKISTAN

BOWLING (continued)

	O	R	W	Avge	Best	5wI	10wM
Shoaib Mohammad	42	113	5	22.60	2- 8	–	–
Tausif Ahmed	1267.2	2888	93	31.05	6- 45	3	–
Waqar Younis	764.3	2373	121	19.61	7- 76	12	2
Wasim Akram	1769.2	4569	186	24.56	6- 62	12	2

SRI LANKA

BATTING AND FIELDING

	M	I	NO	HS	Runs	Avge	100	50	Ct/St
S.D.Anurasiri	13	14	4	24	60	6.00	–	–	3
M.S.Atapattu	2	4	–	1	1	0.25	–	–	–
P.B.Dassanayake	3	4	–	10	25	6.25	–	–	2/4
A.M.De Silva	3	3	–	9	10	3.33	–	–	4/1
P.A.De Silva	37	62	2	267	2478	41.30	6	11	20
H.D.P.K.Dharmasena	2	3	–	5	12	4.00	–	–	–
A.P.Gurusinha	27	45	7	137	1500	39.47	4	4	20
U.C.Hathurusinghe	18	30	1	81	840	28.96	–	5	2
S.T.Jayasuriya	12	19	5	81	568	40.57	–	4	13
R.S.Kalpage	2	4	1	42	48	16.00	–	–	1
R.S.Kaluwitharana	3	4	1	132*	177	59.00	1	–	6
D.K.Liyanage	7	6	–	16	31	5.16	–	–	–
A.W.R.Madurasinghe	3	6	1	11	24	4.80	–	–	–
R.S.Mahanama	23	36	–	153	1276	35.44	3	7	16
M.Muralitharan	9	7	4	19	46	15.33	–	–	4
C.P.H.Ramanayake	18	24	9	34*	143	9.53	–	–	6
A.Ranatunga	45	75	4	135*	2582	36.36	4	17	20
H.P.Tillekeratne	19	29	4	93*	958	38.32	–	9	50
K.P.J.Warnaweera	9	10	3	20	35	5.00	–	–	–
A.G.D.Wickremasinghe	3	3	1	13*	17	8.50	–	–	9/1
G.P.Wickremasinghe	8	11	2	21	88	9.77	–	–	5
P.K.Wijetunge	1	2	–	10	10	5.00	–	–	–

BOWLING

	O	R	W	Avge	Best	5wI	10wM
S.D.Anurasiri	450.1	985	29	33.96	4- 71	–	–
P.A.De Silva	99	334	8	41.75	3- 39	–	–
H.D.P.K.Dharmasena	91	199	2	99.50	1- 29	–	–
A.P.Gurusinha	180.4	515	18	28.61	2- 7	–	–
U.C.Hathurusinghe	238	560	16	35.00	4- 66	–	–
S.T.Jayasuriya	69	247	3	82.33	2- 46	–	–
R.S.Kalpage	71.5	175	4	43.75	2- 97	–	–
D.K.Liyanage	194.5	567	16	35.43	4- 56	–	–
A.W.R.Madurasinghe	66	172	3	57.33	3- 60	–	–
R.S.Mahanama	6	30	0	–	–	–	–
M.Muralitharan	407.4	1046	36	29.05	5-101	2	–
C.P.H.Ramanayake	609	1880	44	42.72	5- 82	1	–
A.Ranatunga	330.2	875	14	62.50	2- 17	–	–
H.P.Tillekeratne	3	6	0	–	–	–	–
K.P.J.Warnaweera	329.5	850	27	31.48	4- 25	–	–
G.P.Wickremasinghe	288	885	22	40.22	5- 73	1	–
P.K.Wijetunge	52	118	2	59.00	1- 58	–	–

ZIMBABWE

BATTING AND FIELDING

	M	I	NO	HS	Runs	Avge	100	50	Ct/St
K.J.Arnott	4	8	1	101*	302	43.14	1	1	4
D.H.Brain	2	4	–	17	28	7.00	–	–	–
E.A.Brandes	3	5	–	8	15	3.00	–	–	1
G.A.Briant	1	2	–	16	17	8.50	–	–	–
M.G.Burmester	3	4	2	30*	54	27.00	–	–	1
A.D.R.Campbell	4	8	1	61	273	39.00	–	2	2
G.J.Crocker	3	4	1	33	69	23.00	–	–	–
A.Flower	4	7	2	115	341	68.20	1	3	7/2
G.W.Flower	4	8	–	96	264	33.00	–	2	1
D.L.Houghton	4	7	1	121	240	40.00	1	–	4
M.P.Jarvis	2	2	1	2*	2	2.00	–	–	1
A.J.Pycroft	3	5	–	60	152	30.40	–	1	2
U.Ranchod	1	2	–	7	8	4.00	–	–	–
A.H.Shah	2	3	–	28	59	19.66	–	–	–
A.J.Traicos	4	6	2	5	11	2.75	–	–	4
A.J.Traicos (SA/Z)	7	10	4	5*	19	3.16	–	–	8

BOWLING

	O	R	W	Avge	Best	5wI	10wM
D.H.Brain	68	247	6	41.16	3-49	–	–
E.A.Brandes	69.4	204	4	51.00	2-49	–	–
M.G.Burmester	72.4	227	3	75.66	3-78	–	–
G.J.Crocker	76	217	3	72.33	2-65	–	–
G.W.Flower	27	108	1	108.00	1-32	–	–
D.L.Houghton	0.5	0	0	–	–	–	–
M.P.Jarvis	75.1	198	4	49.50	3-38	–	–
U.Ranchod	12	45	1	45.00	1-45	–	–
A.H.Shah	31	125	1	125.00	1-46	–	–
A.J.Traicos	190.1	562	14	40.14	5-86	1	–
A.J.Traicos (SA/Z)	268.3	769	18	42.72	5-86	1	–

LIMITED-OVERS INTERNATIONALS CAREER RECORDS

These career records for players registered for first-class county cricket in 1994 are complete to the end of the 1993 season (including Sri Lanka v India and South Africa 1993-94).

BATTING AND FIELDING

	M	I	NO	HS	Runs	Avge	100	50	Ct/St
Adams, J.C. (WI)	10	6	4	27	87	43.50	–	–	–
Ambrose, C.E.L. (WI)	91	49	23	26*	359	13.80	–	–	24
Atherton, M.A.	10	10	1	74	335	37.22	–	3	3
Athey, C.W.J.	31	30	3	142*	848	31.40	2	4	16
Bailey, R.J.	4	4	2	43*	137	68.50	–	–	1
Barnett, K.J.	1	1	–	84	84	84.00	–	1	–

	M	I	NO	HS	Runs	Avge	100	50	Ct/St
Benjamin, W.K.M. (WI)	60	36	7	31	190	6.55	–	–	11
Benson, M.R.	1	1	–	24	24	24.00	–	–	–
Bicknell, M.P.	7	6	2	31*	96	24.00	–	–	2
Bishop, I.R. (WI)	53	25	11	33*	221	15.78	–	–	10
Blakey, R.J.	3	2	–	25	25	12.50	–	–	2/1
Broad, B.C.	34	34	4	106	1361	40.02	1	11	10
Caddick, A.R.	3	2	2	2*	3	–	–	–	–
Capel, D.J.	23	19	2	50*	327	19.23	–	1	6
Cook, N.G.B.	3	–	–	–	–	–	–	–	2
Cork, D.G.	3	1	1	11	11	11.00	–	–	5
Cowans, N.G.	23	8	3	4*	13	2.60	–	–	5
Cummins, A.C. (WI)	29	14	5	24	71	7.88	–	–	3
Curran, K.M. (Z)	11	11	–	73	287	26.09	–	2	1
DeFreitas, P.A.J.	85	54	20	49*	519	15.26	–	–	23
Ellison, R.M.	14	12	4	24	86	10.75	–	–	2
Emburey, J.E.	61	45	10	34	501	14.31	–	–	19
Fairbrother, N.H.	40	38	8	113	1204	40.13	1	9	18
Fowler, G.	26	26	2	81*	744	31.00	–	4	4/2
Fraser, A.R.C.	24	10	4	38*	69	11.50	–	–	1
French, B.N.	13	8	3	9*	34	6.80	–	–	13/3
Gatting, M.W.	92	88	17	115*	2095	29.50	1	9	22
Gooch, G.A.	120	117	6	142	4206	37.89	8	23	44
Haynes, D.L. (WI)	225	224	28	152*	8194	41.80	16	53	54
Hemmings, E.E.	33	12	6	8*	30	5.00	–	–	5
Hick, G.A.	32	31	5	105*	1038	39.92	1	9	18
Hooper, C.L. (WI)	102	89	21	113*	1994	29.32	1	9	55
Hussain, N.	2	2	1	15*	17	17.00	–	–	1
Illingworth, R.K.	18	7	2	14	61	12.20	–	–	8
Jarvis, P.W.	16	8	2	16*	31	5.16	–	–	1
Lamb, A.J.	122	118	16	118	4010	39.31	4	26	31
Larkins, W.	25	24	–	124	591	24.62	1	–	8
Lewis, C.C.	40	29	8	33	251	11.95	–	–	14
Lynch, M.A.	3	3	–	6	8	2.66	–	–	1
Malcolm, D.E.	9	5	2	4	3	3.00	–	–	–
Moody, T.M. (A)	34	32	3	89	751	25.89	–	7	10
Morris, J.E.	8	8	1	63*	167	23.85	–	1	2
Moxon, M.D.	8	8	–	70	174	21.75	–	1	5
Mushtaq Ahmed (P)	70	37	15	17*	192	8.72	–	–	13
Prabhakar, M. (I)	94	64	15	106	1010	20.61	1	4	21
Radford, N.V.	6	3	2	0*	0	0.00	–	–	2
Ramprakash, M.R.	2	2	–	6*	6	–	–	–	–
Reeve, D.A.	24	16	9	33*	225	32.14	–	–	11
Rhodes, S.J.	3	2	1	8	9	9.00	–	–	3
Richardson, R.B. (WI)	185	178	23	122	5306	34.23	5	39	65
Robinson, R.T.	26	26	–	83	597	22.96	–	3	6
Russell, R.C.	26	19	6	50	261	20.07	–	1	26/5
Salisbury, I.D.K.	2	1	1	2*	2	–	–	–	1
Simmons, P.V. (WI)	64	62	4	122	1695	29.22	4	7	21
Small, G.C.	53	24	9	18*	98	6.53	–	–	7
Smith, D.M.	2	2	1	10*	15	15.00	–	–	–
Smith, R.A.	58	57	8	167*	2068	42.20	4	12	18
Stewart, A.J.	51	46	4	103	1278	30.42	1	8	37/3
Taylor, J.P.	1	1	–	1	1	1.00	–	–	–
Thorpe, G.P.	3	3	–	36	89	29.66	–	–	1
Tufnell, P.C.R.	15	7	6	5*	13	13.00	–	–	3
Walsh, C.A. (WI)	111	39	15	29*	203	8.45	–	–	13

	M	I	NO	HS	Runs	Avge	100	50	Ct/St
Waqar Younis (P)	74	32	14	37	236	13.11	–	–	8
Wasim Akram (P)	153	118	22	86	1327	13.82	–	1	29
Wells, C.M.	2	2	–	17	22	11.00	–	–	–
Whitaker, J.J.	2	2	1	44*	48	48.00	–	–	1

BOWLING

	Overs	Runs	Wkts	Avge	Best	4w
Adams, J.C.	7	35	1	35.00	1- 2	–
Ambrose, C.E.L.	826	2852	139	20.51	5-17	8
Athey, C.W.J.	1	10	0	–	–	–
Bailey, R.J.	6	25	0	–	–	–
Benjamin, W.K.M.	539.3	2235	69	32.39	3-21	–
Bicknell, M.P.	68.5	347	13	26.69	3-55	–
Bishop, I.R.	462.1	1874	88	21.29	5-25	8
Broad, B.C.	1	6	0	–	–	–
Caddick, A.R.	33	132	4	33.00	3-39	–
Capel, D.J.	173	805	17	47.35	3-38	–
Cook, N.G.B.	24	95	5	19.00	2-18	–
Cork, D.G.	31	118	1	118.00	1-37	–
Cowans, N.G.	213.4	913	23	39.69	3-44	–
Cummins, A.C.	253.3	996	36	27.66	5-31	2
Curran, K.M.	84.2	398	9	44.22	3-65	–
DeFreitas, P.A.J.	790.1	3104	96	32.33	4-35	1
Ellison, R.M.	116	510	12	42.50	3-42	–
Emburey, J.E.	570.5	2346	76	30.86	4-37	2
Fairbrother, N.H.	1	9	0	–	–	–
Fraser, A.R.C.	222.4	797	23	34.65	3-22	–
Gatting, M.W.	65.2	336	10	33.60	3-32	–
Gooch, G.A.	326.2	1436	36	39.88	3-19	–
Haynes, D.L.	5	24	0	–	–	–
Hemmings, E.E.	292	1294	37	34.97	4-52	1
Hick, G.A.	37	191	4	47.75	2- 7	–
Hooper, C.L.	677.1	2888	95	30.40	4-34	1
Illingworth, R.K.	182.1	760	24	31.60	3-33	–
Jarvis, P.W.	146.3	672	24	28.00	5-35	2
Lamb, A.J.	1	3	0	–	–	–
Larkins, W.	2.3	22	0	–	–	–
Lewis, C.C.	319.1	1412	45	31.37	4-30	2
Malcolm, D.E.	79	363	13	27.92	3-40	–
Moody, T.M.	149	651	16	40.68	3-56	–
Mushtaq Ahmed	569.3	2569	77	33.36	3-14	–
Prabhakar, M.	771.4	3164	119	26.58	4-19	4
Radford, N.V.	58	230	2	115.00	1-32	–
Reeve, D.A.	157.3	671	18	37.27	3-20	–
Richardson, R.B.	9.4	46	1	46.00	1- 4	–
Salisbury, I.D.K.	12	78	2	39.00	2-36	–
Simmons, P.V.	224.5	919	33	27.84	4- 3	1
Small, G.C.	465.3	1942	58	33.48	4-31	1
Taylor, J.P.	3	20	0	–	–	–
Tufnell, P.C.R.	129	528	12	44.00	3-40	–
Walsh, C.A.	998.3	3849	124	31.04	5- 1	6
Waqar Younis	606.1	2526	127	19.88	6-26	11
Wasim Akram	1306.1	4995	215	23.23	5-16	12

FIRST-CLASS CRICKET RECORDS

To the end of the 1993 season
(Including Indian and South African tours of Sri Lanka, July-September 1993)

TEAM RECORDS

HIGHEST INNINGS TOTALS

1107	Victoria v New South Wales	Melbourne	1926-27
1059	Victoria v Tasmania	Melbourne	1922-23
951-7d	Sind v Baluchistan	Karachi	1973-74
918	New South Wales v South Australia	Sydney	1900-01
912-8d	Holkar v Mysore	Indore	1945-46
910-6d	Railways v Dera Ismail Khan	Lahore	1964-65
903-7d	England v Australia	The Oval	1938
887	Yorkshire v Warwickshire	Birmingham	1896
863	Lancashire v Surrey	The Oval	1990
860-6d	Tamil Nadu v Goa	Panjim	1988-89

There have been 26 instances of a team scoring 800 runs or more in an innings, the most recent being by Bombay (855-6d, including 48 penalty runs) v Hyderabad at Bombay in 1990-91. Tamil Nadu's total of 860-6d was boosted to 912 by 52 penalty runs.

HIGHEST SECOND INNINGS TOTAL

770	New South Wales v South Australia	Adelaide	1920-21

HIGHEST FOURTH INNINGS TOTAL

654-5	England v South Africa	Durban	1938-39

HIGHEST MATCH AGGREGATE

2376	Maharashtra v Bombay	Poona	1948-49

RECORD MARGIN OF VICTORY

Innings and 851 runs: Railways v Dera Ismail Khan Lahore 1964-65

MOST RUNS IN A DAY

721	Australians v Essex	Southend	1948

MOST HUNDREDS IN AN INNINGS

6	Holkar v Mysore	Indore	1945-46

LOWEST INNINGS TOTALS

12	†Oxford University v MCC and Ground	Oxford	1877
12	Northamptonshire v Gloucestershire	Gloucester	1907
13	Auckland v Canterbury	Auckland	1877-78
13	Nottinghamshire v Yorkshire	Nottingham	1901
14	Surrey v Essex	Chelmsford	1983
15	MCC v Surrey	Lord's	1839
15	†Victoria v MCC	Melbourne	1903-04
15	†Northamptonshire v Yorkshire	Northampton	1908
15	Hampshire v Warwickshire	Birmingham	1922

†Batted one man short

There have been 26 instances of a team being dismissed for under 20, the most recent being by Surrey in 1983 (above).

LOWEST MATCH AGGREGATE BY ONE TEAM

34 (16 and 18) Border v Natal   East London   1959-60

LOWEST COMPLETED MATCH AGGREGATE BY BOTH TEAMS

105   MCC v Australians   Lord's   1878

FEWEST RUNS IN AN UNINTERRUPTED DAY'S PLAY

95   Australia (80) v Pakistan (15-2)   Karachi   1956-57

TIED MATCHES

Before 1948 a match was considered to be tied if the scores were level after the fourth innings, even if the side batting last had wickets in hand when play ended. Law 22 was amended in 1948 and since then a match has been tied only when the scores are level after the fourth innings has been completed. There have been 53 tied first-class matches, five of which would not have qualified under the current law. The most recent is:

Worcestershire (203/325-8d) v Nottinghamshire (233/295) Nottingham   1993

BATTING RECORDS

HIGHEST INDIVIDUAL INNINGS

499	Hanif Mohammad	Karachi v Bahawalpur	Karachi	1958-59
452*	D.G.Bradman	New South Wales v Queensland	Sydney	1929-30
443*	B.B.Nimbalkar	Maharashtra v Kathiawar	Poona	1948-49
437	W.H.Ponsford	Victoria v Queensland	Melbourne	1927-28
429	W.H.Ponsford	Victoria v Tasmania	Melbourne	1922-23
428	Aftab Baloch	Sind v Baluchistan	Karachi	1973-74
424	A.C.MacLaren	Lancashire v Somerset	Taunton	1895
405*	G.A.Hick	Worcestershire v Somerset	Taunton	1988
385	B.Sutcliffe	Otago v Canterbury	Christchurch	1952-53
383	C.W.Gregory	New South Wales v Queensland	Brisbane	1906-07
377	S.V.Manjrekar	Bombay v Hyderabad	Bombay	1990-91
369	D.G.Bradman	South Australia v Tasmania	Adelaide	1935-36
366	N.H.Fairbrother	Lancashire v Surrey	The Oval	1990
365*	C.Hill	South Australia v NSW	Adelaide	1900-01
365*	G.St A.Sobers	West Indies v Pakistan	Kingston	1957-58
364	L.Hutton	England v Australia	The Oval	1938
359*	V.M.Merchant	Bombay v Maharashtra	Bombay	1943-44
359	R.B.Simpson	New South Wales v Queensland	Brisbane	1963-64
357*	R.Abel	Surrey v Somerset	The Oval	1899
357	D.G.Bradman	South Australia v Victoria	Melbourne	1935-36
356	B.A.Richards	South Australia v W Australia	Perth	1970-71
355*	G.R.Marsh	W Australia v S Australia	Perth	1989-90
355	B.Sutcliffe	Otago v Auckland	Dunedin	1949-50
352	W.H.Ponsford	Victoria v New South Wales	Melbourne	1926-27
350	Rashid Israr	Habib Bank v National Bank	Lahore	1976-77

There have been 106 triple hundreds in first-class cricket, W.V.Raman (313) and Arjan Kripal Singh (302*) for Tamil Nadu v Goa at Panjim in 1988-89 providing the only instance of two batsmen scoring 300 in the same innings.

MOST HUNDREDS IN SUCCESSIVE INNINGS

6	C.B.Fry	Sussex and Rest of England		1901
6	D.G.Bradman	South Australia and D.G.Bradman's XI		1938-39
6	M.J.Procter	Rhodesia		1970-71

TWO DOUBLE HUNDREDS IN A MATCH

| 244 | 202* | A.E.Fagg | Kent v Essex | Colchester | 1938 |

TRIPLE HUNDRED AND HUNDRED IN A MATCH

| 333 | 123 | G.A.Gooch | England v India | Lord's | 1990 |

DOUBLE HUNDRED AND HUNDRED IN A MATCH MOST TIMES

| 4 | Zaheer Abbas | Gloucestershire | 1976-81 |

TWO HUNDREDS IN A MATCH MOST TIMES

| 8 | Zaheer Abbas | Gloucestershire and PIA | 1976-82 |
| 7 | W.R.Hammond | Gloucestershire, England and MCC | 1927-45 |

MOST HUNDREDS IN A SEASON

| 18 | D.C.S.Compton | 1947 | 16 | J.B.Hobbs | 1925 |

MOST HUNDREDS IN A CAREER

| | Total | | 100th Hundred | |
	Hundreds	Inns	Season	Inns
J.B.Hobbs	197	1315	1923	821
E.H.Hendren	170	1300	1928-29	740
W.R.Hammond	167	1005	1935	679
C.P.Mead	153	1340	1927	892
G.Boycott	151	1014	1977	645
H.Sutcliffe	149	1088	1932	700
F.E.Woolley	145	1532	1929	1031
L.Hutton	129	814	1951	619
W.G Grace	126	1493	1895	1113
D.C.S.Compton	123	839	1952	552
T.W.Graveney	122	1223	1964	940
D.G.Bradman	117	338	1947-48	295
I.V.A.Richards	114	796	1988-89	658
Zaheer Abbas	108	768	1982-83	658
A.Sandham	107	1000	1935	871
M.C.Cowdrey	107	1130	1973	1035
G.A.Gooch	106	859	1992-93	820
T.W.Hayward	104	1138	1913	1076
J.H.Edrich	103	979	1977	945
G.M.Turner	103	792	1982	779
E.Tyldesley	102	961	1934	919
L.E.G.Ames	102	951	1950	915
D.L.Amiss	102	1139	1986	1081

Most 400s:	2 – W.H.Ponsford
Most 300s or more:	6 – D.G.Bradman
Most 200s or more:	37 – D.G.Bradman; 36 – W.R.Hammond

MOST RUNS IN A MONTH

1294 (avge 92.42)   L.Hutton   Yorkshire   June 1949

MOST RUNS IN A SEASON

Runs			I	NO	HS	Avge	100	Season
3816	D.C.S.Compton	Middlesex	50	8	246	90.85	18	1947
3539	W.J.Edrich	Middlesex	52	8	267*	80.43	12	1947
3518	T.W.Hayward	Surrey	61	4	219	66.37	13	1906

The feat of scoring 3000 runs in a season has been achieved on 28 occasions, the most recent instance being by W.E.Alley (3019) in 1961. The highest aggregate in a season since 1969, when the number of County Championship matches was substantially reduced, is 2755 by S.J.Cook in 1991.

1000 RUNS IN A SEASON MOST TIMES

28   W.G.Grace (Gloucestershire), F.E.Woolley (Kent)

HIGHEST BATTING AVERAGE IN A SEASON
(Qualification: 12 innings)

Avge			I	NO	HS	Runs	100	Season
115.66	D.G.Bradman	Australians	26	5	278	2429	13	1938
102.53	G.Boycott	Yorkshire	20	5	175*	1538	6	1979
102.00	W.A.Johnston	Australians	17	16	28*	102	–	1953
101.70	G.A.Gooch	Essex	30	3	333	2746	12	1990
100.12	G.Boycott	Yorkshire	30	5	233	2503	13	1971

FASTEST HUNDRED AGAINST AUTHENTIC BOWLING

35 min   P.G.H.Fender   Surrey v Northamptonshire ·   Northampton   1920

FASTEST DOUBLE HUNDRED

113 min   R.J.Shastri   Bombay v Baroda   Bombay   1984-85

FASTEST TRIPLE HUNDRED

181 min   D.C.S.Compton   MCC v NE Transvaal   Benoni   1948-49

MOST SIXES IN AN INNINGS

15	J.R.Reid	Wellington v N Districts	Wellington	1962-63
14	Shakti Singh	Himachal Pradesh v Haryana	Dharmsala	1990-91
13	Majid Khan	Pakistanis v Glamorgan	Swansea	1967
13	C.G.Greenidge	D.H.Robins' XI v Pakistanis	Eastbourne	1974
13	C.G.Greenidge	Hampshire v Sussex	Southampton	1975
13	G.W.Humpage	Warwickshire v Lancashire	Southport	1982
13	R.J.Shastri	Bombay v Baroda	Bombay	1984-85

MOST SIXES IN A MATCH

17   W.J.Stewart   Warwickshire v Lancashire   Blackpool   1959

MOST SIXES IN A SEASON

80   I.T.Botham   Somerset and England   1985

MOST BOUNDARIES IN AN INNINGS

68   P.A.Perrin   Essex v Derbyshire   Chesterfield   1904

MOST RUNS OFF ONE OVER

36   G.St A.Sobers   Nottinghamshire v Glamorgan Swansea   1968
36   R.J.Shastri   Bombay v Baroda   Bombay   1984-85

Both batsmen hit all six balls of an over (bowled by M.A.Nash and Tilak Raj respectively) for six.

MOST RUNS IN A DAY

345   C.G.Macartney Australians v Nottinghamshire Nottingham   1921

There have been 18 instances of a batsman scoring 300 or more runs in a day, the most recent being by N.H.Fairbrother (311*) for Lancashire v Surrey at The Oval in 1990.

HIGHEST PARTNERSHIPS

First Wicket
561 Waheed Mirza/Mansoor Akhtar Karachi W v Quetta Karachi   1976-77
555 P.Holmes/H.Sutcliffe Yorkshire v Essex Leyton   1932
554 J.T.Brown/J.Tunnicliffe Yorkshire v Derbys Chesterfield   1898

Second Wicket
475 Zahir Alam/L.S.Rajput Assam v Tripura Gauhati   1991-92
465*J.A.Jameson/R.B.Kanhai Warwickshire v Glos Birmingham   1974
455 K.V.Bhandarkar/B.B.Nimbalkar Maha'tra v Kathiawar Poona   1948-49

Third Wicket
467 A.H.Jones/M.D.Crowe N Zealand v Sri Lanka Wellington   1990-91
456 Khalid Irtiza/Aslam Ali United Bank v Multan Karachi   1975-76
451 Mudassar Nazar/Javed Miandad Pakistan v India Hyderabad   1982-83
445 P.E.Whitelaw/W.N.Carson Auckland v Otago Dunedin   1936-37
434 J.B.Stollmeyer/G.E.Gomez Trinidad v Br Guiana Port-of-Spain1946-47
424*W.J.Edrich/D.C.S.Compton Middlesex v Somerset Lord's   1948

Fourth Wicket
577 V.S.Hazare/Gul Mahomed Baroda v Holkar Baroda   1946-47
574*C.L.Walcott/F.M.M.Worrell Barbados v Trinidad Port-of-Spain1945-46
502*F.M.M.Worrell/J.D.C.Goddard Barbados v Trinidad Bridgetown 1943-44
470 A.I.Kallicharran/G.W.Humpage Warwickshire v Lancs Southport   1982

Fifth Wicket
464*†M.E.Waugh/S.R.Waugh NSW v W Australia Perth   1990-91
405 S.G.Barnes/D.G.Bradman Australia v England Sydney   1946-47
397 W.Bardsley/C.Kelleway NSW v S Australia Sydney   1920-21
393 E.G.Arnold/W.B.Burns Worcs v Warwickshire Birmingham   1909
† Includes 20 runs credited under ACB playing conditions for 10 no-balls which, under the Laws of cricket, would have produced 7 runs.

Sixth Wicket
487*G.A.Headley/C.C.Passailaigue Jamaica v Tennyson's Kingston   1931-32
428 W.W.Armstrong/M.A.Noble Australians v Sussex Hove   1902
411 R.M.Poore/E.G.Wynyard Hampshire v SomersetTaunton   1899

Seventh Wicket

347	D.St E.Atkinson/C.C.Depeiza	W Indies v Australia	Bridgetown	1954-55
344	K.S.Ranjitsinhji/W.Newham	Sussex v Essex	Leyton	1902
340	K.J.Key/H.Philipson	Oxford U v Middlesex	Chiswick Park	1887

Eighth Wicket

433	V.T.Trumper/A.Sims	Australians v C'bury	Christchurch	1913-14
292	R.Peel/Lord Hawke	Yorkshire v Warwicks	Birmingham	1896
270	V.T.Trumper/E.P.Barbour	NSW v Victoria	Sydney	1912-13

Ninth Wicket

283	J.Chapman/A.Warren	Derbys v Warwicks	Blackwell	1910
251	J.W.H.T.Douglas/S.N.Hare	Essex v Derbyshire	Leyton	1921
245	V.S.Hazare/N.D.Nagarwalla	Maharashtra v Baroda	Poona	1939-40

Tenth Wicket

307	A.F.Kippax/J.E.H.Hooker	NSW v Victoria	Melbourne	1928-29
249	C.T.Sarwate/S.N.Banerjee	Indians v Surrey	The Oval	1946
235	F.E.Woolley/A.Fielder	Kent v Worcs	Stourbridge	1909

MOST RUNS IN A CAREER

	Career	I	NO	HS	Runs	Avge	100
J.B.Hobbs	1905-34	1315	106	316*	61237	50.65	197
F.E.Woolley	1906-38	1532	85	305*	58969	40.75	145
E.H.Hendren	1907-38	1300	166	301*	57611	50.80	170
C.P.Mead	1905-36	1340	185	280*	55061	47.67	153
W.G.Grace	1865-1908	1493	105	344	54896	39.55	126
W.R.Hammond	1920-51	1005	104	336*	50551	56.10	167
H.Sutcliffe	1919-45	1088	123	313	50138	51.95	149
G.Boycott	1962-86	1014	162	261*	48426	56.83	151
T.W.Graveney	1948-71/72	1223	159	258	47793	44.91	122
T.W.Hayward	1893-1914	1138	96	315*	43551	41.79	104
D.L.Amiss	1960-87	1139	126	262*	43423	42.86	102
M.C.Cowdrey	1950-76	1130	134	307	42719	42.89	107
A.Sandham	1911-37/38	1000	79	325	41284	44.82	107
L.Hutton	1934-60	814	91	364	40140	55.51	129
M.J.K.Smith	1951-75	1091	139	204	39832	41.84	69
W.Rhodes	1898-1930	1528	237	267*	39802	30.83	58
J.H.Edrich	1956-78	979	104	310*	39790	45.47	103
R.E.S.Wyatt	1923-57	1141	157	232	39405	40.04	85
D.C.S.Compton	1936-64	839	88	300	38942	51.85	123
G.E.Tyldesley	1909-36	961	106	256*	38874	45.46	102
G.A.Gooch	1973-93	859	70	333	38427	48.70	106
J.T.Tyldesley	1895-1923	994	62	295*	37897	40.60	86
K.W.R.Fletcher	1962-88	1167	170	228*	37665	37.77	63
C.G.Greenidge	1970-92	889	75	273*	37354	45.88	92
J.W.Hearne	1909-36	1025	116	285*	37252	40.98	96
L.E.G.Ames	1926-51	951	95	295	37248	43.51	102
D.Kenyon	1946-67	1159	59	259	37002	33.63	74
W.J.Edrich	1934-58	964	92	267*	36965	42.39	86
J.M.Parks	1949-76	1227	172	205*	36673	34.76	51
D.Denton	1894-1920	1163	70	221	36479	33.37	69
G.H.Hirst	1891-1929	1215	151	341	36323	34.13	60
I.V.A.Richards	1971/72-93	796	62	322	36212	49.33	114
A.Jones	1957-83	1168	72	204*	36049	32.89	56
W.G.Quaife	1894-1928	1203	185	255*	36012	35.37	72
R.E.Marshall	1945/46-72	1053	59	228*	35725	35.94	68
G.Gunn	1902-32	1061	82	220	35208	35.96	62

BOWLING RECORDS

ALL TEN WICKETS IN AN INNINGS

This feat has been achieved on 73 occasions at first-class level.
Three Times: A.P.Freeman (1929, 1930, 1931)
Twice: V.E.Walker (1859, 1865); H.Verity (1931, 1932); J.C.Laker (1956)

Instances since 1945:

W.E.Hollies	Warwickshire v Notts	Birmingham	1946
J.M.Sims	East v West	Kingston on Thames	1948
J.K.R.Graveney	Gloucestershire v Derbyshire	Chesterfield	1949
T.E.Bailey	Essex v Lancashire	Clacton	1949
R.Berry	Lancashire v Worcestershire	Blackpool	1953
S.P.Gupte	President's XI v Combined XI	Bombay	1954-55
J.C.Laker	Surrey v Australians	The Oval	1956
K.Smales	Nottinghamshire v Glos	Stroud	1956
G.A.R.Lock	Surrey v Kent	Blackheath	1956
J.C.Laker	England v Australia	Manchester	1956
P.M.Chatterjee	Bengal v Assam	Jorhat	1956-57
J.D.Bannister	Warwicks v Combined Services	Birmingham	1959
A.J.G.Pearson	Cambridge U v Leicestershire	Loughborough	1961
N.I.Thomson	Sussex v Warwickshire	Worthing	1964
P.J.Allan	Queensland v Victoria	Melbourne	1965-66
I.J.Brayshaw	Western Australia v Victoria	Perth	1967-68
Shahid Mahmood	Karachi Whites v Khairpur	Karachi	1969-70
E.E.Hemmings	International XI v W Indians	Kingston	1982-83
P.Sunderam	Rajasthan v Vidarbha	Jodhpur	1985-86
S.T.Jefferies	Western Province v OFS	Cape Town	1987-88
Imran Adil	Bahawalpur v Faisalabad	Faisalabad	1989-90
G.P.Wickremasinghe	Sinhalese SC v Kalutara	Colombo	1991-92

MOST WICKETS IN A MATCH

19	J.C.Laker	England v Australia	Manchester	1956

MOST WICKETS IN A SEASON

Wkts		Season	Matches	Overs	Mdns	Runs	Avge
304	A.P.Freeman	1928	37	1976.1	423	5489	18.05
298	A.P.Freeman	1933	33	2039	651	4549	15.26

The feat of taking 250 wickets in a season has been achieved on 12 occasions, the last instance being by A.P.Freeman in 1933. 200 or more wickets in a season have been taken on 59 occasions, the last being by G.A.R.Lock (212 wickets, average 12.02) in 1957.

The highest aggregates of wickets taken in a season since the reduction of County Championship matches in 1969 are as follows:

Wkts		Season	Matches	Overs	Mdns	Runs	Avge
134	M.D.Marshall	1982	22	822	225	2108	15.73
131	L.R.Gibbs	1971	23	1024.1	295	2475	18.89
125	F.D.Stephenson	1988	22	819.1	196	2289	18.31
121	R.D.Jackman	1980	23	746.2	220	1864	15.40

Since 1969 there have been 46 instances of bowlers taking 100 wickets in a season.

MOST HAT-TRICKS IN A CAREER

7	D.V.P.Wright
6	T.W.J.Goddard, C.W.L.Parker
5	S.Haigh, V.W.C.Jupp, A.E.G.Rhodes, F.A.Tarrant

MOST WICKETS IN A CAREER

	Career	Runs	Wkts	Avge	100w
W.Rhodes	1898-1930	69993	**4187**	16.71	23
A.P.Freeman	1914-36	69577	**3776**	18.42	17
C.W.L.Parker	1903-35	63817	**3278**	19.46	16
J.T.Hearne	1888-1923	54352	**3061**	17.75	15
T.W.J.Goddard	1922-52	59116	**2979**	19.84	16
W.G.Grace	1865-1908	51545	**2876**	17.92	10
A.S.Kennedy	1907-36	61034	**2874**	21.23	15
D.Shackleton	1948-69	53303	**2857**	18.65	20
G.A.R.Lock	1946-70/71	54709	**2844**	19.23	14
F.J.Titmus	1949-82	63313	**2830**	22.37	16
M.W.Tate	1912-37	50571	**2784**	18.16	13+1
G.H.Hirst	1891-1929	51282	**2739**	18.72	15
C.Blythe	1899-1914	42136	**2506**	16.81	14
D.L.Underwood	1963-87	49993	**2465**	20.28	10
W.E.Astill	1906-39	57358	**2431**	23.76	9
J.C.White	1909-37	43759	**2356**	18.57	14
W.E.Hollies	1932-57	48656	**2323**	20.94	14
F.S.Trueman	1949-69	42154	**2304**	18.29	12
J.B.Statham	1950-68	36999	**2260**	16.37	13
R.T.D.Perks	1930-55	53770	**2233**	24.07	16
J.Briggs	1879-1900	35431	**2221**	15.95	12
D.J.Shepherd	1950-72	47302	**2218**	21.32	12
E.G.Dennett	1903-26	42571	**2147**	19.82	12
T.Richardson	1892-1905	38794	**2104**	18.43	10
T.E.Bailey	1945-67	48170	**2082**	23.13	9
R.Illingworth	1951-83	42023	**2072**	20.28	10
F.E.Woolley	1906-38	41066	**2068**	19.85	8
N.Gifford	1960-88	48731	**2068**	23.56	4
G.Geary	1912-38	41339	**2063**	20.03	11
D.V.P.Wright	1932-57	49307	**2056**	23.98	10
J.A.Newman	1906-30	51111	**2032**	25.15	9
A.Shaw	1864-97	24579	**2027†**	12.12	9
S.Haigh	1895-1913	32091	**2012**	15.94	11

† Excluding one wicket for which no analysis is available.

ALL-ROUND RECORDS

THE 'DOUBLE'

3000 runs and 100 wickets: J.H.Parks (1937)
2000 runs and 200 wickets: G.H.Hirst (1906)
2000 runs and 100 wickets: F.E.Woolley (4), J.W.Hearne (3), W.G.Grace (2), G.H.Hirst (2), W.Rhodes (2), T.E.Bailey, D.E.Davies, G.L.Jessop, V.W.C.Jupp, James Langridge, F.A.Tarrant, C.L.Townsend, L.F.Townsend
1000 runs and 200 wickets: M.W.Tate (3), A.E.Trott (2), A.S.Kennedy

Most Doubles: W.Rhodes (16), G.H.Hirst (14), V.W.C.Jupp (10)

Double in Debut Season: D.B.Close (1949) – aged 18, he is the youngest to achieve this feat

The feat of scoring 1000 runs and taking 100 wickets in a season has been achieved on 305 occasions, R.J.Hadlee (1984) and F.D.Stephenson (1988) being the only players to complete the 'double' since the reduction of County Championship matches in 1969.

WICKET-KEEPING RECORDS

MOST DISMISSALS IN AN INNINGS

9 (8ct, 1st)	Tahir Rashid	Habib Bank v PACO	Gujranwala	1992-93
8 (8ct)	A.T.W.Grout	Queensland v W Australia	Brisbane	1959-60
8 (8ct)	D.E.East	Essex v Somerset	Taunton	1985
8 (8ct)	S.A.Marsh	Kent v Middlesex	Lord's	1991
8 (6ct, 2st)	T.J.Zoehrer	Australians v Surrey	The Oval	1993

MOST DISMISSALS IN A MATCH

12 (8ct, 4st)	E.Pooley	Surrey v Sussex	The Oval	1868
12 (9ct, 3st)	D.Tallon	Queensland v NSW	Sydney	1938-39
12 (9ct, 3st)	H.B.Taber	NSW v South Australia	Adelaide	1968-69

MOST CATCHES IN A MATCH

11	A.Long	Surrey v Sussex	Hove	1964
11	R.W.Marsh	W Australia v Victoria	Perth	1975-76
11	D.L.Bairstow	Yorkshire v Derbyshire	Scarborough	1982
11	W.K.Hegg	Lancashire v Derbyshire	Chesterfield	1989
11	A.J.Stewart	Surrey v Leicestershire	Leicester	1989
11	T.J.Nielsen	S Australia v W Australia	Perth	1990-91

MOST DISMISSALS IN A SEASON

128 (79ct, 49st)   L.E.G.Ames   1929

MOST DISMISSALS IN A CAREER

	Career	Dismissals	Ct	St
R.W.Taylor	1960-88	**1649**	1473	176
J.T.Murray	1952-75	**1527**	1270	257
H.Strudwick	1902-27	**1497**	1242	255
A.P.E.Knott	1964-85	**1344**	1211	133
F.H.Huish	1895-1914	**1310**	933	377
B.Taylor	1949-73	**1294**	1083	211
D.Hunter	1889-1909	**1253**	906	347
H.R.Butt	1890-1912	**1228**	953	275
J.H.Board	1891-1914/15	**1207**	852	355
H.Elliott	1920-47	**1206**	904	302
J.M.Parks	1949-76	**1181**	1088	93
R.Booth	1951-70	**1126**	948	178
L.E.G.Ames	1926-51	**1121**	703	418
D.L.Bairstow	1970-90	**1099**	961	138
G.Duckworth	1923-47	**1096**	753	343
H.W.Stephenson	1948-64	**1082**	748	334
J.G.Binks	1955-75	**1071**	895	176
T.G.Evans	1939-69	**1066**	816	250
A.Long	1960-80	**1046**	922	124
G.O.Dawkes	1937-61	**1043**	895	148
R.W.Tolchard	1965-83	**1037**	912	125
W.L.Cornford	1921-47	**1017**	675	342

FIELDING RECORDS

MOST CATCHES IN AN INNINGS

7	M.J.Stewart	Surrey v Northamptonshire	Northampton	1957
7	A.S.Brown	Gloucestershire v Nottinghamshire	Nottingham	1966

MOST CATCHES IN A MATCH

10	W.R.Hammond	Gloucestershire v Surrey	Cheltenham	1928

MOST CATCHES IN A SEASON

78	W.R.Hammond	1928	77	M.J.Stewart	1957

MOST CATCHES IN A CAREER

1018	F.E.Woolley	1906-38	784	J.G.Langridge	1928-55
887	W.G.Grace	1865-1908	764	W.Rhodes	1898-1930
830	G.A.R.Lock	1946-70/71	758	C.A.Milton	1948-74
819	W.R.Hammond	1920-51	754	E.H.Hendren	1907-38
813	D.B.Close	1949-86			

TEST CRICKET RECORDS

To the end of the 1993 season
(Including Indian and South African tours of Sri Lanka, July-September 1993)

TEAM RECORDS
HIGHEST INNINGS TOTALS

903-7d	England v Australia	The Oval	1938
849	England v West Indies	Kingston	1929-30
790-3d	West Indies v Pakistan	Kingston	1957-58
758-8d	Australia v West Indies	Kingston	1954-55
729-6d	Australia v England	Lord's	1930
708	Pakistan v England	The Oval	1987
701	Australia v England	The Oval	1934
699-5	Pakistan v India	Lahore	1989-90
695	Australia v England	The Oval	1930
687-8d	West Indies v England	The Oval	1976
681-8d	West Indies v England	Port-of-Spain	1953-54
676-7	India v Sri Lanka	Kanpur	1986-87
674-6	Pakistan v India	Faisalabad	1984-85
674	Australia v India	Adelaide	1947-48
671-4	New Zealand v Sri Lanka	Wellington	1990-91
668	Australia v West Indies	Bridgetown	1954-55
659-8d	Australia v England	Sydney	1946-47
658-8d	England v Australia	Nottingham	1938
657-8d	Pakistan v West Indies	Bridgetown	1957-58
656-8d	Australia v England	Manchester	1964
654-5	England v South Africa	Durban	1938-39
653-4d	England v India	Lord's	1990
653-4d	Australia v England	Leeds	1993
652-7d	England v India	Madras	1984-85
652-8d	West Indies v England	Lord's	1973
652	Pakistan v India	Faisalabad	1982-83
.650-6d	Australia v West Indies	Bridgetown	1964-65

The highest innings for other countries are:

622-9d	South Africa v Australia	Durban	1969-70
547-8d	Sri Lanka v Australia	Colombo (SSC)	1992-93
456	Zimbabwe v India	Harare	1992-93

LOWEST INNINGS TOTALS

26	New Zealand v England	Auckland	1954-55
30	South Africa v England	Port Elizabeth	1895-96
30	South Africa v England	Birmingham	1924
35	South Africa v England	Cape Town	1898-99
36	Australia v England	Birmingham	1902
36	South Africa v Australia	Melbourne	1931-32
42	Australia v England	Sydney	1887-88
42	New Zealand v Australia	Wellington	1945-46
42	India v England	Lord's	1974
43	South Africa v England	Cape Town	1888-89
44	Australia v England	The Oval	1896
45	England v Australia	Sydney	1886-87
45	South Africa v Australia	Melbourne	1931-32
47	South Africa v England	Cape Town	1888-89
47	New Zealand v England	Lord's	1958

The lowest innings for other countries are:

53	West Indies v Pakistan	Faisalabad	1986-87
62	Pakistan v Australia	Perth	1981-82
82	Sri Lanka v India	Chandigarh	1990-91
137	Zimbabwe v New Zealand	Harare	1992-93

BATTING RECORDS

HIGHEST INDIVIDUAL INNINGS

365*	G.St A.Sobers	WI v P	Kingston	1957-58
364	L.Hutton	E v A	The Oval	1938
337	Hanif Mohammad	P v WI	Bridgetown	1957-58
336*	W.R.Hammond	E v NZ	Auckland	1932-33
334	D.G.Bradman	A v E	Leeds	1930
333	G.A.Gooch	E v I	Lord's	1990
325	A.Sandham	E v WI	Kingston	1929-30
311	R.B.Simpson	A v E	Manchester	1964
310*	J.H.Edrich	E v NZ	Leeds	1965
307	R.M.Cowper	A v E	Melbourne	1965-66
304	D.G.Bradman	A v E	Leeds	1934
302	L.G.Rowe	WI v E	Bridgetown	1973-74
299*	D.G.Bradman	A v SA	Adelaide	1931-32
299	M.D.Crowe	NZ v SL	Wellington	1990-91
291	I.V.A.Richards	WI v E	The Oval	1976
287	R.E.Foster	E v A	Sydney	1903-04
285*	P.B.H.May	E v WI	Birmingham	1957
280*	Javed Miandad	P v I	Hyderabad	1982-83
278	D.C.S.Compton	E v P	Nottingham	1954
277	B.C.Lara	WI v A	Sydney	1992-93
274	R.G.Pollock	SA v A	Durban	1969-70
274	Zaheer Abbas	P v E	Birmingham	1971
271	Javed Miandad	P v NZ	Auckland	1988-89

270*	G.A.Headley	WI v E	Kingston	1934-35
270	D.G.Bradman	A v E	Melbourne	1936-37
268	G.N.Yallop	A v P	Melbourne	1983-84
267	P.A.De Silva	SL v NZ	Wellington	1990-91
266	W.H.Ponsford	A v E	The Oval	1934
262*	D.L.Amiss	E v WI	Kingston	1973-74
261	F.M.M.Worrell	WI v E	Nottingham	1950
260	C.C.Hunte	WI v P	Kingston	1957-58
260	Javed Miandad	P v E	The Oval	1987
259	G.M.Turner	NZ v WI	Georgetown	1971-72
258	T.W.Graveney	E v WI	Nottingham	1957
258	S.M.Nurse	WI v NZ	Christchurch	1968-69
256	R.B.Kanhai	WI v I	Calcutta	1958-59
256	K.F.Barrington	E v A	Manchester	1964
255*	D.J.McGlew	SA v NZ	Wellington	1952-53
254	D.G.Bradman	A v E	Lord's	1930
251	W.R.Hammond	E v A	Sydney	1928-29
250	K.D.Walters	A v NZ	Christchurch	1976-77
250	S.F.A.F.Bacchus	WI v I	Kanpur	1978-79

The highest individual innings for other countries are:

236*	S.M.Gavaskar	I v WI	Madras	1983-84
121	D.L.Houghton	Z v I	Harare	1992-93

MOST RUNS IN A SERIES

Runs			Series	M	I	NO	HS	Avge	100	50
974	D.G.Bradman	A v E	1930	5	7	–	334	139.14	4	–
905	W.R.Hammond	E v A	1928-29	5	9	1	251	113.12	4	–
839	M.A.Taylor	A v E	1989	6	11	1	219	83.90	2	5
834	R.N.Harvey	A v SA	1952-53	5	9	–	205	92.66	4	3
829	I.V.A.Richards	WI v E	1976	4	7	–	291	118.42	3	2
827	C.L.Walcott	WI v A	1954-55	5	10	–	155	82.70	5	2
824	G.St A.Sobers	WI v P	1957-58	5	8	2	365*	137.33	3	3
810	D.G.Bradman	A v E	1936-37	5	9	–	270	90.00	3	1
806	D.G.Bradman	A v SA	1931-32	5	5	1	299*	201.50	4	–
779	E.de C.Weekes	WI v I	1948-49	5	7	–	194	111.28	4	2
774	S.M.Gavaskar	I v WI	1970-71	4	8	3	220	154.80	4	3
761	Mudassar Nazar	P v I	1982-83	6	8	2	231	126.83	4	1
758	D.G.Bradman	A v E	1934	5	8	–	304	94.75	2	1
753	D.C.S.Compton	E v SA	1947	5	8	–	208	94.12	4	2
752	G.A.Gooch	E v I	1990	3	6	–	333	125.33	3	2

HIGHEST PARTNERSHIP FOR EACH WICKET

1st	413	V.Mankad/Pankaj Roy	I v NZ	Madras	1955-56
2nd	451	W.H.Ponsford/D.G.Bradman	A v E	The Oval	1934
3rd	467	A.H.Jones/M.D.Crowe	NZ v SL	Wellington	1990-91
4th	411	P.B.H.May/M.C.Cowdrey	E v WI	Birmingham	1957
5th	405	S.G.Barnes/D.G.Bradman	A v E	Sydney	1946-47
6th	346	J.H.W.Fingleton/D.G.Bradman	A v E	Melbourne	1936-37
7th	347	D.St E.Atkinson/C.C.Depeiza	WI v A	Bridgetown	1954-55
8th	246	L.E.G.Ames/G.O.B.Allen	E v NZ	Lord's	1931
9th	190	Asif Iqbal/Intikhab Alam	P v E	The Oval	1967
10th	151	B.F.Hastings/R.O.Collinge	NZ v P	Auckland	1972-73

WICKET PARTNERSHIPS OF OVER 300

467	3rd	A.H.Jones/M.D.Crowe	NZ v SL	Wellington	1990-91
451	2nd	W.H.Ponsford/D.G.Bradman	A v E	The Oval	1934
451	3rd	Mudassar Nazar/Javed Miandad	P v I	Hyderabad	1982-83
446	2nd	C.C.Hunte/G.St A.Sobers	WI v P	Kingston	1957-58
413	1st	V.Mankad/Pankaj Roy	I v NZ	Madras	1955-56
411	4th	P.B.H.May/M.C.Cowdrey	E v WI	Birmingham	1957
405	5th	S.G.Barnes/D.G.Bradman	A v E	Sydney	1946-47
399	4th	G.St A.Sobers/F.M.M.Worrell	WI v E	Bridgetown	1959-60
397	3rd	Qasim Omar/Javed Miandad	P v SL	Faisalabad	1985-86
388	4th	W.H.Ponsford/D.G.Bradman	A v E	Leeds	1934
387	1st	G.M.Turner/T.W.Jarvis	NZ v WI	Georgetown	1971-72
382	2nd	L.Hutton/M.Leyland	E v A	The Oval	1938
382	1st	W.M.Lawry/R.B.Simpson	A v WI	Bridgetown	1964-65
370	3rd	W.J.Edrich/D.C.S.Compton	E v SA	Lord's	1947
369	2nd	J.H.Edrich/K.F.Barrington	E v NZ	Leeds	1965
359	1st	L.Hutton/C.Washbrook	E v SA	Jo'burg	1948-49
351	2nd	G.A.Gooch/D.I.Gower	E v A	The Oval	1985
350	4th	Mushtaq Mohammad/Asif Iqbal	P v NZ	Dunedin	1972-73
347	7th	D.St E.Atkinson/C.C.Depeiza	WI v A	Bridgetown	1954-55
346	6th	J.H.W.Fingleton/D.G.Bradman	A v E	Melbourne	1936-37
344*	2nd	S.M.Gavaskar/D.B.Vengsarkar	I v WI	Calcutta	1978-79
341	3rd	E.J.Barlow/R.G.Pollock	SA v A	Adelaide	1963-64
338	3rd	E.de C.Weekes/F.M.M.Worrell	WI v E	Port-of-Spain	1953-54
336	4th	W.M.Lawry/K.D.Walters	A v WI	Sydney	1968-69
332	5th	A.R.Border/S.R.Waugh	A v E	Leeds	1993
331	2nd	R.T.Robinson/D.I.Gower	E v A	Birmingham	1985
329	1st	G.R.Marsh/M.A.Taylor	A v E	Nottingham	1989
323	1st	J.B.Hobbs/W.Rhodes	E v A	Melbourne	1911-12
322	4th	Javed Miandad/Salim Malik	P v E	Birmingham	1992
319	3rd	A.Melville/A.D.Nourse	SA v E	Nottingham	1947
316†	3rd	G.R.Viswanath/Yashpal Sharma	I v E	Madras	1981-82
308	7th	Waqar Hassan/Imtiaz Ahmed	P v NZ	Lahore	1955-56
308	4th	R.B.Richardson/I.V.A.Richards	WI v A	St John's	1983-84
308	3rd	G.A.Gooch/A.J.Lamb	E v I	Lord's	1990
303	3rd	I.V.A.Richards/A.I.Kallicharran	WI v E	Nottingham	1976
301	2nd	A.R.Morris/D.G.Bradman	A v E	Leeds	1948

†415 runs were added for this wicket in two separate partnerships.

4000 RUNS IN TESTS

Runs			M	I	NO	HS	Avge	100	50
10695	A.R.Border	A	147	252	43	205	51.17	26	61
10122	S.M.Gavaskar	I	125	214	16	236*	51.12	34	45
8689	Javed Miandad	P	121	184	21	280*	53.30	23	42
8540	I.V.A.Richards	WI	121	182	12	291	50.23	24	45
8293	G.A.Gooch	E	107	195	6	333	43.87	19	45
8231	D.I.Gower	E	117	204	18	215	44.25	18	39
8114	G.Boycott	E	108	193	23	246*	47.72	22	42
8032	G.St A.Sobers	WI	93	160	21	365*	57.78	26	30
7624	M.C.Cowdrey	E	114	188	15	182	44.06	22	38
7558	C.G.Greenidge	WI	108	185	16	226	44.72	19	34
7515	C.H.Lloyd	WI	110	175	14	242*	46.67	19	39
7250	D.L.Haynes	WI	111	194	24	184	42.64	18	38
7249	W.R.Hammond	E	85	140	16	336*	58.45	22	24
7110	G.S.Chappell	A	87	151	19	247*	53.86	24	31

Runs			M	I	NO	HS	Avge	100	50
6996	D.G.Bradman	A	52	80	10	334	99.94	29	13
6971	L.Hutton	E	79	138	15	364	56.67	19	33
6868	D.B.Vengsarkar	I	116	185	22	166	42.13	17	35
6806	K.F.Barrington	E	82	131	15	256	58.67	20	35
6227	R.B.Kanhai	WI	79	137	6	256	47.53	15	28
6149	R.N.Harvey	A	79	137	10	205	48.41	21	24
6080	G.R.Viswanath	I	91	155	10	222	41.93	14	35
5869	D.C.Boon	A	80	145	16	200	45.49	17	25
5807	D.C.S.Compton	E	78	131	15	278	50.06	17	28
5410	J.B.Hobbs	E	61	102	7	211	56.94	15	28
5357	K.D.Walters	A	74	125	14	250	48.26	15	33
5345	I.M.Chappell	A	75	136	10	196	42.42	14	26
5334	J.G.Wright	NZ	82	148	7	185	37.82	12	23
5234	W.M.Lawry	A	67	123	12	210	47.15	13	27
5231	R.B.Richardson	WI	71	122	10	194	46.70	15	23
5200	I.T.Botham	E	102	161	6	208	33.54	14	22
5138	J.H.Edrich	E	77	127	9	310*	43.54	12	24
5131	Kapil Dev	I	127	180	14	163	30.90	8	26
5062	Zaheer Abbas	P	78	124	11	274	44.79	12	20
4882	T.W.Graveney	E	79	123	13	258	44.38	11	20
4869	R.B.Simpson	A	62	111	7	311	46.81	10	27
4777	M.D.Crowe	NZ	66	112	10	299	46.83	15	16
4737	I.R.Redpath	A	66	120	11	171	43.45	8	31
4656	A.J.Lamb	E	79	139	10	142	36.09	14	18
4555	H.Sutcliffe	E	54	84	9	194	60.73	16	23
4537	P.B.H.May	E	66	106	9	285*	46.77	13	22
4502	E.R.Dexter	E	62	102	8	205	47.89	9	27
4455	E.de C.Weekes	WI	48	81	5	207	58.61	15	19
4415	K.J.Hughes	A	70	124	6	213	37.41	9	22
4399	A.I.Kallicharran	WI	66	109	10	187	44.43	12	21
4389	A.P.E.Knott	E	95	149	15	135	32.75	5	30
4378	M.Amarnath	I	69	113	10	138	42.50	11	24
4334	R.C.Fredericks	WI	59	109	7	169	42.49	8	26
4227	M.W.Gatting	E	74	129	14	207	36.75	9	21
4114	Mudassar Nazar	P	76	116	8	231	38.09	10	17

The highest aggregates for other countries are:

3471	B.Mitchell	SA	42	80	9	189*	48.88	8	21
2582	A.Ranatunga	SL	45	75	4	135*	36.36	4	17
341	A.Flower	Z	4	7	2	115	68.20	1	3

MOST HUNDREDS

							Opponents					
			Inns	E	A	SA	WI	NZ	I	P	SL	Z
34	S.M.Gavaskar	I	214	4	8	–	13	2	–	5	2	–
29	D.G.Bradman	A	80	19	–	4	2	–	4			
26	A.R.Border	A	252	8	–	–	3	4	4	6	1	–
26	G.St A.Sobers	WI	160	10	4	–	–	1	8	3	–	–
24	G.S.Chappell	A	151	9	–	–	5	3	1	6	0	–
24	I.V.A.Richards	WI	182	8	5	–	–	1	8	2	–	–
23	Javed Miandad	P	184	2	6	–	2	7	5	–	1	–
22	G.Boycott	E	193	–	7	1	5	2	4	3	–	–
22	M.C.Cowdrey	E	188	–	5	3	6	2	3	3	–	–
22	W.R.Hammond	E	140	–	9	6	1	4	2	–	–	–
21	R.N.Harvey	A	137	6	–	8	3	–	4	0	–	–
20	K.F.Barrington	E	131	–	5	2	3	3	3	4	–	–

Dashes indicate that the player did not appear against that team.

BOWLING RECORDS

MOST WICKETS IN AN INNINGS

10- 53	J.C.Laker	E v A	Manchester	1956
9- 28	G.A.Lohmann	E v SA	Johannesburg	1895-96
9- 37	J.C.Laker	E v A	Manchester	1956
9- 52	R.J.Hadlee	NZ v A	Brisbane	1985-86
9- 56	Abdul Qadir	P v E	Lahore	1987-88
9- 69	J.M.Patel	I v A	Kanpur	1959-60
9- 83	Kapil Dev	I v WI	Ahmedabad	1983-84
9- 86	Sarfraz Nawaz	P v A	Melbourne	1978-79
9- 95	J.M.Noreiga	WI v I	Port-of-Spain	1970-71
9-102	S.P.Gupte	I v WI	Kanpur	1958-59
9-103	S.F.Barnes	E v SA	Johannesburg	1913-14
9-113	H.J.Tayfield	SA v E	Johannesburg	1956-57
9-121	A.A.Mailey	A v E	Melbourne	1920-21

The best innings analyses for other countries are:

8- 83	J.R.Ratnayeke	SL v P	Sialkot	1985-86
5- 86	A.J.Traicos	Z v I	Harare	1992-93

MOST WICKETS IN A TEST

19- 90	J.C.Laker	E v A	Manchester	1956
17-159	S.F.Barnes	E v SA	Johannesburg	1913-14
16-136†	N.D.Hirwani	I v WI	Madras	1987-88
16-137†	R.A.L.Massie	A v E	Lord's	1972
15- 28	J.Briggs	E v SA	Cape Town	1888-89
15- 45	G.A.Lohmann	E v SA	Port Elizabeth	1895-96
15- 99	C.Blythe	E v SA	Leeds	1907
15-104	H.Verity	E v A	Lord's	1934
15-123	R.J.Hadlee	NZ v A	Brisbane	1985-86
15-124	W.Rhodes	E v A	Melbourne	1903-04

† *On debut.*

MOST WICKETS IN A SERIES

Wkts			Series	M	Balls	Runs	Avge	5 wI	10 wM
49	S.F.Barnes	E v SA	1913-14	4	1356	536	10.93	7	3
46	J.C.Laker	E v A	1956	5	1703	442	9.60	4	2
44	C.V.Grimmett	A v SA	1935-36	5	2077	642	14.59	5	3
42	T.M.Alderman	A v E	1981	6	1950	893	21.26	4	–
41	R.M.Hogg	A v E	1978-79	6	1740	527	12.85	5	2
41	T.M.Alderman	A v E	1989	6	1616	712	17.36	6	1
40	Imran Khan	P v I	1982-83	6	1339	558	13.95	4	2
39	A.V.Bedser	E v A	1953	5	1591	682	17.48	5	1
39	D.K.Lillee	A v E	1981	6	1870	870	22.30	2	1
38	M.W.Tate	E v A	1924-25	5	2528	881	23.18	5	1
37	W.J.Whitty	A v SA	1910-11	5	1395	632	17.08	2	–
37	H.J.Tayfield	SA v E	1956-57	5	2280	636	17.18	4	1
36	A.E.E.Vogler	SA v E	1909-10	5	1349	783	21.75	4	1
36	A.A.Mailey	A v E	1920-21	5	1465	946	26.27	4	2
35	G.A.Lohmann	E v SA	1895-96	3	520	203	5.80	4	2
35	B.S.Chandrasekhar	I v E	1972-73	5	1747	662	18.91	4	1
35	M.D.Marshall	WI v E	1988	5	1219	443	12.65	3	1

200 WICKETS IN TESTS

Wkts			M	Balls	Runs	Avge	5 wI	10 wM
431	R.J.Hadlee	NZ	86	21918	9611	22.29	36	9
425	Kapil Dev	I	127	27250	12619	29.69	23	2
383	I.T.Botham	E	102	21815	10878	28.40	27	4
376	M.D.Marshall	WI	81	17584	7876	20.94	22	4
362	Imran Khan	P	88	19458	8258	22.81	23	6
355	D.K.Lillee	A	70	18467	8493	23.92	23	7
325	R.G.D.Willis	E	90	17357	8190	25.20	16	–
309	L.R.Gibbs	WI	79	27115	8989	29.09	18	2
307	F.S.Trueman	E	67	15178	6625	21.57	17	3
297	D.L.Underwood	E	86	21862	7674	25.83	17	6
266	B.S.Bedi	I	67	21364	7637	28.71	14	1
259	J.Garner	WI	58	13169	5433	20.97	7	–
252	J.B.Statham	E	70	16056	6261	24.84	9	1
249	M.A.Holding	WI	60	12680	5898	23.68	13	2
248	R.Benaud	A	63	19108	6704	27.03	16	1
246	G.D.McKenzie	A	60	17681	7328	29.78	16	3
242	B.S.Chandrasekhar	I	58	15963	7199	29.74	16	2
236	A.V.Bedser	E	51	15918	5876	24.89	15	5
236	Abdul Qadir	P	67	17126	7742	32.80	15	5
235	G.St A.Sobers	WI	93	21599	7999	34.03	6	–
228	R.R.Lindwall	A	61	13650	5251	23.03	12	–
216	C.V.Grimmett	A	37	14513	5231	24.21	21	7
208	M.G.Hughes	A	51	11865	5780	27.78	7	1
202	A.M.E.Roberts	WI	47	11136	5174	25.61	11	2
202	J.A.Snow	E	49	12021	5387	26.66	8	1
202	C.A.Walsh	WI	52	11652	5118	25.33	5	1
200	J.R.Thomson	A	51	10535	5601	28.00	8	–

The highest aggregates for other countries are:

170	H.J.Tayfield	SA	37	13568	4405	25.91	14	2
73	R.J.Ratnayake	SL	23	4961	2563	35.10	5	–
14	A.J.Traicos	Z	4	1141	562	40.14	1	–

HAT-TRICKS

F.R.Spofforth	Australia v England	Melbourne	1878-79
W.Bates	England v Australia	Melbourne	1882-83
J.Briggs	England v Australia	Sydney	1891-92
G.A.Lohmann	England v South Africa	Port Elizabeth	1895-96
J.T.Hearne	England v Australia	Leeds	1899
H.Trumble	Australia v England	Melbourne	1901-02
H.Trumble	Australia v England	Melbourne	1903-04
T.J.Matthews (2)*	Australia v South Africa	Manchester	1912
M.J.C.Allom†	England v New Zealand	Christchurch	1929-30
T.W.J.Goddard	England v South Africa	Johannesburg	1938-39
P.J.Loader	England v West Indies	Leeds	1957
L.F.Kline	Australia v South Africa	Cape Town	1957-58
W.W.Hall	West Indies v Pakistan	Lahore	1958-59
G.M.Griffin	South Africa v England	Lord's	1960
L.R.Gibbs	West Indies v Australia	Adelaide	1960-61
P.J.Petherick	New Zealand v Pakistan	Lahore	1976-77
C.A.Walsh‡	West Indies v Australia	Brisbane	1988-89
M.G.Hughes‡	Australia v West Indies	Perth	1988-89

Hat-trick in each innings. † Four wickets in five balls. ‡ Involving both innings.

WICKET-KEEPING RECORDS

MOST DISMISSALS IN AN INNINGS

7	Wasim Bari	Pakistan v New Zealand	Auckland	1978-79
7	R.W.Taylor	England v India	Bombay	1979-80
7	I.D.S.Smith	New Zealand v Sri Lanka	Hamilton	1990-91
6	A.T.W.Grout	Australia v South Africa	Johannesburg	1957-58
6	D.T.Lindsay	South Africa v Australia	Johannesburg	1966-67
6	J.T.Murray	England v India	Lord's	1967
6†	S.M.H.Kirmani	India v New Zealand	Christchurch	1975-76
6	R.W.Marsh	Australia v England	Brisbane	1982-83
6	S.A.R.Silva	Sri Lanka v India	Colombo (SSC)	1985-86
6	R.C.Russell	England v Australia	Melbourne	1990-91

†Including one stumping.

MOST STUMPINGS IN AN INNINGS

5	K.S.More	India v West Indies	Madras	1987-88

MOST DISMISSALS IN A TEST

10	R.W.Taylor	England v India	Bombay	1979-80
9†	G.R.A.Langley	Australia v England	Lord's	1956
9	D.A.Murray	West Indies v Australia	Melbourne	1981-82
9	R.W.Marsh	Australia v England	Brisbane	1982-83
9	S.A.R.Silva	Sri Lanka v India	Colombo (SSC)	1985-86
9†	S.A.R.Silva	Sri Lanka v India	Colombo (PSS)	1985-86
9	D.J.Richardson	South Africa v India	Port Elizabeth	1992-93

† Including one stumping.

MOST DISMISSALS IN A SERIES

28	R.W.Marsh	Australia v England	1982-83
26 (inc 3st)	J.H.B.Waite	South Africa v New Zealand	1961-62
26	R.W.Marsh	Australia v West Indies (6 Tests)	1975-76
26 (inc 5st)	I.A.Healy	Australia v England (6 Tests)	1993
24 (inc 2st)	D.L.Murray	West Indies v England	1963
24	D.T.Lindsay	South Africa v Australia	1966-67
24 (inc 3st)	A.P.E.Knott	England v Australia (6 Tests)	1970-71
24	I.A.Healy	Australia v England	1990-91

100 DISMISSALS IN TESTS

Total			Tests	Ct	St
355	R.W.Marsh	Australia	96	343	12
272†	P.J.L.Dujon	West Indies	81	267	5
269	A.P.E.Knott	England	95	250	19
228	Wasim Bari	Pakistan	81	201	27
219	T.G.Evans	England	91	173	46
198	S.M.H.Kirmani	India	88	160	38
189	D.L.Murray	West Indies	62	181	8
187	A.T.W.Grout	Australia	51	163	24
179	I.A.Healy	Australia	53	167	12
176	I.D.S.Smith	New Zealand	63	168	8
174	R.W.Taylor	England	57	167	7
141	J.H.B.Waite	South Africa	50	124	17
130	K.S.More	India	49	110	20
130	W.A.S.Oldfield	Australia	54	78	52
114†	J.M.Parks	England	46	103	11
104	Salim Yousuf	Pakistan	32	91	13

The most dismissals for other countries are Sri Lanka 34 (S.A.R.Silva 33ct, 1st in 9 Tests) and Zimbabwe 9 (A.Flower 7ct, 2st in 4 Tests).

† Including two catches taken in the field.

FIELDING RECORDS

MOST CATCHES IN AN INNINGS

5	V.Y.Richardson	Australia v South Africa	Durban	1935-36
5	Yajurvindra Singh	India v England	Bangalore	1976-77
5	M.Azharuddin	India v Pakistan	Karachi	1989-90
5	K.Srikkanth	India v Australia	Perth	1991-92

MOST CATCHES IN A TEST

7	G.S.Chappell	Australia v England	Perth	1974-75
7	Yajurvindra Singh	India v England	Bangalore	1976-77
7	H.P.Tillekeratne	Sri Lanka v New Zealand	Colombo (SSC)	1992-93

MOST CATCHES IN A SERIES

15	J.M.Gregory	Australia v England	1920-21

100 CATCHES IN TESTS

Total			Tests
148	A.R.Border	Australia	147
122	G.S.Chappell	Australia	87
122	I.V.A.Richards	West Indies	121
120	I.T.Botham	England	102
120	M.C.Cowdrey	England	114
110	R.B.Simpson	Australia	62
110	W.R.Hammond	England	85
109	G.St A.Sobers	West Indies	93
108	S.M.Gavaskar	India	125
105	I.M.Chappell	Australia	75

MOST TEST APPEARANCES FOR EACH COUNTRY

			E	A	SA	WI	NZ	I	P	SL	Z
England	117	D.I.Gower	–	42	–	19	13	24	17	2	–
Australia	147	A.R.Border	47	–	–	31	20	20	22	7	–
South Africa	50	J.H.B.Waite	21	14	–	–	15	–	–	–	–
West Indies	121	I.V.A.Richards	36	34	–	–	7	28	16	–	–
New Zealand	86	R.J.Hadlee	21	23	–	10	–	14	12	6	–
India	127	Kapil Dev	27	20	–	25	9	–	29	11	2
Pakistan	121	Javed Miandad	22	25	–	16	18	28	–	12	–
Sri Lanka	45	A.Ranatunga	4	7	3	–	9	11	11	–	–

Six players have appeared in each of Zimbabwe's four Test matches.

MOST CONSECUTIVE TEST APPEARANCES

144	A.R.Border	Australia	March 1979 to August 1993
106	S.M.Gavaskar	India	January 1975 to February 1987

MOST MATCHES BETWEEN APPEARANCES

104	Younis Ahmed	Pakistan	November 1969 to February 1987
103	D.Shackleton	England	November 1951 to June 1963

The longest interval between appearances is 22 years 222 days (March 1970 to October 1992) by A.J.Traicos of South Africa and Zimbabwe.

| 84 | A.R.Border | Australia | December 1984 to August 1993 |

| 55 | H.D.Bird | | July 1973 to July 1993 |

SUMMARY OF ALL TEST MATCHES

To the end of the 1993 season
(Including Indian and South African tours of Sri Lanka, July-September 1993)

	Opponents	Tests	Won by									Tied	Drawn
			E	A	SA	WI	NZ	I	P	SL	Z		
England	Australia	280	89	108	–	–	–	–	–	–	–	–	83
	South Africa	102	46	–	18	–	–	–	–	–	–	–	38
	West Indies	104	24	–	–	43	–	–	–	–	–	–	37
	New Zealand	72	33	–	–	–	4	–	–	–	–	–	35
	India	81	31	–	–	–	–	14	–	–	–	–	36
	Pakistan	52	14	–	–	–	–	–	7	–	–	–	31
	Sri Lanka	5	3	–	–	–	–	–	–	1	–	–	1
Australia	South Africa	53	–	29	11	–	–	–	–	–	–	–	13
	West Indies	77	–	30	–	26	–	–	–	–	–	1	20
	New Zealand	29	–	11	–	–	7	–	–	–	–	–	11
	India	50	–	24	–	–	–	8	–	–	–	1	17
	Pakistan	34	–	12	–	–	–	–	9	–	–	–	13
	Sri Lanka	7	–	4	–	–	–	–	–	0	–	–	3
South Africa	West Indies	1	–	–	0	1	–	–	–	–	–	–	–
	New Zealand	17	–	–	9	–	2	–	–	–	–	–	6
	India	4	–	–	1	–	–	0	–	–	–	–	3
	Sri Lanka	3	–	–	1	–	–	–	–	0	–	–	2
West Indies	New Zealand	24	–	–	–	8	4	–	–	–	–	–	12
	India	62	–	–	–	26	–	6	–	–	–	–	30
	Pakistan	31	–	–	–	12	–	–	7	–	–	–	12
New Zealand	India	31	–	–	–	–	6	12	–	–	–	–	13
	Pakistan	33	–	–	–	–	3	–	14	–	–	–	16
	Sri Lanka	11	–	–	–	–	4	–	–	1	–	–	6
	Zimbabwe	2	–	–	–	–	1	–	–	–	0	–	1
India	Pakistan	44	–	–	–	–	–	4	7	–	–	–	33
	Sri Lanka	11	–	–	–	–	–	4	–	1	–	–	6
	Zimbabwe	2	–	–	–	–	–	1	–	–	0	–	1
Pakistan	Sri Lanka	12	–	–	–	–	–	–	6	1	–	–	5
		1234	240	218	40	116	31	49	50	4	0	2	484

	Tests	Won	Lost	Drawn	Tied	Toss Won
England	696	240	195	261	–	345
Australia	530	218	150	160	2	268
South Africa	180	40	78	62	–	85
West Indies	299	116	71	111	1	154
New Zealand	219	31	88	100	–	109
India	285	49	96	139	1	142
Pakistan	206	50	46	110	–	104
Sri Lanka	49	4	22	23	–	26
Zimbabwe	4	0	2	2	–	1

LIMITED-OVERS INTERNATIONALS RESULTS SUMMARY

To the end of the 1993 season
(Including Indian and South African tours of Sri Lanka, July-September 1993)

	Opponents	Matches	E	A	I	NZ	P	SA	SL	WI	Z	B	C	EA	Tied	NR
England	Australia	55	25	28	–	–	–	–	–	–	–	–	–	–	1	1
	India	29	16	–	13	–	–	–	–	–	–	–	–	–	–	–
	New Zealand	40	20	–	–	17	–	–	–	–	–	–	–	–	–	3
	Pakistan	36	23	–	–	–	12	–	–	–	–	–	–	–	–	1
	South Africa	2	2	–	–	–	–	0	–	–	–	–	–	–	–	–
	Sri Lanka	11	8	–	–	–	–	–	3	–	–	–	–	–	–	–
	West Indies	43	18	–	–	–	–	–	–	23	–	–	–	–	–	2
	Zimbabwe	1	0	–	–	–	–	–	–	–	1	–	–	–	–	–
	Canada	1	1	–	–	–	–	–	–	–	–	–	0	–	–	–
	East Africa	1	1	–	–	–	–	–	–	–	–	–	–	0	–	–
Australia	India	40	–	24	13	–	–	–	–	–	–	–	–	–	–	3
	New Zealand	55	–	37	–	16	–	–	–	–	–	–	–	–	–	2
	Pakistan	38	–	18	–	–	17	–	–	–	–	–	–	–	1	2
	South Africa	1	–	0	–	–	–	1	–	–	–	–	–	–	–	–
	Sri Lanka	24	–	17	–	–	–	–	5	–	–	–	–	–	–	2
	West Indies	69	–	26	–	–	–	–	–	41	–	–	–	–	1	1
	Zimbabwe	5	–	4	–	–	–	–	–	–	1	–	–	–	–	–
	Bangladesh	1	–	1	–	–	–	–	–	–	–	0	–	–	–	–
	Canada	1	–	1	–	–	–	–	–	–	–	–	0	–	–	–
India	New Zealand	29	–	–	16	13	–	–	–	–	–	–	–	–	–	–
	Pakistan	38	–	–	12	–	24	–	–	–	–	–	–	–	–	2
	South Africa	11	–	–	4	–	–	7	–	–	–	–	–	–	–	–
	Sri Lanka	29	–	–	18	–	–	–	9	–	–	–	–	–	–	2
	West Indies	40	–	–	10	–	–	–	–	29	–	–	–	–	1	–
	Zimbabwe	9	–	–	9	–	–	–	–	–	0	–	–	–	–	–
	Bangladesh	2	–	–	2	–	–	–	–	–	–	0	–	–	–	–
	East Africa	1	–	–	1	–	–	–	–	–	–	–	–	0	–	–
N Zealand	Pakistan	28	–	–	–	13	14	–	–	–	–	–	–	–	–	1
	South Africa	1	–	–	–	1	–	0	–	–	–	–	–	–	–	–
	Sri Lanka	26	–	–	–	19	–	–	6	–	–	–	–	–	–	1
	West Indies	14	–	–	–	2	–	–	–	11	–	–	–	–	–	1
	Zimbabwe	5	–	–	–	5	–	–	–	–	0	–	–	–	–	–
	Bangladesh	1	–	–	–	1	–	–	–	–	–	0	–	–	–	–
	East Africa	1	–	–	–	1	–	–	–	–	–	–	–	0	–	–
Pakistan	South Africa	4	–	–	–	–	3	1	–	–	–	–	–	–	–	–
	Sri Lanka	38	–	–	–	–	30	–	7	–	–	–	–	–	–	1
	West Indies	70	–	–	–	–	20	–	–	48	–	–	–	–	2	–
	Zimbabwe	3	–	–	–	–	3	–	–	–	0	–	–	–	–	–
	Bangladesh	2	–	–	–	–	2	–	–	–	–	0	–	–	–	–
	Canada	1	–	–	–	–	1	–	–	–	–	–	0	–	–	–
S Africa	Sri Lanka	4	–	–	–	–	–	1	2	–	–	–	–	–	–	1
	West Indies	7	–	–	–	–	–	3	–	4	–	–	–	–	–	–
	Zimbabwe	1	–	–	–	–	–	1	–	–	0	–	–	–	–	–
Sri Lanka	West Indies	12	–	–	–	–	–	–	1	11	–	–	–	–	–	–
	Zimbabwe	2	–	–	–	–	–	–	2	–	0	–	–	–	–	–
	Bangladesh	3	–	–	–	–	–	–	3	–	–	0	–	–	–	–
W Indies	Zimbabwe	3	–	–	–	–	–	–	–	3	0	–	–	–	–	–
		838	114	156	98	88	126	14	38	170	2	0	0	0	6	26

LEAGUE TABLE OF L-O INTERNATIONALS

	Matches	Won	Lost	Tied	No Result	% Won (exc NR)
West Indies	258	170	80	4	4	66.92
Australia	289	156	119	3	11	56.11
England	219	114	97	1	7	53.77
Pakistan	258	126	122	3	7	50.99
South Africa	31	14	16	–	1	46.66
New Zealand	200	88	104	–	8	45.83
India	228	98	122	1	7	44.34
Sri Lanka	149	38	104	–	7	26.76
Zimbabwe	29	2	27	–	–	6.89
Bangladesh	9	–	9	–	–	–
Canada	3	–	3	–	–	–
East Africa	3	–	3	–	–	–

RECORDS

To the end of the 1993 season
(Including Indian and South African tours of Sri Lanka, July-September 1993)

TEAM RECORDS

HIGHEST TOTALS BY EACH COUNTRY

363-7	(55 overs)	ENGLAND v Pakistan	Nottingham	1992
360-4	(50 overs)	WEST INDIES v Sri Lanka	Karachi	1987-88
338-4	(50 overs)	NEW ZEALAND v Bangladesh	Sharjah	1989-90
338-5	(60 overs)	PAKISTAN v Sri Lanka	Swansea	1983
332-3	(50 overs)	AUSTRALIA v Sri Lanka	Sharjah	1989-90
313-7	(49.2 overs)	SRI LANKA v Zimbabwe	New Plymouth	1991-92
312-4	(50 overs)	ZIMBABWE v Sri Lanka	New Plymouth	1991-92
299-4	(40 overs)	INDIA v Sri Lanka	Bombay	1986-87
288-2	(46.4 overs)	SOUTH AFRICA v India	Delhi	1991-92

HIGHEST TOTAL BATTING SECOND

WINNING:	313-7	(49.2 overs)	Sri Lanka v Zimbabwe	New Plymouth	1991-92
LOSING:	289-7	(40 overs)	Sri Lanka v India	Bombay	1986-87

HIGHEST MATCH AGGREGATE

626-14	(120 overs)	Pakistan v Sri Lanka	Swansea	1983

LOWEST TOTALS BY EACH COUNTRY†

43	(19.5 overs)	PAKISTAN v West Indies	Cape Town	1992-93
45	(40.3 overs)	CANADA v England	Manchester	1979
55	(28.3 overs)	SRI LANKA v West Indies	Sharjah	1986-87
63	(25.5 overs)	INDIA v Australia	Sydney	1980-81
64	(35.5 overs)	NEW ZEALAND v Pakistan	Sharjah	1985-86
70	(25.2 overs)	AUSTRALIA v England	Birmingham	1977
70	(26.3 overs)	AUSTRALIA v New Zealand	Adelaide	1985-86
87	(29.3 overs)	WEST INDIES v Australia	Sydney	1992-93
93	(36.2 overs)	ENGLAND v Australia	Leeds	1975
134	(46.1 overs)	ZIMBABWE v England	Albury	1991-92
152	(43.4 overs)	SOUTH AFRICA v West Indies	Port-of-Spain	1991-92

†Excluding instances when the number of overs was reduced after play began.

LOWEST MATCH AGGREGATE

91-12	(54.2 overs)	England v Canada	Manchester	1979

LARGEST MARGINS OF VICTORY

232 runs	Australia beat Sri Lanka	Adelaide	1984-85
206 runs	New Zealand beat Australia	Adelaide	1985-86
202 runs	England beat India	Lord's	1975
10 wickets	Nine instances		

TIED MATCHES

Australia	222-9	West Indies	222-5	Melbourne	1983-84
England	226-5	Australia	226-8	Nottingham	1989
West Indies	186-5	Pakistan	186-9	Lahore	1991-92
India	126	West Indies	126	Perth	1991-92
Australia	228-7	Pakistan	228-9	Hobart	1992-93
Pakistan	244-6	West Indies	244-5	Georgetown	1992-93

BATTING RECORDS

HIGHEST INDIVIDUAL SCORE FOR EACH COUNTRY

189*	I.V.A.Richards	WEST INDIES v England	Manchester	1984
175*	Kapil Dev	INDIA v Zimbabwe	Tunbridge Wells	1983
171*	G.M.Turner	NEW ZEALAND v East Africa	Birmingham	1975
167*	R.A.Smith	ENGLAND v Australia	Birmingham	1993
145	D.M.Jones	AUSTRALIA v England	Brisbane	1990-91
142	D.L.Houghton	ZIMBABWE v New Zealand	Hyderabad	1987-88
126*	Shoaib Mohammad	PAKISTAN v New Zealand	Wellington	1988-89
121	R.L.Dias	SRI LANKA v India	Bangalore	1982-83
108	A.C.Hudson	SOUTH AFRICA v India	Bloemfontein	1992-93

HIGHEST PARTNERSHIP FOR EACH WICKET

1st	212	G.R.Marsh/D.C.Boon	A v I	Jaipur	1986-87
2nd	221	C.G.Greenidge/I.V.A.Richards	WI v I	Jamshedpur	1983-84
3rd	224*	D.M.Jones/A.R.Border	A v SL	Adelaide	1984-85
4th	173	D.M.Jones/S.R.Waugh	A v P	Perth	1986-87
5th	152	I.V.A.Richards/C.H.Lloyd	WI v SL	Brisbane	1984-85
6th	154	R.B.Richardson/P.J.L.Dujon	WI v P	Sharjah	1991-92
7th	115	P.J.L.Dujon/M.D.Marshall	WI v P	Gujranwala	1986-87
8th	117	D.L.Houghton/I.P.Butchart	Z v NZ	Hyderabad	1987-88
9th	126*	Kapil Dev/S.M.H.Kirmani	I v Z	Tunbridge Wells	1983
10th	106*	I.V.A.Richards/M.A.Holding	WI v E	Manchester	1984

4000 RUNS

		M	I	NO	HS	Runs	Avge	100	50
D.L.Haynes	WI	225	224	28	152*	8194	41.80	16	53
Javed Miandad	P	222	211	40	119*	7233	42.29	8	49
I.V.A.Richards	WI	187	167	24	189*	6721	47.00	11	45
A.R.Border	A	255	237	36	127*	6171	30.70	3	38
D.M.Jones	A	150	147	25	145	5599	45.89	7	42
R.B.Richardson	WI	185	178	23	122	5306	34.23	5	39
C.G.Greenidge	WI	128	127	13	133*	5134	45.03	11	31
Ramiz Raja	P	159	158	11	119*	4915	33.43	8	29
D.C.Boon	A	142	138	10	122	4524	35.34	5	26
M.D.Crowe	NZ	133	132	18	105*	4412	38.70	3	32
G.R.Marsh	A	117	115	6	126*	4357	39.97	9	22
Salim Malik	P	170	158	19	102	4335	31.18	5	24
G.A.Gooch	E	120	117	6	142	4206	37.89	8	23
M.Azharuddin	I	157	144	27	108*	4114	35.16	3	22
K.Srikkanth	I	146	145	4	123	4092	29.02	4	27
A.J.Lamb	E	122	118	16	118	4010	39.31	4	26

The leading aggregates for other countries are:

		M	I	NO	HS	Runs	Avge	100	50
A.Ranatunga	SL	124	117	21	88*	**3201**	33.34	–	21
K.C.Wessels	SA	31	31	2	90	**1134**	39.10	–	9
D.L.Houghton	Z	29	28	–	142	**835**	29.82	1	6

BOWLING RECORDS
BEST ANALYSIS FOR EACH COUNTRY

7-37	Aqib Javed	PAKISTAN v India	Sharjah	1991-92
7-51	W.W.Davis	WEST INDIES v Australia	Leeds	1983
6-14	G.J.Gilmour	AUSTRALIA v England	Leeds	1975
6-29	S.T.Jayasuriya	SRI LANKA v England	Moratuwa	1992-93
5-15	R.J.Shastri	INDIA v Australia	Perth	1991-92
5-20	V.J.Marks	ENGLAND v New Zealand	Wellington	1983-84
5-23	R.O.Collinge	NEW ZEALAND v India	Christchurch	1975-76
5-29	A.A.Donald	SOUTH AFRICA v India	Calcutta	1991-92
4-21	E.A.Brandes	ZIMBABWE v England	Albury	1991-92

HAT-TRICKS

Jalaluddin	Pakistan v Australia	Hyderabad	1982-83
B.A.Reid	Australia v New Zealand	Sydney	1985-86
C.Sharma	India v New Zealand	Nagpur	1987-88
Wasim Akram	Pakistan v West Indies	Sharjah	1989-90
Wasim Akram	Pakistan v Australia	Sharjah	1989-90
Kapil Dev	India v Sri Lanka	Calcutta	1990-91
Aqib Javed	Pakistan v India	Sharjah	1991-92

100 WICKETS

		M	Balls	Runs	Wkts	Avge	Best	4w
Kapil Dev	I	208	10512	6511	243	26.79	5-43	4
Wasim Akram	P	153	7837	4995	215	23.23	5-16	12
Imran Khan	P	175	7461	4845	182	26.62	6-14	4
R.J.Hadlee	NZ	115	6182	3407	158	21.56	5-25	6
M.D.Marshall	WI	136	7175	4233	157	26.96	4-18	6
C.J.McDermott	A	104	5647	3862	155	24.91	5-44	5
J.Garner	WI	98	5330	2752	146	18.84	5-31	5
I.T.Botham	E	116	6271	4139	145	28.54	4-31	3
M.A.Holding	WI	102	5473	3034	142	21.36	5-26	6
S.R.Waugh	A	147	5985	4449	141	31.55	4-33	2
E.J.Chatfield	NZ	114	6065	3621	140	25.86	5-34	4
C.E.L.Ambrose	WI	91	4956	2853	139	20.52	5-17	8
Abdul Qadir	P	102	4996	3364	131	25.67	5-44	6
R.J.Shastri	I	150	6613	4650	129	36.04	5-15	3
Waqar Younis	P	74	3637	2526	127	19.88	6-26	11
C.A.Walsh	WI	111	5991	3847	124	31.02	5- 1	6
M.Prabhakar	I	94	4630	3164	119	26.58	4-19	4
I.V.A.Richards	WI	187	5644	4228	118	35.83	6-41	3
M.C.Snedden	NZ	93	4519	3235	114	28.37	4-34	1
Mudassar Nazar	P	122	4855	3431	111	30.90	5-28	2
S.P.O'Donnell	A	87	4350	3102	108	28.72	5-13	6
D.K.Lillee	A	63	3593	2145	103	20.82	5-34	6

The leading aggregates for other countries are:

J.R.Ratnayeke	SL	78	3573	2865	85	33.70	4-23	1
A.A.Donald	SA	30	1660	1056	45	23.46	5-29	1
E.A.Brandes	Z	19	992	816	26	31.38	4-21	1

WICKET-KEEPING RECORDS

MOST DISMISSALS IN AN INNINGS

5	R.W.Marsh	Australia v England	Leeds	1981
5	R.G.de Alwis	Sri Lanka v Australia	Colombo (PSS)	1982-83
5	S.M.H.Kirmani	India v Zimbabwe	Leicester	1983
5†	S.Viswanath	India v England	Sydney	1984-85
5†	K.S.More	India v New Zealand	Sharjah	1987-88
5	H.P.Tillekeratne	Sri Lanka v Pakistan	Sharjah	1990-91

† *Including 2 stumpings.*

MOST DISMISSALS IN A CAREER

204 (183ct, 21st) P.J.L.Dujon (West Indies) in 169 matches

FIELDING RECORDS

MOST CATCHES IN AN INNINGS

4	Salim Malik	Pakistan v New Zealand	Sialkot	1984-85
4	S.M.Gavaskar	India v Pakistan	Sharjah	1984-85
4	R.B.Richardson	West Indies v England	Birmingham	1991
4	K.C.Wessels	South Africa v West Indies	Kingston	1991-92
4	M.A.Taylor	Australia v West Indies	Sydney	1992-93
4	C.L.Hooper	West Indies v Pakistan	Durban	1992-93

MOST CATCHES IN A CAREER

118 A.R.Border (A) in 255 matches. 101 I.V.A.Richards (WI) in 187 matches.

ALL-ROUND RECORDS

1000 RUNS AND 100 WICKETS

		M	R	W
I.T.Botham	England	116	2113	145
R.J.Hadlee	New Zealand	115	1749	158
Imran Khan	Pakistan	175	3709	182
Kapil Dev	India	208	3672	243
Mudassar Nazar	Pakistan	122	2624	111
S.P.O'Donnell	Australia	87	1242	108
M.Prabhakar	India	94	1010	119
I.V.A.Richards	West Indies	187	6721	118
R.J.Shastri	India	150	3108	129
Wasim Akram	Pakistan	153	1327	215
S.R.Waugh	Australia	147	2916	141

1000 RUNS AND 100 DISMISSALS

		M	R	Dis
P.J.L.Dujon	West Indies	169	1945	204
R.W.Marsh	Australia	92	1225	124

MOST APPEARANCES FOR EACH COUNTRY

Australia	255	A.R.Border	Sri Lanka	124	A.Ranatunga
West Indies	225	D.L.Haynes	England	122	A.J.Lamb
Pakistan	222	Javed Miandad	South Africa	31	K.C.Wessels
India	208	Kapil Dev	Zimbabwe	29	D.L.Houghton
New Zealand	149	J.G.Wright			

ENGLAND v NEW ZEALAND
1929-30 to 1991-92

Captains

Season	England	New Zealand	T	E	NZ	D
1929-30	A.H.H.Gilligan	T.C.Lowry	4	1	–	3
1931	D.R.Jardine	T.C.Lowry	3	1	–	2
1932-33	D.R.Jardine[1]	M.L.Page	2	–	–	2
1937	R.W.V.Robins	M.L.Page	3	1	–	2
1946-47	W.R.Hammond	W.A.Hadlee	1	–	–	1
1949	F.G.Mann[2]	W.A.Hadlee	4	–	–	4
1950-51	F.R.Brown	W.A.Hadlee	2	1	–	1
1954-55	L.Hutton	G.O.Rabone	2	2	–	–
1958	P.B.H.May	J.R.Reid	5	4	–	1
1958-59	P.B.H.May	J.R.Reid	2	1	–	1
1962-63	E.R.Dexter	J.R.Reid	3	3	–	–
1965	M.J.K.Smith	J.R.Reid	3	3	–	–
1965-66	M.J.K.Smith	B.W.Sinclair[3]	3	–	–	3
1969	R.Illingworth	G.T.Dowling	3	2	–	1
1970-71	R.Illingworth	G.T.Dowling	1	–	–	1
1973	R.Illingworth	B.E.Congdon	3	2	–	1
1974-75	M.H.Denness	B.E.Congdon	2	1	–	1
1977-78	G.Boycott	M.G.Burgess	3	1	1	1
1978	J.M.Brearley	M.G.Burgess	3	3	–	–
1983	R.G.D.Willis	G.P.Howarth	4	3	1	–
1983-84	R.G.D.Willis	G.P.Howarth	3	–	1	2
1986	M.W.Gatting	J.V.Coney	3	–	1	2
1987-88	M.W.Gatting	J.J.Crowe[4]	3	–	–	3
1990	G.A.Gooch	J.G.Wright	3	1	–	2
1991-92	G.A.Gooch	M.D.Crowe	3	2	–	1

		T	E	NZ	D
At Lord's		11	5	–	6
At The Oval		8	4	–	4
At Manchester		4	2	–	2
At Leeds		5	3	1	1
At Birmingham		3	3	–	–
At Nottingham		6	3	1	2
In England		**37**	**20**	**2**	**15**
At Christchurch		13	6	1	6
At Wellington		7	2	1	4
At Auckland		13	4	–	9
At Dunedin		2	1	–	1
In New Zealand		**35**	**13**	**2**	**20**
Totals		**72**	**33**	**4**	**35**

The following deputised for the official touring captain or were appointed for only a
minor portion of a home series:
[1]R.E.S.Wyatt (2nd). [2]F.R.Brown (3rd and 4th). [3]M.E.Chapple (1st). [4]J.G.Wright
(3rd).

HIGHEST INNINGS TOTALS

England	in England	546-4d	Leeds	1965
	in New Zealand	593-6d	Auckland	1974-75
New Zealand	in England	551-9d	Lord's	1973
	in New Zealand	537	Wellington	1983-84

LOWEST INNINGS TOTALS

England	in England	158	Birmingham	1990
	in New Zealand	64	Wellington	1977-78
New Zealand	in England	47	Lord's	1958
	in New Zealand	26	Auckland	1954-55

HIGHEST MATCH AGGREGATE

1293 for 34 wickets	Lord's	1931

LOWEST MATCH AGGREGATE

390 for 30 wickets	Lord's	1958

HIGHEST INDIVIDUAL INNINGS

England	in England	310*	J.H.Edrich	Leeds	1965
		206	L.Hutton	The Oval	1949
	in New Zealand	336*	W.R.Hammond	Auckland	1932-33
		227	W.R.Hammond	Christchurch	1932-33
		216	K.W.R.Fletcher	Auckland	1974-75
New Zealand	in England	206	M.P.Donnelly	Lord's	1949
	in New Zealand	174*	J.V.Coney	Wellington	1983-84

111 hundreds have been scored in this series (England 75, New Zealand 36).

HUNDRED IN EACH INNINGS

New Zealand	122	102	G.P.Howarth	Auckland	1977-78

HUNDRED ON DEBUT IN SERIES

England	137	L.E.G.Ames	Lord's	1931
	122	G.O.B.Allen	Lord's	1931
	117	H.Sutcliffe	The Oval	1931
	114	J.Hardstaff, jr	Lord's	1937
	121	J.D.B.Roberston	Lord's	1949
	103	R.T.Simpson	Manchester	1949
	100	P.E.Richardson	Birmingham	1958
	104*	C.A.Milton	Leeds	1958
	126	K.F.Barrington	Auckland	1962-63
	131*	P.H.Parfitt	Auckland	1962-63
	125	B.R.Knight	Auckland	1962-63
	310*	J.H.Edrich	Leeds	1965
	138*	D.L.Amiss	Nottingham	1973
	139	A.W.Greig	Nottingham	1973
	111	D.I.Gower	The Oval	1978
	109	C.J.Tavaré	The Oval	1983
	105	G.Fowler	The Oval	1983
	102*	A.J.Lamb	The Oval	1983
	114	B.C.Broad	Christchurch	1987-88
	151	M.A.Atherton	Nottingham	1990
New Zealand	117	J.E.Mills	Wellington	1929-30
	107*	M.J.Greatbatch	Auckland	1987-88

HIGHEST AGGREGATE OF RUNS IN A SERIES

England	in England	469	L.Hutton	1949
	in New Zealand	563	W.R.Hammond	1932-33
New Zealand	in England	462	M.P.Donnelly	1949
	in New Zealand	341	C.S.Dempster	1929-30

RECORD WICKET PARTNERSHIPS – ENGLAND

1st	223	G.Fowler/C.J.Tavaré	The Oval	1983
2nd	369	J.H.Edrich/K.F.Barrington	Leeds	1965
3rd	245	J.Hardstaff jr/W.R.Hammond	Lord's	1937
4th	266	M.H.Denness/K.W.R.Fletcher	Auckland	1974-75
5th	242	W.R.Hammond/L.E.G.Ames	Christchurch	1932-33
6th	240	P.H.Parfitt/B.R.Knight	Auckland	1962-63
7th	149	A.P.E.Knott/P.Lever	Auckland	1970-71
8th	246	L.E.G.Ames/G.O.B.Allen	Lord's	1931
9th	163*	M.C.Cowdrey/A.C.Smith	Wellington	1962-63
10th	59	A.P.E.Knott/N.Gifford	Nottingham	1973

RECORD WICKET PARTNERSHIPS – NEW ZEALAND

1st	276	C.S.Dempster/J.E.Mills	Wellington	1929-30
2nd	241	J.G.Wright/A.H.Jones	Wellington	1991-92
3rd	210	B.A.Edgar/M.D.Crowe	Lord's	1986
4th	155	M.D.Crowe/M.J.Greatbatch	Wellington	1987-88
5th	177	B.E.Congdon/V.Pollard	Nottingham	1973
6th	134	K.R.Rutherford/J.G.Bracewell	Wellington	1987-88
7th	117	D.N.Patel/C.L.Cairns	Christchurch	1991-92
8th	104	D.A.R.Moloney/A.W.Roberts	Lord's	1937
9th	118	J.V.Coney/B.L.Cairns	Wellington	1983-84
10th	57	F.L.H.Mooney/J.Cowie	Leeds	1949

BEST INNINGS BOWLING ANALYSIS

England	in England	7- 32	D.L.Underwood	Lord's	1969
	in New Zealand	7- 47	P.C.R.Tufnell	Christchurch	1991-92
New Zealand	in England	7- 74	B.L.Cairns	Leeds	1983
	in New Zealand	7-143	B.L.Cairns	Wellington	1983-84

BEST MATCH BOWLING ANALYSIS

England	in England	12-101	D.L.Underwood	The Oval	1969
	in New Zealand	12- 97	D.L.Underwood	Christchurch	1970-71
New Zealand	in England	10-140	J.Cowie	Manchester	1937
		10-140	R.J.Hadlee	Nottingham	1986
	in New Zealand	10-100	R.J.Hadlee	Wellington	1977-78

HIGHEST AGGREGATE OF WICKETS IN A SERIES

England	in England	34	G.A.R.Lock	1958
	in New Zealand	17	K.Higgs	1965-66
		17	D.L.Underwood	1970-71
		17	I.T.Botham	1977-78
New Zealand	in England	21	R.J.Hadlee	1983
	in New Zealand	15	R.O.Collinge	1977-78
		15	R.J.Hadlee	1977-78

ENGLAND v SOUTH AFRICA

1888-89 to 1965

Captains

Season	England	South Africa	T	E	SA	D
1888-89	C.A.Smith[1]	O.R.Dunell[2]	2	2	–	–
1891-92	W.W.Read	W.H.Milton	1	1	–	–
1895-96	Lord Hawke[3]	E.A.Halliwell[4]	3	3	–	–
1898-99	Lord Hawke	M.Bisset	2	2	–	–
1905-06	P.F.Warner	P.W.Sherwell	5	1	4	–
1907	R.E.Foster	P.W.Sherwell	3	1	–	2
1909-10	H.D.G.Leveson Gower[5]	S.J.Snooke	5	2	3	–
1912	C.B.Fry	F.Mitchell[6]	3	3	–	–
1913-14	J.W.H.T.Douglas	H.W.Taylor	5	4	–	1
1922-23	F.T.Mann	H.W.Taylor	5	2	1	2
1924	A.E.R.Gilligan[7]	H.W.Taylor	5	3	–	2
1927-28	R.T.Stanyforth[8]	H.G.Deane	5	2	2	1
1929	J.C.White[9]	H.G.Deane	5	2	–	3
1930-31	A.P.F.Chapman	H.G.Deane[10]	5	–	1	4
1935	R.E.S.Wyatt	H.F.Wade	5	–	1	4
1938-39	W.R.Hammond	A.Melville	5	1	–	4
1947	N.W.D.Yardley	A.Melville	5	3	–	2
1948-49	F.G.Mann	A.D.Nourse	5	2	–	3
1951	F.R.Brown	A.D.Nourse	5	3	1	1
1955	P.B.H.May	J.E.Cheetham[11]	5	3	2	–
1956-57	P.B.H.May	C.B.van Ryneveld[12]	5	2	2	1
1960	M.C.Cowdrey	D.J.McGlew	5	3	–	2
1964-65	M.J.K.Smith	T.L.Goddard	5	1	–	4
1965	M.J.K.Smith	P.L.van der Merwe	3	–	1	2

	T	E	SA	D
Lord's	10	6	1	3
Leeds	8	5	1	2
The Oval	10	3	–	7
Birmingham	3	2	–	1
Manchester	7	3	1	3
Nottingham	6	2	2	2
In England	44	21	5	18
Port Elizabeth	6	4	1	1
Cape Town	15	9	2	4
Johannesburg	23	7	8	8
Durban	14	5	2	7
In South Africa	58	25	13	20
Totals	102	46	18	38

The following deputised for the official touring captain or were appointed for only a minor portion of a home series:
[1] M.P.Bowden (2nd). [2] W.H.Milton (2nd). [3] Sir T.C.O'Brien (1st). [4] A.R.Richards (3rd). [5] F.L.Fane (4th, 5th). [6] L.J.Tancred (2nd, 3rd). [7] J.W.H.T.Douglas (4th). [8] G.T.S.Stevens (5th). [9] A.W.Carr (4th, 5th). [10] E.P.Nupen (1st), H.B.Cameron (4th, 5th). [11] D.J.McGlew (3rd, 4th). [12] D.J.McGlew (2nd).

HIGHEST INNINGS TOTALS

England	in England	554-8d	Lord's	1947
	in South Africa	654-5	Durban	1938-39
South Africa	in England	538	Leeds	1951
	in South Africa	530	Durban	1938-39

LOWEST INNINGS TOTALS

England	in England	76	Leeds	1907
	in South Africa	92	Cape Town	1898-99
South Africa	in England	30	Birmingham	1924
	in South Africa	30	Port Elizabeth	1895-96

HIGHEST MATCH AGGREGATE

1981 for 35 wickets		Durban	1938-39

LOWEST MATCH AGGREGATE

378 for 30 wickets		The Oval	1912

HIGHEST INDIVIDUAL INNINGS

England	in England	211	J.B.Hobbs	Lord's	1924
		208	D.C.S.Compton	Lord's	1947
	in South Africa	243	E.Paynter	Durban	1938-39
		219	W.J.Edrich	Durban	1938-39
South Africa	in England	236	E.A.B.Rowan	Leeds	1951
		208	A.D.Nourse	Nottingham	1951
	in South Africa	176	H.W.Taylor	Johannesburg	1922-23

145 hundreds have been scored in this series (England 87, South Africa 58).

HUNDRED IN EACH INNINGS

England	117	100	E.Paynter	Johannesburg	1938-39
	140	111	C.A.G.Russell	Durban	1922-23
	104	109*	H.Sutcliffe	The Oval	1929
South Africa	189	104*	A.Melville	Nottingham	1947
	120	189*	B.Mitchell	The Oval	1947

HUNDRED ON DEBUT IN SERIES

England	132*	P.F.Warner	Johannesburg	1898-99
	104	L.C.Braund	Lord's	1907
	119	R.H.Spooner	Lord's	1912
	119	J.H.W.T.Douglas	Durban	1913-14
	117 } 100 }	E.Paynter	Johannesburg	1938-39
	106	P.A.Gibb	Johannesburg	1938-39
	163	D.C.S.Compton	Nottingham	1947
	138	P.B.H.May	Leeds	1951
	117	P.E.Richardson	Johannesburg	1956-57
South Africa	No instance – highest scores:			
	in South Africa	93*	A.W.Nourse	Johannesburg	1905-06
	in England	90	P.N.F.Mansell	Leeds	1951

HIGHEST AGGREGATE OF RUNS IN A SERIES

England	in England	753	D.C.S.Compton	1947
	in South Africa	653	E.Paynter	1938-39
South Africa	in England	621	A.D.Nourse	1947
	in South Africa	582	H.W.Taylor	1922-23

RECORD WICKET PARTNERSHIPS – ENGLAND

1st	359	L.Hutton/C.Washbrook	Johannesburg	1948-49
2nd	280	P.A.Gibb/W.J.Edrich	Durban	1938-39
3rd	370	W.J.Edrich/D.C.S.Compton	Lord's	1947
4th	197	W.R.Hammond/L.E.G.Ames	Cape Town	1938-39
5th	237	D.C.S.Compton/N.W.D.Yardley	Nottingham	1947
6th	206*	K.F.Barrington/J.M.Parks	Durban	1964-65
7th	115	J.W.H.T.Douglas/M.C.Bird	Durban	1913-14
8th	154	C.W.Wright/H.R.Bromley-Davenport	Johannesburg	1895-96
9th	71	H.Wood/J.T.Hearne	Cape Town	1891-92
10th	92	C.A.G.Russell/A.E.R.Gilligan	Durban	1922-23

RECORD WICKET PARTNERSHIPS – SOUTH AFRICA

1st	260	B.Mitchell/I.J.Siedle	Cape Town	1930-31
2nd	198	E.A.B.Rowan/C.B.van Ryneveld	Leeds	1951
3rd	319	A.Melville/A.D.Nourse	Nottingham	1947
4th	214	H.W.Taylor/H.G.Deane	The Oval	1929
5th	157	A.J.Pithey/J.H.B.Waite	Johannesburg	1964-65
6th	171	J.H.B.Waite/P.L.Winslow	Manchester	1955
7th	123	H.G.Deane/E.P.Nupen	Durban	1927-28
8th	109*	B.Mitchell/L.Tuckett	The Oval	1947
9th	137	E.L.Dalton/A.B.C.Langton	The Oval	1935
10th	103	H.G.Owen-Smith/A.J.Bell	Leeds	1929

BEST INNINGS BOWLING ANALYSIS

England	in England	8- 29	S.F.Barnes	The Oval	1912
	in South Africa	9- 28	G.A.Lohmann	Johannesburg	1895-96
South Africa	in England	7- 65	S.J.Pegler	Lord's	1912
	in South Africa	9-113	H.J.Tayfield	Johannesburg	1956-57

BEST MATCH BOWLING ANALYSIS

England	in England	15- 99	C.Blythe	Leeds	1907
	in South Africa	17-159	S.F.Barnes	Johannesburg	1913-14
South Africa	in England	10- 87	P.M.Pollock	Nottingham	1965
	in South Africa	13-192	H.J.Tayfield	Johannesburg	1956-57

HIGHEST AGGREGATE OF WICKETS IN A SERIES

England	in England	34	S.F.Barnes	1912
	in South Africa	49	S.F.Barnes	1913-14
South Africa	in England	26	H.J.Tayfield	1955
		26	N.A.T.Adcock	1960
	in South Africa	37	H.J.Tayfield	1956-57

FIRST-CLASS UMPIRES 1994

BALDERSTONE, John Christopher (Paddock Council S, Huddersfield), b Longwood, Huddersfield, Yorks 16 Nov 1940. RHB, SLA. Yorkshire 1961-69. Leicestershire 1971-86 (cap 1973; testimonial 1984). Tests: 2 (1976); HS 35 v WI (Leeds) 1976; BB 1-80. Tour: Z 1980-81 (Le). 1000 runs (11); most – 1482 (1982). HS 181* Le v Glos (Leicester) 1984. BB 6-25 Le v Hants (Southampton) 1978. Hat-trick 1976 (Le). F-c career: 390 matches; 19034 runs @ 34.11, 32 hundreds; 310 wickets @ 26.32; 210 ct. Soccer for Huddersfield Town, Carlisle United, Doncaster Rovers and Queen of the South. Appointed 1988.

BIRD, Harold Dennis ('Dickie') (Raley SM, Barnsley), b Barnsley, Yorks 19 Apr 1933. RHB, RM. Yorkshire 1956-59. Leicestershire 1960-64 (cap 1960). MBE 1986. 1000 runs (1): 1028 (1960). HS 181* Y v Glam (Bradford) 1959. F-c career: 93 matches; 3314 runs @ 20.71, 2 hundreds. Appointed 1970. Umpired 55 Tests (world record – 1973 to 1993), including 3 in Zimbabwe 1992-93 and 4 in West Indies 1992-93. Officiated in 63 LOI (1973 to 1993), including 1975, 1979, 1983 and 1987-88 World Cup finals, 1985-86 Asia Cup and 6 Sharjah tournaments. **Appointed to International Panel 1994.**

BOND, John David ('Jack') (Bolton S), b Kearsley, Lancs 6 May 1932. RHB, LB. Lancashire 1955-72 (cap 1955; captain 1968-72; coach 1973; manager 1980-86; benefit 1970). Nottinghamshire 1974 (captain/coach 1974). 1000 runs (2); most – 2125 (1963). HS 157 La v Hants (Manchester) 1962. Test selector 1974. F-c career: 362 matches; 12125 runs @ 25.90, 14 hundreds; 222 ct. Appointed 1988.

BURGESS, Graham Iefvion (Millfield S), b Glastonbury, Somerset 5 May 1943. RHB, RM. Somerset 1966-79 (cap 1968; testimonial 1977). Tests: HS 129 v Glos (Taunton) 1973. BB 7-43 (13-75 match) v OU (Oxford) 1975. F-c career: 252 matches; 7129 runs @18.90, 2 hundreds; 474 wickets @ 28.57. Appointed 1991.

CONSTANT, David John, b Bradford-on-Avon, Wilts 9 Nov 1941. LHB, SLA. Kent 1961-63. Leicestershire 1965-68. HS 80 Le v Glos (Bristol) 1966. F-c career: 61 matches; 1517 runs @ 19.20; 1 wicket @ 36.00. Appointed 1969. Umpired 36 Tests (1971 to 1988) and 29 LOI (1972 to 1990). Represented Gloucestershire at bowls 1984-86.

DUDLESTON, Barry (Stockport S), b Bebington, Cheshire 16 Jul 1945. RHB, SLA. Leicestershire 1966-80 (cap 1969; benefit 1980). Gloucestershire 1981-83. Rhodesia 1976-80. 1000 runs (8); most – 1374 (1970). HS 202 Le v Derbys (Leicester) 1979. BB 4-6 Le v Surrey (Leicester) 1972. F-c career: 295 matches; 14747 runs @ 32.48, 32 hundreds; 47 wickets @ 29.04. Appointed 1984. Umpired 2 Tests (1991 to 1992) and 1 LOI (1992).

HAMPSHIRE, John Harry (Oakwood THS, Rotherham), b Thurnscoe, Yorks 10 Feb 1941. RHB, LB. Son of J. (Yorks 1937); brother of A.W. (Yorks 1975). Yorkshire 1961-81 (cap 1963; benefit 1976; captain 1979-80). Derbyshire 1982-84 (cap 1982). Tasmania 1967-69, 1977-79. Tests: 8 (1969 to 1975); 403 runs @ 26.86, HS 107 v WI (Lord's) 1969 on debut (only England player to score hundred at Lord's on debut in Tests). Tours: A 1970-71; SA 1972-73 (DHR), 1974-75 (DHR); WI 1964-65 (Cav); NZ 1970-71; P 1967-68 (Cwlth XI); SL 1969-70; Z 1980-81 (Le XI). 1000 runs (15); most – 1596 (1978). HS 183* Y v Sussex (Hove) 1971. BB 7-52 Y v Glam (Cardiff) 1963. F-c career: 577 matches; 28059 runs @ 34.55, 43 hundreds; 30 wickets @ 54.56; 445 ct. Appointed 1985. Umpired 11 Tests (1989 to 1993), including 4 in Pakistan 1989-90, and 5 LOI (1989 to 1992).

HARRIS, John Henry, b Taunton, Somerset 13 Feb 1936. LHB, RFM. Somerset 1952-59. Suffolk 1960-62. Devon 1975. HS 41 v Worcs (Taunton) 1957. BB 3-29 v Worcs (Bristol) 1959. F-c career: 15 matches; 154 runs @ 11.00; 19 wickets @ 32.57. Appointed 1983.

HOLDER, John Wakefield (Combermere S, Barbados), b St George, Barbados 19 Mar 1945. RHB, RFM. Hampshire 1968-72. Hat-trick 1972. HS 33 v Sussex (Hove) 1971. BB 7-79 v Glos (Gloucester) 1972. F-c career: 47 matches; 374 runs @ 10.68; 139 wickets @ 24.56. Appointed 1983. Umpired 10 Tests (1988 to 1991), including 4 in Pakistan 1989-90, and 8 LOI (1988 to 1990) including 1989-90 Nehru Cup.

HOLDER, Vanburn Alonza (Richmond SM, Barbados), b Bridgetown, Barbados 8 Oct 1945. RHB, RFM. Barbados 1966-78. Worcestershire 1968-80 (cap 1970; benefit 1979). Shropshire 1981. **Tests** (WI): 40 (1969 to 1978-79); HS 42 v NZ (P-o-S) 1971-72; BB 6-28 v A (P-o-S) 1977-78. LOI: 12. Tours (WI): E 1969, 1973, 1976; A 1975-76; I 1974-75, 1978-79; P 1973-74 (RW), 1974-75; SL 1974-75, 1978-79. HS 122 Barbados v Trinidad (Bridgetown) 1973-74. BB 7-40 Wo v Glam (Cardiff) 1974. F-c career: 311 matches; 3559 runs @ 13.03, 1 hundred; 947 wickets @ 24.48. Appointed 1992.

JESTY, Trevor Edward (Privet County SS, Gosport), b Gosport, Hants 2 Jun 1948. RHB, RM. Hampshire 1966-84 (cap 1971; benefit 1982). Surrey 1985-87 (cap 1985; captain 1985). Lancashire 1988-91 (cap 1989). Border 1973-74. GW 1974-76, 1980-81. Canterbury 1979-80. Wisden 1982. LOI: 10. Tours: WI 1982-83 (Int); Z 1988-89 (La). 1000 runs (10); most – 1645 (1982). RHB, HS 248 H v CU (Cambridge) 1984. Scored 122* La v OU (Oxford) 1991 in his final f-c innings. 50 wkts (2); most – 52 (1981). BB 7-75 H v Worcs (Southampton) 1976. F-c career: 490 matches; 21916 runs @ 32.71, 35 hundreds; 585 wickets @ 27.47. Appointed 1994.

JONES, Allan Arthur (St John's C, Horsham), b Horley, Surrey 9 Dec 1947. RHB, RFM. Sussex 1966-69. Somerset 1970-75 (cap 1972). Northern Transvaal 1972-73. Middlesex 1976-79 (cap 1976). Orange Free State 1976-77. Glamorgan 1980-81. HS 33 M v Kent (Canterbury) 1978. BB 9-51 Sm v Sussex (Hove) 1972. F-c career: 214 matches; 799 runs @ 5.39; 549 wickets @ 28.07. Appointed 1985.

JULIAN, Raymond (Wigston SM), b Cosby, Leics 23 Aug 1936. RHB, WK. Leicestershire 1953-71 (cap 1961). HS 51 v Worcs (Worcester) 1962. F-c career: 192 matches; 2581 runs @ 9.73; 421 dismissals (382 ct, 39 st). Appointed 1972.

KITCHEN, Mervyn John (Backwell SM, Nailsea), b Nailsea, Somerset 1 Aug 1940. LHB, RM. Somerset 1960-79 (cap 1966; testimonial 1973). Tour: Rhodesia 1972-73 (Int W). 1000 runs (7); most – 1730 (1968). HS 189 v Pakistanis (Taunton) 1967. BB 1-4. F-c career: 354 matches; 15230 runs @ 26.25, 17 hundreds; 2 wickets @ 54.50. Appointed 1982. Umpired 7 Tests (1990 to 1993) and 10 LOI (1983 to 1993).

LEADBEATER, Barrie (Harehills SS), b Harehills, Leeds, Yorks 14 Aug 1943. RHB, RM. Yorkshire 1966-79 (cap 1969; joint benefit with G.A.Cope 1980). Tour: WI 1969-70 (DN). HS 140* v Hants (Portsmouth) 1976. F-c career: 147 matches; 5373 runs @ 25.34, 1 hundred; 1 wicket @ 5.00. Appointed 1981. Umpired 4 LOI (1983).

LYONS, Kevin James (Lady Mary's HS), b Cardiff, Glam 18 Dec 1946. RHB, RM. Glamorgan 1967-77. Tour: WI 1969-70 (Glam). HS 92 v CU (Cambridge) 1972. F-c career: 62 matches; 1673 runs @ 19.68; 2 wickets @ 126.00. F-c umpire 1985-91. Worcestershire CCC coach 1992-93. Re-appointed 1994.

MEYER, Barrie John (Boscombe SS), b Bournemouth, Hants 21 Aug 1932. RHB, WK. Gloucestershire 1957-71 (cap 1958; benefit 1971). HS 63 v Indians (Cheltenham) 1959, v OU (Bristol) 1962, and v Sussex (Bristol) 1964. F-c career: 406 matches; 5367 runs @ 14.16; 826 dismissals (707 ct, 119 st). Soccer for Bristol Rovers, Plymouth Argyle, Newport County and Bristol City. Appointed 1973. Umpired 26 Tests (1978 to 1993) and 23 LOI (1977 to 1993), including 1979 and 1983 World Cup finals.

PALMER, Kenneth Ernest (Southbroom SM, Devizes), b Winchester, Hants 22 Apr 1937. RHB, RFM. Brother of R. (below) and father of G.V. (Somerset 1982-83). Somerset 1955-69 (cap 1958; testimonial 1968). Tours: WI 1963-64 (Cav); P 1963-64 (Cwlth XI). **Tests**: 1 (1964-65; while coaching in South Africa); 10 runs; 1 wicket. 1000 runs (1): 1036 (1961). 100 wickets (4); most – 139 (1963). HS 125* v Northants (Northampton) 1961. BB 9-57 v Notts (Nottingham) 1963. F-c career: 314 matches; 7761 runs @ 20.64, 2 hundreds; 866 wickets @ 21.34. Appointed 1972. Umpired 21 Tests (1978 to 1993) and 18 LOI (1977 to 1993). **Appointed to International Panel 1994.**

PALMER, Roy (Southbroom SM), b Devizes, Wilts 12 Jul 1942. RHB, RFM. Brother of K.E. (above). Somerset 1965-70. HS 84 v Leics (Taunton) 1967. BB 6-45 v Middx (Lord's) 1967. F-c career: 74 matches; 1037 runs @ 13.29; 172 wickets @ 31.62. Appointed 1980. Umpired 2 Tests (1992 to 1993) and 6 LOI (1983 to 1993).

PLEWS, Nigel Trevor, b Nottingham 5 Sep 1934. Former policeman (Fraud Squad). No first-class appearances. Appointed 1982. Umpired 6 Tests (1988 to 1993) and 4 LOI (1986 to 1990). **Appointed to International Panel 1994.**

SHARP, George (Elwick Road SS, Hartlepool), b West Hartlepool, Co Durham 12 Mar 1950. RHB, WK, occ LM. Northamptonshire 1968-85 (cap 1973; benefit 1982). HS 98 v Yorks (Northampton) 1983. BB 1-47. F-c career: 306 matches; 6254 runs @ 19.85; 1 wicket @ 70.00; 655 dismissals (565 ct, 90 st). Appointed 1992.

SHEPHERD, David Robert (Barnstaple GS; St Luke's C, Exeter), b Bideford, Devon 27 Dec 1940. RHB, RM. Gloucestershire 1965-79 (cap 1969; joint benefit with J.Davey 1978). Scored 108 on debut (v OU). Devon 1959-64. 1000 runs (2); most – 1079 (1970). HS 153 v Middx (Bristol) 1968. F-c career: 282 matches; 10672 runs @ 24.47, 12 hundreds; 2 wickets @ 53.00. Appointed 1981. Umpired 19 Tests (1985 to 1993), including 2 in South Africa 1992-93. Officiated in 51 LOI (1983 to 1993), including 1987-88 and 1991-92 World Cups, 1985-86 Asia Cup and 4 Sharjah tournaments. **Appointed to International Panel 1994.**

WHITE, Robert Arthur (Chiswick GS), b Fulham, London 6 Oct 1936. LHB, OB. Middlesex 1958-65 (cap 1963). Nottinghamshire 1966-80 (cap 1966; benefit 1974). 1000 runs (1): 1355 (1963). HS 116* Nt v Surrey (Oval) 1967. BB 7-41 Nt v Derbys (Ilkeston) 1971. F-c career: 413 matches; 12452 runs @ 23.18, 5 hundreds; 693 wickets @ 30.50. Appointed 1983.

WHITEHEAD, Alan Geoffrey Thomas, b Butleigh, Somerset 28 Oct 1940. LHB, SLA. Somerset 1957-61. HS 15 v Hants (Southampton) 1959 and v Leics (Leicester) 1960. BB 6-74 v Sussex (Eastbourne) 1959. F-c career: 38 matches; 137 runs @ 5.70; 67 wickets @ 34.41. Appointed 1970. Umpired 5 Tests (1982 to 1987) and 12 LOI (1979 to 1987).

WIGHT, Peter Bernard, b Georgetown, British Guiana 25 Jun 1930. RHB, OB. Brother of G.L. (West Indies 1949-53), H.A. and N. (all British Guiana). British Guiana 1950-51. Somerset 1953-65 (cap 1954; benefit 1963). Canterbury 1963-64. 1000 runs (10); most – 2375 (1960). HS 222* v Kent (Taunton) 1959. BB 6-29 v Derbys (Chesterfield) 1957. F-c career: 333 matches; 17773 runs @ 33.09, 28 hundreds; 68 wickets @ 33.26. Appointed 1966.

WILLEY, Peter (Seaham SS), b Sedgefield, Co Durham 6 Dec 1949. RHB, OB. Northamptonshire 1966-83 (cap 1971; benefit 1981). Leicestershire 1984-91 (cap 1984; captain 1987). E Province 1982-85. Northumberland 1992. **Tests:** 26 (1976 to 1986); 1184 runs @ 26.90, HS 102* v WI (St John's) 1980-81; 7 wkts @ 65.14, BB 2-73 v WI (Lord's) 1980. LOI: 26. Tours: A 1979-80; SA 1972-73 (DHR), 1981-82 (SAB); WI 1980-81, 1985-86; I 1979-80; SL 1977-78 (DHR). 1000 runs (10); most – 1783 (1982). HS 227 Nh v Somerset (Northampton) 1976. 50 wkts (3); most – 52 (1979). BB 7-37 Nh v OU (Oxford) 1975. F-c career: 559 matches; 24361 runs @ 30.56, 44 hundreds; 756 wickets @ 30.95. Appointed 1993.

RESERVE FIRST-CLASS LIST: P.ADAMS, A.CLARKSON, M.J.HARRIS, M.K.REED, J.F.STEELE.

INTERNATIONAL PANEL: H.D.Bird, K.E.Palmer, N.T.Plews, D.R.Shepherd (England); D.B.Hair, S.G.Randell (Australia); V.K.Ramaswamy, S.Venkataraghavan (India); B.L.Aldridge, R.S.Dunne (New Zealand); Khizer Hayat, Mahboob Shah (Pakistan); K.E.Liebenberg, S.B.Lambson (South Africa); B.C.Cooray, K.T.Francis (Sri Lanka); S.U.Bucknor, L.H.Barker (West Indies); K.Kanjee, I.D.Robinson (Zimbabwe).

See page 64 for key to abbreviations.

PRINCIPAL FIXTURES 1994

* Includes Sunday play
† Reserve days Sunday and Monday

Wednesday 13 April

Fenner's: Cambridge U v Notts
The Parks: Oxford U v Durham

Saturday 16 April

*Fenner's: Cambridge U v Northants
The Parks: Oxford U v Hants

Tuesday 19 April

Uxbridge: Rapid Cricketline
  Champions (Middx 2nd XI) v
  England Under-19 (Four days)

Wednesday 20 April

Fenner's: Cambridge U v Kent
The Parks: Oxford U v Glam

Thursday 21 April

Tetley Bitter Shield
*Lord's: Britannic Assurance
  Champions (Middx) v England 'A'
  (Four days)

Saturday 23 April

The Parks: Combined Us v Glos
  (One day)

Sunday 24 April

Oxford (Christ Church): Combined
  Us v Kent (One day)

Tuesday 26 April

Benson and Hedges Cup
First Round
The Parks: Combined Us v Lancs
Leicester: Leics v Ireland
Lord's: Middx v Northants
Trent Bridge: Notts v Minor Cos
The Oval: Surrey v Somerset
Hove: Sussex v Scotland

Thursday 28 April

Britannic Assurance Championship
*Chesterfield: Derbys v Durham
*Bristol: Glos v Somerset
*Southampton: Hants v Essex
*Leicester: Leics v Northants
*The Oval: Surrey v Worcs
*Edgbaston: Warwicks v Glam
Other Matches
The Parks: Oxford U v Notts
Old Trafford: Lancs v Yorks (Four
  days)

Friday 29 April

Tourist Match
Southgate: England Amateur XI v
  New Zealanders (One day)

Saturday 30 April

*Fenner's: Cambridge U v Middx

Sunday 1 May

Tourist Match
Arundel: Lavinia, Duchess of
  Norfolk's XI v New Zealanders
  (One day)
Other Match
Old Trafford: Lancs v Yorks
  (One day)

Monday 2 May

Tourist Match
The Oval: Surrey v New Zealanders
  (One day)

Wednesday 4 May

Tetley Bitter Challenge
Worcester: Worcs v New Zealanders

Thursday 5 May

Britannic Assurance Championship
Stockton: Durham v Essex
Bristol: Glos v Sussex

240

Southampton: Hants v Derbys
Canterbury: Kent v Notts
Old Trafford: Lancs v Surrey
Lord's: Middx v Surrey
Northampton: Northants v Glam
Edgbaston: Warwicks v Leics

Saturday 7 May

Tetley Bitter Challenge
*Taunton: Somerset v New Zealanders
Other Match
*Fenner's: Cambridge U v Worcs

Sunday 8 May

AXA Equity & Law League
Stockton: Durham v Essex
Bristol: Glos v Sussex
Southampton: Hants v Derbys
Canterbury: Kent v Notts
Old Trafford: Lancs v Surrey
Lord's: Middx v Yorks
Northampton: Northants v Glam
Edgbaston: Warwicks v Leics

Tuesday 10 May

Benson and Hedges Cup
Second Round
Derby: Derbys v Combined Us or
  Lancs
Stockton: Durham v Worcs
Chelmsford: Essex v Leics or Ireland
Southampton: Hants v Yorks
Canterbury: Kent v Glos
Lord's or Northampton: Middx or
  Northants v Warwicks
Trent Bridge or Oxford (Christ
  Church): Notts or Minor Cos v
  Sussex or Scotland
The Oval or Taunton: Surrey or
  Somerset v Glam

Thursday 12 May

Britannic Assurance Championship
Chelmsford: Essex v Kent
Cardiff: Glam v Yorks
Leicester: Leics v Somerset
Trent Bridge: Notts v Durham
The Oval: Surrey v Derby
Hove: Sussex v Hants
Worcester: Worcs v Glos
Tetley Bitter Challenge
Lord's: Middx v New Zealanders

Saturday 14 May

*Fenner's: Cambridge U v Lancs
The Parks: Oxford U v Warwicks

Sunday 15 May

AXA Equity & Law League
Chelmsford: Essex v Kent
Cardiff: Glam v Yorks
Leicester: Leics v Somerset
Trent Bridge: Notts v Durham
The Oval: Surrey v Derbys
Hove: Sussex v Hants
Worcester: Worcs v Glos
Tourist Match
Northampton: Northants v New
  Zealanders (One day)

Tuesday 17 May

Tourist Match
Leicester: Leics v New Zealanders
  (One day)

Wednesday 18 May

The Parks: Oxford U v Leics

Thursday 19 May

TEXACO TROPHY
Edgbaston: ENGLAND v NEW
  ZEALAND
(First Limited-over International)
Britannic Assurance Championship
Derby: Derbys v Worcs
Gateshead Fell: Durham v Glos
Southampton: Hants v Middx
Canterbury: Kent v Lancs
Trent Bridge: Notts v Sussex
Taunton: Somerset v Warwicks
The Oval: Surrey v Northants
Headingley: Yorks v Essex

Saturday 21 May

TEXACO TROPHY
Lord's: ENGLAND v NEW
  ZEALAND
(Second Limited-over International)

Sunday 22 May

AXA Equity & Law League
Derby: Derbys v Worcs
Gateshead Fell: Durham v Glos

Southampton: Hants v Middx
Canterbury: Kent v Lancs
Trent Bridge: Notts v Sussex
Taunton: Somerset v Warwicks
The Oval: Surrey v Northants
Headingley: Yorks v Essex

Tuesday 24 May

Benson and Hedges Cup
Quarter-Finals
Tetley Bitter Challenge
†Southampton or Headingley: Hants or
   Yorks v New Zealanders

†Depending on outcome of B&H Cup
   Second Round

Thursday 26 May

Britannic Assurance Championship
Ilkeston: Derbys v Notts
Gloucester: Glos v Surrey
Southport: Lancs v Somerset
Leicester: Leics v Kent
Lord's: Middx v Warwicks
Hove: Sussex v Glam
Worcester: Worcs v Northants

Saturday 28 May

Tetley Bitter Challenge
*Chelmsford: Essex v New Zealanders
Other Match
The Parks: Oxford U v Yorks

Sunday 29 May

AXA Equity & Law League
Ilkeston: Derbys v Notts
Gloucester: Glos v Surrey
Old Trafford: Lancs v Somerset
Leicester: Leics v Kent
Lord's: Middx v Warwicks
Hove: Sussex v Glam
Worcester: Worcs v Northants

Thursday 2 June

FIRST CORNHILL INSURANCE
TEST MATCH
*Trent Bridge: ENGLAND v NEW
ZEALAND
Britannic Assurance Championship
Chelmsford: Essex v Glos
Swansea: Glam v Surrey
Tunbridge Wells: Kent v Sussex

Lord's: Middx v Worcs
Northampton: Northants v Lancs
Taunton: Somerset v Hants
Edgbaston: Warwicks v Durham
Middlesbrough: Yorks v Notts

Sunday 5 June

AXA Equity & Law League
Chelmsford: Essex v Glos
Swansea: Glam v Surrey
Tunbridge Wells: Kent v Sussex
Lord's: Middx v Worcs
Northampton: Northants v Lancs
Taunton: Somerset v Hants
Edgbaston: Warwicks v Durham
Headingley: Yorks v Notts

Tuesday 7 June

Benson and Hedges Cup
Semi-Finals

Wednesday 8 June

Tetley Bitter Challenge
† Edgbaston or The Oval: Warwicks or
   Surrey v New Zealanders
† Glam to play New Zealanders at
   Swansea if both Warwicks and
   Surrey involved in B&H
   Semi-Finals

Thursday 9 June

Britannic Assurance Championship
Derby: Derbys v Leics
Hartlepool: Durham v Northants
Basingstoke: Hants v Notts
Canterbury: Kent v Middx
Horsham: Sussex v Lancs
Worcester: Worcs v Essex
Bradford: Yorks v Somerset

Saturday 11 June

Tetley Bitter Challenge
*Bristol: Glos v New Zealanders
Other Matches
*Fenner's: Cambridge U v Glam
*The Oval: Surrey v Oxford U
*Glasgow (Hamilton Crescent):
   Scotland v Ireland (Three days)

Sunday 12 June

AXA Equity & Law League
Derby: Derbys v Leics

Hartlepool: Durham v Northants
Basingstoke: Hants v Notts
Canterbury: Kent v Middx
Horsham: Sussex v Lancs
Worcester: Worcs v Essex
Headingley: Yorks v Somerset

Wednesday 15 June

Fenner's: Cambridge U v Essex

Thursday 16 June

SECOND CORNHILL INSURANCE TEST MATCH
*Lord's: ENGLAND v NEW ZEALAND
Britannic Assurance Championship
Cardiff: Glam v Derbys
Old Trafford: Lancs v Hants
Leicester: Leics v Middx
Luton: Northants v Yorks
Trent Bridge: Notts v Glos
Bath: Somerset v Surrey
Hove: Sussex v Durham
Edgbaston: Warwicks v Kent

Friday 17 June

*Worcester: Worcs v Oxford U

Sunday 19 June

AXA Equity & Law League
Swansea: Glam v Derbys
Old Trafford: Lancs v Hants
Leicester: Leics v Middx
Luton: Northants v Yorks
Trent Bridge: Notts v Glos
Bath: Somerset v Surrey
Hove: Sussex v Durham
Edgbaston: Warwicks v Kent

Tuesday 21 June

NatWest Trophy
First Round
Finchampstead: Berks v Kent
March: Cambs v Hants
Bowdon: Cheshire v Durham
Netherfield: Cumberland v Leics
Exmouth: Devon v Yorks
Swansea: Glam v Lincs
Bristol: Glos v Derbys
Old Trafford: Lancs v Scotland
Northop Hall: Minor Cos Wales v Middx
Lakenham: Norfolk v Worcs

Northampton: Northants v Ireland
Jesmond: Northumberland v Notts
Aston Rowant: Oxon v Somerset
The Oval: Surrey v Staffs
Hove: Sussex v Essex
Edgbaston: Warwicks v Beds

Wednesday 22 June

Tourist Match
Fenner's: Combined Us v New Zealanders

Thursday 23 June

Britannic Assurance Championship
Ilford: Essex v Notts
Colwyn Bay: Glam v Lancs
Lord's: Middx v Durham
Northampton: Northants v Warwicks
The Oval: Surrey v Leics
Worcester: Worcs v Sussex
Headingley: Yorks v Hants
Tourist Match
Highclere: Earl of Carnarvon's Invitation XI v South Africans (One day)

Saturday 25 June

Tetley Bitter Challenge
*Derby: Derbys v New Zealanders
*Canterbury: Kent v South Africans
Other Match
*Bristol: Glos v Cambridge U

Sunday 26 June

AXA Equity & Law League
Ilford: Essex v Notts
Colwyn Bay: Glam v Lancs
Lord's: Middx v Durham
Northampton: Northants v Warwicks
The Oval: Surrey v Leics
Worcester: Worcs v Sussex
Headingley: Yorks v Hants

Wednesday 29 June

Tetley Bitter Challenge
Hove: Sussex v South Africans
Varsity Match
Lord's: Oxford U v Cambridge U

243

Thursday 30 June

THIRD CORNHILL INSURANCE TEST MATCH
Old Trafford: ENGLAND v NEW ZEALAND
Britannic Assurance Championship
Derby: Derbys v Middx
Darlington: Durham v Surrey
Bristol: Glos v Glam
Maidstone: Kent v Yorks
Leicester: Leics v Essex
Trent Bridge: Notts v Northants
Taunton: Somerset v Worcs
Edgbaston: Warwicks v Lancs

Saturday 2 July

Tetley Bitter Challenge
*Southampton: Hants v South Africans

Sunday 3 July

AXA Equity & Law League
Derby: Derbys v Middx
Darlington: Durham v Surrey
Bristol: Glos v Glam
Maidstone: Kent v Yorks
Leicester: Leics v Essex
Trent Bridge: Notts v Northants
Taunton: Somerset v Worcs
Edgbaston: Warwicks v Lancs

Wednesday 6 July

NatWest Trophy
Second Round
March or Southampton: Cambs or
  Hants v Berks or Kent
Bowdon or Darlington: Cheshire or
  Durham v Glos or Derbys
Netherfield or Leicester: Cumberland
  or Leics v Warwicks or Beds
Exmouth or Headingley: Devon or
  Yorks v Oxon or Somerset
Cardiff or Sleaford: Glam or Lincs v
  Sussex or Essex
Colwyn Bay or Uxbridge: Minor Cos
  Wales or Middx v Northants or
  Ireland
Lakenham or Worcester: Norfolk or
  Worcs v Northumberland or Notts
The Oval or Stone: Surrey or Staffs v
  Lancs or Scotland
Tetley Bitter Challenge
‡Derby or Bristol: Derbys or Glos v
  South Africans

‡Depending on outcome of NWT First
Round

Friday 8 July

Tourist Match
Comber: Ireland v New Zealanders
  (One day)

Saturday 9 July

†Lord's: *Benson and Hedges Cup Final*

Sunday 10 July

#*AXA Equity & Law League*
Derby: Derbys v Durham
Bristol: Glos v Somerset
Southampton: Hants v Essex
Leicester: Leics v Northants
The Oval: Surrey v Worcs
Edgbaston: Warwicks v Glam
Tourist Matches
Dublin (Malahide): Ireland v New
  Zealanders (One day)
Glasgow (Titwood): Scotland v South
  Africans (One day)

#Matches involving B&H Cup Finalists
  to be played on Tue 12 July

Monday 11 July

Harrogate: Costcutter Cup
  (Three days)

Tuesday 12 July

Tetley Bitter Challenge
Chester-le-Street: Durham v South
  Africans

Thursday 14 July

Britannic Assurance Championship
Southend: Essex v Glam
Portsmouth: Hants v Glos
Canterbury: Kent v Worcs
Blackpool: Lancs v Derbys
Taunton: Somerset v Notts
Guildford: Surrey v Warwicks
Arundel: Sussex v Middx
Harrogate: Yorks v Leics

Saturday 16 July

Tetley Bitter Challenge
*Northampton: Northants v South
  Africans

Sunday 17 July

AXA Equity & Law League
Southend: Essex v Glam
Portsmouth: Hants v Glos
Canterbury: Kent v Worcs
Old Trafford: Lancs v Derbys
Taunton: Somerset v Notts
Guildford: Surrey v Warwicks
Arundel: Sussex v Middx
Scarborough: Yorks v Leics

Thursday 21 July

**FIRST CORNHILL INSURANCE
TEST MATCH**
*Lord's: ENGLAND v SOUTH
  AFRICA
Britannic Assurance Championship
Durham University: Durham v Leics
Abergavenny: Glam v Kent
Cheltenham: Glos v Yorks
Old Trafford: Lancs v Middx
Northampton: Northants v Derbys
Trent Bridge: Notts v Surrey
Hove: Sussex v Somerset
Edgbaston: Warwicks v Essex
Worcester: Worcs v Hants

Sunday 24 July

AXA Equity & Law League
Durham University: Durham v Leics
Ebbw Vale: Glam v Kent
Cheltenham: Glos v Yorks
Old Trafford: Lancs v Middx
Northampton: Northants v Derbys
Trent Bridge: Notts v Surrey
Hove: Sussex v Somerset
Edgbaston: Warwicks v Essex
Worcester: Worcs v Hants

Tuesday 26 July

NatWest Trophy
Quarter-Finals

Wednesday 27 July

Tetley Bitter Challenge
‡Trent Bridge or Old Trafford: Notts
  or Lancs v South Africans

‡Worcs to play South Africans if both
  Notts and Lancs involved in NWT
  Quarter-Finals

Thursday 28 July

Britannic Assurance Championship
Chesterfield: Derbys v Warwicks
Durham University: Durham v Yorks
Swansea: Glam v Somerset
Cheltenham: Glos v Kent
Southampton: Hants v Northants
Uxbridge: Middx v Essex
The Oval: Surrey v Sussex

Saturday 30 July

Tetley Bitter Challenge
*Leicester: Leics v South Africans

Sunday 31 July

AXA Equity & Law League
Chesterfield: Derbys v Warwicks
Durham University: Durham v Yorks
Swansea: Glam v Somerset
Cheltenham: Glos v Kent
Southampton: Hants v Northants
Uxbridge: Middx v Essex
The Oval: Surrey v Sussex

Thursday 4 August

**SECOND CORNHILL INSURANCE
TEST MATCH**
*Headingley: ENGLAND v SOUTH
  AFRICA
Britannic Assurance Championship
Chesterfield: Derbys v Glos
Chelmsford: Essex v Lancs
Canterbury: Kent v Hants
Lord's: Middx v Glam
Northampton: Northants v Sussex
Trent Bridge: Notts v Leics
Taunton: Somerset v Durham
Worcester: Worcs v Warwicks
Other Match
Cardiff: England Under-19 v India
  Under-19 (First Youth Limited-over
  International)

245

Saturday 6 August

Bristol: England Under-19 v India Under-19 (Second Youth Limited-over International)

Sunday 7 August

AXA Equity & Law League
Chesterfield: Derbys v Glos
Chelmsford: Essex v Lancs
Canterbury: Kent v Hants
Lord's: Middx v Glam
Northampton: Northants v Sussex
Trent Bridge: Notts v Leics
Taunton: Somerset v Durham
Edgbaston: Warwicks v Worcs

Tuesday 9 August

NatWest Trophy
Semi-Finals
Other Match
Jesmond: England XI v Rest of the World XI (One day)

Wednesday 10 August

Tourist Match
Torquay: Minor Cos v South Africans (Three days)
Other Match
Jesmond: England XI v Rest of the World XI (One day)

Thursday 11 August

Britannic Assurance Championship
Colchester: Essex v Surrey
Bristol: Glos v Northants
Canterbury: Kent v Durham
Leicester: Leics v Worcs
Lord's: Middx v Somerset
Eastbourne: Sussex v Derbys
Edgbaston: Warwicks v Notts
Headingley :Yorks v Lancs
Other Match
*Taunton: England Under-19 v India Under-19 (First Youth Test Match) (Four days)

Saturday 13 August

Tetley Bitter Challenge
*Pontypridd: Glam v South Africans

Sunday 14 August

AXA Equity & Law League
Colchester: Essex v Surrey
Bristol: Glos v Northants
Canterbury: Kent v Durham
Leicester: Leics v Worcs

Lord's: Middx v Somerset
Eastbourne: Sussex v Derbys
Edgbaston: Warwicks v Notts
Headingley: Yorks v Lancs

Thursday 18 August

THIRD CORNHILL INSURANCE TEST MATCH
*The Oval: ENGLAND v SOUTH AFRICA
Britannic Assurance Championship
Derby: Derbys v Kent
Hartlepool: Durham v Glam
Southampton: Hants v Surrey
Old Trafford: Lancs v Glos
Leicester: Leics v Sussex
Northampton: Northants v Middx
Weston-super-Mare: Somerset v Essex
Kidderminster: Worcs v Notts
Scarborough: Yorks v Warwicks

Thursday 18 or Friday 19 August

Bain Clarkson Trophy
Semi-Finals (One day)

Sunday 21 August

AXA Equity & Law League
Derby: Derbys v Kent
Hartlepool: Durham v Glam
Southampton: Hants v Surrey
Old Trafford: Lancs v Glos
Leicester: Leics v Sussex
Northampton: Northants v Middx
Weston-super-Mare: Somerset v Essex
Worcester: Worcs v Notts
Scarborough: Yorks v Warwicks

Wednesday 24 August

Headingley: England Under-19 v India Under-19 (Second Youth Test Match) (Four days)

Thursday 25 August

TEXACO TROPHY
Edgbaston: ENGLAND v SOUTH AFRICA
(First Limited-over International)
Britannic Assurance Championship
Cardiff: Glam v Leics
Portsmouth: Hants v Durham
Northampton: Northants v Kent
Trent Bridge: Notts v Lancs
The Oval: Surrey v Middx
Hove: Sussex v Warwicks
Worcester: Worcs v Yorks